America's Government

★

America's Government

★

FRED R. HARRIS
University of New Mexico

GARY WASSERMAN

SCOTT, FORESMAN/LITTLE, BROWN HIGHER EDUCATION
A Division of Scott, Foresman and Company
Glenview, Illinois   London, England

Library of Congress Cataloging-in-Publication Data

Harris, Fred R.
    America's government / Fred R. Harris, Gary Wasserman.
        p.   cm.
    Includes bibliographical references.
    ISBN 0-673-39911-7
    1.   United States—Politics and government.   I. Wasserman, Gary.
    II. Title.
JK274.H223   1990
320.973—dc20   89-24381
                                       CIP

1 2 3 4 5 6-VHJ-94 93 92 91 90 89

★

PREFACE

Politics looks different from the inside. *America's Government* is an insider's introduction to politics. It offers the perspective of the participants themselves, their stories, and their insights. The case studies, the peeks behind closed doors, and the excerpts from their writings aim to give students an understanding of America's politics from the representatives, bureaucrats, journalists, pollsters, lobbyists, and citizens who practice it.

The authors have not only spent considerable time involved in politics, they have also lived in non-Western cultures: Fred among Native Americans and Gary in Africa. These societies have a great story-telling tradition of education. Stories are used to pass the insights, values, and experiences of one generation to the young of the next. Narratives often illustrate subtleties that abstract theories do not. They also allow listeners to draw their own conclusions from the actual events. And, because they present people in real-life situations, they often are recalled and their lessons applied.

A similar learning process happens in politics. Politicians will tell stories to each other to convey lessons from their careers. Former Speaker of the House Tip O'Neill was fond of repeating a tale from his first campaign for office. His neighbor, Mrs. O'Brien, had told him the night before the election that she had reservations about voting for him because he hadn't asked for her vote. O'Neill was shocked and replied, "Why Mrs. O'Brien, I've lived across from you for eighteen years, I've mowed your lawn in the summer and shoveled your walk in the winter. I didn't think I had to ask for your vote." She replied, "Let me tell you something: people like to be asked."

One lesson here for a politician is that peoples' votes often depend less on big issues than small civilities. It implicitly cautions younger representatives not to let the "bright lights" of Washington lead them to forget their local roots. The tale gives us a clue to voters' behavior as well as how a seasoned "pol" views that behavior. And it sticks with us.

We have presented in this book some of the experiences we have heard and read and encountered in our political careers. The case studies, for example, are intended to complement and illustrate the concepts discussed in their chapters. But they may also conflict with those ideas. In the chapter on members of Congress (Chapter 11), we stress the importance of constituency influence on how representatives vote. Yet Senator Arlen Spector's vote on Judge Bork's nomination to the Supreme Court indicates that his constituents' opinions were not uppermost in his mind as he made his decision. The chapter on interest groups (Chapter 9) points to the rise of political action committees (PACs) and the amounts of money they increasingly steer into election campaigns. However, the case study in that chapter shows how former Congressman Tony Coelho pressured unwilling PACs to contribute money to cement Democratic control of the House of Representatives. So what's going on here?

The answer is that politics and government involve subtleties and shadings that are difficult to see and more difficult to communicate. Despite our profession's aspiration to teach political *science,* the practice of politics is much closer to a form of art. Truth can be elusive. Voter opinion *is* the single most important influence on representatives, yet a senator facing election only every six years may have considerable room to exercise an independent judgment. PACs *have* increased their influence over policymakers through rising campaign contributions. Yet PAC leaders often have no choice over where they spend this money when approached by powerful committee chairmen with priorities of their own. Complex relationships are difficult to briefly sum up. We hope the insights of insiders will give the beginning student a sense of the shades of gray involved.

The political participants are at least as complex and interesting as the process. The people we have known and worked with in politics are rarely the cynical cartoons by which politicians are often dismissed. If anything sets them off from other fields, besides social skills and a desire to exercise power, it may be their ideals. People in politics often enter it for what sound like naive reasons. They believe in a candidate; they oppose a war; they want to help people; or they want to move the country in a more conservative/liberal direction. These are people with real beliefs engaged in a serious business with important consequences for themselves and our country.

Of course, insiders' stories aren't enough. The two authors—who have divided their working lives between practicing, teaching, and writing about politics—want their book to do at least three things. One, the text should reflect how those in politics actually behave. Politics is presented as its participants understand and play it. Second, students need to be familiar with the history and structure of their system of government. A text should introduce students to the fundamentals of America's government, from the Constitution to congressional committees, and to the language and classic works of political science. Finally, there's no sense writing a book no one wants to read. The cases, illustrations, quotes, and personalities along with a direct writing style attempt to keep the book interesting and the reader awake.

This text, then, is intended for an introductory class in American government and politics. It is organized along traditional lines into four parts and eighteen chapters. Part One, "The Setting," discusses the history of the government's founding, the Constitution, the concept of federalism, and the civil liberties that protect our freedoms.

Part Two, "The Public," begins with public opinion as the ultimate judge of the success or failure of political actions. How groups—from media and political parties to movements and interest groups—organize public opinion to gain influence fills these five chapters. The next two parts are "The Institutions" and "The Policies" of government. Part Three outlines and illustrates behavior in the branches and bureaucracy of the federal government. Part Four examines public policy-making in the arenas of economics and foreign relations.

Other features designed to help students grasp the basic concepts in the text include:

★chapter outlines

★boldfaced key terms with definitions

★numerous charts, graphs, and photographs that highlight the "reality" of day-to-day politics

★quotes from politicians of historical and modern significance

★chapter-opening vignettes that spark the reader's interest and involvement

★case studies in Parts Two and Three that give detailed accounts and analyses of significant events in American government

★end-of-chapter material that includes a summary that puts ideas into perspective, a page-referenced list of key terms, suggested readings, and notes to the chapter text

The text is accompanied by a *Study Guide* that offers the following for each text chapter: a summary, chapter objectives, definitions of terms, self-tests, individual and interactive case studies, and an answer key that refers to text pages and chapter objectives. *STAR (Self Test and Review),* a computerized study guide, is also available. STAR is a self test/diagnostic program that will help assess students' progress learning the material. An *Instructor's Manual* is available that is integrated with the *Study Guide.* It includes information on using case studies in teaching. For each chapter it provides an overview, lecture and discussion suggestions, objective questions, and lists of readings and audiovisual materials. Each part of the book is also summarized, and essay questions are offered for each part and for the entire book. Finally the *Test Bank,* available in print and on computer disk, contains seventy-five multiple-choice questions for each text chapter.

This book can be even better with your contributions. Perhaps you have an interesting political story you would like to share. If so, please send it to:

Political Science Editor
Higher Education Division
Scott, Foresman and Company
1900 E. Lake Avenue
Glenview, Illinois 60025

You are promised the immortality of a footnote.

★
ACKNOWLEDGMENTS

There are many people to thank for their help. Professor Richard Pious of Barnard College provided scholarly aid and comfort throughout the writing; Becky Strehlow with Scott, Foresman transformed thoughts and words into a text; and Naomi Gitlin with Burson-Marsteller spent many hours patiently shaping prose, checking facts, and meeting deadlines. Woodie Woodruff was accurate and resourceful in his research and writing.

In the field of politics no one provided more insights than Bob Beckel. Other participants included Fred Droz on campaigns, Glen Cowan on polling, Les Francis and John Wasielewsky on conventions, Jayne O'Donnell on the Republic's early days, Ed Wasserman and Charlie Clark on the media, and Guy Blynn on all things legal. Scholars who read, commented on, and improved the text include:

Danny Adkison, Oklahoma State University
Peri Arnold, University of Notre Dame
Ed Beard, University of Massachusetts, Boston
John F. Bibby, University of Wisconsin—Milwaukee
Keith O. Boyum, California State University, Fullerton
James T. Chalmers, Wayne State University
Paul Chardoul, Grand Rapids Junior College
Roy Christman, San Jose State University
Anne N. Costain, University of Colorado at Boulder
Donald A. Gross, University of Kentucky
Kenneth Kennedy, College of San Mateo
Margaret Latimer, Auburn University
Michael S. Lyons, Utah State University
Alan Monroe, Illinois State University
George Pippin, Jones County Junior College
Brian F. Rader, Northeastern Oklahoma State University
J. Michael Sharp, Northeastern Oklahoma State University
Beatrice Talpos, Wayne County Community College
William Thurston, Solano Community College
Glynn Tiller, Lee College
Jack Van Aartsen, Grand Rapids Junior College

The editorial team at Scott, Foresman were unfailing in their skills and patience. John Covell first suggested the blending of authors. Bruce Nichols smoothly guided us editorially while Mark Grimes, the Project Editor, and Judy Neighbor, the designer, expertly shaped the final package. Bruce Borland, Scott Hardy, and Karen Bednarski kept a close eye over the process.

As most of those named would quickly agree, none of them is responsible for the final form this product took.

Our families, especially our wives, Margaret and Ann, were saint-like (most of the time) in their tolerance of absent husbands and missing fathers. In partial payment to our children, we dedicate the book to them.

CONTENTS

PART TWO

America's Government: The Public 122

PART THREE

America's Government: The Institutions 310

PART FOUR

America's Government: The Policies   492

America's Government

★

★ The politicians who created America's government had a curious mix of motives. On one hand they were practical men; realists who had earned wealth and fought a war. While standing up for regional interests, they were willing to compromise to shape a union acceptable to their states. They were also men of ideas; intellectuals who could discuss philosophies, debate principles, and draft a declaration of independence and a constitution. They could embrace political ideals while never loosening their grip on the daily necessities for governing.

Their legacy provides the setting for the political discussions that fill the rest of the book. Even if the framers wouldn't recognize everything that goes on under their constitution today, they would certainly understand the language of politics—the conflicts and accommodations, the ambitions and loyalties, the power and bargaining. They might well conclude that on a human level very little has changed.

Chapter One outlines the principles and history lying behind the great documents of the nation's creation—The Declaration of Independence and the U.S. Constitution. Chapter Two discusses the evolution and present meanings of the Constitution. Chapter Three examines federalism, how it was seen in the Constitution and what it has become today. And Chapter Four looks closely at the civil liberties and rights of people, who they protect and how.

Together these chapters set the stage on which the people, their leaders, and their government play politics.

PART ONE

AMERICA'S GOVERNMENT

The Setting

★

CHAPTER 1

The Historical Setting: Present at the Creation

Rum was one of James Madison's reasons for being uncomfortable with democracy. He had seen popular politics played in colonial America and it hadn't left him with much confidence in the process.

Election campaigns in Madison's Virginia often involved candidates supplying potential voters with large quantities of what was called bumbo-rum punch. Along with cookies, ginger cake, and a barbecued pig, it made for a persuasive afternoon's political argument. In one 1757 election, George Washington supplied 160 gallons of alcohol to 391 voters, a fairly stiff one and a half quarts per voter.

This was accepted practice, good enough for Washington, Jefferson, and other founding fathers. But to young Madison it was a "corrupting influence," not in keeping with the "purity of moral and republican principles." Consequently, in his 1779 reelection campaign for the Virginia House of Delegates, he decided to stand up for his beliefs. He refused to provide bumbo.

Madison lost the election—to a tavernkeeper.[1]

Of course Madison would later help write a constitution by which Americans would be guaranteed the right to govern themselves. But that odd mix of democratic impulse countered by a deep suspicion of unrestrained popular power led to the balance found in the Constitution. The complexity of the framers' realism was shaped by the Revolution they had just fought, and the English and colonial heritage they had inherited, as well as their brief experience as independent states under the Articles of Confederation. In writing the Constitution, they would also be influenced by who they were and the political needs of the day that would have to be satisfied if their Constitution was to be accepted.

George III of England. In the Declaration, the colonists wrote that the King had a "history of repeated injuries and usurpations " and that he would only be satisfied with "the establishment of an absolute Tyranny over these States."

THE AMERICAN REVOLUTION

The colonists in America developed a high degree of self-government during the 150 years following the first settlement at Jamestown in 1607. Three thousand miles from England, they had little choice.

Colonial assemblies were established to decide how to provide governmental functions. And colonial merchants, shippers, planters, family farmers, trappers, traders, and land speculators, along with their employees and slaves, created a booming colonial economy. This economic success encouraged widespread political involvement. According to the research of three American historians, "Nowhere else in the world at the time did so large a proportion of the people take an active interest in public affairs."[2]

The relationship between the American colonies and Britain went rather smoothly until the mid-1700s. The two needed each other, at least to counter French Canadian threats to British colonial interests such as the land and fur trade in the Ohio Valley. Accordingly, the Whig Party in Parliament, led by William Pitt the Elder, was willing to give the colonies a large measure of self-rule. In return the colonies were willing to give Britain their loyalty in the struggle with the French over control of North America.

Two major historical events would permanently change this inter-continental attachment: *the French and Indian War (1754–63)* and *the accession of George III to the throne of England in 1760.* The French and Indian War resulted in the defeat of France in America. It also weakened the military ties between the colonies and Britain, since they no longer shared a chief opponent. In addition, the war forced the thirteen colonies to cooperate with each other, train an American officer corps, and make a young George Washington into a true American hero.[3] Most importantly, and ominously for relations with the colonies, Britain developed a large war debt.

Colonists burn stamps in reaction to the Stamp Act of 1765.

In the midst of the war, George III took the throne of England. The new king was a constitutional monarch, limited in his powers by Parliament. But he was also a shrewd politician who insisted on ruling as well as reigning. George wasn't terribly subtle about his way of winning favor with Parliament—he handed out well-paying jobs requiring little work (called sinecures) to those who would support him. He tried to undermine the power of the Whigs by replacing Pitt with the more compatible George Grenville as prime minister.

King George's first act during the Grenville ministry was the **Proclamation of 1763,** a royal decree that closed western America to settlement. The new ruler was trying to stop the dilution of the colonial market through westward emigration. He was also hoping to keep the British monopoly on land speculation.

A series of taxes followed. The Sugar Act of 1764 set up new taxes for the colonists and better overall tax collection. The same year, the Currency Act prevented the assemblies from issuing new paper money and forced them to redeem the old. British merchants were freed from accepting low-value, inflated currency. The Mutiny Act of 1765 made the colonists pay for the British troops permanently stationed in America. Also in 1765, the **Stamp Act** required the colonists to pay a tax on local legal documents, pamphlets, newspapers, and even playing cards and dice.

On one hand, the new laws were a success. They did just what they were intended to do. British revenue from the colonies increased ten-fold from what it was before 1763.

JOIN, or DIE.

The first-Known American political cartoon, at left, was published by Benjamin Franklin in his Pennsylvania *Gazette* May 9, 1754. The cartoon urged the colonies to unite themselves against the French. Below, a portrait of Franklin about 1748.

But politically the laws caused unexpected resistance. Increasingly defiant, the colonists responded with sometimes violent protests. None, however, went so far as to call for a complete break from the homeland. The Virginia House of Burgesses argued that the colonies could be taxed only by their own elected representatives. In 1765, following this line of reasoning, nine colonics scnt delegates to the **Stamp Act Congress** in New York. They agreed to petition the king and Parliament against taxation by other than their local assemblies.

At the time, the demand of *"no taxation without representation"* sounded like a peculiar idea to most Englishmen. Only one in twenty-five of them could vote for members of Parliament. Ireland and entire boroughs in Britain were represented by people whom the citizenry had not even elected.

The colonies and the homeland became locked in a battle of wills. Merchants in a number of American seaports led a colonial boycott that forced Parliament to repeal the Stamp Act. But England replaced it with the more restrictive **Declaratory Act,** giving Parliament complete legislative jurisdiction over the colonies. The battle intensified. New York refused to comply with the Mutiny Act, so Parliament passed a law suspending the New York assembly altogether. Vital imports such as tea, lead, and paint were taxed next. The **Boston Tea Party**—where British tea (which was purposely priced lower than the colonial brew) was dumped in the bay by Bostonians dressed as "Mohawks"—produced another boycott of British goods.

Continuing with his cutting satire, in 1767 Benjamin Franklin had this cartoon made and sent to his friends. It prophesies the plight of England without her American colonies.

Britain responded harshly. Parliament passed the **Coercive Acts,** which closed Boston Harbor and reduced the right of the Massachusetts colony to govern itself. The colonists formed **committees of correspondence** to link the colonies together behind whatever action was taken. In 1774, a **First Continental Congress** was held in Philadelphia. Delegates drew up a list of grievances to be put before the king, agreed upon a united economic boycott of Britain, and prepared for their military defense. They also decided to meet again.

The disagreements spiraled toward violence. British troops marched to Lexington and Concord on April 19, 1775 and exchanged fire with a group of "minutemen." Last-minute attempts at reconciliation by the British came too late to stop the American Revolution. In January 1776, Thomas Paine's pamphlet *Common Sense,* calling for outright rebellion, was read and followed by thousands of colonists. *The war started as an attempt by the colonists to secure their rights as British citizens.* However, in a short time the violence and killing became so severe that there was no alternative to a clean break.[4] (See the box on page 7.)

A DECLARATION OF AMERICAN IDEALS

In June 1776, delegates to the Second Continental Congress in Philadelphia appointed a committee to draft a **Declaration of Independence.** They wanted to state the strongest possible case for independence. It had been a year since the battle of Lexington and Concord and the war was well under way.

The colonists knew they would need help to win the war. The American colonies were far less populated and far less wealthy than Britain. Colonial leaders hoped to sway not only their own people but also world opinion, so that sympathetic countries might offer financial assistance. Consequently, the revolutionary leaders, realistic politicians on the world stage that they were, didn't speak of their rights as Englishmen; they declared their rights as human beings. The Continental Congress's drafting committee, which included Benjamin Franklin, John Adams, and Thomas Jefferson, was charged with proclaiming their human rights and their reasons for rebelling.

Jefferson, an intellectual Virginia planter, wrote the Declaration's

 ## Why Did Americans Fight in the Revolutionary War?

In any war, people fight for a variety of reasons, including the powerful pull of patriotism and the pressures of community opinion. In an interview held years after the Revolutionary War, one old veteran said that he had fought for the right of self-government.

"Why did you? . . . My histories tell me that you men of the Revolution took up arms against intolerable oppressions."

"What were they? Oppressions? I didn't feel them."

"What, were you not oppressed by the Stamp Act?"

"I never saw one of those stamps. . . . I am certain I never paid a penny for one of them."

"Well, what about the tea tax?"

"Tea tax, I never drank a drop of the stuff. The boys threw it all overboard."

"Then, I suppose, you had been reading Harrington, or Sidney and Locke, about the eternal principles of liberty?"

"Never heard of 'em."

"Well, then, what was the matter, what did you mean in going into the fight?"

"Young man, what we meant in going for those red-coats, was this: we always had governed ourselves and we always meant to. They didn't mean we should."

SOURCE: Interview in 1837 with Captain Levi Preston of Danver, Massachusetts, quoted in Charles Warren, *The Making of the Constitution* (Boston: Little, Brown and Company, 1928), p. 4.

first draft. He was chosen by the members of the committee because of his "felicity of expression"—he wrote well. Jefferson didn't look for new principles or arguments. Instead, he sought to reflect the current sentiments of the colonists as straightforwardly as possible, addressing what he called the "common sense of the subject." The three ideals he sought to express and unify in the Declaration were the principles of *human rights, political participation,* and *limited government.*

The First Ideal: Human Rights

"We hold these truths to be self-evident, that all men are created equal, that they are endowed by their Creator with certain unalienable Rights, that among these are Life, Liberty, and the pursuit of Happiness."

With these words, Jefferson expressed the belief in natural rights, rights with which people are born. The principle has two parts: that all "men" are created equal, and all have certain "unalienable" rights.

The equality Jefferson referred to didn't mean all people are the same. Instead, it was the Declaration's recognition of the right to be treated equally under the law. The division of people into "kings" and "subjects" had no natural or religious justification under this theory. The rights people were born with were exactly the same for everyone.

Of course, the Declaration's assertion of equal rights was meant to apply only to white males. Women, blacks, and native Americans were left out. At the time, most American blacks were slaves. Many white colonists were not treated equally either. Those who didn't own property weren't allowed to vote in a typical colony, and some were bound to others as indentured servants.

Jefferson recognized these inconsistencies. He realized his sweeping statement that "all men are created equal" refuted slavery. During his life, Jefferson was torn between his views on equality and his position as a slaveholder. His original draft of the Declaration called the slave trade a crime against liberty, but the Continental Congress deleted the passage from the final draft.

The "unalienable" rights (or inalienable, as we would say today) described in the Declaration are rights so basic that they can't be sold, given up, or taken away. These were the generally accepted rights of English citizens. The colonists believed they inherited the thirteenth-century Magna Carta, which limited the monarch's power, and the seventeenth-century protections contained in the

The Declaration of Independence as drafted by Thomas Jefferson in his handwriting.

A slave auction in colonial America. While the Declaration of Independence declared that "all men are created equal," blacks were being bought and sold.

English Habeas Corpus Act and Bill of Rights. The ideas of English philosopher John Locke (1632–1704) were so well known in the colonies and so accepted among American revolutionary leaders that Jefferson properly regarded them as "common sense."[5]

In his "Second Treatise on Civil Government (1689)," Locke had asserted that all "men" in their natural state are born free and equal. Locke argued that all "men" are created by the same "maker" and are the creator's property. Accordingly, any offense by one man against the life, health, liberty, or possessions of another is an offense against the creator. Locke believed certain inalienable rights were God-given, and no government had the right to take them away.[6]

But what happens when natural rights conflict with majority rule? Can't a majority of people theoretically limit inalienable rights like religious freedom? To Locke, free and independent living—much like the lifestyle of Robinson Crusoe on his island—was the natural state of man. But he recognized that if Crusoe had been joined by twenty more people who built split-level huts and a shopping mall, the new inhabitants might have agreed to give up some freedoms for their mutual benefit. The village council they formed couldn't, according to Locke, justly limit the inalienable rights of Crusoe and the villagers. For example, it couldn't limit the villagers' right to think and speak as they wanted, even if a majority of the villagers believed such actions were necessary for the common good.

In the Declaration of Independence, Jefferson changed Locke's reference to the inalienable rights of "life, liberty and property" to "life, liberty, and the pursuit of happiness." The delegates to the Continental Congress were all property owners, but they assumed owning land was part of a broader right to the pursuit of happiness.

Philosophers have disagreed on the origin of human equality and fundamental human rights—whether they are God-given, utilitarian, customary, or from some other source. Regardless of origin, a belief in these rights remains a cornerstone of America's approach to governing.[7] (See the box on page 10.)

The Second Ideal: Political Participation

" . . . to secure these rights, Governments are instituted among men, deriving their just powers from the consent of the governed . . ."

If people are created equal with the same rights, then it follows that they should govern themselves. They should not be subject to the will of others without their own "consent." This theory was the basis of the Declaration's statement of the ideal of "political participation."

★ Human Rights After Jefferson

John Stuart Mill, writing nearly a century after the Declaration was signed, modified the argument of Locke and Jefferson. He said the right of free speech isn't absolute or God-given. In "Utilitarianism" and "On Liberty," Mill wrote that the right results from its *utility,* or ability to work for the happiness of the greatest number. The determination of what's right and wrong should be guided by this principle, according to Mill. In supporting a right such as free speech, Mill stressed the importance of an open marketplace of ideas. The majority must consider all views when making decisions affecting its own welfare, he said. If free speech were limited, the decisions made by the majority would diminish in quality.

The current theory of fundamental human rights is much like Mill's. The modern approach says that such rights should not be abridged by the majority unless there is a clear showing of danger to society. This is illustrated by the person who falsely shouts "fire" in a crowded movie

theatre. This person cannot exercise absolute free speech because it would endanger people fleeing the theatre.

Politics is the process by which people seek to secure and preserve their share of power or authority. It determines, in Harold Lasswell's memorable phrase, "who gets what, when, and how."[8] Political participation, therefore, is the idea that all "men" should have an equal opportunity to take part in the decisions that affect their lives. The politics described in the Declaration has to do with government—the individuals, institutions, and processes that officially distribute power and authority. Politics affects everyone.

The ideal of political participation is an old one. Jefferson and many other early American leaders became familiar with the idea in their studies of the Greek and Roman philosophers and in Locke's writings. Locke wrote that governments are based on a *social contract*—an implied agreement by all citizens with all citizens. In this theoretical contract, individuals consent to give up some of their rights or powers for the common good.

Thus government rests on a voluntary agreement. To Locke, consent of the governed meant "consent to be governed by the majority." The social contract would form a community that would produce a single authority instead of the multiple wills of the individuals. Locke was also a practical politician. This single authority did not need the unanimous agreement of all citizens, but Locke said the community will and actions of government should be decided by a majority vote (one more than half). Majority rule was the only way Locke thought the system could work in reality.

There were also religious strands woven into the tapestry of belief behind political participation. Following the teachings of John Calvin, the Puritans recognized God's law as supreme and contained in the Bible. They opposed a separation of church and state and advocated a "theocracy," where the rule of God would be administered by his representatives. Puritan practice contained seeds of democracy: local church communities were based on a "covenant," which gave people free choice of whether or not to join; local church communities were free to govern themselves, not subject to central church authority; and governments should have only limited authority.

Despite these practices, in colonial times *democracy was a dirty word.* It was used as a smear, along with *republic,* by British critics who defined both as "mob rule." Many framers of the Constitution agreed (see the box on p. 13). Other colonial leaders such as Roger Williams, Patrick Henry, and Thomas Paine spoke out freely in favor of rule of the people. Most colonial leaders came to prefer the word *republic,* which meant representative government. "For let it be agreed that a government is republican in proportion as every member composing it has an equal voice in the direction of its concerns by representatives chosen by himself, and responsible to him at short periods," wrote Jefferson.[9] Jefferson was referring to a government that was democratic in the sense that the people were the supreme authority, but republican in the sense that the people should govern themselves through representatives.

The extent and form of political participation was not spelled out at the time of the Declaration of Independence, but the two essential elements of political participation had been established. The first element is *democratic process,* which means citizens should have the right to select their governmental leaders. The second is *democratic results,* or governmental policies and practices should reflect the will of the community while protecting human rights. Democracy, then, is both a means justifying an end and an end justifying the means.

The Third Ideal: Limited Government

" . . . whenever any Form of Government becomes destructive of these ends, it is the Right of the People to alter or abolish it, and to institute new Government, laying its foundation on such principles and organizing its powers in such form, as to them shall seem most likely to effect their Safety and Happiness."

John Locke wrote that people give only limited powers to government when they enter into a social contract. The government shouldn't act "arbitrarily" or in violation of "promulgated standing law," based on the common good. Locke didn't think people had a duty to support a government that was not based upon consent. He recognized the right of individual resistance to unjust government. Revolution would occur when a government was so grossly unjust as to destroy the trust between citizens and elected officials. When that happened, peace was unlikely and "God in heaven is the judge," wrote Locke.

The signers of the Declaration held that citizens have a right, even a duty, to rebel against an oppressive and unrepresentative government. People can change the form of their government if it violates these principles. Although some colonial leaders later found the Declaration's language a bit too sweeping in its encouragement to revolt, Jefferson was not one of them. After Shays's Rebellion in 1787, Jefferson declared, "The late rebellion in Massachusetts has given more alarm than it should have done. Calculate that one rebellion in thirteen States in the course of eleven years, is but one for each State in a century and a half. No country should be so long without one."[10]

★ The Framers Against Democracy

It "would be as unnatural to refer the choice of a proper character for chief magistrate [the president] to the people, as it would to refer a trial of colors to a blind man."

James Mason, Virginia

"The evils we experience flow from the excesses of democracy. The people do not want [lack] virtue, but are the dupes of pretended patriots."

Eldridge Gerry, Massachusetts

The people "should have as little to do as may be about the government. They . . . are constantly liable to be misled."

John Sherman, Connecticut

The Declaration of Independence is a political promise. In justifying its revolution, America declared what it stands for. At a minimum this meant respect for human rights, wide political participation, and limited government. When discussing how those with power actually behave, it is often easy to agree with journalist Ambrose Bierce's definition of politics as "a strife of interests masquerading as a contest of principles." While hardly inaccurate, it is incomplete. Countless groups and individuals since the Declaration was written have successfully used these principles as the foundation of their claims for a fairer share in the American promise. And these words have, in turn, restrained and guided the response to these claims by those with power. "It cannot be long ignored or repudiated," Vernon L. Parrington wrote of the Declaration, "for sooner or later it returns to plague the council of practical politics. It is constantly breaking out in fresh revolt . . ."[11]

The Declaration states a set of ideals. The U.S. Constitution establishes a government to carry them out. It took some years of experience in governing to bridge the distance between the Declaration's ideals of politics and the Constitution's processes of government.

EXPERIENCE IN GOVERNING

Winning the New Nation

A statement of principles did not make a new nation. Declaring independence and winning independence were two different things. The Revolutionary War was America's first test of its unity as a nation. It was a test the new nation almost didn't pass. Ultimately, the shared colonial history, the states' own governments, and the results of the ill-fated Articles of Confederation would prove important in eventually uniting the country under the Constitution.

The idea of one nation made up of separate states developed slowly over 150 years of colonial history. The English settlers gradually began to think of themselves as Americans. By the time of the French and Indian War, some common American goals such as defense were recognized. After 1763, opposition to George III's acts caused the colonists to unite behind more shared interests. But even before that, the American colonies collectively sent representatives to foreign countries to negotiate trade and commerce agreements. By the early 1770s, there was a distinct American political community.

Still, only about 40 percent of colonial Americans supported the Revolutionary War. Some 10 percent opposed the war and 50 percent were either indifferent or neutral. When approximately 100,000 British loyalists left the country, forcibly or otherwise, the power of the patriots increased.

Madison and other framers of the U.S. Constitution were to conclude that the state governments were overly democratic: too much power was in the hands of the legislatures, with too little central authority. Yet Americans were enjoying more democracy after the Revolution than would exist elsewhere in the world for many years.

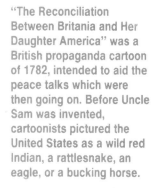

"The Reconciliation Between Britania and Her Daughter America" was a British propaganda cartoon of 1782, intended to aid the peace talks which were then going on. Before Uncle Sam was invented, cartoonists pictured the United States as a wild red Indian, a rattlesnake, an eagle, or a bucking horse.

Articles of Confederation, 1781–1789

Attempts to tighten ties among the colonies during the Revolution met with only limited success. The First Continental Congress in September 1774 had established regular lines of communication among the colonies and had given a focus to anti-British sentiment. The Second Continental Congress, beginning in Philadelphia in May 1775, created the Declaration of Independence. At the same time, a plan for confederation—a loose union among the states—was proposed. **The Articles of Confederation** were ratified by the states by March 1781, and went into effect even before the formal end of the American Revolution in February 1783.

Pointing out the shortcomings of the Articles of Confederation is not difficult. No national government was really set up in the Articles. Instead, they established a "league of friendship" among the states, which didn't have much more authority than the United Nations does today. The center of the federation was a unicameral legislature, called the Continental Congress. Each state had one vote, regardless of its size. Most serious actions required approval by nine states, and amendments to the Articles required approval by all thirteen.

America was still far from operating as one nation. George Washington, then commander of the American army, managed to get financial support from abroad while frequently failing to get the support he needed from the states. France saw the benefits of helping the colonies and weakening Great Britain; so did Spain and the Netherlands. France gave the most, contributing $62 million in aid and $6 million in loans along with naval forces and ground troops.

Even after the war was won, many Americans referred (in the plural) to "these United States of America." When John Adams was in England for commercial negotiations in 1784, English officials asked whether he was there to speak for one nation or thirteen. John Jay later wrote—overlooking native Americans, blacks, and Catholics, among others—that America was "one connected country" with "one united people—a people descended from the same ancestors, speaking the same language, professing the same religion, attached to the same principles of government, very similar in their manners and customs."[12] As historian Ernest Renan once ironically wrote: "What is a Nation? . . . to get one's history wrong."

Governing the New States

The thirteen state governments that took the place of the old colonial governments in 1776 were similar to earlier governments, but very different in operation.[13] Colonial governors had been appointed by the king or his representative; all states, except Pennsylvania, had elected governors. Unlike the royal governors, the state governors didn't have complete veto power over legislative acts. Only three state governors even had a partial veto. The governments retained the executive, legislative, and judicial branches.

Most states had bicameral (two-house) legislatures. The old colonial Governor's Council became in most states an elected senate. The colonial court systems remained virtually intact in the states. The new state governments reflected the revolutionary distrust of centralized authority in the great power given to elected legislatures. In five states, the legislature appointed most state officials; in three, they could even amend the state constitutions without a vote of the citizens.

The states adopted written constitutions, which usually included a bill of rights. The drafters of these constitutions broke new ground by listing human rights that governments were to respect. These lists reflected the colonists' experiences with the British government prior to the Revolutionary War.

Human rights and citizen participation varied widely in the states. New Jersey was the only state to allow women to vote, and the right was soon withdrawn. All states except Georgia and South Carolina prohibited the importation of slaves. Several southern states passed laws encouraging voluntary freeing of slaves. The Massachusetts Supreme Court ruled slavery unconstitutional, and Pennsylvania passed a law calling for the gradual emancipation of slaves. Most states began to recognize the right of religious freedom. Only property owners could vote, voting in all states, but the amount of property needed was so low that this presented little of a barrier. The property requirements were greater for public office holders.

The confederation had no executive branch and no national system of courts. Perhaps most important, the Continental Congress had no ability to tax—it could only *request* funds from the states. Each state retained its "sovereignty, freedom, and independence." Nor did the Congress have any direct authority over citizens, who were subject only to the governments of their states. In short, *the Articles gave Congress no ability to force its will on either states or citizens.*

The Articles did contain a provision for Congress to choose its own president—a president of the Congress, not of the United States. America had fourteen such presidents, some very briefly, before George Washington became the first real chief executive under the Constitution. Nevertheless, a kind of infant executive branch began to grow out of necessity. The Articles provided for a **Committee of the States,** made up of one delegate from each state, to function as a kind of executive committee when Congress was not in session. Separate committees were set up to handle the various tasks of government, such as finance and foreign affairs, and a "secretary" was appointed for each of the committees. Perhaps these committees would have developed into cabinet ministries such as those in the British parliament, where the prime minister and the cabinet come from the legislative body. But the Articles were not given the time to evolve. The Articles of Confederation were to be replaced, not improved.

Despite this, the confederation did have many strengths. Unlike the United Nations, it had the power to declare war, conduct foreign

President Washington and the first—and smallest—cabinet. From left to right: Henry Knox (secretary of war); Thomas Jefferson (secretary of state); Edmund Randolph (attorney general); Alexander Hamilton (secretary of the treasury); and President Washington.

policy, coin money, manage a postal system, and oversee an army made up of the state militias. The Articles were also startlingly democratic in requiring **compulsory rotation** in office. That is, no member of the Congress could serve more than three years in any six. Finally, real accomplishments were made under the Articles, such as the start of a national bureaucracy and the passing of the **Northwest Ordinance,** which established the procedure for admitting new states into the union.

But by 1787, the inadequacies of the Articles were more apparent than its strengths. Too little power had been granted to the central authority. Fears about British, French, and Spanish threats to American territory were widespread. The confederation was in deep financial trouble: not enough funds were coming from the states; the currency was being devalued; and the states were locked in trade wars, putting up tariff barriers against each other. Shays's Rebellion in late 1786, an angry protest by Massachusetts farmers unable to pay their mortgages and taxes, reinforced the fears of many among the propertied elite that strong government was needed to avoid "mob rule" and economic disruption.

THE CONSTITUTIONAL CONVENTION

The Background

Post-Revolution debts made peace nearly as difficult as war. Congress, the states, and individual citizens had all borrowed money. Congress alone owed $34 million to domestic creditors in 1783 when the peace treaty was signed. A few years later it owed another $10 million to foreign creditors.

The national government's low prestige didn't help matters. The states refused to give Congress the power to impose a national tax to help pay its debts. And having the capital in three different places in one year—Princeton, Annapolis, and New York—illustrated the government's low status.

Economic problems were at the forefront. States were issuing their own undervalued paper money because there was no uniform currency. The money issued by Congress was so inflated that few wanted it. When Congress borrowed money, it had to pay very high interest rates. With all these money problems, it was difficult to negotiate adequate trade treaties because it was almost impossible to convince foreigners that the government could enforce them. Some state legislatures even prevented creditors from collecting from debtors.

This situation took Revolutionary leaders like Washington and John Jay by surprise. Washington harbored a grudge over the states' refusal to back the war effort. This lack of support from the states, Washington said, could have caused the "dissolution of any army less patient, less virtuous, and less persevering than that which I have had the honor to command." Others agreed. John Jay wrote, "What a triumph for the advocates of despotism to find that we are incapable of governing ourselves, and that systems founded on the basis of equal liberty are merely ideal and fallacious."[14]

Madison vs. Hamilton

James Madison, John Adams, George Washington, and his aide, Alexander Hamilton, were the key forces behind the Constitutional Convention. Washington, who chaired the proceedings, lent his prestige and popularity to the convention and its resulting constitution. John Adams's analysis of the new state constitutions provided a model for the convention to follow. But it was the dialogue and debate between Hamilton and Madison that to some degree propelled the convention. The ideas, efforts, and arguments of these two rivals largely shaped the final results, though in ways neither entirely agreed with.

These framers went into the convention with their own separate agendas. Hamilton, a bundle of nervous energy, had the bearing of an aristocrat but had grown up in poverty in the West Indies and came to America to make a name for himself. The haughty lawyer-legislator won few friends, but found several framers who shared his low opinion of human nature and the average person. His pessimism helped shape his belief that a strong national government was needed.

Hamilton's experiences in the Revolutionary War as Washington's aide-de-camp were equally important in shaping his views. He, like Washington, was highly critical of Congress's inability to meet the army's needs and cited the doctrine of "implied powers" to make his case. Congress should have simply assumed the undefined powers that were needed to wage the war successfully. Failing this, Hamilton recommended replacing Congress with a strong national government and a powerful chief executive. After the decisive victory at Yorktown in 1781, Hamilton resigned from the army and returned to New York in part to further this goal.

Hamilton, who understood finance as well as anyone in his day, had a clear-cut economic agenda. He thought a strong national government would help improve the country's credit. He also favored a system of national taxation that would provide a dependable, regular payment of interest on the national debt. Hamilton believed this would make the government's bonds such an attractive investment that wealthy people would support it.

In addition, Hamilton was a nationalist. He supported the idea of a "solid coercive union" that could unite the states, regulate trade, and provide for a national army. Without this, he wrote, the states might "cut each other's throats" and the new nation might come to a "speedy and violent end."[15]

James Madison, quieter and less emotional than Hamilton, shared the aristocrat's nationalist views. Madison, whose notes during the convention are the principal source of information on the debates, shared Jefferson's concern about the out-of-control powers of state legislatures, which he called "elective despotism." Madison and Jefferson also agreed about the principles of separation of powers and checks and balances that originated in the writings of Aristotle and Cicero. Madison and Jefferson concurred that democracy could be as threatened by the tyranny of a few in an aristocracy as it could by the tyranny of an unchecked majority in a democracy. Jefferson thought the Virginia government was guilty of giving too much influence to the majority through the legislature.

Madison and Adams shared concerns about the historical persecution of minorities. Madison wrote that people are naturally divided into "different interests and factions, . . . creditors or debtors—rich or poor . . . members of different religious sects . . . inhabitants of different districts . . . etc. . . ."[16] Madison thought the harmful tendency of unrestrained majorities to violate the rights of minorities would be neutralized by the doctrines of separation of powers and checks and balances. A strong national government, which would emphasize the size and diversity of the country, would work against the possibility of one group forming an oppressive majority.[17]

It was Madison who urged the state of Virginia to request that the twelve other states send delegates to a conference in Annapolis. This fall 1786 meeting was called to discuss trade and commerce issues. Underlining the weakness of nationalism, only five states responded. However, at the conference, Hamilton, then a delegate from New York, was able to gain agreement for a meeting of the states—the Constitutional Convention. But numerous revolutionary leaders favored the loose system of government in existence and opposed a strong national government.

A Break with the Past?

The consequences of a depressed economy in New England and elsewhere made the nationalists' case for them. In Northampton, Massachusetts, farmer-debtors who couldn't pay their mortgages took to arms and blocked the local courthouse, preventing judges from foreclosing mortgages and taking their land. In Rhode Island, debtors took over the legislature and issued paper money to make it easier for people to pay their debts. And the New Hampshire legislature was surrounded by several hundred armed men demanding that taxes be returned and paper money issued.

In Boston during the winter of 1786, Daniel Shays, a leader in the Northampton uprising, led a thousand armed men in what came to be known as **Shays's Rebellion.** Propertied men became alarmed that their property rights might be in danger if the disorders were not halted. Others feared that Massachusetts would be unable to restore order alone. But as historian Samuel Morison wrote, "when Massachusetts appealed to the Confederation for help, Congress was unable to do a thing. That was the final argument to sway many Americans in favor of a stronger federal government."[18]

George Washington was convinced by General Henry Knox (who commanded the militia that put down the rebellion in Massachusetts) that the rebellion threatened property rights. In fact, this fear convinced Washington to attend and chair the Constitutional Convention. "There are combustibles in every state which a spark might

set fire to," Washington wrote. "I feel infinitely more than I can express for the disorders which have arisen. Good God!"[19]

The Constitutional Convention did not get a great deal of support from delegates or Congress. Congress did not pass a resolution approving the convention until after seven states had already elected delegates and it was clear it would be held anyway. Congress also tried to restrict the convention to the "sole and express purpose of revising the Articles of Confederation." Rhode Island did not even elect delegates. Of the seventy-four delegates elected by the twelve other states, only fifty-five participated in the convention, and only thirty-nine of the delegates signed the finished document. Some who were most active in its preparation refused to sign.

There is some disagreement among historians over just how great a change the Constitution symbolized. Some authorities have written that it was a "break with mistaken assumptions of the past." From this view it was a hard-headed, *conservative document* that abandoned the democratic ideals of those who wrote and supported the Declaration of Independence. These historians also charge that the preconvention period was not nearly as unsettled as supporters of the Constitution painted it later. Others argue that *the Constitution wasn't as conservative a break with the past* as some scholars claim. They point out that of the forty-three signers of the Declaration who were alive at the time of the convention, thirty supported

Shays's Rebellion in the winter of 1786 convinced many political leaders of the need for a strong central government. At left, Shays's attack on the Springfield arsenal failed because his men were poorly armed and exhausted from marching through the deep snow. At the top, a blacksmith in a Massachusetts town refuses to accept a writ of attachment for his debts. Below, a $20 bill issued by the Continental Congress in 1775 that was "not worth a continental" by the end of the Revolution. This inflation of currency motivated the Rebellion.

the new Constitution (including Jefferson, the chief writer of the Declaration, and Washington, the major symbol of the Revolution). It has also been noted that the principal architect of the Constitution, James Madison, was a friend and disciple of the leader of the liberals, Jefferson.[20]

The year 1913 saw the publication of Charles Beard's influential and controversial book on the motives of the delegates, *An Economic Interpretation of the Constitution of the United States.* Beard viewed the struggle over the Constitution as a "deep-seated conflict between a popular party based on paper money and agrarian interests and a conservative party centered in towns and resting on financial, mercantile, and personal property interests generally."[21]

This view is no longer widely supported by most historians. The two sides Beard described were people on either side of the question of adopting the Constitution. Few would disagree, however, that there was some truth to Beard's assertion that the Constitution was drafted by men whose property interests were at stake. The delegates were the elite of the day, including lawyers, landowners, speculators, merchants, and other commercial people. Along with clear philosophical ideas about how the government should be set up, these delegates weren't about to let their property interests be ignored.

The decision of the delegates to write a sweeping new Constitution led them to keep in mind what the voters wanted. *The Constitution was the product of political bargaining by practical politicians who needed public approval.* A study on the subject found few predictable splits among the state delegations based upon size or special interests. "Each state participated in the core of a winning coalition," which assured that "no major group was radically dissatisfied with the product of the convention's long deliberations."[22]

The delegates submitted the Constitution to popularly elected state conventions for ratification, as opposed to the state legislatures where the Articles had been ratified. In a bold stroke, the framers declared the Constitution would go into effect after only nine of the thirteen states approved it.

Opposition to the idea of a new Constitution was quiet, in part because several well-known liberal leaders were absent from the convention. "I smelt a rat," said the famed orator Patrick Henry, in explaining why he refused to be a delegate. Henry and other Virginia radicals later opposed ratification of the Constitution, but by then it was too late.

The delegates easily agreed the national government should be republican in form, deriving its power from the people. But many other issues were much more controversial, threatening to make a strong union impossible.[23]

THE ISSUES IN PHILADELPHIA

As the temperatures rose in the muggy uncomfortable summer of 1787, so too did the heat of the debates at the Constitutional Convention. One issue was how the power of a strong national government could be reconciled with the carefully guarded sovereignty of often fearful states. Another was how small states could avoid being overruled by large states such as Virginia. Other issues included how to harness the powers of the legislative branch and keep it within reasonable bounds, how to best represent all classes of people within the national government, and what to do about slavery.

To allow full consideration of such issues, some states caucused before the convention to outline the kind of new government they favored. At James Madison's urging, Virginia held such a caucus that passed a series of resolutions called the Virginia Plan.

The Virginia Plan: A Strong Union

One key part of the Virginia Plan, which the delegates to the full convention early on agreed to, was the motion that "a national government ought to be established consisting of a supreme legislative, executive, and judiciary." This clarified that the new government would deal with people, not just with states as the Articles of Confederation did. Furthermore, this new government would be balanced by a separation of powers.

The Virginia Plan called for a two-house "National Legislature," in which members of one house would be elected by the people of each state, and members of the other house would be elected by the first house from a list of people nominated by each state legislature. This national legislature would have the power to "legislate in all cases to which the separate states are incompetent" and the ability to decide when this was true. It would also be able to veto any state laws that, in its opinion, violated the Constitution.

A single "National Executive" would be chosen by the national legislature for one term. There would be a "National Judiciary," with judges chosen by the national legislature to serve during "good behavior," that is, probably for life. A "Council of Revision," made up of the national executive and judges from the national judiciary could examine and reject any law the national legislature passed that violated the Constitution.

Representation in the national legislature would depend on how many people lived in a state or how much a state contributed to the national government. Not surprisingly, Virginia was favored under both tests; it contained the most people and was quite wealthy.

★ Principal Plans Before the Constitutional Convention

	LEGISLATIVE	EXECUTIVE	JUDICIAL	FEDERAL-STATE RELATIONS
Virginia Plan	Bicameral One house popularly elected; second chosen by first from nominees of state legislatures Voting based on money contributions or free population or both Powers of Congress broad	Single executive chosen by Congress for one term only Authority to execute laws and exercise executive rights invested in Confederation Congress	Supreme and inferior courts; judges appointed by Congress for life; Council of Revision to exercise a suspensive veto over acts of the national and state legislatures	Federal government to admit new states and guarantee republican forms of government; federal government to negate state laws incompatible with the Union; also to use force against any state failing to fulfill its duty
New Jersey Plan	Unicameral Delegates to be chosen by state legislatures Each state one vote Powers of Congress enlarged; states to collect taxes but Congress to act if states default	Plural executive chosen by Congress for one term only Authority to execute laws, appoint, direct military operations	Supreme court only; judges appointed by plural executive for life	Acts of Congress and treaties "supreme law of the respective states"; conflicting state laws forbidden; federal executive to use force against non-cooperative states
Hamilton's Plan	Bicameral Assembly elected by people on basis of population; terms, 3 years; Senate elected for life terms by electors chosen by people Congress to have power to pass all laws deemed necessary to common defense and general welfare of Union; Senate alone to declare war, approve treaties and appointments	President elected for life term by electors chosen by people within each state Powers included veto, execution of laws, war, treaties, appointments, pardons	Supreme court appointed by President with consent of Senate for life terms; legislature given power to institute courts in each state	State laws contrary to Constitution are void; governors of states appointed by federal government and have veto over state legislation; a special court provided to hear controversies arising between United States and particular states over territories

SOURCE: John H. Ferguson and Dean S. McHenry, *The American Federal Government*, 14th ed. (New York: McGraw-Hill, 1981), p. 27.

The New Jersey Plan: A Revised Confederation

Delegates from the small states (Delaware, Connecticut, and New Jersey) caucused and came up with an alternative to the Virginia Plan. **The New Jersey Plan,** as it came to be known, was a reform of the Articles of Confederation. Under the plan, "the United States in Congress" would be strengthened, but the states would remain the most important units of government. Congress would continue to be a unicameral legislature as in the Articles, and would have the power to tax and regulate foreign and interstate commerce. Delegates would also continue to be elected by the state legislatures, not the people. Each state would still have one vote in Congress.

Under the New Jersey plan, there would be a "Federal Executive" chosen by Congress for one term. But a majority of the state governors could have Congress remove the federal executive. A "Federal Judiciary," chosen by the executive, would include judges who would serve during good behavior. Although the plan provided that the Constitution, treaties, and laws would be the "supreme law" of the states, it allowed the state courts to enforce this law.

Backers of the New Jersey Plan had one convincing argument on their side. Under the Virginia Plan, the three largest states (Virginia, Massachusetts, and Pennsylvania) could control the national government by voting together. Ratification of a constitution allowing this would be impossible. The small states would not stand for it.

Hamilton's Plan: A British Model

Alexander Hamilton had his own plan, which he advocated in a six-hour speech to the convention. Privately, he thought the states should be abolished because they were dominated by the "avarice, ambition, and interest which govern most people." Publicly, he only advocated reducing the power of the states by making them dependent, administrative units of the national government.

Hamilton permitted "most people" to be represented in one house of the national legislature, based on universal white-male voting rights (with no property ownership requirement). He would, however, keep a check on this house by having a coequal senate (like the British House of Lords) and an "elected monarchy," both chosen for life.

This plan, closely modeled after the British Parliament, was understandably largely ignored by the delegates who had just waged a Revolution against this type of government. It may have helped the convention lean more toward a strong union and less toward a loose confederation.

The Connecticut Compromise: A Federal System

The two major plans—Virginia and New Jersey—posed the basic issue: would there be national sovereignty and *consolidation,* or state sovereignty and *confederation?* The answer was a compromise backing neither option. The delegates decided on a federal system of government with mixed and overlapping national and state sovereignty. As Madison predicted, *the key to resolving the debate was how many votes each state would have in the national legislature.*

At the convention, Dr. William Samuel Johnson of Connecticut presented the Connecticut Compromise, or the **"Great Compromise,"** which held that the states should be considered in two ways: 1) *as districts, or simply areas where individuals lived,* and 2) *as political societies, or units of government.* Representation in the national Congress should embrace both notions, one house representing the people, the other representing the states. This plan was narrowly adopted after lengthy debate on July 16.

Opposition to the Compromise continued even after its passage. Madison thought equal representation for states in the Senate discounted the very notion of a national government. That the Compromise allowed only the popularly elected House to originate tax measures was little consolation for Madison. James Wilson, another critic of the Compromise, wondered for whom the government was being formed. "Is it for men, or for the imaginery beings called States?" Until it became evident there would be no Constitution without the Compromise, many refused to accept it.

The Compromise and later decisions largely satisfied the southern states on *slavery* and *export-trade* issues. Three-fifths of slaves could be counted for purposes of representation in the House of Representatives. Slave importations couldn't be prohibited by the national government for at least twenty years, and slaves couldn't be taxed by more than $10 a head. The southern export trade was also protected by a provision that Congress couldn't tax exports at all and by a requirement that no treaty with a foreign country would become effective until it was ratified by two-thirds of the Senate.

RATIFICATION

We the People of the United States, in Order to form a more perfect Union, establish justice, insure domestic Tranquility, provide for the common defence, promote the general Welfare, and secure the Blessing of Liberty to ourselves and our Posterity, do ordain and establish this Constitution for the United States of America.

FIGURE 1★1
Ratification of the Constitution

VOTE IN RATIFYING CONVENTION

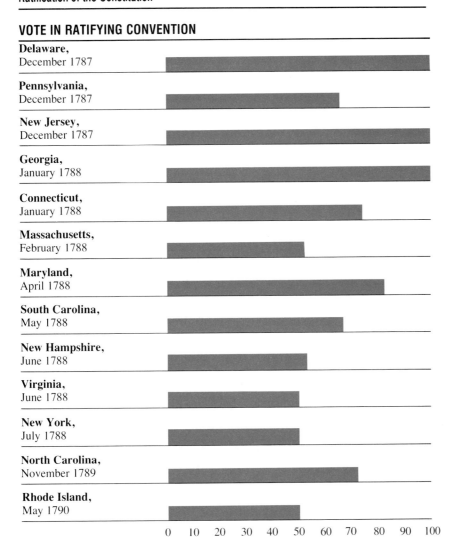

Delaware, December 1787	
Pennsylvania, December 1787	
New Jersey, December 1787	
Georgia, January 1788	
Connecticut, January 1788	
Massachusetts, February 1788	
Maryland, April 1788	
South Carolina, May 1788	
New Hampshire, June 1788	
Virginia, June 1788	
New York, July 1788	
North Carolina, November 1789	
Rhode Island, May 1790	

0   10   20   30   40   50   60   70   80   90   100

The United States Constitution, with this preamble, was signed by the delegates to the convention on September 17, 1787—109 days after they convened. No delegate was totally pleased with the document. Some felt it went too far toward union, others that it did not go far enough. Most concluded it had the most realistic chance of being accepted by the states. "Thus, I consent, Sir, to this Constitution, because I expect no better, and because I am not sure, that it is not the best," Benjamin Franklin told the delegates.

It was now up to the states to decide whether to adopt the Constitution. Congress submitted it to the states for ratification in special state conventions.

Politics prevailed. Supporters of the document, or **Federalists** as they were called, had an advantage. They had a product to sell. The opposing **Antifederalists**—as they were labeled by the Federalists—simply had no better alternative to offer, and "you can't beat something with nothing." Essays written in New York newspapers as propaganda for ratifying the Constitution were collected and called *The Federalist*. Written by Alexander Hamilton, John Jay, and James

---

★ Down with the Constitution

Antifederalists raised a number of serious objections to the proposed Constitution. One of the most outspoken and passionate of the opponents was Patrick Henry, who was the dominant voice of the opposition in the Virginia convention. Here are a few of his objections:

This Constitution is said to have beautiful features, but when I come to examine these features, Sir, they appear to me horridly frightful: Among other deformities, it has an awful squinting; it squints towards monarchy: And does not this raise indignation in the breast of every American? Your President may easily become King: Your Senate is so imperfectly constructed that your dearest rights may be sacrificed by what may be a small minority; and a very small minority may continue forever unchangeably this Government, although horridly defective: Where are your checks in this Government? Your strong holds will be in the hands of your enemies: It is on a supposition that our American Governors shall be honest, that all the good qualities of this Government are founded: But its defective, and imperfect construction, puts it in their power to perpetrate the worst of mischiefs, should they be bad men: And, Sir, would not all the world, from the Eastern to the Western hemisphere, blame our distracted folly in resting our rights upon the contingency of our rulers being good or bad. Show me that age and country where the rights and liberties of the people were placed on the sole chance of their rulers being good men, without a consequent loss of liberty? I say that the loss of that dearest privilege has ever followed with absolute certainty, every such mad attempt. . . .

SOURCE: Reprinted from *THE COMPLETE ANTI-FEDERALIST*, Volume 5, edited by Herbert J. Storing by permission of The University of Chicago Press. Copyright © 1981 by The University of Chicago.

Madison, it was the first major commentary by the framers on the Constitution. This classic of American political thought was written, like much of what the framers did, for very practical reasons, in this case to win approval for their Constitution.

Even supporters of ratification, such as Jefferson, had reservations about the document. In Jefferson's case these involved the lack of a bill of rights. In answer to this concern, Madison proposed that a bill of rights be put before the first Congress. Virginia's George Mason also worried about the lack of a bill of rights and thought the Constitution gave too much lawmaking power to Congress in the "necessary and proper" clause.

In other states, like Massachusetts, the Constitution was narrowly ratified only after legislators were promised that a bill of rights, later to be the first ten Amendments, would be the first order of business of the new government.

Nonetheless, five of the necessary states ratified it within five months, and four more did so six months later. The old Congress under the Confederation was dissolved, the new government was established, and President George Washington was sworn in on April 30, 1789, following his election.

The long ratification fight continued, however. North Carolina didn't join the Union until nine months after Washington's inauguration. Rhode Island (called Rogue Island because of its radical politics) didn't approve the Constitution until May of 1790. With that move, there could finally be a national flag with thirteen stars representing all of the states composing a single nation, the United States of America.

The federal ship *Hamilton*, centerpiece of New York City's grand parade (or what we would today call a political demonstration) celebrating the ratification of the Constitution by the necessary nine states. Three days later, July 26, 1788, New York ratified the Constitution.

WRAP-UP

The American Revolution was fought, in a sense, for the rights of British citizens. Besides their geographical separation from England and their numerous economic conflicts with the mother country, the American colonies justified their revolt by appealing to universal principles. Human rights, political participation, and limited government were the basic American ideals supporting the Declaration of Independence.

After the Revolution, some time was needed before a lasting structure of government could be established. The unity among the colonies would continue to evolve, the state governments would provide models for a national government, and the limitations of the Articles of Confederation would become more and more apparent. Leaders of the new nation such as James Madison and Alexander

Hamilton, worried by debtors' revolts and hoping to preserve vital economic interests, pushed for a Constitutional Convention in 1787. There, a compromise between a big-state proposal, the Virginia Plan, and a small-state one, the New Jersey Plan, resulted in a federal system and a new U.S. Constitution.

It helps to recall that this Constitution of 1787 "is not the sole constitution of our American Liberties. It is not in itself the Living Constitution, but only part of it."[24] Our customs, historical practices, and much of the political behavior discussed in this book compose the "Living Constitution" that unifies and guides the nation. This history and the constitutional document it produced only set the stage for the American political play that follows.

Key Terms

Proclamation of 1763 (p. 4)
Stamp Act (p. 4)
Stamp Act Congress (p. 5)
Declaratory Act (p. 5)
Boston Tea Party (p. 5)
Coercive Acts (p. 6)
committees of correspondence (p. 6)
First Continental Congress (p. 6)
Declaration of Independence (p. 6)

Articles of Confederation (p. 14)
Committee of the States (p. 16)
compulsory rotation (p. 17)
Northwest Ordinance (p. 17)
Shays's Rebellion (p. 20)
The Virginia Plan (p. 23)
The New Jersey Plan (p. 25)
"Great Compromise" (p. 26)
Federalists (p. 28)
Antifederalists (p. 28)

Suggested Readings

Barbash, Fred, *The Founding* (New York: Simon & Schuster, 1987).

Bernstein, Richard B., *Are We to Be a Nation? The Making of the Constitution* (Cambridge: Harvard University Press, 1987).

Kammen, Michael, *The Machine that Would Go of Itself: The Constitution in American Culture* (New York: Alfred A. Knopf, 1986).

Lipset, Seymour M., *The First New Nation* (New York: Vintage Books, 1967).

Morris, Richard B., *Witnesses at the Creation: Hamilton, Madison, Jay and the Constitution* (New York: New American Library, 1989).

Wills, Garry, *Inventing America: Jefferson's Declaration of Independence* (New York: Random House, 1978) and *Explaining America: The Federalist* (New York: Doubleday & Co., 1981).

Endnotes

[1]Fred Barbash, *The Founding* (New York: Simon and Schuster, 1987), p. 131.

[2]T. Harry Williams, Richard N. Current, and Frank Freidel, *A History of the United States to 1877,* 3rd edition, (New York: Alfred A. Knopf, 1969), p. 125.

[3]For an excellent popular biography of George Washington, see James Thomas Flexner, *Washington: The Indispensable Man* (New York: New American Library, 1984).

[4]See Gordon S. Wood, *The Creation of the American Republic 1776–1782,* (Chapel Hill: The University of North Carolina Press, 1969), Part 1.

[5]See Garry Wills, *Inventing America: Jefferson's Declaration of Independence* (New York: Vintage Books, 1978), pp. 168–80.

[6]John Locke, *Two Treatises of Government,* Peter Laslett, ed. (New York: Cambridge University Press, 1965), p. 309.

[7]Morton White, *The Philosophy of the American Revolution* (New York: Oxford University Press, 1978), pp. 213–21.

[8]Harold Lasswell, *Politics: Who Gets What, When, How?* (New York: World, 1936).

[9]Jefferson to Samuel Kercheval, July 12, 1816, contained in Saul K. Padover, *The Complete Jefferson* (New York: Duell, Sloan and Pierce, 1943), p. 288.

[10]Jefferson to James Madison, March 15, 1789, contained in *The Complete Jefferson,* p. 122.

[11]Vernon L. Parrington, *Main Currents in American Thought,* Vol. 3 (New York: Harcourt Brace, 1930), p. 285.

[12]*Federalist,* no. 2.

[13]See Richard B. Morris, *The Forging of the Union* (New York: Harper and Row, 1987), chapter 3.

[14]Charles Warren, *The Making of the Constitution* (Boston: Little, Brown and Company, 1928), p. 18.

[15]Alpheus T. Mason and Richard H. Leach, *In Quest of Freedom: American Political Thought and Practice,* 3rd ed. (Washington, D.C.: University Press of America, 1981), p. 59.

[16]James Madison, *The Federalist,* no. 10.

[17]See Garry Wills, *Explaining America: The Federalist* (New York: Doubleday & Company, 1981), pp. 254–64.

[18]Samuel Eliot Morison, *The Oxford History of the American People* (New York: Oxford University Press, 1965), p. 304.

[19]Quoted in Williams, Current, and Freidel, *A History of the United States to 1877,* p. 181.

[20]For the former view, see Michael Lienesch, "The Constitutional Tradition: History, Political Action, and Progress in American Political Thought, 1787–1793," in *The Journal of Politics,* 42 (1980): 10. For the latter view, see Garry Wills, *Inventing America: Jefferson's Declaration of Independence* (New York: Vintage Books, 1978), pp. 352–53.

[21]Charles A. Beard, *An Economic Interpretation of the Constitution of the United States* (New York: The Free Press), 1965.

[22]Calvin C. Jillson, "Constitution-Making Alignment in the Federal Convention of 1787," in *American Political Science Review,* 75, no. 3 (September 1981): 598–612.

[23]The discussion of the Constitutional Convention is based in part on Max Farrand, *The Framing of the Constitution of the United States* (New Haven: Yale University Press, 1930); James Madison *Notes of Debates in the Federal Convention of 1787* (Athens, Ohio: Ohio University Press, 1976); and for a readable spirited story, see Christopher Collier and James Lincoln Collier, *Decision in Philadelphia,* (New York: Ballantine Books, 1986).

[24]Maury Maverick as quoted in Michael Kammen, *A Machine that Would Go of Itself,* (New York: Vintage Books, 1987), p. 397.

★

CHAPTER 2

The Constitution: The Rules of the Game

The Constitution sometimes plays strange roles in American politics. In his 1975 reelection campaign for the Virginia state senate, Joseph Gartlan was attacked for not supporting a constitutional amendment to end the busing of school children for racial integration. The amendment would have added to the Constitution a ban on busing students from one school district to another. White voters in northern Virginia were dead set against having their children bused to the predominantly black public schools of Washington, D.C. The issue was hurting Gartlan badly, particularly in normally Democratic working-class areas.

On the Friday before the election, Gartlan released a campaign flyer in these areas that turned the issue around. Beneath a picture of the Washington monument with a school bus aimed at it, the brochure's text struck at Gartlan's Republican opponent. "John Watkins believes it is constitutional to bus your children into Washington."

The attack was effective and curiously accurate. Watkins had argued that without such an amendment the courts could not prevent busing. This implied that busing was constitutional. In this bit of constitutional jujitsu the force of the opponent's attack was directed back toward him. The Constitution was being used, though not, perhaps, in the way some Virginians of two centuries before might have intended.[1]

Listening to those debating the issues of the day, one could reasonably conclude that the Constitution must say something about busing, abortion, and school prayer. However, when looking at the surprisingly short document, none of these things can be found. Instead there are amendments forbidding the government to deny "equal protection of the laws," to deprive persons of life, liberty, or property without "due process of law," or to make laws allowing "an establishment of religion."

The framers of the Constitution knew what they were doing. They realized that any document that was to be followed by future generations couldn't possibly anticipate all the issues or problems that would arise. Instead the framers stated the broad principles and procedures that were to be followed, expecting that the details would be filled in through the interpretations of later ages.

This flexibility has made the Constitution a "living thing." Vague phrases such as "general welfare," "necessary and proper," "unreasonable searches and seizures," and "cruel and unusual punishments" have been differently applied from age to age. These *"great generalities of the Constitution"* have had their content and significance altered by different generations, as the phrases have

Court-ordered busing has long been a topic for constitutional debate. Here, school buses head to South Boston High School under heavy police guard.

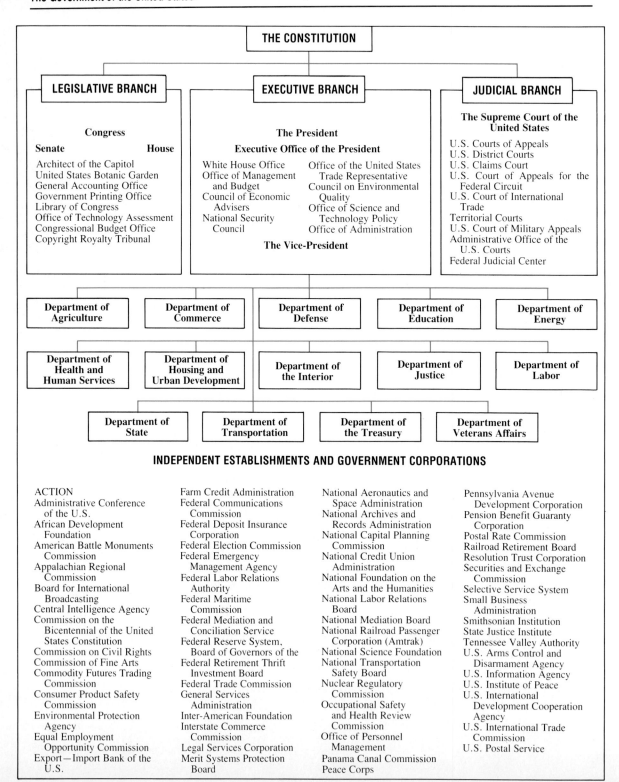

THE CONSTITUTION

LEGISLATIVE BRANCH

Congress

Senate   House

Architect of the Capitol
United States Botanic Garden
General Accounting Office
Government Printing Office
Library of Congress
Office of Technology Assessment
Congressional Budget Office
Copyright Royalty Tribunal

EXECUTIVE BRANCH

The President

Executive Office of the President

White House Office
Office of Management
    and Budget
Council of Economic
    Advisers
National Security
    Council

Office of the United States
    Trade Representative
Council on Environmental
    Quality
Office of Science and
    Technology Policy
Office of Administration

The Vice-President

JUDICIAL BRANCH

**The Supreme Court of the
United States**

U.S. Courts of Appeals
U.S. District Courts
U.S. Claims Court
U.S. Court of Appeals for the
    Federal Circuit
U.S. Court of International
    Trade
Territorial Courts
U.S. Court of Military Appeals
Administrative Office of the
    U.S. Courts
Federal Judicial Center

**Department of
Agriculture**

**Department of
Commerce**

**Department of
Defense**

**Department of
Education**

**Department of
Energy**

**Department of
Health and
Human Services**

**Department of
Housing and
Urban Development**

**Department of
the Interior**

**Department of
Justice**

**Department of
Labor**

**Department of
State**

**Department of
Transportation**

**Department of
the Treasury**

**Department of
Veterans Affairs**

INDEPENDENT ESTABLISHMENTS AND GOVERNMENT CORPORATIONS

ACTION
Administrative Conference
    of the U.S.
African Development
    Foundation
American Battle Monuments
    Commission
Appalachian Regional
    Commission
Board for International
    Broadcasting
Central Intelligence Agency
Commission on the
    Bicentennial of the United
    States Constitution
Commission on Civil Rights
Commission of Fine Arts
Commodity Futures Trading
    Commission
Consumer Product Safety
    Commission
Environmental Protection
    Agency
Equal Employment
    Opportunity Commission
Export—Import Bank of the
    U.S.

Farm Credit Administration
Federal Communications
    Commission
Federal Deposit Insurance
    Corporation
Federal Election Commission
Federal Emergency
    Management Agency
Federal Labor Relations
    Authority
Federal Maritime
    Commission
Federal Mediation and
    Conciliation Service
Federal Reserve System,
    Board of Governors of the
Federal Retirement Thrift
    Investment Board
Federal Trade Commission
General Services
    Administration
Inter-American Foundation
Interstate Commerce
    Commission
Legal Services Corporation
Merit Systems Protection
    Board

National Aeronautics and
    Space Administration
National Archives and
    Records Administration
National Capital Planning
    Commission
National Credit Union
    Administration
National Foundation on the
    Arts and the Humanities
National Labor Relations
    Board
National Mediation Board
National Railroad Passenger
    Corporation (Amtrak)
National Science Foundation
National Transportation
    Safety Board
Nuclear Regulatory
    Commission
Occupational Safety
    and Health Review
    Commission
Office of Personnel
    Management
Panama Canal Commission
Peace Corps

Pennsylvania Avenue
    Development Corporation
Pension Benefit Guaranty
    Corporation
Postal Rate Commission
Railroad Retirement Board
Resolution Trust Corporation
Securities and Exchange
    Commission
Selective Service System
Small Business
    Administration
Smithsonian Institution
State Justice Institute
Tennessee Valley Authority
U.S. Arms Control and
    Disarmament Agency
U.S. Information Agency
U.S. Institute of Peace
U.S. International
    Development Cooperation
    Agency
U.S. International Trade
    Commission
U.S. Postal Service

been used, or ignored, by government and groups arguing for favored policies.[2]

The Constitution is ambiguous. This has allowed for changes in the interpretation of its provisions, especially by the Supreme Court. It has also allowed for a government that has effectively adapted to the varied challenges of different times. Throughout, the Constitution has stood as a symbol of legitimacy for the government under it and a reminder of the values this government was created to pursue.

The Constitution's basic provisions remain the supreme law of the land. Its seven articles and twenty-six amendments have established a generally free, representative, and limited government. How the Constitution established and limited a federal government, what its major principles are and how they shape the branches of government, and how the Constitution is changed and why it has survived are the central questions of this chapter.

THE CONSTITUTIONAL SYSTEM

A written constitution is America's unique contribution to the art of governing. The United States Constitution is the oldest written constitution still being followed today. Despite the tremendous changes that have occurred since the Constitution was first written, the framework of government set down in 1789 has remained essentially the same.

In establishing a system of government, the United States Constitution did three things.

- First, *the Constitution established the structure of government.* It set up three branches of government within a federal system of coexisting central and state authorities. Thus, it gave the country a political framework that has existed to the present.
- Second, *the Constitution distributed certain powers* to this government. Article I gave legislative powers, such as the power to raise and spend money, to Congress. Article II gave executive powers to the president, including command over the armed forces and wide authority over foreign policy. Article III gave judicial power, the right to judge disputes arising under the Constitution, to the United States Supreme Court.
- Third, *the Constitution restrained the government* in exercising these powers. Government was limited by the powers reserved for the states and by the Bill of Rights, for example. This was done so that certain individual rights could be preserved.

The Constitution, then, both *grants* and *limits* the power of government. By its very nature the document *constitutes* the government, not vice versa, and stands above it as the link between the people and their government. Officials of the government derive their power from the Constitution. For officials to substitute their judgment for that of the "people of the United States" as reflected in the Constitution is simply not appropriate. Through a fairly complex process of granting and limiting power, the Constitution sought to ensure that official behavior would remain both "necessary and proper."[3]

★Madison on Government

" . . . If men were angels, no government would be necessary. If angels were to govern men, neither external or internal controls on government would be necessary. In framing a government, which is to be administered by men over men, the great difficulty lies in this: You must first enable the government to control the governed; and in the next place, oblige it to control itself."

—James Madison, *The Federalist Papers* (no. 51).

A closer look at four major constitutional principles illustrates the point. These principles are *separation of powers and checks and balances, federalism, limited government,* and *judicial review.*

MAJOR CONSTITUTIONAL PRINCIPLES

Separation of Powers and Checks and Balances

The 1989 Senate rejection of John Tower to be Secretary of Defense showed one branch checking another, and senators scoring political points in the process. The confirmation hearings before the Senate Armed Services Committee gave senators the opportunity to do several things at once, mostly behind the scenes. With attention focusing on Mr. Tower's drinking and womanizing, the Senate tried to reflect voters' concerns with ethical standards in officials. With the Pentagon weapons procurement scandal still fresh, senators did not want to be accused of any lack of vigilance. Questions were also used to warn the nominee of areas individual senators would follow in the future, such as the promotion of women in the services and keeping certain bases open. These provided the grist for press releases from senators' offices that would please folks back home. Checks and balances worked in political ways.[4]

The principles of separation of powers and checks and balances were demonstrated in the 1989 Senate rejection of John Tower to be Secretary of Defense (shown here testifying before the Senate Armed Services Committee).

The first major constitutional principle actually consists of two—separation of powers, and checks and balances. But the two principles can't be understood apart from each other, and they operate together.

Separation of powers is the principle that the powers of government should be separated and put in the care of different parts of government. Although never exactly stated in the Constitution, this principle had a long history in political philosophy and was in practice in the governments of the colonies. The writers of the Constitution divided the federal government into three branches to carry out what they saw as the three major functions of government. The legislative function—passing the laws—was given to Congress; the executive function—carrying out or executing the laws—was given to the president; and the judicial function—interpreting the laws—was given to the Supreme Court.

Though nice and neat, this principle is probably also unworkable. The purpose of the separation of powers was to allow ambition to counter ambition, to prevent any one authority from monopolizing power. Yet simply dividing the powers of government into these three branches would probably make the legislature supreme, as it did in the colonies. As the starter of the governmental process, the legislature could determine how, or even if, the other branches played their roles. Something else was needed to curb legislative power. That something was checks and balances.

Checks and balances create a *mixture* of powers that permits the three branches of government to limit one another. A *check* is a control one branch has over another's functions, creating a *balance* of power. This principle gives each branch a constitutional means for guarding its functions from interference by another branch. The principle of checks and balances mixed together the legislative, executive, and judicial powers, giving some legislative powers to the executive branch, some executive powers to the legislative branch, and so on, to keep any branch from dominating another.

There are a number of examples of checks and balances in the Constitution. The presidential veto gives the chief executive a primarily legislative power to prevent bills he dislikes from being passed into law by Congress. Congress can check this power by its right to override the veto by a two-thirds vote. The Senate is given an executive power in its role of confirming presidential nominations for major executive and judicial posts. Further, Congress can refuse to appropriate funds for any executive agency, thereby preventing the agency from carrying out the laws.

But the system of separation of powers and checks and balances is even more elaborate. *The way each branch of government is set up and chosen also checks and balances its power.* Their varied procedures for selection and tenure, as well as their duties, were designed to give government officials different interests to defend, varied bases of support, and protection from too much interference by other officials.

The Congress

The Constitutional Convention devoted most of its time to Article I. This article established the Congress and its powers. Not only did the framers separate the executive, legislative, and judical powers, they also divided the legislative powers by making Congress **bicameral.** This means there are two equal houses. No bill can become law unless it is passed by both.

The role of Congress is, of course, primarily legislative. But Congress also "checks and balances" the power of both the judicial and executive branches. Congress can decide how many Supreme Court justices there are and what kind of "inferior" federal courts are established. It determines the budgets for the courts and the salaries of the judges. The Senate must approve judicial appointees before they can take office.

Congressional laws established most of the present agencies of the executive branch, and Congress provides their budgets. This power

FIGURE 2★2
The Different Bases of Support for Separation of Powers: The Original Plan

This model had been substantially democratized. The Seventeenth Amendment (1913) made senators directly elected by popular majorities. Today, the electoral college has become largely a rubber stamp, voting the way the popular majority in each state votes.

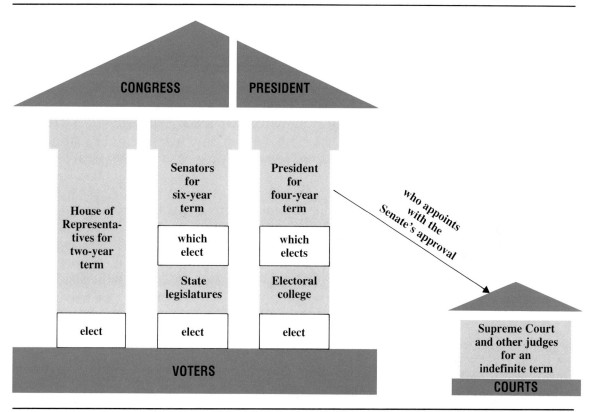

to oversee the executive departments—how the laws are carried out and how the money is spent—is another important check in the system. The principal executive officers cannot be appointed by the president without the consent of the Senate, nor can the president enter into a treaty with a foreign government without ratification by a two-thirds vote in the Senate.

Another way in which Congress is able to check the power of the executive and judicial branches is through **impeachment.** What if an official of the government commits treason, bribery, or "other high crimes and misdemeanors"? Such an official can be impeached (formally accused) by a majority vote in the House of Representatives and tried in the Senate. If two-thirds of the senators present and voting vote to convict, the official is removed from office. When a president is being tried in the Senate, the chief justice of the Supreme

Court presides. Only one president, Andrew Johnson, has ever been tried on impeachment charges, and the vote fell one short of conviction. The House Judiciary Committee in 1974 recommended that Richard M. Nixon be impeached because of his role in the Watergate burglary of the offices of the Democratic National Committee and the cover-up that followed. Nixon resigned the presidency before the House could vote on impeachment.

The House of Representatives. The House of Representatives is sometimes called the lower house of Congress, and the Senate is sometimes called the upper house. Since House members and senators have equal powers, House members object to these phrases. To ensure that the House of Representatives could represent the popular will, the framers limited the term of office to two years. The idea was that members had to frequently go back to the people for approval. The entire membership of the House is up for election every two years.

Any measure having to do with taxes must start in the House. All other bills begin in either house. This provision allowed the house representing the popular will to decide first about taxes and appropriation bills, which deal with spending. But a bill that goes to the Senate after being passed by the House may then be amended in the Senate.

The Senate. The framers of the Constitution wanted to insulate the Senate from control by a popular majority. Thus, the Constitution guarantees every state two senators, regardless of the state's population. The present Senate, then, has only 100 members. All senators are elected for six-year terms, and only one-third of the Senate is elected each two years.

The framers thought senators would be drawn from the educated, wealthy classes. Senators, they felt, should not have to test the political winds on each issue but could vote according to their own judgment. To further insulate senators, the Constitution required them to be selected by state legislatures. This changed in 1913, when the passage of the Seventeenth Amendment required direct popular elections of senators.

The framers expected that the House would be more "liberal" and the Senate more "conservative" in dealing with property, taxes, and social issues. But that has not always proved true. The liberal-conservative pendulum has swung back and forth between the two houses.

In fact the importance of **incumbency** has largely undercut the expectations of the framers. With over 98 percent of those incumbents who choose to run in the House reelected, the House of Representatives is perhaps the least changing of the three branches. Sen-

Richard Nixon performs the last acts of his devastated presidency as he bids farewell to his cabinet, aides, and staff in 1974. Nixon resigned the presidency before the House Judiciary Committee could vote on his impeachment due to his involvement in the Watergate scandal. Nixon said only a man in the deepest valley can know "how magnificent it is to be on the highest mountain."

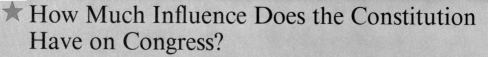

★ How Much Influence Does the Constitution Have on Congress?

In theory, the Constitution is not just for judges. Members of Congress take an oath to "bear true faith and allegiance" to the Constitution. When considering legislation, members—especially the 64 senators and 193 House members who are lawyers—should worry about the measure's constitutionality. They should but they usually don't.

Closer to practice is former Illinois congressman, now judge, Abner Mikva's remark: "The fastest way to empty out the chamber is to get up and say, 'I'd like to talk about the constitutionality of this bill.' Members of Congress believe that's what courts are for." When the Constitution is mentioned in debates it's to bolster other arguments, to serve other conclusions. As another congressman said: "If we happen to be opposed to something, we'll look for respectable reasons to oppose it. The Constitution is a reason. That's politics."

SOURCE: *The New York Times*, June 3, 1988, p. B6.

ators, because they are usually more visible public figures, are more likely to attract well-financed opponents. Consequently, Senate incumbents' chances of reelection are much lower than incumbents in the House.

The Senate has two exclusive powers. Only the Senate has the power of **ratification,** the authority to approve or reject treaties, and the power of **confirmation,** the duty to approve or reject presidential appointees. Including the John Tower vote refusing to confirm him as Secretary of Defense, only nine cabinet nominees have been rejected by the Senate in 200 years.

The President

Just as they did with the Senate, the framers of the Constitution wanted to protect the presidency from popular control. For this reason, they established the **electoral college** to select the president. Each state chooses as many electors as it has senators and representatives combined. These popularly elected electors meet in the states and cast their votes for president and vice-president, who run as a team. Thus, in a presidential election, voters are really voting for electors who are pledged to a specific president/vice-president slate.

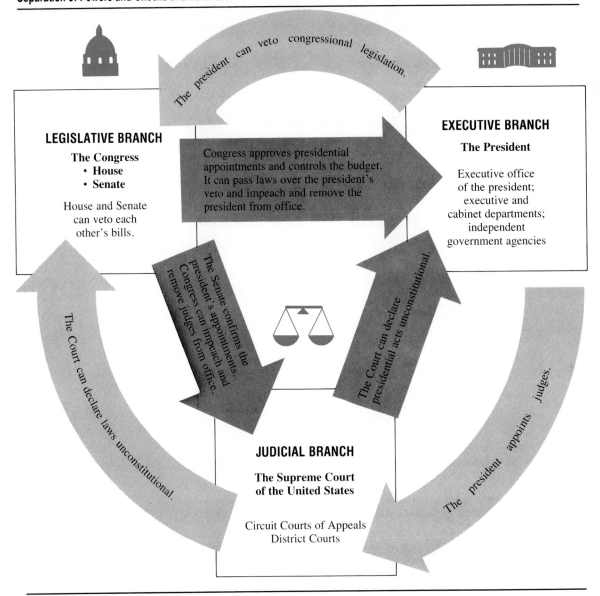

LEGISLATIVE BRANCH

The Congress
- **House**
- **Senate**

House and Senate can veto each other's bills.

The president can veto congressional legislation.

Congress approves presidential appointments and controls the budget. It can pass laws over the president's veto and impeach and remove the president from office.

EXECUTIVE BRANCH

The President

Executive office of the president; executive and cabinet departments; independent government agencies

The Senate confirms the president's appointments. Congress can impeach and remove judges from office.

The Court can declare presidential acts unconstitutional.

The Court can declare laws unconstitutional.

JUDICIAL BRANCH

The Supreme Court of the United States

Circuit Courts of Appeals
District Courts

The president appoints judges.

Until the Twelfth Amendment was adopted in 1804, the presidential candidate receiving a majority of electoral votes became president, and the candidate receiving the next highest number of votes became vice-president. The amendment was passed to prevent a president from being saddled with an opposing presidential candidate as vice-president. If no candidate for president receives a majority of electoral votes, the election is decided from a list of the three highest candidates by a majority vote in the House of Representatives, each state casting only one block vote. This has occurred only twice, in the 1800 election of Thomas Jefferson and in 1824, when John Quincy Adams was elected.

The Constitution does not mention political parties. The framers expected each state to select electors from the "better element" who would then vote without regard for political parties. The candidates would do no campaigning, just like present-day candidates for grade-school class offices. At the time, no one doubted that George Washington would be the first president. But after his two terms, the electoral college system never worked the same way again. Factions developed, and then parties. Today, a president is a party leader, campaigning vigorously for the office as the party's nominee. Electors now cast their electoral votes automatically for the presidential candidate who receives the highest number of popular votes in the state's general election.

The electoral college is like a constitutional appendix—while not functioning as intended, it has the potential to harm the system. The most serious criticism of the electoral college is that it could allow a candidate without the highest number of popular votes to become president through a majority vote in the electoral college. However, this "runner-up candidate" problem has not occurred since 1888, when Benjamin Harrision defeated Grover Cleveland, who had the most popular votes. Many feel that a president without a popular majority chosen by the electoral college would not be considered "legitimate," and that presidential leadership would be dangerously weakened. Consequently, reformers frequently propose that the electoral college be abolished and replaced with direct popular election.

But the electoral college has its supporters. Some of them claim that our system has remained stable over the years because we have not replaced our constitutional institutions, including the electoral college. Others point to the advantages the college gives to the large states with their blocs of electors. Chapter 8 will go into this in more detail.

The president was given the authority to "check and balance" legislative power by using the veto and by calling special sessions of Congress. The president is also required by the Constitution to give Congress "information concerning the State of the Union, and recommend to their Consideration such Measures as he shall judge necessary and expedient. . . ." This last function now has been formalized into an annual message which is followed by numerous other presidential recommendations on the federal budget and new legislation. Particularly since the administration of Franklin Roosevelt, the president has assumed a strong role as chief legislator.

The president also exercises judicial power by appointing (with the advice and consent of the Senate) the members of the Supreme Court and the other federal courts. This power can markedly affect judicial decisions. For example, justices added to the Court under President Reagan have restricted liberal civil-rights and criminal-rights rulings of the Supreme Court.

The Judiciary

Neither the members of the Supreme Court nor the judges of the federal district courts and the circuit courts of appeal are elected. They are appointed and serve for life. The federal judiciary is, therefore, the branch of our government that is least subject to direct popular control.

The Constitution did not make it clear who would determine whether actions by the federal government were consistent with the Constitution. All citizens and all states, according to the supremacy clause, are required to obey the laws passed by Congress, but only if these laws do not violate the U.S. Constitution. But who is to decide?

As will be shown, the Supreme Court used its own authority to declare it had the power of judicial review. Through its rulings in cases brought before the court, the federal judiciary can check the power of other branches of the government. This happens all the time. In early 1989, for example, a federal judge accused the Department of Interior in the executive branch of becoming a "bureaucracy run amok." The Department had ordered wide-ranging and random drug testing for one quarter of all its employees. The district court declared this violated the civil liberties of the employees and ordered it halted.[5] Of course, the executive branch may resent the Court's independence and exercise checks through methods not foreseen by the Constitution. Throughout the postwar period the FBI, under J. Edgar Hoover, used informants and wiretaps to keep posted on the activities of the Supreme Court and liberal justices the Bureau considered insufficiently anticommunist.[6]

The Supreme Court can, in effect, make important political decisions without the direct participation of the people of the country. However, the people participate indirectly through elections and confirmation hearings. In the 1980 presidential campaign, Ronald Reagan pledged to appoint the first woman member of the Supreme Court, a promise made good in 1981 with the appointment of Sandra

Day O'Connor. The 1987 Senate rejection of Robert Bork's nomination to the Court gave various groups the chance to bring public opinion to bear on the makeup and direction of the Court (see the case study in Chapter 11).

Harmony or Frustration?

The institutions that result from this separating and mixing of powers are bodies that in practice share the overall power of government. Each needs the others to make the government work, yet each has an interest in checking and balancing the powers of the others. Nobody claimed that this elaborate scheme of separation of powers and checks and balances was designed as the most efficient form of government. Rather, it was established "to control the abuses of government"—to oblige the government to control itself. It set up a structure that historian Richard Hofstadter has called a "harmonious system of mutual frustration."

Federalism

Which level of government, the federal or the state and local, bears major responsibility for providing civilian (nondefense) services in the United States? The answer is state and local, and by a considerable margin. In fact, when it comes to civilian services, state and local governments together spend more than two and one-half times as much as the federal government. Education, roads, welfare, public health, hospitals, police, sanitation are primarily state and local responsibilities, and their cost falls mainly on state and local sources of revenue.[7]

A second principle, **federalism,** calls for political authority to be distributed between a central government and the government of the states. Both the federal and state governments may act directly on the people, and each has some exclusive powers. Federalism, like separation of powers, spreads out political authority to prevent power from being concentrated in any one group.

Actually, the men who wrote the Constitution had little choice. The loose confederation of states hadn't worked well in their eyes, and centralizing all governmental powers would have been unacceptable to the major governments of the day, those of the states. Federalism, then, was more than just a reasonable principle for governing a large country divided by regional differences and slow communications. It was also the only politically realistic way to get the states to ratify the Constitution.

As we will see in the next chapter, American federalism has always involved two somewhat contradictory ideas. The first, expressed in Article VI, is that *the Constitution and the laws of the central government are supreme.* This was needed to establish an effective government, able to pass laws and rule directly over all the people. The second principle ensures the independence of the state governments: *the Tenth Amendment reserved to the states or the people all powers not delegated to the central government.* These substantial **reserved powers** include control of local and city governments, regulation of business within a state, supervision of education, and exercise of the general "police power" over the safety of the people (see Figure 2.4).

The conflict between the two principles—**national supremacy** and **states' rights**—climaxed in the Civil War, which established the predominance of the national government. That is not to say that the question was settled once and for all—even today, in issues such as school busing and taxes, state governments often clash with the federal government. But the conflict shouldn't be overstated. Even though the Constitution divided the powers of government by federalism, it also clearly set up the basis for national union under the authority of a central government.

Limited Government

The yearbook of Brunswick High School in Brunswick, Maine, was the unlikely site of a fight over free speech. Graduating seniors get to choose a brief quotation to run along with their yearbook picture. One senior had been thinking long and hard about capital punishment. Rather than write "a standard butterfly quote," she chose the following from a *Time* magazine story on capital punishment: "The executioner will pull this lever four times. Each time 2,000 volts will course through your body, making your eyeballs first bulge, then burst, and then boiling your brains. . . ."

While not exactly a joyful farewell to her high school years, she intended to "provoke some of my classmates to think a little more deeply. . . ." The reaction the seventeen-year-old got was more than she could have expected. The students running the yearbook vetoed it as "bad taste," the school principal called it "disruptive," and the school board turned thumbs down on printing it. With the help of the Maine Civil Liberties Union, however, the stubborn student took the school board and the principal to court. The federal judge ruled in favor of the student. He referred to the First Amendment as preventing the government (in this case, the school board) from interfering with people's ability to voice their ideas, no matter how unpopular.[8]

FIGURE 2★4
Federalism

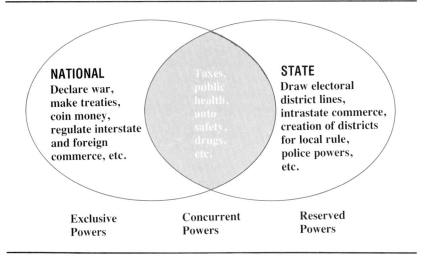

NATIONAL
Declare war,
make treaties,
coin money,
regulate interstate
and foreign
commerce, etc.

Taxes,
public
health,
auto
safety,
drugs,
etc.

STATE
Draw electoral
district lines,
intrastate commerce,
creation of districts
for local rule,
police powers,
etc.

Exclusive   Concurrent   Reserved
Powers   Powers   Powers

SOURCE: Reprinted with permission of Macmillan Publishing Company from *An Introduction to American Government,* 2/e by Erwin L. Levine & Elmer E. Cornwell, Jr. Copyright © 1972 by Macmillan Publishing Company.

The third principle, **limited government,** means that the powers of government are limited by the rights and liberties of the governed. This principle is basic to the very idea of constitutional government: the people give the government listed powers and duties through a constitution, while reserving the rest to themselves. This political compact requires that government actions rest on the rule of law approved, however indirectly, by the consent of the governed. Furthermore, the Constitution sets up procedures, such as separation of powers and federalism, to ensure that the government remains limited to its proper duties and powers. For example, the president may not exercise powers given by the Constitution exclusively to Congress.

However, for this principle to be enforced requires the political will to act on it. During the Vietnam War, many thought that the president had trespassed on congressional powers by waging a war not declared by Congress. Congress, while often taking stands against the war, continued to appropriate funds for the armed services and refused to directly confront the president. The Supreme Court, traditionally reluctant to judge the chief executive's conduct of foreign policy, refused to hear cases questioning his authority. Of course, popular opposition eventually helped lead to the U.S. withdrawal.

The Constitution's exclusive authority to Congress to declare war remained in the document, but whether it was a political fact of life remained in doubt.[9]

Limited government guarantees citizens their rights against the government as well as access to the government. Civil liberties and rights guarantee the openness and competitiveness of the political process. This means not only the right to vote, but also the freedom to dissent, demonstrate, and organize to produce alternatives in order to make the right to vote meaningful. Civil liberties also protect the citizen from arbitrary governmental power. Civil liberties include a citizen's right to have a fair and speedy trial, to have legal defense, and to be judged by an impartial jury. Further, government cannot take life, liberty or property without due process of law, or interfere with a citizen's right to practice religion, or invade his or her privacy. In short, the people who make the laws are also subject to them (see Chapter 4).

Judicial Review

"Judiciary is truly the only defensive armor of the Federal Government, or rather for the Constitution and laws of the United States. Strip it of that armor and the door is wide open for nullification, anarchy, and convulsion."[10]

—President James Madison

"John Marshall has rendered his decision; now let him enforce it!"

—President Andrew Jackson, in bitter disagreement with a Supreme Court decision

An important means of keeping government limited and of maintaining civil rights and liberties is the power of judicial review. **Judicial review,** the last constitutional principle, is the judicial branch's authority to decide on the constitutionality of the acts of the various parts of the government (state, local, and federal).

Although judicial review has become an accepted constitutional practice, it is not actually mentioned in the document. There was some debate in the first years under the Constitution over whether the Court had the power merely to give nonbinding opinions, or whether it had supremacy over acts of the government. Most people at the time agreed that the Court did have the power to overturn unconstitutional acts of the state governments. But opinion was divided over whether this power extended to the acts of the federal government. In 1803, in the landmark case of *Marbury v. Madison,* the Supreme Court actually struck down an act of Congress. Since then, this power has become a firmly entrenched principle of the Constitution.

In *Marbury*, Chief Justice John Marshall ruled that the Court could not force President Jefferson to make an appointment because the legislation under which the case was brought gave the Court jurisdiction not mentioned in the Constitution. He based this power of judicial review on Sections 1 and 2 of Article III of the Constitution. Section 1 reads that the "judicial power of the United States, shall be vested in one Supreme Court and in such inferior Courts as the Congress may from time to time establish." Section 2 states that this "judicial power" extends to all cases "arising under this Constitution, the Laws of the United States, and Treaties. . . ." Marshall took these provisions to mean that the Supreme Court has the final say on what is, and what is not, constitutional. The power of judicial review has been recognized ever since, leading some lawyers to conclude that "the Constitution means what the Supreme Court says it does." Of course the Court must depend on the rest of the government to carry out its rulings, as President Andrew Jackson noted. As will be seen in Chapter 15, *the Court's power of judicial review sails forth in a sea of politics.*

Chief Justice John Marshall wrote several landmark decisions affecting American federalism.

Judicial review has put the Court in the position of watchdog over the central government's actions and has made it the guardian of federalism. Reviewing the acts of state and local governments has in fact been the Court's most important use of judicial review. Though relatively few federal laws have been struck down by the Court, hundreds of state and local laws have been held to violate the Constitution. As Justice Oliver Wendell Holmes said more than fifty years ago, "The United States would not come to an end if we lost our power to declare an act of Congress void. I do think the Union would be imperiled if we could not make that declaration as to the laws of several states."

HOW IS THE CONSTITUTION CHANGED?

To say that the Constitution has lasted 200 years is not to say it is the same document that was adopted in 1789. The Constitution has changed vastly; in practical ways, it bears little resemblance to the original. Most framers would scarcely recognize the political processes that operate today under their Constitution. Changes in the Constitution have been made by four major methods: *formal amendments, judicial interpretation, legislation,* and *custom.*

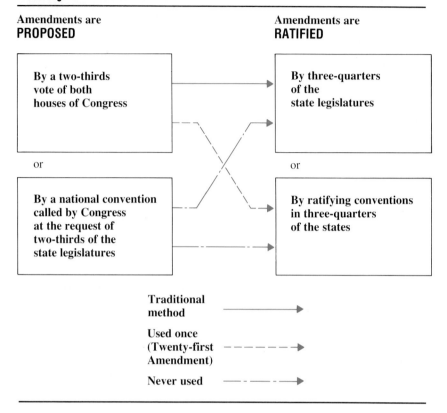

Amendments are
PROPOSED

Amendments are
RATIFIED

By a two-thirds vote of both houses of Congress

By three-quarters of the state legislatures

or

or

By a national convention called by Congress at the request of two-thirds of the state legislatures

By ratifying conventions in three-quarters of the states

Traditional method ———————▶

Used once (Twenty-first Amendment) – – – – – ▶

Never used — – — – — ▶

Amendments

Although the amendment process is the first way we usually think of for changing the Constitution, it is actually the least common and most difficult method. Only twenty-six amendments—including the first ten amendments (the Bill of Rights), which can practically be considered part of the original document—have been adopted. (A twenty-seventh, the Equal Rights Amendment, and a twenty-eighth, the Washington, D.C. Voting Rights Amendment, were proposed by Congress but not ratified.) Though the Constitution's framers recognized the need for change in any such document, no matter how farsighted, they wanted to protect it from temporary popular pressure. Hence, they required unusually large majorities for adopting amendments.

Article V of the Constitution provides a number of methods for adopting amendments (see Figure 2.5). Amendments may be proposed by a two-thirds vote of each house of Congress or (if requested by two-thirds of the state legislatures) by a national convention called by Congress. They must be ratified by conventions in three-fourths of the states, or by three-fourths of the state legislatures (the choice is up to Congress).

Only the Twenty-first Amendment, repealing Prohibition in 1933, was ratified by state conventions. The idea behind this one use of state conventions was that the state legislatures were still full of the same representatives who had passed Prohibition in the first place, and conventions seemed likely to be the fastest way to change it. All other amendments were submitted to the state legislatures for approval. These methods allow the Constitution to be changed without a direct vote by citizens.

The national convention has never been used; all amendments have been proposed by Congress. Recently, thirty-two states of the needed thirty-four had passed resolutions calling for a constitutional convention to draft a new amendment requiring a balanced budget. No other states signed up and the effort seemed to lose its momentum by 1989. (The enthusiasm for an amendment to prevent the burning of the American flag may also decrease as it moves through the obstacle course of adoption.) A major reason that the national convention method has never been used to propose amendments is Congress's jealousy toward another body trespassing on its powers. Some worry over how many other changes might be proposed by such a convention. After all, the Constitution was written by an earlier runaway convention set up only to amend the Articles of Confederation.

House Republicans stand ready to douse any flag burning outside the Supreme Court building. This followed the Supreme Court ruling in July 1989 that stated burning the American flag is protected by the Constitution. The controversial Court ruling started a move for a constitutional amendment banning flag burning.

Judicial Interpretation

If the amendment process is the least-used method of changing the Constitution, interpretations by the Supreme Court are probably the most common. Practically every part of the Constitution has been before the Supreme Court at some time or another. The Court has shaped and reshaped the document. Twentieth-century Court decisions have allowed Congress great scope in regulating the economy, prohibiting legal segregation of races, allowing local communities to define obscenity, and establishing "one man, one vote" as a principle governing election to the House of Representatives. The Court has also given practical meaning to general constitutional phrases such as "necessary and proper" (Article I, Section 8), "due process of law" (Amendments 5 and 14), and "unreasonable searches and seizures" (Amendment 4). No wonder the Supreme Court is sometimes called "a permanent constitutional convention."

Legislation

Although legislation is passed under the Constitution and does not change the basic document, Congress has been responsible for filling in most of the framework of government outlined by the Constitution. Congress has established all the federal courts below the Supreme Court. It has determined the size of the House of Representatives as well as the Supreme Court. The cabinet and most of the boards and commissions in the executive branch have been created by congressional legislation. And most of the regulations and services we now take for granted, such as social security, have come from measures passed by Congress.

Custom

Custom is the most imprecise way in which the Constitution has changed, yet one of the most widespread. Many practices that have been accepted as constitutional are not actually mentioned in the document. The growth of political parties and the influence of party leadership in the government, the presidential nominating conventions, the breakdown of the electoral college, and the committee system in Congress are just a few customary practices not foreseen by the Constitution.

Custom has also changed some practices that seem to have been clearly intended by the framers. The Eighth Amendment, forbidding "excessive bail," has not prevented courts from setting bail for serious offenses that is too high for the accused to raise. Although Congress has the right to declare war (Article II, Section 8), presidents have entered conflicts that looked very much like wars (Korea, Vietnam) without such a declaration. Customs also have been broken and reestablished by law. The custom that a president serves only two terms was created by Washington and cemented by Jefferson. Broken with much debate by Franklin D. Roosevelt in 1940, the custom was made law in the Twenty-second Amendment, adopted in 1951. Despite a half-hearted effort to repeal the law in order to allow Ronald Reagan to run for a third term, it remains an amendment.

WHY HAS THE CONSTITUTION SURVIVED?

All the ways in which the Constitution has been changed to meet different needs at different times do not completely explain why it has lasted for over 200 years. Indeed, many of the framers saw the Constitution as an experiment not likely to survive more than a generation. Various explanations have been put forth for why the Constitution has endured.

One of the chief reasons for the Constitution's durability has been its ability to adapt to the times. Civil rights legislation in the 1960s enforced the protection of constitutional rights. Shown here, club-swinging Alabama state troopers move in on civil rights marchers to disperse them in Selma, Alabama on March 7, 1965.

The major reason it has lasted probably lies not in the Constitution itself, but in *the stability of American society*. Despite disturbances such as the Indian campaigns and massacres, labor strife, and foreign wars, only the Civil War ever seriously threatened the basic constitutional structure of the country. The violence of America's expansion and development has been contained within the same constitutional structure. Whatever social unrest or external enemies the country faced, none went so far as to threaten the constitutionally elected rulers with revolution or upheaval.

The Constitution itself has been adapted to the times. It has been made more democratic to include potentially disruptive groups, like immigrants, former slaves, women, and the poor, that were originally excluded from political participation. The Constitution's *emphasis on procedures* has served it well through the wars and depressions as well as the peace and prosperity of various ages.

Other explanations for the Constitution's durability focus on the document itself. One maintains that it is a work of genius, an original creation by a group of demigods. William Gladstone, a nineteenth-century British prime minister, described it as "the most wonderful work every struck off at a given time by the brain and purpose of man."

Another Englishman, James Bryce, more realistically points to the practices and writings on government the framers inherited from English political institutions. He wrote in his classic study of American government that

> *the American Constitution is no exception to the rule that everything which has the power to win the obedience and respect of men must have its roots deep in the past and that the more slowly every institution has grown, so much the more enduring it is likely to prove. There is little in the Constitution that is absolutely new. There is much that is as old as Magna Carta.*[11]

Incorporating centuries of political traditions as well as the framers' own experience, the Constitution set out the principles and framework of government in concise, well-written phrases.

The *shortness of the document* (only some 7000 words with all its amendments) has contributed to its durability. Although it sets out the basic principles and structures of a government, the Constitution leaves much only generally stated or not mentioned at all. In a word, the Constitution is *vague.* Many of the most enduring Constitutional phrases ("freedom of speech," "due process of law," "all laws which shall be necessary and proper," "privileges or immunities of citizens") leave considerable room for interpretation. Other principles, such as majority rule and individual liberties, sometimes may seem contradictory. It is left to the political players of each age to resolve the conflicts among groups claiming constitutional support. This flexibility has been one of the Constitution's major strengths in adapting to new political pressures and allowing people to reach compromises under competing principles.

WRAP-UP

The Constitution puts forth the fundamental rules of our government. Yet it is a living document, flexible enough to allow new interpretations to meet new challenges. The Constitution has been used to play an important oversight role. It has served to unify the nation, legitimize the government, and protect its citizens.

As it has developed, the Constitution has granted and limited governmental power through four major principles: separation of powers and checks and balances, federalism, limited government, and judicial review. Although these principles remain fundamental, the meaning of the document has been changed vastly by four methods: formal amendment, judicial interpretation, legislation, and custom.

These changes have helped the Constitution to endure. Equally important to its survival have been the English political traditions on which it was based, the stability of American society, and the ambiguity of the key phrases of the document.

Some might too quickly conclude that the flexibility of the document makes the Constitution meaningless, or that so many clearly "unconstitutional" violations of rights have occurred in American history as to make the value of the Constitution somewhat suspect. Perhaps.

All great historical documents, from the Bible on down, have been applied differently at different times. The Constitution is used as an influential symbol over the nation's political behavior. That a president violates the law, as determined by an independent judiciary, does make a difference in whether he stays in power, as President Nixon discovered after Watergate. That Congress can investigate secret foreign-policy dealings can stop arms being sold to our enemies, as Colonel Oliver North found out at the Iran-Contra congressional hearings. And that the press can publish government documents without prior restraint does place limits on the bureaucracy, as the Pentagon Papers detailing the planning for the Vietnam War showed.

Yet the constitutional principles permitting these actions must ultimately rest on existing political relationships. Congress, the courts, and the press must be willing and able to fulfill the functions granted them in the Constitution for those principles to operate. Without political power, Constitutional principles would be empty declarations.

Though rooted in the traditions of the past, the Constitution is supported by the politics of the present. It not only provides guidelines, but declares goals as well. It therefore remains unfinished, as must any constitution setting out to "secure the Blessings of Liberty to ourselves and our Posterity."

Key Terms

separation of powers (p. 37)
checks and balances (p. 38)
bicameral (p. 38)
impeachment (p. 39)
incumbency (p. 40)
ratification (p. 41)
confirmation (p. 41)

electoral college (p. 41)
federalism (p. 45)
reserved powers (p. 46)
national supremacy (p. 46)
states' rights (p. 46)
limited government (p. 47)
judicial review (p. 48)

Suggested Readings

Black, Eric, *Our Constitution: The Myth that Binds Us* (Boulder, Colorado: Westview Press, 1988).

Currie, David P., *The Constitution of the United States: A Primer for the People* (Chicago: The University of Chicago Press, 1988).

Dorsen, Norman, ed., *The Evolving Constitution* (Middletown, Conn.: Wesleyan University Press, 1987).

Friendly, Fred and Martha J. Elliot, *The Constitution: That Delicate Balance* (New York: Random House, 1984).

Endnotes

[1] Christopher Matthews, *Hardball—How Politics is Played—Told by One Who Knows the Game* (New York, Summit Books, 1988), pp. 126–27.

[2] Charles A. Beard, "The Living Constitution," *The Annals* (May 1936), vol. 185, pp. 30–31.

[3] Whether the Constitution meant to prevent or encourage democracy remains a debate. See Robert A. Goldwin and William A. Schambra, eds., *How Democratic Is the Constitution?* (Washington, D.C.: American Enterprise Institute, 1980).

[4] *The New York Times,* February 8, 1989.

[5] *The Washington Post,* February 3, 1989.

[6] *The New York Times,* August 21, 1988.

[7] J. Richard Aronson and John L. Hilley, *Financing State and Local Governments,* 4th ed. (Washington, D.C.: The Brookings Institution, 1986), p. 1.

[8] Nat Hentoff, "One Student's Yearbook Quotation," *The Washington Post,* April 6, 1984.

[9] See Robert A. Goldwin, William A. Schambra, and Art Kaufman, *Constitutional Controversies* (Washington, D.C.: American Enterprises Institute, 1987), Chapter 2, "War Powers and the Constitution."

[10] As quoted by Henry J. Abraham, *The Judiciary,* 3d ed. (Boston: Allyn & Bacon, 1973), p. 129.

[11] James Bryce, *The American Commonwealth* (New York: Macmillan and Company, 1910) Vol. 1, p. 28.

★
CHAPTER 3

Federalism: The States of the Union

The Glen Cove beach, where in 1982 Russian diplomats who lived in the area were banned due to anti-Soviet feelings by area residents.

It was 1985, and peace had finally broken out between Glen Cove, New York, and the Soviet Union. Three years earlier, over strong objections from the U.S. government, the city and its feisty mayor had begun to bar Soviet diplomats who lived in a local residential compound from using the city's public golf courses, tennis courts, and beaches. The city council and mayor generally disliked Communists and resented the fact that the Soviet-owned residential compound was exempt from local taxes.

City officials remained adamant in this policy until a suit was filed against them in federal court by the U.S. State Department (which feared similar actions against U.S. diplomats stationed in the Soviet Union). The mayor and city council finally backed down.

No sooner had the Glen Cove matter been settled than a similar incident occurred. Following the shooting down of a South Korean airliner by the Soviet Union, the governors of New York and New Jersey barred the Soviet Foreign Minister from landing in a Soviet plane at the principal airports in their states, even though he was coming to attend a United Nations session in New York City.

Governors acting against the wishes of the federal government in foreign affairs? A national government suing one of its own cities? A city government defying the orders of its own national government? It must have seemed incredible to Soviet officials that the U.S. national government could not automatically tell one of New York state's cities what to do. It had to go to court.[1]

This federal system protected by the Constitution has preserved separate state and local governments. While strongly rooted in American traditions of decentralized power, it has continued to change as the relations among the governments alter, as the Supreme Court reinterprets the Constitution, and as national challenges arise. Historically, as the chapter will show, power has flowed toward the federal government. But in modern federalism the states and localities remain strong and politically diverse. Recent national policies have shifted more of the "action" from Washington to the states. The country's major problems, however, are likely to remain national in scope and cost, and thus require a national response.

FEDERALISM AND THE CONSTITUTION

The federal system in the U.S. Constitution was a compromise between a unitary government and continued confederation. A *confederation*—such as the governments that existed in America before

★ Characteristics of Federalism

1. There is a constitutional division of governmental functions such that each level is autonomous in at least one sphere of action;
2. Each government is final and supreme in its constitutionally assigned area;
3. Both levels act directly on citizens (unlike a confederation, where only the regional units act directly on the citizens while the central government acts only on the regional governments);
4. Both levels derive their powers from the "sovereign" (i.e., the people or the Constitution), rather than from one another;
5. Therefore, neither can change the relationship unilaterally; and, finally,
6. The regional divisions (i.e., states) exist as of their own right.

SOURCE: Michael D. Reagan and John G. Sanzone, *The New Federalism*, 2nd ed. (New York: Oxford University Press, 1981), p. 9.

the Constitution was written—is a system in which the power to deal with individuals is primarily reserved to the state governments. These constituent governments form a central or national government with only the limited powers they give it. We are the inheritors of this early American compromise. Federalism, a system of shared state and federal power, was the price paid for forming the union (see the box on page 59).

The U.S. Constitution is not a compact among states. It is an agreement among the "people" of the United States. Thus, the preamble of the Constitution reads: "We, the people of the United States, . . ." The framers of the Constitution specified that it should be ratified, not by state legislatures, but by delegates selected by the people. The Constitution created a system of shared sovereignty. Some powers were distributed to the national government, some were left to the states, and some were to be shared by both. These shared powers are called **concurrent powers.**

Powers of the National Government

The national government has only the powers delegated to it by the Constitution, explicitly or implicitly. The listed powers are chiefly those given Congress in Article I, Section 8. These include the power to tax, borrow and coin money, maintain armies and navies, conduct foreign relations, and regulate commerce with foreign nations, Indian tribes, and states.

The same section of the Constitution grants Congress further authority in the *elastic clause* (so called because of the ability of these implied powers to stretch.) This enables Congress to "make all laws which shall be necessary and proper for carrying into execution the foregoing powers. . . ." The "necessary and proper" clause—with liberals stressing the first word to justify actions, and conservatives stressing the second to restrain them—has marked the front lines of the battles before the Supreme Court over expanding national government authority.

The Constitution requires the federal government to guarantee to each state a republican form of government (meaning, at the time, "No Kings"), equal representation in the Senate, and protection in time of war. No new state can be carved out of the territory of an existing state without its agreement, a point violated during the Civil War when West Virginia became a state.

Powers of the States

The state governments retain all powers neither given to the national government nor prohibited to the states. States have the power to supervise schools, regulate commerce within their borders, establish local governments, and borrow money. Each state has a broad "police power" to protect and promote the health, safety, morals, and general welfare of its residents. Under the Constitution, states are the basic units for electing national officials.

Environmental clean-up is often financed by a combination of federal and state funds. Here inmates from a state youth correctional center clean debris from the shoreline in Woodbridge Township, New Jersey.

States also have obligations to other states. Under such *horizontal federalism,* a state must honor the laws and court orders of another state. For example, a state must obey an order from another state to return a stolen automobile. Each state must extend the same "privileges and immunities" to another state's citizens that it gives its own. It must not tax businesses differently because they are owned by citizens of another state (see the box on page 62).

Counties, cities, and towns are considered offsprings of state governments. These local governments gain their powers from their parent governments, and are bound by the same parts of the Constitution that apply to the states.

One question the Constitution did not address was whether a state could withdraw its decision to ratify the document and *secede* from the union. This was answered, in the negative, by a bloody Civil War some seventy-five years later.

Exclusive and Concurrent Powers

The powers of the national and state governments are sometimes **exclusive powers**—reserved solely to one or the other—and sometimes concurrent—shared by both. For example, the national government alone has the power to make treaties, tax imports, and coin money. States also have certain exclusive powers, for example those that relate to domestic relations, such as wills.

Concurrent powers include the power to tax, borrow money, and enact and enforce criminal laws. While the states are supreme in their sphere of activities, the Constitution and national laws are the supreme law of the land when conflicts arise on who has jurisdiction over a certain subject. Since the line of division between state and federal powers is a vague one, it has been left largely to the U.S. Supreme Court to resolve the inevitable clashes. The Court has helped preserve federalism, but there are other reasons why federalism continues.

Why Federalism Continues

Why do we continue to have a federal system today? For one thing, it is *a strong tradition.* In colonial New England, the churches jealously guarded the autonomy of their local congregations against central church authority. Towns and villages exercised considerable authority on their own, separate from the central power of the colonial governments. This tradition of decentralization, nurtured by a distrust of concentrated central power, has continued till today as a strong undercurrent of American politics.

Another basic support for the federal system is the *U.S. Constitution.* The framers of the Constitution at first called the federal system they had created a "compound republic." In *Federalist 51* they described what they meant:

> *In the compound republic of America, the power surrendered by the people is first divided between two distinct governments, and then a portion allotted to each subdivided among distinct and separate departments. Hence a double security arises to the rights of the people. The different governments will control each other, at the same time that each will be controlled by itself.*

Thus, within the federal government and each state government, the framers of the Constitution intended that each of the three branches would check and balance its powers against the others. The framers expected a similar playing off of power between the federal government and each of the state governments.

A final reason the federal system continues is *each state's wish to preserve its own identity.* A state's identity is based on its own particular history, culture, politics, and mix of dominant interests.[2] Citizens within a state tend to identify with their own state, even though the state border may be nearby and the state capital may be far away.

★ Federalism and the States

Guarantees to States	Prohibited to States	Interstate Obligations
Under the Constitution, states are guaranteed:	By the Constitution, a state cannot:	The Constitution requires that states:
1. A republican form of government.	1. Make foreign treaties.	1. Give "full faith and credit" to another state's laws and court orders.
2. Equal representation in the U.S. Senate.	2. Coin money or issue currency.	2. Extend all its "privileges and immunities" to another state's citizens.
3. Protection and defense.	3. Impair private contracts.	
4. Their territorial boundaries.	4. Tax imports or exports.	
	5. Enter into compacts (agreements) with other states without consent of Congress.	

One study of the neighboring cities of Angola, Indiana, Reading, Michigan, and Montpelier, Ohio found that their residents were oriented toward the elections and politics, radio stations and newspapers, jobs and employment in their own states, despite the fact that they lived closer to the other cities across the state borders than to their own state capitals.[3]

THE GROWTH IN NATIONAL POWER

Although federalism has survived down to the present, it is a far different system than the framers could have imagined. The growth of power in the national government has greatly outstripped the power residing among state and local governments. This trend has historically ebbed and flowed (Reagan was an ebb, Lyndon Johnson was a flow). But it has generally been permitted and encouraged by Supreme Court decisions, and impelled by the need to face national economic problems and crises.

Supreme Court Interpretations

The U.S. Supreme Court is the official umpire of the federal system. It decides disputes between states and between states and the federal government. But the historical consequences of its decisions have not been neutral. They have *aided the growth of federal power.*

The first great example of this judicial assist was the constitutional doctrine of **implied powers,** one important basis for enlarged federal powers. It was recognized by the Supreme Court in the 1819 case of *McCulloch* v. *Maryland.* This case arose when the state of Maryland attempted to impose a state tax on a branch of the national bank. The bank's cashier, McCulloch, refused to pay the tax, allowing Chief Justice John Marshall to interpret the Constitution as a flexible instrument, capable of change and growth.

The Supreme Court declared Maryland's tax unconstitutional. In his opinion, John Marshall reasoned this way. First, Congress has the "implied power" to establish a bank because of the "necessary and proper" clause in Article 1, Section 8 of the Constitution. Second, Marshall referred in the opinion to the **supremacy clause.** This holds that a law passed by Congress is superior to a state law that conflicts with it. Such a state law is thus unconstitutional. Finally, Marshall's opinion declared that since "the power to tax is the power to destroy," any attempt by a state to levy a tax on an institution properly created by the national government is invalid.

Marshall reached this conclusion despite the Tenth Amendment. Adopted as part of the Bill of Rights in 1791, it provides: "The pow-

The George Washington Bridge links New York and New Jersey and its administration is an example of interstate cooperation.

ers not delegated to the United States by the Constitution, or prohibited by it to the States, are reserved to the States respectively, or to the people." However, *the Supreme Court held that the federal government not only possesses the stated powers set forth in the Constitution, but that it also has such other "implied" powers as are necessary to carry out the stated powers.* State laws must give way to federal action exercising those implied powers.

In this century, the Supreme Court has taken the view that "the Tenth Amendment states but a truism that all is retained which is not surrendered." Thus, the Tenth Amendment does not add or take anything away from the other provisions of the U.S. Constitution and is no basis for states' rights claims. For example, the Supreme Court has ruled that, under the Fourteenth Amendment, the federal government can act to protect the civil rights of all Americans, whether a particular state approves or not.

Neither Thomas Jefferson nor James Madison believed that the federal government should have implied powers. They were both *strict constructionists.* They had vigorously opposed Hamilton's plan for a national bank. They were equally outraged by Chief Justice Marshall's broad interpretation of the Constitution. However, as president, Jefferson acted contrary to this view when he authorized the Louisiana Purchase, despite the fact that he could not find such power for the president in the Constitution.

The **commerce clause,** (Article 1, Section 8) gives Congress exclusive power to regulate commerce "among the several states." Its broad interpretation by the Supreme Court has greatly enhanced the powers of the national government. Similarly, national powers have been increased by a broad interpretation of the **welfare clause,** a paragraph in the same section that says Congress has the power to provide for the "general welfare of the United States."

Economic Crisis: The Great Depression

The balance of power between the states and the federal government has been further tipped in favor of the federal government during economic crises, notably the Great Depression of the 1930s. The federal government became the prime mover in providing for the well-being of citizens, regulating business and setting economic policy for the nation. As one observer wrote at the time:

> *Where were the states when the banks went under? Powerless Maryland, hysterical Michigan, safety-first New York! Where were the states when all the railroads were on the verge of passing into the hands of bondholders and suspending operation? Where were the states in regulation of power and the control of utilities?*

President Franklin D. Roosevelt significantly expanded federal powers during the Great Depression when the nation was victim to a number of crises. Here a dust storm engulfs Boise City, Oklahoma in 1935.

Where are the states now in regulating insurance companies, with their fake balance sheets and high salaries? In none of these fields affecting economic life was it possible for any state to do anything decisive without driving business out of its jurisdiction into areas where there was no regulation and no control.[4]

The expansion of federal power during the Great Depression was due to Franklin Roosevelt's aggressiveness in a time of great national turmoil. The Supreme Court eventually backed him by reversing earlier rulings and giving a broad and liberal interpretation to the welfare clause and the commerce clause.

With the federal response to the Great Depression, public expectations of what the national government should do have greatly expanded, as have federal taxing, spending, and borrowing activities. These expansions have also been partly a response to social changes—a growing and mobile national population along with increased industrialization and urbanization—leading to huge metropolitan areas with pressing needs that local and state governments cannot meet.

FEDERALISM AND THE CONSTITUENT GOVERNMENTS

Public high schools in Cleveland, San Diego, Boston, or anywhere else in the country are overseen by local school boards. The boards set teachers' salaries and authorize their paychecks. Local school boards make the basic decisions concerning the day-to-day operations of a public-school system. Local taxes on the property in the school district are usually the basic source of public-school funds.

Public education in America is not, however, solely a local government responsibility. The federal and state governments also play important roles in public education, and education accounts for over 14 percent of all federal, state, and local government spending.

State governments provide a large part of the funds for local education. These funds, from state taxes, are partly supplied to school districts according to financial need. This distribution equalizes local revenues from property taxes, which vary widely from poorer to wealthier school districts. In addition, state governments typically control teacher certification, set educational standards for public schools, and approve the textbooks to be used in them. The states have inspection systems to maintain educational standards, and some have done even more (see the box on page 70).

The federal government is also involved in public education. Federal aid programs in education help equalize state funding, just as state funds are used to reduce the differences among local school districts. Some "strings" are attached to these federal funds. For example, no school district that receives federal funds may discriminate on the basis of race in hiring teachers.

As can be seen from the education example, federalism is not neatly layered. The same kind of overlap that exists in the funding and regulation of public education is found in government activities ranging from pollution control and welfare to public health and public roads. *There is virtually no local government function that does not have a parallel federal aid program.*

The federal system is not a three-layered cake, (with the national government as the top layer, resting on the state layer, which rests upon the local government layer). Instead, the American federal system is more like a *marble cake,* characterized by a mingling of differently colored ingredients, the colors appearing in strands and unexpected whirls. As colors are mixed in the marble cake, so functions are mixed in the American federal system.[5]

The system the founders devised clearly separated powers and roles for the states and the national government. What we have today in America might be called **cooperative federalism.** In this system, financing, policy-making, and administration of government programs are shared among the federal, state, and local governments. Few if any policy areas are off limits to the national government, as long as federal action does not hurt the ability of state and local governments to function. Cooperative federalism has resulted from the growth in national power and the importance of federal funds. The state, local, and tribal governments remain important parts of the federal system (see Figure 3.1).

FIGURE 3★1
Administrative Levels Used in Providing Assistance

While this chart simplifies the complex administration of federal programs, the chart gives an idea of the different levels involved.

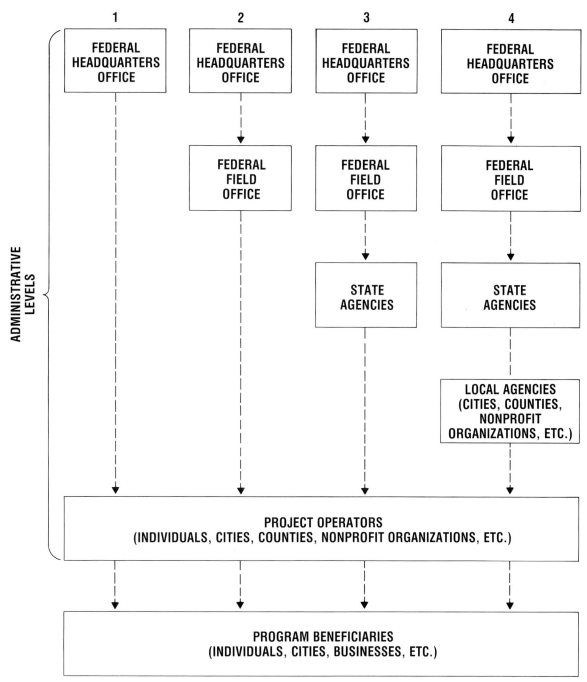

SOURCE: Comptroller General of the United States, *The Federal Government Should But Doesn't Know the Cost of Administering Its Assistance Programs,* GGD-77-87 Washington, DC, U.S. General Accounting Office, 1978, p. 3.

The States

States are the original building blocks of our federal union. Despite their differences in size, population, and income, states share a number of problems in areas such as transportation, welfare, law enforcement, education, and the environment. Yet, as one authority has put it, "the states are 'thriving' in the federal system: . . . their constitutional durability is in little doubt, their activities are greatly expanded, their capacity and authority are increasingly more impressive in relation to those of local governments, they are changing their institutional structures so as to be more effective as agencies of government, and they remain important arenas for the decentralized American party system."[6]

State Constitutions

State constitutions are generally much longer than the U.S. Constitution. They include many details. This detail, which usually sets limits on what a governor or a state legislature can do, tends to make state constitutions inflexible. They are difficult to apply to changing conditions. The work of interest groups lies behind many of the provisions in state constitutions:

> *Taxpayers' groups and property interests have been able to secure strict and detailed limits on state legislatures' taxing, borrowing, and spending powers. The strength of veterans' groups and their lobbyists is revealed in constitutional guarantees of veterans' preference in public employment and even constitutional provisions for bonuses, pensions, tax exemptions, and other privileges. The influence of church groups, sometimes opposed to other church groups, may be measured in constitutional contests. A case in point is the conflict over outlawing bingo as a form of gambling as Protestant groups have urged, or making it legal, as urged by Catholic groups . . .[7]*

Governors

A state governor is the chief executive of the state. Usually, this does not give a governor as much power as a president. Most states, for example, have at least an elected lieutenant governor, secretary of state, attorney general, and state treasurer. In recent years, several states have reduced the number of elected state officials and increased the number appointed by the governors.

Governors are party leaders. Here their power is impressive. They dominate their state party organization and usually prevent it from taking stands that are not to their liking. Governors regularly name the state chairpersons of their parties, and typically lead their party delegations to the national conventions.

New York Governor Mario Cuomo addresses the International Ladies' Garment Workers Union in Hollywood, Florida. Governors wield much power within the state government structure.

A governor also acts as a policymaker. Governors issue executive orders and the departments under their control issue regulations to implement the law. Governors also initiate policy through their influence on legislation. They give a *state of the state message* at the beginning of each session of the legislature, propose a state budget and legislative measures, veto legislation (except in North Carolina), and control considerable patronage. In forty-three states, governors have a power not given to the president—a **line-item veto.** They can veto a particular item in an appropriations (spending) bill without having to veto the whole bill. This allows a state governor extra power over the appropriations process. State governors usually have more political patronage at their disposal than a president does. For example, they can agree to the building of a highway in a particular district in exchange for a legislator's support on other issues.

State Legislatures

All state governments parallel the federal pattern. All have separated the legislative from the judicial and executive functions. All except Nebraska have two-house legislatures. Most states call their upper house the senate, while lower houses are typically called a house of representatives, an assembly, or a house of delegates.

★ A School Takeover

Dissatisfaction with locally run public education is widespread. In May 1988, it led to the state of New Jersey to become the first state to step over a traditional federal division and take over the schools of Jersey City. The state action came after repeated testing in the city schools showed that the many deficiencies in the system had not been corrected. This was in part due to "Political patronage, union pressure and cronyism. . . ." Members of the Board of Education were appointed by the mayor of Jersey City, and they, as well as teachers, were hired and fired based on political loyalties.

Jersey City residents, familiar with the workings of their local political machine, remained skeptical about the changes in the school system. One remarked, "they'll just substitute state politics for local."

SOURCE: *The New York Times,* May 25 and 27, 1988.

Members of state legislatures are usually elected, from single-member districts, to two-year terms for the lower house and four-year terms for the upper house. Most state legislators come from law, farming, or from businesses—such as insurance or real estate—that allow them to take time off for legislative duties. Most state legislatures meet only for short periods each year, so a legislator's job is not thought of as full time. However, legislators are expected to attend committee meetings between legislative sessions, to consult with constituents, and to act on their requests year-round.

In the larger, wealthier states—such as California, Michigan, and New Jersey—there is a greater degree of legislative professionalism than in some of the less populated states such as South Dakota, New Mexico, and Delaware. States such as California provide nearly full-time legislative salaries and adequate staffing for the legislators. Sessions also tend to be longer in these states. States that pay small salaries are less likely to have legislators drawn from certain groups—blue-collar wage earners, women, minorities—who cannot afford to take time off from work to serve.

State legislatures are usually much smaller than Congress. New Hampshire's lower house is the largest, with 400 members. Four other state lower houses have about 200 members, but the rest have 125 or fewer. All of the state senates are small. Minnesota's is the largest, with 67 members. Only four state senates have over 50 members. Most have 30 to 40.

After World War II, America experienced rapid population shifts to the cities and suburbs, called *urbanization* and *suburbanization.* With the exception of Wisconsin and Massachusetts, state legislatures refused to reapportion themselves. That is, they refused to change legislative district lines to reflect the change in population distributions, even though their state constitutions required it. The result was that state legislatures were dominated by rural areas, and cities were underrepresented. Even in states where the membership in one house was fairly well apportioned on the basis of population, the other house was malapportioned. Thus, in 1960, three-fourths of the total population of the state of Maryland lived in the state's four largest counties plus the city of Baltimore, but these areas were represented in Maryland's upper house by only one-third of that body's members.

Then came the landmark U.S. Supreme Court decision of *Baker* v. *Carr* in 1962. Here the Court ruled that malapportionment of a state legislature was a justiciable question, an issue that can be decided by a court, and that it violated the Fourteenth Amendment. Two years later in *Reynolds* v. *Sims,* the Court went further and ordered "one person/one vote"—equal population districts—in both houses of a state legislature. Chief Justice Warren stated that "legislators represent people, not trees or acres." Since these decisions, state legislatures have generally become more open, more modern, and less likely to discriminate against cities.

All state governments have two-house legislatures except Nebraska which has a 49-seat nonpartisan unicameral legislature.

Courts and Judges

The federal system includes parallel state and federal judicial systems.[8] When the federal courts were established by Congress in 1789, it was intended that much of the jurisdiction over civil and criminal cases would still be left to the state courts.

In this century, federal judicial power and jurisdiction has increased. This was especially true when Earl Warren was Chief Justice (1953–69), in cases involving civil rights, reapportionment, and the rights of the accused. The more conservative courts headed by Chief Justice Warren Burger (1969–86) and Chief Justice William Rehnquist (1986–) moved the pendulum back in the other direction. Noninterference from the federal level has become more the norm. The Supreme Court has restricted access to federal courts when people can have their case decided in a state court.

Still, Americans have always been far more likely to appear in a state court than in a federal court. *State courts handle many times more cases than federal courts.* Like federal judges, state judges are involved in conflict resolution, administration of laws, and policymaking. State courts interpret laws and state constitutions, exercising a state "judicial review" power.

State court judgments must conform to the U.S. Constitution as it is interpreted by the U.S. Supreme Court. When a "substantial federal question" is involved in a case, a decision by the state's highest court may be appealed to the U.S. Supreme Court. The U.S. Supreme Court must, of course, think the matter is important enough to accept the appeal. Most state court decisions are not appealed to the U.S. Supreme Court. In those that are, state courts have some discretion in interpreting and implementing the Supreme Court's decision. (See the case study in Chapter 9.)

State Politics

Our federal system fragments power, often confusing popular control of overall government policies. But *federalism also increases the number of access points for political participation and brings this access closer to home.* Active Democrats or Republicans, for example, have a better chance of making their influence felt at a state party convention than at a national convention.

State issues often have as much impact on citizens as national issues. The same may be said of state elections versus national elections. Yet Americans care more about and get more involved in national politics. Local elections produce even smaller turnouts than state elections. The average citizen knows more about the president's last summit meeting than about last week's session of the state legislature. Lower public interest in state and local politics could be the

---

PROPOSED CALL FOR A CONSTITUTIONAL CONVENTION

Explanation of Proposed Call

This proposal deals with a call for a state constitutional convention. The last such convention was held in 1969-70, and a new constitution was adopted in 1970. That document requires that the question of calling a convention be placed before the voters every 20 years. This is your opportunity to vote on that question. If you believe the 1970 Illinois Constitution needs to be revised through the calling of a convention, you should vote YES. If you believe that a call for a constitutional convention is unnecessary, or that changes can be accomplished through other means, you should vote NO.

Punch the number opposite "YES" or "NO" to indicate your choice.

For the calling of a state Constitutional Convention	**YES**	**9 →**
	NO	**11 →**

Referendums have had a great resurgence in recent years, due primarily to state legislatures ducking controversial issues and special interests trying to bypass traditional legislative power.

cause or the result of media attention to national politics. In either case, there is a troubling political paradox: Political participation is lowest where it might be most effective.

Direct Democracy

While there is generally less political participation below the national level, in several states and localities citizens can engage in *direct* democracy through the *initiative, referendum,* and *recall.*

The **initiative** was a reform advocated by the Populist movement around the turn of the century. It is now permitted in twenty-two states, most of them west of the Mississippi.[9] The initiative allows voters to propose a law by getting a sufficient number of signatures on a petition. A direct initiative brings the issue to a vote of the people directly. In the indirect initiative, the measure first goes to the legislature, and then to the voters if the legislature fails to act. In either case, the voters make their own law.

A **referendum** may come up for a popular vote in three ways. In a protest referendum, the people petition for a popular vote on whether a measure passed by the state legislature should be approved. A compulsory referendum, usually involving a proposed constitutional amendment, must be referred to a popular vote by the legislature. In a voluntary referendum, the legislature may decide to refer a legislative proposal to the people, rather than take action on the measure itself.

Initiatives and referendums have had a great resurgence in recent years. In the 1988 elections, 41 states had at least one on their ballots, for a total of 230 propositions, (four more than in 1986). Of these, 54 were on the ballots because of petitions signed by voters. The most common issues started by petition involved the taxing powers of state and local government. *The increase in these propositions comes from a combination of state legislatures ducking controversial issues like taxes and abortion, and special interests seeing referendums as a way of bypassing legislative and administrative power centers.*

One reason for this special-interest preference is that election-spending limits do not apply to referendum campaigns (since the courts see them as an exercise in free speech). A series of propositions on insurance in the 1988 California elections may have cost an astounding $75 million. Of course, overwhelming money is no guarantee of victory. The insurance companies that spent most of these funds ended up losing. Nonetheless, these propositions have already become costly, overused, and complicated. One Berkeley, California political scientist discovered he had sixty-one decisions to make on his November 1988 ballot. Whether this direct democracy now enhances or interferes with representative democracy has become a debatable point.[10]

The **recall** is a kind of "reverse election." It is a way to remove public officials before the end of their terms by petition and popular vote. Only thirteen states permit the recall of state officials, but recall is more widely available at the local level. Recalls are restricted by the large number of signatures required on a recall petition (commonly 25 percent of the eligible voters). Supporters of the recall say that it is an important threat that helps keep public officials on their toes. Opponents argue that it is used mostly as a partisan harassment of officeholders.

The last time a recall was successful at the state level was in 1921 when the governor, attorney general, and secretary of state of North Dakota were recalled. Governor Evan Mecham of Arizona was subjected to a recall in 1988 for campaign finance misdeeds and generally ill-tempered outbursts about blacks and gays. A recall election was set after 300,000 signatures were collected, but he was impeached before it could occur, making Mecham the seventh state governor to be impeached. The recall has been used more often at the local level. In 1977, for example, voters in Madison, Wisconsin, recalled and removed a trial judge who had acquitted a man charged with rape. The judge had said that the dress of today's women provoked such assaults.

Local Governments

For most Americans, the governments closest to them, at least geographically, are local—counties, special districts, and cities or towns. Their grassroots functions often overlap.

Counties

The most common type of government in America is county government. All but three states—Connecticut, Rhode Island, and Alaska—are divided into counties (Louisiana calls its counties "parishes"). There are more than 3000 counties throughout the United States.

The courthouse in each county is at a town called the *county seat*. In early days, the idea behind the location of county seats was that citizens should be able to go by horse from their homes to the courthouse and back in the same day. Today, counties are generally governed by a board of commissioners, a board of supervisors, or something similar elected by the people. Other separately elected county officials include a county treasurer, a county clerk, and a county sheriff. This is called a **plural executive** form of county government. Some of the larger counties have adopted a **county manager** form of government. In this system, the voters elect the county board, which then chooses a county manager. The county manager is responsible for choosing and supervising the other appointed officials of the county. Some counties elect a county executive who performs a similar function. County government has changed very little over the years.

The functions of a county that contains all or part of a large city often overlap with those performed by the city government. In some instances the city and county governments have merged into a metropolitan government, as in Nashville. In other cases certain common functions, such as mass transit, health, police, and fire, have been combined—as in Miami and Dade County. Towns and villages may achieve some local rule by incorporating. When this is done, they can collect taxes and provide basic services for their citizens which otherwise would be performed by the county government.

Special Districts

Within each state and county there are numerous special districts (see Figure 3.2). A water or irrigation district, for example, is supported by local taxes and is governed by a board chosen by the district's voters. The most important local district government is the school district. It is responsible for the public schools, financed by a property tax, and governed by an elected school board. City and county governments usually have little control over school and other district boards (although this wasn't true in Jersey City—as shown on page 70).

This fragmentation of authority means voters must understand how local governments work and show enormous persistence to affect policy. School and other district elections are nearly always

FIGURE 3★2
Layers of Government, Fridley, Minnesota

Believe it or not: A citizen of Fridley, Minnesota, is expected to exercise an informal control, through the electoral franchise, over 11 separate overlapping governments, and is taxed for their support.

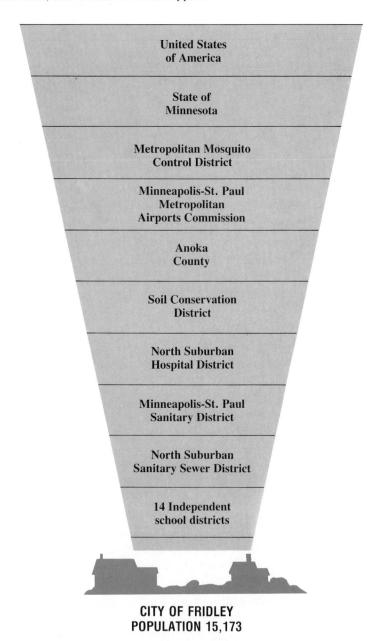

United States
of America

State of
Minnesota

Metropolitan Mosquito
Control District

Minneapolis-St. Paul
Metropolitan
Airports Commission

Anoka
County

Soil Conservation
District

North Suburban
Hospital District

Minneapolis-St. Paul
Sanitary District

North Suburban
Sanitary Sewer District

14 Independent
school districts

**CITY OF FRIDLEY
POPULATION 15,173**

SOURCE: Committee for Economic Development, *Modernizing Local Government* (Washington, DC, 1971).

held on a nonpartisan basis, and voter turnout is typically very low. The result is that *political control of district governments usually resides in a small number of activists or interest groups.*

Cities

The people of ancient Greece thought of themselves, first, as citizens of a city-state like Athens or Sparta. Each Greek citizen was proud of his or her city-state, which was called a *metropolis,* meaning "mother city." America's central cities do not create as much local pride. Urban areas are made up of a central city and surrounding suburbs, which are often separately governed.

Urban problems are among the most difficult of America's domestic issues. (Sometimes they are local manifestations of larger national problems, such as drug abuse.) The spread of these problems accelerated with four major urban developments. First, there was a rapid growth of the cities. Second, there followed "white flight" to the suburbs by the middle classes, leaving behind decay and rising poverty in the central cities. Third, the cities, financially weak to begin with, found their costs going up and their tax bases shrinking. Finally, politics in the central cities has generally been marked by apathy, which stems primarily from citizens' sense of futility. An additional, and more recent, trend has been the "gentrification" process of the late 1970s and early 1980s—a movement of fairly well-off whites back into old houses in the cities, squeezing out poor whites and minorities.

Two-thirds of all Americans live in cities and suburbs, which cover only about 10 percent of the country's land area. From 1860 to 1900, the population of cities doubled. It doubled again during the next 25 years and surged dramatically upward again after World War II. Great waves of immigrants from Europe, American blacks from the rural South, and later, people from Latin America and Asia gathered in the cities.

There has been a decline in the power of old-style city **political machines.** Led by political bosses, and maintained by patronage with a dash of corruption, these machines were fueled by the votes of immigrants. In Chicago, for example, the late Richard J. Daley headed both the party machine in Cook County and served as mayor, maintaining his power with a blend of rewards, loyalties, and penalties. (See the box on page 78.) The Daley machine—one of the last in the country—began to lose its control with his death.

Three factors caused the decline of old-style city politics. The adoption of civil service merit systems removed city jobs from political patronage. Welfare systems based upon need rather than political influence (partly because of federal requirements) reduced the funds available to political bosses. And the rising importance of the mass media, particularly television, allowed candidates to go over the heads of political machines, directly to the people. Local political parties have declined in importance for some of the same reasons. The result is that candidates run primarily as "personalities" or representatives of important ethnic groups.

Most of the large cities in America are governed by a *strong mayor-council* form of government. Under this system, the mayor and city council members are separately elected. The mayor has a great deal of executive authority, in addition to presiding at meetings of the city council. Some large cities have a *weak mayor-council* form of government. In this system, the mayor is more a figurehead than

★ Big-City Machine Politics

During Richard Daley's long reign as mayor of Chicago and boss of the "Machine," he was seldom seriously challenged in an election. One who did run against him was a lawyer named Benjamin Adamowski. Mike Royko, a Chicago columnist, illustrates why he and other Daley opponents didn't get very far:

"The owner of a small restaurant at Division and Ashland, the heart of the city's Polish neighborhood, put up a big Adamowski sign. The day it went up the precinct captain came around and said, "How come the sign Harry?" "Ben's a friend of mine," the restaurant owner said. "Ben's a nice guy Harry, but that's a pretty big sign. I'd appreciate it if you'd take it down." "No, it's staying up."

The next day the captain came back. "Look, I'm the precinct captain. Is there anything wrong, any problem, anything I can help you with?" Harry said no. "Then why don't you take it down. You know how this looks in my job." Harry wouldn't budge. The sign stayed up. On the third day, the city building inspectors came. The plumbing improvements alone cost Harry $2,100."

SOURCE: Mike Royko, *Boss: Richard J. Daley of Chicago,* New York: E. P. Dutton and Company, Incorporated, 1971, pp. 126–27.

a powerful executive. In some cities, the people elect commissioners who choose one of their number from time to time to act as the commission chairperson. The number of cities using the commission system is declining. Some cities have adopted the *council-manager* form of government, under which a professional, "nonpolitical" administrator is hired as the city executive. This system today is mainly used by middle-sized and smaller cities.

Indian Tribes

Indian tribes are not foreign, state, or local governments. They are **tribal governments,** unique in our federal system. States do not generally have jurisdiction over them, unless the federal government delegates such power. While Congress can break Indian treaties—paying just compensation for any property rights thus taken—it has rarely done so. Although the federal government's taxing and regulatory power extends to reservations, states generally have no such power over tribal activities on reservations.

American Indians today are different from other ethnic groups in that their tribes are recognized units of government. From earliest times, the U.S. government dealt with most tribes through treaties, similar to those with foreign nations. These treaties were grants of rights *from* Indian tribes, not grants of rights *to* them. Thus, tribes possess retained powers; they generally include all the powers that the tribes have not given up or that have not been taken away by federal action. American Indians are U.S. citizens. Thus, tribal members have a kind of dual citizenship: U.S. citizenship, from which state citizenship also flows, and citizenship in their own tribes.

Half of all Indians are members of one of nine tribes: Navajo (the largest tribe), Chippewa, Choctaw, Cherokee, Pueblo, Apache, Sioux, Lumbee, and Iroquois. The history, language, customs, traditions, and present tribal governments of these and other tribes vary greatly. Most tribes have an elected tribal council. This council elects the chairperson of the tribe, a number of whom today are women. The Navajo tribe has a tribal council, with members elected by districts, and an executive tribal chairperson, elected by popular vote of the tribe. Aside from the Navajos, most tribal executives are not full-time, paid officials.

The 1.4 million Indians remain one of America's poorest minorities, with a poverty rate more than double the national average. The historical reasons for this stem from the destruction of the traditional Indian culture. More modern explanations were brought out in a recent Senate committee investigation of the administration of nearly $3 billion in government aid to the nation's 500 Indian tribes.

A Sandoval Pueblo tribal council meeting; in most tribes, executive officials are selected by and from the tribal council.

Senate investigators found the programs marred by fraud, corruption, and mismanagement. Tribal leaders and federal officials were reported to have accepted bribes from contractors wishing to do business on Indian lands. One Indian leader described "rampant graft and corruption" among the tribal governments.[11]

Of course many Indian tribes are attempting to improve their economies. Today, tribes own a large portion of America's coal, uranium, and other energy resources. Americans for Indian Opportunity, a national Indian organization, pioneered the idea that Indian tribes are like underdeveloped Third World nations. To develop, they need to regain control over their natural resources from non-Indian corporations, which lease them often for very little. Some are now demanding joint ventures and other arrangements to give them a share of profits and control. Within other tribes, traditional leaders are opposed to resource development on environmental and religious grounds. Economic development on these reservations will proceed, if at all, in ways that the tribes themselves find to be economically, culturally, and environmentally sound.

FISCAL FEDERALISM

Governments have the power to raise revenue—they can tax, collect fees, and borrow money. States and local governments (as well as the federal government) do all three.

Taxation

Generally, state and local taxes are not as *progressive* (based upon the ability to pay) as federal taxes. Most states collect a sales tax, a *regressive* tax that falls heaviest on poor people. The trend has been toward increased reliance on the income tax, however it still accounts for only about 11 percent of total state and local taxes. Unlike the federal government, many states have constitutional budget-balancing requirements that prevent deficit spending. *Because of growing taxpayer opposition to local property taxes, a greater burden for financing public education and other services has been placed on the states in recent years.*

The cities have historically relied on a relatively weak financial base—primarily property taxes and water, sewer, and garbage fees—for operating funds and for bond issues. After World War II, state legislatures began to allow cities to levy other taxes. These were principally local sales taxes, although some cities have also been permitted to use income taxes. Most people who live in the suburbs have been reluctant to be taxed to meet the problems of central cities, even though many of them make their living from jobs in the cities.

By the late 1980s, after several years of surpluses, state and local governments were racking up record deficits (see Figure 3.3). In 1988 these governments had combined deficits of $14.4 billion in their operating budgets. Unwise tax cuts were part of the reason for these deficits, and the decline in federal revenue was another. On the latter point, whereas in 1981, 18 cents of every revenue dollar taken in by states and localities came from the Feds, by 1989 it was down to 13 cents of every dollar. The states, taking their cue from Washington, tried to shift more of the burden to cities and counties, which in turn cut back services. With the economy still prosperous, concerns were expressed about how these governments would weather a recession and the decline in revenue it would bring.[12]

Borrowing

In addition to levying taxes and fees, state and local governments raise revenue through issuing **general obligation bonds,** which pledge the "full faith and credit" of the issuing government. These must be paid through increased taxation, if necessary. States, local governments, and tribes may issue **revenue bonds,** which pledge only the revenues from the particular project to be financed, such as tolls from building a bridge. Under federal law, both general obligation bonds and revenue bonds are called **municipal bonds** and are *tax-exempt.* This federal tax exemption allows state and local governments to borrow money at low interest rates, because investors do

FIGURE 3★3
Sliding Into Deficit

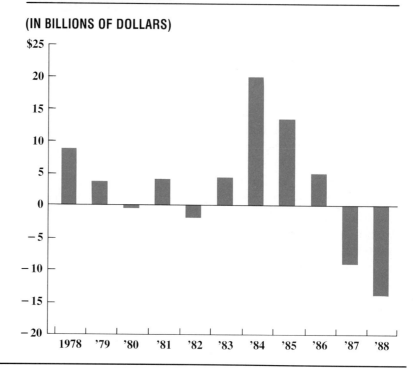

SURPLUS OR DEFICIT OF STATE AND LOCAL GOVERNMENTS EXCLUDING SOCIAL INSURANCE FUNDS

(IN BILLIONS OF DOLLARS)

SOURCE: *The Wall Street Journal,* February 21, 1989.

not have to pay federal income taxes on the bond income. Of course, the tax exemption on municipal bonds gives a special tax break to those wealthy enough to invest in them.

With the cutbacks in federal funds flowing to states and localities in the 1980s, these governments came to depend more on municipal bonds for their *infrastructure* needs (roads, sewers, and housing). At the same time federal officials, largely in the Treasury Department, viewed the tax exemption of these bonds as a subsidy from the federal government. As a result, the 1986 Tax Reform Act limited the number of bonds that state and local governments could issue. A 1988 Supreme Court decision (*South Carolina* v. *Baker*) ruled that the tax exemption of these bonds was not based on the Constitution and could be restricted by Congress. Limits on municipal bonds are likely to increase in coming years as the federal government continues to look for revenues to balance its own budget.

Federal Funds

Federal-state relations are very much affected by the way federal grants-in-aid are provided to lower levels of government. Under these grants-in-aid, the federal government sets a basic policy, but leaves the actual administration of a program to state or local governments. The initial push for such programs has sometimes come from state and local governments, but just as often it comes from the federal government.

Most federal spending involves direct payments to the private sector which are not shared with state or local governments. For example, federal expenditures for defense, foreign aid, and social security go to individuals or to contractors or countries. But when federal policymakers inaugurate a new domestic program, they frequently leave the program administration to localities or states. The feds may say to the states, "If you will administer a new Federal Interstate Highway Program and put up 10 percent of the construction costs, the federal government will pay 90 percent of such costs." The Interstate Highway Program, started during the Eisenhower administration, provided just such an attractive carrot for state participation in a huge, nationwide highway-building project.

Grants may also go directly to local governments, as they do for a program that provides federal matching funds for sewage disposal systems. Frequently, federal grants-in-aid go to both state and local governments. For example, the Law Enforcement Assistance Administration provides federal funds for state and local governments to improve their police departments.

A majority of the funding for the nation's highways comes from the federal government. Here the Edens expressway in Illinois is under construction.

Disaster relief following the Bay-area earthquake in California in 1989 was a combination of federal and state funds. Here, workers dig through the rubble of collapsed highway I-880.

Postwar Trends

From the New Deal days of President Franklin D. Roosevelt in the 1930s to the 1970s, there were a number of trends in fiscal federalism. First, there was *great growth, at all levels, in government spending.* At the federal level, increased spending was especially pronounced during the Great Society years of President Lyndon B. Johnson (1964–1968). Then, growth in the national economy began to slow. Federal deficits rose, as did inflation. With the Vietnam War and the Watergate scandal, public confidence in government declined. This grassroots dissatisfaction, combined with a worsening economy, limited government spending. The growth in real per capita government spending (meaning the amount spent per person, excluding the effects of inflation) stopped first at the local level, in 1974. Then, it stopped at the state level. Finally, it stopped at the federal level, in 1978.[13]

A second trend in fiscal federalism was *the growth of the national government's dominance.* Through increased federal funds, especially as categorical **grants-in-aid,** came a great deal of federal restrictions and guidelines. In 1953, federal funds made up only 10 percent of state and local budgets. By 1973 this figure had doubled to 20 percent. Although it has since declined, one constitutional scholar recently concluded: "Given the practical importance of federal grants today, the power to improve conditions enables Congress effectively to regulate anything it pleases."[14]

A third trend into the 1970s was that *an increased percentage of federal funds went directly to local governments.* In many instances, these went to local community groups and organizations, bypassing the states. From 1960 to 1977, for example, the percentage of grant dollars going directly to local governments tripled.

Federal grants-in-aid were seen as a mixed blessing by state and local governments. These grants created a dependency among state and local governments. They would apply for whatever programs were available—"whatever Washington is calling money this year." In applying for funds, it generally didn't matter what priorities local and state governments might otherwise have set on their own. Federal grants-in-aid did, however, increase the ability of these governments to meet local problems and needs, while allowing them to avoid raising taxes to pay for the new programs. Still, state and local officials regularly complained about the strings attached to federal grants-in-aid. Congress, on the other hand, often felt an obligation to federal taxpayers to set standards, such as no discrimination in hiring, for spending their funds.

A fourth trend, then, was *the development of strong state and local lobbying groups* seeking to influence the dispersal of federal grants. These groups included the National Governors' Conference, the National League of Cities, the U.S. Conference of Mayors, and the National Association of Counties.

Grants-in-aid were criticized because they bypassed elected officials in favor of unelected bureaucrats:

> *Practically all of the new grant programs were functionally oriented, with power, money, and decisions flowing from program administrators in Washington, to program specialists in regional offices, to functional department heads in State and local government—leaving Cabinet officers, governors, county commissioners, and mayors less and less informed as to what was actually taking place. . . .*[15]

States competed for the increased federal funds. Some congressional delegations were more effective than others in securing federal projects in their states. Because of the seniority system in Congress, the

South, as a one-party (Democratic) region sending its senators and representatives back to Washington election after election, was favored with military bases. Federal grant programs based partly or wholly on the degree of poverty in a state also benefited the under-developed South. Arguments can still be heard raging back and forth on whether the *Sunbelt* states of the South or the *Rust Bowl* states of the Northeast and Midwest got unfair advantage from federal spending. Of course, states and localities competed over other resources as well (see the box on page 85).

Nixon and the "New Federalism"

Objections to categorical grants-in-aid, from governors and mayors in particular, led to **block grants** and **revenue sharing** by the Nixon administration. Nixon called it a "New Federalism." It meant more money for state and local governments, but with fewer strings attached.

Block grants, covering both new programs and some conversion of old grants-in-aid, provide federal funds for broad functions but allow state and local officials to determine specific uses. *Revenue*

FIGURE 3★4

Federal Grants to State and Local Governments

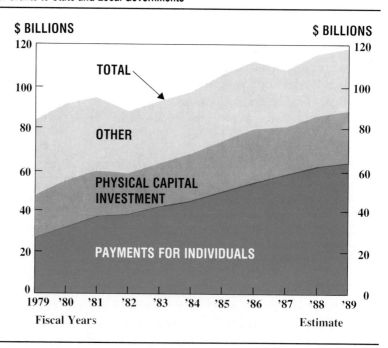

SOURCE: *The Budget for Fiscal Year 1989.*

sharing simply distributed to state and local governments a percentage of federal tax collections with only limited strings attached. For the initial four-year period after 1972, $30.2 billion in federal funds were authorized under the revenue-sharing system. Two-thirds of these funds went directly to local (and tribal) governments; one third went to states.

Jimmy Carter, president from 1977 to 1981, called his fiscal federalism program a "New Partnership." It was basically a blend of the Johnson (categorical grants) and Nixon (revenue spending) programs, but with budget limits. The federal contribution to state and local governments as a percentage of their income from their own sources rose to 31 percent by 1979.[16] Then came the Reagan administration.

Reagan's New "New Federalism"

Reagan's approach to federalism had two sides—**retrenchment** and **devolution.**[17] Retrenchment referred to his efforts to reduce domestic spending, particularly in federal grants-in-aid. His cuts in his first year in office were historic. For the first time in thirty years there was a real dollar decline in federal spending going to state and local governments, amounting to 12 percent (see Figure 3.4).

Reagan's other objective was to devolve power and responsibility from the federal government to the state governments. He favored fewer federal strings, fewer categorical grant programs, and more block grants. Reagan sought to decrease the funds going directly to local governments and to use the states as middlemen for federal funds. He returned to a more traditional federalism, with the states and federal government having separate, less overlapping spheres of authority.

Reagan's "dream," as he referred to it, was to increase the authority of the states, which would then join him in shrinking the size of the government at all levels. Programs such as welfare and social services would be made the responsibility of the states and then reduced in size by states more in tune with conservatism than the federal bureaucracy. Under the president's prodding, Congress consolidated fifty-seven existing federal aid programs into nine new large block grants. Revenue sharing was virtually cut out of existence.

Criticisms were not long in coming. Many in Congress were worried about separating taxing responsibility (federal) from spending (state and local). Certain interest groups, such as cities and minorities, didn't expect to do as well under the states as they had under the feds. Even governors who favored the block-grant approach disliked using it as a cover for a deep, overall cut in federal funds. Arizona's Democratic governor Bruce Babbitt charged that the block

Due to shrinking tax bases or shrinking funds, urban renewal projects, such as this one in New York City, are sometimes left half finished.

multi-level park including play areas, game tables, shaded sitting areas planting and promenades

Department of Housing Preservation and Development
Edward I. Koch, Mayor City of New York
Nathan Leventhal, Commissioner
Andrew Stein, Borough President
Landscape Arch't: Vincent C. Cerasi and Associates
Arch't: Paul Wood and Lee Borrero

Latest "New Federalism"

STATE GOVERNMENTS

"Step right up—everybody gets one star and part of a stripe."

© 1981 by Herblock in *The Washington Post*

grants were "a tactical weapon to cut the federal budget while deputizing the governors to hand out the bad news."

Reagan's new "New Federalism" fulfilled neither its creator's hopes nor its opponents' fears. The shift in accountability to state governments did not lead to the hoped-for cutbacks in domestic programs. As the federal role was reduced, cities and local governments were forced to look more to their state capitals for help. The reforms in federalism stimulated change in state governments. This change led to improvements in states' administrative capabilities and encouraged them to meet needs in areas where the federal government was cutting back. The states employed numerous coping strategies to shift around funds and delay implementing reductions in formerly federal funds. Part of the reason for this was that leaders of civil rights groups and lobbyists for the poor quickly moved their activities to the state level, where they found officials responsive to their appeals.

The results of Reagan's federalism have been called "a paradox of devolution." The president's goals of devolution worked against his goals of social program retrenchment. *The states compensated for the federal cutbacks, in most cases, rather than complementing them.* This trend seems likely to continue under President Bush. As a *National Journal* article concluded, "Conservatives who gleefully assumed that shifting the responsibility for social programs to the states would mean the end of the programs have discovered that state governments were not as conservative as they thought."[18]

WRAP-UP

The framers of the Constitution were pretty clear about their concept of the federal system. Outside of military and foreign relations, the national government was not given great authority. James Madison insisted, "The powers delegated to the Federal Government are few and defined," those "to remain in the State Governments . . . numerous and infinite." This reflected not only the feeling that state governments were better qualified to deal with local problems, but also that a strong central government was a danger to liberty. As a modern constitutional scholar put it, "If the government of a single state falls into bad hands, one can move elsewhere; if the government of the whole nation is oppressive, there is no place to run."[19]

Modern federalism appears to be far different from the original creation. While the Constitution remains an important limit on centralized power, the federal government is much stronger compared to the states. It has complex, overlapping relations with state and local governments. In some ways federalism makes it easier for citizens to participate in decisions because they occur closer to home. In other ways it's more difficult because people need to keep track of separate decisions being made in a variety of places.

Is government best if it is closest to the people? The answer to this question has historically depended in part on how satisfied people have been with the way things are. The growth of national power, while permitted by various Supreme Court decisions, has been motivated by economic changes and popular demands. As the economy became national, the only place to regulate large corporations and unions was on the national level. Other problems such as urban decay, racial discrimination, and environmental pollution seemed to be beyond the states' capacities to solve. Conservatives who have generally opposed government action to meet these needs have felt that more power on the state and local levels would mean less government activity. President Reagan's New Federalism policy, however, caused greater activities by the states, not less. Of course that increase in governments' activities has depended on an equal increase in citizen and interest-group participation at the state and local levels.

In 1908, Woodrow Wilson, a noted political scientist as well as president, wrote that the relations of the states and federal government cannot be settled "by one generation, because it is a question of growth, and every new successive stage of our politicial and economic development, gives it a new aspect, makes it a new question." To see federalism as a flexible arena for representing the varied interests of a large, diverse country within a political tradition of state and local governments is not far from what we have today. Actually, it's not that far from what the framers of the Constitution had in mind.

Key Terms

concurrent powers (p. 59)
exclusive powers (p. 61)
implied powers (p. 63)
supremacy clause (p. 63)
commerce clause (p. 64)
welfare clause (p. 64)
cooperative federalism (p. 66)
line-item veto (p. 69)
initiative (p. 73)
referendum (p. 74)
recall (p. 74)
plural executive (p. 75)

county manager (p. 75)
political machines (p. 77)
tribal governments (p. 79)
general obligation bonds (p. 81)
revenue bonds (p. 81)
municipal bonds (p. 84)
grants-in-aid (p. 84)
block grants (p. 86)
revenue sharing (p. 86)
retrenchment (p. 87)
devolution (p. 87)

Suggested Readings

Beyle, Thad L., ed., *State Government: CQ's Guide to Current Issues and Activities 1988–89* (Washington D.C.: CQ Press, 1988).

Dilger, Robert Jay, *The Sunbelt/Snowbelt Controversy: The War Over Federal Funds* (New York: NYU Press, 1984).

Elazer, Daniel, *Exploring Federalism* (Tuscaloosa, Ala.: University of Alabama Press, 1987).

Hale, George E., and Marian Lief Palley, *The Politics of Federal Grants* (Washington, D.C.: CQ Press, 1981).

Lamm, Richard, *Megatraumas: America at the Year 2000* (New York: Houghton Mifflin Co., 1984).

Endnotes

[1] "In formal terms, federalism in modern usage is to be distinguished from unitary states, which are those in which all regional and local authority derives legally from the actions of the central government and can be taken away by that government at its pleasure, and, at the other extreme, from mere confederations, in which the central government does not reach individual citizens directly—as under the 1783 Articles of Confederation." Michael D. Reagan and John G. Sanzone, *The New Federalism,* 2nd ed. (New York: Oxford University Press, 1981), p. 9.

[2] The pioneer political scientist in this field of state political culture was Daniel J. Elazar. See his *American Federalism: A View From the States,* 3rd ed. (New York: Harper and Row, 1984), especially pp. 109–49.

[3] Cited in Charles R. Adrian, *State and Local Governments* (New York: McGraw-Hill, 1976), pp. 7–8.

[4] Luther Gulick, "Reorganization of the State," *Civil Engineering,* 3 (August, 1933): 421.

[5] Morton Grodzins, "The Federal System," in Irwin N. Gertzog, ed., *Readings on State and Local Government* (Englewood Cliffs, N.J.: Prentice-Hall, 1970), p. 4.

[6] Leon D. Epstein, "The Old States in a New System," in Anthony King, ed., *The New American Political System* (Washington, D.C.: American Enterprise Institute, 1978), p. 366.

[7] Daniel R. Grant and H. C. Nixon, *State and Local Governments in America,* 3rd ed. (Boston: Allyn and Bacon, 1975), pp. 108–9.

[8] Material in this section is based primarily on Herbert Jacob, *Justice in America,* 3rd ed. (Boston: Little, Brown and Company, 1978).

[9] The states are: Alaska, Arizona, Arkansas, California, Colorado, Florida, Idaho, Illinois, Maine, Maryland, Michigan, Missouri, Montana, Nebraska, Nevada, North Dakota, Ohio, Oklahoma, Oregon, Utah, Washington, and Wyoming.

[10] Austin Ranney, "Referendums: Election '88," *Public Opinion,* January/February 1989, pp. 15–17 and W. John Moore, "Election Day Lawmaking," *National Journal,* September 17, 1988, p. 2297.

[11] *The New York Times,* January 31, 1989.

[12] *Wall Street Journal,* February 21, 1989.

[13] Donald H. Haider, "Intergovernmental Redirection," *Annals of the American Academy of Political and Social Science,* Vol. 466 (March 1983), pp. 165–78.

[14] David P. Levine, *The Constitution of the United States* (Chicago: The University of Chicago Press, 1988), p. 28.

[15] U.S. Advisory Commission on Intergovernmental Relations, "Federalism in the Sixties: A Ten-Year Review," *Eleventh Annual Report* (Washington, D.C., Government Printing Office, 1970), p. 2.

[16] See Ronald D. Elving, "The War Between The States (Or Who's Really Getting The Most Money From Congress)," *Governing,* March 1988, pp. 19–23.

[17] Richard P. Nathan and Fred C. Doolittle, and Associates, *Reagan and The States* (Princeton: Princeton University Press, 1987). Much of the discussion of Reagan's federalism is drawn from this comprehensive study.

[18] Jerry Hagstrom, "Liberal and Minority Coalitions Pleading Their Cases in State Capitals," *National Journal* 17, no. 8, February 23, 1985, p. 426.

[19] David P. Currie, *The Constitution of the United States* (Chicago: The University of Chicago Press, 1988), p. 25.

⭐

CHAPTER 4

Civil Liberties and Rights: Protecting People from Power

★

Some years ago, the American Nazis, a small extremist group, announced plans for a May Day parade through Skokie, Illinois, a town containing 7000 survivors of German concentration camps. Skokie officials passed several town ordinances to prevent the march. Among them were prohibitions against public demonstrations by "members of political parties wearing military style uniforms" and distribution of material that "promotes or incites hatred, abuse or hostility" toward any racial, religious, or ethnic group. Town officials then won an Illinois Circuit Court injunction banning the proposed Nazi march, for it would violate all the ordinances.

Because of the free-speech issues involved, the Illinois branch of the American Civil Liberties Union decided to defend the Nazis' civil liberties—an unpopular decision that cost them about 15 percent of their membership. The ACLU argued that the laws were directed against freedom of speech and a symbol (the swastika), rather than at any illegal actions. Therefore the ordinances were violations of the First Amendment.

After more than a year of court cases, the Illinois Supreme Court eventually ruled, in *Village of Skokie* v. *the National Socialist Party of America,* that the Nazis could march and display their swastika, despite the threat of violence from counter demonstrators. Later, a federal court struck down the Skokie ordinances. By this time, the Nazis had decided to move the march because of the strong likelihood of a violent reaction in Skokie. They agreed to march in a park in Chicago if given a permit. A federal district judge, over the opposition of Chicago officials, ruled that the Nazis could march. The march took place without incident.

Should the Nazis have been allowed to march? The ACLU said yes. It argued that the First Amendment freedoms apply to everyone, no matter how unpopular the group or how disgusting its message. The sole function of government was to guard the line of march and prevent violence. If the Nazis are forbidden the right to demonstrate today, which group will be banned tomorrow?

Town officials took a different view. They argued that Skokie had an obligation to preserve the public peace. The requirement that swastikas not be displayed was simply a reasonable regulation to reduce tensions. If the Nazis refused to obey laws designed to protect them, then they gave up their right to march. Shouldn't local governments be able to defend their own streets against anti-democratic bullies?[1]

Nazi leader Frank Collins (speaking into the bullhorn) is shielded from eggs thrown by anti-Nazi counterdemonstrators at the Federal Plaza in Chicago in 1978.

Finding a balance between competing rights and conflicting groups consistent with constitutional principles is at the root of the problem facing decision makers in this and similar cases. Despite the absolute language of these rights—"No state shall make or enforce any law . . ." (14th Amendment)—interpreting and applying civil rights and liberties takes place amid politics. The historical expansion of these rights has taken place as ideas evolved and groups advanced, legally and politically.

CIVIL LIBERTIES AND CIVIL RIGHTS

In America, certain rules govern the relationships between the citizens and their government, and other rules govern the relationships between groups of citizens. The two principles on which these rules rest are straightforward: *the government must not violate the civil rights and liberties of the people; the government must protect citizens from the actions of others who would violate these rights.* These rules are, in the main, based on the Bill of Rights. These liberties have been widened as to whom they cover and deepened as to what they cover.

One general way of looking at the two terms is to see *civil liberties* as *protecting citizens against government actions* and *civil rights* as *protections given citizens against discrimination by other groups.* Civil liberties can be seen as protections given to all citizens (even Nazis) against the government (even of an Illinois town) infringing on rights such as freedom of speech. Civil rights, though granted to all citizens, usually refer to rules preventing discrimination against particular groups because of race, religion, or sex.

Clearly the terms overlap. When a black leader is arrested after giving a fiery speech, his followers may claim that both his civil liberties (freedom of speech) and his civil rights (freedom from racial discrimination) are being violated. The differences, though helpful for understanding, may be difficult to apply in the real world.

Civil liberties are rights of freedom of speech, petition, assembly, and press that protect citizens against governmental actions that would interfere with their participation in a democratic political system. This definition includes various guarantees of due process of law in courtroom proceedings. The underlying principle here is that ours is a government of laws, rather than of arbitrary and unfair action. **Civil rights** are the protections granted in the Constitution recognizing that all citizens must be treated equally under the laws. No racial, religious, or economic group can claim or receive privi-

Below, a group of veterans and their supporters wave an American flag on Michigan Avenue in Chicago in March 1989 during a protest of a controversial student exhibit in the School of the Art Institute. At left, the exhibit, titled "What Is the Proper Way to Display a U.S. Flag?", consists of an American flag placed on the floor to be walked on in front of books in which viewers are invited to comment.

leged treatment. Nor can any group be discriminated against by other groups or by majorities acting through the state or national government.

Examples of these issues are present in all our lives. Civil liberties may involve your rights as a college student: Can school authorities censor the student newspaper? suspend you for demonstrating? prevent you from wearing a political button to class? Other issues involve your right as a citizen to be informed: Can the government prevent a newspaper from publishing a story? Can it require reporters to reveal sources? Can the government censor books dealing with the CIA?

Women, minorities, and everyone else may be affected by civil rights issues: Will you receive equal pay for equal work? Will you be discriminated against in hiring and promotion? And will affirmative-action programs designed to make up for past discrimination against another group lead to "reverse discrimination" against you?

These issues are also becoming more important in American politics. In the last presidential election, prayer in the public schools, abortion, and the right to say or not to say the Pledge of Allegiance were major issues. Of course, the government has not just been a defender of rights, it has also violated peoples' liberties (see the box on page 96). To get a better grip on these current and past issues, it is helpful to look at how these rights and liberties found their way into the Constitution and how they've been expanded since then.

★ Uncle Sam vs. Civil Liberties

Throughout United States history there are uncomfortable reminders of government actions that many would now see as violating the Bill of Rights.

Not many years after the ink had dried on the Constitution, Congress passed the *Alien and Sedition Acts* of 1798. These acts promised heavy fines and imprisonment for those guilty of writing or speaking anything false, scandalous, or malicious against any government official. Such a broad prohibition today would put an end to most political campaigns—which was also the intent then. The conviction of one congressman under the law caused a political uproar.

The slavery issue in 1840 led Congress to pass the "Gag Rule" preventing antislavery petitions from being received by Congress (thus violating a specific First Amendment right). Not to be outdone, President Andrew Jackson called on Congress to pass a bill prohibiting the use of the mails to encourage slave rebellions. The bill didn't pass—not on grounds of free speech, but because the states concerned were already censoring the mails.

Violations of civil liberties continued into the twentieth century. Within five months after the United States entered World World I, every leading socialist newspaper had been suspended from the mails at least once, some permanently. The *Smith Act* of 1940 forbade teaching or advocating the violent overthrow of the government. In 1951, eleven Communist party leaders were convicted under it for activities labeled "preparation for revolution." This "preparation" involved teaching major works of Marxist thought, like the *Communist Manifesto,* which today can be found in any college library. Ten defendants were each sentenced to five years in prison. The Smith Act remains a law to this day.

THE ORIGIN AND EXPANSION OF THE BILL OF RIGHTS

Many of the framers of the Constitution shared Alexander Hamilton's belief that there was no need for a Bill of Rights. In Federalist 84, Hamilton wrote that a Bill of Rights might be necessary to restrict a king, but not a government established by the people. Such a government, he argued, possesses only the powers given to it by the people. "Why, for instance, should it be said that the liberty of the press shall not be restrained, when no power is given by which restrictions may be imposed?" he asked. Adding a Bill of Rights to the Constitution would even be dangerous, Hamilton said. Placing restrictions on powers that had not been granted to the government in the first place might give the government a "pretext to claim more than were granted."

The Philadelphia convention failed to include a bill of rights in the original Constitution, not so much because of opposition to the ideals of the bill, but from a feeling that such a statement was irrelevant. (A proposed bill of rights was voted down unanimously near the end of the convention partly because everyone was worn out and wanted to go home.) *Most of the framers believed that liberty was best protected by procedures,* such as federalism and checks and balances, established by their constitutional government. No matter what ideals were written down, the Federalists argued, support for them would depend on the "tolerance of the age" and the balance of forces established by the Constitution.

These arguments were not shared by other American leaders. Thomas Jefferson supported the Constitution but felt the document needed a bill of rights. As he wrote to James Madison from Paris, "A bill of rights is what the people are entitled to against every form of government on earth . . ."[2] For Jefferson, these natural rights due all people must be honored in their Constitution.

Although the supporters of the Bill of Rights lost the battle in Philadelphia, they soon won the war. Massachusetts and Virginia agreed to ratify the Constitution with the recommendation that a bill of rights be the first order of business of the new Congress. During the first session of Congress, James Madison introduced a series of proposals for amending the Constitution. Harkening back to the Declaration of Independence, he said that it was necessary to make clear that the new U.S. government would not attempt to violate the rights of persons and property, which had been declared "unalienable" by the Declaration. The states ratified ten of twelve proposed amendments approved by Congress. (The two not ratified had to do with compensation for members of Congress and the size of the House of Representatives.) The Bill of Rights became part of the Constitution on December 15, 1791.

Expanding the Bill of Rights

When the Bill of Rights was added to the Constitution, it applied only to the activities of the federal government—Congress and the president. The framers had no intention of restricting the activities of state governments. Since then, the rights guaranteed to citizens under the Bill of Rights have been *widened* as to whom they cover and *deepened* as to what they cover. Perhaps the most significant expansion has been in their application to state governments and individuals.

How can federal courts today apply the Bill of Rights to actions of state officials or of private individuals? The answer rests in the

Fourteenth Amendment, adopted after the Civil War. That 1868 amendment says, in part, "nor shall any State deprive any person of life, liberty or property, without due process of law, nor deny to any person within its jurisdiction the equal protection of the laws." The two key, if vague, phrases are "due process" and "equal protection." They have been used by the courts over the years to both extend and increase the protections granted in the Bill of Rights.

The "equal protection" clause has been used to prevent state officials from engaging in racial or sexual discrimination. It has also prevented discrimination by private individuals when that action: (1) is aided by state action such as a law; (2) furthers a state activity such as an election, or the activities of a political party; or (3) involves a fundamental state interest such as education or public safety. Therefore, though individuals may discriminate in whom they invite to their homes or associate with in private clubs, they cannot discriminate in associations such as private schools, because education involves a fundamental state interest. Private clubs useful for professional purposes that bar women from membership may be forced not to discriminate.

The Doctrine of Incorporation

The "due process" clause of the Fourteenth Amendment echoes similar language in the Fifth Amendment of the Bill of Rights and has been interpreted to extend the regulation of government from the national to the state sphere. The debate over the meaning and application of due process illustrates how the doctrine of incorporation is used in expanding the coverage of the Bill of Rights.

It was not until a 1925 case that the Supreme Court announced the **doctrine of incorporation,** holding that the freedoms of speech and press in the U.S. Bill of Rights were a part of the "liberty" that the Fourteenth Amendment prohibited the states from denying. In *Gitlow* v. *New York,* the court refused to overturn a New York criminal anarchy law, but in an almost casual sentence in the opinion, the court reversed fifty years of refusal to apply the Fourteenth Amendment to the states by stating:

> *For present purposes we may and do assume that freedom of speech and of the press which are protected by the First Amendment from abridgement by Congress are among the fundamental personal rights and liberties protected by the due process clause of the Fourteenth Amendment from impairment by the States.[3]*

Bowing to increased pressure, fraternal organizations and private clubs that were once for men only are now beginning to allow women to join. In 1987, both the Lions Club International and Kiwanis International began to admit women. In July 1989, the Elks Club decided that women would still not be permitted to join. Below, an Elks couple; while women may not join the Elks, they are invited to join an auxilary organization, such as the Does.

Gitlow led to an ongoing debate over how many of the Bill of Rights could be applied to the states. On one side of the debate over due process are the **partial incorporationists.** They see the due process language of the Fourteenth Amendment as meaning that the states must obey some parts of the Bill of Rights, mainly those procedures guaranteeing a fair trial. First Amendment freedoms of religion, speech, and the press might also be included by partial incorporationists as applicable to the states. In other words, the language of the Fourteenth Amendment is a "shorthand" phrase that includes some of the protections of the Bill of Rights and applies them against actions of state officials. Which rights are incorported? That is left for the courts to decide.

An opposing definition of due process is given by judges and lawyers who are **complete incorporationists.** They believe simply that because of the Fourteenth Amendment, every provision of the Bill of Rights should be applied to the states. The complete incorporationists thus do not have to consider which rights to apply when a case comes before them—they apply them all. The partial incorporationists, however, must decide whether to break new ground by moving another right onto their list of those "incorporated" into the Fourteenth Amendment.

For example, take the case of a prisoner held in a state penitentiary who is suing the warden in a federal court. The prisoner charges that two months of solitary confinement for a mess hall riot is a violation of the Eighth Amendment prohibition against cruel and unusual punishment.

A judge who is a partial incorporationist would have to decide whether or not the Eighth Amendment should be incorporated into the Fourteenth Amendment as a limit on state prison officials. He might argue that the "due process" clause of the Fourteenth Amendment applies only to criminal trials in the states. Because the prisoner has already been tried, rights under the Bill of Rights are forfeited once in a state prison.

A judge who is a full incorporationist might argue that the entire Bill of Rights was incorporated into the Fourteenth Amendment and therefore applies to the state prison warden. The judge would then decide whether two months of solitary confinement did indeed constitute "cruel and unusual punishment."

By the 1980s, the Supreme Court had held on a case-by-case basis that the Fourteenth Amendment incorporated most of the Bill of Rights—such as the freedoms of press, of assembly, and of religion—making them apply to state (and local) as well as federal actions (See Figure 4.1). The only Bill of Rights safeguards that have not been specifically incorporated are relatively minor ones: the right to grand jury criminal indictment, the right to trial by jury in civil cases, the right to bear arms, protection against excessive bail and fines, and protection against involuntary quartering of troops in private homes.

To sum up, *the original Bill of Rights declared that the national government could not deprive citizens of certain rights. Now because of courts applying the Fourteenth Amendment, state and local governments (and individuals) cannot do most of the same things, either.*[4]

CIVIL LIBERTIES: PROTECTING PEOPLE FROM THE GOVERNMENT

The framers of the Constitution believed in limited government because they thought that the greatest danger to citizens lay in the abuse of governmental power. For this reason, the most important civil liberties provide protection for those participating in the democratic process. Most of these are called **First Amendment freedoms** because they are derived from the First Amendment, which reads:

> *Congress shall make no law respecting an establishment of religion, or prohibiting the free exercise thereof; or abridging the freedom of speech, or of the press, or the right of the people peaceably to assemble, and to petition the Government for a redress of grievances.*

Without such freedoms, a government might muzzle opposition politicians. Citizens in the minority after one election would have no

In what was later acknowledged as a violation of constitutional guarantees, an emergency order during World War II required Japanese-Americans to relocate to internment camps. At right, Japanese-Americans wait for registration at a Santa Anita, California reception center. Above, a grandfather and his grandsons await their relocation orders in 1942.

FIGURE 4 ★ 1
Incorporation of the Bill of Rights

The U.S. Supreme Court has incorporated most of the provisions of the Bill of Rights under the concept of "liberty" in the Fourteenth Amendment, making them restraints on the states, not just on the federal government.

Freedom of Speech *Gitlow* v. *New York*, 1925	Right to Counsel in Felony Cases *Gideon* v. *Wainwright*, 1963
Freedom of Press *Near* v. *Minnesota*, 1931	Right Against Self-incrimination *Mallory* v. *Hogan*, 1964
Fair Trial *Powell* v. *Alabama*, 1932	Right to Confront Witnesses *Pointer* v. *Texas*, 1965
Free Exercise of Religion *Hamilton* v. *Regents of California*, 1934	Right of Privacy *Griswold* v. *Connecticut*, 1965
Freedom of Assembly *De Jonge* v. *Oregon*, 1937	Speedy Trial *Klopfer* v. *North Carolina*, 1967
Establishment of Religion *Everson* v. *Board of Education*, 1947	Jury Trial for All Serious Crimes *Duncan* v. *Louisiana*, 1968
Public Trial *In re Oliver*, 1948	Right Against Double Jeopardy *Benton* v. *Maryland*, 1969
Unreasonable Searches and Seizures *Wolf* v. *Colorado*, 1949	Right to Counsel in Cases Involving Jail Terms *Argersinger* v. *Ma Hamlin*, 1972
Cruel and Unusual Punishment *Robinson* v. *California*, 1962	

opportunity to win future elections. The First Amendment's "rules of the game" allow democracy to work. The First Amendment freedoms enable people to obtain information and to communicate with their leaders without fear. Without these protections, it would be difficult for the political actors covered in the rest of this book to function. The press, political parties, interest groups, even Congress, would find their ability to "go public" and organize to change government policies very restricted. The Bill of Rights, along with separation of powers and checks and balances, protect a people who have a healthy fear of government.

A famous Supreme Court justice, Oliver Wendell Holmes, once wrote that a democratic society needs competition among ideas as much as an economic marketplace needs competition among producers. "When men have realized that time has upset many fighting faiths," he wrote, "they come to believe . . . that the ultimate good desired is better reached by free trade in ideas—that the best truth is the power of the thought to get itself accepted in the competition of the marketplace . . ." [5] Put another way, how can people be sure their

Americans are constantly voicing their opinions through assemblies, demonstrations, and protests, such as this march on Washington in 1987.

opinions are right unless they hear wrong opinions? How can wrong opinions be changed unless right opinions can be heard?

A look at recent thinking about four of the most important civil liberties will make these points clear. The liberties are *freedom of speech* and *of religion,* which come directly from the First Amendment; *rights of privacy,* which are found in the First and Fourth Amendments; and *due process,* which is stated in the Fifth and Fourteenth Amendments as a support of those liberties in the First. Taken together, they go far in describing the constitutional protections that keep government off the backs of its citizens.

Freedom of Speech

The First Amendment guarantee of **freedom of speech** has been extended to state governments under the Fourteenth Amendment. Its meaning has also been deepened by various court decisions. "Speech" now includes not only speaking, but also gesturing, belonging to organizations, wearing buttons or raising signs, and leafleting passersby. The Supreme Court has upheld laws passed by Congress designed to regulate the Communist party, which make it a crime to conspire to overthrow the government by force. But it has also struck down various convictions of Communists because the government was prosecuting them simply for membership in the party, and not for conspiracy to commit a defined act. Mere belief in the violent overthrow of the government—even a speech about revolution—does not justify laws imprisoning the advocates of these positions. The courts insist that if the government wishes to put these people in prison, it must prove that they conspired to commit a crime.

Clearly Americans have the right of free speech. Just as clearly, the American government has the duty to maintain public order. Neither the individual right nor the governmental power is absolute. Thus, it is up to the courts to balance the two.

But judicial rules about balancing are not clearly defined, and the courts exercise much discretion in applying them. One of the earliest rules, called the *clear and present danger* doctrine, was first announced in a decision by Justice Holmes. It held that speech cannot be restricted unless the words used create a clear and present danger that evil will result before there is time for a full discussion. The classic example of this is in falsely shouting "fire" in a crowded theatre.[6]

In recent cases, *balancing* has become the rule for speech that advocates violation of the law. In such cases, the Supreme Court balances the interests of the government in keeping order and the interests of the individual in exercising First Amendment freedoms. Much depends upon the facts of the particular case, whether the case arises in peacetime or wartime, and what the public mood is. The Supreme Court has used the balancing rule to decide that a person

Drawing by Lorenz © 1985; The New Yorker Magazine, Inc.

"With us tonight are Ray Barris, hiding behind the First Amendment in Chicago; Cathy Tole, hiding behind the First Amendment in San Francisco; and Charles Romero, hiding behind the First Amendment in Detroit."

Mary Beth Tinker sits with her mother as her school board in Des Moines, Iowa meets to decide her case in 1965. Tinker and her brother were suspended from school for wearing black armbands to protest the Vietnam War. The Supreme Court later ruled in favor of the Tinkers, holding that students have a limited right to freedom of speech.

may be punished for urging resistance to the draft or advocating the overthrow of the government. In the Skokie case, it was relevant to the court that the Nazis represented the rantings of a few dozen people rather than a widespread movement.

In general, legislation that attempts to restrict First Amendment freedoms of expression must not be any broader than is necessary to accomplish a legitimate and very important governmental purpose. The Supreme Court has looked with special skepticism at governmental attempts, through laws or enforcement, to impose **prior restraint** on expression—to prevent it from being uttered or printed—rather than punish it afterward.

The Supreme Court has given some protection to what is called "speech plus." This involves various symbolic actions, such as picketing, wearing buttons, burning the flag, but not burning draft cards. One case upheld the right of students protesting against the Vietnam War to wear black armbands in their junior high school. In another case, an antiwar student who entered a courthouse with the words "F_____ the Draft" written on his jacket was held in contempt by a local judge, but the decision was reversed by the Supreme Court. As former Justice John Harlan pointed out, "while the particular four-letter word being litigated here is perhaps more distasteful than most others of its genre, it is nevertheless often true that one man's vulgarity is another's lyric."[7]

However, the First Amendment provides no protection to speech that directly motivates listeners to engage in illegal conduct. In cases in which an individual addresses abuse and "fighting words" to someone, particularly a law enforcement official, the balance may swing toward restriction. The courts have upheld convictions of speakers for incitement to riot, disturbance of the peace, and other criminal acts. When individuals and groups move from *protected speech* to *prohibited action,* the First Amendment shield is unlikely to guard them.

Freedom of Religion

There has never been a complete separation of church and state in America: the armed forces have their chaplains; the Supreme Court chambers have a mural of Moses giving the Ten Commandments; and the dollar bill proclaims: "In God We Trust." But the recent rise in political importance of Christian fundamentalists has led them (along with some Catholics and Orthodox Jews) to try to redefine the nature of church-state relations.

Fundamentalists, who believe that the Bible contains the word of God and is the literal truth, want to permit prayer in schools on the grounds of freedom of speech and religion. Some fundamentalists want to be able to restrict books in the school curriculum or libraries, while others believe that the schools are dominated by "secular humanists" and that Christians must bring their religious values back into the classroom.

Establishment

In these issues, the right to exercise one's religion inevitably gets mixed up in the constitutional prohibition against the establishment of religion. To allow students to pray in school, a position favored by 70 percent of Americans in a 1988 Gallup poll, may seem to be simply an issue of freedom of religion. But if most children in the class are Protestant, should the prayer be Protestant? Will other children feel like outcasts, even if they are excused from the room? If school authorities, in an attempt to avoid favoring one religion, try to compose a bland prayer to God, is that a form of "civil religion"? And do politicians have any business writing prayers? Even a moment of silence has been determined by the Supreme Court to go beyond the church-state boundary.

School prayer cases have caused an enormous outburst of complaints against the Supreme Court. Unsuccessful attempts have been made to amend the Constitution to allow "voluntary" prayer in public schools. In 1984, Senate proponents failed to get the necessary two-thirds vote (56 voted "aye," 44 voted "no") for a proposed constitutional amendment, backed by President Reagan, that would

This nativity scene in Pawtucket, Rhode Island was ruled unconstitutional by a federal judge in 1981 in response to a suit brought by the American Civil Lilberties Union. It was not displayed again until 1984 when the Supreme Court overturned the decision and ruled that city-sponsored creches don't violate the separation of church and state.

have allowed organized prayer in public schools. The decisions continue to stand.

Despite these rulings, prayers are still regularly said. Christian holidays such as Christmas and Easter are still observed in public schools throughout the United States. In a 5–4, 1984 decision, the Supreme Court ruled that a city could include a Christian nativity scene as part of an official Christmas display (which also included reindeer, a Christmas tree, and other seasonal symbols).[8] Since many American schoolchildren come from non-Christian, nonreligious families, many public schools continue to be, in a sense, the parochial schools of the majority. Often, those who might bring lawsuits to challenge these practices are not sufficiently upset, do not want to stand up publicly against strong majority pressure, or do not feel economically able to do so.

The Supreme Court has been fairly lenient in allowing the use of government money for church-run hospitals and colleges. It has been more strict about public funds being used in elementary and secondary schools. The rationale for this difference is that there is little likelihood of religious indoctrination at public expense in colleges and hospitals, as long as the money is not used specifically for religious training or religious buildings. In regard to elementary and secondary parochial schools, the rule is that government may aid the student in certain ways but may not aid the school itself. Similar reasoning was used by the Court in a 1989 ruling that states could not exempt religious publications from paying sales taxes, since that would violate the First Amendment ban on the establishment of a religion.

Free Exercise

Americans have a right to believe in any religion they please. They also have the right not to believe in any religion. A person cannot be required to swear to a belief in God in order to get a job or hold public office. A person can be required to abide by a "valid secular law"—one that applies to everyone—even though such a law may violate the person's religious beliefs. But what is a valid secular law? The test, again, involves a type of balancing. *The courts attempt to measure whether the government's interest in making and enforcing the law is sufficiently strong to override the individual's right to religious freedom.*

For example, the Court has upheld laws that require vaccination of children on the basis that the government's interest in protecting public health overrides conflicting religious beliefs. However, irrespective of presidential campaigns, the government cannot compel a person to salute the American flag. In a famous "flag-salute case,"

★ Jar Wars

Traditionally, rival American politicians have matched wits. In recent elections, some matched urine samples.

President Reagan and his cabinet led many candidates in 1986 in taking drug tests. Testing became the issue of the hour. A presidential commission proposed that all federal government employees be subjected to urine tests. One-fourth of major American companies imposed some form of drug testing.

Supporters of testing argued that drugs harmed worker performance and health, and that companies have a right to expect that their workers will not be stoned. They believed that only random testing could serve as a deterrent to use. Civil liberties groups pointed out that the Constitution's ban on indiscriminate search and seizure of evidence protects the individual's right to privacy. If people are considered innocent until convicted, then employers need probable cause of drug use prior to testing.

With the courts generally against testing, companies began to turn to education and rehabilitation, methods used to reduce smoking. Politicians began to view drug tests as a "fad issue." Four months after calling for a "national crusade against drugs," and two months after the 1986 elections, President Reagan cut $913 million from drug programs.

members of the Jehovah's Witnesses sect would not allow their children to salute the flag, believing that it violated God's commandment against worshipping graven images. In a decision based both on freedom of speech and freedom of religion, the Court acknowledged that the government had an interest in promoting national loyalty but said that it could not require it because freedom of speech includes the right not to speak or make a symbolic expression. That is the present law.

Prohibiting the *establishment* of a religion by the government while permitting its *free exercise* sets up inevitable conflicts, like the one over school prayer. While Americans strongly support freedom of religion, most firmly believe that to avoid religious conflict the government must not favor one religion over another. Balancing these competing values is very difficult. As the Supreme Court itself once confessed, "we can only dimly perceive the lines of demarcation in this extraordinarily sensitive area of constitutional law."

Rights of Privacy

To what extent do citizens have privacy rights against snooping government officials or attempts to regulate their intimate social, sexual, and cultural behavior? The First and Fourth Amendments, along with other parts of the Bill of Rights, are read by the courts as creating a *zone of privacy* that shields individuals from government intrusion into their thoughts, religious beliefs, and some actions. Just as parts of the First Amendment offer protection to individuals in public affairs, so too the Amendment guards against involvement of the state in private matters. The First Amendment not only gives us the freedom to tell the government what we do believe, but also— for example, we need not recite an oath of allegiance—gives us the freedom not to have to say what we don't believe.

The Fourth Amendment states that

> *"the rights of the people to be secure in their persons, houses, papers, and effects, against unreasonable searches and seizures, shall not be violated, and no Warrants shall issue, but upon probable cause, supported by Oath or affirmation, and particularly describing the place to be searched, or the persons or things to be seized."*

This protects an individual's home and person against unreasonable searches. Generally, a search warrant must be obtained from a judge before a search can be conducted. It must specify the place to be searched and the articles to be seized. Random drug testing without "probable cause" is thought by many to be a warrantless search (see the box on page 107). Similar violations include electronic surveillance with wiretaps or bugs, which, except for emergencies involving

The First and Fourth Amendments protect a citizen's home and person against unreasonable searches. Usually a search warrant obtained from a judge is required before a search can be conducted.

national security, also require a warrant from a federal or state judge. The Warren Court (headed by Chief Justice Earl Warren) issued a number of decisions that broadened protection against unreasonable searches. The Burger Court (headed by Chief Justice Warren Burger) generally narrowed these protections.

What can be done if these rules are violated? In federal courts, the judge may exclude the use of illegally obtained evidence against a defendant, called the **Exclusionary Rule.** But the Burger court has reduced somewhat the force of this sanction. In a 1984 opinion, the Supreme Court under Chief Justice Warren Burger adopted an "inevitable discovery exception" to the Exclusionary Rule, holding that when evidence obtained by an illegal search would inevitably have been discovered without police error or misconduct, the evidence is admissible.[9]

Some recent privacy issues have centered on personal sexual conduct between adults. The state, according to the Supreme Court, cannot prevent couples from using contraceptive devices. The state cannot forbid sexual relations between individuals of different races. On the other hand, courts have ruled that individuals of the same sex are not protected from state action if they attempt to have sexual relations, and that homosexual marriages need not be recognized by states (see the box on page 116).

Due Process Rights

Justice Felix Frankfurter said once that court cases generally involve "not very nice people." As a result, the protections they receive are often not very popular. While the complaints heard often have some justifications, these safeguards are meant to protect all of us. Our system rests on the idea that nice people can only be protected when not-very-nice people are also protected.

Many of these safeguards are captured in the constitutional phrase, "due process of law." As mentioned before, the Fifth Amendment prevents the national government, and the Fourteenth Amendment prevents state governments, from depriving citizens of their lives, liberty, or property without "due process of law." **Due process** rights involve fundamental procedural fairness and impartial decision making by government officials, especially in courtrooms. In criminal cases the right to due process would generally include adequate advance notice of the charge, representation by a competent lawyer, the right to confront and cross-examine the accuser, a written record of proceedings, a speedy and fair trial by an impartial judge and jury of one's peers, and the right to appeal the decision to a higher court.

These rights were granted in federal criminal trials by the Fifth and Sixth Amendments. Gradually, as a result of Supreme Court decisions over the years, many of these rights have been established in state criminal trials as well.[10] In the 1970s the federal courts began to require that some of these procedures be introduced into non-court settings. Students could not be transferred, suspended, or expelled from universities without certain kinds of hearings. People on welfare could not be purged from the rolls, nor could tenants in public housing be evicted, without going through due process proceedings.

Consider the case of a student who has received a government loan for college tuition and is then told by some government officials that she is ineligible. Surely she would want all the due process guarantees she could obtain in order to prove to these officials that she had a "right" to the loan. Thus, due process standards serve as a useful check against unfair actions by bureaucrats. Obtaining one due process right often leads to efforts to gain others. Once the right to a "fair hearing" is obtained, the student might demand a lawyer to represent her. Once a lawyer is in the picture, he or she may demand a written transcript and the right to appeal. Often the existence of a fair hearing and the presence of a lawyer will encourage officials to settle issues informally, without a hearing—a money-saving step usually welcomed by all parties.

These due process issues are directly related to First Amendment political freedoms. It does little good to give people the right to protest or to petition the government if officials can retaliate by cutting off essential services or funds to protestors. Students or workers who are politically involved need legal protection from unfair actions by school officials or employers. Due process protects them.

CIVIL RIGHTS: PROTECTING PEOPLE FROM PEOPLE

So far, the chapter has examined relationships between government and the individual. But a large set of civil rights involves the treatment of minorities (including women) by majorities. Here the government becomes potentially a positive force for ensuring that the rights of minorities are protected against unjust actions by majorities and their elected representatives.

Civil rights issues involve discrimination based on classifications such as race, religion, sex, or national origin. A group that believes it is being discriminated against cannot always rely on the private arena for fair treatment. The minority group can try to obtain satisfaction from elected officials, or it may turn to the judiciary to end discrimination practiced against it.

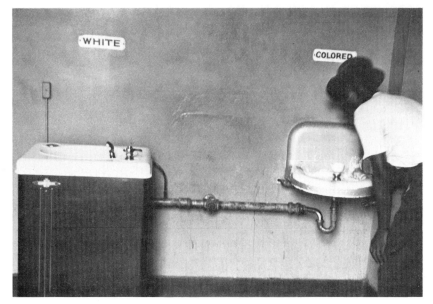

The passage of the Civil Rights Act of 1964 sought to end discrimination in public accommodations in America. The signs in the picture at left do not refer to the complextion of the water.

For example, African-Americans could not purchase homes of their choice in the free market because sellers discriminated against their race. No matter how much they were willing to pay, they could not buy the housing they wanted. They sought a presidential order banning racial discrimination in housing that involved federally financed mortgages. Travelers denied the right to eat in a restaurant or sleep in a motel room because of their race simply could not depend on the free market for relief. To obtain a remedy, they went through the political system—in this case, congressional passage of the Civil Rights Act of 1964 with its provisions for an end to discrimination in public accommodations.

The civil rights conflicts of the past thirty years have involved the struggle for rights by a minority against discrimination by the majority. In recent years more complicated situations arose, at times pitting one group suffering from discrimination against others. The woman who supports affirmative-action programs in order to get a job is in conflict with the black man who thought affirmative action would involve only race. Blacks who want quotas for admission to professional schools came into conflict with Jews who remember that a generation ago such quotas were used to keep them out of these schools. As one group after another receives that status of a "protected class" (to which affirmative-action goals apply), the meaning of affirmative action may be diluted. Dr. Kenneth Clark, a noted black civil rights leader, asked, "Are there now so many protected groups that none are protected?"

Demonstrators march down Constitution Avenue from the Washington Monument to the Lincoln Memorial during the civil rights March on Washington in 1963.

Which People Need Protection?

The right to receive "equal protection of the laws" comes from the Fourteenth Amendment, adopted at the end of the Civil War in 1868. The government can, however, still pass laws applying to some citizens and not to others. The question lies in the limits placed on the ability of national and state governments to classify citizens and pass legislation affecting them. One important limit placed by the courts on government actions is called a **suspect classification.** These are categories the government must show to be necessary. Governments must, when the law or action touches a "suspect class," prove a compelling state interest to justify their action. *A suspect category is one the courts will look at with the assumption that it violates the equal-protection guarantee unless it can be proved otherwise.* Race has become a suspect category in recent times, and sex has verged on becoming one without quite having made it.[11]

Race as a Suspect Classification

For many years the Supreme Court upheld racial segregation. The phrase "equal protection of the laws" was interpreted to mean that facilities (such as schools and public transport) that were racially segregated, but equal, did not violate the Fourteenth Amendment. In practice, even facilities that were not really equal were permitted by the courts. Then, in the 1954 landmark case of *Brown* v. *Board of Education,* the Supreme Court held that schools segregated by race were always unequal, violated the Fourteenth Amendment, and were therefore unconstitutional. In the *Brown* case, a black Kansas school girl sued to go to a white school one block from her house, arguing the social-psychological harm done to blacks by racial segregation. After *Brown,* courts eventually struck down all laws based on racial categories and made race a "suspect classification" when placed in state or national laws.

But do racial classifications always violate the Fourteenth Amendment? Or are there circumstances in which classification by race is a valid exercise of governmental power? Courts have decided that even though racial classifications are suspect, they may be used in laws or in court decisions when they serve to eliminate prior state-sponsored segregation. The courts may use their power to consider the racial makeup of schools and to issue orders for assignment of pupils to new schools based on their race.

In 1978, in *University of California Regents* v. *Bakke,* the Supreme Court was faced with the case of Alan Bakke, a white applicant to medical school who had been rejected for admission while minority students who had scored lower were admitted because sixteen places had been reserved for minorities. While the court struck down the sixteen-place quota and ordered Bakke admitted, it upheld the principle of affirmative action in order to give universities some flexibility in admitting minority students. In 1986, the Court upheld promotion quotas in *Cleveland Firefighters,* where the quotas were narrowly focused on specific practices of past discrimination.

By 1989, the court seemed to be making all racial classifications questionable. In *City of Richmond* v. *Croson,* a set-aside program by which 30 percent of the dollars in city contracts had to go to minority-controlled firms was thrown out. The reasoning was that any official act giving preference to one race over another had to be narrowly tailored and subject to *strict scrutiny* by the courts. It was expected that after the Richmond set-aside case, judicial approval of affirmative action programs would be the exception, not the rule.[12]

Supporters of "benign" quotas argue that there is a difference between a racial classification designed to discriminate against a minority group and a classification designed to help a group by making up for past discrimination. But the opinion of the Supreme Court appears to be evolving back toward the principle stated by Justice Harlan in 1896: "Our Constitution is color-blind, and neither knows nor tolerates caste among citizens. In respect to civil rights, all citizens are equal before the law."

Members of the National Association for the Advancement of Colored People (NAACP) march in New York with a makeshift coffin for voter apathy to promote voter registration in 1984.

Is Sex Suspect?

Until recently, most laws containing classifications based on gender were justified because some supposedly provided benefits to women. Under this reasoning, courts upheld state laws keeping women off juries, barring them from certain professions, and preventing them from assuming certain legal responsibilities involving property or contracts. As Supreme Court Justice Brennan observed, this "romantic paternalism" had the effect of putting women, "not on a pedestal, but in a cage."

In the 1970s, women's groups began attacking these laws in federal courts, arguing that sex should be considered a suspect category. The Supreme Court responded unevenly. Some laws have been upheld and others struck down. The court has allowed state laws granting certain tax benefits to widows but not widowers, and permitting men but not women to serve as guards in maximum security prisons, and has permitted single-sex schools. On the other hand, the court has ruled that men have equal rights to sue for alimony, that the drinking age must be the same for both sexes, and that unwed fathers have rights in deciding whether or not their babies are put up for adoption.

The Supreme Court has gone about halfway in making gender a suspect category. It has allowed the government to reasonably show that sex classifications serve important governmental objectives. Men but not women are required to register for the draft, for example, and the Supreme Court upheld this law in a 1982 decision. In employment, the Court has followed laws passed by Congress in viewing women as a "protected class" able to benefit from affirmative-action programs.

The Court has also decided that victims of sex discrimination must prove that public officials intended to discriminate against them. Merely showing that a law has different effects on each sex is not enough. This "rule of intention, not merely results" favors the government, because often it is hard to prove a deliberate intent to discriminate. The *Equal Rights Amendment* would have outlawed gender classifications so that they would be struck down in much the same way as racial categories were under the Fourteenth Amendment. Although the ERA did not become part of the Constitution, it is likely that more sex-based classifications will fall as a result of the present standards applied by the Courts.

THE BILL OF RIGHTS AND THE PUBLIC

These rights and liberties are applied and argued by various groups in the political arena. Within the government, the courts have been the most important player, although the legislative and executive branches may pass laws, issue executive orders, and monitor developments. Outside the government are a number of organizations that champion the rights of particular groups. *Surrounding these debates is the general public, which ultimately will accept or ignore the applications of these rights.* The politics of civil liberties and rights involves struggles of group against group, as society attempts to strike a balance among competing claims and values.[13]

Judges

Many judges have played a leading role in expanding and deepening civil rights and liberties. These activist judges (who, along with other supporters of civil liberties, are called *civil libertarians*) usually support transferring civil rights cases from state courts to federal courts, where they generally receive more favorable attention. They back **class-action suits,** in which people bring a case to court not only for themselves but on behalf of everyone in a similar situation—perhaps millions of people. To decide a case, they may use not only previous cases and legislative laws, but also the concept of **equity.**

Equitable remedies are used to prevent future permanent damage in situations not covered by existing law. Suppose my neighbor, Jones, decides to cut down a tree in his yard. I see that the tree will crash into my house. My legal remedy is to sue Jones after my house is damaged. My equitable remedy is to obtain an injunction that prevents Jones from cutting down the tree.

Take a school district that has been segregated by race because of state laws and administrative action. Some activist judges have applied an equitable remedy: they have required that the school districts take into account racial imbalances and then come up with plans (some of which involve busing) to overcome the imbalances. (See the case study in Chapter 15.) Other judges are more restrained in cases of civil liberties and rights. They are unsympathetic to class actions. They tend to follow past decisions rather than establishing new rights. Because elected officials are directly accountable to the people, these judges hesitate to impose their own views on the president, Congress, or state legislatures.

The Justice Department

At times the Department of Justice has played a key role in protecting civil rights and liberties. Its lawyers in the U.S. Attorney's offices may prosecute persons, including state or federal officials, accused of violating people's civil rights. Justice Department lawyers may intervene in cases brought by civil rights groups and help argue them in

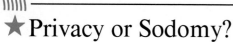

★ Privacy or Sodomy?

In 1986, the Supreme Court ruled that there is no constitutional right for homosexuals to engage in sodomy. In *Hardwick* v. *Bowers,* a Georgia man was arrested in his bedroom for having oral sex with another man. The policeman had entered the house with a warrant for a drinking fine. Georgia outlaws sodomy, gay or straight, with a punishment of one to twenty years in prison. Although the state dropped the charges, the accused filed suit to overturn the law as an unconstitutional invasion of privacy guaranteed under the Fourth Amendment.

The Court held 5–4 that a state may outlaw homosexual sodomy, even if practiced between consenting individuals in the privacy of their home. The majority opinion rejected the view that "any kind of private sexual conduct between consenting adults is constitutionally insulated from state proscription." It pointed to laws against incest and said that laws against homosexuality have "ancient roots." Since the decision, the rarely enforced laws against homosexuality have continued to be rarely enforced.

court. They may draw guidelines for federal agencies to ensure protection of civil rights and liberties.

Under President Reagan, the Department of Justice opposed the goals of civil rights groups. The department intervened in court cases against court-ordered busing and affirmative-action hiring programs, preferring a "color-blind" rather than a "color-conscious" approach to ending discrimination. Under President Bush's Attorney General, Dick Thornbergh, Justice became less likely to actively oppose civil rights groups.

Reagan's Attorney General, Edwin Meese, also offered a novel interpretation of the scope of the Bill of Rights. Meese called for a "jurisprudence of original intention," meaning (1) that the founding fathers intended that most issues would be dealt with by the other branches of government, not the courts and (2) that most of the Bill of Rights can be applied only to the national government, and that the Fourteenth Amendment does not "incorporate" restrictions on state government. This would mean overturning most cases granting federal protection against sex discrimination, permitting abortions, and allowing affirmative actions. Meese's position would have nullified much of the work of the Supreme Court for the past century. It was not widely supported by the judiciary.[14]

"Private Attorneys General"

Various organizations have been created to support the rights of individuals and groups. These are called **private attorneys general** because they act, not for the government, but for groups bringing court cases against the government or against other groups. They are funded in part by foundations and wealthy people, and in part by dues-paying members.

The largest such group is the *American Civil Liberties Union.* The ACLU has a national staff of about 350 in New York City and has 50 state chapters. Its 5000 volunteers handle more than 6000 cases a year. The ACLU was organized in the 1920s to defend individuals against the "red scares" (a period when socialists were persecuted) and has played a part in almost every civil liberties issue since then. It also lobbies for changes in laws involving wiretapping, surveillance, and "dirty tricks" of law enforcement agencies.

The *NAACP Legal Defense and Educational Fund, Inc. (LDF)* was created in 1939 and consisted originally of one lawyer, Thurgood Marshall, who became the first African-American appointed to the Supreme Court. In the 1950s the LDF concentrated on school desegregation suits. Today its efforts are focused on discrimination in employment, housing, and abuses in the judicial system.

Other organizations have been created along the lines of the LDF. In 1968, the *Mexican-American LDF,* or MAL-DEF, was created. With a staff of fifteen, it has brought cases concerning bilingual education, voting rights, and employment. The largest legal organization for women is the *National Organization for Women (NOW) Legal Defense and Education Fund.* It has a number of staff attorneys who work to protect women in gaining equal employment rights.

Implementing Rights

All these organizations use a variety of legal strategies. They conduct research on the problems of their clients, hoping to find a pattern of discrimination or lack of due process. They then write articles for law and bar journals in order to influence thinking in the legal profession. They offer their services to individuals whose rights may have been violated and who cannot afford the hundreds of thousands of dollars it takes to pursue a case all the way through the Supreme Court. Civil liberties lawyers can choose from a large number of complaints until they find a **test case** for their arguments. Such a case offers the group its "best shot" because the violation is so obvious, the damage so great, and the person making the complaint so appealing.

The litigating organization hopes that its case eventually will wind up in the Supreme Court as a **landmark decision,** one that involves major changes in the law. Such a decision creates a new general rule, which is then enforced by lower federal and state courts. These organizations cannot rest after a landmark decision in the high court, but usually must bring dozens of cases in federal district courts to make sure that rights affirmed by the Supreme Court are enforced. *Brown* v. *Board of Education,* which outlawed racial segregation in schools in 1954, is an example of such a landmark decision.

Obeying the Courts

These private organizations may ask judges to do several things. First, they may ask that a law, executive order, or private action be declared unconstitutional, or a violation of the laws of Congress. Second, they may ask that a right be protected by various kinds of judicial action. Of these, the most important are the **injunction,** which prevents someone from taking an action that violates someone else's rights, and the **order,** which requires someone to take a specified action to ensure someone else's rights.

In the event that someone does not comply with an injunction or an order, the judges may issue a citation for contempt of court. They can impose fines or jail sentences. The orders of a federal court are enforced by federal marshals, and if necessary by a state's National Guard—brought into service by the president—or by federal troops. In 1957, when Governor Faubus of Arkansas refused to obey a federal court order to desegregate public schools, President Eisenhower took control of the Arkansas National Guard and then used federal troops to protect black children being sent to white schools.

Often state agencies do not wish to comply with the spirit or even the letter of the court orders. Consider the landmark decision of *Miranda* v. *Arizona* (1966), where a defendant confessed to a rape before his lawyer was present and without being told of his right to a lawyer. The Supreme Court held that once an investigation by police focused on someone, the person had to receive the following warning:

> *You have the right to remain silent.*
> *Anything you say may be used against you in a court of law.*
> *You have the right to be represented by an attorney of your choice.*
> *If you cannot afford an attorney, a public defender will be provided for you if you wish.*

At first, there was only limited acceptance by many police departments of the new rules of the "cops and robbers" game. After all, unless one could put a federal judge into every patrol car, voluntary agreement was the only way such a rule could be effective. Some departments ignored the order; others gave only part of the warnings. Eventually, after hundreds of cases were dismissed by the courts because officials violated these guidelines, most police departments complied with the rulings. But they did so only because the federal and state courts began to apply the *exclusionary rule,* throwing out evidence at trials, including confessions, obtained by unconstitutional means.[15]

Public Acceptance of Civil Liberties

Clearly, *public agreement with a landmark civil liberties or rights decision cannot be taken for granted.* It is precisely because the majority has discriminated against a minority, or because the rights of politically unpopular groups have been violated, that the judicial decision has become necessary. One can assume that the public will oppose the changes that are being implemented and will seek to avoid complying with them (see the case study in Chapter 15). While people generally endorse First Amendment freedoms, large majorities of the public have at one time or another opposed affirmative-action plans, court-ordered busing, and prohibiting prayer in schools. For the courts' decisions to be effective, they must be followed by other parts of the government as well as by the public. As shown in the controversy over abortion, *often a Supreme Court ruling signals the start—not the end—of political debate.*[16]

However, the rightness of judicial action never rests on its popularity. The judiciary is not elected and is not directly accountable to the people. It is accountable to a Constitution that provides for limited government and secures the rights of the minority against certain actions by the majority. Low levels of approval for some judicial decisions may well be evidence that the system is working as intended.

WRAP-UP

Civil rights and liberties are constitutional protections granted all citizens. They protect people against violations of their rights by other people and by the government. Civil liberties usually refer to rights such as freedom of speech and due process, which allow people full participation in a democratic political system. Civil rights guard minorities against discrimination by other groups of citizens. Historically, both sets of rights have been deepened as to what they cover and widened as to whom they cover. Using the vague phrases of the Fourteenth Amendment, the courts have expanded the freedoms in the Bill of Rights to apply not only to the federal government but to states and individuals as well.

A look at some of these rights shows how this expansion has been achieved. The application of civil liberties such as freedom of speech, rights of privacy, and due process has seen gradual growth. Civil rights have similarly been extended with the use of suspect classifications to deal with racial prejudice, although not yet with sexual discrimination. Helping the process along have been judges and private groups whose "test cases" and the resulting landmark decisions have served to change public practices slowly.

While civil rights and liberties protect unpopular groups and opinions, they also protect our system of government. These well-tested values restrain the ambitions of our leaders. They give us traditional standards by which to judge political actions. They outline the means by which politics are to be conducted (no "unreasonable searches and seizures") as well as the ends of the process ("equal protection of the laws"). They underline the historical truth that majorities can be wrong, that leaders can mislead.

Although the Bill of Rights is written in inspiring, absolute language—"Congress shall make no law . . ."—these rights are seldom applied that way. Judges weighing issues of civil liberties and rights (and college students as well) must balance between competing individual rights, the government's obligation to keep order, and what an informed public is willing to tolerate. As shown in the Nazi case, the First Amendment freedoms of speech and assembly are difficult enough to support when the streets are being filled only by the rantings of a few dozen people. At a different time, the balance might seem different to the courts if a mass movement extended its activities to widespread violence. Whatever else it may be, the Constitution is not a suicide pact.

Key Terms

civil liberties (p. 94)

civil rights (p. 94)

doctrine of incorporation (p. 98)

partial incorporationists (p. 99)

complete incorporationists (p. 99)

First Amendment freedoms
(p. 100)

freedom of speech (p. 102)

prior restraint (p. 104)

exclusionary rule (p. 109)

due process (p. 109)

suspect classification
(p. 112)

class-action suits (p. 115)

equity (p. 115)
private attorneys general (p. 117)
test case (p. 117)

landmark decision (p. 118)
injunction (p. 118)
order (p. 118)

Suggested Readings

Adler, Renata, *Reckless Disregard* (New York: Knopf, 1986).

Baker, Liva, *Miranda: The Crime, the Law, the Politics* (New York: Atheneum, 1985).

Lewis, Anthony, *Gideon's Trumpet* (New York: Random, 1964).

McClosky, Herbert and Alida Brill, *Dimensions of Tolerance: What Americans Believe About Civil Liberties* (New York: Russell Sage, 1983).

Witt, Elder, *The Supreme Court and Individual Rights,* 2nd ed. (Washington, D.C.: CQ Press, 1988).

Endnotes

[1] David Hamlin, *The Nazi/Skokie Conflict: A Civil Liberties Battle* (Boston: Beacon, 1980).

[2] Saul K. Padover, *The Complete Jefferson* (New York: Duell, Sloan and Pearce, Incorporated, 1943), p. 121.

[3] *Gitlow* v. *New York,* 268 U.S. 652 (1925).

[4] See Robert A. Goldwin and Robert A. Schambra, eds., *How Does The Constitution Secure Rights?* (Washington: American Enterprise Institute, 1985).

[5] William Cohen and John Kaplan, *Bill of Rights* (Mineola, New York: The Foundation Press, 1976), p. 55.

[6] *Schenk* v. *United States,* 249 U.S. 47 (1919).

[7] *Cohen* v. *California,* 403 U.S. 15 (1971).

[8] *Lynch* v. *Donnelly,* U.S. Reports Slip Opinion, March 5, 1984. See *New York Times* (March 6, 1984), pp. 1, 11.

[9] *Hix* v. *Williams,* U.S. Reports, Slip Opinion, June 11, 1984.

[10] Interesting examples of how due process is actually applied in local courts can be found in James Eisenstein, Roy B. Flemming, and Peter F. Nardulli, *The Contours of Justice* (Boston: Little, Brown, 1988).

[11] See Eric Black, *Our Constitution: The Myth That Binds Us* (Boulder, Colorado: Westview Press, 1988), Part Three, pp. 113–38.

[12] *The New York Times,* January 25, 1989.

[13] See Michael Kammen, *A Machine That Would Go Of Itself* (New York: Vintage Books, 1986), Chapter 12, pp. 336–56.

[14] Goldwin, Schambra, and Kaufman, *Constitutional Cohesiveness,* Chapter 5, "How Should We Interpret the Constitution," pp. 129–62.

[15] See Herbert Jacob, *Law and Politics in the United States* (Boston: Little, Brown and Company, 1986), Chapter 2, "The Law."

[16] See Wilfred Feinberg, "Constraining 'The Least Dangerous Branch,'" in Norman Dorsen, *The Evolving Constitution* (Middletown, Conn: Wesleyan University Press, 1987), pp. 208–26.

★ The "bottom line" is a frequently used term in business. It means money and refers to an ultimate test of viability: Does it make money? In politics, the "bottom line" is the public: Will the public accept it? Through one channel or another, in part or whole, however delayed or distorted, political behavior will be judged by its public acceptance.

Unlike doctors or musicians, those in the political professions do not attain their positions through skill alone. They depend on the strength of their support. And these supporters, be they colleagues, interest groups, the press, party officials, or voters, will somehow connect to a popular base. That popular base may remain uninvolved or manipulated. But, whether or not it chooses to exercise this influence, it is potentially the final determinant of political power.

Part Two deals with the channels through which this public influence is felt. These groups or *intermediaries* can legitimately claim to represent some or most of the public. All of these claims are, as we will see, somewhat flawed.

Chapter Five discusses public opinion directly, how it's formed, how it's measured, and the limits of both. The media, as shown in Chapter Six, is constantly reflecting and shaping public opinion. Chapter Seven shows that elections offer people control over their leaders, but this depends on voters voting and incumbents' money not overwhelming the process. Parties, in Chapter Eight, provide the public with a way of organizing and understanding its electoral choices. Chapter Nine reveals that interest groups depend on their parts of the public for resources while struggling with others for influence. And Chapter Ten examines the political movements that arise as broad sections of the public find that "none of the above" effectively represent them.

For these instruments of power, the public, either its active support or passive acceptance, remains the bottom line.

PART TWO

AMERICA'S GOVERNMENT

The Public

Marchers protest 'legal lynching'

NAACP urges lawmakers: Counter 4 top court rulings

WASHINGTON (AP)—To the somber cadence of muffled drums, an estimated 35,000 people marched Saturday upon the Supreme Court and Congress to protest what NAACP Director Benjamin Hooks called "the legal lynching of black America's hope ... to become full partners in the American dream."

The march, aimed at spurring legislative "remedies" for four recent civil rights decisions by the court,

★ CHAPTER 5

Public Opinion

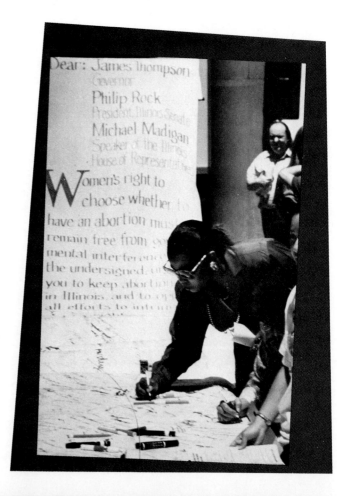

"For almost 40 years I have been active in the political arena, both as a Democrat and as a Republican. I have seen political storms come and I have seen them go, but never, never have I seen the people so incensed over an issue such as this pay raise question."

—Rep. Arthur Ravenel Jr. R-S.C.

It was described as "a firestorm of public outrage." Newspapers ran daily "countdown" stories on the number of days left before Congress got its 50 percent pay raise. Radio talk show hosts organized an informal anti-raise network and encouraged thousands of listeners to send tea bags to their members of Congress as a reminder of the Boston Tea Party. Voters sent congressmen condoms with the message, "For the next time you screw us."

What stirred this uprising in public opinion was the recommendation of a blue-ribbon salary commission that members of Congress (and other high-ranking government officials) should have their salaries raised 51 percent, from $89,500 to $135,000. Further inflaming public resentment was the backdoor way in which Congress seemed to be feathering its own nest. The raise was submitted to Congress on January 9, 1989, and would automatically take effect by February 8th, without a vote.

Whatever the merits of the raise—it would have banned outside income from speeches—and whatever the political protection it had—it was endorsed by both Presidents Reagan and Bush—were swept away by the public backlash. Comedian Jay Leno, guest hosting *The Tonight Show,* remarked, "They say if we give them a 50 percent pay increase they'll stop outside speaking engagements. Maybe if we give them 100 percent, they'll stop talking altogether." Mail flooded the Capitol. Receptionists grew hoarse answering constituents' complaints. A national poll taken in mid-January by *The Washington Post* showed a huge 85-percent majority opposing the pay increase. Members, feeling the heat, started to go public with criticism of the raise, even while they were privately hoping to get the money.

On February 7, the House approved, 380–48, a resolution to kill the pay raise, and the Senate followed suit, 94–6. Inside the Beltway around Washington, most of the press, interest groups, lobbyists, and political leadership had supported the pay raise. Congress itself had only to avoid the issue to collect the money. Yet the force of public protest was irresistible. With national median income at around $20,000, a salary of $135,000 could not be sold to the public. Bowing to public opinion, Congress rejected the pay increase its members clearly wanted.[1]

Protest mail and tea bags piled up at the National Taxpayers Union in 1989 when Congress proposed giving itself a 50 percent pay raise.

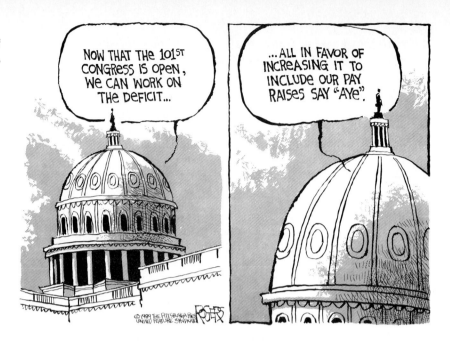

The public reaction to the congressional pay hike was an exception. Usually, public opinion is like a placid stream, indifferent to the politics occurring on it. Politicians find themselves navigating within its boundaries, channeling it in their direction, and perhaps pouring parts of it into containers marked with special-interest labels. Often the problem is gaining any support at all for important issues that drift, ignored, on this body of opinion.

At other times public opinion can become a flash flood, sweeping all before it. It was mainly the fear of this unrestrained popular energy that led the framers of the Constitution to create a government of complex procedures, divided institutions, and individual rights. While these times of an aroused populace are rare, they will often lead to waves of political activity sometimes as creative as the depression-era New Deal, sometimes as embarrassing as the anticommunist hysteria of the 1950s, and sometimes as brief as the 1989 populist reminder that congressional salaries come from taxpayers. With sufficient force behind it, popular opinion will bend any leader—who wishes to continue to lead—in its direction.

The most effective political leaders have a sixth sense when the time is right to arouse public opinion, and an uncanny ability to steer it in their direction. Former President Reagan was a modern master of the art. In 1981 he took a narrow presidential victory (receiving less of a popular vote than Bush won in 1988), with the opposition majority party in control of one house of Congress, and pushed through the largest increase in defense spending, the largest tax cuts, and the greatest cutbacks in domestic programs. There were a number of reasons for Reagan's success, but let his chief opponent, Speaker of the House Tip O'Neill, describe what standing up to a president with public opinion behind him was like at the time:

> *In 1981, I started to receive a tremendous amount of mail—more letters than I had seen in my entire career—asking me to give the president's program a chance . . . There was one week when I received something like fifty thousand letters a day, including many from my own constituents in a fairly liberal district . . . I was afraid the voters would repudiate the Democrats if we didn't give the president a chance to pass his program . . .*
>
> *Many Democrats were scared stiff at the prospect of being out of step with the mood of the country. And for a while there, we were* out of step.
>
> *What I had to get used to in 1981 was being criticized not only by the press but by the man on the street—or, to be more precise, the man in the airport . . . Some shouted insults like "Leave the president alone, you fat bastard.*[2]

Much of this section, and indeed the rest of the book, describes how insiders shape public opinion. In most cases they are operating on a *stable* body of opinion, generally nonparticipants with the values and outlooks sketched out in this chapter. This citizenry will grudgingly vote, reluctantly pay taxes, wholeheartedly embrace national symbols, and occasionally express political opinions. In the following pages it will display mild skepticism toward tax reform, support for the invasion of Grenada, disapproval of womanizing presidential candidates, and partial backing for high-tech means of gaining their backing for political parties.

But Part Two will also show aspects of a *mobilized* public opinion. While not as clear or as detached from its political leadership as in the pay-hike case, this body of opinion will have a role in the actions of government institutions and political actors. Media reporters may broadcast one message, only to find that another one was seen by their audience. Judges may have great difficulty forcing busing programs on resistent parents of schoolchildren. Political movements may ride the crest of public outrage against a war to momentary victories, only to find the support evaporate as quickly as it arose. And certainly all elected officials operate with the fear that they are vulnerable to shifts in the tides and wind of opinion, which they may only be aware of in passing.

Senator Richard Shelby (D-AL) sorts through the massive amounts of mail he has received from his constituents in 1989 expressing their opposition to the Medicare Catastrophic Coverage Act which he had supported. The Act, which was intended to assist the elderly with their medical bills, caused an uproar when some senior citizens found themselves paying hefty surtaxes for benefits.

This chapter will discuss the broad motives and outlines of public opinion in this country. Political socialization describes how people learn and form opinions about politics from family, friends, and experiences. This results in group attitudes, which are in turn influenced by events, media communications, or other messages. All of this is usually measured. Polls both reflect popular sentiment and aid leaders in shaping that opinion. Public opinion, as seen in the case study on abortion, may be a product of social changes having little to do with politics.

POLITICAL SOCIALIZATION

None of us is born with political opinions. Nor are we born political participants. Rather, our political ideas and behavior are learned through a process of political socialization. **Socialization** refers to how we learn our society's traditions and values and how we accept as our own certain cultural patterns. **Political socialization,** therefore, refers to the process of learning about political ideas, about our political system, and about our roles as citizens. What we learn is affected by *who* we are and *when* and *where* we learn about politics. Our political outlook develops consciously and unconsciously. We learn about politics and about our role in the political system from agents of socialization—*families, schools, peers, the media*—and from *events and experiences.*

Family

One of the most influential agents of political socialization is the family. This is especially true if parents agree on and discuss politics. Even young children have a sense of what social class they belong to, what race, and what religion. In addition, they begin to distinguish between groups. Thus a young child learns that some people are white and some are not, that some are Catholics and some are not, and that some are rich and others are not. The family strongly influences a child's loyalty to a political party. Over half of the children in one second grade class said, "I am a Democrat," or "I am a Republican." Even as teenagers, when the family's influence weakens, most students identified with the same party as their parents.[3]

The family has an important impact on children's feelings toward authority. Children idealize the president; to them he is trustworthy and kind. However, positive attitudes toward political figures are

Political socialization begins at an early age. Many political values and ideas develop through the observation of family members. This boy is impatiently waiting for his father to leave the voting booth.

affected by culture and class. A study comparing Appalachian schoolchildren in Kentucky with middle-class children in Chicago concluded, "Children in the relatively poor, Appalachian region . . . are dramatically less favorably inclined toward political objects than are their counterparts in other portions of the nation." The Appalachian children's attitudes toward politics were more affected by their parents' cynicism for government than by their positive feelings toward their parents as authority figures.[4]

Whether a child grows up to be a political participant has much to do with the way the family functions and with the family's attitudes toward participation. American families generally encourage independence and participation in family decision making. A child raised in such a family is likely to develop a greater interest in political participation. For example, members of the student movement of the 1960s tended to come from liberal "activist" families, and their political involvement was not a rebellion against their parents but an attempt to live up to family traditions. Children from lower-income homes generally are taught greater respect for authority than children from upper-income homes.[5]

When children reach adolescence, there is a marked change in their political orientation. They are likely to be less positive toward politics but more knowledgeable. A 1986 survey of seventeen-year-olds found 81 percent knew the freedoms of speech and religion were found in the Bill of Rights, while 43 percent knew the Constitution divides powers between the states and federal government.[6] By late adolescence (ages fifteen to eighteen), young people become more interested in political events, and some begin to participate. The changes reflect the growing influence of other agents of political socialization—schools, peers, and the media.

Schools

While we like to think that **political education** only happens in nondemocratic countries, it also occurs in American schools. There is of course no state-run version of the Boy Scouts indoctrinating youth in a specific ideology and the virtues of the present regime. However, American children are taught to pledge allegiance to the flag, sing the "Star-Spangled Banner," respect the traditions of our government, and to prefer the American form of government over all others. Not surprisingly, a survey of children ages ten to fifteen in several countries showed American youth very positive toward their country (see Figure 5.1).

FIGURE 5★1
The Opinions of Children

7. I am going to make several statements. For each statement please say "yes" if you agree, and "no" if you don't agree.

	JAPAN %	UNITED STATES %	UNITED KINGDOM %	FRANCE %
(My country) is really a good country.				
Yes, I agree	45	89	69	71
No I disagree	21	7	21	17
Don't know	34	4	10	12

SOURCE: *Index to International Public Opinion 1980–81.* Elizabeth H. Hastings and Philip K. Hastings, eds. (Westport, Conn.: Greenwood Press, 1982), p. 612.

American schools also teach indirectly. The teacher is an authority figure who should be obeyed. There are rituals that encourage consensus (such as pep rallies) and reward competitiveness (football) in students. Children also learn to obey majority rule, partly through participation in school elections, and accept that the losers in an election should support the winner. If students are allowed to take part in discussions and to participate in decision making, they are more likely to participate politically as adults.[7]

Peers

Children, like the rest of us, tend to associate with people of similar ages and interests. Our peers (literally, "equals") have a great impact on us. **Peer influence** increases during adolescence. The prevailing teen culture with its language, music, and movies is a witness to the power of peers to exclude other influences. The popular *A Nightmare on Elm Street* horror film series has shifted adults from helping destroy the monster in the early movies to being virtually irrelevant in the latest struggles with the immortal Freddy Kreuger.

College friends seem to have a greater impact on political attitudes than college classes. Membership in groups increases peer influence and political involvement even more. Even members of a nonpolitical organization are likely to be more politically involved than those who belong to no organization. This is as true for adults as it is for young people. When a person moves up in the social scale, there is a tendency to adopt the views of the new peer group. The union member who moves to the suburbs may find himself agreeing with new Republican neighbors that property taxes are too high. Those who move downward on the social scale, however, usually continue to hold their former views.

The political socialization process continues throughout a person's life. Entering a new occupation provides peers who can change political outlooks. This probably explains why women who work outside the home usually become more politically active than those who do

---

 ★ How to Tell a Liberal from a Conservative

Here are some of the political beliefs likely to be preferred by liberals and conservatives.

	Liberals	Conservatives
On Social Policy:		
Abortion	Support "freedom of choice"	Support "right to life"
School prayer	Are opposed	Are supportive
Affirmative action	Favor	Oppose
On Economic Policy:		
Role of the government	View government as a regulator in the public interest	Favor free-market solutions
Taxes	Want to tax the rich more	Want to keep taxes low
Spending	Want to spend more on the poor	Want to keep spending low
On Crime:		
How to cut crime	Believe we should solve the problems that cause crime	Believe we should stop coddling criminals
Defendants' rights	Believe we should respect them	Believe we should stop letting criminals hide behind the laws

---

not. At different ages, socialization may have different results partly because of changes in peer groups. For example, while the party loyalty young people acquire is likely to continue through adulthood, people do change their party. People develop strong political views around the age of thirty, as they assume roles of taxpayers, parents, and community members. Retirement may be another critical period of socialization. The American Association of Retired People's (AARP) successful efforts to mobilize older citizens behind issues like social security reflect this new activism.

Media

Nearly everyone "knows" that the media—newspapers, magazines, radio, and television—affect our attitudes and beliefs, but not enough is known about how this comes about and what its result is. For example, Daniel Patrick Moynihan, now a Democratic Senator from New York, wrote in the early 1970s that journalists had become so critical of presidents that they "set a tone of pervasive dissatisfaction with the performance of the national government, whomever the presidential incumbent may be and whatever the substance of the policies."[8] During the Vietnam War and the scandals of the Nixon administration, Americans may have had good reason to be cynical and distrustful, regardless of the media.

This is not to dismiss the influence of the media. For example, take television. Most people get their news from television. Those with the least interest in politics are likely to be the most affected by television, simply because they have fewer other sources of political information. But television entertainment programs, not just the news, have an impact on political socialization.

One study found that the beliefs of heavy television viewers differ from those of light viewers. Crime in prime time is at least ten times as prominent as in real life. Among heavy viewers, this tends to "heighten perceptions of danger and risk" and leanings toward "repressive measures and apparently simple, tough, hard-line" solutions. Heavy viewers are more likely to call themselves politically "moderate" and less likely to call themselves "liberal" or "conservative." Their mainstream "bends to the right on issues dealing with minorities and personal rights, reflects the anxieties and mistrust of television's violent 'mean world' and tilts to expansive populism on some welfare and economic issues." Heavy television viewers, whatever their politics, are alike in saying the government does not spend too much on health, welfare, and blacks, and spends too little on crime and drug abuse.[9]

FIGURE 5★2
Distrust of Government, 1964–1986

Bars show the percentage of people who said they "trust the government in Washington to do what is right" no more than "some of the time." [Findings from 1964 through 1982 are from the Institute for Social Research at the University of Michigan; those for 1985 and 1986 are from *Washington/ABC News* polls.]

QUESTION.   How much of the time do you trust the government in Washington to do what is right: just about always, most of the time, or only some of the time?

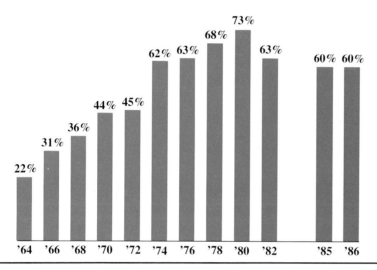

SOURCE: Barry Sussman, *What Americans Really Think* (New York: Pantheon, 1988), p. 69.

Political Events and Experiences

New ideas, events, and experiences can change political orientations. This is especially true of dramatic events such as the Great Depression of the 1930s, the Vietnam War, and Watergate. The civil rights and anti-Vietnam War years of the 1960s and 1970s caused young people to be more politically active than their elders, which is unusual.

The effects of Watergate and other serious problems of the time lowered people's faith in government. In 1976, 63 percent of the adults surveyed said they believed that government could be trusted "only some or none of the time"; ten years earlier, only 31 percent had felt that way. Kids showed mistrust of presidents. Thus, because of political events and people's own experiences, many Americans who grew up during this period tended to be cynical about politics (see Figure 5.2).

The spread of AIDS in the 1980s and the fear that accompanied it caused some people to attack the rights of AIDS victims. Here, parents picket outside the Board of Education building in Brooklyn over AIDS children attending New York City schools.

RESULTS OF POLITICAL SOCIALIZATION

What do Americans believe? Efforts have been made to study American attitudes toward *democratic values, political ideology, the American system of government,* and *political participation.*

In principle, almost all Americans support democratic values such as freedom of speech and the right of periodic elections. But when these principles are put to specific tests—when the question is whether an atheist or a communist should be allowed to speak publicly, for example—Americans show less support for democratic values.[10]

Support for civil liberties increases markedly with education level. Yet regardless of education, people may temporarily express "antidemocratic" attitudes. The recent fear of the AIDS plague has led otherwise reasonable citizens to call for the forcible quarantining of AIDS victims. It helps to remember that some of the attitudes people express do not reflect deeply held beliefs. An overall belief in democratic values may be a greater restraint on behavior than it is on instant verbal expressions of attitudes.

Although Americans have always had a healthy suspicion of authority, they have usually expressed support for the political system. A study done in 1963 showed that 85 percent of the people in America were proud of America's political institutions, while only 46 percent of the people in Great Britain and 7 percent in Germany said that they were proud of their political institutions. When asked what they were most proud of about their country, Americans were twice as likely to mention the political aspects of American society such as the Constitution, political freedom, and democracy. Similarly, a 1981 survey showed that popular confidence in public institutions—such as the armed forces, schools, and the legal system—was considerably higher in the United States than in Europe.[11]

In political ideology, a majority of Americans do not like to call themselves liberal. (The **liberal** view sees a positive role for government regulation and services in helping the disadvantaged and dealing with society's complex problems. The **conservative** view argues for government's limited role both because its programs don't work well and because a bigger government is also large enough to take away individual liberties. See the box on page 131.) More people call themselves *moderate* than anything else. This has not changed significantly in recent years. There has been no conservative trend in the 1980s. As the chart of CBS/New York Times polls indicates, political self-identification has not changed much in the 1980s (see Figure 5.3).

Americans remain *theoretical conservatives*—the way they express their general political philosophy is conservative. Yet, Americans also seem to be *operational liberals*. Despite the fact that more Americans call themselves conservative than liberal, more Americans favor liberal social welfare programs than oppose them. Political scientist Everett Carll Ladd found in 1978 that 67 percent of Americans favored a national health-insurance program, 85 percent felt the gov-

★ Woody Allen on Political Apathy

"I'm not a political activist. If anything, I'm an uninformed coward, totally convinced that a stand on any issue from subway fares to the length of women's skirts will ultimately lead me before a firing squad.

I prefer instead to sit around in coffeehouses and grouse to loved ones privately about social conditions, invariably muttering imprecations on the heads of politicians, most of whom I put in a class with blackjack dealers.

Take a look, for instance, at the Reagan Administration. Or just at the President himself. Or the men hoping to become President. Or the last cluster of Presidents. These characters would hardly inspire confidence in the average bail bondsman."

SOURCE: *The New York Times,* January 28, 1988.

FIGURE 5★3
Conservative and Liberal

Note: Question wording varied before 1985. The first asking in each year is shown. From 1985 on that occurred in January. Surveys by CBS News/New York Times, latest that of January 1988.

QUESTION. How would you describe your views on most political matters? Generally, do you think of yourself as liberal, moderate, or conservative (1985—present)?

PERCENT

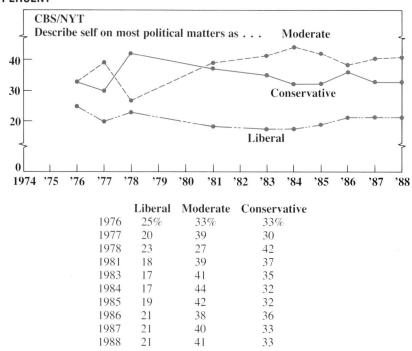

	Liberal	Moderate	Conservative
1976	25%	33%	33%
1977	20	39	30
1978	23	27	42
1981	18	39	37
1983	17	41	35
1984	17	44	32
1985	19	42	32
1986	21	38	36
1987	21	40	33
1988	21	41	33

SOURCE: *Public Opinion,* November/December 1988, p. 30.

ernment should assure low-cost medical care, 77 percent believed that the government should assure a job for everyone who wants to work, and 61 percent favored government-imposed wage and price controls. By mid-1986, Americans were looking favorably toward government powers. From 1982 to mid-1986 the number believing "the federal government has too much power" dropped from 38 percent to 28 percent. Those wanting the government to use its powers more vigorously jumped from 30 percent to 41 percent. President Bush's call for a "kinder, gentler nation" accurately reflected the country's more liberal attitudes at the end of the Reagan presidency.

American public opinion occupies the liberal end of the scale on a number of social and economic issues.[12]

Finally, how do Americans feel about political participation? On a theoretical level, most people mention active participation in political affairs as key to being a "good citizen." But political participation may be affected by people's feelings of **political efficacy,** that is, the degree to which people believe that being politically active can make a difference.

One striking difference between voters and nonvoters is that nonvoters feel more serious changes are necessary than are possible through electoral politics. A major reason for the decline in voting since 1960 has been a decline in efficacy—a reduction in the feeling that the system will respond. Voting is the only political activity that more than one-third of American citizens say they have performed, and, generally, lower-income groups and minorities are less likely to understand the political process or wish to participate in it, a position comedian Woody Allen illustrates (see the box on page 135).

POLITICAL COMMUNICATION

Opinions about political issues are based on sets of beliefs derived from political socialization. Opinions develop from a communication process that involves, in addition to the message, three other elements: *the source of the message, the means of communication,* and *the recipient.* Each has a role in the communication of opinion.

Sources and Means of Communication

How we get information can dramatically influence its effect on us. Does it come to us by word of mouth? How close is the person who brings the message? Does it come to us from public officials? Does the message come from newspapers, television, or radio—and are they just transmitting it or did they also generate it?

Person to Person

Communications from one person to another are more likely to change an opinion than media communications are. There are a number of reasons for this. First, personal contacts are usually "nonpurposive." They are not "sales pitches" and they usually do not create the "sales resistance" media contacts sometimes do. Second, person-to-person contacts have greater flexibility. The speaker can tailor the message to fit the recipient and change it as he or she sees the reactions. Third, in personal meetings, there is a kind of "reward" system. The recipient of the information receives expres-

A Republican central committee member shows how effective personal contact is in politics by recruiting a voter during a door-to-door voter registration drive in 1984.

sions of personal approval in return for various kinds of reactions. Fourth, there is usually more emotional involvement in person-to-person exchanges than in presentations by the media.

Government Officials

Government can affect public opinion in the United States by helping shape what people think are "proper" beliefs, what they think are the "facts," and what their expectations of the future are. The government, for example, can provide cues as to which nations are our enemies and which are our friends. It can also influence public opinion by deciding what information to release and what "spin" or presentation to give it. Government officials often "leak" certain information to the press in order to influence public opinion on a particular issue. For example, around the time increased military spending is being considered by Congress, government leaks about threatening Soviet military weapons often find their way into print.

Media

The media's most important role in forming opinion lies in setting the public agenda—helping decide what issues the public will focus on. They do this by the types of issues they cover. The public considers most important the issues the media emphasizes. This **agenda-setting** role begins in the political socialization process, in which people acquire their political attitudes.

In setting this agenda, the media tend to emphasize stability and moderation—the viewpoints of the elite institutions, of which the national media is one. Part of the reason for this lies in the dependence of reporters on officials as the source for news.

Other criticism of the media's role focuses on news reports that are *too personal* ("President Bush extends hand to Senate Democrats"), *emotionally dramatic* ("House Democrats jockey for slots at feverish pace"), and *badly fragmented* ("Chinese students demonstrate. NATO in disarray. Mayor's drug program attacked. News at ten."). Underlying causes of events often get lost in the dramatization of the news, while news fragmentation makes it difficult for people to see the connection among issues. The television networks and national media are frequently called *too liberal.* This may come from the Eastern big-city origins of most news gathering, as well as from reporters who often sympathize with the causes of the left. However, their employers, the owners of the media, are clearly conservative, and the criticism of the press as liberal usually surfaces during a heavily criticized conservative administration.

Of course, neither government efforts to influence public opinion nor media messages (including news reports and advertising) can propagandize everyone to accept certain views. The reason for this is that the effect of the mass media depends on the *preconceptions* and the *social setting* of the intended receiver of the media message.

The Recipient

Preconceptions

Preconceptions may produce *selective exposure* to the message. A person with no interest in politics may simply ignore political news. In addition, just as Republicans do not generally attend Democratic rallies, they may also avoid reports about Democratic candidates. Of course, people sometimes listen to messages that contradict what they believe. *But the basic influence of the mass media is to reinforce opinions.* V. O. Key, Jr., has said that ". . . the major influence of the media upon political attitudes is by and large a reinforcement of the status quo."[13] In other words, people pay attention to the candidates and positions they already support.

Preconceptions can cause the receiver to distort a message. In one interesting study of **selective perception,** a white person was shown a picture of a white man holding a razor and having an argument with a black man. The first person was then asked to pass along this "rumor" to another person who had not seen the picture. The story was then passed on to others. In more than half of the cases, those telling the gossip reversed the roles of the attacker and the victim: It became a report about a black man holding a razor and having an argument with a white man.[14] Through selective perception, then, individuals may use propaganda for their own purpose, not for the purpose of the propagandist.

Social Setting

The social setting of the receiver of a media message can significantly influence the message's effect. This may be because of the group to which a person belongs, the influence of opinion leaders, and the person's class status, occupation, age, sex, place of residence, race, religion or ethnicity, and party identification.

If the message a person receives does not conform to the clearly stated views of a *closely knit group,* (such as a family or peers), to which the person belongs, the receiver is likely to reject it. For these groups, **opinion leaders**—avid listeners to or readers of the media, at least in matters that interest them—become an important part of the effect of the media message. They receive the message and then pass it along to others who are less avid. Thus, the influence media exerts on people is the result of two steps: the media message is first received by opinion leaders (who may be different for each issue) and then relayed to others. These opinion leaders act as information filters.

Occupation can be an important factor in the formation of political opinions. This may in part reflect a similar class status as well as the reinforcement of a closely knit group's influence. Professional training and a shared outlook may also shape an occupational group, as shown in the chart of the significantly conservative opinions of military officers (see the box on page 141).

Sex is increasingly important in the formation of American public opinion. From the early 1980s, public opinion polls began to show a persistent "gender gap" on certain political issues. This worked against former President Reagan and spelled trouble for then-Vice-President George Bush in 1988. In an August 1988 poll in which Bush ran six points behind Dukakis (45 percent to 51 percent), he ran 16 percent behind among women (40 percent to 56 percent).[15] The gender gap did not just relate to so-called "women's issues." For example, a 1988 Gallup poll showed that while 40 percent of male voters felt their own economic futures were very secure, only 27 percent of women did. This greater sense of economic vulnerability among women was reflected in the answers to whether they had personally benefited from the Reagan administration's policies. Among men, 55 percent said they had benefited; among women, only 40 percent said they had benefited.[16]

Residence—where people live— can make a difference in their political opinions. For example, the suburbs are growing larger and more conservative than the cities. In a 1988 poll, only 39 percent of those in the central city supported Bush, while 48 percent in the suburbs did. Since a large percentage of the nation's poor people and minorities live in central cities, it can be seen that some categories of social setting, such as class, race, and residence, overlap. In other words, people in the cities tend to be more liberal than those in the suburbs partly because of socialization and partly due to the filtering influences of the groups among whom they live.

Race, religion, or ethnicity can influence opinions. This is partly a result of history. Catholics, for example, first came to the United States in large numbers at a time when the Democratic party was more willing than the Republican party to act on social and economic needs. Because of their history, members of racial, religious, or ethnic groups may continue to maintain distinctive political opinions even after they have been integrated into the larger society and gained in education, income, and status. Thus, Catholics still tend to be more liberal than Protestants, even though Catholics have now more than caught up with Protestants in income and status. Religious beliefs themselves can affect opinions. The fact that people

★ Opinion of Military Officers

Do you have a favorable or unfavorable opinion of the following American institutions and personalities:

	FAVORABLE	UNFAVORABLE	DON'T KNOW
The news media	32%	59%	9%
Congress	44%	50%	6%
Ronald Reagan	97%	2%	1%
Jimmy Carter	15%	78%	7%
Labor unions	19%	70%	11%
The Pentagon	81%	9%	10%
Jesse Jackson	24%	64%	12%
The CIA	81%	9%	10%
Richard Nixon	46%	44%	10%
Nuclear-freeze movement	8%	88%	4%
The Moral Majority	31%	54%	15%

Interviewed by telephone for this poll were 257 Army, Navy, Air Force, and Marine generals and admirals.

SOURCE: "Opinion of Military Officers," *Newsweek* July 9, 1984, p. 37. Copyright © 1984 by Newsweek, Inc. All Rights Reserved. Reprinted by permission.

are members of a religious faith can have considerable influence on how they feel about issues such as abortion or pornography.

Not surprisingly, African Americans generally support government action on social and economic problems. They show a "group consciousness" and "racial evaluation" on political issues, parties, and candidates. For example, in mid-1984, a poll showed that only 11 percent of blacks had a favorable opinion of President Reagan, compared to 64 percent of whites.[17]

MEASURING PUBLIC OPINION

Determining public opinion on a political issue is not a straightforward process. A few years ago, a California polling organization demonstrated the power of pollsters to make public opinion. By asking the "same" question two different ways, the pollster got a perfect reversal of percentages; contradictory responses were supported by the same number of people. The first version of the question, concerning academic freedom, was asked to half the sample. The other half got the second version.

The first question was: "Professors in state-supported institutions should have the freedom to speak and teach the truth as they see it. Do you agree or disagree?" (Agree: 52 percent; Disagree 39 percent.)

The second question asked: "Professors who advocate controversial ideas or speak out against official policy have no place in a state-supported college or university. Do you agree or disagree? (Agree: 52 percent, Disagree: 39 percent.)[18]

In these two instances a majority agreed with seemingly appropriate sentiments. Besides being easier to agree than disagree with a question, each version has "hot" or "loaded" words. Phrases such as "freedom to speak" and "teach the truth as they see it" are more attractive concepts than "advocate controversial ideas" and "speak out against official policy." These value-laden words influenced the interviewees in one way or another. They graphically illustrate that the way a question is asked may shape the response. They also leave us a bit uncertain about public opinion on this issue, as well as others.

While we may doubt the accuracy of measuring public opinion, few would question its importance. *Success in political life is often determined by a leader's ability to generate, guide, and respond to public opinion.*

How do we measure public opinion? Very often, it's done informally. Public officials usually cannot afford to pay for scientific opinion polls conducted on a regular basis. So, most of them use the "ear-to-the ground" approach: they get a general "sense" of public opinion from their mail, from telephone conversations, and from visits to their home states. This method of measuring public opinion, however, is far from accurate.

Another approach used to measure public opinion, begun by some American newspapers in the 1800s, is the **straw poll.** This, too, is unscientific. The straw poll uses written ballots or call-ins to ask questions of people who have *not* been randomly selected by a scientific process. For example, a Cleveland TV station might ask viewers to phone in to answer, "Who is your choice in next Tuesday's election for mayor?" This type of poll would obviously be weighted in favor of the opinions of people who happened to be watching the particular program, and would give no weight to those who were not. Maybe it was a rock-and-roll show or a news discussion program, both with narrow audiences. Thus, straw polls are a poor method of accurately measuring public opinion.

Scientific Polling

In the 1930s, a number of people became interested in **scientific polling.** They began to develop a methodology that could produce reliable measurements of public opinion. The American Institute of Public Opinion was formed in 1933 to promote and improve scientific polling.

A scientific poll is an attempt to sample the opinion of a particular population, or *universe*. Are we interested in the views of the students in Political Science 200? Do we want to know what adults in New York City think about a particular candidate? Or are we interested in the opinions of farmers in the state of Iowa?

If the universe is small enough—the fifty students who are enrolled in Political Science 200, say—the public opinion of the universe can be measured by interviewing each member of it. Usually, though, the universe is too large. In that case, the measurement of public opinion depends on a **representative sample.** Representative sampling involves two questions: Who will be interviewed? How will they be interviewed?

Random sampling is the method most often chosen to determine who will be interviewed. **Random sampling** involves interviewing a randomly selected number of people within a particular geographical area. In a random sample, a pollster tries to select interviewees so that each member of the universe has an equal chance of being chosen for an interview. Federal census tracts (units used in taking the national census) are frequently the basic geographical unit within which scientific pollsters sample opinions. The census provides information about the people who live in a particular tract. For example, it includes statistics on race, income, and age.

Drawing by Lorenz; © 1988 *The New Yorker Magazine,* Inc.

"And as the campaign heats up, the latest poll shows the Dan Rather news team running slightly ahead of the Peter Jennings news team, with the Tom Brokaw team just two points back and gaining."

An alternative to sampling is the **quota method.** This approach involves interviewing a certain number of people from various ethnic, religious, age, sex, and other groups. But the quota method is generally not as reliable as random sampling because it leaves too much discretion to the interviewer in choosing which people will be interviewed within each quota.

Sample size is an important consideration in scientific polling. People are usually surprised to find that a sample can be representative even though it is relatively small. For the whole United States—some 245 million people—a properly selected random sample of only 1500 to 1600 persons will produce accurate responses (results that can be repeated) within three percentage points 95 percent of the time. The Gallup poll uses a national sample of 1500; Louis Harris uses 1600. To reduce the sampling error of 3 percent to 1 percent, it would be necessary to increase the size of the sample to 9500 persons.

The method pollsters use to conduct interviews can affect the accuracy of the responses. The most reliable method is the face-to-face interview. An interviewer can evaluate the person being interviewed and can ask immediate follow-up questions if the truthfulness or intensity of the opinion expressed is in doubt. It is also much more difficult for a person to evade a question when it is asked face-to-face. A telephone interview is generally less reliable than a face-to-face interview, but is usually more reliable than a poll by mail.

In scientific polling, the wording of questions and the form of the answer allowed are highly important. Scientific pollsters attempt to word questions in a way that will not indicate a bias or a desired answer. As shown in the California academic freedom poll example, that can be difficult.

The type of answers allowed in a poll can help measure intensity of feelings. If a poll asked only for a "yes" or "no" answer to the question, "Do you favor quotas to aid minority hiring?," it will be impossible for a person to tell from the poll results how strongly the respondent feels about the issue. If, on the other hand, the people being interviewed are given a choice between "strongly opposed" or "strongly in favor," with several levels in-between as well as a "no opinion" option, it will be possible to tell much more about the intensity of their opinions.

How reliable are the polls? The best are fairly reliable. For example, polls have shown a remarkable consistency in interview responses on a variety of issues through the years. However, polls taken during a political campaign claim to measure opinion only at the time the poll is taken; thus they do not necessarily predict the eventual election results.

★ Wired to the Public Pulse

The following describes how President Reagan's pollster, Richard Wirthlin, refined the White House's ability to measure public opinion:

In the second term, Wirthlin began to incorporate into the daily operations of the White House a novel system that he had pioneered during the 1984 campaign. Called "speech pulse," it allowed him to market test every presidential phrase. He would gather forty to eighty people (usually drawn from the heartlands) in a room where they were each handed sensitive, computerized dials that enabled Wirthlin to chart their instant response to presidential speeches moment by moment. The system could measure their positive or negative reaction, interest or boredom, understanding or confusion, as well as their view of the speaker's credibility. The information, once processed, was printed out with the text of the president's speech in one column and a number measuring second-by-second approval ratings in the other. So precisely calibrated was the system, Wirthlin exulted, that "it's not just phrase by phrase, it's word by word!"

Wirthlin analyzed the results to determine something called a "speech rate," which measured the effect of the rhetoric on the audience's mood. He also found what he called "power phrases" or "resonators," the lines most effective in altering public feeling. His system was useful, he said, because "it tells us what themes we can play after the speech, what phrases we can use again, and the tonality of speech that makes sense." It also allowed the White House to "do some pretesting so that we can fine tune the [president's] message."

SOURCE: Jane Meyer and Doyle McManus, *Landslide: The Unmaking of the President, 1984–1988 (Boston: Houghton Mifflin Company, 1988), p. 44.*

Polls and Elections

During the 1980 presidential campaign, ABC News tried to do "instant polls" immediately after the Carter-Reagan television debate. ABC provided two "900" numbers, and for 50 cents viewers could call to record who they thought won. Alas, some partisans set up phone banks to "stuff the ballot box" for their candidate. After some controversy pointing out the unrepresentative nature of the sampling, ABC dropped the project.

Dr. George Gallup helped his mother-in-law get elected to a state office by conducting an experiment—public opinion polls for her in 1932. Thomas Dewey, who ran unsuccessfully for President as a Republican in 1944, may have been the first presidential candidate to have access to polling data. Franklin D. Roosevelt started taking regular polls and used government employees to do it. Ronald Reagan may have perfected using a pollster to literally "wire" people to take continuous public opinion soundings (see the box on page 145). Today, candidates and public officials rely heavily—some say too heavily—on public opinion polls for deciding campaign strategy and even for making policy decisions once in office.

Although the publication of opinion polls during a campaign may not have a direct effect on the voters—that is, not create a direct "bandwagon" or "underdog" effect on the mind of the voter—published poll results certainly can have an *indirect* influence. A candidate who is running well in the polls will have a much better chance of raising funds and getting campaign volunteers than will a candidate who is running poorly in the polls. In addition, campaign strategy can be influenced by the polls. Presidential candidates, for example, may decide to bypass states where poll results are unfavorable to them and campaign instead in states where the polls are favorable. Polls may even be the ultimate judge of a campaign: a bad poll may cause a person to decide not to run or may cause a candidate to withdraw.

Polls have an additional influence because they are taken seriously by the press. They become self-fulfilling prophecies. As one pollster has said, "It becomes a chicken-and-egg syndrome. If the polls say you aren't a major candidate, you can't get good coverage. But if you don't get the coverage, you can't become a major candidate."

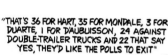

"THAT'S 36 FOR HART, 35 FOR MONDALE, 3 FOR DUARTE, 1 FOR D'AUBUISSON, 24 AGAINST DOUBLE-TRAILER TRUCKS AND 22 THAT SAY YES, THEY'D LIKE THE POLLS TO EXIT"

© 1984 by Herblock in *The Washington Post*

THE ROLE OF PUBLIC OPINION

The writers of the *Federalist* declared that "all government rests on opinion." Much earlier, Niccolò Machiavelli had written that public opinion is important even for the government of a nondemocratic state. He said that a ruler "who has the masses hostile to him can never make sure of them, and the more cruelty he employs the feebler will his authority become; so that his best remedy is to try and secure the good will of the people."[19] In the United States, where we stress that government is based on consent of the governed, public opinion is even more important. James Bryce, a perceptive English observer of the American scene in the late nineteenth century, wrote that "public opinion stands out in the United States as the great source of power, the master of servants who tremble before it."[20] V. O. Key, Jr., defined public opinion as "those opinions held by private persons which governments find it prudent to heed."[21]

If we are to call our system democratic, we must be able to say that public opinion *is in some way* reflected in government policy and the decisions made by public officials. As has been shown, Thomas Jefferson felt that "governments are republican only in proportion as they embody the will of their people, and execute it." To what degree must the actions of a public official in a democracy "embody the will" of the people?

Public opinion is basic to the instruments of power discussed in the next chapters of this section. It is to the public that the various interest groups, parties, and government officials look for justification and approval of what they do. It is public opinion that will render their activities effective or embarrassing.

Public opinion is the audience before which all these political actors must eventually perform. Yet in our media-dominated society, the public is much more than an audience. It is also involved in selecting the cast, writing the script, and, at times, canceling the show. It may be led by skillful performances into playing an onstage role or in shifting the spotlight from one group to another.

Power and the People

All the instruments of power are linked in some way to a popular base. The *media* make the most immediate claim to reflect public opinion. They can reach the public almost instantly, and by so doing their messages often preempt any other claim to public opinion. Merely publicizing certain messages gives the media tremendous political force. As seen in the Gary Hart case in Chapter 6, the press's decision to focus on his extramarital affairs was sufficient to end his campaign for president.

Voters were not given the chance to pass judgment on Hart (although he reentered the race with halfhearted campaigns in several early primaries). Voting is the authorized sanction the public retains to influence the political process. It is also the only political activity in which most people participate. The *parties* that compete for voters have strengthened their organizations and techniques to gain popular support and elected office for their candidates. Regular *elections* provide the battlefields where the parties' candidates compete using a modern mastery of media backed by old-fashioned resources of money. Elections allow ritual uprisings in public opinion to "throw the rascals out" or "stay the course."

Interest groups represent parts—usually well-heeled, well-organized parts—of public opinion. They allow economic and ideological groupings to continually monitor and pressure government decision makers. They link organized opinion groups to the government, but do little for others without the same clout. *Political movements* have periodically filled these gaps. They represent groups whose ideas do not fit readily into the prevailing consensus. Through a variety of activist tactics, causes like the black civil rights and student antiwar movements have elbowed their way onto the political stage.

In short, to get elected, to keep a political party operating, to sell newspapers, to gain support for an interest group's bill, and to recruit volunteers for a movement's boycott means dealing with public opinion. How these political players deal with each other within the boundaries set by public opinion is what American politics, and this book, is about.

Whether these instruments of power are the most effective linkages between public opinion and public policy can be argued. There is some indication of a general consistency between public opinion and policy decisions, though clearly the process is complicated and convoluted.[22]

Future Forms of Participation

Prophets of the communication revolution foresee that technology will soon allow a new age of direct democracy. Innovations like two-way television receivers, satellite-transmitted meetings, and electronic polling can allow nearly instant access and direct citizen input. Intermediate organizations claiming to channel public opinion into the policy process may lose their functions. Public opinion can be turned into immediate participation and direct control over policy. Who needs representative democracy? As John Naisbitt puts it in *Megatrends:*

> *We created a representative system two hundred years ago when it was the practical way to organize a democracy. Direct citizen participation was simply not feasible, so we elected people to go off to the state capitals, represent us, vote, and then come back and tell us what happened. . . . But along came the communication revolution and with it an extremely well-educated electorate. Today, with instantaneously shared information, we know as much about what's going on as our representatives and we know it just as quickly.*

Protest is one of the most active vehicles for public opinion. One of the most recent issues to become the object of protest is apartheid in South Africa. Here, a trustee of Amherst College is met by demonstrators demanding that the college divest itself of ties to all corporations which do business in South Africa.

The fact is we have outlived the historical usefulness of representative democracy and we all sense intuitively that it is obsolete.[23]

Predictions are always risky. The future has not yet arrived nor is it likely to undermine all the existing processes and intermediaries. Leaving aside people's willingness to participate more often than they now seem to vote, there is a curious lack of politics in this vision of electronic democracy. Government is not simply about counting citizens' raised right hands in order to decide an issue. Some have longer arms than others. Changing the techniques of representation is unlikely to alter greatly this distribution of power. This vision neglects the public's need for leadership and direction to be mobilized to act.

Besides the pressure of custom and comfort, this "electronic commonwealth" would not necessarily be more democratic than the "eighteenth-century" representative forms it aspires to replace. Take polling, for example.

Even the most scientific of polling is only a very partial kind of democratic participation. Immediate responses tend to separate public *opinion* from public *debate*. There is no reasoning together, no exchange of views, and no collective deliberation that ought to be present in the democratic process. Polling doesn't give the respondent much information with which to make judgments or much time to think of a response. Information and time are essential for making judgements on policy and, eventually, for generating citizen activity on behalf of that policy. Instant opinion from a private respondent is not the same as citizens engaging one another in a public debate and hammering out policy positions.[24]

Abortion and Public Opinion

Public opinion is not just produced by political leaders, nor are peoples' opinions completely separate from the political process. Public opinion may move as a consequence of social changes having little directly to do with the issue at hand. This movement of public opinion can be seen in Americans' more tolerant attitude toward abortion over the last few decades. Modern views toward abortion have resulted from a number of social changes, including acts of government.

Pro-lifers pass the Supreme Court building during a March for Life in 1989.

The Polls on Abortion

Between 1976 and 1987, the National Opinion Research Center of the University of Chicago, in its annual survey, asked Americans about their views on legalized abortion (see Figure 5.4). The results during this period came out pretty much the same. Four in ten people approved of abortion on demand; one in ten opposed abortion in all circumstances; and the rest of the people, about half, approved of

abortion in certain unfortunate situations.[25]

For example, eight in ten say abortion should be legal if "there is a strong chance of serious defect in the baby." Nine in ten favor abortion "if the woman's health is seriously endangered." However, almost six in ten say abortion should *not* be legal for a woman who is married and does not want any more children. The public divides evenly in the case of a

poor family that "cannot afford any more children."

While these views have been remarkably consistent since the mid-1970s, the polls don't reveal that tremendous social changes in the 1960s led to more permissive attitudes toward abortion. Interestingly, the Gallup poll did not even ask about abortion until 1962, either because it was not much of an issue or it was too sensitive to discuss.

In that year, an Arizona woman, Sherri Finkbine, went to Sweden for an abortion because she couldn't get one legally here. She had taken the drug thalidomide and feared having a deformed baby. A bare majority, 52 percent, approved of what she had done. This is a vast difference with the 82 percent who today approve of abortion if there is a chance of a serious defect in the baby. By 1965, fewer than one person in five approved of abortion on demand. More than one in four opposed abortion in all circumstances.

But in the mid-1960s, a social and sexual revolution was underway. Liberal attitudes toward abortion were linked to more educated young people, less concern for religion, and greater support for the women's movement. As some states passed laws allowing abortions, women traveled to them to end unwanted pregnancies, and the debate in the media intensified.

Greater education led young people to turn away from their parents' religions and introduced them to feminism. In 1972, 54 percent of college graduates favored abortion on demand compared to only 34 percent of people without high-school degrees. Among people saying religion should have *less* of a role in national life, three out of five supported abortion. Among those who believed religion should have a *greater*

FIGURE 5★4
The Social Revolution and Abortion
Changing Attitudes, 1965–1987

There has been a massive easing in public thinking about abortion since the social revolution of the 1960s, as these findings show. The slight decline in support in the 1980s is considered a minor one having no bearing on the overall trend.

QUESTION. Please tell me whether or not you think it should be possible for a pregnant woman to obtain a legal abortion in the following circumstances (percentages show those favoring legal abortions in each instance):

If she is not married and does not want to marry the man.

If she is married and does not want any more children.

If the family has a very low income and cannot afford any more children.

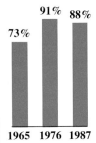

If the woman's own health is seriously endangered by the pregnancy.

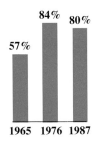

If there is a strong chance of serious defect in the baby.

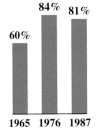

If she becomes pregnant as a result of rape.

role, only one in five backed abortion on demand.

Catholics have shown an especially striking change. In the 1962 survey, 33 percent of the Catholics interviewed supported Finkbine. Since 1972, surveys have shown 77 percent

supporting abortion where there is a strong chance of a serious defect in the baby.

Government Role

In 1973, the Supreme Court legalized abortion in the first

three months of a pregnancy (*Roe* v. *Wade*). Not only did this decision reflect how much public opinion had changed since the mid-1960s, but it helped move that opinion further. Surveys showed that in the 1972–74 period there were increases of 6 percent in the number of people supporting a single woman's right to an abortion. Similar support for abortion was registered in other situations. As one pollster concluded:

"That jump in support after the court decision was sharper than in any other two-year period of polling; it signified a switch in position for some ten million adult Americans."[26]

In the 1980s, President Reagan's frequent speeches against abortion may have led to a slight decline in support for abortion in some situations. But the decline is minor in light of the trends of the last twenty-five years. Opinion has

A pro-choice march in 1989.

moved far from the days when opposition to abortion on demand was the dominant view.

The Court's July 3, 1989 ruling in *Webster* v. *Reproductive Health Services* placed some limits on the right to abortion. The initial reaction to the decision was to increase membership and donations to groups on both sides of the issue. Pro-choice groups, feeling more threatened, may have seen a more dramatic increase.[27] A complete Supreme Court

reversal of its 1973 decision would probably lead to an uproar of popular opposition. At the same time, such a Court decision would probably lower the general public's support for abortion. The government cannot overwhelm public opinion, but it can nudge it in other directions.

The growing acceptance of legal abortion over the last three decades was a result of a vast social change in attitudes. An increase in premarital sex, decreasing support for religion (which continues even today), a better-educated youth, and a growing women's movement all led to abortion as an acceptable method of birth control. First state governments, and then the Supreme Court, supported this trend. To now outlaw abortions would require more than a Supreme Court decision, passing a bill in Congress, or even a Constitutional amendment. It would seem to require a social revolution similar to the one that began in the 1960s.

WRAP-UP

None of us is born with political opinions. We gain them as a result of political socialization, which begins at an early age and continues throughout our lives. Family, school, peers, the media, and political events and experiences may affect our beliefs about politics. Americans from upper-class backgrounds often receive a different kind of socialization than Americans from lower-class backgrounds. Low status, with low feelings of political efficacy, largely explains the low rates of political participation among poor people and minorities.

While not always clear, public opinion plays an important part in the formation of public policy in America. The quality of public opinion largely depends on the quality of the information on which the opinion is based. The impact of public opinion on public officials largely depends on its intensity. Opinion that is intensely held—even by small groups, which may or may not represent the majority view—can be more influential than vaguely held majority opinions. To influence public policy, citizens' opinions, if they are to be effective, are usually channeled through the instruments of power made available to them. They may act through interest groups and political movements; they can become involved with political parties; and they may speak with special authority in the voting booth. Whatever they do, if their activities have an impact, they will be carried, amplified, and changed by the media, as Chapter 6 will show.

Key Terms

socialization (p. 128)
political socialization (p. 128)
political education (p. 129)
peer influence (p. 130)
liberal (p. 135)
conservative (p. 135)
political efficacy (p. 137)
agenda-setting (p. 138)

selective perception (p. 139)
opinion leaders (p. 139)
straw poll (p. 142)
scientific polling (p. 142)
representative sample (p. 143)
random sampling (p. 143)
quota method (p. 144)

Suggested Readings

Conway, M. Margaret, *Political Participation in the United States* (Washington D.C.: Congressional Quarterly, 1985).
Dawson, Richard E., et al., *Political Socialization,* 2nd ed. (Boston: Little, Brown, 1978).

Ferguson, Thomas, and Joel Rogers, *No Right Turn* (New York: Hill & Wang, 1986).

Ginsberg, Benjamin, *The Captive Public* (New York: Basic, 1986).

Lippmann, Walter, *Public Opinion* (New York: Harcourt, Brace, 1922).

Endnotes

[1] See *National Journal,* February 11, 1989, pp. 261–67 and *Newsweek,* February 6, 1989.

[2] Tip O'Neill, *Man of the House* (New York: St. Martin's Press, 1987), pp. 412, 418, 420.

[3] David Easton and Jack Dennis, *Children in the Political System* (Chicago: University of Chicago Press, 1980).

[4] Dean Jaros, Herbert Hirsch, and Frederic J. Fleron, Jr., "The Malevolent Leader: Political Socialization in an American Subculture," *American Political Science Review,* 62 (1968): 575.

[5] See Kenneth Keniston, *Young Radicals* (New York: Harcourt, Brace and World, 1968).

[6] Diane Ravitch and Chester E. Finn Jr., *What Do Our 17-year-olds Know? A Report on the First National Assessment of History and Literature* (New York: Harper & Row, 1987), pp 263–69.

[7] See Gabriel A. Almond and Sidney Verba, eds., *The Civic Culture Revisited* (Boston: Little, Brown, 1980).

[8] Daniel Patrick Moynihan, "The Presidency and the Press," *Commentary* (March 1971), p. 44.

[9] George Gerbner, Larry Gross, Michael Morgan, and Nancy Signorielli, "Charting the Mainstream: Television's Contributions to Political Orientations," *Journal of Communications* (Spring 1982), Vol. 32, no. 2:102 and "Political Correlates of Television Viewing," *Public Opinion Quarterly,* Vol. 48, no. 1B (Spring 1984):298.

[10] See Herbert McClosky and Alida Brill, *Dimensions of Tolerance: What Americans Believe About Civil Liberties* (New York: Russell Sage, 1983).

[11] Almond and Verba, *The Civic Culture* and Richard Rose, "Public Confidence, Popular Consent: A Comparison of Britain and the United States," *Public Opinion* (February/March 1984), p. 11.

[12] Louis Harris, *Inside America* (New York: Vintage Books, 1987), p. 305.

[13] V. O. Key, Jr., *Public Opinion and American Democracy* (New York: Alfred A. Knopf, 1961), p. 396.

[14] See Ralph K. White, *Nobody Wanted War: Misperception in Vietnam and Other Wars* (Garden City, NY: Doubleday and Company, 1970), pp. 262–64.

[15] *Business Week,* August 22, 1988, p. 32.

[16] *The Wall Street Journal,* September 23, 1988.

[17] *The New York Times,* June 10, 1984.

[18] Reported in James B. Lemert, *Does Mass Communication Change Public Opinion After All?* (Chicago: Nelson-Hall, 1981), pp. 46–47.

[19] Niccolo Machiavelli, *The Discourses* (New York: Random House, Modern Library Edition, 1940), p. 162.

[20] James Bryce, *The American Commonwealth,* Vol. 1 (Putnam, Capricorn Books, 1959), p. 296.

[21]V. O. Key, Jr., *Public Opinion and American Democracy.*

[22]Alan D. Monroe, "Consistency between Public Preferences and National Policy Decisions," *American Politics Quarterly,* January 7, 1979, pp 3–19.

[23]John Naisbitt, *Megatrends: Ten New Directions Transforming Our Lives* (New York: Warner Books, 1982), p. 160.

[24]For more on this discussion see Jeffrey B. Abramson, et al., *The Electric Commonwealth* (New York: Basic Books, 1988), Chapter 5.

[25]This discussion is adapted from Barry Sussman, *What Americans Really Think,* 1988, pp. 192–99.

[26]Ibid. p. 196.

[27]Carol Matlock, "Mobilizing for the Abortion War," *National Journal,* July 15, 1989, pp. 1814–15.

CHAPTER 6

Mass Media

During the 1984 presidential campaign, Lesley Stahl, a CBS reporter, prepared a critical commentary on how President Reagan used television. In her blunt report, Stahl described how Reagan used television images to obscure his own political record.

The script charged the president with manipulation, if not hypocrisy. He will appear at the Special Olympics or the opening ceremony of a senior housing facility, but no hint is given that he cut the budgets for the disabled and for subsidized housing for the elderly. He will also distance himself from bad news, Stahl reported. After he pulled the marines out of Lebanon, he flew off to his California ranch, allowing others to make the announcement.

To illustrate her piece, Stahl put together an array of Reagan's video clips. There was Reagan greeting handicapped athletes in wheelchairs, cutting the ribbon at a home for the elderly, mingling with black inner-city children, relaxing on his ranch in jeans, and paying tribute at Normandy to American GIs who had died in World War II.

"I thought it was the single toughest piece I had ever done on Reagan," Stahl said. She worried about White House reaction.

After the piece aired, the phone rang. It was a senior White House official. Stahl thought, "here it comes." She recalls the conversation:

"And the voice said, 'Great piece.'

"I said, 'What?'

"And he said, *'Great piece!'*

"I said, 'Did you listen to what I said?'

"He said, 'Lesley, when you're showing four and a half minutes of great pictures of Ronald Reagan, no one listens to what you say. Don't you know that the pictures are overriding your message because they conflict with your message? The public sees those pictures and they block your message. They didn't even hear what you said. So, in our minds, it was a four-and-a-half-minute free ad for the Ronald Reagan campaign for reelection.'

"I sat here numb . . . None of us had figured that out. All of us were proud of that piece 'cause we thought we had done a good, tough job, and then"—She broke into laughter. "They loved it. They really did love it."[1]

Ronald Reagan at his California ranch.

Few would argue that the media are not powerful political forces. How we understand politics and what we think is important are greatly affected by what we read in the newspapers and see on television. Politicians recognize that reality and, as Lesley Stahl

© 1981, Raleigh News & Observer. Reprinted by permission of Los Angeles Times Syndicate

learned, they influence the media at least as often as they are influenced *by* the media.

The other point illustrated in this introductory tale is the complexity of these instruments of power. The consequences of their use is often unpredictable, even to the cult of experts claiming mastery over the medium. The media is both an actor and an arena in American politics. As an *arena* it is a setting, though hardly a neutral one, in which all the country's major political conflicts are eventually played out. As an *actor,* the media may at times act coherently with enormous power to influence political events, as is shown in the case study on Gary Hart on page 174.

The media have been labeled "the fourth branch of government," rivaling the three official branches in political power. Although this overstates the matter (the press can't actually *do* what the executive, legislature, and judiciary can), mass media's major role in shaping the actions of government make it vital to understand. This chapter addresses the following questions: What are the media? What do the media do? Who controls the media? How do the media affect politics? How are they influenced by the government and other political players?

WHAT ARE THE MEDIA?

Media are means of communication that permit messages to be made public. Media such as television, radio, magazines, books, and newspapers provide links connecting people to one another. But these are links with an important quality—they have the ability to communicate messages from a single source to a great many people at roughly the same time.

With more than 125 million television sets in the United States and 97 percent of U.S. households possessing at least one set, television dominates the mass media. Its political influence is illustrated not only by an exceptional event, such as the presidential debates watched by more than 100 million Americans, but also by the networks' evening news programs, which reach more than 45 million people each night (see Figure 6.1).

Television is in turn dominated by the three major networks, CBS, NBC, and ABC. These **networks** each own seven television stations (the legal limit). But the *networks* function mainly as agencies that produce and sell programs with advertising to local broadcast stations called **affiliates.** (In 1988, NBC had 207 television affiliates; ABC, 220; and CBS, 204.) The networks have contracts with their affiliates that enable them to buy or produce programs and to sell time to advertisers on a national basis. They then offer these programs, with ads, to their affiliates, which can sell time locally to advertisers—"and now a word from our local stations." The affiliates get the shows, and the networks get the national coverage, which allows them to sell time at more than $1 million for six minutes of advertising during prime evening viewing hours.

In recent years, the television networks have been challenged by a number of new technologies that are widening the choices available to viewers. Some 40 percent of the nation's nearly 84 million television households get their signals not over the air but through cables. News organizations such as CNN (Cable News Network) and C-SPAN (Cable-Satellite Public Affairs Networks) have appeared to fill the enormous appetite of a technology that already can provide

FIGURE 6★1
Audiences Reached by Leading Media, 1988

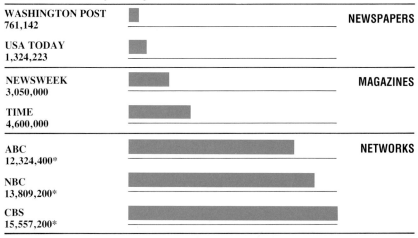

SOURCE: Data on newspapers from American Newspaper Publishers Association, *Facts About Newspapers '88,* April 1988. Data on the three networks from A. C. Nielsen Company. Used by permission of A. C. Nielsen Company.

★ All the News That's Fit for Pictures

Television network news shows are in trouble. In Chicago, only half the viewers watch network news. In San Francisco, more people watch "Wheel of Fortune" than the two competing CBS and ABC nightly news programs combined. Just as bad, the game show attracts younger people, especially women, whom advertisers want to reach, while people over fifty watch the news. Adding to the problem is that local stations' news programs are muscling out network news with earlier headlines and larger audiences.

Some of the blame may lie within the shows. While losing an estimated $20 million in a recent year, CBS News still managed to pay its anchor, Dan Rather, a reported $2.3 million annually. Today's broadcasts stress lighter news with shorter explanations and more emphasis on exciting pictures. Often the technology has produced absorbing visual content without really informing the viewer. But supplying serious information is not the bottom line. That lies in the networks' battle for the largest audience,

which frequently seems to rest on selling the personality of their anchors.

upward of eighty channels per household. And nearly 100,000 American homes are connected to two-way cable systems, which allow them not only to *receive* television programs but to transmit messages as well. They can order goods from stores, transact business with their banks, and respond to opinion polls.

Radio has made a great comeback. There are some 8600 radio stations, and each American family has an average of five radios. There are around 10,000 magazines and other periodicals available in the U.S., but about one-fifth of America's adult population accounts for three-fifths of all magazines sold, and most of the magazines are specialized in their audience appeal. Only one magazine, *Reader's Digest* (with a circulation of 18 million) is a mass-circulation magazine with general appeal to middle America. More important in the formation of public opinion—especially because they are read by opinion leaders—are the weekly newsmagazines *Time, Newsweek,* and *U.S. News and World Report.*

Newspapers are even more varied. Some 60 million copies of newspapers are distributed each day, but the top twenty-five newspaper companies account for over half of the daily circulation. Newspapers range in quality from the top of the elite media, *The New*

York Times, which carries national and international news collected by its own reporters, to small-town dailies that relay crop reports and describe local fires but provide sketchy coverage of national events reprinted from the wire services. (Wire services are specialized agencies such as the *Associated Press (AP)* and *United Press International (UPI)* that gather, write, and sell news to the media that subscribe to them.) Many local newspapers pay for reports from one of the more influential dailies like *The Washington Post* and *The Los Angeles Times.*

Newspapers are also becoming less numerous and less competitive. At the turn of the century there were 2600 daily papers in the United States. By 1987, though the population had tripled, there were only 1645. The same period has seen a decline in the number of cities with competing newspapers. In 1910, more than half the cities and towns in the United States had dailies owned by two or more companies. Today, only 4 percent of U.S. communities have competing newspaper ownerships. Of our major cities, only New York has more than two separately owned daily papers. The reasons for this trend lie in the economic nature of the media.

THE MEDIA MARKETPLACE

Media are privately owned economic assets bought and sold to make a profit. Profitability, and often, lack of profitability, has led to the increasing concentration of media ownership. The decrease in competition among newspapers has been reflected in the increase in **chains,** companies that combine different media in different cities under one owner. More than 70 percent of the nation's newspapers today are owned by chains, as are many television and radio stations.

Some media companies and newspaper chains are not only involved in more than one media market or locality but are also involved in all three of the major media—newspaper, radio, and television. Newhouse Publications, one of the largest chains, owns twenty-six daily papers, seven television stations, seven radio stations, three cable systems, a major book publisher (Random House), and twelve national magazines including *Vogue, The New Yorker,* and *Parade.*

Some people fear that chain ownership breaks the link between the owner (called the *publisher*) and the community that historically had helped maintain the quality of local newspapers. Reduced competition has given rise to a concern among some about concentrated media power. Ben H. Bagdikian, a media critic, worries that "fifty men and women, chiefs of their corporations, control more than half the information and ideas that reach 220 million Americans."[2]

Marketplace calculations led to drastic changes in the television networks' ownership in 1985. Early that year, ABC was bought by another media company, Capital Cities Communications. In December, NBC's parent company, RCA, was acquired by General Electric for over $6 billion, making it at the time the biggest buyout of a non-oil firm. In between these two mergers, CBS had to bring in an outside investor to buy large amounts of stock to keep from being acquired by corporate raiders. Many reasons for these merger activities lay outside the industry, but within the industry the networks had been hit by competition from cable, video cassettes, and independent stations, all of which had reduced their audiences and their shares of advertising dollars. This caused the price of the networks' stock to drop and they became vulnerable to takeovers.

None of this should leave the impression that the media industry is not very profitable. A 100-percent return on investment each year for a television station in a major city is not uncommon. Network advertising revenues have climbed beyond $8 billion. Newspapers, though not as profitable, earn even more than the television industry—bringing in advertising revenues of almost $30 billion in 1987. Although customers pay for newspapers, most of the papers' costs are covered by advertising.

Unlike other Western democracies such as Britain and France, where state ownership and financing of the national mass media are dominant, the private marketplace is key in America. As one current study concluded: "The history of the mass media in the United States thus records an almost total triumph of commercialization—the dominance of private ownership and advertiser financing."[3] This means that networks fiercely compete for a larger audience in order to gain advertising dollars. This leads to similar shows on all three networks and limited time devoted to less-popular news programs. It may also encourage "objective," balanced newscasts designed to avoid antagonizing the audience and advertisers.

WHAT DO THE MEDIA DO?

The media provide three major types of messages. Through their *news reports, entertainment programs,* and *advertising,* the media help shape people's attitudes about many things, including politics.

News

In news reports, the media supply up-to-date accounts of what journalists believe to be the most important, interesting, and newsworthy events, issues, and developments in the nation and the world. But

Due to intense media exposure, Lieutenant Colonel Oliver North became a "national figure" for his role in the Iran-contra affair. Here, North arrives at the Senate to testify before a congressional committee in 1987.

the influence of news reports goes well beyond relaying facts. The key to this power is **selectivity.** By reporting certain things (President Reagan's naps) and ignoring others (President Roosevelt's wheelchair), the media suggest to us what's important. Media coverage gives status to people and events—a national television interview or a *Time* magazine cover creates a "national figure." As shown in the box on page 165, most news stories originate in settings controlled by government officials or in information from these officials.

There are, of course, limits. When he was running for president in 1984, Ohio Senator John Glenn, a former astronaut, was thought likely to benefit from the release of a movie, *The Right Stuff,* based on the exploits of the early astronauts and featuring Glenn as a hero. The movie bombed, however, as did the Glenn campaign. And that was without the kind of intense scrutiny that is a part of media attention to serious presidential candidates.

Perhaps the most important function the media perform has been called **agenda setting:** *putting together an agenda of national priorities—what should be taken seriously, what lightly, and what ignored altogether.* "The media can't tell people what to think," as one expert put it, "But they can tell people what to think *about.*" The attention the media give to the nuclear arms race, environmental pollution, or unemployment will largely determine how important most people think these issues are. How the problems are presented will influence which explanations of them are more acceptable than others, and which policies are thought to be appropriate responses. Whether inner-city crime is associated with the need for more police or with cutbacks in urban welfare programs will help shape public debate. Likewise, if layoffs in the auto industry are linked to imports of Japanese cars—and not to the failure of U.S. automakers to modernize their factories—the result may be trade barriers rather than industrial aid.[4]

Over time, public concern for political problems such as civil rights and inflation closely reflects changes in the attention paid them by national media. Dramatic events such as student demonstrations in China or a gang attack on a jogger in New York City's Central Park may also move public opinion above and beyond the volume of coverage devoted to them. Nonetheless, media provide a lens that can magnify or reduce the importance of these events.

In setting this agenda of importance, the national media may also alter the criteria by which viewers judge government performance. In one experiment, viewers were asked to evaluate President Carter after they were exposed to a steady stream of stories on the nation's energy problems. The ratings of presidential performance on energy became more influential in the participants' evaluation of Carter's overall standing as president. Thus, in delivering their reports, news programs set standards by which presidents and governments are judged.[5]

Entertainment

Entertainment programs offer amusement and also give people images of "normal" behavior. Certain standards are upheld by heroes, who are rewarded, and violated by outlaws, who are punished. Whether or not this television behavior offers socially acceptable models is another question. Soap characters such as Alexis of "Dynasty" and J. R. Ewing of "Dallas" engage in immoral business practices that result in great wealth and power. These television experiences may substitute for learning from life's more complex experiences. As one analyst of television observed: "If you can write a nation's stories, you needn't worry about who makes its laws. Today, television tells most of the stories to most of the people most of the time."[6]

Advertising

The programs and news that media present are built around a constant flow of advertisements. Television programs are constructed to reach emotional high points just before commercials so that audiences will stay put during the advertisements. Newspapers devote much more space to ads than to news (over 62 percent in 1987), leading English author G. K. Chesterton to define a *journalist* as "someone who writes on the back of advertisements." The ads generally show well-off Americans enjoying the material rewards that come from conforming to the norms of society. Whether this image is true is a very debatable and very political question.

★ A Study of News Sources of *The Washington Post* and *The New York Times*

The vast majority of news stories (from 70 to 90 percent, depending on how they are categorized) are drawn from situations over which newsmakers have either complete or substantial control. Here is the breakdown of the contexts from which the *Times* and *Post* drew their information:

CONTEXT	PERCENT
Press conferences	24.5
Interviews	24.7
Press releases	17.5
Official proceedings	13.0
Background proceedings	7.9
Other nonspontaneous events	4.5
News commentary and editorials	4.0
Leaks	2.3
Nongovernmental proceedings	1.5
Spontaneous events	1.2
Reporter's own analysis	0.9

Government officials (either domestic or foreign) were the sources of nearly three quarters of all news, and only one sixth of the news could be traced to sources outside the government. The breakdown of news sources looked like this:

SOURCE	PERCENT
U.S. officials, agencies	46.5
Foreign, international officials, agencies	27.5
U.S. state, local government officials	4.1
Other news organizations	3.2
Nongovernmental Americans	14.4
Nongovernmental foreigners	2.1
Nonascertainable	2.4

Less than *1 percent* of all news stories were based on the reporter's own analysis, while over *90 percent* were based on the calculated messages of the actors involved in the situation.

SOURCE: Leon V. Sigal, *Reporters and Officials: The Organization and Politics of Newsmaking* (Lexington, Mass.: Heath, 1973), pp. 122–24. Reprinted from W. Lance Bennett, *News: The Politics of Illusion* (New York: Longman, 1983), pp. 53–54.

Advertisers approach media with certain expectations. They want their ads to be seen or read by as many people as possible; they want the people seeing the ads to be potential customers; and they don't want the surrounding programs or articles to detract from the ads.

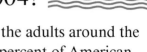

★ Fred Flintstone for President in 2004?

An international study has shown that although only half the adults around the world could identify a picture of their national leader, 90 percent of American three-year-olds could identify a photograph of cartoon character Fred Flintstone.

Another survey asked four- to six-year-olds which they preferred, "television or daddy?" Forty-four percent replied, "Television."

As a result, *advertising encourages media content—whether news or entertainment—to be as conventional and inoffensive as possible in order to keep the customer satisfied.* Tobacco companies have contracts that keep their ads away from articles linking cigarette smoking to health hazards. Airlines have standard arrangements with most newspapers that provide for their ads to be pulled from editions that carry news of airline disasters. A talk-show host once had a list of possible guests that was cut by a third by his sponsor because of the political views some guests held. One of television's biggest advertisers, Procter & Gamble, has a censorship code that reads in part: "Members of the armed forces must not be cast as villains."

MEDIA AND GOVERNMENT

Government officials have a number of formal and informal means for regulating and influencing the media. Their formal powers include the requirement that radio and television stations renew their broadcast licenses with the Federal Communications Commission every six years. Although this is a formality, the threat of losing a license can be an effective means of pressuring broadcasters that are hostile to a particular administration or policy. Until 1987, the FCC tried to enforce its **fairness doctrine,** which required that contrasting views on controversial issues be presented. If stations did not give balanced presentations, they would have to provide air time to correct the balance. The doctrine was sometimes used against certain political views. President Johnson used it in 1964 to intimidate radio stations favorable to his Republican challenger, Senator Barry Goldwater. But the Reagan administration's FCC abolished the fairness doctrine because it interfered with an unregulated marketplace. It felt that broadcast journalism should be treated like print journalism, with no fairness doctrine.

Packaging Politics

For campaigning politicians, the media are both opportunity and adversary.[7] Between 50 and 60 percent of the campaign money in presidential races goes to advertising. Considerable effort also goes into engineering events that will be considered "newsworthy" and will capture free media coverage. Some of these activities have been called **pseudoevents**—not real events at all, but staged in order to be reported.

Michael Dukakis spent the day before Labor Day 1988 at Ellis Island in front of the Statue of Liberty, marking the seventy-fifth anniversary of his father's arrival in America (his patriotism had been questioned by Vice-President Bush). George Bush, a week before, had visited Boston Harbor (in Dukakis's back yard) to note its severe pollution (Bush's support for the environment had been questioned by Dukakis).

The examples of government leaders informally pressuring media are numerous. As seen in the box on "Dealing with the Media" (page 170), the Nixon administration took a very hard line toward the media, with poor results. Most of the time presidents try to get on the good side of the media by giving favored reporters exclusive "leaks" of information and by controlling information going to the public through television, radio, and newspapers. This is called **news management.**

Press conferences have been used by presidents since Theodore Roosevelt to give the media direct contact with the chief executive. With radio, and then television, such conferences have allowed presidents to bypass journalists and present their views directly to the public. Franklin Roosevelt's radio "fireside chats"—which were briefly revived on television, with less success, by President Carter—were a skillful use of direct communication during the Great Depression. Television and presidents can also make uneasy partners. In 1960, presidential candidate Richard Nixon's streaky makeup, dull suit, and heavy beard made a poor impression in the first-ever televised candidates' debate. (His opponent was John Kennedy).

Presidents generally have large staffs of media experts, speech writers, and public-relations people to perfect their images. As a former movie actor, professional speaker, and radio and television personality, Ronald Reagan understood the importance of television news to his image—and the importance of "visuals" to television news. His cheerful waves to the camera and smiling gestures to reporters became common on newscasts, regardless of the substance of the report the film illustrated. Said Sam Donaldson, ABC News White House correspondent: if confronted with hard questioning

Democratic presidential nominee Michael Dukakis poses in a tank in Sterling Heights, Michigan in 1988. The event, staged for the media shortly before the November 8 election, was widely derided as making the governor look faintly ridiculous.

Richard Nixon wipes his face during the first televised presidential debate with John F. Kennedy in 1960, a debate that may have lost him the election.

from reporters, Reagan may "just jolly us along with a joke, point to his watch, or wave. The viewer sees a good-natured guy being nice about being pestered, but what Reagan's really done is duck another question."

Ronald Reagan's polish in front of the cameras did not come easily. He spent up to ten hours a week rehearsing speeches. (Jimmy Carter, by contrast, averaged three hours or less.) The result of Reagan's skill as "The Great Communicator" was an ability, unrivaled in recent presidents, to look and sound absolutely honest and forthright. Remarked Bob Landers, a top commercial announcer: "You'll notice that when Ronald Reagan makes a mistake, he says the wrong word with the same sincere fervor as the right one. That's the skill of a professional communicator; it comes from years and years of "being sincere.'"

Mediating Elections

Despite President Bush's evident dislike at being "packaged" for the media, he still enjoys the deference that comes with the office. Journalists, among others, often cozy up to those in power. Bush, first as vice-president and then as a candidate for president, was generally given fairly rough treatment by the press. He was portrayed as a preppie wimp who stood up for nothing in the Reagan White House and could not win an election on his own. With his electoral victories came his transformation into a tough winner, sportsman, and regular guy. Sixteen months before he entered the White House, *Newsweek* pictured Mr. Bush in his power boat to illustrate a cover story called "Fighting the 'Wimp Factor.'" Two weeks before his inauguration, a picture of Bush fishing from the back of a motor boat illustrated "The 'Liberation' of George Bush." As Barbara Walters of ABC TV said shortly before the inauguration, "It's as if Clark Kent became Superman."[8]

Of course, media gets its licks in too. As shown in the Gary Hart case, media can make or break a political career. While the argument of bias by the national media—it's too liberal, too critical—is far from proven (see Chapter 5) the media does influence the way politicians seek power. The extraordinary media attention given to the early primaries in presidential-election years has made New Hampshire into a "winner-take-all" primary. A winner in New Hampshire is instantly transformed into the "front-runner," with his face on the cover of *Time* magazine and money and support pouring in.

A more negative example of media influence on elections lies in the *exit polls* conducted by television networks that project winners before balloting ends. In 1980, these projections appeared before the polls closed in many states, and President Carter publically conceded over an hour before voting ended in California. Many prominent Democratic senators and congressmen blamed their defeat on the reduced turnout caused by these media events. Turnout did seem to have been reduced significantly among potential voters who either heard the projections or the concession speech.

During his candidacy for president, George Bush worked hard to change his image to that of an all-American sportsman, family man, and regular guy. His image improved vastly when he became president.

★ Dealing With the Media

A Nixon aide's ideas for fighting media "bias" against the Nixon administration: "Plant a column with a syndicated columnist which raises the question of objectivity and ethics in the News media. . . .

"Arrange for an article on the subject in a major consumer magazine authorized by Stewart Alsop, [William F.]Buckley or [James J.] Kilpatrick. . . .

"Have Rogers Morton [Chairman of the Republican National Committee] go on the attack in a news conference. . . . Have him charge that the great majority of the working press are Democrats and this colors their presentation of the news. Have him charge that there is a political conspiracy in the media to attack this Administration. . . .

"Arrange for an 'expose' to be written by an author such as Earl Mazo or Victor Lasky. Publish in hardcover and paperback. . . .

"Have outside groups petition the FCC and issue public statements of concern over press objectivity.

"Generate a massive outpouring of letters-to-the-editor.

"Have a Senator or Congressman write a public letter to the FCC suggesting the 'licensing' of individual newsmen. . . ."

SOURCE: 1970 memo from Jeb Magruder to other White House staff members, in Thomas Whiteside, "Annals of Television: Shaking the Tree," *The New Yorker,* March 17, 1975, p. 46.

MEDIA IMPACT

It is easy to overstate the impact of media on the public. The facts about television watching alone seem to make it a pervasive influence. The average set is on seven hours a day; the average male viewer watches television for nine full years (3000 days) by the age of sixty-five; and the average eighteen-year old has spent 20,000 hours in front of the TV—more time than in classrooms, churches, and all other educational and cultural activities *combined.*[9]

Yet there is a case to be made that media has a rather **minimal impact** on public opinion, especially in relation to politics. For starters, television seems to be often on but not so often watched. As much as 40 percent of the time the TV set is operating no one is in the room or watching it. Even when someone is watching, during almost one-third of the time TV viewing is secondary to talking, eating, dancing, reading, as well as some less-mentionable pursuits.

Television news ranks near the bottom of programs not watched. The news is also little remembered. Ratings for television news run much lower than ratings for entertainment programs. Audiences are generally one-half to two-thirds the size of those for prime-time programs.

And those watching are not watching very closely. One telephone survey in the San Francisco area found that people could recall, on average, only one of some twenty stories covered on the news earlier in the evening. Even with prompting, by running down a list of the day's headlines, half of the stories were completely forgotten. Still, television is considered the most objective and complete source of news by most people. Americans also overwhelmingly assert that they get most of their information about national events from television, not newspapers.

The impact of most political messages is significantly diminished simply because relatively few people are paying attention. Except for the special political event—a presidential address on prime time, or election-night coverage—continuing attention to political content on the media is uncommon. Even the rare event, like a presidential debate that may be more closely watched, seems to generally lead to **reinforcement** of previous attitudes as the dominant effect on the audience.[10]

However even where partisan predispositions are immediately reinforced, media may have the last word. In the first presidential debates of 1984 between Walter Mondale and Ronald Reagan, polls taken right afterward showed people narrowly picking Mondale as having done better. Following this, TV and press accounts focused on Reagan's poor performance and whether he was too old to be president. Subsequent polls only two days later showed how dramatically such coverage had influenced the public. As Figure 6.2 on page 172 illustrates, Mondale was now seen as the winner by wide majorities. Of course, since Reagan won the election by a landslide, exactly who had the last laugh—the public or the media—is left in some question.

Clearly, media does at times have considerably more than a minimal impact. During moments of crisis, presidents have used patriotic symbols and the media to rally support, as President Reagan did following the Grenada invasion (see Chapter 13). Also, over time the **cumulative impact** of media in changing attitudes can be impressive. Opposition to the war in Vietnam grew as the casualties increased and as the coverage given the war amplified the violence. During the Watergate scandal, as new revelations of White House misconduct were reported in the press day after day, President Nixon's popularity irreversibly declined. While media appear to be everywhere, their impact may be difficult to measure and apparent only over time.

MEDIA POLITICS

Political scientist E. E. Schattschneider pointed out that the "definition of alternatives is the supreme instrument of power." By "definition of alternatives" he meant the ability to set limits on political

FIGURE 6★2
The Media Effect:
Presidential Debates, 1984

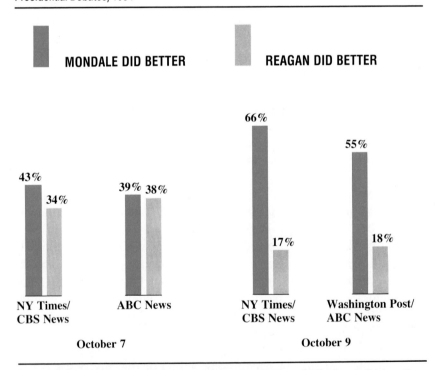

SOURCE: Barry Sussman, *What Americans Really Think and Why Our Politicians Pay No Attention* (New York: Pantheon Books, 1988), p. 214.

debates, to define what is politically important and what is not, and to make certain solutions reasonable and acceptable and others not. Media, to a great extent, have this power. Who influences the exercise of this power is another question.

Certainly editors, newscasters, producers, and reporters have an important role in shaping political views. It was these managers who Nixon's former Vice-President Spiro Agnew saw as too powerful and attacked as "the nattering nabobs of negativism." The owners of media, whether television networks or newspaper chains, play a part in selecting who will handle the day-to-day running of the press and what the general "slant" of the media they own will be. Advertisers, by buying space in some programs or papers and not in others, affect the messages the public gets. *Government and politicians have a whole catalogue of laws and tactics to pressure media into conforming to their political priorities.* And the public, by watching or not watching certain programs, by buying or not buying certain papers, or by demanding or not demanding access to the means of free speech, can help shape the output of mass communications.

No matter who controls the media, the messages the media provide usually reflect the power of those in the political game. Government officials, through press conferences, paid public-relations experts, and news releases, can be fairly sure of reaching the public through the media. Using paid advertising, those with wealth can claim media time to persuade the public to act in certain ways— usually by buying the goods they produce, but sometimes (like oil companies) simply by thinking well of them. The ability of nonelite groups to address each other, as well as their political representatives, is far more limited. The practice of giving air time to community groups has not gotten very far in this country (certainly not as far as in the Netherlands, where any group with enough members is entitled to a certain amount of time on television each week to present its programs). Free speech without broader access to the *means* of free speech remains a limited right for most Americans.

Even citizens with little interest in politics were riveted by media coverage of the events that led to President Nixon's resignation in 1974.

Gary Hart and the Press: The Politics of a Sex Scandal

At the beginning of May 1987, Democrat Gary Hart's four-year effort to become president was undone by rumors of extramarital affairs, a blonde model named Donna Rice, and a fifty-two-foot sloop called "Monkey Business." The power of the press to transform a presidential front-runner, almost overnight, into a posterboy for supermarket tabloids raised many questions about what the press sees as newsworthy and why.

A Rising Star

Based on his strong showing in 1984, when he almost beat former Vice-President Walter Mondale for the Democratic nomination, Gary Hart emerged as the early favorite for 1988. Nonetheless, Hart and his staff recognized that having front-runner status would mean intense press scrutiny. They worked hard to dispel old charges against Hart. Reams of position papers were issued to answer the 1984 question about Hart's new ideas, "Where's the beef?"

What Hart did not anticipate was that old rumors about unfaithfulness to his wife during the 1984 campaign would be printed as part of the public assessment of his "character" for 1988. Rather than focusing on Hart's proposals, reporters asked whether Hart was still a "womanizer." A Hart adviser from the 1984 campaign gave his own response to *Newsweek:* "He's always in danger of having the sex issue raised if he can't keep his pants on."[11] Hart denied the rumors. He even challenged the press to follow him around. "If anybody wants to put a tail on me, go ahead," Hart told the *New York Times,* "they'd be very bored."

The Miami Herald Story

Unfortunately for Hart, *The Miami Herald* took him up on his offer. Following an anonymous tip that a Miami woman was flying to Washington to spend the weekend with Hart, a five-person stakeout team formed to watch Hart's Capitol Hill townhouse. At about 9:30 P.M. Friday night, May 1, a *Herald* reporter observed a blonde woman emerge from the house with Hart. The two left and then reentered the house about two hours later.

The reporters next saw Hart and the woman about twenty-four hours later, at 8:40 P.M. on Saturday night. Had Hart spent Friday night and all day Saturday alone with the woman? Interviewed on his doorstep, Hart said no. The woman, whom he identified as Donna Rice, had left by the back way Friday night and had spent the night three blocks away with her friend Lynn Armandt, at the home of Hart acquaintance Bill Broadhurst, an attorney.

Unable to speak to Rice to confirm Hart's claim, the *Herald* reporters interviewed attorney Broadhurst. According to Broadhurst, he, Rice, and Armandt had picked Hart up in front of Hart's townhouse on Saturday and the four had driven over to Alexandria, returning Saturday night. While later acknowledging gaps in their late-night stakeout of the rear entrance to Hart's townhouse, the *Herald*

Donna Rice is photographed sitting on the lap of smiling Gary Hart on the cover of the June 2, 1987 issue of the *National Enquirer.*

team was confident that no one had come in or left the front of the house all day Saturday as Broadhurst had stated.

Based on this rather stark conflict of events, the *Herald* went ahead with the story that Gary Hart had spent the night alone in his townhouse with a young woman. The story ran with a banner headline on Sunday May 3, 1987.

"Mr. Hart has suggested the press follow him to disprove the (recent) allegations on womanizing," explained *Herald* Executive Editor Heath Meriwether. "The womanizing issue [was] a major one . . . because it raise[d] questions

concerning the candidate's judgment and integrity. That's why we reported on this story."[12]

The Gary Hart-Donna Rice story would remain on the front pages of the nation's newspapers for five more days. At the end, Hart would be out of the presidential race.

The Hart Campaign Reacts

Hart's campaign acted as if the best defense was a good offense by aggressively attacking the press. Bill Dixon, Hart's campaign manager, questioned the ethics of the *Herald,* accusing the paper of character assassination. Hart went further, dubbing the *Herald*'s tactics of "hiding in bushes [and] peeking in windows" as "outrageous".

The Hart camp also tried to limit the number of days of coverage by getting the whole story out quickly. On Monday, however, further interviews revealed that the same foursome (Hart, Rice, Armandt, and Broadhurst) had sailed to Bimini in April, staying overnight on the chartered boat, "Monkey Business." The Bimini story served to undercut Hart's contention to the *Herald* that his relationship with Rice was limited to a few telephone calls. Hart's credibility was further strained when Bimini officials rebutted Hart's claim that the group had been

Gary Hart, with his wife Lee, announces his withdrawal from the Democratic presidential race on May 8, 1987.

forced to stay the night because the customs office there was closed. Disturbed by the new revelations, Hart campaign manager Dixon quietly resigned.

Undeterred by the mushrooming Rice story, Hart pursued his offensive. In a speech on Tuesday to the American Newspaper Publishers Association, Hart challenged the press to ask "searching questions" about its conduct in covering what he termed a "mistake in judgment." The speech was generally well received. But a press conference the next day, designed to end the matter once and for all, backfired. Hart curtly refused to answer reporters' direct questions about whether he had ever committed adultery. The dramatic exchange was prominently featured both by the network news that night and by most newspapers the next morning.

By Wednesday, an atmosphere of disarray emerged in the Hart campaign. New poll results showed a severe erosion of Hart's lead among Democratic voters. Long-time Hart congressional supporters declined to speak up for their candidate. Even worse, key fundraisers were closing their checkbooks.

Hart's Withdrawal

What little hope remained for continuing the Hart candidacy evaporated on Wednesday night. *The Washington Post* informed Hart's press secretary of evidence of another Hart liaison with a Washington woman. The *Post* was prepared to report that this partic-

ular affair had been going on for months. The crippling effect of such a story on Hart's presidential bid—and his wife and family—was immediately obvious to Hart officials. Would the *Post* hold off publication, they asked, if Hart withdrew from the race? *Post* Executive Editor Ben Bradlee said yes.

Thirty-six hours later, Gary Hart stood before a small crowd of his Denver supporters and announced his withdrawal. (Although he would attempt a comeback six months later; underfunded and understaffed, Hart would lose badly in the few primary contests he entered.) Hart's defiant speech laid the blame for his demise on the press. In Hart's view, presidential press coverage overlooked important issues for more appealing, sensational stories:

"We're all going to have to seriously question the system for selecting our national leaders, for it reduces the press of this nation to hunters and the presidential candidates to being hunted. That has reporters in bushes ... photographers peeking in our windows. ... [13]

Conclusion

Prior to the Donna Rice affair, several American presidents (including John F. Kennedy and Franklin D. Roosevelt) had carried on extramarital affairs the press knew about but did not report. Presumably, reporters considered these private indiscretions to be irrelevant to the more basic issues of public qualifications and job performance. Many in the press believe that these old rules still apply. "Generally, private lives ought to remain private," says Norman Pearlstien, managing editor of *The Wall Street Journal,* "(unless) the private life is so much at variance with public posturing that it goes to the character of the candidate." Did Hart's behavior reveal a dark character flaw?

For many, the most disturbing aspects of the Hart case did not involve reporting known indiscretions. Worse was the news treatment of unproven rumors about Hart's "womanizing." By printing these rumors before the Rice linkage had been made, many argued that the press had set an unfortunate precedent. Any past allegations about a candidate's "character" were now fair game, true or not. In the rough-and-tumble world of presidential politics, this increased the opportunities for shrewd political operators to manipulate press coverage of candidates. Within weeks of Gary Hart's departure, references could be found to rumors of infidelity concerning other presidential candidates. In the 1988 general election, false rumors of Michael Dukakis's health problems were widely publicized. And later, press reports of members of Congress's "ethics" damaged or ended a few more careers in 1989.

The Hart case also points to the expanded role of the press in elections. Modern media now have assumed some of the roles formerly played by the old-time political bosses in evaluating candidates for office. With the reduced power of the parties to select candidates, this "winnowing" function (reducing the number of serious candidates running for office) has fallen to the press. The media now test—and in Hart's case, fail—candidates seeking the presidency.

★ Are Private Lives Private?

Oliver Sipple was in the right place at the right time, as far as President Gerald Ford was concerned. But, after the fact, he clearly wondered whether being a hero was worth his privacy.

Sipple was credited with deflecting a handgun held by Sara Jane Moore when she fired it from a crowd at Ford in San Francisco on September 22, 1975. An ex-Marine who served in Vietnam, "Bill" Sipple was widely profiled in the media as an all-American hero. In their coverage, the press said Sipple was homosexual. He filed a $15 million suit for invasion of privacy against several California news organizations, but it was dismissed by the courts who said his homosexuality was known to "hundreds of people" (although not to his family). While Sipple lost his case, the question of whether his sexual orientation was a proper subject for news coverage was widely debated by the press.

Following his bout with fame, Sipple was treated for drug and alcohol abuse. His death in February 1989 was listed as due to "natural causes" because of a history of heart ailments. He was forty-seven.

SOURCE: *The Washington Post,* February 4, 1989.

WRAP-UP

The framers of the Constitution believed that a free flow of information from a great many sources was basic to maintaining the system of government they set up. Ideas would compete with one another without restraint in the "marketplace of ideas." Fearing that the greatest enemy of free speech was the government, the framers added the First Amendment forbidding government officials from "abridging the freedom of speech, or of the press." The phrase has since been interpreted to include radio and television. The principle, however, remains the same, as Judge Learned Hand wrote:

> *Right conclusions are more likely to be gathered out of a multitude of tongues than through any kind of authoritative selection. To many this is, and always will be folly; but we have staked upon it our all.*

The ability of media to fulfill the goal of presenting a variety of opinions, representing the widest range of political ideas, has, to no one's surprise, been limited in practice. It is limited both by what the media are and by what the government does. As economic assets competing for audience and advertising, media provide political information as a secondary function. However, through their news, entertainment shows, and advertising, media help shape public opinion. Government officials using leaks, staged events, and clever visuals can use media to get their own messages across. How much impact any of these media messages has remains, in the end, debatable.

Key Terms

media (p. 158)	fairness doctrine (p. 166)
networks (p. 159)	pseudoevent (p. 167)
affiliates (p. 159)	news management (p. 167)
chains (p. 161)	minimal impact (p. 171)
selectivity (p. 163)	reinforcement (p. 171)
agenda setting (p. 163)	cumulative impact (p. 172)

Suggested Readings

Diamond, Ed and Stephen Bates, *The Spot: The Rise of Political Advertising on Television*, revised ed. (Cambridge: MIT Press, 1988).

Ellerbee, Linda, *"And So It Goes"* (New York: Putnam Publishing Group, 1986).

Halberstam, David, *The Powers That Be* (New York: Knopf 1979).

Hertsgaard, Mark, *On Bended Knee: The Press and the Reagan Presidency* (New York: Farrar, Straus & Giroux, 1988).

Hess, Stephen, *The Washington Reporters* (Washington, D.C.: The Brookings Institution, 1981).

Hewitt, Don, *Minute by Minute* (New York: Random House, 1985).

Joyce, Ed, *Prime Times, Bad Times* (New York: Doubleday, 1988).

Leonard, Thomas, C., *The Power of the Press: The Birth of Modern Political Reporting* (New York: Oxford University Press, 1987).

Endnotes

[1] Adapted from Hedrick Smith, *The Power Game,* 1988, pp. 413–14.

[2] Ben H. Bagdikian, *The Media Monopoly,* 2nd ed. (Boston: Beacon Press, 1987), p. xxiii. Also see David Halberstam, *The Powers That Be* (New York: Dell, 1979).

[3] Jeffrey B. Abramson, F. C. Arterton, and G. R. Orren, *The Electronic Commonwealth* (New York: Basic Books, 1988), p. 84.

[4] See Shanto Iyengar and Donald Kinder, *News That Matters: Television and American Opinion* (Chicago: University of Chicago, 1987).

[5] Donald R. Kinder and David O. Sears, "Public Opinion and Political Action," in Gardner Lindzey and Elliot Aronson, *The Handbook of Social Psychology* (New York: Random House, 1985), pp. 711.

[6] *The New York Times,* August 23, 1987.

[7] Don Donafede, "Blame the Scribes?" in *National Journal,* July 9, 1988, pp. 1803–06.

[8] *The New York Times,* January 22, 1989.

[9] Kinder and Sears, *Handbook,* pp. 708–10. The research on media impact is adapted from this chapter.

[10] John P. Robinson and Mark R. Levy, *The Main Source* (Beverly Hills: Sage Publications, 1986), pp. 231–36.

[11] *The New York Times,* May 9, 1987.

[12] *The Washington Post,* May 4, 1987.

[13] *The New York Times,* May 9, 1987.

In the 1988 presidential campaign, George Bush attacked Michael Dukakis for vetoing a Massachusetts bill requiring teachers to lead their classes in the Pledge of Allegiance. Dukakis's reply that the State Supreme Court had an "advisory opinion" against the bill was widely considered a weak, legalistic response. The Bush attack was designed to show Dukakis as a far-out liberal and separate him from more conservative working-class voters.

Political reporter David S. Broder offered Dukakis a more political response aimed at Bush's weak spot: the widespread perception of him as a "patronizing patrician." Although Dukakis never gave these remarks, Broder illustrated how politicians can turn issues to their advantage in a campaign and win support from key groups of voters. Broder's suggested speech was:

George Bush used the Pledge of Allegiance in the 1988 presidential race to attack Michael Dukakis's patriotism. It seemed to work.

"I am sorry my opponent has chosen to inject this question, because there are far more important things to discuss. But since it has come up, let me just say this, and then I do not intend to return to it.

"My name may be Mike Dukakis, but I do not need lessons in patriotism from George Herbert Walker Bush . . .

"And I want to say" (here he starts to turn the issue from an attack on Michael Dukakis to an attack on all the common people) "that the voters who elected me as their governor, the people of Malden and Chicopee and Lexington and Concord" (if you got it, flaunt it), "are every bit as patriotic as the people with whom George Bush grew up in Greenwich and Kennebunkport.

"My parents came as immigrants to America early in this century, long after some other people's ancestors arrived. But they, like millions of other immigrants, imbued their children with a love of this country, and its flag, second to none. We do not measure patriotism in America by the date of your arrival or the ship on which you came. The sons and daughters of those who came in chains on the slave ships love America." (Hear that, Jesse?) "The children of the steerage passengers from Ireland and Italy and Poland and Greece love America. The love of our country shines in the faces of our newest immigrants, from Vietnam and Cambodia, the Pacific, from Mexico and Central America" (Are you counting your losses in Texas and California, Mr. Bush?)

"I want to add just one word . . . to my opponent. You do not prove your love of the flag, Mr. Bush, by tromping on the Constitution of the United States . . . any more than you prove your love of the Bible . . . by sending a Bible as a good-will offering to a terrorist Iranian dictator who has held innocent Americans hostage."

(Very calm now, very presidential.) "There is no issue of patriotism between my opponent and myself. So let us address ourselves to the real questions the American people want discussed."[1]

Perhaps if Michael Dukakis had followed David Broder's advice to run a more "political" campaign he would be president today, for elections are contests of political skills. They test the ability of competing candidates to appeal to the logic, emotions, and prejudices of a voting majority. The rules of the game may vary, the techniques of campaigning may be modernized, and the issues, voters, and candidates remain in constant flux, but the essence of elections in America remains the same. They are *a competitive struggle for the people's vote through which leaders acquire governmental power.*[2]

This chapter looks at the electoral system and how it has evolved and shaped the electorate—who votes and what affects how they vote, who doesn't vote and why. The modernization of campaigning, the character of candidates, and a case study of a day in the life of a fictional candidate for the Senate also contribute to this chapter's examination of the electoral system.

THE ELECTORAL SYSTEM

Elections serve several important functions. First, they allow citizens to choose who will govern. Second, they increase citizen involvement in government. By voting, people can influence public officials. As one student of voting, V. O. Key, Jr., has written, "The wishes and probable actions of a vast number of people at the polls must be taken into consideration in the exercise of public power."[3] Third, elections enable citizens to show their support for the political system. This symbol of unity may be a reason why, interestingly, the suicide rate goes down in the months before U.S. presidential elections.[4]

Voting Barriers

Voting is a right in America. For years, that right was denied to many. But legal barriers to voting based upon sex, age (down from twenty-one to eighteen), property, ability to pay poll taxes, literacy, and race have been removed. The last five of these were used mainly in the South to keep large numbers of blacks from voting. Residency requirements for voting have been greatly reduced by the Voting

Registering voters is an important part of the electoral process. Here, women sponsor a voter registration drive aimed at women.

Rights Act of 1970 and by Supreme Court decisions. (In effect, you need to reside in a place no more than fifty days in order to be eligible to vote.)

Today state registration laws are the major remaining legal barrier to voting. Voter registration laws spread at the turn of the century, and were justified as a way to prevent fraud. Some states have periodic registration systems that require registration at frequent intervals, usually just before elections. Others have permanent registration systems under which voters continue to be registered unless they fail to vote in a certain number of elections.

By requiring voters to make a special effort to vote, registration laws screen people out. This screening affects some more than others. People with high incomes are more likely to register—and vote—than those with low incomes. Unregistered voters are more likely to be Democrats than Republicans. As a result, Democratic candidates spend a good deal of effort trying to get supporters registered to vote and, later, getting them to the polls.

Suggestions have been made for reforming the registration system. Nineteen states allow their citizens to register by mail. The U.S. House of Representatives passed a bill in 1976 to mandate such a "postcard" registration system in all of the states for *federal* elections, but the bill went nowhere in the U.S. Senate. President Carter recommended to Congress the Universal Voter Registration Act, which would allow voters to register and vote simply by showing proper identification at the polls on election day. A similar system, had it been in effect in 1972, would have increased voting by nine percent or 12 million voters, based on the experience of states that have such a system. (Minnesota, Wisconsin, and North Dakota now have such systems in operation at the state level.) Postcard registration while widely supported has not been adopted on the national level. Not surprisingly, Democrats are more supportive of it than Republicans.

The Electoral College

Except for the election of the president, American elections are direct. Voters simply vote for one of the candidates. But in a presidential election they cast their ballots for **presidential electors** who are pledged to a candidate. Each state chooses as many electors as it has U.S. Senators and Representatives.

The **electoral college** is a controversial feature of our Constitution.[5] It originated at the Constitutional Convention as a compromise between simpler plans such as direct election by the people or selection by Congress. James Madison later admitted that the plan for the electoral college was adopted in the final stages of the Convention and "was not exempt from a degree of the hurrying influence produced by fatigue and impatience."

Opponents of this institution criticize the *unit rule,* or the **winner-take-all** practice by which all of a state's electoral votes are cast for the candidate who receives the most popular votes in that state. This *multiplier effect* often turns close popular votes into landslides. George Bush in 1988 won a 54-percent majority of the popular vote. But, he won *all* the electoral votes in the 38 states in which he ran first, giving him 426 electoral votes to Dukakis's 112.

Another criticism of the electoral college is that it violates the principle of "one person, one vote." Voters in the large states and in the smallest states have more weight than voters in the middle-sized states. This bias in favor of the smallest states is because each state, no matter how small, gets one elector for each of its two U.S. senators. The bias in favor of the large states—especially for minority-bloc voters, such as Hispanics, within these states—results from the winner-take-all practice. A candidate will give much more attention to large states such as New York and California, because picking up 50,000 additional popular voters there—if that puts the candidate out front—means far more in electoral college votes than gaining the support of 50,000 additional voters in a state like Oklahoma.

The most serious criticism of the electoral college is that it is possible for a candidate without the highest number of popular votes nationwide to become president through a majority vote in the electoral college. This last happened in the election of 1888. However, if Gerald Ford had received 5559 more votes in Ohio and 3687 more votes in Hawaii in 1976, he would have run first in those states, gained a majority in the electoral college, and been elected president—despite trailing Jimmy Carter by 1.7 million popular votes. This is the *runner-up candidate* problem. The fear is that such a president would not be considered "legitimate" and that his leadership would be dangerously undermined.

Supporters of the electoral college argue that it favors a strong two-party system. Abolition of the electoral college, they insist, would give rise to a number of new parties, fragmenting our political system. Some claim that our system has remained stable over the years precisely because we have not replaced constitutional institutions like the electoral college.

By favoring large states like New York, California, and Texas, the electoral college also supports minorities like blacks, gays, and Hispanics who live there and whose issues might otherwise be ignored. Furthermore, it makes candidates discuss specific states' issues as they concentrate in these key states. The idea of minorities having more power than majorities is not exactly unconstitutional. In the U.S. Senate, for example, senators from Vermont and Wyoming can outvote California 4 to 2, even though California has about thirty times their population.

Some have suggested abolishing the electoral college altogether and replacing it with a direct popular election. The American Bar Association has backed such a constitutional amendment. So far, however, it has failed to gain sufficient support in the U.S. Congress.

THE VOTERS

Pollster: Do you think people don't vote because of ignorance or apathy?

Respondent: I don't know and I don't care.

Americans believe in voting.[6] They just don't always act on their beliefs. Among all the ways of participating—voting, campaigning, or making a campaign contribution—voting is the easiest, yet the United States ranks last among the world's major democracies in voter turnout. European national elections, for example, bring out 70 to 80 percent of eligible voters, compared to America's 49 percent in 1988 (the lowest since 1924). (See Figure 7.1.) Even smaller percentages of Americans vote in off-year congressional elections (33 percent in 1986) than in presidential elections. Fewer vote in statewide elections than in national elections, and fewer still vote in local elections. Why don't people vote, and who are the nonvoters?

Americans learn political behavior at an early age. Here, high school students root for Republican presidential candidate Robert Dole during a mock convention held during the 1988 New Hampshire primary.

FIGURE 7★1
Participation of the Eligible Population in Elections, 1924–1988

PERCENTAGE OF VOTING-AGE POPULATION VOTING

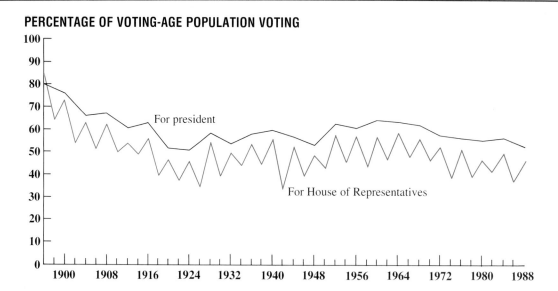

SOURCE: For data up to 1930, *Historical Statistics of the United States* (Washington, D.C.: Government Printing Office, 1975), part 2, 1071, 1078–79, 1084. For 1930–1980, see U.S. Bureau of the Census, *Statistical Abstract of the United States, 1980* (Washington, D.C.: Government Printing Office, 1981), 248. For post-1980 data, see *Congressional Quarterly Election 1984* (Washington, D.C.: Congressional Quarterly, 1984) and *Congressional Quarterly Weekly Report,* April 13, 1985.

Why Don't People Vote?

There are **electoral barriers** to voting in America, such as the previously discussed registration requirements that exist in most of the states. *These requirements make voting inconvenient.* Election day in the United States is not a national holiday, as it is in many European countries, nor are the polls open as late here (they are open until 10:00 P.M. in England). A relaxation of these "inconvenience" barriers in America could make a difference; voter turnout is an average of 9 percent higher in states where the law requires that workers be given time off from their jobs in order to vote. Absentee voting in the United States is usually difficult. There is also the problem of "ballot fatigue." There are so many officials to vote for at each level of government that people get turned off.

Besides being complicated, American registration procedures are restrictive for another critical reason. The U.S. government stands virtually alone in not taking any responsibility for helping citizens cope with voter registration. In other countries people are either automatically eligible to vote when they come of age, or government canvassers come door-to-door to register voters before an election.

Not surprisingly, in 1980 more than 60 million people were unregistered out of almost 160 million eligible voters. Two out of three of these unregistered voters lived in households with incomes below the median. However, *once people are registered they overwhelmingly vote.* More than 80 percent of those registered voted in 1980, and turnout was only marginally lower among those with very little education and income. Consequently, while voter turnout in the U.S. is practically the worst among democracies, turnout *for registered voters* is about the same as in other countries.[7] (See the boxes on pages 187 and 188.)

 ★ Voter Turnout Percentages in Democratic Nations
(Most Recent Major National Elections as of 1983)

1.	Belgium	95
2.	Australia	94
3.	Austria	92
4.	Sweden	91
5.	Italy	90
6.	Iceland	89
7.	New Zealand	89
8.	Luxembourg	89
9.	West Germany	87
10.	Netherlands	87
11.	France	86
12.	Portugal	84
13.	Denmark	83
14.	Norway	82
15.	Greece	79
16.	Israel	78
17.	United Kingdom	76
18.	Japan	74
19.	Canada	69
20.	Spain	68
21.	Finland	64
22.	Ireland	62
23.	**United States**	**53**
24.	Switzerland	48

SOURCE: Harvard/ABC News Symposium (1984:7) from Frances Fox Piven and Richard A. Cloward, *Why Americans Don't Vote* (New York: Pantheon Books, 1988), pp. 5, 8. Turnout for the United States is based on the voting-age population; for other countries, it is based on registered voters. Apart from the United States, registration is more or less universal.

★Voter Turnout in Democratic Nations as a Percentage of Registered Voters

(Most Recent Major National Elections as of 1983)

1.	Belgium	95
2.	Australia	94
3.	Austria	92
4.	Sweden	91
5.	Italy	90
6.	Iceland	89
7.	New Zealand	89
8.	Luxembourg	89
9.	West Germany	87
10.	Netherlands	87
11.	**United States**	**87**
12.	France	86
13.	Portugal	84
14.	Denmark	83
15.	Norway	82
16.	Greece	79
17.	Israel	78
18.	United Kingdom	76
19.	Japan	74
20.	Canada	69
21.	Spain	68
22.	Finland	64
23.	Ireland	62
24.	Switzerland	48

SOURCE: Harvard/ABC News Symposium (1984:7) from Frances Fox Piven and Richard A. Cloward, *Why Americans Don't Vote* (New York: Pantheon Books, 1988), p. 19.

Another external factor that tends to reduce voter turnout in America is *lack of competition betweeen candidates and parties.* Where the outcome of an election appears to be a foregone conclusion, as in a one-party state or when the television networks have already announced (as a result of exit polling) a "projected winner" before the polls close, voter turnout is discouraged. The same is true when a potential voter is never contacted on behalf of any candidate. Campaign activities increase turnout. Furthermore, when potential voters can see no policy differences between the candidates (and candidates sometimes try to conceal where they stand), they will see less sense in voting.[8]

Ask any first-year American government class why they think so many Americans do not vote, and their answer will be similar to the following: "They don't think it will make any difference." In this case at least, common sense about nonvoters is backed by political studies. This is a *lack of political efficacy*—a lowered sense that the government will respond to the needs of the voter.

The "makes no difference" reason can also result from the fact that some people have not been socialized to political efficacy (as discussed in Chapter 5). Therefore, they do not consider politics relevant to their lives; or do not identify with a political party; or do not understand how the system works; or do not believe it will respond; or some combination of these. One study has shown that weakened party identification and decreased belief in government responsiveness alone account for at least two-thirds of the decline in presidential election turnout between 1960 and 1980.[9]

Of course the belief that government will not respond is not merely a result of faulty socialization. Government may *not* be responsive to peoples' needs. After Vietnam, Watergate, inflation, the Iran-Contra scandal, and huge deficits, newspaper headlines stressing government gone amok reinforce this view. Even the system of voting may hinder government responsiveness. Political parties that assume that poor people will not vote because of a difficult registration system or their own apathy are unlikely to champion their causes. Parties adapt their positions to the narrowed electorate, and then reinforce the barriers to voting by ignoring the needs of the people beyond them.

Who Are the Nonvoters?

Nonvoters in the United States are usually young or poor or both. Youth characterizes many nonvoters. Those between the ages of eighteen and twenty-four are the least likely to register and the least likely to vote. In 1984 those under thirty had a 49-percent voting turnout; those over thirty showed 70 percent voting. Young people, as shown in Chapter 5, have weaker ties to parties. They also change residences more, making registration and voting more difficult. One reason for the recent decrease in the percentage of voting was the lowering of the voting age to eighteen. But voter turnout has declined for all age groups, so it cannot be blamed solely on youth.[10]

For all age groups, lower voter turnout is linked to *lower socioeconomic status.* The lower a person's income, the less likely that person is to vote. Related to socioeconomic state are level of education and job status. The greater a person's education, the more likely that person is to vote, perhaps because educated people have an easier time figuring out how the system of voting works and because they are socialized to believe that their votes make a difference. Blue-collar workers are less likely to vote than white-collar workers.

A lower percentage of blacks vote than do whites, but differences of race disappear when voting by blacks and whites of the same income levels is compared. Rates of black voting have been increasing in recent years—probably reflecting some increase in black income levels and also an increase in get-out-the-vote efforts. A lower percentage of Hispanic-Americans than black Americans vote, but this may be due to a large proportion of this population not being citizens.

One might think that those who need government's help most—the unemployed, for example—would be motivated to take a more active part in politics, change government policy, and help themselves. This is not the case. "Economic adversity reduces voter turnout . . ."; people who lose their jobs spend what time and emotional resources they have left in "holding body and soul together," and thus, "When economic adversity strikes, withdrawal from politics is the likely result."[11] This can be called a **paradox of democracy:** those who most need the government to improve their lives participate the least and are the least influential.

This paradox does not affect the two major parties equally. As shown in Chapters 6 and 8, the lower a person's socioeconomic status, the more likely that person will have liberal economic views and identify with the Democratic party. Democrats have an advantage over Republicans in the ratio of party identifiers. But when "who is likely to vote" and "who is not likely to vote" is factored in, the Democratic advantage shrinks.

Liberal organizations have launched registration drives in state offices where low-income people line up for government assistance. Minorities have also shown a willingness to vote when they have a minority candidate to vote for, as Jesse Jackson's campaigns for president illustrated. A Washington-based low-income registration group, Project Vote, filed lawsuits in 1984 to force certain Republican governors to allow such registration efforts in government offices.

To offset Democratic registration efforts the Republican National Committee and other Republican groups have undertaken sophisticated registration efforts aimed at people most likely to vote Republican. (See the case study in Chapter 9.) Similarly, conservative groups such as the National Association of Realtors, the U.S. Chamber of Commerce, and the Moral Majority sponsored their own registration drives.

Handicapped voters in Chicago cast their votes at a polling place that has been set up to allow them easier access.

Still, the people most likely to vote are white, middle-aged or older, and better paid and better educated than the average citizen. In addition, people who have been contacted personally by a campaign are more likely to vote. Voters are less likely than nonvoters (40 percent to 60 percent) to agree with the statement: "The country needs more radical change than is possible through the ballot box." They are more likely than nonvoters to believe that their political participation will make a difference.

Factors in How People Vote

Why do voters vote the way they do? The same factors are at work in the making of a voter's electoral decision as those discussed in Chapter 5 in connection with the formation of public opinion in general. The voter may have certain *preconceptions* that can filter—or even cause a rejection of—a campaign message. The *social setting* of the voter is also important. The opinion of the group the voter belongs to can influence the effect of a campaign message, as can the two-step flow of a campaign message through an opinion leader. Another important factor is *age.* Younger voters are more likely to support equality for women and minorities and a clean environment. They are less likely to identify with a political party. *Gender* has, in recent years, become a factor in how people vote. The "gender gap" involves not only a different percentage of women and men favoring so-called "women's issues," but also a difference on "war and peace issues." In 1988, this translated into lower support among women for President Bush (50-percent support) than among men (57-percent support).

Place of residence can make a difference in the way people vote. The central cities generally are more liberal and Democratic than the suburbs and the rural areas (this may also involve differing incomes). The sunbelt states of the South and West are generally more conservative and Republican than the snowbelt states of the North. People are influenced in how they vote by their *class, occupation,* and *religion.* For example, college-educated voters were more positive than grade-school-educated voters toward President Reagan. Although voting differences among Catholics, Protestants, and Jews seem to be lessening somewhat, Catholics still tend to be more liberal than Protestants, and Jews tend to be more liberal than Catholics.

Identification with a political party is an important part of a voter's choice. Some elections reflect the importance of party ties more than others. The influence of party affiliation on voting in the 1976 presidential election (Jimmy Carter versus Gerald Ford) was greater

"Pressing the flesh" is still part of every campaign. Democratic presidential candidate Michael Dukakis shakes hands with Hassidic Jews in New York City in 1988.

than in preceding elections. In 1980 (Jimmy Carter versus Ronald Reagan), however, partisanship was less important than dissatisfaction with President Carter.[12] Still, party identification is the single most important predictor as to how a person will vote. *Issues* also have a great affect on how people vote. There are indications of an increase in issue voting in America with its importance gaining steadily since 1956.[13] When we add up all the general demographic factors, we should also not forget, as one scholar put it, "Voters think about politics. They are not just inherited loyalties. They think about the public good and try to promote it in their choice of candidates."[14]

Voting decisions do not take place in a vacuum. All these factors interact with each other and with a candidate's campaign. How these candidates campaign and who they are also influence voting decisions.

THE CAMPAIGN

Campaigning affects how people vote, but how much and in what way is not clear. **Voter contact** through phone, mail, or in person is a central part of the campaign operation. The idea is simple enough. Identify your supporters, convince those who are undecided, and make sure both groups get out to the polls. Increasingly sophisticated techniques underlie election campaigns.

Voter targeting uses census and voting patterns to identify groups who are likely to support a candidate. Therefore, devoting resources, like phone banks and mail, to reach these voters tends to be the most effective use of time and energy. How people voted in a past election is the best indicator of how they will vote in the next election. Keeping names, addresses, and phone numbers of these voters updated requires extensive computer operations. In the 1988 presidential race, Republicans spent some $33 million for voter-contact activities.[15]

Direct mail specialists use census data and polling information to target computer-produced letters to voters. They are keyed to issue positions (such as gun control or support for a nuclear freeze) that the recipient is likely to hold. Direct mail specialists may use computerized lists allowing them, for example, to contact middle-aged, upper-middle-income registered Democrats who probably voted for Ronald Reagan and who have Eastern European surnames. They can also target fundraising appeals to those most likely to contribute.

Polling helps establish the strategy of a campaign. It shows the standing of the candidates. More importantly, it can show what issues are most important to the voters, what aspect of the candidate's image is most appealing, and what about the opponent is most vulnerable to attack.

Focus groups are small groups of targeted voters who are interviewed as a group. They complement polls and are used to get more detail on voters' intensity of feelings on particular issues. In 1988, Republicans found through polls and focus groups that the Massachusetts furlough program by which criminals were released for the weekend received a very negative reaction from voters. This was used by George Bush in his TV ads to illustrate Governor Dukakis's alleged softness toward crime.

College student volunteers do the grunt work by phone for the Bush campaign in 1988.

Tracking polls, taken nightly by telephone, can measure the daily effect of events, advertisements, debates, and mistakes—and allow next-day corrections. Such changes would include special targeting of voters where support is lagging. Governor Dukakis, for example, tried to counter the "soft on crime" charges by incorporating his own family's experience as victims of crime and by publicizing the endorsements of his candidacy by police unions.

Canvassing voters involves sending workers—sometimes candidates—door-to-door to talk with voters directly. The workers are given "walking lists" of the names of the people who live in each house on the block they are to canvass. Canvassers are carefully instructed about what to say and do. Reports are made on each voter who is contacted. Some voters may already support the candidate for whom the canvassing is being done or may be "leaning" toward the candidate. Others may be undecided. On election day, campaign workers make a special effort to get known supporters to the polls.

Consultants

In 1980, Lee Atwater was running Ronald Reagan's presidential primary campaign in South Carolina. Atwater, who would later manage George Bush's successful presidential effort in 1988, was supporting Reagan against Bush and former Texas Governor John Connally in the Republican primary. A group of black ministers came to his office and suggested that if Reagan was willing to spend some money on black mobilization they could turn out votes. Atwater dismissed the idea that blacks would vote for Reagan but sensed an opportunity. "We're broke" he told the ministers, "but John Connally is loaded with Texas money. He's the one you ought to be talking to."

As soon as the ministers left, Atwater was on the phone quietly getting out the message to the Bush headquarters that "Connally's buying the black vote." Soon the Bush and Connally campaigns were at each other's throats over charges of vote buying. Connally's campaign manager later concluded that they had fallen into the trap of fighting the wrong guy. Reagan went on to crush both candidates.[16]

A few years ago, everyone knew who the "pros" were in a political campaign. These were the experienced party operatives who could call on a network of contacts and their own intuition to win elections. Now the "pros" are **political consultants,** skilled at using media, polls, the mails, computers, and organization to win elections for those who hire them. Many operate nationwide. Some of these, like Harrison Hickman, specialize in polling and work only for Democratic candidates, the same thing Robert Teeter does for Republicans. Some, like Robert Squier, a Democrat, and Roger Ailes, a Republican, are media specialists. Others, like Democrat Joe Napolitano or Republican Stu Spencer, are generalists and run the total campaign from top to bottom, hiring individual, trusted specialists as needed. Democrat Matt Reese, also a generalist, can create an "instant organization" for a candidate by using census data, polls, and computer mailings.

Some people are concerned about the manipulation of voters by political consultants. Others point out that there have always been "hired guns" in campaigns; the modern ones are just more scientific. These defenders say the public is best served when both sides have the best consultants to help get their messages across, just as justice is served when both sides in a lawsuit have the best lawyers available. Consultant Joe Napolitano has, a little defensively, said, "A political consultant is a specialist in political communication. That's all there is to it—it's not very Machiavellian."[17]

It is also arguable that the rise of consultants is connected to the decline in voter turnout. As consultants have become more adept at manipulating images, people have grown more cynical about the political messages that they are getting. If candidates can be packaged like breakfast cereal, the ability to make an informed choice appears to many to be limited. The effective use of *negative advertisements* to diminish support for an opponent also tends to turn off voters toward the electoral process. By the end of October 1988, after weeks of negative ads by presidential candidates Bush and Dukakis, polls showed that voters by nearly two to one were dissatisfied with their choices and wished someone else were running. The ironic contrast between the rise in the amount of money spent on campaigns with fewer and fewer people bothering to vote may, in this curious way, be linked.[18]

Campaign Communications

Campaigns use public appearances, rallies, printed materials, buttons, the mass media, and the mail to communicate their messages. Much of the television news about campaigns focuses only on the "horse-race" aspects—on who's in the lead at that moment and why. But television coverage is important because it is most Americans' major source of news. Television also has led to much discussion about the candidate's *image.*

It is probably not true, as some have said, that Abraham Lincoln could never be elected president today because a candidate's "looks" on television are so important. Neither Richard Nixon nor Lyndon

The 1988 presidential campaign was notable for its negative attack ads. Pictured below is convicted murderer and rapist William Horton Jr., who was used by George Bush supporters to portray Michael Dukakis as soft on crime. Under the Massachusetts furlough program, Horton was released from prison even though he was serving a life sentence. In 1987, during his tenth furlough, Horton fled to Maryland, twice raped a woman, and assaulted her fiance. Republicans denied that racism was part of their calculation in using this very scary photo.

Johnson exactly sparkled on TV, yet both won the presidency by landslides. "Clearly, images depend on what a candidate represents—his party, his actions, his policies—and just as clearly on how a voter feels about what the candidate represents—his party, past actions, future policies. For almost every voter, a candidate's image depends on these two realistic factors and not on whether he looks good or bad on television."[19] Nevertheless, candidates spend much time and money projecting a desired image with the help of consultants.

This desired image is made up of several elements. One of these is honesty. This means more than not lying, cheating, or stealing. Candidates must also appear open and straightforward on the issues. They must be willing to "take a stand." Candidates also want to appear to be "one of us," to give the impression that they have the same problems that we do. They want to be "on our side" on the issues (while often avoiding a stand on the more controversial ones). In addition, candidates must appear qualified to handle the duties of the office. This is especially important in a campaign for the presidency, or as shown in the focus on Dan Quayle's qualifications, for the vice-presidency. Voters are always concerned about which candidate is the most disciplined, most in command of himself, and thus, best "able to govern."

There are good reasons why presidential campaigns spend by far the largest part of their advertising budgets on television. Television can go a long way in shaping and, at times, creating an attractive image for a candidate. Prior to the general election campaign in mid-1988, George Bush had a largely unfavorable public image. As Reagan's vice-president he was seen as a weak leader (*wimp* was the term used), a preppy Yalie who garbled his sentences. In the course of his campaign, Bush's image was "born again" largely through the creative use of TV. He attacked his opponent as an out-of-touch liberal and in so doing demonstrated his own toughness as a campaigner. He also tried to give voters positive reasons for supporting him.

In building their image campaign the Bush people used *sound-bites* to get their messages across on TV. This reduced the candidate's daily message to a brief, catchy phrase, usually with an attractive visual, that would then almost inevitably end up on the TV news that evening. The Republican's visit to Boston Harbor to denounce it as the dirtiest in America was an irresistible visual for television, and shifted the focus away from Bush's own criticized record on the environment.

★ What Do Granddaughters Have to Do with Elections?

Children are a favorite technique in political ads on TV. They play to viewers' feelings of hope, innocence, and vulnerability. In 1964, Lyndon Johnson's media experts ran a devastating ad. It showed a little girl picking daisies with a voice counting down "10–9–8–7 ..." followed by a nuclear explosion. It aimed to arouse fears of Barry Goldwater's alleged trigger-happy foreign policy.

George Bush had a TV ad in 1988 called "The Future." It began with a close-up of one of Bush's granddaughters running across a field. Cut to the Republican convention; cut to family scenes; cut to a Bush close-up. "I want a kinder and gentler nation ..." Bush says. Cut to the granddaughter as she reaches her grandfather and is swept

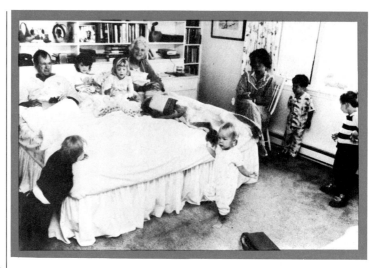

high in his arms. The frame freezes and the words read: "EXPERIENCED LEADERSHIP FOR AMERICA'S FUTURE."

This emotional appeal, run early in the campaign when Bush was not well liked, was designed to show the human side of a candidate often perceived as remote and elitist. It illustrated his concern for the future in a very personal way through his grandchild. It also offered the viewer a warm emotional bond with George Bush as a caring grandfather.

Negative *attack ads* were designed to reduce support for Governor Dukakis among undecided voters or weak supporters. George Bush's repeated attacks on his opponent over whether the Pledge of Allegiance should be recited in school used patriotic symbols to detach blue-collar voters from the Democratic nominee. What are called "soft and fuzzy" TV ads were used to change images more positively through emotional appeals. The use of kids in visual advertisements often has that impact, as George Bush's granddaughter ad shows. (See the box on page 197.)

The stars are out as Republican presidential candidate George Bush is surrounded by Hollywood glitter at a fund-raiser at the home of comedian Bob Hope.

Campaign Financing

Money is often the key to an election. Candidates do not necessarily have to have as much money as their opponents to get elected, but a successful campaign requires at least enough money to communicate the basic message about the campaign, the candidate, and the issues. Campaigns have become very expensive, particularly because of the greater use of television. An estimated $458 million was spent in campaigns to elect the 101st Congress in 1988. However, by way of comparison, Procter & Gamble spent $213 million advertising its products in only the first quarter of 1988. The $30 million each presidential candidate spent in political advertising is roughly comparable to the $31 million Procter & Gamble spent in 1987 on Crest, an already well-established toothpaste.[20]

Where does the money come from? Candidates use several methods. Soliciting friends is one. Soliciting large contributions from people with particular interests is another. Candidates can contribute to their own campaigns, sometimes borrowing money to do so. In recent years, concerts and personal appearances by entertainers have become commonplace in national elections (Barbra Streisand for Dukakis and Bob Hope for Bush). Direct-mail requests for contributions are a very important means of campaign fundraising, but this method requires spending a considerable amount of money in advance.

There are a number of reasons why people contribute to a campaign. Friendship is one. Some people simply enjoy having the opportunity to associate with candidates who are, or may become, famous or powerful. People holding strong opinions about political issues are increasingly important campaign contributors. And those who have "axes to grind"—interests to protect or push—give money to secure access and influence. (See Congressman Barnes's story at the beginning of Chapter 9.)

An increasingly large part of this axe-to-grind money in federal campaigns is coming from *political action committees* (PACs)—which, as will be discussed in Chapter 9, have increased vastly in numbers and monies contributed since the mid-1970s. The law restricts individual contributions to any one candidate to $1000, while the limit for contributing to a PAC is $5000; PACs can give $5000 per election to any number of candidates. A majority of PACs are business-oriented, sponsored by corporations, trade associations and others. Most of their contributions go to incumbents in a position to help them, and increasing amounts have gone to Democrats. (See the case study in Chapter 9.)

The people who are the least likely to vote are also the least likely to contribute money. Hence, people with low incomes are again at a disadvantage in influencing government. Americans may endorse the principle of "one person, one vote," but it is clear that the political influence of those with money to contribute to campaigns goes far beyond their single vote.

The *1974 Campaign Reform Act* contains provisions that were intended to lessen the influence of money. The law limits contributions and spending in federal campaigns, requires all candidates for federal office to disclose all the financial aspects of their campaigns, and provides a public financing system for presidential campaigns.

The reforms have failed to live up to the hopes behind them, especially for congressional campaigns. For one thing, the prohibition of private contributions to presidential nominees has diverted that money into Senate and House races. Campaign expenditures for the U.S. House and Senate have grown at an astounding rate. No system of public financing exists for congressional candidates, and efforts to pass such legislation have been unsuccessful. Citizen lobby groups like Common Cause have continued to apply pressure for public financing of congressional campaigns.

The 1974 Campaign Reform Act limits the public financing of party presidential nominees to the candidates of parties that received 5 percent or more of the total vote in the previous general election. At first, this requirement was only met by the Republican party and the Democratic party. A minor party's candidate who receives 5 percent or more of the total vote in a presidential general election, as John Anderson did in 1980, is paid after the election for campaign expenses. Thereafter, the presidential candidate for such a minor party is entitled to prior campaign financing as long as the party nominee continues to receive at least 5 percent of the national vote.

The Supreme Court has opened two loopholes in the 1974 Campaign Reform Act. First, the Court held that the government cannot limit congressional candidates' contributions to their own campaigns. However, if there was public financing for congressional campaigns, candidates who accepted it could be limited in their personal contributions. Second, the Court ruled that the government cannot restrict spending by supporters not connected with the campaign who make no prior arrangements with the candidate. These *independent expenditures* were upheld on the basis of freedom of speech.[21]

An even more serious loophole in presidential campaigns was called **soft money.** In 1988 the presidential campaigns of the two nominees were publically financed to the tune of $46 million each. While private contributions were illegal, "soft money" contributors were encouraged to donate to state parties, which could make unlimited expenditures for "party-building" activities in election years, including advertisements encouraging votes for the party's candidate. Both presidential efforts collected some $25 million each from this indirect funding for their campaigns, and at least 375 people contributed $100,000 or more to the Democrats or Republicans. This was more large contributors than in the Watergate year of 1972 and, despite the reforms, led one reporter to conclude that the "fat cats were back."[22]

THE CANDIDATES

Candidates for office are usually politicians—if they aren't when they start, they are if they win. Yet Americans are ambivalent about politicians. Each year political figures dominate the lists of most-admired people. The president and first lady are inevitably near the top. Other polls reflect a low general opinion of politicians. The House ethics scandals of 1989 reinforced the popular view that the general run of politician was not to be trusted. The public seems to say that while it's good to be an elected official, it's bad to do the campaigning necessary to win office. That seems neither consistent nor fair.[23]

None of this keeps politicians out of politics. Those who seek full-time employment in politics do show similarities just like people in other professions, such as doctors, may share certain skills and personalities. Some see politics as financially rewarding; others are attracted to the intellectual challenge; still others have a deep commitment to a set of ideas or their community. Political scientists like Harold Lasswell have characterized politicians as people of low self-esteem. They enter politics to overcome childhood feelings of deprivation and powerlessness. Private motives are transferred to public objects and rationalized in terms of public advantage. These psychological problems need not necessarily produce poor leaders, as seen in Abraham Lincoln with his feelings of inferiority and periods of depression.[24]

The world of politics screens out those who can't survive an ego-busting process. Anyone making it to the level of president or Congress has climbed a very steep pyramid. Those who rise in this world develop unusual abilities to cope with unusual stresses.

In this highly competitive business the successful politician is not necessarily "your basic nice guy." The demands of a political life are likely to produce a single-minded drive, leaving little room for other activities and softer emotions. The higher up the politician gets the greater the stakes and, often, the risks of failing. Members of the House of Representatives who want to be in the Senate have to give up their usually safe seats to run. If they lose, they're out of both.

One might not necessarily agree that the best survive the process. The contrasting view, that the worst of the lot survives, is reflected in H. L. Mencken's definition of a politician: "A sturdy rogue whose principal, and often sole aim in life, is to butter his parsnips." Yet the self-confidence needed to take the risks, the public exposure of records of performance, and the ever wider constituencies who will sit in judgment do make it likely that those least fit for high office will be weeded out in the process.

Fred R. Harris campaigns for the Democratic party's nomination for president in 1976.

The Candidate: A Day in the Life

Morning

The phone jars her awake. For a moment, she cannot remember where the phone is—or even where she is. It is still dark outside. But months ago, she started leaving the light on in the bathroom of each motel she stayed in so that she could quickly get her bearings when, like this morning, she woke up disoriented.

"Yes?" she asks raspingly into the mouthpiece, her voice slightly hoarse from too many speeches.

"Time to get moving, boss," an aide's voice says. There is an important breakfast meeting this morning with a teachers' group.

She has learned to travel light and dress quickly. Her short functional haircut is ready as soon as it dries. She is ready when the aide knocks on her motel door, just thirty minutes after the wake-up call. As she settles into the backseat of her mid-size American-made car, she tries to recall what brought her to the southeast part of the state for two days of campaigning.

Her schedule is done by regions. To save travel time and money she does events in neighboring communities. The two good-sized towns she will be in today offer her enough voters to make her stay worthwhile—not to mention money and media. Every day must include a money event in the community being visited. And of course if you don't get media on a trip, you weren't there.

Her thoughts are interrupted by the car stopping. Waiting to greet her is a long-time party official. Before he can give her his kiss of welcome, she reaches out her hand for a firm shake and a direct look in the eyes. She doesn't see party officials kissing her opponent, the general, so she sees no reason to act any differently.

She works the crowd, prodded by an aide's earlier reminders of the key names, spouses, and previous times she has met them. As she eases into her seat at the head table, she turns to the aide for her purse, which reminds her of an argument at the beginning of the campaign.

Should she carry a purse? Her campaign manager said no. Why should a candidate for the U.S. Senate carry a purse? It was a bother, and easy to forget. But if she didn't hold it, who would? That wasn't even the worst of the very special problems facing women running for office. How feminine should she look? Does she wear dresses or suits? jewelry? lipstick? Do heels make her look too tall or do people want to look up at their next senator?

At the breakfast, she tries to eat the by-now-cold eggs because she has been losing weight and her face is looking haggard on television. Her major campaign promise is a cut in income taxes, but she assures the teachers that savings in management will still allow for a cost-of-living increase in educational salaries.

There is a ten-o'clock press conference at the local press club. A reporter rides with her. He is doing a story about her family life. "But don't you feel bad about having to be away from your children so much?" he asks. It is a question she has fielded a hundred times before.

Unsuccessful Democratic vice-presidential candidate Geraldine Ferraro holds a news conference in 1984.

"My husband is very good with them," she says, "and then Betsy, who's eleven, and Henry, who's fourteen, are very much involved in the campaign themselves, and they feel that what we are all doing together is very important."

The press conference goes smoothly. She reads the prepared statement, which explains how much the proposed income tax cut will mean for an average family. During the last two weeks of the campaign, she will issue two such statements each day, one for the morning newspapers and one for the afternoon papers. But the main hope is that one of them will get a minute segment on the nightly news. Television news is the key to a successful statewide campaign, and she has planned her campaign accordingly. In this case she is well under the 2:00 P.M. deadline for the 6:00 local news.

Afternoon

At noon, she visits a senior citizen's center, where hot lunches are served to about sixty older people each day. Unfortunately the local college student serving as her driver gets lost. She is late. This happens once a week.

After lunch, she goes back to her motel room for some urgent fundraising. She learns that she could lose some vital last-week TV advertising spots unless she can come up with $30,000 before the day ends. At the motel, two wealthy friends are waiting. She has another cup of coffee, pours them a beer, and makes the pitch. "I know you've given more than you should be asked to give, but we've got to raise the money for these spots." She always finds this a little demeaning. One of the men is a large dairy producer. The other is a highway contractor. What will they want when she becomes senator?

The two friends write checks for another $1000 each and leave. She talks to more prospective contributors on the telephone, as each is dialed in turn by an aide. A number of these are directors of PACs in Washington, D.C. "Did you see the *Tribune* poll?" she asks. "We're really coming up, but these spots are crucial." With all but $4000 of the needed money raised (which will probably be picked up through an aide's follow-up calls), she changes clothes and heads for a low-budget café to film the TV spots.

The café is crammed with television lights, reflectors, cameras, technicians, and spectators anxious to get into the picture. The candidate briefly studies a script, which will take forty-five seconds to recite. With the café and its customers as backdrops, she looks into the camera on cue and begins, "In the closing days of this campaign, ordinary people have increasingly been joining with me in demanding a cut in income taxes . . ."

"Hold it!" the producer says. "We're getting a buzzing

on the sound track from the ice machine."

She starts again. "In the closing days of this campaign . . ."

"Wait a minute," the producer interrupts. "We're getting some kind of funny shadow on her face."

The lights are adjusted, and she begins again—and again and again. A minute spot takes two hours to film.

After filming the TV spot, she hurries to two "coffees" in supporters' homes, one at 4:30 and one at 5:15. She makes a brief opening statement at each coffee, and then answers questions. At the end of each session, she asks those who are willing to help with telephoning, canvassing, stuffing envelopes, or other campaign chores to sign a pledge sheet. After she leaves, her hosts make a pitch for money. Almost $1200 is promised at the two coffees.

Evening

Back at the motel, she takes the phone from an aide and responds to a pre-arranged, live radio interview for fifteen minutes. She spends twenty minutes with her campaign manager going over the latest poll results. "We're cutting down the general, but I'm worried about the increase in your 'negatives'; maybe we should soften our attack a little," the manager says. She knows that her attacks on an opponent will also increase voters' negative feelings toward her. She nods agreement.

"Then there's the son question. Our focus group shows it doesn't bounce back on you." She had hoped to avoid dealing with this. The general's son had been arrested a few years ago in a park restroom with another man on a vice charge. It had been dismissed out of court, but the police records were sent anonymously to the campaign. The temptation to use the records is increased not only by the closeness of the race but also by the general's snide attacks on her for "ignoring" her children. Their release will embarrass and distract the general and there is, arguably, a legitimate issue as to whether he had used his influence to get the charges dropped.

She has never liked any of this, which is why she eagerly followed the staff suggestion to quietly see how a focus group reacted to the issue. She can imagine the impact of the news on the son who is now married and living in another state. What does this have to do with public service, she wonders. But as her husband said to her, she has worked and sacrificed too much not to do everything she can to win. Including this? She decides to talk with her husband about it and tells her manager she'll let him know in the morning.

Her stomach tightens as she begins to think ahead to the last of the day's activities, a televised "debate," with the other senatorial candidates before a League of Women Voters audience. Too tense to eat, she turns down a sandwich and goes over her notes. "Should I be rough with the general or not?" she asks nobody in particular.

Riding back to the motel after the debate, she feels good. She is sure that the local news tomorrow evening will make a "sound-bite" out of her statement, "The general may want to be a senator as an honor to cap off his career, but I want to be a senator because I feel deeply about what we ought to be doing for our people."

She talks to her husband and one of the children by telephone; the youngest child is already asleep. Her husband is enthusiastic about the debate, and that is a good note to end the day on. Maybe that's why she doesn't raise the issue of the general's son, or maybe she's just too tired to remember. Just before she gets into bed, she calls the motel desk. "Would you ring me in the morning at five o'clock?"

★ Vice-Presidential Candidate Lloyd M. Bentsen's Campaign Schedule for Wednesday, September 14, 1988

This is a summary of the actual schedule put together by advance people for a candidate's day.

7:05 A.M.   Depart family home
7:15 A.M.   Arrive Senate fundraising breakfast
8:15 A.M.   Depart Senate fundraiser
9:05 A.M.   Arrive Confederate Air Force
            Event: Remarks and Plane Inspection
9:10 A.M.   Proceed to address audience
9:30 A.M.   Conclude remarks
9:35 A.M.   Inspect WWII bomber plane
NOTE: LMB will don a bomber jacket and proceed to view a BT 13. LMB will be greeted at the BT 13 by two young cadets who will ask him about the plane. LMB will climb into the plane and start the engine.
10:00 A.M. Hold for filming television spot
11:20 A.M. Depart Confederate Air Force
11:30 A.M. Board plane
12:50 P.M. Wheels down to DFW [Dallas-Fort Worth] International
1:00 P.M.   Depart airport
1:30 P.M.   Arrive LTV, Inc.
1:35 P.M.   Proceed to view HVM missile display
1:50 P.M.   Address employees
2:35 P.M.   Proceed to motorcade
2:40 P.M.   Depart LTV, Inc.
3:15 P.M.   Arrive Adolphus Hotel/Dallas
NOTE: Downtime for LMB
4:15 P.M.   Depart Hotel
4:30 P.M.   Arrive Dallas Times Herald Editorial Board
5:15 P.M.   Depart Dallas Times Herald Editorial Board
5:30 P.M.   Downtime/Dinner
7:45 P.M.   Arrive Senate fundraiser
8:45 P.M.   Depart fundraiser
9:00 P.M.   Arrive Adolphus Hotel

WRAP-UP

Elections bring candidates before the voters. They force voters to listen to candidates, but they also force candidates to listen to voters. These electoral encounters between citizens and their leaders are shaped by a number of conditions including the rules of the electoral system, who votes and who doesn't, the skillfulness of the campaigns, and the candidates' own strengths or weaknesses.

These factors overlap and are affected by each other. State registration systems tend to keep the less-educated poor and the mobile young away from the polls. This in turn slants voter turnout toward higher income groups and encourages campaigns to speak to their concerns. Campaigns use modern technology both to raise money and put across their messages in the most attractive way possible. But, as was shown, the candidate is in many ways the message.

Elections choose, restrain, guide, punish, and legitimate leaders. Citizens' decreasing willingness to vote, incumbents' increasing ability to make themselves invulnerable to challengers, and campaigning's modern means of manipulating the vote have placed constraints on all these functions of democratic elections. Yet the position of honor and importance given elections by virtually all political participants indicates a process that retains greater consequences than mere ritual.

Key Terms

presidential electors (p. 184)
electoral college (p. 184)
winner-take-all (p. 184)
electoral barriers (p. 186)
paradox of democracy (p. 190)
voter contact (p. 192)
voter targeting (p. 192)

direct mail (p. 193)
polling (p. 193)
focus groups (p. 193)
tracking polls (p. 194)
canvassing (p. 194)
political consultants (p. 194)
soft money (p. 200)

Suggested Readings

Alexander, Herbert E. and Brian A. Haggerty, *Financing the 1984 Election* (Lexington, Mass.: Lexington Books, 1987).

Gerald M. Pomper, *et. al., The Election of 1988: Reports and Interpretations* (Chatham, New Jersey: Chatham House Publishers, Inc., 1989).

Faw, Bob and Nancy Skelton, *Thunder in America: The Improbable Presidential Campaign of Jesse Jackson* (Austin, Texas: Texas Monthly Press, 1988).

Furgurson, Ernest B., *Hard Right: The Rise of Jesse Helms* (New York: Norton, 1986).

Hagstrom, Jerry, *Beyond Reagan: The New Landscape of American Politics* (New York: W.W. Norton & Co., 1988).

Loomis, Burdett, *The New American Politician: Ambition, Entrepreneurship and the Changing Face of Political Life* (New York: Basic Books, 1988).

Reichley, A. James, ed., *Elections American Style* (Washington D.C.: The Brookings Institution, 1987).

Endnotes

[1] *The Washington Post,* September 11, 1988.

[2] Joseph Schumpeter, *Capitalism, Socialism and Democracy* (New York: Harper and Row, 1942), p. 269.

[3] V. O. Key, Jr., *Politics, Parties and Pressure Groups,* 5th ed. (New York: Thomas Y. Crowell, 1964), p. 622.

[4] See Myron Boor, "Reduction in Deaths by Suicide, Accidents, and Homicide Prior to United States Elections," *Journal of Social Psychology* (1982), Vol. 118, pp. 135–36.

[5] For an appraisal of the electoral college, see Nelson W. Polsby and Aaron Wildavsky, *Presidential Elections: Strategies of American Electoral Politics,* 6th ed. (New York: Charles Scribner's Sons, 1984), pp. 246–56.

[6] Nine out of ten people in a survey disagreed with the statement: "So many other people vote in the national elections that it doesn't matter much to me whether I vote or not." Center for Political Studies, University of Michigan. Also see Fred I. Greenstein and Frank B. Feigert, *The American Party System and the American People,* 3rd ed. (Englewood Cliffs, NJ: Prentice-Hall, 1985), Chapter 2.

[7] Frances Fox Piven and Richard A. Cloward, *Why Americans Don't Vote* (New York: Pantheon Books, 1988), pp. 17–18.

[8] See an important book on the subject of the rationality of voting: Anthony Downs, *An Economic Theory of Voting* (New York: Harper and Row, 1957), Chapter 14.

[9] See Paul R. Abramson and John H. Aldrich, "The Decline of Electoral Participation in America," *American Political Science Review* (September 1982), Vol. 26, no. 2: 502–21.

[10] See Frank J. Sorauf and Paul A. Beck, *Party Politics in America,* 6th ed. (Boston: Little, Brown, 1988), pp. 195–98, 229.

[11] Steven J. Rosenstone, "Economic Adversity and Voter Turnout," *American Journal of Political Science:* 26, no. 1 (February 1982): 25–46.

[12] Gerald M. Pomper, "The Presidential Election," in Gerald M. Pomper et al., *The Election of 1980* (Chatham, NJ: Chatham House, 1981), pp. 65–96.

[13] William Crotty, *American Parties in Decline,* 2nd ed. (Boston: Little, Brown, 1984), pp. 45–48.

[14] See Gerald M. Pomper, *Voters, Elections and Parties* (New Brunswick: Transaction, 1988), p. 25.

[15] James A. Barnes, "Taking Aim," *National Journal,* October 8, 1988, pp. 2520–23.

[16] *The Washington Post,* January 20, 1989.

[17] David Chagall, *The New King-Makers* (New York: Harcourt Brace Jovanovich, 1981), p. 19.

[18] *The Washington Post,* October 28, 1988.

[19]Thomas E. Patterson and Robert D. McClure, "Political Campaigns: TV Power Is a Myth," *Psychology Today* (July 1976), p. 90.

[20]*The Washington Post,* March 5, 1989 and *BAR/LNA Multimedia Service AD 4 Summary,* January-March 1988, Leading National Advertisers, New York 1988, p. 73.

[21]See Herbert E. Alexander, *Financing Politics: Money, Elections and Political Reform* (Washington, D.C.: Congressional Quarterly Press, 1980).

[22]David Ignatius, "Return of the Fat Cats," *The Washington Post,* November 20, 1988.

[23]Stephen Hess, *The Presidential Campaign,* 3rd ed. (Washington, D.C.: The Brookings Institution, 1988), Chapter 2, pp. 5–15.

[24]Hess, quoting *The Political Writings of Harold D. Lasswell* (Free Press, 1951), p. 12.

★

CHAPTER 8

Parties

For America's political parties, it is the best of times, it is the worst of times. For the party organizations the last decade has brought reform and revitalization. The professionals of the national parties have made great strides in using modern campaign technology to raise money and support candidates. While both parties remain "fragmented organizations," the national committees, especially the Republicans, have become stronger than their state and local parties.

Despite these organizational successes, neither party has been winning any popularity contests, except against each other. The parties have shown even less of a grip on public opinion than they formerly had. Fewer Americans publicly align with either party, and those who do show less commitment to their party. And, of course, an emerging majority of citizens doesn't even bother to vote for the parties' candidates.

These opposite trends of *strengthening organizations* and *weakening popularity* have led to confusion about the prospects for parties. One book from the early 1970s by a well-known reporter, *The Party's Over,* was answered recently by another called *The Party's Just Begun.*[1] Being in the middle of change is usually confusing.

The elephant as a symbol of the Republican party made its first appearance in print in this 1874 cartoon by Thomas Nast.

Without getting too confused ourselves, this chapter will first review the traditional characteristics of American parties by focusing on their loose, decentralized structures paralleling the federal system. The Party-in-the-Electorate section looks at the differences in the two parties' voting strength and the alignments, realignments, and dealignments they go through. The party organization section assesses the parts of the parties, from local organizations to national conventions to elected officials. Finally, a case study shows the Republicans "getting their act together" in a Rocky Mountain high-tech voter registration drive.

CHARACTERISTICS OF AMERICAN PARTIES

A **political party** is a group organized to run candidates in elections in order to control government. American parties are unusual in a number of ways. They are decentralized and fragmented. Membership is by self-identification only. The party organization does not control party nominations. There is little party discipline requiring elected officials to follow their party's line. And ours is a two-party system, not a multi-party system.

Decentralization and Fragmentation

In some ways, there is no such thing as the Democratic party or the Republican party. The federal principle of divided powers between the states and the federal government means that each party has a national organization and separate state and local organizations. In addition, the separation of powers in the government is paralleled by a separation within the parties—each party has informal congressional and presidential wings. A political party does not have a single position on issues for all the branches in either the federal or a state government. In America, then, *there is a decentralization and fragmentation of political parties parallelling the divisions of power within the political system.* By contrast, power in European governmental systems is usually more centralized, and thus there is less fragmentation within their political parties.

Membership by Self-Identification

Membership in an American political party may not mean much. An American might say, "I am a Democrat," even though he or she might never have attended a party gathering, might never have paid any party dues, and might seldom vote. Such a person may register as a Democrat in order to vote in a primary election, which nominates the party candidates, but that registration requires no approval by a Democratic party organization. Similarly, people can change their party registration without getting party approval. American political parties have no control over who is a member. It is purely by self-identification.

Uncontrolled Party Nominations

Early twentieth-century America witnessed a number of party reforms. Among the reforms was the **direct primary election** as a method of nominating party candidates. In a direct primary election, the voters of the party, rather than leaders or delegates, decide which candidate will be nominated. Even in many states that still have conventions for selecting party nominees for state offices, unsuccessful candidates can get their names on the primary election ballot by getting a certain number of signatures on a petition or votes at the convention. This procedure allows candidates to go around the party organization. Presidential nominees are selected in national conventions, but most of the delegates at such conventions are elected by popular vote. This convention approves the selections made in those state primaries and caucuses. The bottom line is the same: *party organizations do not control their party's nominations.*

Lack of Party Discipline

A political party cannot require an elected official to vote for the party position on an issue. In Great Britain, on the other hand, prime ministers who do not follow the wishes of a majority of their party members in the House of Commons cannot continue in office. In addition, members of the British House of Commons who do not follow their party platform face the possibility of being refused the party's nomination at the next election, because the party organization controls nominations. In the United States, members of Congress who vote against a plank in their party platform can be renominated by going directly to the people in a primary election. This undermines party discipline. The party organization is unable to require that public officials elected under the party label support the organization's positions on issues.

TWO-PARTY SYSTEM

The U.S. Constitution did not mention political parties. George Washington warned against them, and John Adams declared that there was nothing he dreaded as much as the division of the country into "two great parties." Dreaded or not, they sprang up almost at once. The strong ones prevailed two at a time.

In most other countries with competing political parties, there are several, and sometimes many, parties. In contrast, America has a two-party system—there are two parties that are nationally competitive. This two-party system has been an enduring feature in our history. Since the early 1800s, with few exceptions, two major political parties have accounted for about 90 percent of the total popular vote in the country.

Why just two? Why not three, four, or more? No one is quite sure. But there are three reasons that seem most persuasive: *historical dualism, institutional structures,* and *political culture.*[2]

Historical Dualism

In part, the two-party system exists simply because the United States has always had two major political parties. The first political division among Americans was dual, or two-sided, between Federalists and Anti-Federalists. This original two-sided political battle established the tradition of two-party domination.

The first political party in the United States was the *Federalists*— the party of the Constitution, which, despite its name, favored a strong national government backed by people of wealth. It was led by Alexander Hamilton. Soon there was an opposition party, led by

Thomas Jefferson, which was less a party of privilege and more a defender of the power of the states. The Jefferson party was called the *Democratic-Republican party,* confusing students everafter. It was a coalition of farmers, laborers, and slave owners. Segments of this party eventually developed under Andrew Jackson as the *Democratic party,* the oldest continuously functioning political party.

Soon, as the federalists faded, anti-Jackson elements formed the *Whig Party* and the formal party structures that exist today—national nominating conventions and national and state committees—were organized. *The Republican Party* was founded in 1854. It opposed slavery and came to include not only financiers, industrialists, and merchants who left the declining Whig Party, but also workers, farmers, and newly freed slaves. Except for Grover Cleveland's two terms as president (1885–89 and 1893–97), the Republicans dominated the presidency from 1860 until 1912. Not until 1932, when Herbert Hoover was defeated by Franklin Roosevelt, were the Democrats able to put together a national coalition that has lasted, in weakened form, till today (see Chapter 13).

Institutional Structures

The structure of our electoral system encourages two-party dominance. We elect one representative from a district to Congress, which is called election by **single-member districts.** The winning candidate is the one who gets the most votes, or a plurality. (A *majority* of votes means more than 50 percent of the votes cast; a *plurality* simply means more votes than anyone else.) Similarly, in presidential elections the party with a plurality in a state gets all the electoral votes of that state. This system makes it difficult for minor-party candidates to win elections. Without election victories, parties fade fast.

Many countries with multi-party systems, such as Israel, elect representatives by *proportional representation.* That is, each district has more than one representative, and each party that receives a certain number of votes gets to send a proportionate number of representatives to the legislature. For example, in a single-member district, a minor party that received 10 percent of the vote would not be able to send its candidate to Congress. In a multi-member district the size of ten congressional districts, however, that 10 percent of the vote would mean that one out of ten representatives sent from the district would be a minor party member.

Another institutional reason lies in the *separation of powers* system. Separation of powers means just that. For presidents (and governors) there is no sharing the power of the office. In parliamentary democracies, such as France, Italy, and Great Britain, the parliament elects the prime minister. Except in Great Britain, governments are usually elected by a coalition of two or more parties, because no one party has a majority of the parliament. A minor party, though unable to gain majority control of the parliament, may have influence. It may even be awarded a cabinet position in return for being a member of the major coalition. In an unusual case, a premier of Italy in the early 1980s came from a party with less than 3 percent of the parliamentary seats. No such opportunity for coalitions and minor-party influence exists in American politics.

Political Culture

In all of America's history, only five political parties have attained major nationwide standing. The Republicans won fifteen and Democrats eleven of the twenty-four presidential elections from 1888 to 1988. In all but seven of these contests, a shift of only 10 percent of the popular vote would have changed the outcome. Elections to the House of Representatives have been even closer nationwide. From 1932 to 1982, the median spread in the vote between the Democratic and Republican candidates for the House was only 6.2 percent. In national campaigns, the trend has been toward greater competition between the two major parties.

This two-party dominance is partly due to the moderate views of the American voter. Unlike some democracies with radical political parties, American politics tend to stay toward the center. Americans may be moderate because their political party system forces them to choose between two moderate parties, or American parties may be moderate because Americans do not want to make more extreme political choices. As with the chicken and the egg, it is tough to know which came first.

Minor Parties

Minor parties, sometimes called third parties, have always been present. Some have been based on ideology, such as the Socialist Workers party and the Libertarian party. Others, like Theodore Roosevelt's Progressive party of 1912, George Wallace's American Independent party of 1968, and John Anderson's National Unity party in 1980, have been organized around individuals. Several, such as the Prohibition party, focused on particular issues. Many of these parties have lasted for a long time, although with little influence.

American Independent party candidate George Wallace, governor of Alabama, campaigns for president in 1968.

Others have lasted for only a short time. Most have been more like interest groups than parties, seeking to influence public opinion and government policy rather than to win elections.

The Democratic and Republican parties have continued to dominate national politics because they are flexible enough to adopt some of the programs proposed by third parties, and thus win over third party supporters. The Socialist party in America, even during its strongest period, always had difficulty achieving national support partly because the Democratic party was able to co-opt, or win over, the support of most organized labor with pro-labor economic programs. The Republican party lured voters away from Alabama Governor George Wallace's American Independent party (AIP) by emphasizing law and order in its 1968 presidential campaign.

What then do we mean by "political parties" in America? Each of our two major political parties is a group that seeks to elect people to government offices under a specific label. This simple definition obscures the two faces of the major political parties. American political parties exist two ways: among citizens who identify and support their party there is the *"party-in-the-electorate"*; then, as a permanent machinery with its elected officials, there is the *party organization*.

THE PARTY-IN-THE-ELECTORATE

When someone says, "I am a Republican," that person is probably a part of the Republican party-in-the-electorate. The **party-in-the-electorate** is made up of citizens who identify with the party. Party identification often begins at an early age.

Origins of Party Loyalty

Families are important factors in party loyalty.[3] A majority of us inherit our party loyalty, especially if both parents were in agreement. For example, a survey by the University of Michigan showed that over 64 percent of those whose parents were Democrats identified with the Democratic party, and that nearly 60 percent of those whose parents were Republicans identified with the Republican party. Children whose parents had mixed loyalties or were Independents were found more likely to call themselves Independents. Eighty percent of those whose parents (both) considered themselves Independents were likely to do so also.

People do not keep their party identification only out of blind family loyalty. They do so partly because, as they grow older, that original identification is reinforced by other agents of socialization such as peers. (As shown in Chapter 6, people are more receptive to reinforcing, rather than contradictory, messages.) But, since not all of us still have the same party identification as our parents, it is obvious that some people do change loyalties. A change in peer groups (as when a person from a low-income background becomes a doctor), a significant event such as the Great Depression, or an important time in a person's own life (such as an extended period of unemployment) may cause a change in party loyalties.

A Bush supporter expresses her party loyalty at the Republican National Convention in New Orleans in 1988.

Are Democrats Different from Republicans?

No matter how people acquire their party identification, there is a definite relationship between party loyalty and income. People with lower incomes are likely to be Democrats; people with higher incomes are likely to be Republicans (see Figure 8.1).

In any classification of Americans—such as blue-collar workers, or Protestants, or suburban dwellers—there is a mixture of Democrats, Republicans, and Independents. Nobody fits into one category alone. A person might be, for example, a Protestant blue-collar worker who lives in the suburbs. It is true, though, that those who live in the suburbs are more likely to be Republicans and those who live in the central cities are more likely to be Democrats. People with college educations are more likely to be Republicans, while those with only grade-school educations are more likely to be Democrats. These categories are also tied to *class.* People who have college educations and those who live in the suburbs are more likely to be of higher socioeconomic status than those with a grade-school education or those who live in central cities.

FIGURE 8 ★ 1
Who's for Whom? The Party Identification of Various Groups of Americans

Some groups are fairly evenly split–people who live in rural areas and homemakers are examples. But many groups are solidly Democratic or Republican—more than 80 percent of blacks, for example, are pro-Democratic. Note that "conservatives" are solidly Republican and people who call themselves "very liberal" are solid Democrats.

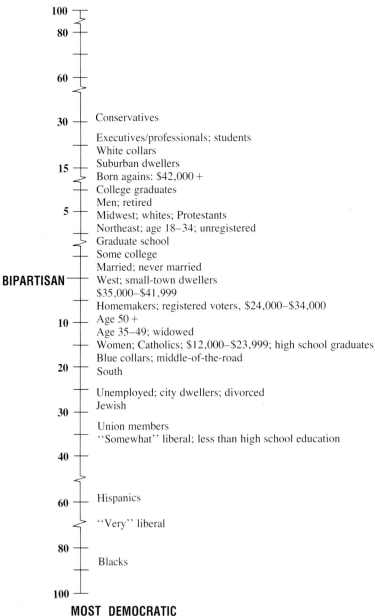

MOST REPUBLICAN

- 100
- 80
- 60
- 30 — Conservatives
- Executives/professionals; students
- White collars
- 15 — Suburban dwellers
- Born agains: $42,000 +
- College graduates
- Men; retired
- 5 — Midwest; whites; Protestants
- Northeast; age 18–34; unregistered
- Graduate school
- Some college
- Married; never married
- **BIPARTISAN** — West; small-town dwellers
- $35,000–$41,999
- Homemakers; registered voters, $24,000–$34,000
- 10 — Age 50 +
- Age 35–49; widowed
- Women; Catholics; $12,000–$23,999; high school graduates
- Blue collars; middle-of-the-road
- 20 — South
- Unemployed; city dwellers; divorced
- 30 — Jewish
- Union members
- "Somewhat" liberal; less than high school education
- 40
- 60 — Hispanics
- "Very" liberal
- 80
- Blacks
- 100

MOST DEMOCRATIC

SOURCE: Larry Sabato, *The Party's Just Begun* (Glenview, Ill.: Scott, Foresman/Little Brown, 1988), 125.

Through the years, blacks (heavily) and Catholics and Jews (not so heavily) have been Democrats. This, too, has some economic connection. A greater percentage of blacks are at lower economic levels than the rest of the population. They are concentrated in central cities. Both statements were once true of Catholic and Jewish immigrants too. The fact that the modern Democratic party has more strongly supported federal policies against discrimination than has the Republican party also explains these party loyalties (see the box on page 222).

There is also a difference between Democrats and Republicans in the way they think of themselves and certain issues. In one study, Republicans were found to think of themselves as conservatives, while most Democrats considered themselves moderate or liberal. In 1984, only 6 percent of the people who identified themselves as "strong" Republicans favored more government spending on services, while 25 percent of the "strong" Democrats did. Only 17 percent of the Republicans favored a government role in providing jobs and a good standard of living. Almost half of the Democrats, however, were in favor of such action. In response to the 1980 question, "Do you feel close to the poor?" 67.4 percent of the Democrats said yes, while 77 percent of the Republicans said no.[4]

Party Identification and Voting

A number of things can be said about party identification. First, since 1940, a large and stable percentage of Americans—usually between 42 and 48 percent—have identified themselves as Democrats.[5]

This identification is affected by the popularity of leaders of the party. For example, in 1946, when Harry Truman's public approval was at a low point (before he bounced back to win reelection against Thomas E. Dewey in 1948), the Gallup poll found that the percentage of Americans who called themselves Democrats was down to 39. By 1948, that figure was back up to the more usual 45 percent. Democrats hit the high of 53 percent in 1964, when former President Lyndon Johnson was winning big over highly conservative Republican Senator Barry Goldwater of Arizona. Then in 1972, when the very liberal Democratic Senator George McGovern of South Dakota was being trounced by Richard Nixon, the percentage of Americans who called themselves Democrats ebbed to 43 but soon rose back up (see Figure 8.2).

Second, from 1960 through 1983, fewer than 30 percent of Americans identified themselves as Republicans—and, at various times in the 1960s and 1970s, Democrats outnumbered Republicans two to one. As might be expected, Republican self-identifiers varied with the fortunes of their party's presidential candidates. The high point of the 1970s for the Republicans was 1972, the big Nixon reelection year. But Gallup found that following the Watergate scandal, Nixon's resignation, Gerald Ford's presidency, and his defeat by Jimmy Carter, the percentage of Republicans declined to 21 in 1977.

During the early-1970s administration of President Nixon, Republicans prophesied an "Emerging Republican Majority," with a realignment of party loyalties based on the appeal of a conservative Republican party. Nixon's disgrace dashed those hopes, but Republicans found their champion in Ronald Reagan. Right-wing GOP strategists had all along advocated the building of a conservative coalition that would not just be based on the traditional business-oriented, conservative economic philosophy of the Republican party, but also on reduced government, lower taxes, and less inflation. The new coalition was to include a *populist* thrust emphasizing socially conservative issues, such as prayer in the schools and opposition to abortion and busing, as well as an appeal to rising nationalism

FIGURE 8★2
Party Identification Through 1988

Note: Slight variation in question wording over time. In earlier years question was: "Do you consider yourself: (A Republican, Democrat, Socialist, or Independent/Democrat, Republican, Progressive, or Independent)? For comparison purposes "Other," "Socialist," and "Progressive" calculated out. Figures for January-March 1971 through October-December 1979 and January-March 1982 through January-March 1983 based on combined results of several surveys.

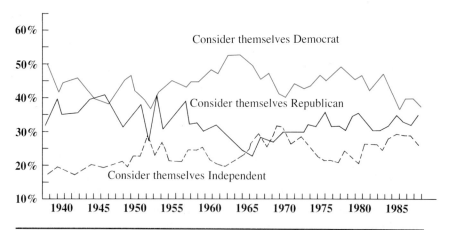

SOURCE: Surveys by the Gallup Organization, latest that of January 13–16, 1984. Reprinted from *Public Opinion* (April/May), p. 32; 1984–87 from *Gallup 1987,* p. 237, "Selected National Trends"; 1988 from *The New York Times*/CBS News Polls, *The New York Times,* November 10, 1988.

Labor unions demonstrate for Jimmy Carter in 1980.

through increased defense budgets and "standing up to" the Soviet Union.

To some, the Reagan election in 1980 seemed a victory of this appeal. But analysis showed that the voters had not so much approved Reagan's policies as they had simply rejected Carter.

Republican Realignment?

The elections of the 1980s led some political analysts to conclude that a Republican realignment had occurred similar to the Democratic one of the 1930s. This **party realignment** would be a permanent shift in the ratio of Democratic and Republican voters with a new majority party emerging. By the 1986 elections, with the Democrats once again winning control of the Senate, talk of realignment diminished. Then came 1988.

George Bush's victory reignited the debate. The Republicans again convincingly won the presidency with 53 percent of the popular vote and the electoral votes of forty states, making it their fifth victory in six elections. And this time Democrats couldn't blame Ronald Reagan's unique personality for their loss. Voters' identification with the two parties was about equal, with 37 percent Democrats and 35 percent Republicans. Complicating the analysis a bit was the fact that the Democrats were in the majority just about everywhere besides the presidency. They added seats to their majorities in the House and Senate, picked up strength in the state legislatures, and gained governorships. So has a party realignment occurred or not?

George Bush, showing he's not about to coddle Massachusetts criminals, receives an endorsement from the Boston Police Patrolmen's Association during the 1988 campaign.

★ Party Identification by Group and Region, 1966 and 1987

GROUP IDENTIFICATION	1966			1987		
	D	R	I	D	R	I
Overall party identification—all voters	50%	26%	24%	42%	29%	29%
Sex						
Men	49	25	26	38	31	31
Women	52	26	22	46	28	26
Race						
White	47	28	25	38	32	30
Nonwhite	x	x	x	x	x	x (black 73 08 19; hisp 53 25 22)
Religious Affiliation						
Protestant	41	35	24	41	33	26
Catholic	60	16	24	47	25	28
Jewish	x	x	x	x	x	x (not asked in '87)
Age						
Under 30	46	22	32	34	31	35
30–49 year	53	22	25	42	27	31
50 and older	50	30	20	49	30	21
Region						
East	49	28	23	43	20	37
Midwest	45	30	25	36	28	36
South	58	16	26	47	29	24
West	49	31	20	40	31	29
Education						
College	38	34	28	35	35	30
High school	50	25	25	44	27	29
Grade school	58	22	20	53	22	25
Occupation						
Professional and business	42	30	28	34	36	30
White collar	48	29	23	42	30	28
Farmers	50	33	17	x	x	x (not asked in '87)
Manual workers	54	21	25	x	x	x (skilled 42 25 33; unskilled 46 23 31; blue collar 44 24 32)

SOURCE: Gallup Opinion Index, February 1966, p. 14, and *The Gallup Poll,* "Public Opinion 1987," pp. 235–37.

Clearly there has been a realignment in the loyalties of major voting groups and the balance of power between the two parties. In presidential elections the south is as solid for whoever the Republicans nominate as it once was for the Democrats. Republicans run just about on an equal basis against Democrats for most offices in most of the states of the former Confederacy.[6] Most blue-collar workers, once reliably Democratic, voted for Reagan twice and split evenly between Bush and Dukakis in 1988.

The youngest voters swung toward the Republicans. In 1980, young people 19–29 had narrowly supported Jimmy Carter, while the nation supported Reagan 51 to 41 percent. By 1984, the young gave Reagan the same 59 percent of their vote as the electorate as a whole. In 1988, the youth vote again paralleled voters in general, giving Bush 52 percent of their votes.[7] Throughout most of the 1980s, a majority of all voters found the Republicans better able to manage the economy, keep the country prosperous, and even balance the budget. The percentage of Americans viewing the GOP as a credible governing party was larger than at any time since the Depression.

This realignment did not make the Republicans a new majority party. Despite GOP strength in presidential politics, the Democrats still controlled Congress and a majority of state legislatures (see the box on page 225). Republican gains in voter identification have brought them to **party parity;** they are now equal to the Democrats on the national scene. *Rather than a realignment similar to 1932, where a new majority party took power, the period ahead looks to be one of partisan balance.* A stable majority-minority party relationship such as existed in the 1920s (with Republicans ruling) and the 1930s (with Democrats dominating) seems unlikely.[8]

Reinforcing this was the volatility of an electorate that refused to identify with either party. **Dealignment** came to be a common buzz word, reflecting a decaying loyalty to both parties among voters. This led to split control (one party dominating at least one house of the legislature, another controlling the executive) in the national government and in most state governments. The early 1990s appear to be a period of divided party rule, with the outcome of the competition likely to be determined by the health of the economy.

Independents: The Nonaligned

There is also a large percentage of Americans who call themselves *Independents* and who are not significantly tied to either Republicans or Democrats. This percentage was in the low 20s in the 1950s and 1960s, rose to almost one-third of voters in 1968, and has stayed in the high 20s ever since. The increase in the percentage of Independents came mostly in the 1960s and 1980s. During the same period, there was a corresponding decline in the percentage of Democratic and Republican identifiers who called themselves "strong" Democrats or "strong" Republicans (see Figure 8.2).

Who are the Independents? The increase of Independents and the decline of strong partisans came about not so much because of hostility toward the parties, but because of increasing neutrality. People just did not think parties held any meaning for their lives. Not long ago, political scientists held that Independents were less politically active and less informed than members of political parties. After the mid-1960s, however, there was a rapid increase in Independents among upper-status and younger voters. These "new Independents" were more likely than the "old Independents" to analyze issues and make informed electoral choices. They were probably as politically knowledgeable as partisans. While Independents had less faith in electoral politics and little belief in the values of the major parties, they still had to choose between the candidates of the two major parties.

This stable body of Independents and weak partisans, taken together with an increase in "issue voting," meant that voters were more "volatile." They were more likely to swing from one party's candidate to the other, more responsive to personality and issue appeals in a campaign, and somewhat less predictable. Lastly, it should be noted that *party identification was still the single most important predictor of how a person voted in a general election.*[9]

Independent presidential candidate John Anderson holds up a campaign sticker in an attempt to persuade voters that they are not "wasting their votes" on him in 1980.

★ Divided Government in Washington Since World War II

	PARTY IN POWER AT WHITE HOUSE		PARTY IN CONTROL OF CONGRESS
1945–46	Democrats	Franklin Roosevelt, Harry Truman	Democrats
1947–48	Democrats	Truman	Republican
1949–50	Democrats	Truman	Democrats
1951–52	Democrats	Truman	Democrats
1953–54	Republicans	Dwight Eisenhower	Republicans
1955–56	Republicans	Eisenhower	Democrats
1957–58	Republicans	Eisenhower	Democrats
1959–60	Republicans	Eisenhower	Democrats
1961–62	Democrats	John Kennedy	Democrats
1963–64	Democrats	Kennedy, Lyndon Johnson	Democrats
1965–66	Democrats	Johnson	Democrats
1967–68	Democrats	Johnson	Democrats
1969–70	Republicans	Richard Nixon	Democrats
1971–72	Republicans	Nixon	Democrats
1973–74	Republicans	Nixon, Gerald Ford	Democrats
1975–76	Republicans	Ford	Democrats
1977–78	Democrats	Jimmy Carter	Democrats
1979–80	Democrats	Carter	Democrats
1981–82	Republicans	Ronald Reagan	Split
1983–84	Republicans	Reagan	Split
1985–86	Republicans	Reagan	Split
1987–88	Republicans	Reagan	Democrats
1989–90	Republicans	George Bush	Democrats

SOURCE: Ruth K. Scott and Ronald J. Hrebenar, *Parties in Crisis: Party Politics in America,* 2nd ed. (New York: John Wiley and Sons, 1984), p. 18. Updated to 1989.

THE FORMAL PARTY ORGANIZATION

A more tangible part of parties is their formal organization. On one hand, parties are like interest groups: they enable people to participate in politics and they link the people and their government. Yet parties are also different. Their principal aim is to contest elections and, unlike interest groups, the party label is on the ballot. Parties fill government positions with people who are more or less committed to the party's programs. An interest group seeks to influence the government, but a political party seeks to control it.

Functions and Structures

Like our federal system, each party has a national organization and separate state and local organizations that operate with a great deal of independence from each other. The chair and members of the Texas Democratic State Central Committee, on one hand, and the chair and members of the Democratic National Committee, on the other, have much the same independence in dealing with each other as the Texas governor and members of the Texas state legislature have in dealing with the president and the Congress.

Party organizations can be classified as "strong" or "weak" depending on whether they are active in recruiting candidates to run for public office, they take a leading role on issues, they engage in public opinion polling, they offer services and funds to their party candidates, they sponsor voter mobilization programs, and they have regular headquarters, adequate budgets, and professional staffs.

How representative of popular opinion are the issue positions of party officials? The answer depends on which party you have in mind and which level of party organization. Republican party organization officials at all levels—county chairs, state chairs, national committee members, and national convention delegates—are a fairly similar group and fairly conservative. They are more conservative than the public and even a bit more conservative than Republican party members in the electorate. Almost none of them answer to the label "liberal."

The Democratic elites are different. Few call themselves "conservative." They range from moderate to liberal and are closer to their party members and the general public than are the Republican elites. They are a more heterogeneous group, with more liberal views the higher in the party they are. The most liberal are the delegates to the Democratic National Convention.

The unsuccessful Equal Rights Amendment (ERA), for example, which would amend the Constitution to prohibit discrimination on the basis of sex, is supported by 70 percent of the American public, 70 percent of Democrats, and 66 percent of Republicans. What about the views of the party organization elites on this issue? On the Democratic side, ERA is supported by 92 percent of the DNC members and state chairs, 91 percent of the national convention delegates, and 67 percent of the county chairs. In contrast, on the Republican side, ERA was opposed by 73 percent of the national convention delegates and 79 percent of the county chairs. Unsurprisingly, the 1988 Democratic National Convention endorsed ERA, while the 1988 Republican Convention did not.

What about the question of cutting federal spending? Democratic party officials were more likely (ranging from 30 percent of the county chairs to 58 percent of the national convention delegates) to say defense was the place to cut than were Republican party officials (only 5 to 6 percent). Republican party officials were much more likely (57 to 62 percent) than Democratic officials (only 15 to 26 percent) to say that the federal government could best cut education, health, and medicare programs.

These findings prompted the study's authors to conclude that "the Democrats are the liberal-to-moderate alternative and the Republicans are clearly the conservative option in American politics. We do not have . . . pure ideological differences . . . , but we do have dramatic differences between the two parties. There are almost no liberals in the Republican Party and very few conservatives at the leadership level of the Democratic Party."[10]

Local and State Party Organizations

Party organizations reflect a variety of forms usually matching the voting districts of their individual states. Generalities here will only generally be true.[11]

The smallest geographical unit of American party organizations is the **precinct.** It is also the smallest unit for voting and registration. Theoretically, every precinct has a party committee for each of the major parties. Each committee in turn is headed by a precinct chairperson. In reality, a large percentage of the party precincts have no officers and very little activity—rarely even a meeting except at election time.

Each county has a *county central committee* headed by a county chairperson. In the cities, there are usually *ward committees,* the ward being a city council district. The larger cities have city-wide party committees. Each of the major parties has a *state central committee,* directed by state party chairpersons. Many states also have party committees at the congressional district level, between the county and state level (see Figure 8.3).

The process of selecting state and local party officials begins with meetings in the precincts. The time and date for the precinct meetings are frequently set by state law. The parties now have rules requiring standards of fairness in conducting these meetings. Some states provide for the election of party officials by the voters in primary elections. In others, state party officials are chosen in conventions. Each level of the state and local party machinery is not necessarily dependent for its election upon the level below.

FIGURE 8⋆3
A Typical State Party Organization

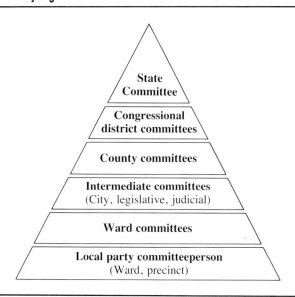

State Committee

Congressional district committees

County committees

Intermediate committees
(City, legislative, judicial)

Ward committees

Local party committeeperson
(Ward, precinct)

SOURCE: Sarouf and Beck, *Party Politics in America,* p. 78.

What do the officers do in nonelection years? Their duties primarily depend upon whether they are the *in-party* or the *out-party.* The basic job of out-party officials is to show that the party is still alive. They may have booths at fairs, issue press releases criticizing public officials of the other party, and conduct voter registration drives. But all political activity takes money, which out-parties have difficulty raising. Systems for collecting regular contributions have been only modestly successful. State parties typically sponsor "Jefferson-Jackson Day" dinners (Democrats) or "Lincoln Day" dinners (Republicans). The success of these dinners is often limited without the "clout" of a party member in a powerful public office.

Party activists attend party caucuses, take part in primary campaigns, and vote in primary elections. Studies have consistently found that less than 10 percent of Americans have ever attended a political meeting or worked for a candidate.[12]

The in-party—the party with more of its own members in important government positions—presumably has more power than the out-party. This isn't necessarily so. It is the public official, rather than the party, who actually exercises the power of the office. The government official uses the party organization, rather than vice versa. *If a party elects one of its own to a powerful public office, the organization often becomes a tool of the public official.* For example, a governor usually names the state party chairperson, who generally serves as a voice of the governor.

Party Machines

There are still some party machines, principally in cities. These machines have declined sharply in modern times. The old party machines, headed by "bosses," were powerful because they could control party nominations for public office. Then, by electing these officials, they could control **patronage,** the power to appoint supporters to public jobs. They also controlled welfare programs and influenced who would get government contracts. The government became an arm of the party machine.

Machine influence still exists. In New York City, many young lawyers get involved in party activities to gain appointments as judges. A weakened Democratic machine still exists in Chicago. After the death of the machine's boss, Richard J. Daley, who was both the mayor of Chicago and the chairperson of the Cook County Democratic party, an insurgent black congressman, Harold Washington, became the Democratic nominee and was elected mayor over the opposition of the old Daley machine. Even though Daley's son, Richard M. Daley, was elected mayor in 1989, the politics of race—with whites and blacks voting over 90 percent for the candidate of their race—seemed more important than loyalty to the machine.

Richard M. Daley, son of the famous mayor and now mayor himself, campaigns for mayor in Chicago in 1988.

Party machines have lost much of their power for several reasons. First is the *primary election.* This allows the party-in-the-electorate, rather than the party organization, to select party nominees. In addition, the machines' bad image because of past corruption has led to stricter *laws to prevent fraudulent voting,* which was one of their main levers of power. Perhaps the most important reason is that *civil service* systems have taken many of the old patronage jobs away from the politicians. As a leader of New York's Tammany Hall said around the turn of the century about civil service:

> *"This civil service law is the biggest fraud of the age. It is the curse of the nation. There can't be no real patriotism while it lasts. How are you goin' to interest our young men in their country if you have no offices to give them when they work for their party?"*[13]

Many jobs that can still be passed out through political patronage are unattractive because of their low status or because they require skills that the politically faithful don't have. *Welfare laws* now base eligibility on need rather than on influence. The *mass media,* particularly television, gives voters their political information directly without as much need for local precinct workers. The *rise of interest groups* and their willingness to finance costly campaigns has also displaced another machine function.

Modern Machines

Using new technologies of fundraising and direct mail campaigns, issue-oriented **modern machines** have appeared in both the Democratic and Republican parties. On the left is the Los Angeles-based machine named after its founders Congressmen Henry A. Waxman and Howard L. Berman. The *Waxman-Berman machine* (which calls itself an "alliance") differs from the traditional machine in several ways. It is informal, centered on candidates (rather than the party), uses impersonal communications media and technologies (rather than patronage and ward committee members), and concentrates on influencing national and local policies by electing congressional candidates (rather than solely local politics). The machine uses money from the entertainment industry in Hollywood to elect dozens of allies to congressional and local posts. In the 1984 elections Waxman gave some $140,000 to Congressional and Senate candidates, probably increasing his own leverage within the House.

On the right, Republican Senator Jesse Helms of North Carolina uses his *Congressional Club* for direct mail fundraising. In North Carolina, the club recruits, trains, and finances dozens of candidates for state legislative and congressional races. Though the state party is uneasy with the Club, this ideologically based machine is an important factor in state politics, even though Helms' candidates took a pasting in recent elections.

The Helms and Waxman-Berman type of modern machines based on ideology and technology appear to have more of a future than older machines based on ethnicity and patronage. Or, perhaps, some combination of the two will yet emerge.[14]

National Party Organizations

Each of the major parties is headed by a *national chairperson* elected by the party's national committee. The chairperson's role varies. Within the president's party he or she will be a loyal link to the White House. If in the opposition party, the chairperson must be congenial with all factions and knowledgeable about organizational nuts and bolts.

The **Republican National Committee (RNC)** is made up of two committee persons from each of the state parties. The Democratic party has an expanded national committee with over 300 members. The **Democratic National Committee (DNC)** now includes the chairperson and the next highest ranking officer of the opposite sex from each of the states, 200 other members apportioned from the states on the same basis as delegates to the national convention, and assorted Democratic officials.

The national parties divide into a *presidential wing* and a *congressional wing.* The parties' national committee represents the presidential wing. Its outlook is national, and its principal goal is the election of a party member to the presidency. The congressional wing of each of the parties is composed of the party leaders, the party members in each house, and the campaign committees of the House and the Senate. Nothing requires these different parts of the party to work together. In practice, there is more cooperation between the Republicans in Congress and the Republican National Committee than there is among the Democrats.

The activities of the national committee vary depending on whether it represents an in-party or an out-party. At the national level, the party that has a president in the White House is the in-party. Its national committee is dominated by the president. John F. Kennedy, for example, named John Bailey to head the Democratic National Committee and made the committee a political arm of the White House. President Bush followed the Kennedy example and had his campaign manager, Lee Atwater, elected Chairman of the Republican National Committee. *Since presidents prefer to seem "above politics," they sometimes use the national committee as a par-*

Ron Brown, Chairman of the Democratic National Committee.

tisan voice to criticize the other party. In addition, presidents may use their national party committees to raise funds for presidential activities that have a political character. As a rule, presidents do not welcome being advised on issues by the national committee of their party.

The national committee has more flexibility when it represents an out-party. In this case, the national committee may choose its own chairperson. Following President Carter's defeat in 1980, the Democratic National Committee elected California Attorney Charles T. Manatt as its chairperson, without regard to Carter's wishes. The out-party typically attempts to "rebuild" from the party's recent defeat. The Democratic National Committee did this in 1985 by selecting a new chairman, Paul Kirk. After its presidential setback in 1988, the DNC elected Ron Brown, a black lawyer long active in the party.

When the national committee represents the out-party, it frequently runs into trouble with the party leaders of the House and Senate by attempting to speak out on issues. The congressional leaders feel that this is their turf. Congressional leaders prefer the national committees to deal only with "nuts and bolts" projects, such as voter registration and voter turnout.

The party's professional staff have gained power through their understanding of the modern technology of campaigning and the complicated laws governing how money is raised and spent. The Republican staff is much larger than the Democratic staff because the Democrats contract out much of their work (such as direct mail fundraising) to campaign consultants. The Republicans have also taken the lead in reforming and strengthening their national party.

The Republicans have a strong party organization. The Democrats' organization at present can only be called moderately strong.

In fundraising and organization, the Republicans have gotten a head start on the Democrats. In the 1985–1986 election cycle, the Republicans raised over $190 million, nearly five times the $38 million raised by the Democrats. In the 1981–1982 election cycle, the Republicans' postage bill alone—$7.5 million—almost equaled half the entire operating budget of the Democratic National Committee. It is of course easier to raise money with your party in the White House. By the mid-1980s, the Republican party had become the single most important source of money in American politics.

These funds were used to support the party's candidates and pay for expensive campaign technology. The large amounts of money the Republicans gave to their candidates tended to concentrate power in the national organization and produced loyalty in party members' votes in Congress on the president's program. Besides increasing party discipline, the funds were spent on sophisticated media and computerized mail campaigns to register Republican voters. Although the Democrats remained the majority party and have mounted more sophisticated fundraising in recent elections, the Republicans had the advantage in money and technology in turning out their voters (see the case study). The power of both national parties is likely to increase as the formerly weak parties strengthen their central organizations.[15]

Party-in-Government

The parties are also organized within government at the local, state, and federal levels, and in the executive and legislative branches. The people who hold office under a party label make up the **party-in-government.** They are, however, pretty independent of each other within their own areas. The president can't tell a state governor what to do even if he is in the same party, and may have trouble getting party members in Congress to follow his program.

This party-in-government is an important source of strength for the party and can at times act with some coherence. In the executive branch, the president or governor becomes the leader of his or her national or state party. His or her "coattails" may help elect legislators, and patronage can provide rewards or punishments for party members.

Given the party's lack of control over who runs under the party label, there is a surprising degree of party coherence in Congress and state legislatures. The division between the two parties remains "the chief lines in American legislative voting behavior."[16] Nevertheless, as the chapters on Congress will show, this cohesion may be a product of factors other than the orders of party leaders. For example, most liberal Democrats representing inner-city districts may see an issue the same way because of the constituencies they represent, regardless of party preferences.

It's easy to overstate this party unity. When former House Speaker Tip O'Neill declared "all politics is local," he was accurately estimating legislators' predominant concerns with the people who elected them. Legislators' constituents have more influence over whether they stay in office than does the national party. Similarly, a president means something to his party's officeholders, but not everything. The decentralized nature of party power and competing demands from interest groups, other parts of the government, legislative leaders, and the media all may push legislators in different directions than their party (see the case study in Chapter 11).

Presidents, too, react to pressures other than party influence. The civil service system and legislative checks on appointment powers restrict governors and presidents in helping the party faithful. Chief executives' own personal appeal, friendly interest groups, and frequent wishes to be "leader of all the people" may cause them to distance themselves from their own party.

THE PARTY IN GENERAL ELECTIONS

How does a person become the nominee of the party? The prenomination procedure in most states requires only the filing of a petition with a certain number of signatures. Party nominations may either be by *primary election* or by *convention.* The convention method provides for nomination by a vote of party delegates who have been selected for that purpose. Presidential nominations are made by national conventions.

The primary election method of nomination gives party voters a choice among competing party candidates. Primary elections are usually decided by a *plurality of the vote* (at least one more vote than any other candidate). A few states provide for a run-off primary between the two highest party candidates if no one achieves a majority in the first primary. In a **closed primary,** party voters may only choose among candidates of their own party. Republican voters only receive Republican ballots and are not allowed to vote on the Democratic nominees. An **open primary** allows voters—whether registered Republicans or Democrats or Independents—to choose to vote either in the Democratic or Republican primary. The open primary tends to dilute party members' votes and can allow non-party members to select candidates not representing party positions. Most states have closed primaries, allowing no crossover voting.

National Conventions

There are two sides to a national convention. Traditionally, the national convention is the *party's ultimate authority.* The convention approves the rules and operation of the party. It also ratifies the party's philosophy and its positions on important issues. This **party platform** represents what the party promises to do if it controls the government. At its climax, the convention formally nominates party candidates for president and vice-president.

The platform represents more than merely "campaign promises" adopted and soon forgotten. Platform *planks*—positions on specific issues—are hammered out after special hearings before each party's convention. This allows for a public testing of opinions that has some educational value for officeholders. Platforms also affect government policy. Gerald Pomper concluded that most platform promises were kept. He found that 72 percent of the platform pledges made between 1944 and 1964 and 63 percent of those made between 1964 and 1976 were fulfilled. A similar study for the period from 1960 to 1980 drew the same conclusions.[17]

While still carrying out these traditional functions, the modern national convention is usually something less than meets the eye. *The presidential convention is basically a media event.* Staged and managed by the staff of the candidate who has won the most delegates in the spring primaries and caucuses, the convention politically functions as a media launching pad for the general election campaign. Everything is geared toward maximizing three nights of free television exposure (see the box on page 236). The speeches, the platform, and the nominating process are shaped to cast the party and its nominee in the most appealing light to the public.

Fights over rules and debates over platform planks still go on at conventions, but the major contest over who will be the partys' nominees for president has already been resolved by the voters. Not since 1952 has either party's battle for the nomination gone past the first *ballot* (or *roll call*) of the delegates. The convention basically *ratifies* the decisions of the voters and the rules put forward by the new party leadership, led by its nominee.

The delegates, although usually party activists, are elected pledged to one candidate or another. These candidates control their delegates at the convention. The candidate with the most delegates controls the convention and wins the nomination. Behind the scenes, *floor whips* in each of the state delegations make sure that the delegates stay in line and do not disrupt the proceedings. Keeping the nominee's message and supporters in front of the TV during prime time is a major task of the convention's managers. The Democrats' 1972

★ Are Conventions Really TV Miniseries?

Don Hewitt, executive producer of CBS's "60 Minutes," made the following remarks about political conventions:

"There is no doubt whose convention this really is. The politicians meeting there are now extras in our television show. . . .

When I first went to political conventions, we were observers and reporters. Now we're participants. And there's something a lot wrong with that.

In the old days, before the primaries took the steam out of political conventions, you could watch a good credentials fight or a good platform fight— even though a week later no one could remember what they were fighting about. Today, if you want to see a good fight at a political convention, let CBS News's sign be an inch bigger than NBC's. Now you'll see a fight at a convention. All hell breaks loose.

It's time we gave the politicians back their convention. Tell them it's nothing but a big commercial and that it's not Rather, Brokaw, or Jennings' job to be the emcee of their commercial."

SOURCE: *The New York Times,* February 28, 1986. Reprinted in Sorauf and Beck, *Party Politics,* 1988, p. 350.

experience, when their nominee, George McGovern, began his acceptance speech at 2:45 A.M. (with only one-fifth of the TV audience still watching) because of lengthy debates over the platform, stands as a warning to nominees not to let the conventioneers control the convention.

Both parties, starting with the Democrats, have reformed the way they select delegates. Beginning after their conflict-ridden 1968 convention in Chicago, the Democrats, led by Chairman Fred R. Harris (this book's coauthor), appointed a series of reform commissions. These commissions "democratized" party procedures and ensured that women and minorities were adequately represented.

Following Reagan's 1980 victory, the Democrats worried that these reforms had led to liberal special-interest control and backed away a bit from them. The party installed a **superdelegate** system by which uncommitted elected officials could be represented at the convention while maintaining the gains in delegates by minorities and women. The Republicans never went as far in their reforms as the Democrats, and therefore didn't have to backtrack as much in the 1980s.

Party reforms have forced presidential candidates to start campaigns earlier to win primaries. That is also the effect of the presidential campaign financing reform laws of 1974, which, as discussed, provided federal money for major presidential campaigns.[18] **Matching funds** are only available to candidates who have raised at least $5000 in each of at least twenty states, counting no more than $250 from any single contributor.

Taken together, these party reforms have led to the increased use of presidential primary elections. Candidates, encouraged by matching funds, the need for early media attention, and the chance to get more mileage from limited funds in small states like Iowa or New Hampshire, have concentrated on states that choose their delegates early in the election year. With the momentum gained from these primary victories, a couple of candidates emerge—Dukakis and Jackson for the Democrats in 1988—or just one comes out—George Bush for the Republicans.

Either way, the selection of a majority of delegates is dominated by the presidential candidate. The conventions are populated by activists whose ideologies and issues often don't reflect the views of the party members watching on TV. The conventions have in turn declined in importance. Even as staged media events, their ever-smaller TV audiences reflect popular indifference toward the parties and their role in America's government.

Getting Out the Vote

Elections bring all the elements of the party together. Once the party nominees have been chosen, they must compete against the other party's nominees. To a great extent the role played by the party organization is decided by the nominee. Candidates may merge their campaign organization into the party, taking over the party and naming a new party chairperson. Or they may keep the organizations separate. As seen in Chapter 7, party candidates are usually more concerned about media, money, interest groups, and scheduling than they are about party support.

The following case study gives a clear example of the type of support a modern party can give its candidates. The continuity and skills a party organization retains within its walls can be decisive in elections when developed and used effectively.

★ CASE STUDY

A Party Goes High Tech

In the spring of 1984, voters in several western states were called by a computer. A tape-recorded voice said the following:

"Good evening. This is Reagan-Bush '84 calling you on a special computer that is capable of recording your opinion. Your answers to two short questions are very important and will take less than a minute of your time. Please answer after the tone.

Question No. 1: If the election for president were held today, would you vote for President Reagan or the Democratic candidate? (Tone).

Question No. 2: There are a number of unregistered voters in your neighborhood. Is there anyone in your household who needs to register? (Tone).

Thank you and good night."

In some areas the telephoned person replied to the questions by pressing a button on his or her push-button phone—five to indicate support for the president, and six to indicate opposition. If six was pushed the computer terminated the interview.

Merging and Purging

This was just a sample of the Republican party's answer to the Democrats' advantages in finding and registering new voters. Since nonvoters were concentrated in lower-income and minority groups that overwhelmingly voted Democratic, Republican efforts to register new voters had to be selective. Money and technology were the core of the Republican strategy to register supporters.

In computer terms this became the "merging and purging" of multiple lists. To find the relatively affluent people who were most likely to support Republican candidates and who had not registered, the party's computers ran through a range of lists: mail-order buyers from upscale stores, licensed drivers, homeowners, new utility hookups, and subscribers to *The Wall Street Journal,* to name just a few. The 1984 Republican effort in Colorado was a good example of how well technology could be employed in the service of the party.

Rocky Mountain High Tech

The state GOP effort to build voting support began with a list of registered Colorado voters, purchased from the State for $500. Party workers (paid $3.50 an hour) first merged this by computer with a list of all licensed drivers over age 18. They then "purged" all drivers registered to vote, leaving the names of 800,000 unregistered voters who were licensed drivers.

This list was then cut to 120,000 names by eliminating all unregistered drivers who lived in precincts and zip codes with strong Democratic voting patterns. The list of 120,000 was then matched with names and phone numbers on a list put out by a commercial firm. About half of the names produced a match of a phone number that corresponded with a name and address on the party list.

These 60,000 names were the base from which the phone bank with the computerized message operated. The 60,000

Campaign workers use computers at the campaign headquarters of Michael Dukakis in 1988.

had been filtered down from 1.2 million registered voters and 2.2 million licensed drivers in Colorado. The goal of the phone survey was to further reduce the names to a list to 20,000 solid Republican prospects.

For those 20,000 making the final cut, the computer automatically generated a letter from the Colorado state GOP chair giving them the address of the nearest county clerk where they could register. In addition, the names were sent to their local county Republi-can executive committee and the campaigns of the president and senator who was running that year. Someone was then assigned to make sure the person actually registered.

GOP Targeting

The computer operation allowed even greater targeting for purposes other than registering likely Republican voters. Using polling, phone bank, and census information, the party could produce clusters of voters most likely to be interested in specific issues.

For example, a Republican candidate for the Senate might find from his polls that he was running poorly among women forty-five and older who were single heads of households. He might also discover from polling that this group was particularly concerned about crime. The party lists enabled the candidate to locate the names and addresses of, say, 25,000 women in this category. A letter centering on crime and what the candidate proposed to do about it could then be generated by computer and sent only to this group.

A similar sophisticated targeting effort allowed the Republicans to identify potential supporters among an ethnic group that tended to be strongly Democratic. The Republican National Committee developed a list of about 12,000 Hispanic last names. Tapes with those names were run against voter registration lists, then cross-tabbed against real estate tax lists. Doing this allowed the party to identify unregistered Hispanics who were homeowners. That list could then be run against car-buyer names, subscribers to financial newspapers, and Hispanic business owners in the search for upper-income Hispanics.

The goal of the high-tech outreach identifying potential Hispanic Republicans was put this way by the Colorado GOP political director: "Our initial target has to be the upwardly mobile Hispanic who has a vision of the future that is similar to Ronald Reagan's. That takes a very sophisticated effort. . . ."

It also took considerable money. In 1984, the GOP paid an estimated $7 for every new registered voter, with a cost to the party of up to $10 million. The Democratic efforts, on the other hand, depended on generally nonpartisan organizations registering the poor and minorities in grassroots drives.

These were neither controlled nor usually paid for by the Democratic party. As a result, no one could be sure that the new Democratic registrants actually voted on election day.

The Republicans, for their part, had this problem covered by computers and more traditional party techniques as well. A state GOP official commented: "We are not going to pay $5 for every new Republican and then let that person stay at home on Election Day. We are going to check those names against our computers all day on November 6, and if some guy hasn't shown up by 6 p.m., we'll carry him to the polls."[19]

WRAP-UP

Someone once described the camel as a horse designed by a committee. American parties, though not designed by any one set of hands, have evolved into a peculiar species of horseflesh. Party members don't pay dues and often feel little obligation even to vote for the party's candidates. For their part, the candidates seldom depend on the party for their nomination or election and, unsurprisingly, the party is far from a dominating influence over them once in public office. The party's structure is as dispersed as the government's, with separate national, state, and local units as well as detached legislative and executive parts.

Led by the Republicans, both parties have modernized and strengthened their organizations. As the Colorado case showed, the effective use of money and technology can be an advantage at election time. However, the parties have continued losing their popular appeal. More people declare themselves Independents and fewer are strong partisans of either party. While Republicans claim that recent presidential victories have shown a "realignment" in the electorate, others declare that "dealignment" more accurately reflects less loyalty to either party.

Yet the two parties are likely to be with us a while longer. They provide a clarifying link between citizens and their government and a crucial means of organizing elected officials in government. They have shown great flexibility in reforming their own rules and in adapting to the demands of new political groups, whether Hispanics, women or Christian fundamentalists. Their labels on the ballot simplify the choices voters must make at elections and indicate directions policy will take after elections. The parties' shortcomings largely reflect those of the unwieldy government and country they serve.

Key Terms

political party (p. 211)
direct primary election (p. 212)
single-member districts (p. 214)
party-in-the-electorate (p. 216)
party realignment (p. 221)
party parity (p. 223)
dealignment (p. 223)
precinct (p. 227)
patronage (p. 229)
modern machines (p. 230)

Republican National Committee
  (RNC) (p. 231)
Democratic National Committee
  (DNC) (p. 231)
party-in-government (p. 233)
closed primary (p. 234)
open primary (p. 234)
party platform (p. 235)
superdelegates (p. 236)
matching funds (p. 237)

Suggested Readings

Blumenthal, Sidney, *Rise of the Counter-Establishment: From Conservative Ideology to Political Power* (New York: Times Books, 1986).

Herrnson, Paul S., *Party Campaigns in the 1980s* (Cambridge: Harvard University Press, 1988).

Kayden, Xandra and Eddie Mahe, *The Party Goes On: The Persistence of the Two-Party System in the United States* (New York: Basic Books, 1985).

Kuttner, Bob, *Life of the Party: Democratic Prospects in 1988* (New York: Penguin, 1988).

Mazmanian, Daniel, *Third Parties in American Politics* (Washington, D.C.: The Brookings Institution, 1974).

Price, David, *Bringing Back the Parties* (Washington, D.C.: Congressional Quarterly, 1984).

Rapoport, Ronald B., Alan I. Abramowitz, and John McClennon, *The Life of the Parties: Activists in Presidential Politics* (Lexington: University Press of Kentucky, 1986).

Endnotes

[1] David S. Broder, *The Party's Over: The Failure of Politics in America* (New York: Harper and Row, 1971) and Larry J. Sabato, *The Party's Just Begun* (Glenview, IL: Scott, Foresman, 1988).

[2] For a discussion of these three reasons for the two-party system, see Robert J. Huckshorn, *Political Parties in America,* 2nd ed. (Monterey, CA: Brooks/Cole Publishing, 1984), pp. 37–39.

[3] Except as otherwise indicated, this discussion is based on Frank Sorauf and Paul Allen Beck, *Party Politics in America,* 6th ed. (Boston: Little, Brown, 1988), chapter 6.

[4] Sorauf, *Party Politics in America,* 5th ed., p. 157, and Sorauf and Beck, *Party Politics,* 6th ed., p. 185.

[5] William J. Keefe, *Parties, Politics, and Public Policy in America,* 4th ed. (New York: Holt, Rinehart, Winston, 1984), p. 114 and Gallup polls through the years cited there.

[6] See Alexander P. Lamis, *The Two-Party South* (New York: Oxford University Press, 1988).

[7] See *The New York Times,* November 10, 1988; *Public Opinion,* January/February, 1989.

[8] This discussion owes much to Everett Carll Ladd, "Party Time, Realignment," in Roger H. Davidson and Walter J. Oleszek, *Governing* (Washington, D.C.: Congressional Quarterly Press, 1987), pp. 114–18.

[9] See William Crotty, *American Parties in Decline,* 2nd ed. (Boston: Little, Brown, 1984), pp. 45–58.

[10] John S. Jackson III, Barbara L. Brown, and David Bositis, "Herbert McClosky and Friends Revisited: 1980 Democratic and Republican Elites Compared to the Mass Public," *American Politics Quarterly* (April 1982), Vol. 10, no. 2., pp. 158–80.

[11] See Sorauf and Beck, *Party Politics,* Chapter 3.

[12]Fred I. Greenstein and Frank B. Feigert, *The American Party System and the American People,* 3rd ed. (Englewood Cliffs, N.J.: Prentice Hall, 1985), p. 12.

[13]George Washington Plunkett in William L. Riordan (ed.), *Plunkett of Tammany Hall* (New York: E.P. Dutton, 1963), p. 11.

[14]Sabato, pp. 97–98.

[15]See Frank J. Sorauf, *Money in American Elections* (Glenview, IL: Scott, Foresman, 1987).

[16]Sorauf and Beck, p. 392

[17]Gerald M. Pomper, *Elections in America: Control and Influence in Democratic Politics,* rev. ed (New York: Longman, 1980), p. 163 and Alan D. Monroe, "American Party Platforms and Public Opinion," in *American Journal of Political Science* (February 1983), Vol. 27, no. 1:36.

[18]Herbert Asher, *Presidential Elections and American Politics,* rev. ed., (Homewood, IL: Dorsey Press, 1980), p. 283.

[19]Thomas B. Edsall and Haynes Johnson, "Colorado's High-Tech Republicans," in Roger H. Davidson and Walter J. Oleszek, *Governing* (Washington, D.C.: Congressional Quarterly Press, 1987), pp. 108–13.

CHAPTER 9

Interest Groups

As a congressman, I had plenty of phone calls from political directors of PACs, in which the conversation went something like this:

"Mike, we're getting ready to make our next round of checks out, and just want to let you know that you're right up there at the top. We really think we can help you with a nice contribution."

"Gee, that's great. Really appreciate it. Grateful to have your help."

"Oh, by the way, Mike, have you been following that bill in Ways and Means that's going to be coming to the floor next week? It's got an item in there we're concerned about—the amendment by Congressman Schwartz. You know, we'll be supporting that and we hope you'll be with us on that one. Hope you'll take a good look at it, and if you need any information about it, we'll send that up to you . . ."

You have to make a choice. Who are you going to let in the door first? You get back from lunch. You've got fourteen phone messages on your desk. Thirteen of them are from constituents you've never heard of, and one of them is from a guy who just came to your fundraiser two weeks earlier and gave you $2,000. Which phone call are you going to return first?[1]

—former Congressman Michael Barnes of Maryland

INTEREST GROUPS AND DEMOCRACY

The problems caused by interest groups that concern modern members of Congress are not all that different from what troubled the Constitution's framers 200 years ago. In *Federalist 10,* James Madison worried about interest groups, which he called "factions." "By a faction, I understand a number of citizens who are united and actuated by some common impulse of passion, or of interest, adverse to the rights of other citizens, or to the permanent and aggregate interests of the community." He went on to say that "the most common and durable source of factions has been the various and unequal distribution of property." Although Madison deplored the existence of factions (interest groups), he felt they were "sown in the nature of man." To guard against the evils of interest groups, Madison helped design a republic in which power was fragmented between the state and the federal levels, and among three branches of the federal government.

Alex de Tocqueville, in his famous *Democracy in America,* took a kinder view of interest groups and marveled at the American instinct to form them. "Americans of all ages, all conditions, and all dispositions constantly form associations," he wrote in the 1830s. "They have not only commercial and manufacturing companies, in which all take part, but associations of a thousand other kinds—religious, moral, serious, futile, extensive or restricted, enormous or diminutive."[2]

Whether denounced as "special interests" or praised as many of "a thousand points of light," Americans down to the present have varied in their views of interest groups. Their influence in politics makes it important to know more about what they are, the roles they play, and the tactics they use. Of special interest are the *Political Action Committees (PACs)* they set up, how they operate, and how much power they have. The case study on page 274 shows that PACs are not only influential but influenced as well.

Characteristics of Interest Groups

Party organization and the electoral system are based on geographic divisions. Senators and representatives represent us on the basis of the state or the district in which we live. But within one district there might be important group interests that are not represented. People of different religions, races, ethnic backgrounds, income levels, or occupations may have different political concerns. Interest groups have developed to give Americans with common causes a way to express their views to political decision makers.

Interest groups may try to influence the outcome of elections, but unlike parties, they do not compete for public office. Although a candidate may be sympathetic to a certain group, or may be a member of that group, he or she does not run for election as a candidate of that group.

Interest groups are usually more tightly organized than political parties. They are often financed through contributions or dues-paying members. Organizers communicate with members through newsletters, mailings, and conferences. Union members, for example, usually receive regular correspondence from the union leadership informing them about positions they are expected to support.

Interest groups have three principal characteristics. First, an interest group is *organized*. It is not just a population group, such as all blacks or all women. It has leaders and goals and some means of raising money to meet the group's goals. Second, an interest group may not agree on every issue, but it does *agree on the goals* of the organization. Third, an interest group acts to *influence public policy*. It tries to push government in its direction.

Gene Basset, *The Atlanta Constitution*

The Advocacy Explosion

Tocqueville said that Americans successfully used associations more than any other people in the world. That is probably still true. One study found that 56 percent of Americans said they would form an informal group in order to protest an unjust law, compared to only 34 percent in Great Britain, 13 percent in Germany, and 7 percent in Italy.[3]

Why are people so willing to join groups? Some people join because they are interested in particular causes. Others do it to further their economic interests. People also become members of groups for companionship. Peer pressure may push people into groups. In some communities people may say, "Everyone who is anyone belongs to the Chamber of Commerce." Finally, some people join groups because they have to. If labor and management at a plant agree to maintain a "union shop," the workers will be required to join the union (unless state law prohibits it).

In recent years, there has been what one observer calls an "advocacy explosion" in America.[4] Washington remains a "city of lawyers," a number of whom make their living by lobbying. The nation's capital has more lawyers than Los Angeles, which is three times larger. The number of Washington lawyers increased from 11,000 to 38,000 between 1972 and 1983. The number of political action committees (PACs) formed to raise campaign contributions for political candidates increased from 608 in 1974 to 4211 in 1987 (see Figure 9.1).

FIGURE 9★1
The Growth of PACs

It is impossible to know how many interest groups there are since no one keeps a precise count. The growth in the number of Political Action Committees (PACs) registered with the Federal Election Commission (FEC) is one good indicator of the interest group explosion. This is the FEC's annual count since 1974.

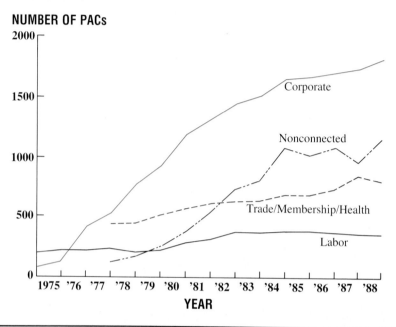

NUMBER OF PACs

SOURCE: Federal Election Committee, *Record,* March 1989, vol. 15, no. 3, p. 5.

Why has there been such an increase in interest groups pushing causes? For one thing, Americans are not a homogeneous people. A black person may also be a military veteran, a parent of a school child, a feminist, and a disgruntled taxpayer. Such a person might join more than one interest group in order to advance several separate interests. For another thing, our Constitution fragments government—between federal and state (and local) levels and, among the executive, legislative, and judicial branches. Unitary governments such as that of Great Britain have given rise to only one group representing one interest—a single farm organization representing all farmers, for example, unlike the U.S. situation.

Social and economic change spawned interest groups. Industrialization led to unionization. In the 1960s, the civil rights movement set the pattern for movements by women, Native Americans, Hispanics, environmentalists, and consumer advocates. Events such as the Vietnam War triggered a wave of organizing. *Expanding govern-*

*ment social programs and economic regulation caused both benefi-
ciaries of programs and targets of regulation to organize to protect
their interests.* All this was happening at the same time as the weakening of political parties, which people might otherwise have turned
to for help.

Advocacy by one group often led to a reaction by another. The
consumer movement in the 1960s stimulated increased business
attention toward government policy. The *techniques* of organization
have improved, and as one group used new methods its rivals felt
pressured to match its efforts. The availability of skilled organizers,
patrons with money to spare for a good cause, and new methods such
as direct mail solicitation of funds also aided the explosion of interest groups.

Interest Groups: The Pro

Many people think of interest groups as an evil, if inevitable, influence. Others view interest groups as a good and necessary part of
democracy. Beginning with the positive side there are four functions
that interest groups perform.

First, interest groups serve as *links between the people and policymakers,* bridging individual needs and government actions.
According to this view, interest groups help the government identify
opinions to which it must respond.

Second, interest groups *increase political participation.* They
inform their members of government decisions, explain how members can influence such decisions, and encourage them to use this
influence. Membership in interest groups further encourages political participation by increasing a person's sense of efficacy.

Third, advocates argue that interest groups improve *official representation.* As members of a group, individuals feel they have more
of an impact on a federal agency's actions—a sense of "strength in
numbers." People who would not testify before a congressional committee or write to a representative, or contribute to an election campaign, may be represented in the process through an interest group.
This representation function can be seen throughout the policy process—from helping put issues on the public agenda to evaluating
their implementation.

Finally, supporters of interest groups claim that they help *resolve
conflicts in our society.* Some even argue that policy is the product of
the competition and compromises among interest groups, with the
government simply giving approval to decisions that have already
been reached outside the government. This theory of how democracy
works is called **pluralism.**[5]

Politicians, including
presidents, need to keep
interest groups happy. One
of the most powerful
interest groups is the
Veterans of Foreign Wars.
Here, George Bush puts on
a VFW ceremonial cap
when speaking at the VFW
convention in Chicago in
August 1988.

Interest Groups: The Con

Criticism of interest groups centers on several counts. First, all Americans are *not equally represented* by interest groups. Although 62 percent of the people in one study said that they belonged to an organization, only about 40 percent were active in an organization, and only 31 percent belonged to an organization in which political discussions took place. Eight percent belonged to political groups, such as Democratic or Republican clubs, or to political action groups, such as voters' leagues.[6]

Members of these organizations had more education than non-members. Fifty-nine percent of Americans who had attended college were active in at least one organization, while only 43 percent of the high-school graduates and 27 percent of those who did not graduate from high school were active. Minorities and poorer people were less likely to be members of interest groups. E. E. Schattschneider wrote that the "pressure system" of interest groups is "skewed, loaded and unbalanced" in favor of a small fraction of Americans.[7] So, it is argued, democracy cannot be explained in terms of pluralism and competition among groups because many people never even get to play the game.

A second criticism of interest groups is that a few leaders dominate undemocratic organizations. This has been called the "iron law of oligarchy."[8] (*Oligarchy* is the rule of the few rather than the many.) Critics claim that the groups are dominated by an active minority. This is not just true of interest groups that lobby for their own economic interests; it also holds for "citizens' lobbies" such as Common Cause or Public Citizen, Ralph Nader's fundraising organization. Public Citizen, for example, makes it clear when it asks for funds by mail that members will not receive reports on the organization's activities. Clearly, interest groups are not always able to speak for all their members and may sometimes take positions with which members disagree.

A third criticism of interest groups is that *they are not really accountable* to anyone except their members (and not always to them). Interest groups are not as responsible to the general public as are elected public officials, who must account for their actions, at least at election time.

Finally, opponents of interest groups argue that competition and compromise among various groups *do not necessarily result in coherent government policy.* Instead, they often produce government stalemate. Theodore J. Lowi criticized interest groups and pluralism, saying "Government that is formless in action and amoral in intention (i.e., ad hoc) is government that can neither plan or achieve justice."[9]

Critics point out that the interest group-pluralism model views politics as a process very similar to the adversarial relationship in court, although with more than two sides. All the interests are represented, not by lawyers but by interest groups. However, critics point out, some lawyers/interest groups are more skilled than others. Some lawyers are not really controlled by those whom they are supposed to represent. Moreover, some of the interests are not even represented. Finally, the compromises worked out among the contending lawyers may result in action that is not in the public interest.

We are left, then, with *James Madison's dilemma: the freedoms of speech and assembly guarantee Americans the right to lobby their government, but how can some groups be kept from having too much influence?* Madison thought that a fragmented government system would balance their powers against each other. The fragmented system may itself encourage the formation of more interest groups to take advantage of the many points of access. Despite the criticisms leveled at it, the pluralism model of democracy offers added encouragement for greater participation in politics. It remains the most available cure for too few having too much power over too many.

TYPES OF INTEREST GROUPS

The largest and probably most important type of interest group is the *economic interest group*: business, professional, labor, and farm. *Issue-oriented groups* are motivated primarily by causes or ideology rather than material gains. Minority and women's groups like the NAACP (the National Association for the Advancement of Colored People) and NOW (the National Organization for Women) can also be considered interest groups. *Governments,* including local and state as well as foreign, often act as interest groups in their lobbying in Washington.

Economic Groups

The most influential interest groups in the making of public policy are those which aim to gain economic benefits for their members. These include business, professional, labor, and farm organizations.

Business

Nearly 3000 business organizations and trade associations—about one-third of all national interest groups—maintain headquarters in Washington. The two principal business groups are the *National*

★ A Few Interest Groups

NAME (DATE OF FOUNDING)[a]	HEADQUARTERS	MEMBERSHIP	STAFF	PUBLICATION
Economic Groups				
National Association of Manufacturers (1895)	Washington, D.C.	13,000	220	*Enterprise*
Air Line Pilots Association, Int'l. (1931)	Washington, D.C.	33,000	250	*Air Line Pilot*
AFL-CIO (1955)	Washington, D.C.	13,800,000	500	*American Federationist; Free Trade Union News*
National Consumers League (1899)	Washington, D.C.	2500	7	*Bulletin*
American Farm Bureau Federation (1919)	Park Ridge, Ill.	3,297,224	102	*Farm Bureau News*
American Mushroom Institute (1955)	Jennet Square, Penn.	300	5	*Mushroom News*
Equality Groups				
National Association for the Advancement of Colored People (1909)	Washington, D.C.	500,000	132	*Crisis; Report*
National Urban League (1910)	New York	50,000	2000	*The Urban League Review; State of Black America*
National Women's Political Caucus (1971)	Washington, D.C.	75,000	15	*Women's Political Times*
Energy/Environment Groups				
American Petroleum Institute (1919)	Washington, D.C.	7500	500	b
Sierra Club (1892)	San Francisco, Ca.	350,000	185	*Sierra; National News*
Other Groups				
Veterans of Foreign Wars (1899)	Kansas City, Mo.	1,965,000	250	*VFW Magazine; Washington Action*
Common Cause (1970)	Washington, D.C.	250,000	152	*Common Cause*
American Medical Association (1847)	Chicago, Ill.	250,000	b	*Journal; American Medical News*

[a]All data based on reports from individual groups

[b]No data reports

SOURCE: Denise Akey, ed., *Encyclopedia of Associations, 1985* (Detroit: Gale Research Company, 1984).

Association of Manufacturers (NAM) supported by about 13,000 member companies and a 100-employee national staff, and the *United States Chamber of Commerce* (with 400 people in its Washington office and 80,000 member chambers, companies, and individuals). A third important business group, the *Business Roundtable,* is composed of the chief executive officers of the top 200 American corporations.

The largest business corporations, such as American Express and Mobil, have individual lobbying operations in Washington. They and others also join in specialized trade associations that serve their separate industry interests. These trade associations range from the Grocery Manufacturers of America, to the American Bankers Association, to the American Petroleum Institute.

Business interest groups do not, of course, always agree on government policy. Some, such as those which make computers or trade in grains, may favor free trade among nations because foreign sales are important to them. Others, such as the auto companies, favor restrictions on foreign imports because their market is primarily in the U.S. and they want to protect it. Business interest groups are, however, united on some issues like lowering business taxes, lessening government regulation, and weakening labor unions.

Professional

Professional associations are also influential. They include groups like the *American Bar Association* (ABA) and the *American Medical Association* (AMA). The ABA is the professional organization for lawyers. The federal and state governments regularly ask it for recommendations on presidential and gubernatorial nominees for judicial positions. The American Medical Association has considerable power on health-care issues, particularly those that threaten the independence and income of doctors. The AMA remains opposed to a national health insurance system for all Americans, because, it believes, it would lower the quality of health care (see the box on page 252).

Another influential professional organization is the *National Education Association* (NEA), which has nearly 700 staff members headquartered in Washington. NEA represents schoolteachers. Like many other professional organizations, NEA has become more directly involved in political campaigns in recent years.

Labor

On economic issues, organized labor is America's most influential liberal group. Its major national organization, the *American Federation of Labor-Congress of Industrial Organizations (AFL-CIO)*, has an excellent research staff to support labor arguments. However, labor is not as powerful as it has been. Recruiting new workers into unions has lagged in recent years. Also, union strength has fragmented into several national organizations. The AFL-CIO was formed in 1955 by the merger of two rival organizations: the AFL represented crafts (such as carpenters, plumbers, and welders) and the CIO represented industry-wide unions (such as those of the steelworkers and automobile workers). Marked differences still exist in the political outlook of union leaders in the two halves of the AFL-CIO, and two major national unions (the United Mine Workers and the railway brotherhoods) are not affiliated with the AFL-CIO. Many laborers remain unorganized.

Labor's support is central to legislative success on liberal issues such as tax reform, health, housing, and civil rights. But on some issues, particularly international questions, the AFL-CIO is conservative. Its leaders favor restrictions on free trade, and are hardliners in U.S.-Soviet relations. On civil rights, although the AFL-CIO has led the battle to eliminate racial discrimination, it has differed with rights groups by upholding the seniority rights of union workers when these rights have been threatened by affirmative action for minorities.

Farm

Agricultural interest groups are also not as influential as they once were, mainly because there are not as many farmers as there once were. Mechanization and unstable farm prices have taken their toll. Still, a number of interest groups (with sometimes conflicting positions) represent agriculture. The largest (and most conservative), the *American Farm Bureau Federation,* has about three million members. *The Farm Bureau,* representing generally large farms, is aligned with agribusiness and supports less federal regulation. The national *Grange,* the oldest farm organization, provides help for farm families through cooperatives. Its half-million membership has been declining in numbers. The *National Farmers Union* was created as a liberal-leaning labor union for farmers. Two militant interest groups

AFL-CIO president Lane Kirkland (center) walks the picket line with other members of the AFL-CIO executive committee outside of the Eastern Airlines office in Miami in support of Eastern machinists in 1989.

are the *National Farmers Organization* (1956) which provides farmers with collective bargaining on the sale of their products and the *American Agriculture Movement* (1978) which is a more radical movement that favors government intervention to protect family farmers.

In addition to these general farm organizations, there are many others more specialized, some of which are like trade associations, such as the National Corn Growers Association, and some of which are cooperatives, such as the Associated Milk Producers. These groups formed to handle marketing and pricing of their farm products.[10]

Issue-Oriented Groups

A large number of interest groups have been started in recent years to champion causes not covered by others. They do not principally offer their members the prospect of material benefits. These ideological organizations include environmental groups, citizen lobbies, church groups, and "single-issue" groups.

Environmental Groups

The 1970s saw the environment suddenly placed on the public agenda. Environmental interest groups were both a cause and a consequence of the environmental movement. *The Sierra Club,* founded in 1892, is typical of the older interest groups that adopted a more activist stance. Newer interest groups include *Friends of the Earth* and *Environmental Action.* These groups and their supporters were instrumental in lobbying successfully for new environmental programs.

Political attention to environmental issues decreased in the 1980s. However, environmentalists were able to preserve clean air, water, and other environmental programs from the strong attack of the Reagan administration. They were largely responsible for the resignations of James Watt as Secretary of the Interior and Anne Burford as head of the Environmental Protection Agency in the Reagan administration, both of whom were seen as turning back earlier advances.[11] More recently, media attention on the greenhouse effect, acid rain, and oil spills in Alaska have increased public concern for the environment.

Citizen Lobbies

Public interest is how groups of liberal reform organizations describe what they do. These organizations seek to represent the interest of the general public in the policy-making process.

Common Cause, with 250,000 members, Ralph Nader's *Public Citizen,* with 65,000 members, and the *League of Women Voters,* with about 200,000 members, are **citizen lobbies.** They are issue-oriented groups not concerned with a single issue, such as abortion, or a single set of issues, such as the environment, but rather with a range of "good-government" and consumer matters.

Common Cause was formed in 1970 under the leadership of a former Secretary of Health, Education and Welfare, John Gardner. Although it initially received some seed money from wealthy donors, it now depends on members' dues. Common Cause concentrates on "process" issues such as public meetings in Congress and the executive branch, and reform of campaign financing and lobbying regulations.[12]

Probably the best-known citizen lobbyist is Ralph Nader. He became famous in the late 1960s after criticizing the unsafe features of a General Motors car. GM hired a private detective to find information to discredit him. GM was unsuccessful, the company's efforts were exposed, and Nader became a celebrity. He sued GM for damages and collected. Since then, he has formed organizations that have analyzed Congress and numerous federal agencies, lobbied Congress for new consumer-protection laws and recently organized a boycott against Exxon because of the 1989 Alaska oil spill. Nader's operations were initially funded by the money from his lawsuit against General Motors. Today they are financed by Nader's lecture fees and contributions from individuals. Local Nader-affiliated *Public Interest Research Groups (PIRGs)* which push consumer and environmental issues are financed by student activity fees.

Citizen lobbies are weaker than economic interest groups. The financing of citizen lobbies is precarious. It is difficult to organize people and keep them involved enough to pay dues. In addition, donors cannot deduct their contributions for tax purposes if they give to organizations that try to influence legislation. This leads to low salaries and high staff turnover.

Of course, it is difficult to maintain general citizen interest in day-to-day government decisions. In contrast, specific economic groups are always intensely interested in any government action that affects them. In spite of these disadvantages, citizen lobbies have often been highly successful.

Church Groups

Despite the traditional separation of church and state, there is another tradition of religious involvement. Many of America's major political efforts, such as the antislavery movement, civil rights, and antiabortion, have religious underpinnings. Not surpris-

Before it was disbanded in 1989, the Moral Majority exerted significant influence on the American political agenda. The leader of the Moral Majority, Jerry Falwell, is shown on TV hosting the PTL Club while a counselor takes donations and prayer requests over the phone.

ingly, at present a number of religious interest groups—usually liberal on social issues and peace-oriented—have been active at the national level. These include *Friends* (Quakers), the *National Catholic Conference,* and the *National Council of Churches.* The National Conference of Catholic Bishops frequently releases major statements, such as one calling for more fairness in U.S. economic policy and another calling for a freeze in nuclear weapons.

Catholic groups have become active in recent years in support of antiabortion laws. They have been joined by the Moral Majority and other fundamentalist Protestant organizations. The *Moral Majority,* founded by the Reverend Jerry Falwell, not only lobbied for prayer in public schools and against abortion, but also for increased military spending and other conservative causes that, some argued, were not directly connected with religion. It was disbanded in 1989.

An advertisement for the National Rifle Association (NRA).

Single-Issue Groups

Some issue-oriented groups have such a narrow focus that they are labeled **single-issue groups.** People have always grouped around issues they feel intensely about. The *National Rifle Association* (NRA) is a single-issue organization that has lobbied quite successfully against gun control, although its 1989 effort against California's restrictions on semi-automatic weapons met defeat. It has influence because its members are spread throughout the United States and they feel strongly about their issue. They are helped by not scattering shots, so to speak, across a broad range of subjects. Another intense single-issue group is the *Right to Life* organization, which concentrates on ending legal abortions by a constitutional amendment. Members of this and similar antiabortion groups picketed and harassed the Democratic presidential candidate, Mike Dukakis, throughout his campaign. They have increasingly rejected politics-as-usual and, by defining abortion as a sin, have left little room for compromise.[13]

Governments

Local and state, as well as foreign, governments often act as interest groups—powerful ones. As mentioned in Chapter 4, local and state governments lobby Washington directly through such national organizations as the *National Municipal League* and the *National Governors Conference.* In 1985, they focused heavily on defeating President Reagan's budget cuts of federal monies to state and local governments. Similarly, state legislatures have become lobbies, both through their own separate Washington offices and through the *National Conference of State Legislatures.*

Foreign governments and interests are important lobbyists. From Japan to South Africa, governments are among the biggest purchasers of lobbying influence in Washington. In one year South Africa paid Ronald Reagan's former campaign manager, John Sears, over $500,000 for representing its interests. The Japanese corporation Fujitsu paid former Democratic party chairman Robert Strauss's Washington law firm a half million dollars for legal services in 1987. There are also groups of semipermanent interests such as the "Japanese lobby" or the "Israel lobby." These will mobilize around special issues such as import restrictions on computer software or military assistance to the Middle East, bringing a great deal of domestic and foreign pressure to bear on policymakers. Lobbyists acting as agents of foreign governments must register with the Department of Justice.[14]

INTEREST GROUP TACTICS

Some interest groups, especially the issue-oriented ones, use direct-action tactics such as demonstrations, boycotts, and sit-ins. Direct-action tactics will be more fully examined in the next chapter. Here, the focus is on the tactics more commonly used by interest groups and more directly electoral in nature. These include *litigation, public relations, grassroots pressure, political campaign activity,* and *lobbying.*

Litigation

Activists are frequently frustrated by the political system's fragmentation. Favorable action by one branch of the federal government does not guarantee success. But this very fragmentation of power can also be of help. When one branch will not act, citizens may turn to another. Take the NAACP's struggle for civil rights in the 1950s. For a long time, Congress would not act on civil rights legislation. Southerners were very powerful, and in the Senate they blocked passage of such legislation. The NAACP turned to the courts, with great success. As the Supreme Court said, "For such a group, association for litigation may be the most effective form of political association."[15]

Litigation—the process of bringing lawsuits—has become a highly effective tactic for issue-oriented groups. They have filed suits to protest utility-rate increases and have brought court actions against federal agencies. Litigation offers a way to protect citizen rights inde-

★MADD Grassroots Lobbying

MADD (Mothers Against Drunk Driving) was founded by a California housewife, Mrs. Carrie Lightner, after her thirteen-year-old daughter was killed by a drunk driver. The group pushed for mandatory sentences for drunk drivers and for raising the minimum drinking age, pointing out that while teenagers made up 10 percent of the nation's drivers, they accounted for 21 percent of alcohol-related deaths. By June 1984, MADD had gotten a bill before Congress that would reduce federal highway funds to states that failed to enact a minimum drinking age of twenty-one.

At first, the measure was given little chance of passing. President Reagan opposed it and Senate conservatives saw it as federal interference in states' rights. MADD dramatized the drunk-driving statistics in repeated appearances by victims and their relatives on television and before Congressional committees. The group gathered the support of twenty-six other organizations, including the national PTA, the American Medical Association, and Allstate Insurance. The groups met constantly, concentrated on key senators, and had their grassroots supporters write and telephone their congressmen.

In short order, the president reversed himself and the bill passed both houses of Congress overwhelmingly. Why? The president apparently saw a popular campaign issue on which he was on the wrong side. And in Congress it had become "an apple pie issue," which few dared oppose. MADD demonstrated it had changed popular and political opinion, and official Washington had little choice but to follow.

pendent of Congress or the executive department. It is a form of self-help. Now not only citizen lobbies but economic interests as well are forming tax-exempt foundations to fight government regulations in the courts. President Reagan's controversial former secretary of the interior, James Watt, was appointed to that post after having headed up a conservative legal foundation which, among other things, opposed environmental groups.

Public Relations

Interest groups can mount advertising campaigns and **public relations** to affect public opinion. Individual corporations buy paid advertising on public issues. Mobil spends one-third of its $16.5 million annual advertising budget, not to sell gasoline, but to propangandize on public issues that affect its business.[16] Often the most effective advertisements are those in which economic interests are not identified. For example, companies that make bottles and cans may advertise through a "front" organization, telling people not to litter and urging them to pick up bottles and cans. The implication is that there would be no need for legislation prohibiting no-return bottles if people refrained from littering.

Interest groups also spend lots of money on public relations for favorable media coverage shaping public opinion. In 1982, in their successful campaign against a withholding of income taxes on interest and dividends similar to what is already done for wages, the American Bankers Association launched a large propaganda campaign. As reported in the *Washington Monthly:*

> *By November the Bankers News Weekly was offering ABA members complimentary kits, wrapped in plastic, with all the tools to tickle the public glands. The kits contained posters for bank vestibules ("CONGRESS WANTS A PIECE OF YOUR SAVINGS. WHAT THEY NEED IS A PIECE OF YOUR MIND"), sample press releases ([name], [title], of [name of bank], told the [name of organization] that the new withholding provision is a "consumer volcano that's about to erupt"), sample speeches ("Literally, the government will be picking the taxpayers' pockets . . ."), advertisements, sample letters to congressmen ("As a senior citizen . . . I think this is an invasion of my privacy!"), letters to the editor from bankers and consumers, and a pre-fab op-ed piece ("This should be retyped on your bank's letterhead and sent with a personal note to your newspaper's editor"). An enclosed order blank allowed bankers to send away for zillions of preprinted, preaddressed postcards for depositors to send to their members of Congress.[17]*

Advertising and other forms of mass communication designed to influence public opinion are very expensive. Thus, public-interest groups are generally less able to use mass propaganda than are special-interest groups. As Chapter 10 will show, minority, women's, and other issue-oriented groups are left to demonstrate to dramatize their demands and gain media coverage for free.

Grassroots Pressure

Many interest groups launch **grassroots campaigns** in which group members flood their representatives with appeals to back a certain position. These appeals sometimes contain threats that the representative will not be reelected if he or she opposes the group's position. A telephone conversation with a public official or a key assistant is even more effective than a letter. *A personal conversation is the most effective.* (See the box on page 259.)

Interest groups often arrange to have constituents talk to their member in Washington. This method demonstrates intensity of feeling, and it can provide persuasive information on the impact of an issue in the member's home district or state. Personal lobbying of this kind is often applied to members of Congress while they are visiting their districts. It is often easier to see members of Congress while they are at home, and many constituents feel more confident on their home ground than they do in Washington.

Widespread geographic distribution of group members can make the grassroots pressure more powerful because more representatives can be contacted by their own constituents. Other groups use technologies including computers and laser printers in direct mailings targeted to rented mailing lists. In one impressive case, the Motion Picture Association—in an unsuccessful lobbying effort to force home video manufacturers to pay copyright royalties to movie makers—delivered an estimated 20,000 letters to congressional offices within a few weeks. The letters looked as if they had been individually written on the constituent's own letterhead.

Another example of grassroots pressure occurred on the 1986 tax reform bill. Its early drafts contained major restrictions on tax-exempt municipal bonds. The interest group representing bankers handling these bonds, the Public Securities Association (PSA), organized a grassroots campaign in the districts of key members of the House Ways and Means Committee. It hired Robert Beckel, former campaign manager for Walter Mondale's presidential effort, to use campaign techniques to organize in the districts of these members.

Beckel sent his organizers into the districts to mobilize people who benefited from the bonds. Local public officials, hospital administrators, construction unions, and businesspeople developing downtown areas were informed of the provisions and how they would be economically harmed. They were asked to contact their representative. Direct mail campaigns were targeted at people who bought these bonds. The results, while not a complete victory for PSA, was a substantial moderation in the original proposals affecting municipal bonds.[18]

Political Action Committees (PACs)

Ninety percent of what goes on here during a session is decided on the previous election day. The main drift of legislation is decided then: it is out of our control. There is simply no substitute for electing the right folks and defeating the wrong folks.[19]

—a lobbyist

One of the principal arenas for interest groups are political campaigns. Political campaigns require money, lots of it. The more powerful the office, the more money it takes to run. One California political figure, the late Jesse Unruh, said that "*Money is the mother's milk of politics.*" Political campaigns depend on contributions, often from interest groups. Campaign contributions are a legal instrument of influence over elected public officials.

Corporations and labor unions are prohibited from using regular operating funds for donations. But both corporations and unions can set up separate **political action committees (PACs)** to solicit voluntary funds for political campaigns. Business and unions contribute large sums of money to political campaigns through these "voluntary" contributions. In both cases, pressure may be applied for the contributions.

PACs are not new in American politics. Their model was created in 1955 when the newly formed AFL-CIO started the Committee on Political Education (COPE). Through its national and local units, COPE not only contributed money to pro-union candidates, but also organized get-out-the-vote drives and sought to politically educate its members.

The expansion in business PACs occurred in the late 1970s as an unintended result of campaign financing reforms. These laws, backed by labor, put strict limits on individual donations and provided for public disclosure. Before this legislation, money could legally go into campaigns in large amounts as individual donations

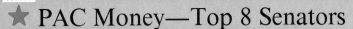

★ PAC Money—Top 8 Senators

(1987–1988 Election Cycle)

1. Lloyd Bentsen (D-TX) $2,596,145
2. Pete Wilson (R-CA) $2,403,240
3. David Durenberger (R-MN) $1,772,900
4. Frank Lautenberg (D-NJ) $1,642,990
5. James Sasser (D-TN) $1,634,765
6. Donald Riegle (D-MI) $1,529,940
7. Jeff Bingaman (D-NM) $1,423,742
8. John Heinz (R-PA) $1,408,912

SOURCE: *Common Cause News,* March 1989, pp. 5–6.

from wealthy corporate leaders. There was thus little need for business PACs.

The reforms backfired, however. Rather than reducing the influence of large "special-interest" contributions, they have increased them. Corporations and trade associations organized PACs that more effectively channeled their money and influence into campaigns than individuals had been able to do. The number of PACs mushroomed, from 608 in 1974 to 4211 in 1987. There were five times as many corporate and trade association PACs, compared with union PACs. Spending also skyrocketed. In 1974, interest-group donations to congressional candidates totaled $12.5 million. By the 1988 elections, PAC contributions to House and Senate candidates reached over $151 million. Some 29 percent of the funds raised by all federal candidates in 1985–86 came from PACs. Whereas union PACs had outspent corporate PACs in the 1976 elections, by 1980 business and trade donations were far greater, and the gap has grown. One estimate showed business groups outspending labor by three to one in 1986.[20] (See Figure 9.1 on page 248).

Every election cycle brings more expensive congressional elections. In 1986, candidates for the House and Senate spent a record $450 million, a 20-percent rise from 1984. (They spent $458 million in 1988.) To win a seat in the Senate cost about $3.1 million, and getting to the House cost around $355,000. (Of course, money doesn't guarantee victory. The biggest spender in 1986 for a Senate seat—from California—spent $11.8 million and lost. In 1988, the biggest spender was also for the Senate in California. Pete Wilson spent $13 million and kept his seat.) PACs gave a good deal more to incumbents than to challengers. (See the box on page 263.) Incumbents in both houses got nearly $90 million from PACs; challengers got $19.2 million. This meant that *some 70 percent of PAC money went to incumbents, thereby decreasing the competitiveness of election campaigns.*[21] In part because there were more Democratic incumbents than Republicans, the Democrats depended more on PACs than did Republicans, and spent more than Republicans. As this chapter's case study will show, the Democrats were very active in encouraging PACs to look in their direction.

Causes of PACs

The rapid growth of PACs was caused by several factors. Clearly the campaign reform law in 1974, making it more difficult to raise large gifts from a handful of wealthy supporters, forced candidates to broaden their financial bases. PACs became an important way of reaching potential contributors. The weakened condition of political parties left gaps that PACs could fill. Like traditional parties, PACs now represent certain loyal constituencies; they fund primary and general elections; and they even "discipline" the votes of representatives by grouping them around a consistent set of interests.

The growth of PACs reflect a basic fact: there are today simply more groups seeking government's attention. *As government programs grow, more interests are affected and the response is to organize to lobby for or against these programs.* The more groups there are, the weaker the impact of any single one. PACs seem to help by providing more direct access to an elected official than do broad based political parties. And PACs can focus all their attention on single issues with the backing of narrow but devoted constituencies.[22]

PACs have ways to contribute over the $5000 limit to any congressional candidate. For example, AMPAC, the PAC of the American Medical Association, sponsors polls for candidates (and discounts their value) and does "opposition research" on the candidate's opponent. All this is over and above the $5000 cash contribution. After a campaign, a successful candidate is likely to get a call from a lobbyist offering to help pay any leftover campaign debt. Another way to channel money to officials is to pay them speaking fees. Senator Robert Dole (R., Kan.), Minority Leader of the Senate, has said jokingly about such *honoraria,* or speaking fees, "Some of us are uncomfortable taking honoraria. I am uncomfortable taking campaign contributions. So, I compromised; I decided to take both."[23] (See Chapter 11.)

Consequences of PACs

What does this money buy? It at least buys access, the right to talk to the official. For example, a prominent Washington lobbyist, Robert C. McCandless, has said, "We don't just want to give money to people. We want to get them involved in a dialogue. The only way you get a favorable hearing is to deal with his problem. What he or she has is two problems, getting reelected and having an income supplement for his children."[24]

The implicit threat of using money against an incumbent can also have a strong negative influence. Incumbents do not like hard reelection campaigns. When a wealthy interest group supports one side of an issue, money may affect how members vote, even if no money actually changes hands. If a member votes "wrong," the interest group might finance a serious opponent in an upcoming election. Thus, the implied *threat* of money being used against an incumbent and the implied *offer* of a financial contribution to the incumbent may both affect decision making.

Reform of PACs

An attempt at campaign reform occurred in 1987 when then-Majority Leader Robert Byrd of West Virginia pushed a bill that would have provided federal funds to Senate candidates who voluntarily accepted a ceiling on the campaign funds they raised. The bill would have put a cap on PAC contributions as well. The measure was bitterly opposed by Republicans, who filibustered it. The last of a record seven attempts to end the debate—by cloture vote—failed and the measure died.

The Republicans came up with their own reform on June 29, 1989. President Bush proposed to eliminate corporate, union, and trade PACs, allow ideological PACs (but reduce their contribution limits from $5,000 to $2,500), and enhance the role of political parties in spending money on congressional campaigns. Democrats responded that the package was just designed to help Republicans, it would hurt Democratic incumbents' advantages in raising money from PACs, and it would emphasize the role of parties (where Republicans had the advantage). Few thought the Bush proposals were going to become law anytime soon.[25]

Clearly the increased spending by PACs has affected Congress. One member remarked, "It is a simple fact of life that when big money enters the political arena, big obligations are entertained." There also may be relatively little that can be done to block the impact of money and the creative ways campaigning politicians use to get it. As one lobbyist cynically concluded, "Trying to cleanse the

★ The Five Commandments of Lobbying

In meeting with elected officials, lobbyists follow a set of "informal rules":

1. *Demonstrate a constituent interest.* One of the best ways to ensure attention is to show the impact on the representative's voters.

2. *Be well informed.* Officials want information in return for the time and attention they give.

3. *Be well balanced.* Compromise is inevitable in legislation. The lobbyist who presents both sides leaves the official with the impression that he or she has looked at all sides of the question and then arrived at a conclusion.

4. *Keep it short and sweet.* The challenge is to present the greatest amount of relevant information in the shortest time in the nicest way.

5. *Leave a written summary of the case.* It relieves officials of the necessity of taking notes and ensures that the correct information stays behind.

SOURCE: Adapted from Lester Milbrath, *The Washington Lobbyists* (Rand McNally, 1963), pp. 220–26.

political system from the evils of money is like writing a law ordering teenagers not to think about sex . . . You don't need a law, you need a lobotomy."

Federal law already prevents corporations from using regular operating funds to contribute to a candidate for federal office. Federal laws also prohibit labor unions from spending money that members have not voluntarily donated for political candidates. In the past, there were many violations of these laws. Former President Nixon received over three quarters of a million dollars in illegal corporate funds for his 1972 reelection campaign. Corporations **"laundered"** this illegal corporate money by giving extra "bonuses" to their officers and then requiring them to make campaign contributions. Federal laws have been tightened to prevent such abuses.

Less successful efforts have been made to restrain PAC influence. Various bills have sought to limit the amount a candidate could receive from all PACs in an election and the amount each PAC could give to a candidate. Their sponsors worried that corporations in the same industry (say, steel or energy) could separately contribute to a candidate. When combined, these contributions would be extremely large and would give the industry great influence.

The previous reforms designed to reduce the influence of wealthy interest groups have clearly failed. The role of such groups through PACs has increased. As long as these PACs are *a* factor in financing political candidates rather than *the* factor, they have a legitimate role to play. When they cross this narrow line, as many fear their rapid growth indicates, then more restrictions on their spending will be needed to keep democratic access open to the rest of us.

Lobbying

Those seeking to influence state legislatures used to gather in the lobbies just outside of the legislative chambers. They came to be called "lobbyists," and their activity was called "lobbying." **Lobbying** is the effort to influence the decisions of government.

Interest groups influence policy decisions in a variety of ways. They may help people sympathetic to their interests get appointed to administer programs important to them. They may quietly get involved in the election of officers of the House and Senate. In addition, interest groups may promote studies and seminars on government policies. Access is key for an interest group. A campaign contributor will often say: "I don't want any special promise from you; all I want is the right to come and talk to you when I need to." This seemingly modest request may well prove critical. *Access is power.*

Who are the lobbyists? Whether lawyers or consultants, many of the top ones have worked in the executive or legislative departments. As a recent congressional report stated: "a survey of former Members of both houses of Congress showed that 80 are currently registered as lobbyists. But of registered lobbyists with congressional experience, nine in ten are former staff members, primarily committee staff members."[26]

Effective lobbyists value their networks of contacts. These may develop into **subgovernments,** made up of *iron triangles* of interest groups, bureaucrats, and members of Congress on particular committees or subcommittees, all focused on one set of issues (see the box on page 269). Usually the less public a decision, the more power these triangles of networks have over it.

In a farewell address shortly before leaving office, President Reagan described an "iron triangle" a bit differently. He denounced the alliance of interest groups, congressional committees, and **the media** for preventing any action against the deficit. The president's noteworthy change in the traditional definition was to replace executive agencies, over which he presided, with the media, a traditional rival

New York's Senate lobby is filled with lobbyists discussing the day's legislation as newsmen and tourists look on.

of chief executives. This, of course, reduced the president's responsibility.[27]

The lobbying influence of an interest group depends on several factors. Its grassroots effort, propaganda, and political campaign activity are essential to its lobbying. But other things make a difference, too. *Size* can be very important. The AFL-CIO, for example, can mobilize its large constituency on labor legislation.

The *intensity* of the interest group can compensate for size. Even a relatively small group can be effective if its members are intensely committed and narrowly focused. One of the reasons why the National Rifle Association is so powerful is that its members are vigorously and bitterly opposed to any form of gun control. An interest group that speaks only on limited issues of special concern to its members will have great influence in its narrow arena. Often large groups cannot act at all on issues that divide their members. The National Association of Manufacturers, for example, cannot lobby on free trade because its members disagree on this issue.

Geography can influence the effectiveness of interest groups. Some interest groups, such as importers, are so concentrated in specific regions that they wield little influence with most members of Congress who have few importers in their home states or districts. On the other hand, when Chrysler was seeking government loan guarantees, Lee Iaccoca successfully followed Tip O'Neill's advice to make sure that each member of the House and Senate was lobbied by people from his or her own home district (see the box on page 272).

Reliable information enhances an interest group's influence. The relationship between a lobbyist and a policymaker is not a one-way

★ The Military Veterans' Iron Triangle

The military veterans' lobby is a showcase "iron triangle." In annual congressional hearings, "veterans present their legislative 'wish lists' in an atmosphere so friendly that it is hard to tell the congressmen from the witnesses" one reporter noted. And it's a bountiful harvest that Congress approves.

The newest cabinet department, Veterans' Affairs, has a $26 billion annual budget. Only the Defense Department and Postal Service have more employees. The VA's hospital system is the nation's largest. Preference in federal jobs, the "GI Bill" education program, pensions, and subsidized life insurance and home loans illustrate the benefits.

The first leg of the triangle is 27 million veterans and their powerful lobbying groups, the American Legion and the Veterans of Foreign Wars. The vets' organizations enjoy free office space in VA facilities.

In Congress, veterans' committees are chaired by senior members who anchor the congressional leg of the triangle. Veterans' bills come to the House floor under rules that ward off amendments, so members must vote for the committee—which they do overwhelmingly with little debate—or vote "against" veterans.

Though often blasted as a massive bureaucracy by veterans entangled in it, the Department of Veterans' Affairs completes the triangle. The VA is often headed by a former national commander of a veterans' organization.

The veterans' triangle of lobbyists, congressional committees, and executive departments easily fights off challenges. Several years ago, the National Academy of Sciences called for merging VA hospitals into the community hospital system. The proposal was hammered from all sides. The NAS staff director said ruefully, "I didn't really appreciate . . . how powerful the veterans' organizations turned out to be."

SOURCES: Bill Keller, "The Veterans' Lobby as an 'Iron Triangle,'" reprinted from *Congressional Quarterly Weekly Report* June 10, 1984, pp. 1627–34; Tom Watson, "Veterans' Lobbies Showing New Unity on Hill,' *CQ Weekly Report,* Sept. 12, 1987, pp. 2181–84.

street. The lobbyist may achieve something from the relationship—the policymaker's support for the interest group position. But the policymaker may also get something from the relationship—reliable information. Some interest groups do first-rate research on issues. Information is used by policymakers in making decisions and in justifying positions already taken. The Chamber of Commerce staff in Washington is highly regarded for using reliable information to their advantage.

LIMITS ON INTEREST GROUP POWER

Interest groups are powerful but far from being all-powerful. *Events, leaders, media,* and the *laws* all limit the power of interest groups.

The combined impact of events and leaders can be seen in the first years of President Lyndon Johnson's administration. After Johnson took office following John F. Kennedy's assassination on November 22, 1963, Congress adopted a number of proposals that had been gathering dust for years. This flurry of legislation was partly due to

In 1965, President Lyndon B. Johnson signed into law the Medicare legislation that had previously been proposed by President Truman (right) and President Kennedy.

the national mood of sympathy for the slain president's recommendations, especially his civil rights proposals. But it was also due to Johnson's skill as a former Senate majority leader, in getting Congress to follow his leadership. For example, Kennedy had recommended health care for the elderly to Congress in 1961 in the form of medicare, but medical and insurance groups blocked its passage. The same groups still fought the proposal after Johnson became president. Yet Johnson was able to get medicare passed. A strong reformist government with a united party behind it could, and did, limit the power of interest groups.

A more recent example of events overwhelming the power of interest groups can be seen in the Exxon *Valdez* oil spill off the coast of Alaska in spring 1989. The massive 10 million gallon spill and the bumbling clean-up efforts produced a change in public opinion. Proposed legislation to open up the Arctic National Wildlife Refuge to expanded oil drilling was a casualty of the spill. It became, as one senator put it, "politically foolish to push legislation now. . . ."[28]

Reforms such as open meetings of public agencies and full disclosure of financial information by public officials allows the press to be a watchdog, alerting the public to questionable practices by interest groups. But ironically, public exposure is a two-edged sword. For example, during congressional consideration of the 1986 tax reform bill, holding committee meetings in public frequently resulted in posturing by representatives and stalemates. Members who had made promises to various interest groups could not make the compromises needed to get the legislation passed while the lobbyists were watching them. Only when the Senate Finance and House Ways and Means committees went behind closed doors were the chairmen able to control their committees and forge a consensus. Here what seemed to be a "reform"—public committee meetings—was used by the special interests it had aimed to weaken. (See the case study in Chapter 12.)

The law regulating lobbying has little effect. This law, first adopted in 1946, only requires interest groups to register with the House and Senate if lobbying is their "principal purpose." The legal definition is also restricted in another way: a lobbyist is defined as "one who solicits, collects, or receives contributions where one of the main purposes is to influence the passage or defeat of congressional legislation and the intended method of accomplishing that purpose is through conversation with members of Congress."

Such narrow definitions prompted one observer to say that federal lobbying laws have "more loopholes than a spiral notebook."[29] Furthermore, the Supreme Court has held that grassroots lobbying is not

★ Tip O'Neill's Advice on Lobbying

When a few years ago Lee Iacocca, chairman of Chrysler, found his company in deep financial trouble, he appealed to the government for loan guarantees. One of his first visits seeking support was to House Speaker Tip O'Neill. Although O'Neill was a liberal Democrat who might be expected to oppose a "bailout" of big business, he offered Iacocca the following advice:

"Tell me, how many people in my district work for Chrysler or one of its suppliers?"

"I have no idea," [Iacocca] replied.

"Find out," I told him. "That's the key to this thing. And do the same for every district in the country. Make up a list, and have your employees and dealers in each district call and write letters to their own member of Congress. You've heard my famous phrase that all politics is local. A lot of jobs will be lost if Chrysler goes under and believe me, no member wants to see something like that happen in his district."

SOURCE: Tip O'Neill, *Man of the House* (New York: St. Martin's, 1987), p. 388.

covered by the act. Most economic interest groups are not formed for the primary purpose of lobbying. Labor unions, trade associations, and chambers of commerce, for example, are formed to provide largely nonpolitical services to their members. Many interest groups, then, argue that lobbying is not their principal purpose. Hence only about 2000 bother to register. Virtually all interest groups take advantage of the exemption for grassroots lobbying, which is always a large part of any major interest group's activities.

In November 1988, President Reagan vetoed an ethics measure that would have widened the number of elected and appointed officials forbidden to engage in "revolving-door" lobbying for companies they had dealt with while in the government. For the first time, members of Congress were to be covered. Numerous Reagan administration officials, including Reagan's own Attorney General, Edwin Meese III, had been investigated for real or apparent conflicts of interest. These larger problems motivating the vetoed bill remained.

New laws regulating lobbying are needed if there is to by any regulation at all. The old law is an empty shell. Only four cases have ever been prosecuted under it. Congress is faced with the alternative of continuing an ineffective law or adopting a new one that will give an accurate picture of the influence of interest groups in the American political system. The recent ethics scandals in Congress may have set the stage for another round of reforms. But, as the following case illustrates, the role of interest group money is unlikely to be eliminated.

★ CASE STUDY

PACs Under Pressure

For Tony Coelho, politics is big business. As Chairman of the Democratic Congressional Campaign Committee ("the D triple C"), the campaign organization for Democrats in the House of Representatives, he pushed business PACs to back Democrats despite their fondness for Republican policies. Congressman Coelho's success lends a new twist to a common perception of PACs and how they supposedly buy and control Congress. As players in the political game, PACs are not only *pressure* groups, they are *pressured* groups as well.[30]

Coelho to the Rescue

In 1980, Coelho was an ambitious junior congressman from California. In his youth he had wanted to become a priest. He was the first in his Portuguese immigrant family to go to college, where the death of John F. Kennedy prompted Coelho to pursue a career in helping people. In 1964 he was diagnosed as having epilepsy, and Church law prohibited epileptics from becoming priests. Coelho's handicap led him, through a job with comedian Bob Hope, to politics. Beginning as a

Tony Coehlo

young intern, Coelho rose to become the chief aide of his local congressman and eventually ran for the seat when his mentor retired.

Coelho had demonstrated his fundraising abilities in the 1980 elections, both for himself and for fellow Democrats. The defeat for reelection of the DCCC chairman left the position empty, and the party's defeats in 1980 had left its treasury bare. Majority Leader Jim Wright nominated the second-term congressman for the position of DCCC chairman.

The Democratic setbacks in the 1980 Reagan victory (losing thirty-three seats in the House) ironically helped Coelho raise money: "Demo-

crats were afraid that with the polling, television, and mail that money could buy, Republicans might topple them from power at last." (p. 52) The Democratic majority in the House was in danger and the leadership gave Coelho their full backing.

Coelho's first task was to make the DCCC competitive with its Republican opposition—the NRCC (National Republican Congressional Committee). Traditionally, both parties had relied on a small number of wealthy individuals for financial support. With the 1974 campaign reforms, Republicans eagerly embraced aggressive fundraising. They built up their donor base with sophisticated direct-mail tactics, targeting specific groups to maximize their efforts. They also worked the business PACs. By 1980, the NRCC income was thirteen times as great as the DCCC's. House Democrats were in trouble.

To keep majority control in the House, Democrats had to slow the flow of business money to Republican challengers. In the 1980 elections, challengers—almost all Republicans—received $5.9 million from corporate PACs and $3.7 million from ideological PACs. Business interest groups were clearly growing more numerous, wealthier, and bolder, especially where they sensed political weakness. One leading PAC, the National Association of Realtors, gave $1 million to Republican candidates in 1980—more than double the funds given to Democrats.

Coelho's strategy assumed that business PACs were more interested in their businesses than in the Republican party. Even though the Republicans might be closer to the ideological positions of the corporate PAC leaders, they were still the minority party. Thus they were in no position to look after business interests. Democrats were.

Tony Coehlo (right) prepares to speak on behalf of the homeless.

PACs Date Democrats

Coelho reorganized the DCCC to market Democrats to PACs. He created a new position responsible for getting more money to candidates. He established forums where PAC directors could informally talk with candidates. To these "meat markets" (named after the college mixers they resembled), Coelho invited influential Democrats like House Ways and Means Committee Chairman Dan Rostenkowski. His presence made the point that the Democratic leadership was interested in what happened to the junior, more endangered candidates of the party. The message was clear—be nice to our vulnerable candidates and we incumbent power brokers will be good to business.

Coelho's marketing campaign fell short in 1982. The Reagan tide from 1980 was still too strong. In the 1982 elections, the Republican candidates received more from PACs and the Democrats got less than in 1980. Despite PAC money, the 1982 recession was more important to voters. Unemployment reached double digits and support for Republican candidates dwindled. Republicans lost twenty-six seats in the House, and the business PACs, which had overinvested in Republican candidates, were left exposed backing the wrong horses in Congress.

Coelho turned up the pressure. He emphasized that he would offer the PACs honest assessments of political races, unlike what the Republicans had done in promising victories in 1982. He also reminded business PACs that there was no getting around the Democrats. As one business PAC leader said: Coelho's ". . . argument is that we should always go with the winner, that we should never do anything that isn't related to our business interests." (p. 77)

The 1984 election brought good news for Coelho. Even though the economy was rebounding and Reagan was up in the polls, business PAC support for Republicans declined. The realtors' PAC, for example, decreased the amount of money given to Republicans slightly, but it increased amounts to Democrats by 73 percent, to $877,349. Coelho summed up the situation after the 1984 elections this way: "'At the same time they (business PACs) were killing us they were coming to us for legislative solutions. . . . Democrats are going to retain control of the House for the remainder of this century. . . . We have the advantage. We're the incumbents. They have to beat us.'" (p. 80)

By the 1986 elections, the success of Coelho's game plan was clearer. The Democrats recaptured the Senate. PACs had given $84.4 million to House candidates and Democrats got 63 percent of that total. House Democratic incumbents who ran for reelection in 1986 received $41 million from PACs compared to the $25 million received by the Republicans. (By 1988, House Democrats received double the amount from PACs as Republicans did.) PACs had helped keep Democrats in office, in the majority, and in the chairmen's seats of vital committees. PACs as a group remained more interested in keeping on the right side of those with power than in promoting the Republicans' free-market ideas.

A Shakedown?

The PACs almost seem to have been blackmailed by incumbent politicians. According to a study conducted by the Center for Responsive Politics after the 1986 elections, PAC directors and lobbyists complained privately that they felt victimized by the system of campaign financing. The study indicated that the PACs did not like fundraising, "yet the fear of losing access compels them to continue. . . ." One lobbyist quoted a senator saying: "I've had people who contribute to my campaign, and they get access; the others get good government." (p. 89)

This is not to say that the results are a no-win situation for the PACs. The donors have become a "second constituency" for House members, helped not by virtue of their residence but by virtue of their currency. Does this mean representatives are selling their votes? Coelho denies this but admits that donors affect legislation:

Take housing. Take anything you want. If you are spending all your time calling up different people that you're involved with, that are friends of yours, that you have to raise $50,000, you all of a sudden, in your mind, you're in effect saying, 'I'm not going to go out and develop this new housing bill that may get the Realtors or may get builders or may get the unions upset. I've got to raise the fifty thousand; I've got to do that.' That isn't a sellout. It's basically that you're not permitted to go out and do your creativity. I think that's bad. (pp. 108–9)

The final chapter in this story of money and members may have occurred at the end of May 1989. After reports in the press surfaced that he had benefited from a loan by a banker interested in legislation before Congress, Tony Coelho resigned his seat. A few days later the man who had appointed him to head the DCCC, James Wright, resigned as Speaker of the House. He had been accused of financial misconduct.

WRAP-UP

The First Amendment safeguards the rights of Americans to organize and to petition their government. Participation in interest groups is an important way for citizens to exercise those rights. The fragmentation of power in our governmental system—designed to prevent the concentration of political power in too few hands and to restrict majority control—is one reason why there are so many interest groups in this country. Another reason is the increasing complexity of modern life, and the consequent increasing role of government in the economy and in our lives.

There are a wide range of interest groups using a variety of tactics, with arguable impacts on American politics. Clearly PACs have increased the amounts of money going into election campaigns and have reinforced the ability of incumbents to remain incumbents. It's not as clear that their lobbyists now call the shots in the halls of power. The case study suggests that these PACs serve the interests of elected officials at least as much as the reverse is true. This is more due to power limiting power rather than any adequate legal regulation on lobbying or PAC campaign spending.

Interest groups are probably not as powerful or evil as their critics maintain. They perform important functions of linking some citizens to the political system. They have increased their influence as the power of others, such as political parties, has decreased. The flaw of these groups lies outside them, in the interests not represented at all or with very unequal influence when they are represented. Interest groups are an instrument of power remaining in the hands of the powerful.

Key Terms

interest groups (p. 246)
pluralism (p. 249)
citizen lobbies (p. 256)
single-issue groups (p. 257)
litigation (p. 259)
public relations (p. 260)
grassroots campaigns (p. 261)

political action committees
 (PACs) (p. 262)
"laundered" money (p. 266)
lobbying (p. 267)
subgovernments (p. 267)
the media (p. 267)

Suggested Readings

Berry, Jeffrey, *The Interest Group Society* (Glenview, Ill.: Scott, Foresman, 1984).

Ciglar, Allan J. and Burdett A. Loomis, *Interest Group Politics,* 2nd ed. (Washington, D.C.: Congressional Quarterly Press, 1986).

McFarland, Andrew S., *Common Cause: Lobbying in the Public Interest* (Bridgeport, Conn.: Chatham, 1984).

Montgomery, Kathryn C., *Target: Prime Time: Advocacy Groups and the Struggle Over Entertainment Television* (New York: Oxford University Press, 1989).

Vogel, David, *Fluctuating Fortunes: The Political Power of Business in America* (New York: Basic Books, 1989).

Endnotes

[1]As quoted by Philip M. Stern, *The Best Congress Money Can Buy* (New York: Pantheon Books, 1988, pp. 100–101.

[2]Alex de Tocqueville, *Democracy in America,* Vol. 2, Henry Reeve, trans. (New York: Schocken Books, 1961), p. 128.

[3]Gabriel A. Almond and Sidney Verba, *The Civic Cultures: Political Attitudes and Democracy in Five Nations* (Princeton, NJ: Princeton University Press, 1963), pp. 194, 203.

[4]This section owes much to Jeffrey M. Berry, *The Interest Group Society,* 2nd ed., (Glenview, IL: Scott, Foresman, 1988).

[5]See David B. Truman, *The Governmental Process* (New York: Knopf, 1951), p. 37 and Robert A. Dahl, *Who Governs?* (New Haven, CT: Yale University Press, 1961).

[6]See Sidney Verba and Norman H. Nie, *Participation in America* (New York: Harper and Row, 1972).

[7]E. E. Schattschneider, *The Semisovereign People* (New York: Holt, Rinehart and Winston, 1960), p. 35.

[8]See Robert Michaels, *Political Parties: A Sociological Study of the Oligarchical Tendencies of Modern Democracy,* Eden and Cedar Paul, trans. (New York: The Free Press, 1966).

[9]Theodore J. Lowi, *The End of Liberalism,* rev. ed. (New York: Norton, 1979) p. xvi.

[10]See Norman J. Ornstein and Shirley Elder, *Interest Groups, Lobbying and Policymaking* (Washington, D.C.: Congressional Quarterly Press, 1978).

[11]An interesting case involving environmental issues can be found in Christopher J. Boss, *Pesticides and Politics,* (Pittsburgh: University of Pittsburgh Press, 1987).

[12]Andrew S. McFarland, *Common Cause: Lobbying in the Public Interest* (Chatham, N.J.: Chatham House, 1984), pp. 93–107.

[13]Marjorie Randon Hershey, "Direct Action and the Abortion Issue," in Burdett A. Loomis and Allan J. Ciglar, *Interest Group Politics,* 2nd ed. (Washington, D.C.: Congressional Quarterly Press, 1986), pp. 27–45.

[14]See Edward Tivnan, *Lobby: Jewish Political Power and American Foreign Policy* (New York: Simon & Schuster, 1987).

[15]*N.A.A.C.P.* v. *Button,* 371 U.S. 415 (1963).

[16]See Robert G. Meadow, "Political Advertising as Grassroots Lobbying: New Forms of Corporate Political Participation," *Social Science Journal* (October 1983), Vol. 20, no. 4:49–63.

[17]*Washington Monthly* (May 1983), Vol. 15, no. 3, p. 38.

[18]Gary Wasserman, co-author of the book, worked in Mr. Beckel's firm on this campaign.

[19]Donald R. Mathews, *U.S. Senators and Their World* (Chapel Hill, NC: University of North Carolina Press, 1960), p. 193.

[20]P. M. Stern, p. 24 and *The Washington Post,* March 5, 1989.

[21]David S. Broder, "Three Keys to Incumbent Lock," *The Washington Post,* December 7, 1988.

[22]Herbert E. Alexander, "The PAC Phenomenon," Ed. Zuckerman, *Almanac of Federal PACs, 1988,* (Washington, D.C.: Amward Publications, 1988), pp. vi–x.

[23]*The Wall Street Journal,* April 24, 1984.

[24]*Ibid.*

[25]See *Congressional Quarterly,* July 1, 1989, pp. 1648–49.

[26]*Post-Employment Restrictions Act of 1988, Report together with additional and supplemental views.* (Report on HR 5043), p. 57.

[27]*The Washington Post,* December 14, 1988.

[28]*The Washington Post,* April 10, 1989.

[29]Charles Peters, *How Washington Really Works* (Reading, MA: Addison-Wesley, 1980), p. 4.

[30]The case study is adapted from Brooks Jackson, *Honest Graft* (Alfred A. Knopf, New York, 1988). The page numbers in the text refer directly to this book.)

CHAPTER 10

Political Movements

In late 1964, despite the passage of the historic Civil Rights Act, hundreds of thousands of blacks in the Deep South still could not vote. Only 19 percent of voting-age blacks were registered to vote in Alabama while a mere 6 percent were registered in Mississippi. Judicial solutions were slow in coming. In his 1965 State of the Union Message President Johnson promised to submit voting legislation, but its timing and eventual passage was uncertain. Dr. Martin Luther King, Jr., a young minister from Atlanta who as head of the Southern Christian Leadership Conference led the civil rights movement, wished to assure its speedy enactment.

Voting was the immediate goal of the civil rights movement at the time, and civil disobedience was the chosen method. The movement saw nonviolence as likely to cause a violent reaction from southern officials. Through the media this would touch the conscience of the North and bring in the coercive power of the federal government against racial injustice. Selma, Alabama was chosen as the site of King's voting campaign in part because Sheriff Jim Clark was noted for his lack of self-control in beating demonstrating black people.

On January 19, 1965, confronting a demonstration of blacks attempting to register at the county courthouse, Sheriff Clark flew into one of his rages. He roughed up a local black leader and arrested sixty-seven demonstrators. That night demonstrators voted Clark an honorary member of their movement.

In the following weeks the protests peaked. King was arrested, attracting national attention. A delegation of congressmen visited Selma. King flew to Washington where President Johnson promised a voting rights bill "very soon." The shooting death by a state trooper of a black demonstrator led King to announce the climax of his campaign—a fifty-four-mile protest march from Selma to the state capital of Montgomery.

Governor George Wallace banned the march. But on Sunday, March 7, 600 marchers set off for Montgomery. Alabama state troopers confronted the marchers on Edmund Pettus Bridge, gave them two minutes to disperse, and then attacked them with tear gas and clubs. Fleeing back to Selma, the marchers met Jim Clark's posse, which was being urged on by its leader's cry, "Get those god-damned niggers." Bloody Sunday, televised for the evening news, outraged public opinion in the North creating a powerful, instant demand for a new voting law. The demonstration had mobilized public opinion and moved political leaders to action.

A week later President Johnson went on TV to emotionally plead for passage of the bill, using the words of the civil rights

The protest march led by Martin Luther King, Jr., from Selma to Montgomery, Alabama.

movement, "we shall overcome." After setbacks including protests from black militants against his nonviolent tactics, King led 25,000 marchers, under the protection of the federalized Alabama National Guard, into Montgomery. The Voting Rights Act was signed into law on August 5, 1965.

POLITICAL MOVEMENTS

In organizing people for certain goals, parties and interest groups have left gaps in the political process. Political movements fill some of the gaps. Movements allow underrepresented groups to unite and press their demands for change. They have historically provided a means for Americans to use mass support in place of massive amounts of money to influence the political direction the country is taking.

What Is a Political Movement?

Three main characteristics set political movements apart from political parties or interest groups. First, the *structure* of political movements is *flexible and unstable.* Movements rarely have a permanent form; they center on activists creating new flexible organizations. This often makes them hard to identify. Sometimes parts of a movement are permanent organizations, or become permanent, taking the form of interest groups. Parts of the civil rights movement of the 1950s and 1960s, such as the still-active Southern Christian Leadership Conference (SCLC), became stable interest groups. Other parts, such as the NAACP (founded in 1910), had been active as interest groups long before the civil rights movement. Other groups registered voters in the South or participated in sit-ins and demonstrations, but never became formal organizations.

Second, the issues championed by movements are *proposals for major changes in society.* Political movements generally demand change in who gets what, when, and how, and in who gets to participate in political decision making. The civil rights movement aimed at winning for black Americans (who) the same rights and liberties enjoyed by white Americans (what) as quickly as possible (when) through nonviolent protest (how). There was also a thrust in the movement to change the process of decision making so that blacks could control the institutions that affected their communities.

Third, movements depend for their success on their *ability to mobilize as many people as possible.* The success of the student anti-Vietnam War movement rested on the number of supporters directly involved in the movement's activities. A Washington demonstration with 500,000 people got wide media attention and underlined popular discontent with the war. Widespread support shows political decision makers that the movement's goals are popular, and puts pressure on them to give in to some of the movement's demands.

The Rise and Fall of Political Movements

Movements develop out of a combination of ingredients.[1] The first is discontent caused by **relative deprivation.** Political movements are fueled by supporters who feel deprived compared to someone else. That American blacks in the 1960s had more opportunities than blacks earlier in the century did not lessen their discontent. Indeed, it may have increased it as they gained confidence from previous achievements and recognized the barriers that remained. Similarly, because American women are more equal to men than women in other societies does not reduce their feeling of deprivation. Groups are deprived relative to others in their own environments.

A second ingredient needed for a political movement to ignite is a **historical moment** or *spark.* This is an event or situation that focuses a group's general feeling of discontent and moves it to action. It might be a severe depression or a war. A brief event like the Chinese army attack on students at Tiananmen Square in Beijing may prove to be the spark leading to a long-term political movement. The Vietnam War clearly presented the student movement with an ideal opportunity to recruit supporters. The Montgomery bus boycott of 1955 began when a black woman, Rosa Parks, refused to give up her seat for a white man. It was one of the sparks that set the civil rights movement in motion. Such historical moments activate people: They see that their discontent is caused by identifiable causes and that, by organizing together, they can change their common conditions.

Targets and Leaders

The third and fourth ingredients are **leaders** and **targets.** Leaders present at the historical moment help people connect their discontent, a political target, and realistic goals. Often the target is a member of the elite who is accused of being responsible for people's conditions. Once the target is identified, leaders develop strategies and tactics to achieve the change they desire. Movements are well-known for the nonviolent and sometimes violent demonstration tactics (sit-ins, teach-ins, and strikes) they use to draw attention to their causes. But movements use many other tactics, and other political actors (labor unions, for example) use demonstration tactics, so it is misleading to identify movements by tactics alone.

The tactics themselves may draw attention away from the issue they are advancing and become the issue instead. Whether acts of civil disobedience are justified was a frequent debate during the civil rights movement. A more dramatic question of tactics occurred in the early 1970s, when an anti-Vietnam-War group in New York City announced that a coming noon rally would feature the burning of a

Policemen chase crowds of antiwar demonstrators on the campus of Columbia University in New York in 1968.

puppy. The aim was to bring the horror of napalm bombs home to an indifferent citizenry. After a few days of free publicity and expressions of outrage, the rally was held before an unusually large if somewhat angry crowd. The puppy was of course released unharmed. Whether the tactic had worked remained clouded.

The selection of targets results from a blend of pragmatism and ideology. Columbia University students in 1968 accused their school of involvement in the Vietnam War because of the Defense Department contracts held by some faculty members. They chose the university for a target as much because of its convenience for organizing student rallies as its contribution to the war effort. In a more recent example, animal-rights groups targeted research labs as a symbol of human exploitation of animals. Though these activists may oppose hunting and the raising of animals for food, focusing attention on "scientific" research allowed for dramatic "animal-liberation" actions. Breaking into labs to videotape and free suffering animals enabled these activists to publicly and graphically pose the question of what rights animals have.[2]

Animal rights activists protest outside of New York University in 1988.

Decline and Fall

Movements may lose their force if the authorities (1) do something to cure the discontent (such as passing a Voting Rights Act), (2) alter policies to reduce the "historical moments" (ending segregated seating on Alabama buses), (3) eliminate the movement leadership (arresting demonstrators), or (4) remove the target of movement activity (President Johnson deciding not to run for reelection after antiwar protests).

Even with no response from authorities, movements often lose momentum. *It is difficult to keep large numbers of people involved in continual political activity.* The leadership may split, with more radical leadership pushing demands that divide the members and antagonize public opinion. Frustration from bold, if unrealistic, attempts to change society is a constant companion. The rewards of movement activity are often few and far between.

STRATEGY AND TACTICS

What movements do is as varied as what movements are. The general strategies and specific tactics they pursue derive from their membership and its resources, the political environment they face, their objectives, and the skills and experience of their leaders. Two general types of strategies employed by political movements are *civil disobedience* and *legal direct actions.*

Police try to remove one of 100 antiabortionists blocking the door to a Planned Parenthood clinic in St. Paul, Minnesota in 1988.

Civil Disobedience

Civil disobedience involves breaking the law in an open, deliberate, nonviolent manner. The people who employ tactics of civil disobedience are willing to suffer the consequences of their acts in order to make a public protest. A sit-in at a lunch counter where service to blacks has been refused is an example of civil disobedience. The people who practice civil disobedience intend that only they will suffer the penalties for their acts. By contrast, people who advocate violence as a tactic (terrorists) intend to cause harm to others' persons, property, or both.

Civil disobedience has a long history in America. Its earliest major advocate was Henry David Thoreau, an antiwar activist and tax resister who wrote *Civil Disobedience* (1849). In the 1950s and 1960s, Martin Luther King and other civil rights activists used civil disobedience successfully to fight racial discrimination in America.[3] More recently this tactic was used by anti-abortion groups to block entrances to abortion clinics.

Civil disobedience may have a significant propaganda effect. People perform acts of civil disobedience to call public attention to what they believe are immoral laws. People have deliberately provoked an arrest in order to be able to question in court the constitutionality of the law under which the arrest was made. Of course, no one has the "right" to break the law in America, even if the lawbreaker believes that the law is unjust.

In 1984, even a state governor advocated civil disobedience against nuclear weapons (although it caused a storm of controversy). Wisconsin governor Anthony S. Earl, in a university lecture, said: "Speeches are not going to turn the trick here. What may be required is a program of action—mass demonstrations of the type we have been seeing in Europe, and a carefully thought-out campaign of civil disobedience. These have been the models . . . which have carried the great moral issues of the 20th century and they can work again."[4] Perhaps because governors are in awkward positions to lead movements, few demonstrations resulted from this call to arms.

Legal Direct Action

Ralph Nader leads a group of activists to a General Motors stockholders' meeting to protest certain management practices. The residents of Westwood, California, outraged about utility rate increases, stage an electricity boycott. Women in a public housing development organize a rent strike to protest the lack of affordable day-care facilities. All of these are **legal direct actions** organized by political movements or others. They are self-help efforts to directly affect conditions that people want changed. *These actions are aimed not so much at gaining political decisions (such as legislation or court rulings) as at directly motivating the targets of the actions.*

Activist Ralph Nader holds a press conference about fruit juices in 1988. Nader argued that companies should be required to list on the products' labels the amount of real fruit juice used, as opposed to chemical substitutes.

Many political movements and community organizations have used techniques first developed in the 1930s by Saul Alinsky, a Chicago neighborhood organizer. Alinsky believed that confrontation was necessary for two reasons. First, it would get the attention of the people who make the decisions. Second, it would "radicalize" community members, making them more conscious that wrongs could be righted.[5]

This "transforming effect" on the people who organize themselves has long been recognized by political movement leaders. As Dr. King said about the Montgomery bus boycott, "our real victory is not so much the desegregation of the buses as it is a new sense of dignity and destiny."[6] Similarly, another citizen activist states, ". . . in the course of their struggles, people develop a critical world view, and they come to believe in their own ability to act. They are transformed by their experience."[7]

It is not easy to organize direct action. There is often a lack of money available to start organizations and other activities, and organizing often requires more effort and more commitment than some people are willing to give. Organizing direct action requires several steps. First, someone must identify an issue that involves basic human concerns and set reachable goals. Second, the issue must be stated in terms that give it legitimacy in the community; such phrases as "it's only fair" or "health care is a right" are often used. Third, the issue must be politically drawn so that people take sides; organizers must present the issue in a way that highlights the differences between the powerful and the powerless, the "haves" and the "have-nots."

Specific direct-action tactics may include **boycotts** like the electricity boycott in Westwood, California. Direct-action campaigns may also use a **strike,** a tactic borrowed from the labor movement. For instance, tenants in housing projects have organized rent strikes, refusing to pay increased rents. **Demonstrations** can take the form of sit-ins, picketing, paying bills in pennies, blocking traffic, marching, candlelight vigils, and holding up signs at busy intersections.

Direct-action strategy almost always involves using the media. Finding ways to embarrass those with the power to change things can be quite effective. *The ability to embarrass, coupled with access to the media, may be the only tools available to people with little power.*[8] "Awards" may be given to slumlords for "Worst Neighbor of the Year." Well-publicized petitions may be delivered to direct-action targets. Garbage cans may be taken to the mayor's office to dramatize that garbage is not picked up in poor neighborhoods. Thus, publicity (and the ability to embarrass) aimed at forcing government or corporations to respond, is often the most important goal of a direct-action campaign.

The three modern movements discussed in this chapter have used these strategies, and their tactics followed most of these patterns. Blacks, women, and student activists have organized themselves to seek broad social goals. Their intensity, their frequently radical aims, and the persistence required to pursue "the struggle" have separated movement members from more conventional political activities. While all three movements almost inevitably fell short of their goals, all substantially expanded the boundaries of their political worlds. They not only challenged the political limits of the day, they changed them.

THE BLACK CIVIL RIGHTS MOVEMENT

Unequal from the Start

Blacks have been in America from the beginning. The first African Americans to arrive in Jamestown were indentured servants, as were many of the first whites who came to America. An indentured servant was bound to an employer for a certain number of years. But soon inherited slavery—classifying the children of slaves as slaves themselves—became the rule for blacks.

There were black revolts in America from early colonial days to the Civil War, but they were scattered and unsuccessful. The Civil War brought freedom in name only for most African Americans. Although the weed of slavery had been chopped down, the roots of racism remained. Congressional proposals for federal aid to education, aimed principally at upgrading education for the former slaves, were defeated. So, too, was a proposal to provide "forty acres and a mule" for freed slaves. Former slaves had little opportunity to acquire capital—particularly land and the means of working the land—or educational skills. Thus, although the Thirteenth Amendment guaranteed *legal* freedom, former slaves were in reality neither free nor equal.

Throughout the South **Jim Crow laws,** segregation laws taking their name from a black-face minstrel song, were passed to prohibit blacks from using the same public facilities as whites.[9] These state laws required segregated schools, hospitals, prisons, restaurants, toilets, railways, and waiting rooms. Some communities passed "Sundown Ordinances" that prohibited blacks from staying in town overnight. Blacks and whites could not even be buried in the same cemeteries.

There seemed to be no limit to the absurdity of segregation. New Orleans required separate districts for black and white prostitutes. In Oklahoma, blacks and whites could not use the same telephone booths. In North Carolina and Florida, school textbooks used by black children had to be stored separately from those used by white children. In Birmingham, the races were specifically prohibited from playing checkers together.

Ending Segregation

Changes in racial laws came from "above" in government policy and from "below" in the growth of a black civil rights movement. In the 1930s and 1940s federal courts began to weaken segregation laws. They were pushed by cases brought by the National Association for the Advancement of Colored People's (NAACP) Legal Defense Fund. The fund was headed by Thurgood Marshall, later to become the first black Supreme Court Justice. In the 1940s, presidents issued executive orders banning discrimination in government employment and in the army. Although Congress, dominated by southern conservatives, was unable to pass civil rights measures, by 1954 the Supreme Court was ready to act. In that year a unanimous decision written by Chief Justice Earl Warren (*Brown* v. *Board of Education*) held that segregation of schools violated the equal protection guaranteed by the Fourteenth Amendment. The Court followed this with decisions outlawing other forms of racial discrimination.

White students look on as heavily guarded black students climb the steps en route to classes at Central High School in Little Rock, Arkansas in 1957.

It was one thing for the Supreme Court to make a ruling and quite another to have it enforced. Throughout the South, white officials girded up for "massive resistance" to the Court decisions, and they were backed by white public opinion. Highway billboards went up demanding the impeachment of Earl Warren. Even President Eisenhower, who had appointed Chief Justice Warren, said privately that the Court had gone too far.

But Eisenhower felt bound by his constitutional duty to "take care that the laws be faithfully executed." After the Court had ruled that its *Brown* decision had to be implemented "with all deliberate speed," a major state-federal government confrontation arose in Little Rock, Arkansas in 1957. The governor of that state, Orval Faubus, called out the Arkansas National Guard to block integration in Little Rock's Central High School. The lines were clearly drawn. To use one of Eisenhower's phrases, it was time to "fish or cut bait." Though he did not want to do so, Eisenhower felt that he had no alternative but to nationalize the Arkansas National Guard and to use it (and U.S. Army paratroopers) to enforce the Supreme Court decision.

Resistance to the Court's decisions persisted through the South. President Kennedy sent federal marshals to Oxford, Mississippi in 1962 to enforce the right of a black student, James Meredith, to attend that state's university. Kennedy also nationalized the Alabama National Guard in 1963 to thwart an attempt by Alabama's governor, George Wallace, to block school integration in that state.

The Rise of the Civil Rights Movement

Pushing the federal government and paralleling it were the actions of the civil rights movement. From the time of the Montgomery bus boycott in 1955, touched off by the courage of Rosa Parks (who refused to move to the back of the bus), the black civil rights movement had increasingly been marked by demonstrations that were heavily covered by the media. Blacks were no longer willing to rely solely on the courts. The *Southern Christian Leadership Conference (SCLC)*, led by Dr. King, was central to these efforts, which also won white support in the North. The *Congress of Racial Equality (CORE)*, headed by James Farmer, and the *Student Non-Violent Coordinating Committee (SNCC)*, led first by John Lewis (now a congressman), were also active and usually more militant than the older leaders of SCLC.

Lunch-counter sit-ins by young African Americans swept southern cities, starting in Greensboro, North Carolina in 1960.[10] Black and white "freedom riders" tried to ride public buses through the

President Lyndon B. Johnson meets with Martin Luther King, Jr., and other civil rights leaders at the signing of the Civil Rights Act of 1964.

South. Even before the *Brown* decision, the Supreme Court had declared that blacks had the right to use public transportation. What the freedom rides proved, though, was that there was no such right in the South. Freedom riders were brutally beaten and one bus was burned. In Birmingham, Alabama in 1963, Police Commissioner Eugene "Bull" Connor unleashed his police with cattle prods and fire hoses on civil rights marchers. As the marchers sang "We Shall Overcome," he set police dogs on them. Dr. King was jailed as a leader of this demonstration.

The televised brutality of the Birmingham police aroused public sympathies. To protest the lack of federal action in support of civil rights, black leaders organized a "March on Washington" in August 1963. Nearly a quarter of a million people—black and white—filled the area in front of the Lincoln Memorial. It was here that Dr. King made his inspiring "I Have a Dream" speech: "From every mountainside, let freedom ring," he concluded, ". . . to speed up that day when all God's children, black and white men, Jews and Gentiles, Protestants and Catholics, will be able to join hands and sing in the words of that old Negro spiritual, 'Free at last! Free at last! Thank God Almighty, we are free at last!'"[11]

The freedom of which Dr. King spoke so movingly did not come easily. Most American cities saw black demonstrations that summer. Four black girls were killed when a bomb exploded in a black church in Birmingham. President Kennedy proposed a sweeping civil rights bill to a Congress that showed no willingness to pass it. Then, in November 1963, Kennedy was assassinated in Dallas. His successor,

Lyndon Johnson, appeared before a joint session of Congress and, in the name of the slain president, called for passage of the civil rights legislation, dramatically invoking the familiar words of the movement's anthem, "We Shall Overcome." After a long filibuster, the first one ever broken on a civil rights bill, the **Civil Rights Act of 1964** was passed and signed into law. The new law prohibited discrimination in public places such as hotels and restaurants, in voting, and in jobs, and empowered the executive branch to enforce it.

The following year, the **Voting Rights Act** was pushed through a suddenly responsive Congress, in part due to the civil rights movement's activities in Selma, Alabama. Federal examiners were appointed to stop discrimination in voter registration in the South. Voter-registration drives were mounted among blacks. Despite stubborn white resistance, these efforts were markedly successful. At the same time, black impatience grew.

Frustration and Violence

As Johnson's War on Poverty program began to reach out and organize poor people in the 1960s, it became clear that racism was not just confined to the South. After World War II, millions of African-Americans had left the South for what they hoped would be better lives in large cities in the rest of the country. What they usually found were poor or nonexistent jobs and segregated slums. In the North and West, where they had already had the right to vote, blacks saw that the new civil rights laws had done nothing to improve their lives.

The civil rights movement and Johnson's Great Society programs aroused great expectations, many of which were not fulfilled. Some of the president's programs provided increased training for jobs without providing jobs. There was encouragement to organize and get into the system, but often the system did not respond. And all-white television programs showed that "blondes had more fun" and that white middle-class families were living happily ever after. "Why are we on the streets with no jobs?" blacks wondered. "Why are we living in this tenement where the toilet won't flush and the rats bite our babies?" Minor improvements seemed to produce more frustrations, heightening the sense of relative deprivation.

In the summer of 1965, rioting, burning, and looting erupted in Watts, a black area of Los Angeles. Hundreds of people were hurt and thirty-four were killed. Property damage was in the tens of millions of dollars. A citizens commission, headed by noted (white) leader John McCone, investigated. The commission members tried to call the nation's attention to the high unemployment in Watts, especially among young blacks, and to the inadequate health and housing there. Their report said that the lack of public transportation made it almost impossible for many Watts residents to get to jobs elsewhere in the city.

Few Americans paid much attention to the McCone Commission report entitled "Violence in the City—an End or Beginning?" Perhaps that's why the Watts riots proved to be a beginning. The next summer, there were disorders in black sections of Cleveland, Chicago, and eighteen other cities. Young black leaders pushed the black movement beyond the mild slogan of "Black is Beautiful" (which focused on improving self-image) toward the more aggressive concept of "Black Power." It was time, they said, for blacks to organize and demand their rights as Americans.

During the "long, hot summer" of 1967, there were riots in black sections of Plainfield and Newark, New Jersey; Detroit and Grand Rapids, Michigan; Atlanta, Georgia; Buffalo, New York; Cincinnati, Ohio; Milwaukee, Wisconsin; Tampa, Florida; and Cambridge, Maryland. Twenty-eight other cities had disorders, and ninety-two had smaller outbreaks of violence. In Newark, twenty-five people were killed; twenty-one were black. In Detroit, thirty-three blacks and ten whites died.

Looters run through the streets during the Watts riots in Los Angeles in 1965.

To determine the causes of the disorders and to find out how to prevent more, Johnson appointed the National Advisory Commission on Civil Disorders. This committee, which came to be called the **Kerner Commission** after its chairman, Otto Kerner (then Governor of Illinois), declared in its report of February 1968: "What white Americans have never fully understood, but what the Negro can never forget, is that white society is deeply implicated in the ghetto. White institutions created it, white institutions maintain it and white society condones it." The Commission found that no organized conspiracy had caused the riots. Instead, frustration and powerlessness had created a situation so volatile that a random incident could spark an explosion. "Our nation is moving toward two societies, one black, one white—separate and unequal," the Commission Report concluded.[12]

While the Kerner Report was being publicly debated, Dr. King was assassinated on April 4, 1968 in Memphis. Riots broke out again in over 100 cities. In Washington, D.C., riots occurred within blocks of the White House.

Stirred by Dr. King's death and armed with the Kerner Commission Report, Congress passed a bill on April 16, 1968 prohibiting discrimination in the sale or rental of private housing. Equal employment and other civil rights laws had been strengthened, and various federal agencies and departments continued to enforce the new laws. But by 1968 the major thrust of the movement no longer pushed for legislation to remove discrimination. The civil rights movement ended, or at least moved into other phases.

The Aftermath of the Civil Rights Movement

Compared to the violence of the 1960s, the decades that followed were a quiet period for civil rights. Liberal political attention shifted first to protests against U.S. involvement in the Vietnam War, then to concerns about the environment. With conservatism dominant and federal programs benefiting blacks reduced by cuts in government spending, America's interest in civil rights waned. Blacks continued to work in different settings for their rights.

The phrase *civil rights* does not adequately describe the current direction of African American political activities. The achievement of real voting rights underwritten by intense voter registration drives helped produce 5700 black elected officials in 1988 and black mayors in 250 cities including Los Angeles, Philadelphia, Detroit, Atlanta, Birmingham, and Washington, D.C. The courts through the 1980s generally supported busing and affirmative action programs to reverse historical patterns of discrimination.

But the problems confronting African Americans were no longer characterized in political and media circles by phrases like "racial discrimination," "police brutality," and "inadequate opportunities." The black community now was labeled, and burdened, by phrases like "underclass," "drug culture," and "street violence." Responsibility, or blame, focused increasingly on unwed teenage mothers, on families without fathers, and on black ghettos plagued by crime, drugs, and unemployment. Solutions no longer seemed as clear even within the community. Increasing numbers of middle-class blacks could now participate in the broader society's affluence, but those left behind on inner-city streets seemed trapped in a continuing cycle of poverty.

Leaders such as Jesse Jackson have pushed solutions ranging from self-help motivational programs to keep teenagers off drugs to political coalitions with other minorities backing Jackson's presidential candidacy. Whatever the solutions, black leaders have seen that legal and political equality, while important, cannot fully remove the causes of inequality without greater economic advances. Martin Luther King realized this earlier than most. Prophetically, his last trip to Memphis in 1968 had been to support the economic demands of low-paid black sanitation workers.

Jesse Jackson is one of the most visible leaders of the black community, having run for the office of president in 1980, 1984, and 1988.

THE WOMEN'S MOVEMENT

A Half-Free People

While John Adams was in Philadelphia in 1776, helping draft the Declaration of Independence, his wife, Abigail, wrote to him: "I desire that you would Remember the Ladies, and be more generous and favorable to them than your ancestors. Remember all Men would be tyrants if they could. If particular care and attention is not paid to the Ladies, we are determined to foment a Rebellion, and will not hold ourselves bound by any laws in which we have no voice, or Representation." Adams' reply qualifies him as an FFCP— A Founding Father Chauvinist Pig. He called his wife "saucy" and added, "We know better than to repeal our Masculine system." Indeed, neither the Declaration ("all *men* are created equal") nor the Constitution recognized women as free and equal citizens.

Women are not a minority. In the United States, they represent 51 percent of the population and some 52 percent of voters. Yet they have often been treated as a minority. Throughout American history, they have suffered from discrimination because they are women. This form of discrimination is called **sexism.** Women's historical reaction against discrimination has taken many forms.

Women march for the right to vote in the 1880s.

During the 1830s, women who were active in the movement to abolish slavery began to realize their own inequality. They were, for example, not even allowed to speak at antislavery meetings. The women's movement took organized form during the 1880s as part of the general stirring of philosophical thought about human rights.

Today, it is common to think of this early women's movement as merely a movement to secure the right to vote (*suffrage*). However, it represented far more than that. It is true that these early feminists objected to being bound by laws they could not participate in passing. But they also objected to unequal pay for the same work, lack of educational and professional opportunity, lack of equality in the courts, and subjection to a different moral code. In the Declaration of Sentiments (which was modeled after the Declaration of Independence) of the 1848 Women's Rights convention at Seneca Falls, New York, feminists protested the subjugation of their lives to men. These men, they declared, sought to destroy the confidence of women in their own powers, lessen their self-respect, and make them "willing to lead a dependent and abject life."[13]

From Discontent to the Vote

Little by little, this early movement was converted into a single-issue cause. *Partly to gain respectability, the movement focused on the vote for women.* The movement suffered a major disappointment after the Civil War, when the Fifteenth Amendment granted black men—but not women, black or white—the right to vote. During the centennial celebration of the Declaration of Independence, Susan B. Anthony, one of the leading suffragists, pointed out that ". . . the women of this nation, in 1876, have greater cause for discontent, rebellion, and revolution than the men of 1776."

Slowly, some progress was made. In 1890, women were granted the right to vote in the new state of Wyoming, which was seeking women to help fill its unpopulated land. By 1917, eight other states had followed suit. After World War I, women convinced President Woodrow Wilson to support the Nineteenth Amendment. It was approved by Congress and ratified by the states in 1920. Two feminist authors have written that when this goal was finally achieved, "so much energy had been expended . . . that the women's movement virtually collapsed from exhaustion."[14]

The women's movement did not die. Many saw clearly that even though they could vote, inequalities remained. *From their earliest years, children continued to learn from family and schools that men and women were expected to assume very different roles in life.* For example, it was acceptable for boys, but not girls, to hope to become doctors or lawyers. Girls were encouraged to become housewives and mothers or, if they hoped to work outside the home, to become secretaries or nurses.

The Women's Movement Sitrs

The civil rights, student, and antiwar movements of the 1960s produced large numbers of young women activists. Like the women in the earlier movement against slavery, they began to recognize their own inequality. By the 1970s, they had established what came to be known as the **Women's Liberation Movement.**

An early response to increased lobbying by women was President Kennedy's creation of a Commission on the Status of Women in 1961. The Commission's report deplored the fact that women continued to be second-class citizens in America. It led to the establishment of similar commissions at the state level, a national advisory council, and the passage of the Equal Pay Act in 1963.

In 1966, Betty Friedan, author of *The Feminine Mystique*,[15] helped form the first important national feminist organization in America since Susan B. Anthony's National Woman Suffrage Association. The new organization was called the *National Organization for Women (NOW)*. It continues to be a vocal force in America on such issues as employment opportunities for women, full legal equality, and the rights of lesbians.

Members of NOW march in front of the White House for the Equal Rights Amendment in 1969 (note that this occurred before *Roe* v. *Wade* legalized abortion in 1973).

ERA opponent Phyllis Schlafly holds a STOP ERA rally in the Illinois State Capitol.

In 1967, pressured by NOW, Lyndon Johnson formally prohibited sex discrimination in federal employment and by those doing business with the federal government. The 1964 Civil Rights Act was amended to include sex as a prohibited grounds for discrimination in private employment. In 1969, Richard Nixon set up a presidential task force on the status of women. It found that women had not achieved equality. In higher education, for example, less than 12 percent of doctoral degrees awarded in 1969 in the United States went to women. Only 8 percent of U.S. medical students were women, and less than 6 percent of law students were women.[16]

In 1972, Congress proposed the **Equal Rights Amendment (ERA)** for the needed approval of three-fourths of the states. March 1979 was set as the deadline for ratification. The Equal Rights Amendment had been first proposed in the Congress nearly fifty years before. It states: "Equality of rights under the law shall not be denied or abridged by the United States or by any state on account of sex." The words seem fairly plain, but they have caused many conflicting arguments.

Opponents did not want women to become subject to a military draft. Supporters, however, argued that women with children to care for could be given special exemptions and some women could be given special kinds of military jobs. Opponents feared that divorced women would lose their rights to alimony and child support if the

Armed with broad slogans and an empty crib, antiabortionists gather in 1989 in front of a Planned Parenthood office in Schenectady, New York to mark the sixteenth anniversary of the U.S. Supreme Court decision legalizing abortion.

amendment passed. Supporters, on the other hand, said that marriage partners should be equal. They advocated equal child-rearing responsibilities for men and women, and insisted that alimony and child support should be awarded on the basis of the financial capabilities of each partner. In addition, they pointed out that only 44 percent of women were awarded child support, and less than half of these women actually received such payments regularly.

By 1978, momentum toward ratification of the ERA had slowed. Although 35 of the necessary 38 states had ratified the amendment, efforts to win three more states ran into opposition from some church groups, housewives, and conservative state legislators. As the ratification deadline neared, feminist organizations lobbied through Congress a three-year extension of the ratification period to 1982. Once again, the fight shifted to the state legislatures. But for the supporters of the ERA it was a loss. The ERA was not ratified.

Other Issues, Other Victories, Other Setbacks

In 1973, the Supreme Court held that a woman has a right to an abortion during the first three months of pregnancy and that no state can interfere with this right (*Roe* v. *Wade*). Throughout the 1970s and 1980s, men and women organized themselves in "Right-to-Life" groups to seek (unsuccessfully) a constitutional amendment to overturn this decision and to lobby Congress (successfully) to prohibit federal welfare funds from being used for this purpose. Supporters of abortion countered that the issue was a private one of a woman's right to choose. Opponents asked who would represent the fetus, and pointed to ambiguous scientific evidence as to when life began.

Women continued to inch toward parity with men in the high-paying and influential professions. Their share of law degrees went from 15 percent in 1975 to 38.5 percent in 1985; engineering degrees went from 2.2 percent to 12.5 percent and the number of medical school graduates rose from 13.1 percent to 30.4 percent over that same period.[17]

But what women got paid for that work remained only about two-thirds of what men got paid for roughly the same type of work, with men getting a median $419 a week in 1986 and women getting only $290. This was the pattern up and down the ladder of skills: the 8.5 million male executives, administrators, and managers got a median of $32,000 per year, and the 5.2 million females in those jobs got $19,000; 7.6 million men in the "professional" category got $32,000 a year while 8 million women got $18,000; 7 million male service workers got $9000 a year and 10,000 female service workers got $5000.

An increasing percentage of women work outside the home, including 65 percent of mothers. But the median annual earnings for year-round, full-time women workers in 1986 were only 64 percent of those for men, according to the U.S. Bureau of Labor Statistics. A central reason for this is the clustering of women in "pink-collar" fields such as nursing, elementary school teaching, and secretarial work, which do not pay as well as the fields in which men predominate.

While working to open up the better-paid fields, women also pushed for the adoption of **comparable worth.** This controversial concept goes beyond the widely accepted "equal-pay-for-equal-work" idea to demand equal pay for different jobs that are of comparable value. A law based on this concept would assign points to different kinds of jobs, and those of comparable value such as book-keeping (usually done by women) and accounting (usually done by men) would result in comparable pay. Republican administrations opposed the concept, and the practical difficulties in implementing it (who decides and how?) led to it being shelved as a major issue.

The Impact of the Women's Movement

Over the last two decades the women's movement has had a dramatic effect. It has raised the awareness of millions of American women by increasing their self-esteem and their expectations of themselves. A strong majority of women supports the goals of the movement.[18] The movement has also caused a lot of men to change both their attitudes and their roles. Many men now realize that women have been exploited and limited in their opportunities. Men can no longer make sexist comments about women without hearing objections; old jokes portraying women as flighty, disorganized, and unable to drive cars correctly are no longer generally accepted. All major textbook publishers now have guidelines to eliminate sexism from their books in order to avoid stereotypes that narrow students' expectations. Politicians struggle to say "representative" instead of "congressmen"; city ordinances refer to "police officers" instead of "policemen"; and men in many businesses hesitate to ask the "girls in the office" to make the coffee.

An increasing number of feminists are making it clear, too, that homemaking ought to be recognized as a very important profession. Many women who start a sentence with "I'm no women's libber, but . . ." endorse such causes as government assistance for child care, equal education, professional and job opportunity, and equal pay for equal work. The movement's goals remain to expand the choices available to all women. Much remains to be done.

STUDENTS FOR A DEMOCRATIC SOCIETY (SDS)

Student activism in the 1960s provides a vivid example of the rise and fall of a political movement. Here, student groups employed grassroots tactics and ideas to make their demands heard outside of existing institutions. Here, too, key people and events at first propelled a small movement toward broad popular support, only to be caught later in a decline brought on by the movement's internal divisions as well as external pressures from forces beyond its control.

Emergence of the Student Movement of the 1960s

Hippies burning draft cards, marches to end the Vietnam War, drugs, sit-ins, and protest songs—these are the usual images of the student movement of the 1960s. But the roots of the "New Left" movement reach back to the 1950s Cold War era, a time when school bombing drills were regularly held to prepare for nuclear attack by the Russians. Along with their concern for ending the arms race, children of the prosperous 1950s were also influenced by the civil rights movement—its idealism, leadership, and tactics.

The election of a reform-minded president also seemed to signal the beginning of a new era. Campaigning for the presidency in 1960, John F. Kennedy had delivered a rousing speech at the University of Michigan supporting the creation of the Peace Corps. The young candidate had thus dramatically endorsed the idea that students had much to offer the world. "A New Frontier" was at hand.

Students for a Democratic Society (SDS) was first organized in 1960 by graduate students at the University of Michigan and supported by the League for Industrial Democracy, a socialist labor group founded in 1905. The League viewed SDS as a training ground for a new generation of union organizers. The first student leaders, however, wanted SDS to help develop radical alternatives to what they saw as an inadequate society.[19]

This vision soon attracted Tom Hayden, the editor of the campus paper. Arriving at Michigan in 1957, Hayden had found the open intellectual atmosphere of campus life quite a change from his parochial-school upbringing. He was particularly taken with the ideas of C. Wright Mills, the author of *The Power Elite.*[20] Mills's writings painted a sad picture of a new "mass society" where most citizens had become "cheerful robots" under the spell of advertising, television, and the power of faceless bureaucracies. However, Mills was skeptical of the traditional Marxist emphasis on the working class as the sole agent of social change.

Burning a draft card was a common form of protest during the 1960s.

SDS leader Jerry Rubin speaks at a Black Panther Rally at Yale University in 1970.

This question of which group in society could take the lead in pushing for social change had long plagued the American Left. With seemingly conservative unions dominating labor, workers did not look like the group to lead the "revolution." SDS leaders wondered, who could? Their eventual answer—that students could—came to them in newspaper headlines from the South. In the spring of 1960, four black college students from North Carolina A&T held a non-violent sit-in in Greensboro to protest white-only lunch counters. Their effort spawned mass sit-ins throughout the South. To SDS, the Greensboro action became a model for direct student involvement.

SDS had to spell out its ideas to provide guidance for a movement that would put students at the vanguard of social change. United by such ambitious goals as promoting civil rights, ending the nuclear arms race, and championing what they called "participatory democracy," fifty-nine people traveled to a United Auto Workers camp at Port Huron, Michigan in June of 1962 to hash out the SDS manifesto.

Working from a forty-nine-page draft prepared by Hayden, the SDS delegates spent three days refining their ideas (see the box on page 303). The resulting document, the **Port Huron Statement,** would soon become a major rallying focus for the student movement. Over 10,000 copies of the statement were distributed throughout the country. The Port Huron delegates represented perhaps 500 members of SDS nationwide. Six years later, SDS would claim a membership of 100,000.

Building the Movement

Most SDS organizing activity was centered at first in Ann Arbor, in the basement of Tom Hayden's apartment. The group's initial goal was "to be a grand coalition of labor, minorities [and] progressives." From their cluttered office, the members of the Ann Arbor chapter coordinated efforts to support civil rights activists, sending food, bail money, and student volunteers to the South.

But SDS leaders also wanted to organize projects of their own. In September 1963, SDS launched the Economic Research and Action Project (ERAP). ERAP involved organizing projects, primarily in the ghettos of Newark and Cleveland. In a sense, reflects one former ERAP participant, the project was also "built on guilt." Attempts were made to organize the unemployed, to form tenants' councils, and to register voters among welfare recipients. ERAP had some successes. By the summer of 1964, it could claim 125 organizers at work in nine cities.

Less outstanding were the Cleveland project's efforts to expand **participatory democracy.** Sharing living quarters and expenses, the SDS-Cleveland organizers believed that *all* the group's decisions had to be made through consensus—a simple majority was unacceptable. This democracy by exhaustion was a source of pride: one ERAP pamphlet even declared that "freedom is an endless meeting." At one point, a twenty-four hour meeting was needed before the group could agree to take a day off to go to the beach.

But it was an event beyond the control of the student movement—Vietnam—that provided SDS with its greatest organizing opportunities.

Vietnam: The Movement Mushrooms

Although united against growing U.S. military involvement in Vietnam, SDS's leaders were divided over how to act. Meeting in December 1964, after Congress had passed the Gulf of Tonkin resolution, SDS's National Council rejected a proposal to send medical supplies to the North Vietnamese. Such an action risked charges that the SDS was pro-communist.

★ The Port Huron Statement

We are the people of this generation, bred in at least modest comfort, housed now in universities, looking uncomfortably to the world we inherit . . .

Our work is guided by the sense that we may be the last generation in the experiment with living . . .

While the world tumbles towards the final war . . . America is without community impulse, without the inner momentum necessary for an age when societies cannot successfully perpetuate themselves by their military weapons, when democracy must be viable because of its quality of life, not its quantity of rockets.

We seek the establishment of a democracy of individual participation, governed by two central aims: that the individual share in those social decisions determining the quality and direction of his life; that society be organized to encourage independence in men and provide the media for their common participation.

It was then suggested that SDS sponsor a march on Washington. Opponents of the idea, including Hayden, argued that a march would divert too many resources from SDS's projects among the poor. But after spirited debate, the Council approved a plan for SDS to sponsor a national march in April (majority rule still governed national-level decisions).

SDS invited interested groups to join it. Leftist groups quickly agreed; liberal mainstream organizations, fearful that support for the communists in Hanoi would divide their constituency, at first declined. But in February, when President Johnson announced an increase in U.S. troops being sent to Vietnam, momentum for the march grew. The April 1965 march became a major success.

Suddenly, SDS found itself at the forefront of a national movement against the war. Teach-ins were used to recruit new campus members into the antiwar movement. Around the country, teachers and students held these loose-knit seminars, some of which ran all night, examining U.S. involvement in Vietnam. With a growing number of university professors against the war, the movement grew fast.

Then in the fall of 1965, SDS leader Paul Booth, a clean-cut Swarthmore student, was featured sympathetically on the national news describing why he supported draft resistance. Soon national exposure made Booth and other SDS leaders such as Hayden into overnight celebrities. The stories also stimulated a rapid growth in SDS membership—to 10,000 in 1966 and about 100,000 two years later. Campus organizers appealed to students in graphic terms: ". . . if you're tired of the Vietnamese eating napalm for breakfast, if you're tired of the blacks eating tear gas for dinner, and if YOU'RE tired of eating plastic for lunch, then give it a name: Call it SDS and join us."[21] SDS membership soon became something of a status symbol at many U.S. colleges. This very success was to prove SDS's undoing.

The Roots of Disintegration

Fresh from the success of the April 1965 march, 500 SDS delegates returned to Port Huron in June to chart the future path of the organization. SDS was changing. A new, more radical guard was emerging, suspicious of the older SDS leaders. *This new group opposed any form of authority or hierarchy.* Decision by consensus—the Cleveland model for participatory democracy—quickly replaced the loose parliamentary rules that had governed earlier national SDS gatherings. Workshop leaders were picked at random, and the office of national secretary (the chief administrative post) was abolished.

At the national office (now in Chicago), this new antielitist attitude meant that all staffers had to share administrative responsibilities of xeroxing, envelope stuffing, and even chairing meetings. It didn't work. At precisely the time when new membership applications were arriving in droves, the organization was in a state of near chaos. Participatory democracy, it seemed, worked better as a slogan for the movement than as a guide for managing a growing organization.

Internal tensions grew even more pronounced at the next two national SDS meetings. "Elder statesmen" like Paul Booth (age 23) and Tom Hayden (27) gave up all claims to titles within the organization. The December 1965 conference also brought to light conflicts between male and female members. Upset by male domination of SDS meetings, the SDS women spent part of the conference meeting alone, to the shock of male SDS leaders. Some consider this the starting point of the contemporary women's movement.

Internal dissension continued to grow over the choice of protest tactics. Although SDS helped stage the successful October 21, 1967 March on Washington, more radical new members believed that such nonviolent demonstrations were unproductive. Many SDS members were urging an alliance with the *Progressive Labor Party (PL)*, a Maoist organization that supported a worker-student alliance to overthrow the capitalist system. PL supporters argued against the need for any national organizational structure, thus further weakening the SDS national leadership. SDS was deteriorating into a loose national network of increasingly radical independent local chapters.[22]

The organization was also increasingly plagued by FBI informants, who often pushed for more drastic resistance tactics to expose SDS to police action. The U.S. government began investigations into SDS activities; SDS leaders' own actions and posturings also served to hurt the organization. In March of 1965, for example, SDS's national office sent out march-song lyrics that said: "And before I'll be fenced in, I'll vote for Ho Chi Minh, and go back to the north and be free." In December 1965, Hayden traveled to Hanoi at the invitation of the North Vietnamese government. Besieged by the Progressive Labor Party on the left and FBI informants pushing them to excess, SDS was disintegrating.

Tom Hayden became an overnight celebrity as a leader of SDS and remains politically active today.

The Whole World Is Watching

In 1968, America experienced a level of domestic violence seldom seen since the Civil War. Everything seemed to be falling apart. Martin Luther King was assassinated in April, which led to outbreaks of rioting. Two months later, Robert Kennedy, who was running for the

Democratic presidential nomination on an antiwar platform, was assassinated in Los Angeles. Between January and May of 1968 there were ten bombings or burnings of ROTC facilities on college campuses. SDS leaders, although they denounced the use of violence, were nonetheless tainted.

SDS led a takeover of the Columbia University campus in New York City in April 1968 to protest the war. Columbia was high drama for the network news, featuring radical speeches and a rowdy conclusion (forcible removal of the students by the police). To Middle America, Columbia was evidence that things had gotten out of hand. After Columbia, SDS's leadership was overtaken by events and other groups. Antiwar protests at the Democratic Convention in Chicago in August of 1968 highlighted the newly formed Youth International Party. The "Yippies" joked about putting the drug LSD in Chicago's water supply and sending an elite force of "sexy yippie males" to seduce the wives of convention delegates. Their new style—"symbolic politics"—was designed to both attract press attention and the reaction of authorities. The Yippies succeeded on both counts. Americans watched Mayor Richard Daley's police commit, in the words of a presidential commission which investigated the event, "a police riot."[23]

SDS itself splintered apart for good in June 1969, when the Progressive Labor Party completed its takeover of the national organization. Several factions emerged, including the radical *Weathermen* group. Far from the original SDS ideal of peacefully promoting social change through student activism, the Weathermen (and women) promoted working-class revolution through violence, such as their 1969 Days of Rage (a four-day spree of glass breaking and police confrontation). The Weathermen sect came to an abrupt end on March 2, 1970, when three members of the group were killed after a bomb they were working on exploded prematurely.

Although discredited by the Weathermen violence, the New Left movement continued (without SDS) into the 1970s. National protests against the U.S. invasion of Cambodia were held in May 1970. Four students were killed by authorities at Kent State, and two were killed at Jackson State. But as the war began to de-escalate and the drafting of students ended, so too did student activism. By 1972 it was over.

The Legacy of the Student Movement

The student movement began in 1960 as a grassroots call for reform. Despite its concern for domestic change, the movement's rapid emergence was propelled by the Vietnam War. But with growth also came threats. *The internal conflicts between the movement's ideals ("participatory democracy" and a suspicion of authority) and the movement's organizational needs (a structure to manage its growth) helped undermine the New Left.* The winding down of the war, pressures from authorities, and the rise of radical factions all sped up the decline.

However naive the New Left now appears, it did leave its mark. SDS's tradition of activism can be seen in today's women's movement, pro-environment groups, and in recent student protests against issues ranging from South African investments to Nicaraguan involvements. And former SDS members remain involved, such as Tom Hayden (formerly married to actress Jane Fonda) who is a controversial California state legislator. The roots of activism remain alive just below the political surface.

WRAP-UP

I know you are asking today, "How long will it take?" I come to say to you this afternoon, however difficult the moment, however frustrating the hour, it will not be long, because truth pressed to earth will rise again. How long? Not long, because no lie can live forever.

How long? Not long, because you still reap what you sow. How long? Not long. Because the arm of the moral universe is long but it bends toward justice.

How long? Not long, cause mine eyes have seen the glory of the coming of the Lord . . .[24]

When Dr. Martin Luther King, Jr. spoke these words in Montgomery, Alabama in 1965, he summed up both the lofty ideals and the frequent frustrations of political movements. Seeking broad social change by mobilizing mass support from underrepresented groups, these movements arise and grow only in certain settings. Starting with groups' recognition of their relative deprivation in society, they need the right historical moment, focused targets, and accepted leaders. In the American context their tactics will take forms of civil disobedience and legal direct actions, which require discipline and persistence with the rewards uncertain at best.

This uncertainty can be seen in the three movements examined in this chapter. The civil rights movement, in overcoming southern terrorism to gain integration and political rights in the 1950s and 1960s, had perhaps the most success. Yet the movement splintered, violent riots overtook the people it sought to lead, and its economic goals were suddenly out of reach. The women's movement has channeled its energies into legal and cultural arenas while women slowly take positions of power and equality in society. The student movement had the most defined history. It rose and fell in the 1960s. Aiming at broad change, it focused on stopping American involvement in the Vietnam War and fell apart due to internal weaknesses and external pressures.

Movements are a political system's necessary reminders. They remind satisfied leaders of ideals not attained and of people barely touched by society's affluence. They point the country's politics closer to its public purposes. And even if these movements do not share in the fruits of the policies they motivate, their presence offers participation to those least touched by America's government.

Key Terms

relative deprivation (p. 283)
historical moment (p. 283)
leaders (p. 284)
targets (p. 284)
civil disobedience (p. 286)
legal direct actions (p. 287)
boycott (p. 288)
strike (p. 288)
demonstrations (p. 288)
Jim Crow laws (p. 289)
Civil Rights Act of 1964
  (p. 292)

Voting Rights Act (p. 292)
Kerner Commission (p. 294)
sexism (p. 295)
Women's Liberation Movement
  (p. 297)
Equal Rights Amendment (ERA)
  (p. 298)
comparable worth (p. 300)
The Port Huron Statement
  (p. 302)
participatory democracy (p. 303)

Suggested Readings

Branch, Taylor, *Parting the Waters: America in the King Years* (New York: Simon & Schuster, 1988).

Garrow, David, *Bearing the Cross: Martin Luther King Jr. and the Southern Christian Leadership Conference 1956–1968* (New York: William Morrow & Co., 1986).

Gitlin, Todd, *The Sixties: Years of Hope, Days of Rage* (New York: Doubleday/Bantam, 1987).

Gwaltney, John, *The Dissenters: Voices from Contemporary America* (New York: Random House, 1986).

Harris, Fred and Roger Wilkins, *Quiet Riots: Race and Poverty in the United States* (New York: Pantheon, 1989).

Mansbridge, Jane, *Why We Lost the ERA* (Chicago: University of Chicago Press, 1986).

McGlen, Nancy and Karen O'Conner, *Women's Rights: The Struggle for Equality in the Nineteenth and Twentieth Centuries* (New York: Praeger, 1983).

Endnotes

[1] A deeper explanation of revolution can be found in Crane Brinton, *The Anatomy of Revolution,* rev. ed. (New York: Prentice-Hall, 1952), pp. 278–83.

[2] Steven Zak, "Ethics and Animals," in *The Atlantic,* Vol. 263, No. 3, March, 1989, pp. 68–74.

[3] See Martin Luther King, Jr., "Letter from Birmingham Jail," in Staughton Lynd, ed., *Nonviolence in America: A Documentary History* (Indianapolis: Bobbs-Merrill, 1966).

[4] Pacific News Service, reprinted in *Today* (February 10, 1984), p. 6.

[5] See Saul D. Alinsky, *Reveille for Radicals* (New York: Vintage Books, 1969); *Rules for Radicals* (New York: Vintage Books, 1971).

[6] As quoted by Harry Boyte, *The Backyard Revolution* (Philadelphia: Temple University Press, 1980). p. 28.

[7] Celene Krauss, "The Elusive Process of Citizen Activism," *Social Policy:* 14, no. 2 (Fall 1983), p. 53.

[8] Nancy Amidei, "How to Be an Advocate in Bad Times," *Public Welfare:* 40, no. 3 (Summer 1982): 37–42.

[9] C. Vann Woodward, *The Strange Career of Jim Crow* (New York: Oxford University Press, 1968).

[10] See generally, Allen J. Matusow, *The Unraveling of America* (New York: Harper and Row, 1984), p. 185.

[11] James M. Washington, ed., *A Testament of Hope: The Essential Writings of Martin Luther King, Jr.* (New York: Harper & Row, 1986), pp. 217–20.

[12] Report of the National Advisory Commission on Civil Disobedience (Washington, D.C.: Government Printing Office, 1968). (Also in paperback by Bantam Books.)

[13] See generally Anne Firor Scott and Andrew Mackay Scott, *One Half of the People: The Fight for Woman Suffrage* (Urbana, IL: University of Illinois Press, 1982).

[14] Judith Hole and Ellen Levine, *Rebirth of Feminism* (New York: Quadrangle Books, 1971).

[15] Betty Friedan, *The Feminine Mystique* (New York: Dell Publishing Company, 1974).

[16] National Commission of the Observance of International Women's Year, *To Form a More Perfect Union* (Washington, D.C.: U.S. Government Printing Office, 1976).

[17] All citations from the U.S. Department of Commerce Bureau of the Census, *Statistical Abstract of the United States 1988* (Washington, D.C.: United States Government Printing Office, 1987 ed.), pp. 151, 394–95.

[18] See *Washington Post* National Weekly Edition (August 6, 1984).

[19] See James Miller, *Democracy Is in the Streets* (New York: Simon and Schuster, 1987). Much of this section is based on Miller's book.

[20] C. Wright Mills, *The Power Elite* (New York: Oxford University Press, 1959).

[21] Quoted by Matusow, p. 337.

[22] See Kirkpatrick Sale, *SDS* (New York: Vintage Books, 1973).

[23] See William L. O'Neill, *Coming Apart* (New York: Quadrangle Books, 1979).

[24] *The New York Times,* March 26, 1965.

★ Arguably America's government *is* its institutions. The formal bodies of government are what the Constitution established and what the groups in the public arena try to influence. These institutions are both powerful weapons in competitive politics and valued prizes of the competition. They provide symbols of our national union and vital means for achieving political and economic goals.

Given their importance, it is not surprising that these institutions inspire contradictory public reactions. We have already encountered some of these debates in discussing their constitutional origins in Part One and their roles as "targets" of public participation in Part Two. Here we will look at the institutions from the inside, how they've changed, how they now function, and why people respond to them like they do.

Chapter Eleven looks at representatives in Congress, who they are, how they got there, and what influences them once they're there. Chapter Twelve discusses how Congress gets its work done and why it sometimes doesn't. Chapter Thirteen focuses on the president, the superstar of American politics, the resources and limits of the office, its impact on its occupants, and their impact on us. The bureaucracy, as shown in Chapter Fourteen, is, in theory, under the chief executive and is, in reality, most of the government which we deal with in our daily lives. Chapter Fifteen shows the courts operating the judicial system under the law yet not at all detached from politics.

Together these are the institutions around and through which the politics of America's government swirl.

PART THREE

AMERICA'S GOVERNMENT

The Institutions

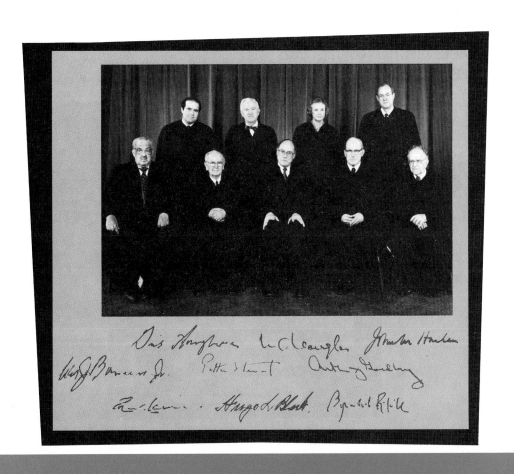

The division between the next two chapters helps in starting to analyze how the legislative branch operates. This chapter will focus on the "good" half—the individual representatives and senators. Who are they? How do they get to Congress and stay there? What do they do? And how are they influenced? This chapter also features a case study of a senator balancing pressures from his party, his constituents, and his conscience in voting on a controversial Supreme Court nomination.

MEMBERS OF CONGRESS

The U.S. Congress has 535 members—100 in the Senate and 435 in the House. Senators serve six-year terms and are elected by the population of an entire state. Every two years, one-third of the Senate seeks reelection. The other senators do not run because they are only one-third or two-thirds of the way through their terms.

Members of the House of Representatives (called "congressmen," even though Congress includes both the Senate and the House, and of course women) serve two-year terms. They are elected from congressional districts within states. Each state is assigned a number of representatives on the basis of its population. States with large populations have many congressmen; smaller states have fewer. Every state has at least one House member. (Washington, D.C. and four American territories—Puerto Rico, the Virgin Islands, Guam, and American Samoa—have non-voting members.) Congressional districts are drawn up by state legislatures, and no congressional district ever crosses state borders.

Any American who has been a citizen for at least nine years and who is at least thirty years old is eligible to serve in the United States Senate. Any American who has been a citizen for at least seven years and is at least twenty-five years old may serve in the United States House of Representatives. But these constitutional qualifications of age and citizenship do not tell the story of who gets to Congress.

WHO ARE THEY?

A closer look at our national representatives underlines the fact that they are not, strictly speaking, "representative" of the U.S. population (see the box on page 316). Although women constitute more than 50 percent of America's population, there were only two women, Nancy Landon Kassebaum (R-Kan.) and Barbara Mikulski (D-Md.) among the Senate's 100 members in 1989 and only 26 women among the 435 representatives in the House. There were no

black or Hispanic members of the Senate. The House included only 24 blacks (counting a non-voting delegate from the District of Columbia) and 12 Hispanics (counting one non-voting delegate from Puerto Rico and one from the Virgin Islands).

Senators and House members usually come from "high-status" occupations. Lawyers predominate; they made up nearly half of the total members of Congress in 1989. Each body also contains many people with backgrounds in business and banking, the second largest group at 166. A majority of the members of Congress (321) are, as would be expected from the religion of the general public, Protestant—244 from the four Protestant denominations: Baptist, Methodist, Episcopal, and Presbyterian. The number of Catholic and Jewish members has been growing in recent years, with 139 Catholics (the largest single denomination) and 39 Jews.

Are they religious? A study found that three-quarters of Congress said they attended a church or synagogue at least once a month, compared to only 50 percent of the general public. Considerably more members of Congress (90 percent) reported that they were members of churches or synagogues than was true for the rest of Americans (67 percent). But the authors of the study wrote that "There may not be any meaningful difference here. Being a member of a church is helpful: People expect it and raise their eyebrows if they find that a candidate is not a church member."[2]

★ Composition of the 101st Congress

MEMBERS	HOUSE	SENATE
	435	100
Average Age	52.1	55.6
Race (%)		
White	91	98
Black	5	0
Hispanic	3	0
Asian-American	1	2
Sex (%)		
Male	95	98
Female	5	2
Occupations (%)		
Actor	.5	0
Aeronautics	.5	2
Agriculture	4	4
Business/Banking	31	28
Clergy	.5	1
Education	10	11
Engineering	1	0
Journalism	4	8
Labor Officials	.5	0
Law	42	63
Law Enforcement	2	0
Medicine	1	0
Military	0	1
Professional Sports	1	1
Public Service/Politics	1	1

SOURCE: *Congressional Quarterly Weekly Report,* Nov. 12, 1988, pp. 3295–97.

Senators and representatives are different from average citizens in their education and, naturally, in their experience in political office. Some 94 percent of the members of the Senate have attended college, compared to only 24 percent of the general adult population in America. Most senators have held more than one previous political office. Today, however, with television, it is easier to get elected to Congress without prior political experience, especially for celebrities. The U.S. Senate includes a former astronaut, John Glenn (D-Ohio) and the House has former "Love Boat" actor Fred Grandy (R-Iowa).

Members of Congress have to work hard to stay in touch with people. Their salaries alone put them among the top 1 percent of all Americans in income. The salaries of both senators and representatives were raised to $89,500 in 1987 and would have been increased another 50 percent in 1989 if there had not been such a public outcry. Perquisites of congressional office—*perks*—include free stationery, free postage (called the "franking privilege") for official business, cut-rate life insurance, gymnasiums and health facilities, a free medical clinic, special beauty and barbershops, allowances for telephone and telegraph, trips home, staff and other professional assistance, and free offices in Washington and back home.

What does it mean that senators and representatives are not strictly typical of the average American citizen? If you were a young Hispanic woman, say, with a grade-school education, you might feel that the interests, outlooks, and opinions of this kind of Congress differ considerably from your own. And you would probably be right. But must members of Congress be exactly like us to represent us? For example, is an educated lawyer unable to represent the interests of working people? Not necessarily, but many Americans might feel closer to members of Congress—particularly in regard to race and sex—were they more similar to America's general population.

HOW DO THEY GET THERE—AND STAY?

There's a saying around Capitol Hill that before you can be a *good* congressman you have to be a congressman. Becoming, or staying, a member of Congress requires winning an election. Being an effective representative doing a competent job should be a crucial factor. But how voters see that is influenced by three key factors. Whether he or she is already there, **incumbency,** is most crucial. **Apportionment,** or the type of electorate represented, is important. Third is **campaign finances;** the ability to raise money for a modern expensive campaign is often the first question to be answered in running for election.

Incumbency

The most important factor in being elected to Congress is already being there. Over 90 percent of the incumbent House members who run for reelection are successful. In 1988, a record 98.5 percent of the incumbents running returned to the House. Of the 409 incumbents who sought reelection in 1988, 402 won. More than 75 percent of the incumbent members of Congress occupy so-called *safe seats,* where they repeatedly win reelection by more than 60 percent of the general election vote. The number of safe seats in the House, as well as the Senate, has been steadily increasing (see the boxes on pages 318–19).

Senate incumbency is not as much of an advantage as House incumbency, although about 80 percent of the senators who run for reelection win. (Twenty-three of twenty-seven incumbents won in 1988, an 85 percent reelection rate.) Fewer than half of the seats in the Senate can be considered safe. In part this reflects the smaller size of the Senate and the greater attention given to it in the media. This makes it harder for senators to duck controversial issues. The Senate's higher prestige may also attract stronger challengers.

The reasons for the growing advantage of incumbency are not difficult to find. As the section on apportionment shows, redistricting after each census usually helps House incumbents. State legislatures often draw district lines in a way that protects vulnerable incumbents. More important is that members of Congress have been placing greater emphasis on constituency service and the effective use of the perks of office. Incumbents have a public record; they can call

★ House Incumbents

U.S. HOUSE OF REPRESENTATIVES

YEAR	RETIRED	TOTAL SEEKING REELECTION	INCUMBENTS DEFEATED IN PRIMARIES	INCUMBENTS DEFEATED IN GENERAL ELECTIONS	REELECTED AS PERCENTAGE OF THOSE SEEKING REELECTION
1962	24	402	12	22	91.5
1964	33	397	8	45	86.6
1966	22	411	8	41	88.1
1968	23	409	4	9	96.8
1970	29	401	10	12	94.5
1972	40	390	12	13	93.6
1974	43	391	8	40	87.7
1976	47	384	3	13	95.8
1978	49	382	5	19	93.7
1980	34	398	6	31	90.7
1982	40	393	10	29	90.1
1984	9	411	3	16	95.5
1986	17	391	2	6	98.0
1988	11	409	1	6	98.5

SOURCES: For 1962–1980: *Vital Statistics in Congress, 1982.* pp. 42, 46–47. For 1982–1984: *National Journal,* November 6, 1982, p. 1881; and Congressional Research Service, Library of Congress. Updated and reprinted from Thomas E. Mann and Norman J. Ornstein, eds. *The American Elections of 1982* (Washington, D.C.: American Enterprise Institute, 1983), pp. 159–60, 164–65. For 1986: *1986 CQ Almanac,* Congressional Quarterly Press, Washington, D.C., 1987, pp. 11B–15B. For 1988: *Congressional Quarterly Weekly Report,* Nov. 12, 1988, pp. 3266–68 and Oct. 15, 1988, p. 2878.

attention to particularly popular votes they have cast. They are also more visible to constituents than their opponents because of their free mail, their public appearances, and their travel through the district. As one member of Congress put it:

> *The most effective campaigning is done when no election is near. During the interval between elections you have to establish every personal contact you can, and you can accomplish this through your mail as much as you do it by means of anything else. At the end of each session I take all the letters which have been received on legislative matters and write each person telling him how the legislative proposal in which he was interested stands.*
>
> *Personally, I will speak on any subject. I am not nonpartisan, but I talk on everything whether it deals with politics or not. Generally, I speak at non-political meetings. I read 48 weekly newspapers and clip every one of them myself. Whenever there is a particularly interesting item about anyone, that person gets a note from me. We also keep a complete list of the changes of offices in every organization in our district. Then when I am going into a town I know exactly who I would like to have at the meeting.[3]*

★ Senate Incumbents

U.S. SENATE		TOTAL SEEKING REELECTION	INCUMBENTS DEFEATED IN PRIMARIES	INCUMBENTS DEFEATED IN GENERAL ELECTIONS	REELECTED AS PERCENTAGE OF THOSE SEEKING REELECTION
YEAR	RETIRED				
1962	4	35	1	5	82.9
1964	2	33	1	4	84.8
1966	3	32	3	1	87.5
1968	6	28	4	4	71.4
1970	4	31	1	6	77.4
1972	6	27	2	5	74.1
1974	7	27	2	2	85.2
1976	8	25	0	9	64.0
1978	10	25	3	7	60.0
1980	5	29	4	9	55.2
1982	3	30	0	2	93.3
1984	4	29	0	2	93.1
1986	6	28	0	7	75.0
1988	6	27	0	4	85.1

SOURCES: For 1962–1980: *Vital Statistics on Congress, 1982*, pp. 44, 48. For 1982–1984: *Congressional Quarterly Weekly Report,* November 6, 1982, pp. 2789–91; and November 10, 1984, pp. 2923–30. For 1986–1988: Stuart Rothenberg, "The House and the Senate," in *Public Opinion,* Jan.-Feb. 1989, p. 9.

Senator Charles H. Percy (R-Ill.) was one of two Senate incumbents to lose in 1984. Percy, shown here thanking campaign supporters, narrowly lost to Democratic Representative Paul Simon. Simon charged that Percy had fallen out of touch with his constituents as Chairman of the Senate Foreign Relations Committee.

Incumbents can enhance their visibility to narrow national audiences through televising floor proceedings (see the box on page 321). One cable network, C-SPAN, gives gavel-to-gavel coverage of House and Senate sessions, and networks regularly use clips of speeches on nightly news programs. Members may send clips of their speeches to stations back home. The House and Senate control the cameras, so that they usually don't pan around a near-empty chamber or focus on a member dozing. In addition to televised floor debate, members take full advantage of canned announcements that are produced very cheaply for them in congressional studios and regularly sent to their local stations.

Incumbents also have paid staffs and offices. None of the perquisites of office is supposed to be used for political or campaign purposes, but the line is a hard one to draw. "I don't see the out-party able to get in, when incumbents flood their districts with questionnaires and staff," one Republican representative has said. Incumbents also find it easier to raise campaign money than do challengers, especially from PACs. Members of Congress are known quantities, likely to be elected, and contributors to them see their donations as investments in future access. Indeed, one expert on elections has written that "Incumbents can raise whatever they think they need," adding that "the stronger the challenge (operationally, the more the challenger raises and spends), the more the incumbent raises and spends."[4]

Casework

Incumbent members of Congress benefit from the ability to perform constituent service. This is called **casework.** It involves helping constituents solve individual problems or claims. A veteran who has been turned down for a disability pension may turn to his or her member of Congress as a "court of last resort." A surviving child may ask a senator for help on a Social Security claim. Nothing in the law requires members of Congress to give this kind of service, but many members view casework as an important way to make government policies more humane and get themselves reelected.

The constituent service expected of an individual legislator in Congress may conflict with the lawmaking function of Congress as an institution. For example, a zealous member of Congress, pressing a particular constituent's claim, may ask for a generous ruling by a federal agency, such as a liberal definition of disability. If this definition were followed in every case, it would result in a different national policy than that laid down by Congress as a whole.

Local Advocates

When Representative Neal Smith (Democrat of Iowa) sat down on a House-Senate conference committee to resolve differences in a bill to fund the Commerce, Justice, and State departments for 1989, his focus was on smaller things than the $15.3 billion spending total. During several lengthy negotiations Congressman Smith kept demanding that $7.5 million be inserted into the bill to pay for expanding a technology center at Iowa State University in Ames.

Even though the Ames project had been considered but rejected by the National Science Foundation, it was clear that this powerful member of the House Appropriations Committee wasn't going to let the massive bill get through until his project was approved. Finally an agreement was reached to shift money from other places to fund the project located in Smith's central Iowa district and the funding bill passed.[5]

"I regret that I have but one country to give to my congressional district," only slightly overstates the priorities of many members of Congress. Their local representation requires members to serve as "lawyers" for the interests of their district or state. For example, a member of Congress may feel that he or she must fight to get a dam

★ TV or Not TV

In June 1986, the Senate opened its sessions to television. This followed by seven years the House's allowing televised floor debates. While some Senate committee hearings had been televised before, notably the McCarthy-Army hearings in the 1950s and the Watergate hearings in the 1970s, there was opposition to allowing television on the Senate floor. The fear was that members would grandstand by putting on dark suits (which show better on televison) to give partisan speeches for a national audience.

By the time of the Senate's television debut, there was more of a fear that the House was overshadowing the Senate; that people could see the House in action but did not know what the Senate was doing. Television had helped make the former House Speaker, Thomas P. (Tip) O'Neill the most visible speaker in history. It had also helped keep congressmen better informed by allowing them to follow floor debates from their offices. After several years experience, television did not seem to have made much of a dent in much of the Senate's behavior.

built back home or prevent a military base from closing, even though the legislator—and his or her constituents—also favor the idea of cutting back on federal spending generally. Whether this local advocacy conflicts with the overall lawmaking goals expected of Congress is not a question most congressman are called on to answer by voters.

The power of congressional incumbency, especially evident in the House, tends to maintain stability (see Figure 11.1). It makes sudden changes in government policy less likely to occur through elections. One's attitude toward this trend depends largely upon whether or not one is satisfied with the way things are. Some political observers believe that the Republicans, the minority party in the House, may find it difficult to soon win enough seats to become a majority party there. This "permanent" Democratic majority in the House changes the system of checks and balances by allowing the Democrats to control legislation no matter who occupies the other branches. Furthermore, congressional elections may no longer be serving their original purpose of permitting voters to protest policies every two years by "throwing the rascals out."

Apportionment

At the beginning of each decade, the Bureau of the Census counts the nation's population, and the House of Representatives is reapportioned to reflect the change in each state's population. Between 1970 and 1980 the population had not only grown, but had also shifted toward the South and West. Because the number of seats in the House is limited by law to 435, after the 1980 census seventeen seats switched to the Sunbelt. New York, for example, lost five seats, while Florida gained four. After the states are allocated their seats the state legislatures shape the new districts, combining them in states losing population and splitting up districts in states gaining voters. This usually leads to intense fights between the two parties.

Until the Supreme Court decided *Wesberry* v. *Sanders* in 1964, the number of people who lived in different congressional districts varied considerably. Before Court-ordered reapportionment, a study showed that in twenty-one of the forty-two states with more than one congressional district the largest district had twice the population of the smallest district. In effect, a vote in the largest district was worth only one-half as much as a vote in the smallest district. The *Wesberry* case corrected this imbalance by holding **malapportionment** to be unconstitutional and requiring all congressional districts to be approximately equal in population.

FIGURE 11★1
The Incumbency Factor in Congressional Elections

PERCENTAGE OF INCUMBENT CANDIDATES ELECTED

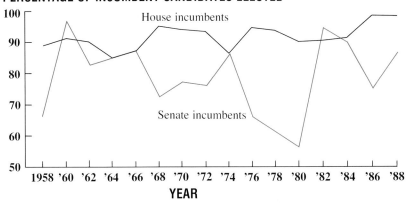

SOURCE: Norman J. Ornstein, Thomas E. Mann, and Michael J. Malbin, *Vital Statistics on Congress, 1987–1988* (Washington, D.C.: American Enterprise Institute, 1987), and *Congressional Quarterly Weekly Report,* November 2, 1988. Figures reflect incumbents running in both primary and general elections.

The *Wesberry* decision followed an earlier landmark case concerning state legislatures. In *Baker* v. *Carr,* the Supreme Court held that the courts could decide legislative apportionment matters, which had previously been considered "political" questions. Chief Justice Earl Warren said that the *Baker* decision was the most important Supreme Court ruling during his tenure. The rule is now "one person, one vote," and congressional districts today contain approximately 550,000 people.

While keeping each district approximately equal in population, state legislatures can still draw boundary lines in a way that favors particular candidates, incumbents, or parties. This practice is called **gerrymandering.** The name comes from Massachusetts Governor Elbridge Gerry, who in 1812 helped to draw a long, misshapen district composed of a string of towns north of Boston. The story goes that one critic observed, "Why, that looks like a salamander!" and another retorted, "That's not a salamander, that's a gerrymander." (See Figure 11.2.) The two most common forms of gerrymandering are "packing" and "cracking." *Packing* involves drawing up a district so that it has a large majority of your supporters, to ensure a "safe" seat. *Cracking* means splitting up your opponents' supporters into minorities in a number of districts to weaken their influence.

FIGURE 11★2
Twelfth Congressional District of New York, 1950s

"There are very few Republicans in Brooklyn, and distributed in ordinarily shaped districts they would never make a majority anywhere. But the Republican legislature strung G.O.P. areas into a district winding through the borough, and the result was Republican victories until this year."

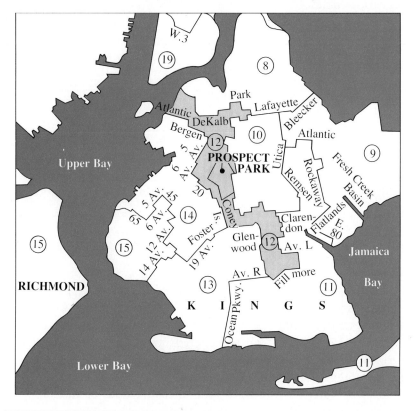

SOURCE: "Twelfth Congressional District of New York, 1950," from *The New York Times,* November 27, 1960 by Anthony Lewis. Copyright © 1960 by The New York Times Company. Reprinted by permission.

When the U.S. Supreme Court ruled malapportionment unconstitutional, it did not hold that gerrymandering was unconstitutional. In a 1986 ruling the Supreme Court upheld a gerrymander by the Republican-controlled Indiana state legislature. At the same time the Court held that redistricting to give an advantage to the majority party may sometimes violate the Constitution, but it couldn't decide what standard to use to judge such gerrymandering. The result of this confusing decision is to place gerrymanders in limbo.

Nationwide, any effort to limit gerrymanders will probably work against the Democratic party. The Democrats control a majority of state legislatures and there is some justification to Republican charges that the Democrats have gerrymandered them out of their true congressional strength. The Republican National Committee has made a special effort to win party control of state legislatures in order to influence the shape of congressional districts. Despite considerable funds spent on state legislative races, the Republican gains have been very limited. The results of the 1990 census can be expected to set off partisan struggles in many state legislatures and, often, the courts. Both parties have put considerable money into making sure apportionment in the early 1990s works in their favor.

Campaign Finances

If one receives, as I did in my last election in 1980, over $100,000 from labor PACs, and then if one were contemplating running for reelection in 1986—which I did not—then when a labor vote is coming up, I'd have to weigh the legitimacy and the merits of that particular vote versus a funding source that I might be looking forward to in the future. It so happens that my philosophical views tie in very closely with the AFL-CIO on a whole range of domestic social issues. But nonetheless, a vote or two or three might come along and I'd say, "I can't make up my mind on this issue," and my staff would tell me, "Well, let us remind you that labor's keenly interested in this issue and we're looking forward to labor's support next time."[6]
—Senator Tom Eagleton (D-Missouri) shortly before his retirement in 1987

Campaigns for Congress cost a great deal of money—more every election year. In 1988 the 66 Senate candidates spent a total of $190 million—nearly 6 percent more than the 1986 candidates who spent $179 million. But there were wide swings inside those totals: Senate winners averaged $3.7 million in expenditures, a 22-percent increase over 1986; Senate losers spent $1.8 million, a 20-percent *decrease* from 1986. Overall spending in Senate races has increased almost five-fold in the past dozen years, from $38.1 million in 1976. In California, incumbent Pete Wilson (R) and Lt. Gov. Leo McCarthy (D) spent a total of more than $21 million in their race alone, making that contest 1988's most expensive. For the first time, winning candidates in Senate races averaged over $1 million in political action committee (PAC) contributions to their campaigns.[7]

In the House, the average seat cost almost $360,000 to win or keep. PACS made record contributions to incumbents, giving them a total of $82.2 million compared to $9 million for the challengers. PACs favored incumbents over challengers by a ratio of more than 7 to 1 on average, one reason why in the 1988 general elections only six incumbents lost House races. One analyst said, "Members of the House are now less vulnerable politically than members of the Soviet Politburo."[8] Total expenditures on House races were $204 million, about 6 percent higher than the $194 million spent by House candidates in 1986. As in the Senate races, the modest overall increases masked a larger increase for incumbents and a decrease in spending for challengers (see the box on page 329).

Successful candidates for Congress do not have to have more money than their opponents. But an adequate amount of money to tell the candidate's story is essential. Early campaign money is much more important than late money. (One fundraising effort for women candidates is called "EMILY's List," with the initials standing for "Early Money Is Like Yeast.") Early money "is seed money for the entire campaign effort" and allows a candidate "to organize, plan, and raise more money."[9] Republican party committees are more likely to provide adequate campaign funds than Democratic party committees, and they are more likely to provide it early.

Among the changes suggested for reforming the present system of financing congressional campaigns, the most basic is to provide federal financing similar to what is done in presidential campaigns. Most Americans favor the idea of federal financing of congressional campaigns, with private contributions barred. A 1987 Gallup poll found that 50 percent of those polled said this was a good idea; 42 percent said it was a poor idea; and 8 percent expressed no opinion. The percentage of respondents in favor of federal financing has dropped steadily from a peak of 65 percent in 1973.[10] Since incumbents find it easier to raise money than do challengers, the incumbent members of Congress have blocked any such reform (see Figure 11.3).

HOW ARE THEY EXPECTED TO ACT?

Occasionally, there are manifestations of mass disrespect for a colleague who has exhibited some undesirable personality traits. One senator recalled an instance in which the session had extended into the early evening and Mike Gravel of Alaska arose to make a floor speech. "At that point," the senator recollected, "forty senators decided that it was time to have dinner."[11]

FIGURE 11★3
Sources of Receipts
All Congressional Candidates, January 1987–September 1988
Note: Charts do not reflect funds received prior to 1987–88.

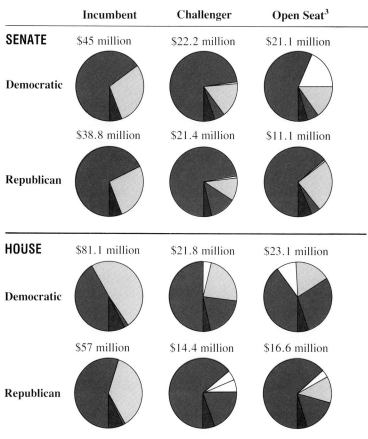

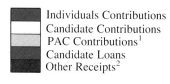
Individuals Contributions
Candidate Contributions
PAC Contributions[1]
Candidate Loans
Other Receipts[2]

	Incumbent	Challenger	Open Seat[3]
SENATE			
Democratic	$45 million	$22.2 million	$21.1 million
Republican	$38.8 million	$21.4 million	$11.1 million
HOUSE			
Democratic	$81.1 million	$21.8 million	$23.1 million
Republican	$57 million	$14.4 million	$16.6 million

Note: Charts do not reflect funds received prior to 1987–88.
     [1]PAC contributions include contributions from other candidate committees and from any other political committees that are not part of national or state party organizations.
     [2]Other receipts include, for example, party committee contributions, interest and dividends earned on investments, and offsets to expenditures.
     [3]Herbert Kohl's contributions to his Wisconsin senatorial campaign account for 98 percent of the contributions made by Democratic Senatorial candidates to their own seat races.

Speaker of the House Jim Wright announces his resignation before Congress in 1989 after being charged with unethical conduct.

Each house of Congress has its own informal, unwritten rules of conduct called **norms.** These norms describe "the way thing are done around here." They are learned by new senators and representatives in a socialization process that involves other members, senior colleagues, experienced staff assistants, and reporters. If members wish to have influence in the House or Senate, they must respect these norms. When he was Speaker of the House, Sam Rayburn regularly told new House members, "If you want to get along, you must go along."

Since norms are informal rules of conduct, sanctions for ignoring them are usually informal, though very real—less influence and respect. For bringing discredit on the "good name" of the House or Senate, sanctions may sometimes be more formal—removing a person as chair of a committee, voting censure or reprimand, or (in very rare cases) expulsion.

Among the most important congressional norms is that of *institutional loyalty.* This norm, which is a little stronger in the Senate than in the House, means generally that members should be loyal to their own House against the other and to Congress against interference from the president, the bureaucracy, or the judiciary. Members should avoid public criticism of the Congress (except, perhaps, when running for election), and should refrain from behavior that might bring the Congress into disrepute.

The norm of *courtesy and accommodation* means that a member of Congress should be courteous to other members—"disagreeing without being disagreeable," should be cooperative and willing to compromise where principle and back-home sentiment will allow, should refrain from excessive partisanship, and, because virtually all agreements between members are oral, should keep his or her word. When Representative Newt Gingrich (R-Georgia) first attacked the Democratic Speaker of the House for unethical conduct, many Republicans were shocked at what seemed a violation of norms. Jim Wright's resignation as Speaker in June 1989 led GOP members to a greater willingness to undercut norms of restraint that they felt helped keep them the minority party in the House.

The norms of **specialization** and **reciprocity** work together. Specialization means that once assigned to a committee or subcommittee a member is expected to become an expert in that area. Especially in the House, members are not expected to follow all legislation equally, or speak out on widely varying issues. That's where reciprocity comes in. Members are involved in the mutual recognition of the expertise of other members, particularly members of the committee with jurisdiction over the subject being considered. Legislators seek guidance on how to vote from their party's members on the committee specializing in the area.

These norms do not operate as strongly in the Senate. Senators serve on more committees and subcommittees, giving them broader interests. There are fewer senators and more wide-open floor debates, and senators are more likely to be national figures with national ambitions encouraging them to speak on any and all sub-

---

★ Top Ten House and Senate Fundraisers, 1988

SENATE

		TOTAL RECEIPTS
1.	Senator Pete Wilson (R-CA), incumbent winner	$14,511,755
2.	Senator Lloyd Bentsen (D-TX), incumbent winner	9,332,939
3.	Mayor George Voinovich (R-OH), challenger loser	8,278,013
4.	Senator Howard Metzenbaum (D-OH), incumbent winner	8,065,744
5.	Senator Frank Lautenberg (D-NJ), incumbent winner	8,033,550
6.	Peter Dawkins (R-NJ), challenger loser	7,739,164
7.	Herbert Kohl (D-WI), open seat winner	7,576,541
8.	Lt. Governor Leo McCarthy (D-CA), challenger loser	6,938,143
9.	Senator David Durenberger (R-MN), incumbent winner	6,807,046
10.	Senator John Heinz (R-PA), incumbent winner	6,104,682

HOUSE

1.	Robert Dornan (R-CA), incumbent winner	$1,731,888
2.	Gary Hart (D-CA), challenger loser	1,550,232
3.	Joseph DioGuardi (R-NY), incumbent loser	1,489,942
4.	Tom Campbell (R-CA), open seat winner	1,445,772
5.	Joseph Kennedy (D-MA), incumbent winner	1,410,821
6.	Nita Lowey (D-NY), challenger winner	1,338,150
7.	John Miller (R-WA), incumbent winner	1,328,979
8.	Jim Moody (D-WI), incumbent winner	1,281,491
9.	Robert Lagomarsino (R-CA), incumbent winner	1,226,234
10.	Jim Courter (R-NJ), incumbent winner	1,211,064

SOURCE: *Common Cause News,* March 2, 1989, pp. 5–6; March 28, 1989, p. 5.

jects. Even in the House, the recent increase in subcommittees, backed by ever-larger congressional staffs pushing their own proposals, has resulted in more hustling for votes and less automatic reciprocity.

Seniority

Lastly there is the norm of **seniority,** one of the most influential unwritten traditions in Congress. Seniority determines that the chair of any committee would be the majority-party member who has served the longest consecutively on the committee. The ranking minority member is selected by identical criteria from the minority party. The rankings within the committee run from the most senior to the most junior in a strict hierarchy based on time served on the committee.

For most of this century the custom of seniority was never broken. Then in the fall of 1974, Wilbur Mills, chairman of the House Ways and Means Committee, was involved in several public incidents with a striptease dancer, including an appearance on stage in a Boston burlesque house. This behavior, later attributed to a drinking problem, led to Mills's forced resignation from his chairmanship, which went to the next most-senior Democrat on the committee. Two years later another sex scandal occccurred. Wayne Hays, chairman of the House Administration Committee, was accused by a secretary of keeping her on the committee payroll for services beyond the call of duty. In spite of his seniority, the Democratic party caucus quickly acted to force Hays's resignation.

For the next decade, Democrats routinely elected their committees' most senior members as chairmen. However, in 1985 Les Aspin of Wisconsin deposed Melvin Price of Illinois as chairman of the House Armed Services Committee, winning the position over several more senior members. This breach in seniority worked against Aspin in 1987, when he was challenged by other committee members for the chairmanship and barely retained it.

While these challenges have not overturned seniority, they have made congressional leaders more vulnerable, and thus more cooperative and less authoritarian. In the smaller Senate, where seniority is not as important in participating in decison making, the seniority tradition has not been subject to the same attacks as in the House.

The seniority system (sometimes called the "senility system") has been attacked as out of date and undemocratic. It favors members from one-party regions like the South and urban North and the inner cities of the Northeast, where the same person is reelected to Congress time after time. But it also allows minorities in the Democratic party and moderates in the Republican party to gain positions of power, which they would never win on a vote of their parties. In spite of its presumed rigidity, seniority ensures that experienced people will become chairmen. It also provides *a predictable system of succession* that prevents constant fights over control of the chair. Whether seniority's influence continues to weaken will largely depend on the junior members of Congress who must serve apprenticeships under the system. Their incentives to try to undercut the system will probably decrease as they themselves gain seniority.

HOW ARE THEY INFLUENCED?

The goals motivating members of Congress are pretty straightforward. The first is *reelection*. Most members wish to keep or increase the support of their voters and thus ensure their tenure in office. The second is adding to their *influence in the House or Senate*. Congressmen will act so that their power is enhanced in the body in which they serve. The final goal is contributing to *good public policy*. However filtered through ideological or partisan perspective, members generally justify their actions as being in the best interest of the nation.

The mix or intensity with which these three goals are pursued varies with the influence other important political players can bring to bear on particular issues. The influences on members' votes come from six major sources: 1) *constituency*, 2) *colleagues*, 3) *political party*, 4) *interest groups*, 5) *presidency and executive branch*, and 6) *congressional staff*.

Congressmen have an obligation to keep in touch with the people. Here, Senator Edward Kennedy speaks with victims of a flood that devastated Albright, West Virginia. Kennedy, while born into a wealthy and powerful family, has championed the interests of the poor and underprivileged throughout his career.

Constituency Influence

There are two opposing concepts of how elected representatives should respond to their constituents. In between the two lies a more accurate picture of how most of them do behave.

On one hand, some legislators think of themselves as **delegates.** They feel they must vote with the majority opinion in their district or state. Their job becomes one of being an ambassador: Find out what the "folks back home" want and *re-present* that view in Congress. As one Congressman put it: "I am here to represent my district. This is part of my actual belief as to the function of a congressman. What is good for the majority of my district is good for the country. What snarls up the system is these so-called statesmen-congressmen who vote for what they think is the country's best interest."[12]

This opposing "statesman-congressman" view sees legislators as **trustees.** Here representatives are obligated to vote as their judgment and conscience demand. The great conservative English philosopher

---

★ Top Speech Fee Recipients

TOP SENATE SPEECH FEE RECIPIENTS IN 1987

Bob Dole (R-Kan)	$106,050
Ernest F. Hollings (D-S.C.)	$99,400
Don Reigle (D-Mich)	$86,750
Orrin Hatch (R-Utah)	$79,926
Richard G. Lugar (R-Ind)	$71,485
Alan K. Simpson (R-Wyo)	$71,425
Thomas Daschle (D-S.D.)	$60,450
Dave L. Boren (D-Okla)	$59,175
Daniel Patrick Moynihan (D-N.Y.)	$55,575
Bob Packwood (R-Ore)	$50,500

TOP HOUSE SPEECH FEE RECIPIENTS IN 1987

Dan Rostenkowski (D-Ill)	$245,000
William H. Gray III (D-Pa)	$119,038
Bill Gradison (R-Ohio)	$96,250
Dick Cheney (R-Wyo)	$79,350
Tony Coelho (D-Calif)	$78,500
Henry Waxman (D-Calif)	$76,400
Bill Frenzel (R-Minn)	$70,650
Robert H. Michel (R-Ill)	$61,250
Thomas A. Luken (D-Ohio)	$59,700
Robert Matsui (D-Calif)	$55,950

SOURCE: *Congressional Quarterly Weekly Report,* June 11, 1988, pp. 1572–73.
NOTE: Fees over the allowed 30–40 percent of annual salaries cannot be kept by members and are usually donated to charities.

Edmund Burke, who distinguished between delegates and trustees, came down strongly in favor of the latter. He believed he was elected to exercise his judgment, and that a representative body was a place for deliberation and formulating policy in the interest of the nation as a whole. A less-elevated view of this maintains that legislators are not very accountable to their constituents for how they vote. "The people back home don't know what's going on. Issues are not most important so far as the average voter is concerned."[13]

Most members of Congress can realistically be called **politicos.** They are sometimes delegates and sometimes trustees. Depending on the importance of the principle involved and the intensity of constituency feeling about an issue, the members may be swayed one way or the other. As a member of Congress has said, "I am sent here as a representative of 600,000 people. I try to follow my constituents—to ignore them would be a breach of trust—but I use my judgment often because they are misinformed. I know they would vote as I do if they had the facts that I have."[14]

These concepts of representation are not necessarily very helpful in analysing how or why a member votes a certain way. While constituency influence may well be the most important factor in a member's vote, the influence often comes in different forms with varying effects.

For example, *in general, the more visible an issue, the greater the input from constituents.* At the least members know they will have to explain the vote to their voters. But *intensity* of feeling by constituents is equally relevant. Very few representatives will vote against the vital interests of a key industry back home. In most cases constituency influence acts to constrain behavior; members know that some votes will be costly to them by arousing opposition. *Constituency influence makes some votes highly unlikely.*

Colleagues' Influence

Members of Congress cannot become experts on every subject before them. Each session, they must vote on hundreds of bills and thousands of proposed amendments. Many of these involve matters on which there may be no back-home sentiment or about which they may not feel strongly. Members of Congress frequently rely upon voting **cues** from other members. For example, a senator may ask a colleague while riding over to the Senate chamber for a roll-call vote, "What's this?" The colleague may reply, "It's the Miller amendment," referring to another member of the Senate. "Oh, an easy 'no' vote," the first member might say, knowing Miller to be his opposite on most matters.

In other words, senators and House members often get a cue on how to vote by learning who is for and against the question. Cues have special weight when they come from people who are considered experts on the issue involved, or members representing similar districts or like-minded colleagues from the same party. One senator illustrated this reliance in a comment about a former senator from Massachusetts:

> *When Leverett Saltonstall was whip I'd turn to him. One time I went to see him on a bill, and he said to me, "I'm going to vote for this bill, but you shouldn't where you come from." I believed what he told me.*[15]

In some ways congressional colleagues are perfect lobbyists. They are fellow politicians knowing the ropes of the trade, they may be from the same state or region, and they are usually available with little fanfare at the time of the vote. Most importantly, members have a free choice as to who to ask, whose judgment they trust, and whose knowledge they respect. For advice on how to vote congressmen will often go to someone whose voting record closely matches their own.

Party Influence

On most major conflicts, most Democrats vote against most Republicans. If their constituency will allow it, most members will tend to follow their party line in voting. This is not to say that the parties are unified voting blocs. With regional coalitions, state delegations, defense hawks vs. doves, and conservative Democrats opposing liberals, there are numerous alignments other than parties. But the party label does make a difference, despite the rather weak structures of the parties and the lack of leverage this gives party leaders.

As shown in Chapter 9, being a Democrat or a Republican generally reflects a certain policy orientation and political philosophy. Democrats tend to be more liberal, Republicans more conservative. Being elected as a Democrat also tends to give a member a similar demographic base and supporting coalitions as other Democrats, like unions and minorities. Members will also rely on party colleagues for advice on voting. And, of course, every elected member has experienced running against the other party's candidate which builds in a certain partisan antagonism once in office.

On bills that congressmen don't care about, they will tend to listen to their party's senior committee members and party leaders. As we will see in Chairman Dan Rostenkowski's activities on tax reform,

leaders also have political resources in dealing with members (see the case study in Chapter 12). They can control the scheduling of bills, speaking on the floor, committee assignments, and whether a member's interests are reflected in committee bills passing under their gaze. In short, there is always a cost to opposing the party leadership.

Interest Group Influence

Gentlemen may find ways to do each other favors. Take the example of Senator Olin Johnston of South Carolina, and Reader's Digest. *Senator Johnston, as chairman of the Senate Post Office and Civil Service Committee, had tremendous power over the postage rates to be paid by newspapers, magazines, and other periodicals;* Reader's Digest *was, and is, among the big users of the mail in distributing its product. Obviously, accommodations were in order. About every six years—when he came up for reelection—the senator's by-line appeared in their magazine over stories tending to do great credit to his public record.*[16]

As previously discussed, interest groups can influence Congress through campaign donations and hired lobbyists. Much of the information representatives and their staffs get on an issue comes from interest groups involved in a fight over it. They often do much of a legislator's work. Interest groups also use other techniques of pressure day in and day out on members of Congress. Three of the most common are (1) *grassroots pressure,* (2) *speaking fees,* and (3) *ratings and endorsements.*

Grassroots Pressure via Modern Technology

This is a sample of a letter sent to constituents in a mass-mailing campaign. All the voter has to do is sign the letter and put it in a pre-addressed stamped envelope.

HOWARD K. SKOLNIK

Senator Dennis DeConcini
U.S. Senate
Washington, D. C. 20510

Dear Senator DeConcini:

I, for one, think the Reagan administration has gone too far. In the face of an overwhelming pro-family planning majority in this country, the administration is still insisting on the minority position. Having failed at home to end family planning programs and alter the legality of abortion, President Reagan has taken his ideological quest to the developing world.

The point of contention here is the so-called "Mexico City" or anti-abortion clause that has been inserted without any legislative authority into cooperative agreements between the U.S. Agency for International Development (AID) and agencies that work with foreign non-governmental providers of family planning services. In order to receive AID funds, overseas providers must sign a clause which requires the provider to break all ties with any program involved in abortion counseling, advocacy, referral or services—although these programs do not use U.S. Government dollars.

The policy must be repudiated when the Foreign Assistance bill comes before Congress. As a member, you have an important opportunity to reject the "Mexico City" policy and send a clear message to the White House: This is a Democracy and the will of the majority will not be held at bay or stifled by a small extremist faction!

Please, do your part to reverse the "Mexico City" policy.

Respectfully,

Howard K. Skolnik

Howard K. Skolnik

210 S. Darling Avenue   **Tucson, Arizona   85710**

Some of the most effective grassroots pressure comes from groups whose rank and file members live in the home states or districts of many members of Congress. Interest groups such as beer wholesalers, home-builders, or automobile dealers can organize members throughout the country and target their efforts toward selected members of key committees. Grassroots pressure can be greatly enhanced by modern technology. Tens of thousands of seemingly personal letters can be produced for constituents by an interest group using computers and laser printers. Several thousand letters from voters cannot be lightly dismissed (see Figure 11.4).

Interest groups pay fees, or *honoraria*, to members for speeches to their organization, or sometimes for just attending an industry seminar. In 1984, Congress (with the reluctant agreement of the Senate, whose better-known members have usually made the most from public speaking) agreed to limit these fees to 30 percent of House salaries and 40 percent of Senate salaries. Speaker Jim Wright's effort to get around these limits through large royalties from a book of speeches helped lead to his resignation from Congress. These fees have, however, continued to nicely supplement members' salaries (see the box on page 332).

These fees are not paid just to hear a good speech. One year the billboard industry, which wants to weaken federal laws restricting

---

★ Congressional Staffers Cover Up the Goofs

Congressional staffers are said to be indispensable. Senator Strom Thurmond (R-South Carolina) found that out when he went to read the opening statement at a committee hearing. The situation went something like this: Thurmond's staff had provided him with his statement and list of questions for his hearing. When he arrived at the hearing, he began reading his statement, and then continued on, uninterrupted: "If the first witness answers 'Yes,' then ask him so and so . . . If the witness answers 'No' or 'I'm not sure,' then ask him such and such." Although Thurmond did not seem to realize what he was saying, his audience did. An aide hurried over to Thurmond's side and took the paper from him.

SOURCE: Morris Udall, "Some Political Laughs for an Unfunny Week," *The Washington Post,* October 25, 1987.

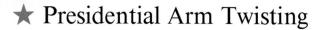

★ Presidential Arm Twisting

Senator Robert Byrd, who has had his arm twisted by presidents of both parties, offered an imaginary dialogue of what a White House phone call is like:

"Hello, Mr. President."

"Bob, I have been wanting to talk to you about something . . . I know you have some moneys in the appropriations bill for the Gallipolis Locks and Dam."

"Yes, sir."

"The people of West Virginia, in my opinion, are to be complimented in having you as their Senator. I know you have worked hard for that funding. . . . By the way, Bob, we have this piece of legislation that is going to be coming up in the Senate in a few days to authorize moneys for the contras in Central America. Gee, I wish you would support that, Bob. . . . It will be used only for food and medicines. . . . I respect you for your opposition to that funding, but I wish you would see your way to vote with us next time on that. Can you do it?"

"Well, I will certainly be glad to think about it, Mr. President. . . ."

"Well, Bob, I hope you will. And by the way, that money for the heart research center in Morgantown that you have worked for, I will bet your people love you for that."

"Yes, Mr. President. There is a lot of support for that in West Virginia."

"Bob, I have given a lot of thought to that. Be sure and take another look at that item we have, funds for the contras."

SOURCE: *The New York Times,* Friday July 26, 1985, p. A10. Copyright © 1985 by the New York Times Company. Reprinted by permission.

highway signs, paid some $67,000 to twenty-five senators and twenty-four House members. A dozen major defense industries paid $60,000 to nine members of the House Appropriations Committee. While some suggest that these fees smack of bribery, their real importance is to give interest groups access to key members of Congress.

From labor's AFL-CIO to business's U.S. Chamber of Commerce, interest groups issue *ratings of members' voting records* at the end of each session. These ratings, along with the organization's endorsements, show predictable conservative-liberal patterns in Congress. Republicans support business issues more frequently than Democrats, while most Republicans, not surprisingly, win little support from labor unions. These endorsements can help or hurt in raising campaign contributions. One senator remarked that the lack of an endorsement by the Chamber of Commerce cost him $150,000 in contributions from other business groups.

Presidential and Executive Branch Influence

As the story by Senator Byrd (in the box on page 338) makes clear, a presidential request can be a fearsome thing. A popular president skillfully using the resources of his office behind his legislative program can often prove unstoppable. Certainly Lyndon Johnson's "Great Society" program of the mid-1960s and Ronald Reagan's early budgets illustrate this point. As Figure 11.5 shows, presidential success with Congress often comes early in an administration when presidential popularity is the greatest. But more often, on less-visible measures, the influence of the executive branch on congressional votes is difficult to measure and hard to see.

FIGURE 11★5
Presidential Success on Votes in Congress

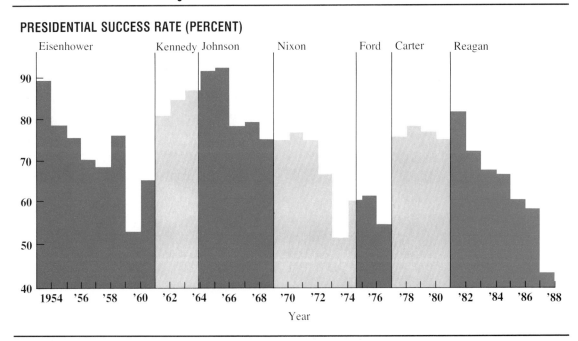

SOURCE: George C. Edwards, III, *At the Margins: Presidential Leadership of Congress* (New Haven, Conn.: Yale University Press, 1989), Table 2.1.

The constitutional separation of powers encourages a certain jealousy between the branches of government. Congress is wary of any trespassing on its turf, and congressmen as a rule distrust bureaucrats. Viewing the executive branch as another lobbyist, members of Congress often pride themselves in standing up to administration requests. Members of the president's party are, naturally, more likely to follow their leader. And, of course, a president's prestige, his ability to grant or withhold favors, and his hold over public opinion are not to be dismissed lightly. But in deciding how to vote on an issue, a member of Congress is likely to allow the executive relatively little influence over his or her decisions (see the case study on page 342).

Congressional Staff Influence

As the workload of Congress has grown, so has the staff. Congress is the most heavily staffed legislature in the world. Its more than 31,000 employees contrast with the British House of Commons where 650 members get by with about 1000 employees.[17] Other than voting, a member's staff is likely to do everything he or she does. Staff will organize hearings, negotiate agreements with other members' staffs, write questions of witnesses at committee hearings, research propos-

Senator Alfonse D'Amato with members of his staff. The staff perform important functions that range from helping senators maintain their packed schedules to lobbying them for bills.

als, speak with constituents, and promote legislation for which its bosses can take credit (see the box on page 337). Lobbyists understand the importance of the staff and thus spend much of their time cultivating relations with them. Staffers will often initiate proposals and then "sell" them to their bosses.

The influence of the staff is best exercised quietly. Staff are hired with an eye for their agreement with the member, and can be quickly fired in case of disagreement. An effective staffer will operate as part of a member's decision-making team. This makes it difficult to assess staff influence. As the trusted eyes and ears of many an overworked member, and often able to focus on particular issues more deeply, staff influence is always present if only partially visible.

A Senator Decides: The Battle Over Robert Bork

President Reagan's July 1, 1987 nomination of Judge Robert Bork to a U.S. Supreme Court vacancy brought on the Senate's most furious battle over a court nominee in memory. Both sides agreed on the issue. The Bork selection would tip the liberal-conservative balance of the Court in a conservative direction—*if* the Senate would "advise and consent."

The Senate Judiciary Committee had the initial role in the process, holding lengthy hearings and then voting on whether the nomination should go to the full Senate floor. Within the committee, enormous crosspressures were put on moderate senators, notably liberal Republican Senator Arlen Specter of Pennsylvania, widely viewed as a decisive swing vote in a close fight. Specter's decision on Bork's confirmation illustrates the varying importance of the factors surrounding a senator's vote—constituents, colleagues, staff, party, the White House, and interest groups—as well as one other factor sometimes overlooked—the member's own beliefs.

President Ronald Reagan nominates Judge Robert Bork to the U.S. Supreme Court on July 1, 1987.

Setting the Stage

The long summer recess between the July 1 nomination and the early-October committee vote gave the members and staff time to look over Judge Bork's extensive writings. Liberal interest groups, knowing Bork was a likely nominee for the Court, had been preparing to fight him for years; the recess gave them time to gear up.

The recent Supreme Court nominations of William Rehnquist (to Chief Justice) and Antonin Scalia (to the seat Rehnquist's promotion opened) had encouraged official Washington and the public to accept the president's nominees to the Court as a debatable political issue. Reagan called Bork's appointment his "top priority." News analysis suggested that the Bork confirmation had "thrust electoral politics and public opinion into the Supreme Court confirmation process more deeply than ever before."[18]

Bork himself was a respected judge on the U.S. Court of Appeals for the District of Columbia Circuit, and a former Solicitor General in the Justice Department. He was also a conservative, opinionated law professor. He first entered public view in 1973 when, as Solicitor General and the third-ranking Justice Department official, he followed President Richard Nixon's order to fire Watergate special prosecutor Archibald Cox in the famous "Saturday Night Massacre." Bork did this after his two immediate superiors resigned rather than carry out Nixon's wishes. That Nixon was clearly trying to stop Cox's investigation from discovering the president's involvement in the burglary of Democratic offices only made Bork look like he was part of the cover-up.

An Undecided Republican

Senator Specter, as the only Republican on the Judiciary Committee whose vote was in doubt, became a key target of grassroots pressure throughout the summer. He said later that "the hearings brought a record 140,000 letters and calls to my office. Wherever I went it seemed that everyone had a strong opinion. The pressure was pervasive."[19]

Anti-Bork partisans in Pennsylvania purchased their own media advertising in the state to influence Specter. The pro-Bork forces put on an "ambush" that was described this way by the *Washington Post:* ". . . more than 60 members of the College Republicans chapter at the University of Pennsylvania . . . waited to ambush Specter here Saturday at a meeting of the Republican State Committee. . . . The students unfurled their signs— one said 'Don't be a Dork; Confirm Bork.'" Specter's office estimated at that point that phone calls and postcards were running about two to one in favor of confirming Bork.[20]

But Specter had resources to stand against the tide if he chose. He had won a respectable 56 percent reelection in 1986—a difficult year for incumbent Republicans—in a state with a Democratic majority. He was more secure than most GOP senators, at least until his term ended in 1992.

Specter's willingness to listen to the White House was muddled by a somewhat difficult relationship. His 1985 vote to build the MX missile had meant reversing himself and voting with the administration after heavy pressure from the White House that included a threat to cut off fund-raising help in his 1986 reelection campaign. The pub-

licity given the threat led Specter to refuse help from the White House. His victory without White House fundraising had made him less vulnerable to administration pressure. Now, Specter told a reporter, the White House had "modulated" its approach to him. This new approach included two lengthy meetings with Reagan's chief of staff, former Senate Majority Leader Howard H. Baker, Jr. Specter remained "undecided."

Meanwhile, interest groups in the anti-Bork coalition coordinated by the Leadership Conference on Civil Rights organized early, worked hard, and focused attention on the nominee's most controversial statements. Groups such as the ACLU and the NAACP Legal Defense Fund had a close relationship with Specter's staff (one of whom described himself and the rest of the staff as more liberal than the liberal senator). These groups answered questions about Bork's positions on specific topics. Providing substantive legal information on matters of concern to the senator and his staff was considered these groups' most powerful influence. The responses from pro-Bork lobbyists were little and late.[21]

The Committee Decides

Within the committee, the process of deliberation and the

influence of colleagues had an effect. Democrat Joseph Biden of Delaware, the new Judiciary Committee chair, got high marks from many observers for an even-handed examination of Bork's qualifications. But it was noted that Biden "carefully structured the scheduling of witnesses and gave selective emphasis to Judge Bork's published views, in an effort to dominate the news and appeal to undecided senators and the constituencies on which they depend." Specter, for his part, had "made a career" out of being an undecided member of the Judiciary Committee, as *Congressional Quarterly* put it.

The committee held its September hearings in the midst of groups struggling to define the landscape against which the vote would take place. Some worked on shaping the "facts" by presenting the staff with information from interest groups and hometown media. Others pushed mail and phone calls from constitutents to provide ammunition to alter the electoral arithmetic of the vote. Through the media, the anti-Bork forces seemed to win the struggle over the agenda. Senators were able to justify a rejection of a "rubber-stamp" comfirmation in favor of a genuine "advise and consent" role. The issue of Bork's *politics* as well as his judicial *qualifications* became a legitimate basis for decison.

For example, during the hearings Specter made statements affirming his "open mind" and won significant praise for his tough questioning of witnesses. The *Philadelphia Inquirer* called it "his finest hour." Specter said later that he was troubled by the likelihood that Bork would cast a deciding vote on some close questions involving individual rights, such as free-speech cases. Specter also noted that he had read all of Bork's articles, opinions, and other evidence of his judicial philosophy.

The anti-Bork forces in the Senate, media, and interest groups had rewritten the script. Rather than the story of a popular president who deserved his own way on a Supreme Court nomination, it became "... a lame-duck President should not be able to use his appointment power to further a social agenda that he cannot get through Congress, especially at a time when the Court is so closely balanced ..." as *The New York Times* outlined it.[22]

With the battle described in those terms, senators could openly focus on Bork's judicial philosphy. And for Specter, the eventual deadlock of public opinion in his home state left him free as another senator put it, "to make a substantive decision."

A Specter staffer remembered Specter saying "he always considers his constituents' views on issues, but this was not an issue where he

Supreme Court Justice nominee Robert Bork testifies before the Senate Judiciary Committee holding his confirmation hearings in September 1987.

thought these views would necessarily control; he wasn't running a tally."[23] With the agenda focused on the nominee's judicial philosophy, a divided constituency, and a White House that Specter felt little debt to, the senator could later argue that his decision was free of politics: ". . . . my goal was to figure out what impact Judge Bork would have on the people who came to the Supreme Court in search of their constitutional rights. . . . My substantial doubts persisted, and so I decided to vote no."[24]

The Judiciary Committee, after thirty hours of hearings, voted 9–5 against the nomination, with Specter the only one of six Republicans voting "no." On Oct. 23, 1987, the full Senate voted 58–42 against naming Bork to the Supreme Court.

Conclusion

Motives, especially those of politicians, are never easy to determine. Yet there is no reason to dispute the senator's explanation that he made a decision on the merits of the appointment. That is not to say that the organizing and pressures from interest groups, constituents, colleagues, and the press had no effect. In fact, the anti-Bork groups had created a situation that a Specter staffer described as "no political plus either way." This was, in fact, a considerable *political* achievement. It meant that the partisan pressures of constituents, party, and president were neutralized for the Republican senator. And it meant that Specter, a liberal from a liberal state, could vote agianst Bork, a conservative jurist whose positions he opposed.

WRAP-UP

Members of Congress are generally overworked, popular, high-status professionals. A typical member is a white Protestant male lawyer. Most are there because they're already there and, as incumbents, are regularly reelected. Apportionment of House districts helps to create safe constituencies, and campaign financing by PACS and others overwhelmingly favors incumbents.

Within Congress, members follow unwritten norms, from specializing on certain committees to deferring to seniority in voting for committee chairmen. In deciding how to vote they follow other unwritten channels of influence. Their home state or district, which can take their jobs away, tends to be their first priority. If the message from the constituency isn't clear, a member will listen to friendly colleagues. The opinions of party leaders are important, and interest groups will weigh in, as will the executive branch agencies and the member's own staff. The politician's craft comes in balancing and sorting out these often competing pressures, which may allow members, at the end of the day, to vote their own preferences, as Senator Specter apparently did.

Professor Richard Fenno quotes a congressman saying, "People don't like Congress, but they do like their own man."[25] The reason they do is that most members have lived up to James Madison's hope that "a local spirit" would prevail in these elected officials. The most direct link between voters and their government lies in these individual members. They represent the essence of representative goverment.

Key Terms

incumbency (p. 317)	specialization (p. 328)
apportionment (p. 317)	reciprocity (p. 328)
campaign finances (p. 317)	seniority (p. 330)
casework (p. 320)	delegates (p. 332)
malapportionment (p. 322)	trustees (p. 332)
gerrymandering (p. 323)	politicos (p. 333)
norms (p. 328)	cues (p. 333)

Suggested Readings

Fenno, Richard, *The Making of a Senator: Dan Quayle* (Washington, D.C.: Congressional Quarterly Press, 1988).

Kennedy, John F., *Profiles in Courage* (New York: Harper & Row, 1956).

Malbin, Michael, *Unelected Representatives* (New York: Basic Books, 1982).

Mayhew, David R., *Congress: The Electoral Connection* (New Haven, Conn.: Yale University Press, 1974).

Miller, James A., *Running in Place: Inside the Senate* (New York: Simon & Schuster, 1986).

Moynihan, Daniel P., *Came the Revolution: Argument in the Reagan Era* (New York: Harcourt Brace Jovanovitch, 1988).

Ornstein, Norman, and Shirley Elder, *Interest Groups, Lobbying, and Policymaking* (Washington, D.C.: Congressional Quarterly Press, 1978).

Endnotes

[1] Adapted from Fred Barnes, "The Unbearable Lightness of Being a Congressman," in *The New Republic,* February 15, 1988, p. 20.

[2] Peter L. Benson and Dorothy L. Williams, *Religion on Capitol Hill: Myths and Reality,* (New York: Harper and Row, 1982), p. 80.

[3] Quoted in Charles L. Clapp, *The Congressman: His Work As He Sees It* (Washington, D.C.: The Brookings Institution, 1963), p. 332.

[4] See Gary C. Jacobson, "Money in the 1980 and 1982 Congressional Elections," in Michale J. Malbin, *Money and Politics in the U.S.* (Chatham, N.J.: Chatham House, 1984), p. 57.

[5] *The Washington Post,* May 30, 1989.

[6] As quoted by Hedrick Smith, *The Power Game.*

[7] "The Winning Edge," Common Cause Press Release, March 2, 1989.

[8] Stuart Rothenberg, "Election '88: The House and the Senate," in *Public Opinion,* January/February 1989, pp. 8–11, 59.

[9] Gary C. Jacobson, *The Politics of Congressional Elections* (Boston: Little, Brown, 1983), pp. 58–59.

[10] Lawrence Erlbaum, *The Gallup Report: Public Opinion 1987,* Camden, N.J., 1987.

[11] Ross K. Baker, *Friend and Foe in the U.S. Senate,* p. 246.

[12] Quoted in Lewis Anthony Dexter, "The Representative and His District," in Robert Peabody and Nelson W. Polsby, *New Perspectives on the House of Representatives* (Chicago: Rand McNally, 1969), p. 6.

[13] Charles L. Clapp, p. 421.

[14] Charles O. Jones, "The Agriculture Committee and the Problem of Representation," in Peabody and Polsby, *New Perspectives,* p. 168.

[15] Ross K. Baker, *Friend and Foe in the U.S. Senate,* p. 200.

[16] Bobby Baker and Larry King, *Wheeling and Dealing* (New York: W. W. Norton and Company, 1978), p. 51.

[17] *The Wall Street Journal,* March 21, 1988.

[18] Stuart Taylor, Jr., *The New York Times,* September 28, 1987, and Elizabeth Drew, "Letter from Washington," *The New Yorker,* September 2, 1987, p. 153.

[19] Arlen Specter, "Why I Voted Against Bork," *The New York Times,* October 9, 1987.

[20] *The Washington Post,* September 29, 1987.

[21] June, 1988 interview transcript, Jeff Robinson, former Judiciary Committee subcommittee staffer to Senator Specter, provided by Bork project, The Advocacy Institute.

[22] *The New York Times,* September 28, 1987.

[23] Robinson Transcript.

[24] *The New York Times,* October 9, 1987.

[25] Richard Fenno, *Home Style* (Boston: Little, Brown, 1978), p. 165.

★

CHAPTER 12

Congress: The Institution

★

In some ways, being in Congress is more like being in high school than anything I've done since high school—I mean the way the structure is. Nobody in the House of Representatives can give any other member an order. The speaker is more influential than a new Republican from Texas, but he can't order anybody to do anything. Nobody can fire anybody. So what that means is that you become influential by persuading people, being likable, and having other people respect you but not resent you. That's why it's like high school . . .

"Everybody's got the same networks—your class, the people you were elected with. That's like your high school class. Then the people from your region, they're like the people whose neighborhood you live in. And then, the people whose committee you're on, they're like the other students you used to go to class with. Those are the three networks that everybody has. And you may be able to pick up some over and above that.[1]

—Barney Frank (D-Massachusetts)

The United States Congress is not just a collection of its members. It is also an institution with a life of its own.

The framers of the Constitution saw Congress as the central branch of the federal government. They had had enough of kings and dictatorial colonial governors. Therefore, while giving few responsibilities to the president, they gave many detailed powers to the Congress. Of course, some of their reasons for detailing these powers were also to *restrain* the branch they saw as likely to grab too much power. Article I, Section 1 declares, "All legislative Powers herein granted shall be vested in a Congress of the United States, which shall consist of a Senate and House of Representatives." Article I goes on to give Congress the power to levy taxes, borrow money, raise armies, declare war, determine the nature of the federal judiciary, regulate commerce, coin money, and "make all Laws which shall be necessary and proper for carrying into Execution the foregoing powers. . . ."

Until well into the twentieth century Congress played the leading role in shaping the nation's policies. Before the Civil War, members of Congress such as Daniel Webster, Henry Clay, and John C. Calhoun molded the major issues of their time from within the legislature. After the Civil War, Congress took the lead on reconstruction in the South and in meeting the regulatory challenges brought by the industrialization of late nineteenth-century America. By the end of that century, Woodrow Wilson could proclaim, "Congress is the dominant, nay, the irresistible power of the federal system."

President Wilson was later to change his mind, and with good reason. The twentieth century brought vast growth and complexity to the economy. It also brought a Great Depression and wide differences between rich and poor. Two world wars made the country a great power with an active role overseas. *A larger, more diverse society wanted more than representation from its government.* People demanded services, regulation, protection, and leadership. And they looked to the president and the bureaucrats under him for these expanded governmental functions.

Congress went along with this growing power of the executive branch. Congress has often enhanced the executive's policy-making role by delegating part of its law-making function to that branch. For example, when Congress passed a new law to clean up the nation's rivers and lakes, it allowed the Environmental Protection Agency to fill in the details of the new program by issuing regulations. In other cases, such as foreign affairs, Congress, at least in the past, has been relatively passive in developing policy, thus leaving it to the executive branch. Policy-making is clearly not exclusively exercised by Congress.

In an age saturated by the mass media, Congress has been further weakened by its inability to speak in a single coherent voice. The very nature of a representative body filled with time-consuming, confusing, and conflicting public debate made Congress often appear to be an obstacle to solving the nation's problems. The presidency appeared unified and purposeful, while Congress looked divided and chaotic. Not only does a president speak with one voice, but the decisions leading up to his announcements are usually made in private and then explained at a time and in a manner enhancing his position.

Despite this shift in balance toward the executive branch and the advantages that branch brings to policy conflicts, Congress remains a strong legislative body, perhaps the most powerful in the world. Its majority party dominance, seniority, and committee system make it a bit more organized than Congressman Frank's analogy to high school might suggest. Its legislative and nonlegislative powers are numerous and important; its organization is partisan and complex; and the process by which bills become laws is difficult and political, as the case study of tax reform before the House Ways and Means Committee shows.

CONGRESSIONAL POWERS

To carry out its functions, Congress has certain powers that come from the Constitution, long-accepted interpretations and practices by Congress itself, and from various decisions by the United States Supreme Court.

Among the powers exercised by one house or both are the *fiscal power, commerce power, foreign policy power, impeachment power, investigative power,* and *confirmation power.*

Fiscal Power

The "power of the purse" is Congress's most important power. Only by an act of Congress can money be raised to pay for the government's operation; only by an act of Congress can money be spent by the government. This **fiscal power** derives from Article I, Section 8 of the Constitution, which gives Congress the power to "lay and collect taxes," and Section 9, which states that "No money shall be drawn by the Treasury, but in consequence of appropriations made by law." The Sixteenth Amendment adopted in 1913 gave Congress the right to collect income taxes.

★ How Deficits Grow

On the next to last day of its 1972 session, Congress completed action on an omnibus social security bill that (among its many provisions) entitled victims of kidney failure to medicare benefits. The provision was added to the bill by a Senate floor amendment, without prior committee hearings or review and without any consideration of the issue in the House. When it adopted the amendment by an overwhelming margin, the Senate had no reliable cost estimates and only a fuzzy notion of how expanded medicare coverage would affect future budgets. During brief floor debate, Senator Vance Hartke, the amendment's sponsor, implored the Senate to put health care ahead of budgetary concerns: "How do we explain," he asked, "that the difference between life and death is a matter of dollars." Hartke estimated that the new benefits would cost $75 million in the first year and perhaps $250 million in the fourth. Annual expenditures turned out to be much higher—about one billion dollars by the end of the 1970s. By then, however, the entitlement of kidney patients to medicare was inscribed in law and the budget routinely labeled these expenditures as "uncontrollable."

SOURCE: Allen Schick, as quoted by Aaron Wildavsky, *The New Politics of the Budgetary Process* (Glenview, IL: Scott, Foresman and Company, 1988), p. 318.

These taxing, spending, and borrowing powers are vitally important. Congress has the authority to raise or lower taxes, to decide which people or corporations will pay what share of federal taxes, to borrow money by issuing government bonds, to decide how much the federal government will spend, and to decide how the money will be spent. Congress's fiscal policies have an important impact on the economy. For example, Congress can stimulate the economy by increasing spending or slow the economy by raising taxes (see Chapter 17).

The responsibility for putting together a comprehensive government budget and national economic policy has generally rested with the president for most of this century. In 1974, however, Congress passed the *Budget Act* (the Congressional Budget and Impoundment Control Act). The Budget Act enabled Congress to propose a coherent alternative to the president's budget based on an examination of all spending and tax measures and the overall needs of the economy. Rather than merely debating the merits of individual government programs, Congress could now examine formerly isolated parts of the budget and evaluate them for their influence on the economy and other spending priorities (see the box on page 352). The Budget Act did this in several ways.

The Budget Process

The act set up House and Senate Budget committees. The committees guide Congress in setting total spending, tax, and debt levels. Aiding the two Budget committees is the *Congressional Budget Office (CBO)* established by the Act. The nonpartisan CBO provides experts to analyze the president's budget proposals and to match up Congress's numerous spending decisions with the established budget targets.

The budget works its way through Congress on a series of deadlines. The goal is to have a completed budget by the beginning of the government's fiscal year, October 1. Essentially, the process starts when the president submits his budget to Congress in January. All the committees in Congress then submit their estimates and views of the budget to the Budget committees, which shape them into a **first resolution.** Congress must vote on this resolution, which sets overall spending and tax levels, by April 15. The various parts of this resolution then go back to the standing committees concerned with the particular subject or program. By mid-June the standing committees' recommendations have gone back to the Budget committees, which draw up a reconciliation bill that is then voted on by

FIGURE 12★1
United States Budget History

The red ink of federal deficits from Washington to Bush is shown in this figure, where deficits in the federal budget are shown as revenues failing to come up to equal rising expenditures. (Turn the chart over to get a better idea of how deficits have risen.) The first big deficits came in the World War II administration of Franklin D. Roosevelt. There was a large deficit, too, during the Nixon recession. No deficits have come close to those of the Reagan administration. The budget for 1990 is estimated.

IN BILLIONS OF DOLLARS

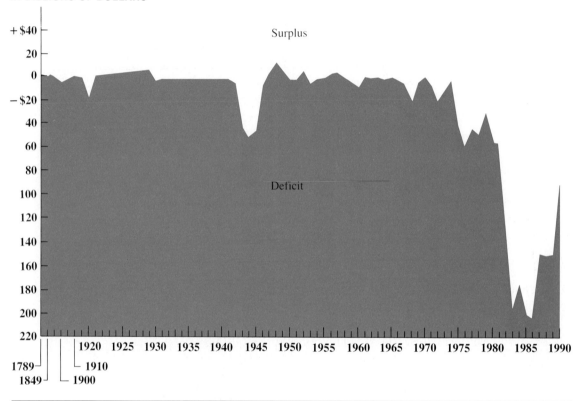

SOURCE: Cited in *Today* (March 2, 1984), p. 7, and *The New York Times,* March 26, 1989, p. 4-1.

Congress. This part of the process is called **reconciliation** because it attempts to balance the separate standing committees' decisions with the targets set by the first resolution.

By 1985 it was as clear as the record $220 billion deficit that the budget process was not working (see Figure 12.1). The government was spending $24 for every $19 it raised in taxes, and the White House was deadlocked with Congress over whether the solution was to cut programs or raise taxes. In a radical attempt to lower the deficit, Congress passed an antideficit measure called **Gramm-Rudman** in late 1985. The law required five years of federal deficit reductions of $36 billion a year, resulting in a balanced budget (zero deficits) by fiscal 1991. These reductions, by less spending or more taxes, would take place in the normal budget process but—and this was the radical part—if Congress failed to meet the deficit target, automatic across-the-board cuts would be made in defense and nondefense programs. Although some programs, such as social security, were exempt, the automatic cuts were designed to be so harsh that Congress and the president would reach agreement to avoid them. As Senator Warren Rudman (R-N.H.), one of the bill's sponsors said, Gramm-Rudman was "a bad idea whose time has come."

The verdict on the bill has been mixed. In 1986 the Supreme Court ruled that the mechanism imposing automatic cuts was unconstitutional. Even without the automatic cuts Congress tried to keep to the Gramm-Rudman deficit reduction schedule. It cut the defense build-up, reduced farm aid, and slowed down government spending to less than 1 percent annual growth. However, Congress also "cooked the books" by some questionable practices like selling government holdings, which resulted in one-time gains but sacrificed future income, and making overly optimistic assumptions about the economy. Critics called the bill "a charade" to avoid the hard decisions on cutting programs or raising taxes. By 1989 the law had become a vague statement of purpose that few in Congress would oppose, or follow.

Senators Warren Rudman (left), Phil Gramm (center), and Ernest Hollings, the original sponsors of the Gramm-Rudman law, hold a press conference in 1986 in response to the Supreme Court ruling that found parts of Gramm-Rudman to be unconstitutional.

Commerce Power

Article I, Section 8, of the Constitution, states that Congress shall have the power "to regulate Commerce with foreign Nations, among the several States, and with the Indian tribes." From the republic's beginnings, this **Commerce Clause** was used for public works projects, some of which fell under the category of "pork barrel" legislation (see the box on page 357). Regulating commerce was another matter. Congress did tax foreign imports with vigor, in the form of tariffs, right from the start of the new nation. But its power to regulate domestic business grew more slowly.

In 1824 Chief Justice John Marshall, in a Supreme Court opinion, wrote Congress a broad mandate to regulate commerce between the states, but not within them—hence, the phrase, "interstate commerce." *The Interstate Commerce Act* established the commission of the same name in 1887 and transportation of goods became the legislators' first real foothold in regulating domestic business. When railroads and trucking were added to the control of navigation, Congress tried with the 1890 Sherman Act to use its Commerce Clause power to bust the monopoly trusts. The Supreme Court eventually went along and the whole "stream of commerce"—manufacturing, finance, and similar commercial areas—came under the Sherman Act and later trust-busting laws. Finally, the Depression and the New Deal saw the high court approve the extension of Congress's regulatory powers into labor relations, upholding the National Labor Relations Board as a legitimate exercise of congressional authority under the Commerce Clause.

Foreign Policy Power

Presidential and congressional powers overlap on foreign policy. Article I, Section 8 gives Congress the exclusive power to declare war, but Article II, Section 2 declares that the president is the commander in chief of the nation's armed forces. Abraham Lincoln, for example, claimed the power to call out troops at the beginning of the Civil War without waiting for legislative authorization. "Are all the laws but one to go unexecuted and the government itself to go to pieces lest that one be violated?" he asked.[2] President Truman sent troops to war in Korea, calling it a "police action." Presidents Johnson and Nixon justified, increased, and finally ended America's involvement in the Vietnam War. Both Korea and Vietnam were fought without any formal declaration of war by Congress. However, Congress supported both conflicts by appropriating money for the armed forces.

★ Patriotic Pork

Pork barrel legislation, the practice of public spending for parochial legislation, is as old as the Republic. The first Congress in 1789 took on itself the general task of maintaining lighthouses, and then proceeded to order a specific one for the Chesapeake Bay. Similar bills with lists of specific locations for lighthouses, roads, and canals continued into the next century.

The phrase *pork barrel* came from the practice of rewarding slaves with salt pork and referred to their eagerness to crowd around the barrel to grab as much as possible for themselves. Dividing between "pork" and "progress"—whether a project was in the national interest or just that of a few local voters—is not always easy. However, the 1870s and 1880s seem to be justly called the "Golden Age of Pork." Here, periodic river and harbors bills allowed a long parade of members, usually serving local party bosses, to add their own projects without opposition.

The coming of the automobile brought new demands for roads and new opportunities for Congress. Although Congress adopted a rule, still in existence, that general legislation on roads could not contain "any provision for any specific road," the rule has been frequently bypassed. A 1987 highway bill, for example, included more than 120 special "demonstration" projects. As is said in Congress, "It's just makin' bacon."

Power over foreign policy in peacetime is equally fragmented under the Constitution. Although Congress must ratify treaties and confirm appointments of ambassadors and other officials before they can become effective (Article II, Section 2), it is the president who negotiates treaties and nominates people for federal office. At times, presidents have entered into executive agreements with foreign governments—obligating themselves to defend a foreign country, for example—without submitting the agreements to the Senate for ratification as treaties.

In recent years, Congress has reasserted its foreign policy power. In 1973, at the height of public anger over Vietnam, Congress passed the **War Powers Act** over former President Nixon's veto. This law recognizes the power of the president to order military action for defense, but it requires the president to terminate any such troop commitment within sixty days unless Congress specifically approves it. The Act did not keep President Reagan from sending marines to Lebanon, or from invading Grenada, or from sending warships to the Persian Gulf. President Reagan denounced the War Powers act as an unconstitutional expansion of congressional powers. Yet the president avoided a confrontation with Congress by either getting the troops out before the deadline or defining the situation as one not involving hostilities. Its effectiveness today remains a bit uncertain (see Chapter 18).

The Senate Watergate committee in the early 1970s investigated Richard Nixon's abuses of White House power.

Impeachment Power

Article I, Section 3 of the Constitution established the impeachment power of Congress. By majority vote, the House of Representatives may *impeach* (or charge) any officer of the executive or judicial branches of the federal government, including the president. If the House votes to impeach, the Senate conducts the trial, which requires a two-thirds vote for conviction. When the impeachment proceeding involves the president, the chief justice of the United States presides over the trial in the Senate. The Constitution provides that an officer may be impeached for treason, bribery, and other "high crimes and misdemeanors." The punishment for conviction is removal from office.

The House of Representatives has impeached fourteen federal officers. Most were federal judges; one justice of the U.S. Supreme Court and one secretary of state have been impeached. (The fifteenth and sixteenth impeachments, of federal judges from Florida and Mississippi, were recommended by a House Judiciary subcommittee in March 1989.) One former president, Andrew Johnson, was impeached by the House but acquitted in the Senate trial because the vote for conviction was one less than the required two-thirds majority. Richard Nixon was the first president to resign. He did so after impeachment charges had been voted by the House Judiciary Committee, but before there had been a full vote in the U.S. House of Representatives.

Investigative Power

Under its broad legislative authority, Congress has investigative power. If Congress, or a committee (or committee chairman), decides that something is being done wrong, an investigation may be launched. The subject might be foreign-policy decision making in the executive branch, price fixing by private industry, or the power of organized crime. In other words, Congress can investigate whatever it wishes.

Congressional investigations in recent years have covered a wide range of matters, such as possible conspiracy behind the assassinations of President John F. Kennedy and Dr. Martin Luther King, Jr. Congressional investigations can sometimes endanger civil liberties. In the 1950s, Senator Joseph McCarthy's Permanent Investigations Subcommittee and the House Un-American Activities Committee ruined the reputations of many people, forced able persons out of government service, and drummed up fear throughout the country with often-unfounded charges of disloyalty.

Congressional investigations are not welcomed by executive departments, for they allow Congress to influence executive behavior. Colonel Oliver North candidly illustrated this attitude when, in testifying in 1987 on the Iran-Contra scandal, he explained why he shredded documents by saying, "I didn't want to show Congress a single word on this whole thing." The Iran-Contra hearings embarrassed the White House and led to the conviction of Colonel North on relatively minor charges of lying to Congress and destroying government documents.[3]

Most presidents have claimed *executive privilege* to withhold certain information from congressional committees. Presidents have justified the use of this privilege by asserting the need for secrecy in diplomatic affairs and for receiving frank advice from their staffs without making them fear that what they say may later be disclosed. Sometimes executive privilege has been used to withhold information that might reflect unfavorably on the president. One legal authority has pointed out that the right of executive privilege is not granted in the Constitution. He sees it as a myth created by a succession of presidents to suit their own interests.[4]

Nevertheless, presidents have claimed the right to withhold information on certain occasions, and there has never been a final showdown with Congress on this issue. During the Watergate scandal (in *U.S.* v. *Nixon* 1974), the Supreme Court did force President Nixon to hand over tapes and records to a district court for use in criminal proceedings. It is clear that if Congress firmly resists such withholding of information, it has certain sanctions it can use. For example, Congress could stop funding for any programs about which the president or his appointees refused to give full information.

Confirmation Power

Although presidents "nominate" or name cabinet members, ambassadors, Supreme Court justices, and other federal officials, they can only appoint them "by and with the advice and consent of the Senate." This confirmation power is not shared with the House of Representatives. Since 1789, the Senate has rejected only nine of the president's cabinet appointees with John Tower's unsuccessful nomination to be secretary of defense in 1989 being the most recent. Before that it last occurred thirty years ago.

Most presidential appointments within the executive branch are routine. There is a tendency in the Senate to agree that the president

---

★ Major Differences Between the House and the Senate

HOUSE	SENATE
Larger (435)	Smaller (100)
Shorter term of office (2 years)	Longer term of office (6 years)
More procedural restraints on members	Fewer procedural restraints on members
Narrower constituency	Broader, more varied constituency
Policy specialists	Policy generalists
Less press and media coverage	More press and media coverage
Power less evenly distributed	Power more evenly distributed
Less prestigious	More prestigious
Briefer floor debates	Longer floor debates
Less reliant on staff	More reliant on staff
More partisan	Less partisan

SOURCE: Walter J. Oleszck, *Congressional Procedures and the Policy Process*, 3rd ed. (Washington D.C., C.Q. Press, 1989), p 24.

has a right to have the persons he wishes working with him. The "behind-the-scenes" pressure of Senate dissatisfaction undoubtedly causes presidents not to make certain unpopular nominations in the first place. Also, the Senate takes a more active role in presidential appointments to the independent regulatory commissions and the Supreme Court, as shown by the successful opposition to President Reagan's nomination of Robert Bork to the Supreme Court (see the case study in Chapter 11).

The Senate also acts to guard local party influence over appointments by following a custom called **Senatorial Courtesy.** This means that the recommendations made by particular senators for the nominations of federal judges, district attorneys, and district marshals in their home states will have a strong influence on appointments. Under Senatorial Courtesy, the Senate will not confirm an appointment if the senators of the president's party from the state concerned refuse to endorse it.

HOW IS CONGRESS ORGANIZED?

Congressional organization sometimes appears to be a contradiction in terms. With power dispersed among two houses, two parties, several congressional leaders, many informal caucuses, numerous committees, and 535 elected members, it often appears that no one is in charge and nothing will get done. Given recent deadlocks and squabbling over budgets, deficits, ethics, and taxes, there may be some truth to this.

But there is a method to this seeming madness. The organization of Congress reflects the intentions of the framers of the Constitution. The dispersing of power in Congress was not designed to make government operate more efficiently. It was aimed at preventing the accumulation of too much power in any one set of hands. Congress's organization is also a product of its own history. The traditions of party rule, of the division of labor into committees, and of each house's own rights have evolved as ways of smoothing out what can be a rough legislative process. And finally, Congress reflects the large, complex society it serves. Its deadlocks and lukewarm compromises may accurately represent the lack of agreement on critical issues found in the nation and government.

The House and Senate are very different from each other (see the box on page 360). But both are organized around three focal points: *the parties, congressional leadership, and committees.* All three are interdependent, providing both structure and leadership to the legislative branch.

The Parties in Congress

The very physical division of the House and Senate chambers illustrates the importance of the political parties in organizing Congress. A central aisle runs from the rear of each chamber up to the desk of the presiding officer in front. Looking from the rear of the chamber toward the desk, one sees that all the Democratic members of the House of Representatives (who are in the majority) sit on the left side of the aisle, and all of the Republicans sit on the right side. (Every member of the House and Senate was elected as a candidate of one of the two major parties.) Similarly, looking from the back of the Senate chamber toward the desk of the presiding officer, all Republican members of the Senate (who are in the minority) sit on the right side of the central aisle. All the Democrats sit to the left.

Other physical divisions in Congress are based on party. When committees and subcommittees meet, members are seated according to their party. There are two "cloakrooms," or places for informal discussion, just off the floor of each chamber, which are separately assigned to each party. The "Senators' Private Dining Room" is composed of two separate rooms where senators rigidly segregate themselves by party.

Each "Congress" lasts two years—and a "session" is held each year. At the beginning of each Congress, the party caucuses or conferences meet to vote on party leaders and to approve decisions on committee chairs and committee membership. To participate in the caucus, a member must simply be willing to vote with party members on matters of formal organization. Thus, in the *Senate Republican Conference* the *House Republican Conference,* the *Senate Democratic Conference,* and the *House Democratic Caucus,* a senator or representative achieves membership simply by saying, "I am a Republican" or "I want to be a member of the Senate Democratic Conference." No one asks why.

The organization of Congress is based on the political parties. The **majority party** in each house is the one with the greatest number of members. *The majority party is important because that party chooses the leaders of that branch of Congress, controls debate on the floor, selects all committee chairs, and has a majority on all committees.* For most of the last thirty years, the Democratic party has been the majority party. In the 1980 elections the GOP won control of the Senate for the first time in twenty-eight years. However, in the 1986 election the Democrats regained control of the Senate, and are now the majority party in the House and Senate.

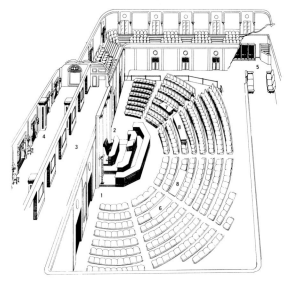
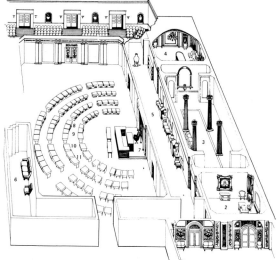

1. The Mace
2. Speaker of the House
3. Speaker's Lobby
4. Members' Reading Rooms

5. Republican Cloakroom
6. Democratic Leadership Table
7. Republican Leadership Table
8. Committee Tables

1. Senate Reception Room
2. Vice-President's Room
3. The Marble Room
4. The President's Room
5. Senate Lobby
6. Republican Cloakroom

7. The Presiding Officer
8. Democratic Whip
9. Democratic Leader
10. Republican Leader
11. Republican Whip

A diagram of the House and Senate chambers and their surrounding rooms.

Congressional Leadership

The first order of business of the party caucus or conference at the beginning of each new Congress is the election of officers. The leaders and their powers differ in the two houses.

House Leadership

In the House of Representatives, the majority party chooses the **Speaker of the House.** (All members of the party *must* vote for their party's choice.) The Speaker does not have to be the oldest or longest-serving member, but is likely to have served a long apprenticeship in other party posts. Around the turn of the century, House Speakers like Thomas B. Reed and his successor, Joseph Cannon, held almost dictatorial powers. Strong party leadership kept committee chairmen in line and allowed for coherent party government. "King Caucus" was eventually dethroned in 1915 by reformers, with power flowing back to committees and their chairmen. The Speaker still retains considerable power by presiding over debate on the House floor, recognizing members who wish to speak, and interpreting procedural questions. He also influences membership on committees. The present speaker is Thomas Foley, Democratic congress-

House Speaker Jim Wright vows to fight charges the House ethics committee was expected to bring against him concerning his financial dealings in April 1989. Supporting Wright at the news conference are (from left) Rep. Tony Coelho (D-Cal.), Rep. Thomas Foley (D-Wash.), and Rep,. David Bonior (D-Mich.). Despite being a strong Speaker, Wright resigned in June 1989.

man from Washington, who became Speaker in 1989 when James Wright of Texas, the Speaker since 1987, resigned under an ethics cloud. The 1989 scandal involving Wright's questionable financial dealings with wealthy friends showed how quickly power can be lost when members feel that public opinion has turned against their leaders.

The *caucus* of each political party in the House or Senate is simply a gathering of all the members of that party serving there. In recent Congresses the majority-party caucus has grown more assertive. The House Democratic caucus has shown a willingness to influence committee and floor action on legislation, to remove committee chairmen from their positions, and to attempt to unite Democrats around the leadership of the Speaker.

The majority-party caucus also chooses a *majority leader* who is second in command to the Speaker, and in recent years has succeeded to the speakership. The majority leader works closely with the Speaker and schedules legislation for debate on the House floor. Tom Foley was majority leader when he succeeded Jim Wright. Richard Gephardt of Missouri is now majority leader.

The Speaker and majority leader are assisted by *majority whips.* (The word *whip* comes from English fox hunting, where the "whipper-in" keeps the dogs from running away.) The whips help coordinate party positions on legislation, pass information and directions between the leadership and other party members, make sure party members know when a particular vote is coming, try to persuade wavering representatives to vote with the leadership, and conduct informal surveys to check the likely outcome of votes. Being at the center of the congressional process, all these party leaders possess more information than other legislators, which adds to their power.

The minority party in the House, currently the Republicans, have a caucus, known as a *conference,* in which a *minority leader* and *minority whips* are selected. Like the majority party's leader and whips, their duties are to coordinate party positions. The minority leader is usually his or her party's candidate for Speaker should it become the majority party.

The Democratic and Republican caucuses in the House run their affairs in slightly different ways. The Democratic party chooses a *Steering and Policy Committee* to function as an executive committee of the caucus. The Steering Committee helps chart party policy in the House. It assigns Democratic members to committees, with the advice of the committees' chairmen and senior members. It also nominates committee chairmen, although the nominations must be approved by the full caucus. The approval used to be a formality, but in 1975 the House Democratic caucus rejected three nominees for chairmen: the incumbent heads of the Armed Services, Banking, and Agriculture committees. The increasingly important role of the Steering Committee has also enlarged the power of the House Speaker, who, as leader of the congressional Democrats, is chairman of the committee. On the other hand, it has weakened the ability of committee chairmen to act independently of the wishes of their party caucus.

Republican party committee assignments in the House are made by a *Committee on Committees.* This group contains a member from each state with Republican party representation in the House. These members have as many votes in the committee as their state's Republican delegation does in the House.

Senate Leadership

The Senate has no Speaker. The **president of the Senate** is the vice-president of the United States. He has the right to preside over the Senate chamber and to vote in case of a tie. Presiding is a rarely exercised function, one he fills only when an important vote is scheduled. However, shortly after taking office Vice-President Dan Quayle announced that he would preside frequently over the Senate. And in November 1983, then Vice-President Bush cast the deciding vote in favor of funding for nerve gas.

The honorary post of *president pro tem* (from *pro tempore,* meaning "for the time being") of the Senate is given to the senator from the majority party who has served longest in the Senate—currently Robert Byrd (D-West Virginia). He is third in line of succession for the presidency but his only power is to preside in the absence of the vice-president. Because the majority of Senate work takes place in committees, the job of presiding over a Senate chamber that may be dull and nearly vacant usually falls to a junior senator, who is asked to do so by the **Senate majority leader.**

The majority leader of the Senate is the nearest equivalent to the Speaker of the House. He (1) schedules debate on the Senate floor, (2) assigns bills to committees, (3) coordinates party policy, and (4) appoints members of special committees. Maine Democrat George Mitchell was elected majority leader at the start of the 1989 session. The Senate majority leader is assisted by a *whip* and *assistant whips.* The minority party in the Senate selects a *minority leader* (who is now Robert Dole, R-Kansas) and a *minority whip,* both of whom coordinate party positions and manage floor strategy.

In the Senate the Democrats have a *Steering Committee,* which makes committee assignments, and a *Policy Committee,* which charts legislative tactics. The Senate Democratic leader chairs the Democratic caucus (called the *Democratic Conference*), the Steering Committee, and the Policy Committee, giving him, like the House Speaker, influence over legislation and committee assignments. Senate Republicans are organized in much the same way. A *Committee on Committees* assigns members to committees; a *Policy Committee* coordinates strategy; and the *Republican Conference* consists of all Republicans in the Senate. One difference from the Democrats is that these groups are chaired by leading Republican senators, rather than by the Senate Republican leader.[5]

The Leverage of Leaders

[Former Senate Majority Leader] Bob Byrd did not get to his present job based on his personal popularity. He got there by dint of prodigious work. He is able. He learned the institution. If I were Majority Leader I would want him as the whip. He loves the floor. He loves the detail. He'll stay there endless hours with all of the mechanics that would bore me to death—working out schedules and making sure that people are there. But he's a guy who didn't get where he is based on personality by a long shot. I can't think of a single one of my colleagues who would count Bob as one of their personal friends.[6]

—A Democratic senator

★ The Senate Is Not What It Used to Be— Good or Bad?

To some the Senate just isn't what is used to be—the old gentlemen's club. It has lost its civility, its comradery. Long-time Senator Thomas Eagleton of Missouri, who retired in 1986, sums up his view of the Senate this way: "We went through an economic boom that lasted from the end of World War II through the early '70s. America ruled the world—and it all went to our heads. . . . And we became a selfish society, a self-absorbed society. The United States Senate, today, is a reflection of that society."

Former Senator William Proxmire of Wisconsin remembers the old days differently, "The day I came here, it was the end of the session in 1957, and Strom [Thurmond] was then finishing what was to be one of the longest filibusters in history. It got pretty boring, and I decided to duck into the Secretary of the Senate's office. And there were all my heroes, men I had dreamed about serving with. Most of them were dead drunk, just staggering around. I thought I was being thrown into a drunk tank." Proxmire adds that such behavior is rare today and that civility among members has improved.

SOURCE: Tim Hackler, "What's Gone Wrong with the U.S. Senate?" *American Politics,* January 1987, pp. 7–8.

Congressional leaders are powerful. They know the rules of the body in which they serve, and they know how to use them to their advantage. Leaders in both houses have some control over tangible goodies like committee assignments, foreign trips, and assistance in reelection campaigns. They can help or hinder legislation in which a member may be interested. They can let the word get around that a member is a "comer" or is out of favor with the leadership. Lastly, they possess more information than the average member about when decisions will be made. They dominate the channels of communication.

The power and influence of particular House and Senate leaders also depend upon their personalities and persuasiveness. Lyndon B. Johnson was the most powerful Senate majority leader in modern times. On the other hand, his successor, Mike Mansfield of Montana, saw his job as being more like that of a "shepherd" than a "drover." While Johnson worked at persuading senators to go along with leadership positions on issues, Mansfield believed that individual senators should be allowed to do pretty much what they please.

Informal Caucuses

Before there were political parties, there were *informal caucuses* in the U.S. Congress. Today, these factional and regional groups of members are more numerous than ever before (more than seventy). Liberal Democrats in the House formed one of the oldest when the *Democratic Study Group* was begun in 1957 to do research for members and to be sure all liberal members were informed on important votes. The *Wednesday Group* was started in the House by liberal Republicans for similar reasons.

These two groups were the models for informal House caucuses. Today, others include the Snowbelt Caucus, the Women's Caucus, and the Steel Caucus. These caucuses have staffs, do research, and are financed by members' staff allowances and outside contributions. Most are bipartisan and are limited to one chamber. A good many are tied in with interest groups. All serve to organize and influence individual members of Congress around common regional, economic, ethnic, or ideological interests. Grassroots economic concerns have made *regional divisions* in the 101st Congress over issues like offshore drilling and airline service to rural areas more important than traditional liberal-conservative splits.

The Committee System

The basic work of the House and Senate is done in committees. President Woodrow Wilson called them "little legislatures," and wrote that "Congress in session is Congress on exhibition, whilst Congress in its committee rooms is Congress at work."[7]

The most important congressional committees are **standing committees,** which are permanent. They handle most of the legislative, appropriations, and investigative work. In 1989 there were sixteen standing committees in the Senate and twenty-two standing committees in the House (see the box on page 369). Almost all of these standing committees have subcommittees, which have jurisdiction over parts of a full committee's work. Although both houses have periodically reduced the number of committees and subcommittees, they have tended to multiply again after the reforms. The growth of subcommittees, with their chairmanships often going to junior members of Congress, was a dramatic and decentralizing change in Congress in the 1970s. It gave more members a "piece of the action."

Suppose you have just been elected to the United States Senate, and you want to become a member of the powerful Senate Finance Committee. Or suppose you have been elected to the United States

Congressional Committee Chairmen

1989 SENATE COMMITTEE LEADERS (ALL DEMOCRATS)

Agriculture, Nutrition, and Forestry	Patrick J. Leahy, Vt.
Appropriations	Robert C. Byrd, W.Va.
Armed Services	Sam Nunn, Ga.
Banking, Housing, and Urban Affairs	Donald W. Riegle, Jr., Mich.
Budget	Jim Sasser, Tenn.
Commerce, Science, and Transportation	Ernest F. Hollings, S.C.
Energy and Natural Resources	J. Bennett Johnston, La.
Environment and Public Works	Quentin N. Burdick, N.D.
Finance	Lloyd Bentsen, Texas
Foreign Relations	Claiborne Pell, R.I.
Governmental Affairs	John Glenn, Ohio
Judiciary	Joseph R. Biden, Jr., Del.
Labor and Human Resources	Edward M. Kennedy, Mass.
Rules and Administration	Wendell H. Ford. Ky.
Small Business	Dale Bumpers, Ark.
Veterans' Affairs	Alan Cranston, Calif.

1989 HOUSE COMMITTEE LEADERS (ALL DEMOCRATS)

Agriculture	E. "Kika" de la Garza, Texas
Appropriations	Jamie L. Whitten, Miss.
Armed Services	Les Aspin, Wis.
Banking, Finance, and Urban Affairs	Henry B. Gonzales, Texas
Budget	Leon E. Panetta, Calif.
District of Columbia	Ronald V. Dellums, Calif.
Education and Labor	Augustus F. Hawkins, Calif.
Energy and Commerce	John D. Dingell, Mich.
Foreign Affairs	Dante B. Fascall, Fla.
Government Operations	John Conyers, J., Mich.
House Administration	Frank Annunzio, Ill.
Interior and Insular Affairs	Morris K. Udall, Ariz.
Judiciary	Jack Brooks, Texas
Merchant Marine and Fisheries	Walter B. Jones, N.C.
Post Office and Civil Service	William D. Ford, Mich.
Public Works and Transportation	Glenn M. Anderson, Calif.
Rules	John Joseph Moakley, Mass.
Science, Space, and Technology	Robert A. Roe, N.J.
Select Intelligence	Anthony C. Beilenson, Calif.
Small Business	John J. LaFalce, N.Y.
Standards of Official Conduct	Julian D. Dixon, Calif.
Veteran's Affairs	G. V. "Sonny" Montgomery, Miss.
Ways and Means	Dan Rostenkowski, Ill.

House of Representatives, and you would like to be a member of the equally powerful Ways and Means Committee. How do you go about it? Who makes these committee assignments?

Several factors determine who is chosen to fill the committee vacancies. House and Senate *leaders* influence the selections. *Seniority* in the House or Senate can play a part; a senior member usually has a better chance of getting a good committee assignment than a junior member. The need for regional or *geographical balance* on a committee may be a factor. Some strong-willed *committee chairs* "recruit" new members with whom they ideologically agree or who they feel will follow their leadership. Then they urge the appropriate leaders and appointing authority to approve their choices. Special-interest groups may have a behind-the-scenes influence on committee assignments too.

★ Fighting for Your Committee's Turf

Sen. Edward Kennedy was said to have been on the receiving end of a reprisal as the result of a usurpation of jurisdiction. The retribution grew out of a series of hearings that Kennedy held as chairman of the Subcommittee on Administrative Practices and Procedures. The hearings involved a particularly attractive issue—that of airline deregulation. The colleague upon whose jurisdiction Kennedy was encroaching was Howard Cannon (D.-Nev.), chairman of the Aviation Subcommittee of the Commerce, Science, and Transportation Committee. Cannon might have protested in vain at this infringement of jurisdiction, but he had more at his disposal than wrath; he was also chairman of the Rules and Administration Committee, which has jurisdiction over such matters as staff and office space. Cannon retaliated by being extremely uncooperative when the Massachusetts senator wished to increase the size of his staff. Cannon ultimately provided the staff, but not without prolonged dilatory tactics.

SOURCE: Ross K. Baker, *Friend and Foe in the U.S. Senate* (New York: The Free Press, 1980), pp. 244–45.

Once you become a member of the committee, how do you get to be the chairman of the committee or subcommittee? First, you must be a member of the majority party. Then, it is primarily a matter of seniority on the committee or subcommittee. If you have served longer than any other member of your majority party on a particular committee, you will almost automatically become the chairman. The senior minority party member of the committee becomes the *ranking minority member*. These positions are very important because the chair can decide when hearings will be scheduled and when votes will be taken. In return, he or she is expected to guard the committee's powers against other committees' encroachments (see the box on page 370). The chair, too, can choose the majority committee staff. The ranking minority member chooses the minority staff. In recent years, the influence of individual members of committees and subcommittees over scheduling and choice of staff has increased. In the House, majority members of a subcommittee may vote on the selection of the chairman.

Major Committees in the House

With the coming of the budget process and the political focus on the deficit, power centered even more than it had on committees shaping the taxing and spending policies of the government. In the old days, power came through seniority to all committee chairmen. While this still has some truth, power is now concentrated in the members of a few elite committees. Members of less-fortunate committees spend a good deal of time trying to get help from members of the key committees. The key House committees, besides Budget, are *Rules, Ways and Means, Appropriations,* and *Energy and Commerce.*

Almost all legislation approved by committees in the House must pass through the *Rules Committee* before reaching the House floor. The Rules Committee's name comes from its function: If the committee approves a bill for transmission to the House floor, it assigns a "rule" to that bill setting the terms of a debate. The Rules Committee can, for example, assign a "closed rule," which forbids any amendments and forces the House into a "take it or leave it" position. Thus the Rules Committee acts as a traffic cop. It has the power to delay or even stop legislation; it can amend bills or send them back to committee for revision; and it can decide in cases where two committees have bills on the same subject which one gets sent to the floor. Since 1975 when the Speaker was given the power to nominate the Democratic members and the chairman, the Rules Committee has acted as a powerful arm of the Speaker.

The *Ways and Means Committee* deals with tax legislation, or the *raising* of revenue for the government. Because all money-raising bills begin in the House, any tax legislation goes first to the Ways and Means Committee.

As shown in this chapter's case study, Ways and Means under Chairman Dan Rostenkowski (D-Ill.) is a central power in Congress. Its jurisdiction covers a large number of *entitlement programs*—where money comes directly from the program itself—such as social security, unemployment compensation, and Medicare. In recent crises, it has been the lead committee handling taxes, welfare reform, catastrophic health insurance, and trade restrictions. In "reconciliation," it and the Senate Finance Committee are key in deciding where the Budget Committee's spending cuts will fall.

The Ways and Means Committee handles tax bills to raise money; the *Appropriations Committee* deals with how government *spends* that money. When the federal budget is presented to Congress by the president each year, it is sent to the House Appropriations Committee and its thirteen subcommittees as the first stage in congressional review. Because the power to tax and spend is the power to make or break programs, areas, and individuals, the importance of the Ways and Means and Appropriations committees and their subcommittees is clear. While Appropriations is limited by the budget process on overall spending, it can still decide *where* it will spend money or make cuts. It has become a key place for doing favors for other members.

The *Energy and Commerce Committee* is an exception to the trend of the flow of power following the budget process. Under its assertive chairman, John Dingell (D-Mich.), the committee has expanded its reach to include regulatory agencies, nuclear energy, toxic wastes, and telecommunications. It has the largest staff and budget of any House committee.

Major Committees in the Senate

The most important committees in the Senate (besides Budget) are *Appropriations, Finance,* and *Foreign Relations.* The Senate *Appropriations Committee* receives appropriations bills after they have been passed by the House. Its procedures are very much like those of its House counterpart, with the important distinction that the Senate committee tends to act as a "court of appeals," adding money to or subtracting it from the amounts granted by the House. If passed by the House, tax legislation then goes to the Senate *Finance Committee,* the Senate's equivalent to Ways and Means in the House.

The Senate *Foreign Relations Committee* is a watchdog over the president's dominant position in foreign policy. Its importance

comes from the Senate's role in confirming appointments of ambassadors and approving or disapproving treaties. It was recently influential in developing policies toward the Philippines and South Africa. It is also considered a helpful publicity forum for senators with presidential ambitions.

The Senate also has a Rules Committee, but it is much less important than its House counterpart. The Senate has fewer than one-fourth as many members as the House. Thus, the problem of coordination is not as great and the Senate simply decided that it did not need to set up a strong committee to aid the Senate majority leader in screening and scheduling legislation.

THE DANCE OF LEGISLATION

Once begin the dance of legislation, and you must struggle through its mazes as best you can to the breathless end—if any there be.

—Woodrow Wilson

Ninety-five percent of the almost 20,000 bills introduced into Congress never become law. Most die in committee. The bills that are introduced may be part of the president's program, may be drafted by individual members, may come from committees with jurisdiction over the subject, or may be a result of alliances between Congress, the executive bureaucracy, and private interests. The present

THE HOUSE OF REPRESENTATIVES		THE SENATE
"Revenue-raising" bills must be introduced in the House first; bills may be sponsored by any member or members.	**Introductory Stage**	Bills may be sponsored by any member or members; except for "revenue-raising" bills, they may originate in either chamber, or in both at the same time.
Bills are referred to the appropriate committee . . . and then to a subcommittee for hearings, "mark-up," and vote . . . and then are sent back to the full committee for hearings, "mark-up," and vote.	**Committee Stage**	Bills are referred to the appropriate committee . . . and then to a subcommittee for hearings, "mark-up," and vote . . . and then are sent back to the full committee for hearings, "mark-up," and vote.
Once approved by a committee, bills are sent to the House Rules Committee, which determines rules governing consideration by the whole House . . . and places them on a calendar scheduling House floor debate and vote. Bills approved by a majority vote in the House are then introduced in the Senate (if both chambers have considered a bill at the same time and the finally approved versions are identical, it goes directly to the President for approval of veto).	**Floor Action**	Once approved by a committee, bills are placed on a calendar scheduling Senate floor debate and voting. Bills approved by a majority vote in the Senate are then introduced in the House (unless both chambers have considered and approved identical bills, which are then sent to the President).
	Conference Stage	

If a bill approved by one chamber differs from the version approved by the other chamber, select members of each meet to agree upon a compromise, which must then be reconsidered in each chamber for final approval.

If both the House and the Senate approve identical versions of a bill (with or without a conference), it is sent to the President for approval or veto; if vetoed, a bill can still become law if the veto is overriden by two-thirds votes in both the House and the Senate.

Democratic control of both houses of Congress with Republican control of the presidency makes it uncertain which party will introduce most of the legislation passed by Congress.[8]

The difficulty any bill encounters in being passed by Congress can be appreciated by reviewing the four stages through which a bill becomes a law: *introduction, committee, floor,* and *conference* (see Figure 12.2).

The Introductory Stage

The booklet which caused me wry amusement was entitled "How a Bill Becomes a Law." It traced the sixteen steps from introduction through assignment to the appropriate committee for hearings, and on until the president signs it into law. Not that it wasn't accurate in the strict civics class sense: it just failed to tell the whole truth. What is left out was how the winnowing processes work: the tradeoffs and the private agreements or understandings between politicians. Often the merits or demerits of a bill have little or nothing to do with whether it becomes law. If certain people in power reach a private trade or accommodation, then it likely will become law. If not, then it may not. . . .[9]

—Bobby Baker, former Secretary of the Senate

The legislative process begins when a bill is introduced in either the House or Senate. Most bills can begin their life in either house, as long as there is at least one House or Senate sponsor. The principal sponsor of a bill will generally try to secure cosponsors in order to demonstrate that it has wide support. Under the Constitution, "revenue-raising" bills—those having to do with taxation—can originate only in the House; and, by custom, the same is true of appropriation bills. The special power of the House to originate taxation and appropriation bills is not very important. The Senate can and does freely amend bills that come to it from the House, sometimes adding wholly new items to them (subject, of course, to later agreement). Thus, the Senate may, in effect, originate such proposals of its own.

Bills are often introduced for their symbolic value. By introducing bills, members can demonstrate their position on certain issues to their constituents. For example, members of Congress may cosponsor a bill to limit deficit spending by the federal government, even though they know that the measure has no chance of being adopted by Congress. Bills may also be introduced to give a representative or senator publicity for an issue, or for themselves.

The Committee Stage

After a bill is introduced, it is immediately printed. This gives members of Congress a chance to study it. The bill is then referred to a committee. Since the rules of the House and Senate are specific concerning the jurisdictions of committees, it is usually a simple matter for the presiding officer in each body to decide which standing committee should receive the newly introduced bill.

Senate and House committees are not required by the rules to take any action at all on a bill that has been referred to them. But seldom-used procedures exist in both houses for floor votes to force a committee to act on a bill or to release it for full floor action.

A bill is usually referred to a subcommittee for public hearings. These hearings, which are announced in advance, offer a public forum for anyone who has an opinion about a bill. These hearings allow members to test the political climate toward the bill, gather information and support, and modify their views accordingly. They also allow interest groups to organize grassroots pressure to influence a bill. Hearings give various groups and representatives the chance to publicize through the media the virtues or vices of the legislation. Following the public hearings in the subcommittee, there is usually a subcommittee **mark-up session,** where decisions are made concerning amendments and the final wording of the bill. After the mark-up session in the subcommittee, there is a mark-up session in the full committee.

Prior to recent reforms, mark-up sessions in the Senate and House committees were normally closed to the public. Committees now regularly hold open mark-up sessions unless—for national security reasons or otherwise—members of the committee publicly vote to close the session. This reform tends to make committees and their members more accountable to the public. However, tax and appropriations measures are usually marked up out of public view. Certainly in most cases the crucial wheeling and dealing surrounding all major legislation is inevitably private (see the case study).

When the bill is "reported," or acted upon by the committee, it is printed again, showing any amendments made in committee. In addition, the committee staff prepares a **committee report,** which accompanies the bill to the full House or Senate. This report is important. If, later on, a court cannot tell exactly what Congress intended from the words of the bill, it may try to discover the "legislative intent" by referring to the committee report and the records of debate.

In the Senate, once a committee has taken final action on a bill, it is ready for floor action. It is listed on the **calendar,** which indicates the bills that are ready for full Senate consideration. The Senate leadership consults with the committee chairperson and decides when the bill will be scheduled for debate.

In the House, there is a step between the committee report of a bill and the listing of the bill on the House calendar. This step

★ A Congressman's Vote: The View from the Floor

"This was the day of the vote on whether the government should guarantee a loan to rescue Lockheed Aircraft from its financial troubles. . . . The final vote was very close. . . .

"Bill Steiger hadn't answered on the first roll-call vote. Yet he had been standing on the floor and obviously had heard his name called. Bill is a party man; he's careful to play the game by the established rules. He knew the Lockheed loan wouldn't be popular in his district. Hence he wanted to vote against it. But at the same time he's close to the Republican leadership. They wanted him to vote aye. So he intended to vote for the loan only if it developed that one or two votes were needed to pass it. . . .

"Once the roll has been called twice, those who haven't yet voted or who wish to change their votes can stand in the well and be recognized for that purpose. Because Democrats control the House, the Democratic side of the well is the first to be "cleared." Democrats are recognized before Republicans—and women are recognized before men.

"When the Democrats had voted, the clerk turned toward the dozen or so Republicans who were waiting to be recognized. Steiger was standing in the far corner of the well so he could vote at the end of the line and be absolutely certain that his vote was needed. . . .

"At this point, only four or five members remained in the well. The margin of ayes was big enough to let Steiger vote no, and with a look of obvious relief on his face, that's exactly what he did. The bill passed by three votes, 192 to 189."

SOURCE: Donald Riegle, *O Congress* (New York: Doubleday, 1972), pp. 98–99.

involves action by the House Rules Committee. With 435 members, the House has more restrictive rules and procedures than the smaller Senate. These rules include limits of debate and amendments on the floor, and they are largely applied by the Rules Committee.

The Floor Stage

Except for tax and appropriations bills, which must be voted on first, in the House, floor action on a bill may start in either chamber. Senators have more freedom of action on the floor than members of the House. Senate rules are far more liberal, and senators may freely

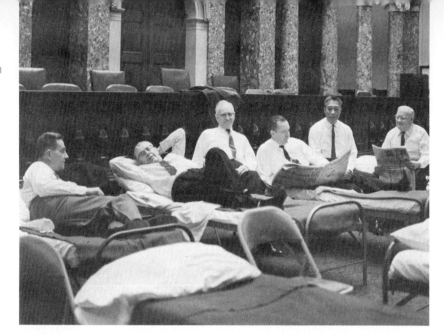

The Senate stayed in session around the clock in attempting to exhaust a long fillibuster of a civil rights bill in 1960. Minorities in the Senate have traditionally used the fillibuster to delay or stop legislation supported by the majority.

offer and vote upon amendments. Debate is usually unlimited, unless senators unanimously agree on time limits, which they usually do. Senate rules also provide for a filibuster, a practice not allowed in the House.

A **filibuster**—an attempt to "talk a bill to death"—may be used by senators to prevent a final vote. In the Senate, this is politely called "extended debate." Senators resort to the filibuster when they are in a minority and want to block the adoption of a measure by a majority of senators. Senators who oppose certain provisions in a bill can also use the filibuster to force changes in it before the bill is allowed to come for a vote. To stop a filibuster, three-fifths of the Senate membership can invoke **cloture**—that is, end debate. This three-fifths requirement—sixty senators—is rather stiff. Basically, it permits a minority of senators to block a majority in the Senate from passing a measure.

The filibuster rule came under its greatest attack when southern senators succcessfully used it in the 1950s to prevent passage of civil rights legislation. Senator Strom Thurmond of South Carolina still holds the individual filibuster record of 24 hours, 18 minutes in seeking to block a civil rights bill in 1957.

Today filibusters are routinely threatened by Republicans in the Senate to force compromises on legislation. With the Democrats holding a 54–46 majority (six votes short of the number needed for cloture), Republicans have used the threat of filibuster to change or kill legislation they dislike. Most of the action takes place behind the scenes with disputed bills being temporarily withdrawn for private negotiations.

Passage of a bill in the House or Senate requires a majority vote of those present and voting. One more than half the members constitutes a **quorum** needed to operate in both houses of Congress in most instances. Noncontroversial bills, however, are sometimes adopted by unanimous consent, without a formal vote. When the House and Senate pass a bill in exactly the same form, congressional consideration of the measure is complete. It is then sent to the president for approval or disapproval.

The Conference Stage

If the House and Senate versions of a bill differ, each house must appoint conferees to resolve their disagreements. Each set of conferees is expected, at least initially, to support the bill approved by its own house. Before a **conference committee** report can be adopted, a majority of the House conferees *and* a majority of the Senate conferees must support it.

The purpose of the conference is to reach an agreement. But this would not be possible if all the conferees from each house refused to make concessions. After some give and take, a majority of the conferees from each house usually agrees on a compromise version of the bill. The conference can put in measures not part of the House or Senate bills. If no agreement is reached, the bill cannot become law.

Once a conference report has been written, the bill then must go back to both the House and Senate for votes on the revised version. Either house may turn down the report and ask for an additional conference. When both houses have agreed to the conference bill, it is sent to the president. If the president signs the bill, it becomes law. If the president vetoes the bill, it cannot become law unless the House and Senate again pass the bill, this time by a two-thirds vote.

Inside the Ways and Means Committee: Enter Tax Reform

Looking at how the House Ways and Means Committee tackled a major tax reform bill shows how Congress works, revealing party control in congressional committees, the bargaining that moves the legislative process, and the importance of a key individual, in this case the Committee's chairman, Dan Rostenkowski.[10]

Setting the Stage for Tax Reform

It was May 1985 and the Democrats had a problem. The unfairness of the tax code had long been a staple part of Democratic speeches. Pointing out, for example, that General Electric, with profits of $9.5 billion over four years, paid no Federal income tax and had actually gotten refunds was good politics. But doing something about tax reform involved wholly different political calculations.

The tax code represented years of delicately balanced compromises among powerful economic interests. And these interests were in a position to make their voices heard. In 1985, a nonelection year, the thirty-six members of the Ways and Means Committee had received some $7 million for their campaigns. One Congressman remarked that the ". . . only reason it isn't considered bribery is that Congress gets to define bribery."

But now President Reagan's Treasury Department had come up with a radical tax reform plan that accepted the desirability of lower tax rates for everyone in return for removing tax loopholes favoring wealthy interests. The plan also accepted that every corporation and individual should pay some minimum tax. Not the least important motive behind the plan was the Republicans' political hope that tax reform could become a populist realigning issue, by which the GOP would bring blue collar voters into the party.

Democrats were stunned. While Democratic leaders were skeptical of reform—especially its chances in beating the special interests—they had no choice but to embrace the effort. As Dan Rostenkowski put it: "I thought Ronald Reagan was trying to outpolitic us. I am not a reformer. But I'm a Democrat. And if the Democrats are for reform, then I'm a reformer."

Indeed, few people would call Dan Rostenkowski a reformer. A product of Mayor Richard J. Daley's Chicago machine, he had entered politics much like someone would join a family business. His father was the ward committeeman from a Polish section of Chicago and he "inherited" the position. In 1958, at the age of thirty, he was elected to Congress, where he faithfully served the machine, becoming chairman of Ways and Means in 1981. Along the way he acquired a reputation as a hardball politician with a long memory for anyone who crossed him. He could also bully liberals on his committee as sissy "blow-dried types."

Enter the Committee

The new Treasury Secretary, James Baker, a Texan and savvy former White House

Chief of Staff, realized that getting the bill through Ways and Means was key to its passage and that Rostenkowski was the key to Ways and Means. Treasury's plan was designed to be revenue neutral—the amount of money lost by lowering rates would be matched by the amount gained by closing loopholes. The staff of Ways and Means soon concluded that Treasury's revenue estimates were not realistic, and some of the proposals did not stand a chance of passing Congress. The Texan Secretary had left the oil companies with virtually all their tax breaks and had given bigger cuts to upper-income taxpayers than to the middle class. Both were difficult political sells in the Democratic House.

In confronting tax reform, Rostenkowski's first task was to keep control of his committee. His chief instrument for doing that was the Democratic majority on the committee, tied to him in various ways. Some owed their seats on the committee to the chairman's timely intervention. Others found that Rostenkowski's attendance at their fundraisers was worth thousands of dollars to their campaigns. And still others who had defied him in the past saw their pet projects squashed. The pattern of rewards and punishments was clear to all.

One of the best-financed lobbying efforts sought to save

Rep. Dan Rostenkowski confers with Treasury Secretary James Baker.

the deduction for state and local taxes. By *not* allowing taxpayers to subtract what they paid in these taxes from what they owed the federal government, the reform bill gained some $150 billion over five years. But it also threatened high-tax states' ability to fund programs and raised the cost of living there. Led by New York, a coalition of state officials, businesses, and public-employees' unions raised $1.5 million to organize grassroots campaigns in the districts of committee members. They declared that their position was not open to compromise.

The Bill's Mark-up

After holding public hearings on the bill across the country during the summer, the committee began drafting sessions called "mark-ups" on October 1st. These were held behind closed doors, with neither press nor lobbyists. The bill was soon in trouble. By mid-month an amendment favoring banks was adopted that tore a gaping hole in the bill. It actually widened a loophole and cost so much revenue that tax reform seemed on the brink of defeat.

Rostenkowski at this point chose an interesting strategy. He was pushing, in his words, "the bill that nobody wanted." At the same time, no one wanted to be seen as selling out to special interests by opposing "reform." So for the chairman, the worse the bill did at first, the worse the publicity for the members and the more of a chance reform would eventually have to pass. As one staff aide put it: "The last thing that any of these guys want is for it to be written that tax reform dies in the Ways and Means Committee because sleaze-bag politicians want to take care of First National City Bank so the average public gets screwed."

The "don't-let-this-dog-die-on-my-doorstep" theme helped push the legislation along at every stage. But shame alone was not going to get the bill out of committee. The chairman realized that there were too many interests lined up against it. The oil interests from the Southwest (which found the committee's bill raising their taxes) were forming an alliance with the high-taxed states of the Northeast to kill the bill. They concentrated their efforts on keeping the deduction for state and local taxes. Some groups backed the deduction because their states needed the monies; others backed it because they believed they could destroy the entire reform measure. Soon Rostenkowski was presented a list of nearly half of the 435-member House who declared they would vote against any reform tampering with the deduction.

To cut a deal on the state and local deduction Rostenkowski needed the help of the staff. The president had committed himself to a top rate no

Dan Rostenkowski

higher than 35 percent. If the deduction was retained, this rate would have to rise to compensate for the lost revenue. This was the box the chairman was in. What the staff suggested was to leave the rates alone but to lower the income levels at which they took effect. So rather than have 35 percent as the tax rate for income above $60,000 (with a lower rate below that), start the 35% rate at, say, $45,000. This had the same effect as raising rates but was less noticeable.

The chairman's offer to the New Yorkers leading the deduction charge was direct. In return for their support of him he would retain the state and local deduction. They agreed. Rostenkowski then went to the sponsor of the disastrous banking amendment and asked him, "What can we do to get you to back off?" When the chairman asked a member for a favor it could not usually be ignored. Eight days after the

initial disaster, the new compromise was passed with the support of the state and local backers. It was a key vote. The chairman had his core of supporters and for the first time a vote that indicated they might just pass a tax reform bill.

Trading Off Obstacles

Night after night in sessions lasting into the early hours of the morning, Rostenkowski steered the bill around and over numerous interests. The Committee divided into smaller working groups dominated by allies of the chairman to take up issues like real estate and municipal bonds.

One sticky problem was the write-off for business meals and entertainment. A powerful coalition including American Express, sports teams, unions, hotels, and the tourist industry opposed reducing the deduction. Without the deduction the New York Mets baseball team claimed they'd have to sell star pitcher Dwight Gooden. Others threatened that thousands of jobs in restaurants would be lost. At the end of a heated debate, the chairman spoke of the unfairness of the present system. He said that any reform that allowed the average guy to take his lunch to work in a pail, while a big-shot down the road went to a fancy restaurant and deducted his meal, would not gain the trust of the public.

Rostenkowski then backed up his populist words and gruff personality with a pointed reminder: *transition rules* were to be doled out toward the end of November and he would decide who got what. These rules were supposed to ease the change from present law to the new one. In fact, they functioned as targeted benefits for companies and home districts that the chairman could dispense as he saw fit. These tax breaks included tax-exempt bonds for a new stadium for the Miami Dolphins football team, a tax break for a new headquarters for Merrill Lynch in New York, and a $200 million benefit for Commonwealth Edison in Illinois. More than $5 billion of these favors were given out with the chairman seated behind his desk asking each member, "What do you need?"

For whatever reason—ideals or transition rules—the committee went along with its chairman and voted to reduce the business deduction for entertainment.

After all the smaller deals had been cut, the committee still had to make sure that the overall package made sense— that the bill was revenue neutral, that the middle and working classes would benefit, and that Republicans would find enough in it to support. In fact, all of these points were questionable.

Ahead would lie a hundred changes and a dozen near disasters as the bill worked its way through the House floor, the Senate Finance Committee and Senate floor, and then back to Rostenkowski's line of sight in the Conference Committee. Rostenkowski himself thought the bill would die in the Senate, where at least there would be the Senate's majority-party Republicans' fingerprints on the gun.

But by 3:30 Sunday morning on November 24, 1985, an exhausted Dan Rostenkowski could emerge from his committee room to declare that his committtee's work was completed. One Republican remarked of Rostenkowski, "He's played the committee like Yehudi Menuhin plays the Stradivarius." The chairman more modestly said, "We have not written a perfect law. Perhaps a faculty of scholars could do a better job. . . . But politics is an imperfect process."

Conclusion

The saying that "victory has many fathers while defeat is an orphan," applies here. Certainly the president who rallied the country behind tax reform and the press that kept the pressure on have reason to take credit. But the Chairman was the critical ingredient to what happened in Ways and Means. Seeing that he did not have the votes to pass a bill, Rostenkowski first cut out the largest opposition by surrendering on state and local deductions. In doing so he demanded its supporters' backing for the rest of the bill. While generally ignoring the Republicans, he "horse-traded" with the Democratic majority. Rostenkowski knew that most congressmen needed sweetheart amendments for interests in their districts. The chairman would offer them these particular items in exchange for their support of the whole bill. In the end it was the force of Chairman Rostenkowski's personality, skill, commitment, and dogged determination that allowed the most significant tax reform in a generation to move through Ways and Means.

WRAP-UP

Congress was designed to be the democratic centerpiece of the federal government. Although the executive branch has in the twentieth century grown vastly, congressional powers remain extensive. Of these the fiscal power, the "power of the purse," is the most important. But its roles in commerce, foreign policy, investigations, and confirmations of presidential appointments give Congress a vital role to play in governing.

Its decentralized organization frequently undercuts Congress's capacity to use these powers effectively. With contending parties and congressional leaders and a multitude of fairly independent committees, Congress doesn't operate that badly for a representative body. That bills do get through the legislative process is testimony to the political skills of the participants. The case study of how laws are made illustrates Chairman Rostenkowski's talents in passing tax reform through his Ways and Means Committee. It also is a reminder of former German Chancellor Otto Bismarck's remark that lovers of sausages and laws should not watch either being made.

Nelson Polsby, a political scientist at the University of California at Berkeley, said once, "The fact is that Congress is the most powerful and most effective legislative body in the world. It you don't think it's efficient, it's because democracy isn't efficient."[11] Clearly the making of laws is not a tidy business. Congress operates best when it reminds the rest of government where its support and money ultimately rest. But that in turn means reflecting the country's diversity of interests, a diversity that often leads to stalemates or watered-down compromises. The art of leadership lies in making a legislative body representative and effective, or as near to both as politically possible.

Key Terms

fiscal power (p. 352)
first resolution (p. 353)
reconciliation (p. 354)
Gramm-Rudman (p. 355)
Commerce Clause (p. 356)
War Powers Act (p. 357)
Senatorial Courtesy (p. 361)
majority party (p. 362)
Speaker of the House (p. 363)
president of the Senate (p. 365)

Senate majority leader (p. 366)
standing committees (p. 368)
mark-up session (p. 376)
committee report (p. 376)
calendar (p. 376)
filibuster (p. 378)
cloture (p. 378)
quorum (p. 379)
conference committee (p. 379)

Suggested Readings

Redman, Eric, *The Dance of Legislation* (New York: Simon & Schuster, 1973).

Reedy, George, *The U.S. Senate: Paralysis or a Search for Consensus* (New York: Crown, 1986).

Reid, T. R., *Congressional Odyssey: The Saga of a Senate Bill* (San Francisco: W.H. Freeman & Co., 1980).

Sinclair, Barbara, *Majority Leadership in the U.S. House* (Baltimore: John Hopkins, 1983).

Smith, Steven S., and Christopher J. Deering, *Committees in Congress* (Washington, D.C.: Congressional Quarterly Press, 1984).

Endnotes

[1] As quoted by Hedrick Smith, *The Power Game, How Washington Works* (New York: Random House, 1988), pp. 53–54, 101.

[2] Edward S. Corwin, *The President: Office and Powers, 1787–1957* (New York: New York University Press, 1957) p. 64.

[3] See Jane Mayer and Doyle McManus, *Landslide: The Unmaking of the President 1984–1988* (Boston: Houghton Mifflin Company, 1988).

[4] Raoul Berger, *Executive Privilege: A Constitutional Myth* (Cambridge, MA: Harvard University Press, 1974), p. 1.

[5] See George E. Reedy, *The U.S. Senate* (New York: New American Library, 1986).

[6] Ross K. Baker, *Friend and Foe in the U.S. Senate* (New York: The Free Press, 1980), p. 191.

[7] Woodrow Wilson, *Congressional Government,* 15th ed. (Boston: Houghton Mifflin, 1900), pp. 69–70.

[8] See Walter J. Oleszek, *Congressional Procedures and the Policy Process* (Washington, D.C.: Congressional Quarterly Press, 1989).

[9] Bobby Baker, *Wheeling and Dealing* (New York: W. W. Norton, 1978), p. 97.

[10] The case study is adapted from Jeffrey Birnbaum and Alan S. Murray, *Showdown at Gucci Gulch, Lawmakers, Lobbyists and the Unlikely Triumph of Tax Reform* (New York: Random House, 1988).

[11] *The Wall Street Journal,* March 21, 1988.

★

CHAPTER 13

The Presidency

President John F. Kennedy was assassinated on November 22, 1963. In the days that followed, two political scientists interviewed college students for their reactions. The following comments by three students reflect a deep personal attachment between people and the president.[1]

" . . . It was not so much that Kennedy was dead, but that I was without a friend and a leader, and so was the whole country. It had become sort of queer. Well, my mother's been in the hospital recently, you know, and kind of ill. In a kind of a way I felt that it would be better if she had died rather than Kennedy."

"I was on my way to go to class. I remember . . . thinking, what should I do? Where should I go, what should I do? And then almost immediately thinking this is ridiculous. Obviously there's nothing left for me to do but go to [class], because there's nothing I can do about it anyway. And we got to the room and there was a feeling among four or five people in the class that the class should be called off. And I remember reacting to that suggestion with something awful close to . . . anger. The idea that we can't let this thing upset us that much. You know, we've got to have our class. There's no point in letting this destroy the social order."

"The thing that really hit me was watching a tape of the morning before it happened . . . he came outside and cracked a joke about Jackie as he does a lot of times, or as he did a lot of times, and then he went out and shook hands with the people. Then you see him walking back in the way he walks with that sort of jaunty look back over his shoulder, smiling and waving to everyone, just obviously loving the public, obviously loving being out in it . . . You see the Kennedy that's become a fixture in this country. . . . Then, all of a sudden, boom, he's gone."

The funeral procession for John F. Kennedy in 1963.

In 1967, President Johnson's efforts were bent toward reenforcing the country's commitment to Vietnam. As the number of troops passed the half-million mark and the war continued to expand, the agencies of government worked up new tactics to make the policy work. But the policy wouldn't work, and by March 1968 Johnson had changed his mind. A key person involved in this change was the Secretary of Defense, Clark Clifford.

Clifford was a preeminent Washington player. He had served presidents of both parties for two decades since Truman had brought him into his administration. He dressed, talked, and acted like a family lawyer from the pages of an English novel, yet he possessed one of Washington's shrewdest minds, and he was skilled in the art of "manipulating a monarch."

When Clifford was appointed to head the Defense Department, replacing Robert McNamara who had developed qualms about the war, he asked leading strategic thinkers what it would take to bring peace. Their answer—a military victory requiring an invasion of North Vietnam—went far beyond the resources then being employed. Given that the nation was already being torn apart by the present policy, the alternative seemed to be to get out. Clifford quickly grasped that the idea of punishing the enemy until they were ready to "make a deal" would not work. He brought the president around to this idea with great care and skill.

Clifford had been assigned the role of briefing the cabinet on the war. He used these briefings to conceal his own position and to subtly present a view of the war from which those listening could not fail to draw the correct conclusion. As one participant put it:

President Lyndon Johnson listens to a tape of Vietnam soldiers recounting their battle experiences.

> There were at least two more meetings before I realized what was happening. He was presenting the weakest possible case for staying in Vietnam, but presenting it in such a manner that he could not be accused of opposing the general policy. Furthermore, he spoke in soothing tones that sent everyone into a half-doze where they absorbed his words on a virtually subliminal basis. Over a period of time, they would come to recognize the holes in the rationale and would almost certainly turn against the war— and think it was their own idea. I do not know how he worked on the president directly when they were alone, but there is little doubt in my mind that he turned LBJ around in such a way that LBJ decided it was his own idea. . . .[2]

These two tales illustrate two very different levels on which presidents operate. The grief over President Kennedy's death shows the emotional tie Americans have to their president. Here the president is an almost religious symbol of national stability, a larger-than-life figure personalizing the government. But presidents also head up the executive branch of that government, as the Johnson story underlines. This view of the Vietnam decision reminds us that when we read, "The president said today. . . ." we cannot always be sure who is speaking. A president in his actions may be reflecting major bureaucracies, powerful interest groups, or influential aides. Even strong presidents, like Johnson, will be playing messy games of politics inside the White House with no assurance, despite their public posture, of emerging as the winner.

Presidents are both real and symbolic national leaders. Like monarchs, presidents are **heads of state,** representing the nation at symbolic and ceremonial occasions. Like prime ministers, presidents are also **heads of government,** with actual political responsibilities and powers, including the responsibility of leading the executive branch of the government. In England the positions are divided between the queen and the prime minister. In America, both positions are combined in the president of the United States (see the box on page 393).

While it is not clear what Americans expect from their president, it is clear they expect too much. Thomas Cronin has pointed out a number of these paradoxical expectations.[3] Americans want a president to be both tough and gentle—tough enough to stand up to a foreign adversary but gentle enough to be concerned about less fortunate people ("A kindhearted son of a bitch," Cronin put it). They want a president to have strong convictions on issues but to be flexible enough to make compromises when necessary. They expect a president to both lead and listen, to initiate new ideas but not to get too far ahead of the people.

Americans also want their presidents to inspire the country to high ideals, yet they believe that presidents should not promise more than they can deliver. Americans want presidents to work well with Congress and other officials, but also to have the courage to stand up for deeply held principles. They want presidents to be "above politics" but to be political enough to put together a coalition that can govern. They like a president who is ordinary enough to be "one of us," but extraordinary enough to lead and be admired.

These popular contradictions, as well as the historical evolution of the office and its central importance to the government, make discussion of the presidency (not to mention *being* a president) difficult. Analysts of the chief executive have tended to take the most recent president and project his flaws or strengths onto the office. Students of the office in the early 1960s saw Eisenhower as too detached and nonpolitical, and wrote approvingly of Kennedy's vigorous leadership style. By the early 1970s, Johnson and Nixon led scholars to

FIGURE 13★1
Public Approval of Reagan Through Eight Years

Based on sixty-two New York Times/CBS News Polls and five New York Times Polls. When two polls conducted in the same month gave identical results, only one value is shown. Wording of final poll in January 1989: "Do you approve or disapprove of the way Ronald Reagan has handled his job as President since 1981?"

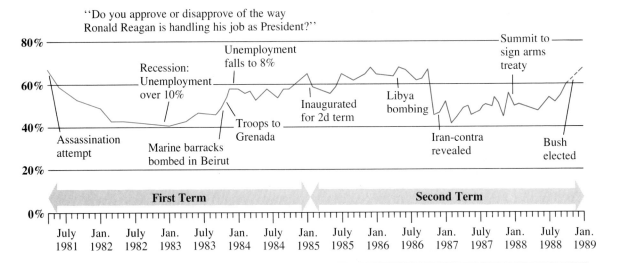

SOURCE: The New York Times/CBS News Poll, January 13, 1989.

warn of an imperial presidency leading to wars abroad and endangered liberties at home. By the early 1980s, Carter's tenure had influenced writings about an "imperiled" presidency and raised questions about whether anyone could fill the job.

Today the glow of the Reagan years has restored much of the luster of the presidency (see Figure 13.1). Yet George Bush's cautious low-key style and his confrontations with looming deficits and deadlocks in Congress have served as warnings to keep a balanced view of the presidency. Presidents *can* fail. Their influence *is* limited.

PRESIDENTIAL LEADERSHIP

In being both "a king and a prime minister," as Theodore Roosevelt described his office, a president must be both a real and a symbolic national leader. The president must retain national popularity while administering the executive branch of the government. In fulfilling the tasks of the office, a president's power is shaped by three overlapping factors. First is the constitutional grant of powers and the historical evolution of these powers in the practices of past presidents. This inheritance is molded by the political environment in which a president serves, particularly the strength of the interests that support him. Finally, his own personality, skills, and goals will go far in explaining the success or failure of his administration.

The Presidential Inheritance

What did the framers of the Constitution want when they established a "president" to head the new United States of America? It is difficult to say. The framers themselves had doubts about the nature of the presidency. There was no office like it in any government in the world at the time. They had rebelled once against a king, and they certainly did not want another one. Thus, the news that came from the secret meetings of the Constitutional Convention in Philadelphia in 1787 was: "Tho' we cannot, affirmatively, tell you what we are doing; we can, negatively, tell you what we are not doing—we never once thought of a king."

In its very beginnings, the presidency involved a search for balance, an office with somewhere between "too much" and "not enough" power. Too much power would produce an executive tyrant; not enough would mean ineffective government.[4] The framers did not spell out the president's duties and limits for two reasons. They held conflicting attitudes toward the chief executive's role, and they were sure that George Washington, a man universally trusted, would become the first president. As a result, Article II, Section I begins with the words, "The Executive power shall be vested in a President of the United States of America." But "executive power" is never defined.

The framers did make some important decisions concerning the presidency. For example, they decided to have a single executive. Some at the convention preferred a plural executive, fearing that one executive would lead to monarchy. But a majority decided in favor of a "single magistrate, as giving most energy, dispatch, and responsibility to the office." The convention also decided against having the president elected by Congress. This plan had been proposed to make the presidency an instrument for carrying out the will of the legislature. Instead, the framers gave the office of president independence from Congress. Most did not see a *political* role for the president. They pictured him as a gentleman-aristocrat who would stand as a picture of national unity. Congress, not the president, was to be central.

Historical Growth

Forty-one men have been president of the United States, from George Washington, who took office in 1790, to George Bush, who began his term in 1989. The powers of the president have expanded far beyond the brief words of the Constitution. At times weak presidents and popular sentiment reduced executive power, so only with hindsight does this growth seem relentless. *The expansion of presidential powers is due to a number of factors: the actions and outlooks of individual presidents; the expanded federal role in domestic and economic affairs; the emergence of the United States as a world power in the nuclear age; and a rise in public expectations concerning the presidency in an era of mass communications.*

Individual presidents have turned the presidency into an office of national leadership. George Washington sent troops to put down a rebellion among farmers in western Pennsylvania who were angered by a tax placed on whiskey. Washington's action in the Whiskey Rebellion was later claimed as a precedent for a president's **residual power** (also called *inherent power,*) power not spelled out in the Constitution but necessary for the president to be able to carry out other responsibilities. The third president, Thomas Jefferson, had fought against establishing a strong executive in the Constitution. Yet by negotiating and signing the Louisiana Purchase, gaining the approval of Congress only after the fact (perhaps inevitable in an age of slow communication), Jefferson weakened the principle of checks and balances. He had acquired territory even though the Constitution is silent on whether the national government has that power. Congress played no role in doubling the size of the country, and couldn't easily reverse the president's action.

Andrew Jackson's veto of a bill to recharter the Bank of the United States brought him into confrontation with Congress. The Bank had become especially unpopular in the rural West because it had foreclosed many mortgages during the depression of the 1820s. The veto helped mold the independence of the office. Before Jackson, the veto was used as a means of preventing unconstitutional legislative expansion. Jackson made it a tool of a president's policy preferences.

No president in America's history stretched the limits of the Constitution as much as Abraham Lincoln did during the Civil War. As one historian wrote, "It is indeed a striking fact that Lincoln who stands forth in popular conception as a great democrat, the exponent of liberty and of government by the people, was driven by circumstances to the use of more arbitrary power than perhaps any other

★ Comparison of President and British Prime Minister

PRIME MINISTER	PRESIDENT
Appointed by legislature	Elected
Budget prepared by executive or head of state	Prepares proposed budget
Has free hand to appoint cabinet	Cabinet must be confirmed by Senate
Usually resigns upon vote of no confidence	Must be impeached
Constitution in common law; can be interpreted by P.M. and ruling party	Constitution governs actions and is interpreted by judicial branch
Can dissolve Parliament	Cannot dissolve Congress
Must respond to legislature's questions	Can be investigated by Congress
Top role in foreign policy	Has top foreign policy role, except that Congress reserves right to declare war
Averages 3½ years in office	Averages 5½ years in office
Averaged 25 years service in Parliament since 1885	Less than half served in Congress in this century

SOURCES: *Parliaments of the World: A Reference Compendium,* DeGruyter, New York, 1976; Rasmussen, Jorgen, "Executive and Legislative Roles," in Hodder-Williams, Richard and James Ceaser *Politics in Britain and the United States: Comparative Perspectives* (Durham, N.C.: Duke University Press, 1986), pp. 1–27.

president has seized."[5] Lincoln believed that his highest duty was to save the Union. Thus, he "carried his executive authority to the extent of freeing the slaves by proclamation, setting up a whole scheme of state-making for the purpose of reconstruction, suspending the habeas corpus privilege, proclaiming martial law, enlarging the army and navy beyond the limits fixed by existing law, and spending public money without congressional appropriation." Lincoln recognized that most of the steps he took involved powers not proper for a president to exercise. Still, the memory of the presidency as an activist office lingered after the Civil War crisis.

President Franklin D. Roosevelt expanded the powers of the presidency by increasing the role of the federal government in domestic affairs. Here he initiates work on the Whiteface Mountain Memorial Highway.

Theodore Roosevelt used the presidency as a "bully pulpit" for rallying the nation. Before his own election, Woodrow Wilson expressed his idea of the president as a leader of the nation: "The nation as a whole has chosen him, and is conscious that it has no other political spokesman. He is the only national voice in affairs. He is the representative of no constituency, but of the whole people."[6]

Franklin D. Roosevelt established the pattern for modern presidents. He asserted the authority of the president to represent the will of the whole nation, instead of the will of Congress, more vigorously than any other chief executive. Coming to office during the Great Depression of the 1930s, when a third of all Americans were out of work, he won "social acceptance of the idea that government should be active and reformist."[7] As he said to the Democratic Convention that nominated him, "I pledge you, I pledge myself, to a new deal for the American people." Roosevelt's New Deal inaugurated the expanded federal role in domestic and economic affairs in this country. One authority described Roosevelt's first term as follows:

> Headline writers could barely keep pace with lawmakers . . .
> subsidies to farmers . . . codes for business, relief for unemployed,
> loans for homeowners, safeguards of "truth in securities,"
> promises of the Tennessee Valley Authority. Amid the
> Congressional fireworks, some Senators fretted over the long-
> range implications of this carnival of Presidential initiatives. But
> Harry Hopkins, who would become Roosevelt's closest counselor,
> once snapped the retort: "People don't eat 'in the long run.' They
> eat everyday."[8]

From Franklin D. Roosevelt on, the policy questions the federal government dealt with became far more complex. Congress became increasingly willing to leave the details of new policies and programs to the various executives agencies and departments under the president. *The expanded federal role in domestic affairs, therefore, expanded the power of the presidency.* But it also expanded the power and discretion of the executive agencies, which presented a challenge to the president's ability to control the bureaucracy formally under him.

The presidency gained enormous power from America's emergence as a world power. Following World War II, a Cold War developed between the United States and the Soviet Union. A Cold War view of the world justified executive activities in virtually every part of the globe. With some pride, Americans came to think of the president of the United States as the "leader of the free world." National security seemed to require the president to be able to act in an emergency, without waiting for congressional approval.

These circumstances inflated public expectations of the president. They also glorified the presidency in a mass media era. As one expert has pointed out, "When George Washington announced his retirement, his words, in print, without any image, took 4 days to reach New York and 10 days to reach outlying regions. When Lyndon Johnson made the same announcement in 1968, he faced an audience of 75 million people."[9] Television coverage and newspaper reports have caused the presidency to seem larger than life. This media attention has encouraged Americans to feel that a president of the United States can and must do something about nearly all the problems we face.

The Political Environment

The historical expansion of presidential power should not conceal each president's dependence on political coalitions. These shifting coalitions of powerful groups (labor, blacks, small business, and southern conservatives) act as the dominant influence over the federal government during broad periods of American history. They rise, rule, and decline and in the process they affect the ability of the president to govern. Generally, the longer a coalition rules the more it weakens, with the interests composing it quarreling among themselves.

The strength and age of a political coalition will affect the presidential leadership within the period. Stephen Skowrenek, Professor of Political Science at Yale University, has studied these political regimes at three different stages of rule. The first stage is that of *con-*

struction. Here the new regime comes to power by removing an old ruling coalition and takes over the institutions of government the president now leads. The second stage is regime *management*. Here a president needs to maintain the coalition while facing increasing division within the ranks. Finally comes the regime *decline*. Presidents face divided coalitions and a declining popular belief in this old order's right to rule.[10]

In this century we can see these stages by considering three Democratic presidents who governed over the **New Deal coalition:** Franklin D. Roosevelt, 1932–45, who founded it following the political upheaval caused by the Great Depression; John Kennedy, 1960–63, who managed the coalition under the increasing divisions between southern conservatives and northern liberals; and finally Jimmy Carter, 1976–80, who governed during its decline and was caught leading a coalition that no longer had the unity to govern.

The election of 1932 reflected the collapse of the Republicans as the ruling party in the face of their perceived lack of response to the Great Depression. Roosevelt, as president, *constructed* a new majority coalition and shaped the government's services to meet the needs of a collapsing economy. He reached out to southern conservatives, incorporated big business into New Deal programs, and supported the interests of organized labor, the poor, the elderly, and small business. While facing some setbacks, Roosevelt reformed and expanded government to meet the needs of his coalition. His sweeping reforms consolidated an activist regime and the support of the majority coalition Roosevelt established and represented.

John F. Kennedy's presidency reflected the *management* stage of this New Deal coalition. His narrow election victory in 1960 resulted from the awkward unity between northern liberals and southern conservatives. From the beginning, Kennedy's task was to balance these increasingly opposed interests. His choice of Lyndon Johnson for vice-president, to appease the South, was balanced by his attempt to meet the liberal demand for civil rights through executive action. While his Justice Department supported black voter registration, Kennedy also appointed segregationist judges in the South. The administration cautioned civil rights leaders and pursued a nationalist foreign policy—both, in part, to avoid a southern withdrawal from the coalition. However, by the end of his brief administration, Kennedy had made his moral choice. He introduced strong civil rights legislation and saw his popularity in the South plummet.

By 1976, the Democrats' New Deal coalition had shattered into groupings of special interests. Jimmy Carter offered the Democrats an outsider's anti-Washington platform capable of bringing his southern region back to a Democratic party dominated by liberals. But the coalition in *decline* could not support many substantive policies. Instead Carter emphasized improving the efficiency of the bureaucratic machinery and bypassed Congress with symbolic appeals to the nation. The core constituencies of blacks and labor found little in government reorganization meeting their concerns. At the same time, Carter's conservative opponents likened him to a traditional New Deal liberal for whom they felt little sympathy. Carter was caught in a paradox, trying to represent the people's alienation from government while tied to the government by his party's control of it. The Democrats tore themselves apart in a revolt against him with Ted Kennedy's 1980 candidacy. This and the Reagan victory only underlined the New Deal coalition's decline.

The political situation in which a president rules helps determine the influence of the office. Whatever the inherited powers or political skills of the chief executive, he will be constrained by the interests he represents and the historical viability of their coalition. Roosevelt was able to shape his presidency and coalition almost anew; Kennedy inherited a coalition needing reinforcement and skillful balancing of factions; and Carter assumed the head of a declining regime, neither unified nor clear of its goals in governing. The accomplishments of these presidents depended, in part, on the political environments they faced.

A somewhat similar pattern can be seen in Bush's inheritance of the Reagan coalition in 1988. Here the clear ideas and political force behind Reagan appeared less clear and less powerful under the management of his former vice-president. Instead George Bush stressed moderation in his dealings with Congress, reached out to liberal groups like blacks and environmentalists, and downplayed the verbal conservatism of Ronald Reagan. Whether he was in the management stage of the Reagan regime or in that of its decline remained for the record of the Bush administration to make clear.

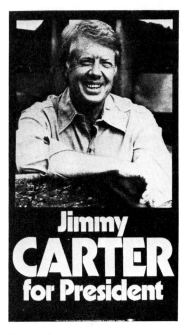

Jimmy Carter won the presidency in 1976 by campaigning as an anti-Washington outsider.

Presidential Personality and Skills

Of course, once in office, a president is more than the powers he has inherited and more than an instrument of his backers. Woodrow Wilson said, "The President is at liberty, both in law and conscience, to be as big a man as he can."[11] And a large factor in how one president's administration differs from another's is the personality of the person who occupies the office.

One popular attempt to classify presidents by personality is the work of political scientist James David Barber.[12] Barber's work, called by some a "psychobiography," also seeks to predict what kind of president a candidate might become.

Barber first divides presidents into *active* and *passive* categories based on how much energy they bring to the job. Comparing Lyndon Johnson to Calvin Coolidge, Barber says:

> *Lyndon Johnson, clearly one of the most active politicians ever, went about his job like a human cyclone. He spent half the day and night calling up people, shaking hands, working very hard at the job. In contrast—undoubtedly the most striking contrast—is Calvin Coolidge. Calvin Coolidge slept about eleven hours a night, and he still needed a nap in the middle of the day.*"[13]

Barber then divides presidents by *positive* and *negative* attitudes about presidential duties. He bases these classifications on whether or not these people enjoy what they have to do.

> *Today-it-was-fun was Franklin Roosevelt's attitude. He had fun being president. He liked dealing with people in that way of his. For contrast, take Herbert Hoover. . . . Hoover discouraged the presence of people in the White House. He did not like the servants in the hall, so when he walked down the halls the servants would jump into the closets and close the doors, so you had the waiters and waitresses crowding in there with trays. Hoover exuded a sense of suffering, of having a rough time of it rather than enjoying it.*[14]

Barber argues that the country is better off when the president is active-positive. Of modern presidents, Barber placed Franklin Roosevelt, Truman, Kennedy, Ford, and Carter in that category, while Ronald Reagan was a passive-positive president, an easily influenced, agreeable, non-assertive chief executive (see Figure 13.2).

Barber believes that the worst kind of personality to have in the White House is the active-negative, a classification he assigned to both Nixon and Johnson. This type of driven personality is likely to turn rigidly inward in the face of political setbacks. When Lyndon Johnson came under severe attack because of Vietnam, he became more rigid, and, as he put it, "hunkered down like a heifer in a hailstorm." Even before Watergate, Barber had prophetically written of Nixon: "The danger is that crisis will be transformed into tragedy. . . . The loss of power to forces beyond his control would constitute a severe threat. That would be a time to go down, if one must, in flames."[15]

	Active	Passive
Positive	Roosevelt Truman Kennedy Carter	Taft Harding Reagan
Negative	Johnson Nixon Hoover Wilson	Eisenhower Coolidge

SOURCE: From *The Presidential Character* by James David Barber. © 1972 by James David Barber. Published by Prentice-Hall, Inc., Englewood Cliffs, NJ 07632.

Barber has been justly criticized for oversimplifying and overemphasizing presidents' personalities. Putting presidents in one of four categories leaves considerable room for debate—was General Eisenhower really passive? Was Abraham Lincoln that negative? These two examples also serve as reminders that personality does not always determine how successful a president's tenure is. A healthy political personality—like Carter—may turn out to be a mediocre president, while a more passive political personality—like Reagan—turns in a better performance in the Oval Office. A president's staff, his policies, the alignment of political forces outside his office, and the tenor of the times in what is demanded of presidents may be more important in determining presidential results. Personality, as Barber would agree, is not all that matters in presidents.[16]

The President as Politician

All the people who have been elected president of the United States in modern times have actively sought the office. Since Franklin D. Roosevelt, all presidents except one have been professional politicians. The one exception was Dwight D. Eisenhower, who gained national fame as an army general. Five modern presidents first served as vice-president: Truman, Nixon, Johnson, Ford, and Bush. Four had previously served in the United States Senate: Truman, Kennedy, Johnson, and Nixon. Five had served in the U.S. House of Representatives: Ford, Johnson, Nixon, Kennedy, and Bush. Three had been governors: Roosevelt, Carter, and Reagan.

It's been said that we elect politicians, not prophets. Politicians tell us what we want to hear; prophets tell us what is right. Presidents need the skills of politicians to mobilize popular support, accommodate existing power centers, and, of course, to become president in the first place. The White House is no place for amateurs. This was true for Abraham Lincoln the politician, and equally true for George Bush the politician. A historian has written:

> Behind that facade of humble directness and folksy humor, Lincoln was moving steadily toward his object; by 1860, he had maneuvered himself into a position where he controlled the party machinery, platform, and candidates of one of the pivotal states in the Union. A Chicago lawyer who had known Lincoln intimately for three decades summarized these pre-presidential years: "one great public mistake . . . generally received and acquiesced in, is that he is considered by the people of this country as a frank, guileless, and unsophisticated man. There never was a greater mistake . . . He handled and moved men remotely as we do pieces upon a chessboard."[17]

This view of Lincoln as a politician takes nothing away from him. Government requires politicians.

Jimmy Carter, whatever his virtues as a campaigner, was by most accounts a poor politician. He neither projected a forceful image nor seemed able to effectively lobby for his objectives. His soft-spoken, "cool" demeanor did not produce the fighting skills needed to lead his party and Congress. As one Congressman said about Carter and his staff a couple years into his administration: "They still haven't learned horse-trading."

Lyndon Johnson, for all his arrogance, sensitivity to criticism, and preoccupation with secrecy, was a superb politician. Described by a colleague as "driven by demons," LBJ put his enormous skill, energy, and compulsions into dominating everyone around him. His legendary ability to gain support for his positions was refined in the years he served as Senate Majority Leader. This relentless verbal manipulation, known as the Johnson Treatment, was described this way:

> The Treatment could last ten minutes or four hours. It came, enveloping its target, at the LBJ Ranch swimming pool, in one of LBJ's offices, in the Senate cloakroom, on the floor of the Senate itself—wherever Johnson might find a fellow Senator within his reach. Its tone could be supplication, accusation, cajolery, exuberance, scorn, tears, complaint, the hint of threat. Its velocity was breathtaking, and it was all in one direction. Interjections from the target were rare. Johnson anticipated them before they

could be spoken. He moved in close, his face a scant millimeter from his target, his eyes widening and narrowing, his eyebrows rising and falling. From his pockets poured clippings, memos, statistics, mimicry, humor, and the genius of analogy that made The Treatment an almost hypnotic experience and rendered the target stunned and helpless.[18]

"Presidential *power* is the power to persuade," wrote Richard Neustadt in a classic sentence in his classic work, *Presidential Power.*[19] The written grants of formal powers given the presidency are no guarantee of leadership. Although at times the president can legally command obedience, most often this is only one of his tools of persuasion. To operate all the tools of influence connected with the office requires political skills of the highest order. *To convince bureaucrats, congressmen, and other influentials that what the president wants is also in their interest to a great extent describes what chief executives do with their days.* It also explains why our greatest presidents are inevitably our best politicians.

Senate Majority Leader Lyndon B. Johnson gives "The Treatment" to Senator Theodore Francis Green.

THE EXECUTIVE BRANCH

The Constitution makes the president the manager of the executive department, the head of government or **chief executive.** Article II, Section 3, declares that the president of the United States shall "take care that the Laws be faithfully executed." Among other things, this provision means that the president is our principal law enforcer. The chief executive, then, has the job of seeing that the Constitution, laws passed by Congress, and decisions of the courts are carried out.

Of course, no one person can be responsible for everything involved in administering the executive branch. Day-to-day responsibility must be delegated to subordinates. According to Article II, Section 2 of the Constitution, the president has broad appointive powers to choose who will assist him in carrying out the law. The principal positions prescribed by the Constitution or by law must be filled "by and with the Advice and Consent of the Senate." Although the Senate rejects very few presidential appointments, the failure of John Tower to win Senate confirmation as Defense Secretary in 1989 clearly underlined this power. The White House staff, however, is not subject to Senate confirmation. This power of appointments gives the president preeminence in the executive department.

Immediately after being elected in November, a president-elect makes plans for taking office in January. Today, the law provides special federal funds for the *transition* from one president to another. During this transitional period, a widespread talent search is conducted. In most government agencies and departments, only the principal positions are subject to presidential appointment and removal.

As chief executive, the president presides over the Executive Office of the President which includes the White House staff, as well as the cabinet departments, independent agencies, and regulatory boards and commissions. Every modern president has also relied to some degree on his vice-president. A president's family members and spouse can also have an important influence on government.

The Executive Office of the President

The **Executive Office of the President** was established in 1939 to advise the president and assist him in managing the bureaucracy. It has grown steadily in size and influence; today it includes eight agencies and some 1400 people. Four of the most important agencies of the executive office are the *White House Office,* the *Office of Management and Budget,* the *Council of Economic Advisers,* and the *National Security Council.*

The White House Office

The **White House Office** is a direct extension of the president. The staff, who often come from the president's campaign organization, are not subject to Senate approval. Some may be chosen for their expertise on certain subjects or for dealing with Congress. The staff help schedule the president's time and provide advice on policy, public relations, and dealing with the media. The staff also includes a group of lawyers under the White House Counsel. These lawyers, called "the most powerful little law firm in the nation's capital," review every presidential decision or action to determine its legal consequences.

In recent years the centralization of executive power has increased the authority of the White House staff at the expense of the cabinet officers—and even the president, as shown by the Iran-contra hearings. Under Ronald Reagan, the **chiefs of staff** in his second term—Donald Regan followed by former Senator Howard Baker—became powerful by controlling access to the president and by their hands-on management of the Executive Office.

Soon after taking office, George Bush's chief of staff, John Sununu, became the butt of criticism for his abrupt manner and inexperience in dealing with Congress. This underlined one important function of the position—to steer attacks away from the chief executive and toward the staff.[20]

Another criticism aimed at the White House office is that the president has taken on the trappings of a monarch and his staff has become a *palace guard*. The staff effectively isolates the president through its deference. As George Reedy, former Special Assistant to President Lyndon Johnson, commented, "... A president moves through his days surrounded by literally hundreds of people whose relationship to him is that of a doting mother to a spoiled child. Whatever he wants is brought to him immediately ..."[21] Reedy adds, "An occasional 'go soak your head' or 'that's stupid' would clear the murky, turgid atmosphere of the White House. ..."

The Office of Management and Budget

The **Office of Management and Budget (OMB)** was created by President Nixon in 1970 as a renamed, reorganized Bureau of the Budget. Departments of the executive branch submit competing claims for shares in the federal budget to the OMB. Besides preparing the budget, OMB is an important general-management arm of the president. It helps him control the executive branch by overseeing all the agencies and their success in accomplishing their programs. Preparing and administering the annual budget (which is then submitted to Congress for approval) gives OMB tremendous power within the

---

★ President Bush's Cabinet—1989
(With Dates When Positions Were First Created)

Secretary of State: James A. Baker, III (1789)
Secretary of the Treasury: Nicholas Brady (1789)
Secretary of Defense: Richard Cheney (1789; was Department of War until 1947)
Attorney General: Dick Thornburgh (1789)
Secretary of Interior: Manuel Lujan (1849)
Secretary of Agriculture: Clayton K. Yuetter (1889)
Secretary of Commerce: Robert Mosbacher (1913)
Secretary of Labor: Elizabeth H. Dole (1913)
Secretary of Health and Human Services: Louis Sullivan (1953; was Department of Health, Education, and Welfare until 1979)
Secretary of Housing and Urban Development: Jack Kemp (1965)
Secretary of Transportation: Samuel Skinner (1966)
Secretary of Energy: Adm. James Watkins (1977)
Secretary of Education: Lauro Cavezas (1979)
Secretary of Veterans Affairs: Edward Derwinski (1988)

★ Painting Pictures for Presidents

President Reagan's first Director of OMB, David Stockman, frequently—and usually unsuccessfully—battled Secretary of Defense Caspar Weinberger over cutting the Defense budget. Stockman describes how Weinberger briefed an often-disinterested president on his requests for defense:

His briefing was a masterpiece of obfuscation. Incredibly, Weinberger had also brought with him a blown-up cartoon. It showed three soldiers. One was a pygmy who carried no rifle. He represented the Carter budget. The second was a four-eyed wimp who looked like Woody Allen, carrying a tiny rifle. That was—me?—the OMB defense budget. Finally, there was G.I. Joe himself, 190 pounds of fighting man, all decked out in helmet and flak jacket and pointing an M-60 machine gun menacingly at—me again? This imposing warrior represented, yes, the Department of Defense budget plan.

It was so intellectually disreputable, so demeaning, that I could hardly bring myself to believe that a Harvard-educated cabinet officer could have brought this to the President of the United States. Did he think the White House was on Sesame Street?

SOURCE: David A. Stockman, *The Triumph of Politics* (New York: Avon Books, 1987), p. 315.

government. It imposes a budget procedure over the executive agencies, reviews and usually lowers their budget requests, and gives clearance on legislation affecting the budget. David Stockman, Reagan's first director of OMB, was architect of the administration's proposals for some $50 billion in spending cuts in its first budget. Richard Darman, now head of OMB, has the tricky task of lowering spending, not raising taxes, and getting Congress to pass a budget.

The Council of Economic Advisers

The **Council of Economic Advisers** is another advisory body of the executive office. It is a three-member council of economic experts, appointed with Senate approval, that helps the president form a national economic policy and gives him advice on economic developments. Presidents have varied on how much they use the chairman of the Council who is, in theory, his principle economic adviser.

The **National Security Council (NSC)** was established early in the Cold War (1947) to help the president coordinate American military and foreign policies. These policies mainly involve the departments of State and Defense, which are represented on the council. (The Central Intelligence Agency, though an executive agency, also falls under the authority of the NSC). Presidents have varied in how much they wished to use the NSC. Kennedy preferred more informal ways of getting advice on national security matters, but Nixon restored the council to a dominant role over policy, when Henry Kissinger served as his special assistant for national security affairs under the NSC. From his position as NSC adviser, Kissinger controlled the flow of communications on international relations to the president. His skill in formulating policies gave him more influence than the Secretary of State and eventually he assumed that position.[22]

The NSC adviser has often rivaled the Secretary of State in influence over foreign policy. Under President Reagan, NSC staffers such as Oliver North took on operational duties including hostage negotiations, antiterrorist actions, and funding guerrillas abroad. When these activities, which had been performed by the NSC to keep them secret from Congress, were publicized in the Iran-Contra hearings in the summer of 1987, the NSC was forced back into a narrower advisory role (see Chapter 18).

The Cabinet Departments

The **cabinet** departments, created by Congress, are the major agencies of the federal government. How much the president uses the cabinet as a whole is strictly up to him, for the cabinet has no power as a body. Its authority comes neither from the Constitution, nor from legislation. Sometimes *cabinet councils,* consisting of several cabinet secretaries, work on problems cutting across departmental boundaries. Although many presidents, including Reagan and Bush, entered office promising to give the cabinet policy-making authority, *power has usually ended up flowing back toward the White House staff.* There is a story about President Lincoln being opposed by his entire cabinet on an issue and remarking, "Seven nays, one aye; the ayes have it."

There are several reasons presidents have not given greater power to the cabinet. First, when a decision must be made, presidents turn to advisers with special experience in that field. Asking the secretary of transportation, for example, to comment on a national security matter at a cabinet meeting would be viewed by most presidents as a waste of time. Second, presidents often choose a cabinet member because of the appointee's independent stature and following. Thus presidents may feel obliged to appoint a person acceptable to organized labor as secretary of labor, or a prominent woman to fill another cabinet position. But since presidents are generally not so worried about how White House staff appointments will look, they give greater consideration to loyalty and expertise.

Third, cabinet officials often develop independence from the White House because of their positions. Cabinet officials have a dual responsibility, to the president and federal government, on one hand, and to their departments and the constituents of their departments, on the other. These agencies are large, fairly independent worlds of their own with their own agendas and constituencies. *The responsibilities of cabinet officers extend in two directions—upward toward the president and downward toward their own department.* Fourth, cabinet officials are removed from day-to-day involvement with the president because of their physical separation from the White House. Cabinet officials must usually go through the White House staff to talk to the president (the physical closeness of the staff to the president increases their influence; the physical distance of cabinet officials limits their influence). For all these reasons, presidents have come to feel that cabinet officials are not as loyal or as supportive as they should be. As the remarks by Former OMB Director David Stockman indicate, this doesn't mean that cabinet members knowing how to manipulate their boss can't have great influence (see the box on page 404).

Vice-President Dan Quayle meets with officials in El Salvador in 1989.

The Vice-President

Vice-presidential nominees are generally chosen for political reasons. Presidential candidates may select the vice-presidential nominee to balance out regional, religious, or other factors and thus to add strength for the general election. The 1988 choice of Lloyd Bentsen, a Texas conservative with long Washington experience, as Democratic vice-presidential nominee for Michael Dukakis, a New England liberal governor, illustrates the process. The choice of Dan Quayle, while it befuddled many at the time, was clearly an attempt by Bush to calm the right wing of his party without promoting past rivals to the important post.

The major constitutional duties of the vice-president are to preside over the Senate and to succeed to the presidency if the office should become vacant. (The Speaker of the House of Representatives and the president pro tem of the Senate are next in line.) Traditionally, the vice-presidency has been seen as a limited, frustrating office. Harry Truman, Franklin Roosevelt's vice-president, said that vice-presidents " . . . were as useful as a cow's fifth teat." But the fact that fourteen vice-presidents have become president, and that four of our last six presidents were vice-presidents at some time, has increased the political importance of the office.

Today scholars speak of a "new vice-presidency."[23] In recent years, vice-presidents like Walter Mondale and George Bush have played key roles in their presidents' administrations. They have represented the chief executive at cabinet meetings and in diplomatic visits oversees. They have lobbied for him in Congress, campaigned in midterm elections as a partisan voice for the president, and served as a top presidential adviser. With large staffs of their own (George Bush as vice-president had some seventy aides), they have become a vital part of the presidential team. Provided they keep the confidence of the president, and give him all the credit, they are likely to continue to be used as "deputy presidents."

ADMINISTRATIVE STYLES

How do presidents deal with the agencies and staff of the executive department and how do they make decisions? Some presidents have encouraged a military chain of command, with the president at the top of the pyramid. Eisenhower was like this; perhaps because of his military background, he preferred to deal personally only with those questions that could not otherwise be resolved and to have reports boiled down to short memos. Reagan also delegated wide responsibility. Nixon preferred to see and talk with only a small number of his White House staff members. His chief of staff, Bob Haldeman, cut off most officials' access to the president. Carter originally made a point of not having a White House chief of staff. But increasingly, Hamilton Jordan began to perform the functions of the position and was eventually named to it officially.

Franklin Roosevelt, Lyndon Johnson, and, now, George Bush have a more freewheeling style of administration. They wanted to be in personal contact with a wide number of government officials and others outside the government. As a result, only they had a clear understanding of much that was being done or discussed in the government. Unlike other recent presidents, George Bush encourages controversy and debate among his advisers as a management tool. It is his way of choosing the best alternative among a number of options, and a means of gaining the most complete information. This is called **multiple advocacy**, where top aides argue out policy in front of the president.

How does a president get the necessary information on which to base decisions? Much of it is filtered through the White House staff. Some of it comes to him in conversations. Other information comes in the form of written memoranda from staff members and officials. Some presidents prefer one over the other, but they all have to do a considerable amount of reading. George Bush has favored the phone for both information and politicking, with impressive results. As one Democrat remarked, "There's just something magnificently intoxicating about having the President on the line."[24]

Typical presidential reading involves a lengthy memorandum listing proposals and alternatives, with a one- or two-page summary at the front. Presidents can read the summary and, if necessary, read more of the whole memorandum, noting decisions or instructions on the front and returning it to the appropriate staff member. Carter was criticized for involving himself in too many small details of programs and proposals, although the box on page 409 on Nixon indicates Carter was hardly unique in this. Reagan regularly relied on his staff and other administration officials to handle details (causing a scandal when it was revealed that he had apparently not been informed by his NSC advisor that funds from Iranian arms sales were being illegally channeled to contra fighters in Nicaragua).

Some presidents seek more outside information—beyond what their closest advisers and White House staff members give them—than others. Lyndon Johnson made a fetish of keeping up with news reports. He had three television sets in his office, which allowed him to see all three network newscasts simultaneously. George Bush has made a point of avoiding White House aides in communicating directly with people close to issues of interest to him.

Security arrangements, heavy duties, and the reverence given the office tend to insulate presidents from the public and from ordinary experiences. It is very easy for a president to become isolated from the outside world and to receive only the information and advice that comes through the White House staff. This may be one reason why recent First Ladies have become so influential. Spouses like Nancy Reagan and Barbara Bush are clearly not afraid that speaking their minds will cause them to lose their husbands' confidence.

A president must guard against the "chilling effect" that the awesome nature of the presidency has on those who talk with him. Advisers tend to refrain from being direct or honest with the president. The staff reinforces what they think the president wants, and the bureaucrats reinforce a decision once it is made and accepted by them. White House meetings are not debating contests, testing all the options available. They usually center on helping the president get

★ Nixon's Absorption in Detail

The Watergate investigation brought to light aspects of presidential behavior previously hidden from the public. Here, an aide testifies concerning President Nixon's peculiar involvement in the most minor of details. "He was deeply involved in the entertainment business, whom we should get, for what kind of group, small band, big band, black band, white band, jazz band, whatever. He was very interested in meals and how they were served and the time of the waiters and was usually put out if a state dinner was not taken care of in less than an hour or an hour's time. . . . He wanted to view the musical selections himself. He was very interested in whether or not salad should be served and decided that at small dinners of eight or less, the salad course should not be served. . . .

He was interested in the plants in the south grounds and whether or not we should retain the tennis court or move it. Memorandums went on about the tennis court for over a year's time. . . . And Washington, D.C.—he even did a memorandum in Yugoslavia and Belgrade, having been impressed by the fine restrooms along the way there, or at least the structures along the way, and having the feeling that back here on the Mall, we had some rather shabby wooden restrooms which he had seen during the time of those demonstrations . . ." SOURCE: Testimony of Alexander Butterfield before the House Impeachment Committee as quoted by Larry Berman, *The New American Presidency,* (Boston: Little, Brown, 1987), pp. 266, 268–269.

his way and winning favor by overcoming difficulties in how the policy choices can be accomplished. *The president's staff can thus become his greatest barrier to reality.*

PRESIDENTIAL ARENAS

Presidential powers are exercised in three major relationships: *with Congress, with foreign countries,* and *with the American public.* A president's skills and mastery of the executive branch will be tested by being applied in these main arenas. Popular support can be converted to congressional victories, success abroad can lead to a rise in public opinion, and congressional backing may help negotiations with foreign countries. This of course works in reverse, with failures in one arena echoing loudly in the others.

The President and Congress

Despite the principle of separation of powers, the historian James McGregor Burns wrote that "The classic test of greatness in the White House has been the chief executive's capacity to lead the Congress. . . ."[25] It is often remarked that while the Capitol and the White House are only a mile and a half apart, politically it can be a very long way to travel. The truth is that the president and Congress share powers. There are few major pieces of legislation in which the president is not deeply and constantly involved with Congress. The Constitution gives the president both positive and negative powers to deal with the Congress.

Article I, Section 7, of the Constitution gives the president a negative power—the **veto.** When the president vetoes or rejects a bill passed by Congress, the measure cannot become law unless approved by a two-thirds vote in both the House and Senate. Since Congress cannot usually muster that kind of a vote, the president generally prevails. Most often the president uses the *threat* of the veto to gain compromises on a bill before it is passed.

If the president neither signs nor vetoes a bill within ten working days after Congress has passed it, the bill becomes law without his signature. If, during this ten-day period, Congress adjourns and the president fails to act on the bill, it is killed by a **pocket veto.** Presidents do not have the power of an **item veto,** which in some states allows the governor to veto a particular item in a bill passed by the state legislature. President Reagan unsuccessfully asked Congress to propose a constitutional amendment allowing for an item veto. Now Presidents must either accept or reject an entire legislative measure, whether or not they like every item in it.

Presidents also have affirmative or positive legislative powers. Article II, Section 3, states:

> *He shall from time to time give the Congress Information of the State of the Union, and recommend to their Consideration such measures as he shall judge necessary and expedient.*

All presidents now give a *State of the Union address* at the beginning of each congressional session. They also send a barrage of legislative proposals to Congress. The proposed federal budget that presidents submit to each Congress is particularly important. It outlines the president's priorities on policies and expenditures. There is of course no constitutional requirement that Congress go along with any of the president's proposals.

The president's legislative powers put him in the middle of the Congress's activities (and the same goes for Congress's involvement in the executive's responsibilities). And given the executive branch's resources, the president's people have the leverage to bargain as former Secretary of Treasury Baker discovered when he needed Republican votes to pass the 1986 tax reforms on the floor of the House (see the box on page 414).

Representing different constituencies, the two branches see things differently. The president tends to view things nationwide, while members of Congress must pay close attention to local interests. Time horizons also differ. Members of Congress, especially those in positions of power, tend to serve longer than presidents and may not feel quite the same sense of urgency to pass legislation. As a saying heard on Capitol Hill puts it: "Presidents come and go, but the Congress remains."

Despite these obstacles, more than anyone else it is the president who determines Congress's agenda. To successfully exercise influence on Congress, one might suggest a *Ten Commandments* for presidential leadership.[26]

I. *Know Congress,* its leaders and procedures. George Bush may prove to be one of the best in this, as seen in his inaugural address and his budget reconciliation efforts. Jimmy Carter never mixed informally with Congress and suffered as a result.

II. *Timing is everything;* know when to lead, when to pause. After Kennedy's assassination and following the 1964 elections that increased the Democratic majority, President Johnson could push through a historic civil rights law that had been bottled up for years.

III. *Establish priorities;* one cannot fight on all fronts at once. President Nixon had little luck with Congress because he proposed so much without indicating which bills he thought most important. George Bush was accused of a similar sin in his first year.

IV. *Listen to your party leaders.* One reason Carter had so much trouble with Congress is that in his first year he introduced several controversial issues that divided members of his own party.

V. *Follow-through is vital.* By keeping in contact with members about the administration's program at every stage of the legislative process, the president demonstrates earnestness. President Bush earns high marks for this.

VI. *Hire the best legislative liaison staff.* Communications with Congress go two ways. Richard Nixon ignored his staff, with poor results. Bush's staff was initially not rated as highly as the one put together by Reagan.

VII. *Respect Congress.* Presidential attacks on Congress generate resentment. Ronald Reagan was one of the few to violate this commandment and prosper. On the other hand, Ford issued numerous vetos and still was overwhelmed by Congress.

VIII. *Seek bipartisan support.* Successful presidents put together coalitions across party lines, as President Reagan did in gaining conservative Democrats' (the Boll Weevils') support for his first budget proposal in 1981.

IX. *Know when to compromise,* not giving up too early or holding out too long. George Bush quickly got rid of unpopular Reagan positions on increased defense spending, military aid to the Nicaraguan contras, and acid rain, so he could focus on his own issues.

X. *Present a good program:* good technique cannot, and should not, save a badly prepared program not anchored to the public good. President Reagan's last budgets were pronounced DOA—Dead-On-Arrival—because they were unrealistic in their cuts and assumptions.

Combined with some level of popularity with the public, a president following these commandments can take the initiative and influence legislative policy-making.

The President and the World

"The Two Presidencies" is how one political scientist described the differences between presidential power in domestic affairs and his power over foreign policy. *Whereas a president is often limited by the separation of powers and strong political actors in the domestic arena, on foreign relations he is dominant.* One study done before the Vietnam war showed that on domestic proposals before Congress presidents won about 40 percent. But in foreign policy all of the presidents' major initiatives passed.[27] More recently and largely because of Vietnam, Congress has reduced this imbalance. It has become more assertive in foreign affairs with the restrictions on aid to the Nicaraguan contras and the Iran-Contra hearings being examples of Congress enforcing its will when the executive balks. The Grenada case at the end of the chapter underlines the power of the president to act independently when he can marshall the resources at his command.

This presidential preeminence in foreign affairs stems from the constitutional grants of power establishing the dual roles of chief diplomat and commander in chief. Although these powers are shared with Congress, authority is concentrated in the chief executive.

Chief Diplomat

Article II, Section 2, of the Constitution allows the president to negotiate and sign treaties with foreign countries, but treaties do not go into effect until *ratified* by a two-thirds vote in the U.S. Senate. The president may appoint U.S. ambassadors to foreign countries, but these officials cannot take office until confirmed by a majority vote in the U.S. Senate. The president may make agreements with foreign nations, but such agreements cannot proceed if they require money until such funds have been appropriated by Congress. Yet the president clearly dominates foreign affairs. Although the Senate must ratify a treaty, only the president can negotiate it. The Senate cannot name a U.S. ambassador, it can only approve or disapprove presidential nominees, and it almost always approves.

The Supreme Court has upheld the President's implied power to enter into **executive agreements** with foreign nations, without submitting them to the Senate for approval. Since the early 1970s, Congress has resisted the use of secret executive agreements. In 1971, Congress passed a nonbinding resolution stating that such agreements should be submitted to the Senate for approval. In addition, the Case Act requires the secretary of state to submit to Congress any international agreement made by the executive branch within sixty days after it is signed. This legislation, however, does not require congressional approval of these agreements; it merely means Congress must be kept informed.

In addition to congressional limitations, the president is subject to the broad constraints of public opinion on foreign policy. But presidents can shape public opinion, as Nixon did when he visited the People's Republic of China in 1972. It is difficult for Congress to challenge the president without public opinion behind it. And it is difficult to win public opinion away from the president's influence, as the case study on the invasion of Grenada shows.

Though limited by Congress, the president clearly dominates U.S. involvement in foreign affairs. Here, President John F. Kennedy looks into East Berlin across the Communist wall that divides the German city in 1963 during a European tour.

Commander in Chief

Article II, Section 2, of the Constitution provides that "The President shall be Commander in Chief of the Army and Navy of the United States, and of the Militia of the several states, when called into the actual service of the United States." The president appoints the officers of the armed forces, but the war-making powers are divided between the executive and legislative branches. In Article I, Section 8, the framers gave Congress the power to "provide for the common Defence," declare war, and raise and support armies. Since the Constitutional Convention gave to Congress the power to "declare" war, leaving to the president only the authority to "make"

★ The White House Looks for Votes

In influencing Congress, the president's people have to wheel and deal like anyone else. They usually have more to offer as this story of the White House trying to get Congress's support for tax reform in 1986 illustrates.

Members who were still sitting on the fence saw this as an opportunity to swap their votes for favors from the White House, and they began horse trading. Eager to get fifty supporters, the administration team was more than willing to deal. Representative Steven Gunderson of Wisconsin said he would support the tax bill if President Reagan would promise to sign the farm legislation his rural district needed; the White House agreed. Representative George Gekas of Pennsylvania said he would change his vote if the administration would take a look at his proposal to have staggered filing dates for tax returns; [Secretary of State James] Baker agreed. Representative Nancy Johnson of Connecticut promised to switch if the cabinet would consider placing import quotas on machine tools; Baker promised to look into that as well. One congressman asked Baker to come to his state and help in his reelection campaign; Baker said he would. "Boy, they weren't bashful," Baker recalls.

SOURCE: Jeffrey Birnbaum and Alan S. Murray, *Showdown at Gucci Gulch,* 1988, p. 172.

war, Alexander Hamilton probably expressed the opinion of the framers when he said that the power of the commander in chief "would amount to nothing more than the supreme command and direction of the military and naval forces, as First General and Admiral of the Confederacy."[28]

Historically presidents have made greater use of this than their power as commander in chief. America was involved in the Korean and Vietnam Wars without any formal declaration of war. The Korean War was called a "conflict." American troops were sent there in response to a United Nations resolution. Kennedy sent troops to Vietnam as military "advisers" and Johnson greatly escalated America's involvement. Congress later passed the *Tonkin Gulf Resolution,* a nonbinding measure that stopped short of a declaration of war.

In both the Korean and the Vietnam Wars, Congress could have ended U.S. military involvement. It could have cut off all funds, or it could have adopted a joint resolution prohibiting the further use of American troops. But Congress did neither. Eventually criticism of the president's role in Vietnam led to the passing of the 1973 *War Powers Act* over Nixon's veto. This law requires the president to report to Congress within forty-eight hours after committing any armed forces to foreign combat. It provides that combat must end within sixty days, unless it is specifically authorized by Congress.

The present effectiveness of the War Powers Act remains uncertain. President Reagan felt that Congress had put too many restraints on his national security powers and, essentially, ignored the War Powers Act as an unconstitutional restriction. Following the 1987 attack on the USS Stark by an Iraqi plane, the Reagan administration claimed that the Act did not apply to the U.S. Navy escorting tankers through the Persian Gulf.

Congress avoided confrontations with Reagan and found more subtle ways of limiting his foreign policy powers. When Congress agreed to some foreign policy or national security measure the president wanted, it was likely to add certain restrictions. In its frequent votes on contra aid, for example, Congress often made assistance conditional on progress toward a negotiated settlement. This has been described as **conditionality.** One Reagan aide commented, "For everything there are conditions now. What you read in the headlines is that Reagan 'won' on X vote. What you don't read in the headlines—or watch on network news—are the conditions that Congress incorporated in the Reagan win.... Congress always likes to have a little bit of a hedge, a little bit of a hook, to keep their jurisdiction.[29]

The President and the Public

The Reykjavik summit of 1986 offers another example of how the press elevates political skill over policy substance in its coverage of arms control. President Reagan left his meeting with Soviet premier Mikhail Gorbachev grim—and, on television, grim-faced—with disappointment over his failure to reach an agreement on nuclear weapons. In a post-summit press conference, Secretary of State George Shultz called the meeting a "failure."

But as Air Force One headed back to Washington, Reagan's advisers decided that the situation was salvageable, at least politically: all the White House had to do was start smiling and declare victory. The summit had not failed, according to the new administration interpretation. Instead, Reagan had stared down the Soviets on the Strategic Defense Initiative ("Star Wars") and established the framework for a better arms agreement in the near future. To sell this argument, Shultz, Chief of Staff Donald Regan, national security adviser John Poindexter, and other administration officials spent a solid week appearing on television news shows and talking to journalists—smiling, upbeat, and aggressive all the while. The press, marveling at the audacious shrewdness of this exercise in "spin control," changed the emphasis in its coverage from "Failure at Reykjavik" to "President Stands Tall."[30]

Face to face: President Ronald Reagan and Soviet leader Michael Gorbachev take a walk in Red Square in 1988.

President George Bush holds his first prime-time nationally televised news conference from the East Room of the White House on June 8, 1989.

Much of what the modern president does is designed to gain the understanding and support of public opinion. Presidential trips, speeches, and news conferences are aimed at keeping the public backing a president needs to govern. Even President Bush's informality and spontaneous chats with reporters are calculated to politically benefit him. This "public presidency" rests on popular support; without it the exercise of other powers is muted and weakened. Popular support, in turn, depends on the president's access to the public through the media (see Figure 13.3).

As the story of the Reykjavik summit reflects, presidents have a great deal of influence over the media. On live television the president can speak directly to the nation, bypassing news reporters. TV can further insulate the president. Television becomes a "one-way street"—he speaks to the public without any communication coming back to him. Presidents may also get their messages across through selected interviews with favored reporters and commentators. The *spin control* mentioned earlier simply consists of the president's agents putting the best possible interpretation on events for reporters' benefit.

The news *leak* is widely used to further presidential objectives. By this method, the president or some unnamed source sends up a "trial balloon" to gauge the public's acceptance of an administration policy. Thus, news stories often begin: "A high-level administration spokesperson today announced that the administration is considering a new policy concerning. . . ." News reporters regularly agree to this "not-attributable-as-to-source" reporting because they can get a story that they might not otherwise obtain. For the administration, the leak serves to avoid a head-on debate.

The media are also likely to base their stories on White House handouts. One study over a twenty-five year period found that there were two favorable stories about the president during that period for every unfavorable story.[31] Pictures were even more favorable because the White House can control "photo opportunities," as they are called, even more than the news. Richard Nixon's White House was especially adept at "PR" (public relations), or "managing the news," as it was called by his detractors. Jimmy Carter, trying to avoid the Nixon example, ran a much more open presidency. Some say this hurt him and helped bring about his defeat in 1980.

President Reagan was the most skillful chief executive at using the media. Trained as an actor, "The Great Communicator" spent up to ten hours a week rehearsing speeches. His years of public speaking gave him the unrivaled ability to look and sound absolutely honest and forthright. Mr. Reagan's skill at avoiding responsibility for potentially damaging failures (such as Marine deaths in Beirut and

FIGURE 13★3
Average Yearly Presidential Approval

For years the Gallup Poll has asked Americans, "Do you approve of the way _____ is handling his job as president?" Notice that all presidents seem to be most popular when they first enter office. Note also that most recent presidents, even Reagan, have lower approval rates than earlier chief executives.

PERCENTAGE APPROVING

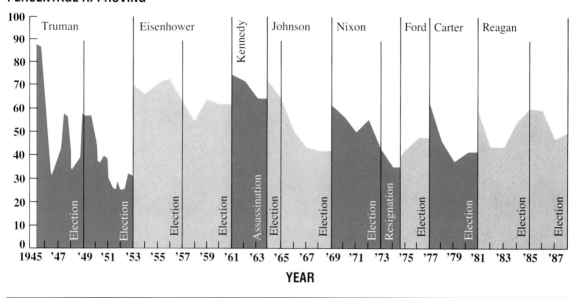

SOURCE: Gallup Poll; Bush figure is from *National Journal,* May 13, 1989, p. 1208.

record deficits) led critics to speak about his "Teflon presidency." His "nonstick" talent saw him through a second term with high public support and grudging admiration from the press. Compared to most recent presidents, this was a remarkable achievement.[32]

In fact there is and should be a tension between the president and the press. The president is an advocate of certain policies while the press is communicating and interpreting those policies to the public. Presidents seldom feel they are getting a fair shake from the press. George Bush, like most presidents before him, saw his relations with the press flounder, in the administration's failure to aid an unsuccessful military coup in Panama and in early dealings to release American hostages in Lebanon. Following an initial "honeymoon" period, presidents' relations with the press decline. That's because both the president and the press are doing their jobs. As former presidential press secretary George Reedy admitted, ". . . I do not think our country has ever been hurt by a skeptical and rambunctious newspaperman."

Presidential Management and Marketing: The Grenada Invasion

On October 25, 1983 the U.S. military invaded the small Caribbean island of Grenada. The invasion illustrates the wide range of relationships a chief executive must manage in order to implement a decision. The political actors—the bureaucracy, press, Congress, and ultimately public opinion—all figured in the president's successful exercise of the powers of his office.

Background to a Crisis: Cubans, Communists, and Citizens

In March 1979, Maurice Bishop seized control of the East Caribbean government of Grenada in a bloodless coup and suspended the country's constitution. Bishop, a Marxist, established formal diplomatic relations with Cuba. By early 1983, the hundreds of Cubans on the island, completing construction of a new 9000-foot jet airfield, were beginning to worry the Reagan administration. Reagan publicly warned of "the Soviet-Cuban militarization of Grenada." According to Reagan, the Soviets planned to use the Grenada airfield as a strategic link for supplying arms to Latin American revolutionaries.

Reacting to this pressure, Maurice Bishop came to Washington in July 1983 in order to patch up deteriorating relations. At the meetings, Bishop assured U.S. officials that his government planned to use the new airfield only for tourism and economic development. Returning home, Bishop found extremists accusing him of selling out to the Americans. In quick order, he lost control of his ruling party and was arrested. On October 19, Bishop was executed.

The outbreak of violence potentially threatened the safety of nearly 1000 U.S. citizens, mostly medical students, living in Grenada. Moreover, the brutal rise of the radicals undercut their popular support both on Grenada and on neighboring islands. Reagan's top crisis-planning teams set to work.

Building the Bureaucratic Consensus to Act

On October 20, Vice-President Bush convened the Special Situations Group. Representatives of the National Security Council, the Departments of State and Defense, and the CIA attended the 6:00 PM meeting. At first, the president's advisers were divided. Some pushed for a "surgical rescue" of the American students on the island. The staff of the National Security Council supported a full-scale invasion of the island, to rescue the students and remove the radicals from power. An invasion would also demonstrate to Nicaragua and other nations in the region that the United States was no "paper tiger." CIA Director William Casey and Secretary of State George Shultz agreed. "Let's dump these bastards," argued Casey.[33]

The Joint Chiefs of Staff initially resisted a limited rescue because of a lack of intelligence about Cuban strength on the island. The chairman of the Joint Chiefs soon signed on to the idea that an effective rescue operation would require control of the entire island, since Americans were dispersed in several locations. In agreeing, each of the services (Army, Navy, Air Force, and Marines) demanded participation in the invasion. Grenada, they expected, would be a useful test of troops, equipment, and strategy under real military conditions. With his advisers in agreement, Reagan approved the initial plan of invasion two days later on Oct. 22.

Managing Public Reaction

Administration officials knew that they had a tough selling job facing them. Since Vietnam and the aborted Iranian hostage rescue, public opinion had generally opposed the use of U.S. troops in battle conditions. Press and congressional reaction would be even more skeptical. Other than an airport runway, firm evidence of Soviet-Cuban intentions for Grenada was not available, and there was no specific violence against U.S. citizens justifying a full-scale invasion.

Partial public relations "cover" to the charge of U.S. gunboat diplomacy was pro-vided by the pro-American Organization of Eastern Caribbean States, coincidentally meeting on October 21 in Barbados. A message was sent to the OECS leader, Eugenia Charles of Dominica, stating that U.S. intervention in neighboring Grenada would only take place if the OECS requested action. By day's end, the OECS had forwarded a written plea for the U.S. to "restore order and democracy" in Grenada.

On October 25, U.S. forces invaded Grenada under cover of darkness—and a total press blackout. Perhaps sensitive to public reaction to further scenes of U.S. casualties (the Beirut barracks bombing that killed 241 Marines had occurred just two days earlier), the military task force took the unprecedented step of denying press requests to accompany troop landings. Reporters who reached the island by charter boat were arrested.[34]

Criticism of the media blackout was easily overshadowed by the success of the mission. In three short days the island was in U.S. hands and the students were safe. America had finally won one. The invasion, Reagan told the nation, had prevented another Iranian hostage "nightmare." Public opinion polls showed overwhelming support for the president. In just one instance, mail ran ten to one against

U.S. Army troops invade Grenada in 1983.

John Chancellor's NBC News commentary criticizing the press ban. Without media coverage, the public's perception was largely shaped by the government.

Dealing with Congress

Besides the need to "shape" press coverage, a parallel concern for the Reagan administration involved managing congressional reaction to the surprise invasion. On the eve of the invasion, leaders of Congress had been briefed by the White House and had expressed approval. In the few days after the invasion, support had split along party lines, with Republicans generally in favor, and Democrats generally questioning the mission. For example, House Speaker Tip O'Neill expressed fear over Reagan's apparent preference for using "gunboat diplomacy." Concerned with the troop presence in Grenada, both the House and the Senate invoked the War Powers Act. Reagan had sixty days to remove U.S. forces from Grenada if he did not gain congressional approval.

Faced with these criticisms, administration officials moved to demonstrate to Congress and the public that Grenada was indeed, in Reagan's words, "a Soviet-Cuban colony being readied . . . to export terror." Speaking on national televi-

Congress presents its report on the Grenada invasion in 1983.

sion two days after the invasion, President Reagan took pains to emphasize that "we got there just in time." The next day, the administration stated that captured documents revealed that the Cubans planned to take the students hostage and to place a force of 341 officers and 4000 reserves on the island. Officials also claimed that enough weapons were captured to support attacks on neighboring islands.[35]

The strategy was effective. Favorable public opinion isolated congressional critics of this use of force. A congressional fact-finding mission a week after the invasion discovered that the majority of Grenada's citizens approved of what the islanders called a "rescue operation." Thomas Foley, the third-ranking House Democrat, returned from Grenada convinced that "the President acted correctly to protect American lives." Few voices opposed to the invasion were heard in Congress after that.

Public Opinion Backs the President

For many, the Grenada victory was the zenith of President Reagan's first term in office. Scenes of American medical students triumphantly returning home—and foreign citizens actually welcoming the American presence—stood in stark contrast to the more tragic American reversals in Iran and Lebanon. Post-invasion public opinion polls showed that President Reagan had the highest approval rating (62 percent) in two years. Americans enthusiastically believed the president when he said: "Our days of weakness are over. Our military forces are back on their feet and standing tall."

With congressional critics of Reagan's foreign policy temporarily silenced, the administration pushed through $24 million in new aid to the Contras in Nicaragua and $19 million for Grenada. Expanded foreign aid was also directed to Dominica, home of OECS leader Eugenia Charles. Debate over the press blackout continued for several months. Eventually the Reagan administration compromised. In the future, a pool of reporters would accompany U.S. troops ashore as observers. Public reports would be delayed, if necessary, to preserve mission secrecy.

Conclusion

President Reagan's triumph in Grenada took in far more territory than the area covered by that small island. It reflected the successful management of his own bureaucracy and the selling of their actions to the Congress, press, and public. The constitutional powers of the commander in chief allowing decisive and dramatic action in foreign affairs combined with the president's standing as the representative of the nation gave the White House all the necessary tools. Reagan's own skills of communication and his use of national symbols quickly placed the invasion beyond political debate.

WRAP-UP

From a slender grant of executive powers in the Constitution the presidency has irregularly grown into a position of leadership of the government and nation. This historical development has been influenced by the crises presidents have faced, the political coalitions they have led, and the skills and personalities they have brought to the office. The vastly expanded executive branch bureaucracy they head has both broadened their powers and, at times, hindered them in reaching their goals. In dealings with Congress, the world, and the American public, their own political talents have largely determined the success of their policies, as seen in the Grenada case study.

Conclusions on presidential power—too much? too little?—largely flow from opinions of the recent occupants of the office. Weakness encourages calls for added strength; strength leads to fears of too much power. The very growth of presidential powers has to some degree produced forces restraining this influence. The same bureaucracy that extends presidential power frustrates it by the very size, complexity, and inertia of the agencies through which the president must operate. The media that enhances the chief executive's stature also investigates his staff and exposes his blemishes. The Constitution's checks and balances are not the only ones limiting the concentration of power found in the presidency.

Key Terms

heads of state (p. 389)
heads of government (p. 389)
residual power (p. 392)
New Deal coalition (p. 396)
chief executive (p. 401)
Executive Office of the
   President (p. 402)
White House office (p. 402)
chiefs of staff (p. 402)
Office of Management and
   Budget (OMB) (p. 403)
Council of Economic Advisors
   (p. 404)

National Security Council
   (NSC) (p. 405)
cabinet (p. 405)
multiple advocacy (p. 407)
veto (p. 410)
pocket veto (p. 410)
item veto (p. 410)
executive agreements (p. 413)
War Powers Act (p. 414)
conditionality (p. 415)

Suggested Readings

Anderson, Martin, *Revolution* (San Diego: Harcourt Brace Jovanovitch, 1988).

Boller, Paul F., *Presidential Campaigns* (New York: Oxford University Press, 1985).

Donovan, Hedley, *Roosevelt to Reagan* (New York: Harper & Row, 1983).

Greenstein, Fred I., *The Hidden-hand Presidency: Eisenhower as Leader* (New York: Basic Books, 1982).

Kearns, Doris, *Lyndon Johnson and the American Dream* (New York: New American Library, 1976).

Patterson, Bradley H. Jr., *The Ring of Power: The White House Staff and Its Expanding Role in Government* (New York: Basic Books, 1988).

End Notes

[1] Fred I. Greenstein, "College Students' Reactions to the Assassination," in Bradley S. Greenberg and Edwin B. Parker, eds., *The Kennedy Assassination and the American Public* (Stanford: Stanford University Press, 1965), pp. 220–39.

[2] Adapted from George Reedy, *The Twilight of the Presidency* (New York: NAL Books, 1987), p. 147.

[3] Thomas Cronin and Rexford G. Tugwell, eds., *The Presidency Reappraised* (New York: Praeger, 1977), pp. 3–23 and Cronin, *The State of the Presidency,* rev. ed. (Boston: Little, Brown, 1980).

[4] Max Farrand, *The Framing of the Constitution of the United States,* vol. 2 (New Haven: Yale University Press, 1913), p. 52.

[5] See James G. Randall, *Constitutional Problems Under Lincoln* (Urbana, IL: University of Illinois Press, 1963), pp. 513–22.

[6] Woodrow Wilson, *Constitutional Government in the United States,* quoted in James MacGregor Burns, *Presidential Government* (Boston: Houghton Mifflin, 1965), p. 96.

[7] Edward S. Corwin, *The President* (New York: New York University Press, 1957), p. 311.

[8] Emmet John Hughes, "FDR: The Happiest Warrior," *Smithsonian,* 3, no. 1 (April 1972), pp. 30–33.

[9] William W. Lammers, *Presidential Politics: Patterns and Prospects* (New York: Harper and Row, 1976), p. 49.

[10] Stephen Skowrenek, "Presidential Leadership in Political Time," in Michael Nelson, ed., *The Presidency and The Political System,* 2nd ed. (Washington, D.C.: Congressional Quarterly Press, 1988), p. 115–60.

[11] Quoted in Emmet John Hughes, "Presidential Style," *Smithsonian,* 2, no. 12 (March 1972), pp. 28–36.

[12] James David Barber, *The Presidential Character,* 3rd ed. (Englewood Cliffs, N.J.: Prentice-Hall, 1985).

[13] James David Barber, "Predicting Presidential Character," in Charles W. Dunn, ed., *The Future of the American Presidency* (Morristown, N.J.: General Learning Press, 1975), p. 316.

[14] *Ibid.,* p. 317.

[15] Barber, *The Presidential Character,* pp. 441–42.

[16] See Michael Nelson, "The Psychological Presidency," in Nelson, ed., *The Presidency and the Political System,* 2nd ed., 1988, pp. 185–206.

[17] David Donald, "A Lincoln Politician," in Aaron Wildavsky, ed., *The Presidency* (Boston: Little, Brown and Company, 1969), p. 125.

[18] As quoted by Robert Donovan, *Nemesis: Truman and Johnson in the Coils of War in Asia* (New York: St. Martin's Press, 1984), pp. 10–11.

[19]Richard E. Neustadt, *Presidential Power* (New York: John Wiley, 1960), p. 10.

[20]See Donald T. Regan, *For The Record* (New York: St. Martin's Press, 1988), Part 3.

[21]Reedy, *Twilight,* p. 45.

[22]See Seymour M. Hersh, *The Price of Power* (New York: Summit Books, 1983).

[23]Paul Light, *Vice Presidential Power* (Baltimore: Johns Hopkins, 1983).

[24]*The New York Times,* January 31, 1989.

[25]James MacGregor Burns, *Roosevelt: The Lion and the Fox* (New York: Harcourt, Brace, 1956), p. 186.

[26]Adapted from Reo M. Christenson, "Presidential Leadership of Congress," in Thomas E. Cronin, ed., *Rethinking the Presidency* (Boston: Little, Brown, 1982), pp. 255–70.

[27]Aaron Wildavsky, "The Two Presidencies," *Trans-Action* (December 1988), reprinted in *Readings in American Government* (Guilford, CT: Dushkin Publishing, 1975), p. 75.

[28]*Federalist,* no. 69.

[29]*The Washington Post,* reprinted in *Today* (September 28, 1984).

[30]James Fallows, "The Presidency and the Press," in Michael Nelson, *The Presidency and the Political System* (Washington, D.C.: Congressional Quarterly Press, 1988), pp. 298–99.

[31]Martha Joynt Kumar, Michael Baruch Grossman, and Leslie Lichter-Mason, "Images of the White House in the Media," in Doris A. Graber, ed., *The President and the Public* (Philadelphia: Institute for the Study of Human Issues, 1982), pp. 85–110.

[32]See Michael K. Deaver, *Behind the Scenes* (New York: William Morrow, 1987).

[33]Bob Woodward, *Veil* (New York: Simon and Schuster, 1987), p. 289.

[34]See Peter M. Dunn and Bruce Watson, *American Intervention in Grenada* (Westview Special Studies in Military Affairs, 1985).

[35]A CIA assessment, prepared five days after the invasion, contradicted many of these claims. The assessment found, for example, that arms captured on the island were not sufficient or intended for use in attacking neighboring islands. The assessment was never made public. See *Veil,* p. 209.

The need for cuts in government spending is a constant theme in speeches from Washington. That more is said than done has a lot to do with how bureaucracies play politics to protect themselves. One favored tactic is for a threatened agency to translate general budget reductions into specific bad news for members of Congress in a position to reverse the general cuts. The following incident occurred a few years ago.

Amtrak, which depends on federal monies to operate its passenger rail lines, was threatened with a budget cut. It immediately announced that it would be forced to close the following routes:

1. San Francisco-Bakersfield, running through Stockton, the home town of the chairman of the House Appropriations subcommittee;
2. St. Louis-Laredo, running through Little Rock, Arkansas, the home of the chairman of the Senate Appropriations Committee;
3. Chicago-Seattle, running through the homes of the Senate Majority Leader and the chairman of the Senate Commerce Committee;
4. and (getting four with one track), Norfolk-Chicago, running through the states of the chairman of the Senate Appropriations transportation subcommittee, the chairman of the Senate Commerce surface subcommittee, the chairman of the House Commerce committee, and the Senate Majority Whip.

Senator Byrd of West Virginia was then Senate Majority Whip, and the effectiveness of the bureaucrats' tactics was illustrated a few days later by a story in the *Charleston Gazette:*

Continued Rail Service Byrd's Aim

Senator Robert C. Byrd, D-WV, has announced that he intends to make an effort today to assure continued rail passenger service in West Virginia.

Byrd, a member of the Senate Appropriations Committee, said he will "either introduce an amendment providing sufficient funds to continue the West Virginia route or try to get language adopted which would guarantee funding for the route for Amtrak."[1]

As this example illustrates, the agencies of government are something more than mere instruments for carrying out elected officials' policies. They contain seasoned political players stirring the primordial broth out of which policy evolves. There's a good argument that the bureaucrats may be the most important of all the actors.

The executive branch has been described as three million people, one of whom has been elected. (It would be two if you count the vice-president). The rest are political appointees who, except for the White House staff, are soon absorbed into the operations of their agencies. To assume that this bureaucracy is an arm of the president is to declare victory in an ongoing fight that most modern presidents seem fated to lose.

This chapter discusses bureaucracy, how it developed, how it is structured, and how it behaves, as well as examining how bureaucrats act in the real world and how people and politicians have attempted to influence them. Controlling and using the bureaucracy is a large part of the power of political leaders. Everything that administrative agencies do must conform to the law, yet making this instrument both effective and responsive remains a major goal of democratic government.

WHAT IS A BUREAUCRACY?

Bureaucracy is a large administrative system with four basic characteristics.[2] First is *job specification:* each employee in a bureaucracy performs a specific job. Second is the *hierarchy of authority,* or chain of command, within the bureaucracy from top to bottom. Third, a bureaucracy has a *system of rules* that defines its operations. Finally, a bureaucracy is characterized by *impersonality.* Employees are expected to treat all persons fairly and impartially.

Although these characteristics should provide for the most efficient operation of a bureaucracy, they also give rise to the most severe criticisms. We want government officials to treat all citizens alike, but when we are personally involved, we would appreciate a little consideration. We expect the bureaucracy to keep within the bounds of the law, but we also worry about unreasonably following the letter of the law.

Former President Reagan drew laughs when he said, "Bureaucrats favor cutting red tape, lengthwise," and added that he was for "busing some of the bureaucrats in Washington out in the country to meet real people."[3] (See the box on page 431.) While often this criticism is justified, some form of organization is necessary to carry out the complex tasks of government. For example, most Americans would agree that any institution that receives tax funds, such as a hospital or a university, should not practice racial discrimination. Yet the passage of a law is not enough to carry out that policy. Some-

how, compliance with the law has to be ensured. Historically, bureaucracies have served this function.

Among the complaints about governmental bureaucracy there are common misperceptions:

1) *All bureaucracies are not governmental.* Each large corporation or private institution has its own large bureaucracy.

2) *Most of the governmental bureaucracy exists not at the federal level but at the state and local levels.* There are fewer than three million federal civilian employees but nearly five times that many state and local employees. More than seventeen million people, or nearly one person out of every six in the U.S. labor force, are employees of some government (see Figure 14.1).

3) *The federal bureaucracy has not recently experienced runaway growth.* From 1958 to 1988, federal civilian employment grew more slowly than the overall labor force, dropping from about 4 to about 3 percent of it, and dropped from being nearly a third of all government employment to being about one-sixth of it. The number of state and local employees for every one thousand Americans increased from about twenty-six to almost fifty-seven, an increase of over 100 percent. But federal, state, and local government employment generally were outstripped by the growth of the U.S. labor force, though state and local government grew slightly faster than the workforce until its rate of growth peaked in about 1978. In 1989, as President Bush's term began, there were 12.4 federal employees for every 1000 Americans, up from a 1982 low of 11.9 but still lower than the high of 14.7 in 1967–68, at the height of the Vietnam War.

4) *Most federal employees do not live and work in Washington, D.C.* In fact, only about 11 percent of them do.

5) *Most federal employees do not work for social welfare agencies; only about 5 percent do.* Two-thirds of federal employees are in three major agencies: the Postal Service, the Department of Veterans Affairs, and the Defense Department. Still, the number of federal agencies keeps growing. While the number of federal employees has not been mushrooming, it hasn't been shrinking either and there were more people working for the federal government at the end of Reagan's term than at the beginning. Despite President Reagan's vow to eliminate the Departments of Energy and Education, those departments are still around. In addition, the Department of Veterans Affairs had been created, giving the Veterans Administration its long-sought cabinet status.[4] (See Figure 14.2.)

The Development of Bureaucracy

Perhaps we should blame the Chinese. They developed the first government bureaucracy over 2000 years ago, including written examinations for career employees. In the West, it was hundreds of years

FIGURE 14★1
Government Civilian Employment

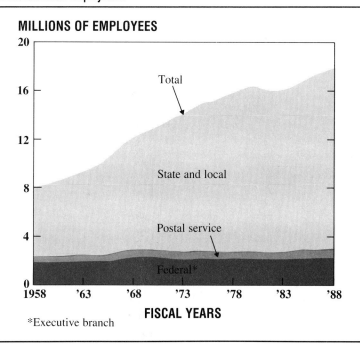

MILLIONS OF EMPLOYEES

Total

State and local

Postal service

Federal*

1958   '63   '68   '73   '78   '83   '88
FISCAL YEARS

*Executive branch

SOURCE: *The Budget for Fiscal 1990: Special Analysis,* U.S. Government Printing Office, Washington, D.C., 1989, p. 12

FIGURE 14*2
Organization of the Executive Branch

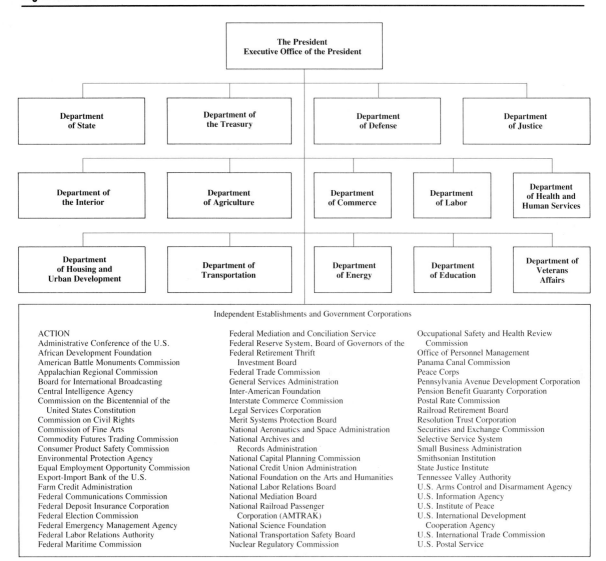

The President
Executive Office of the President

Department of State | Department of the Treasury | Department of Defense | Department of Justice

Department of the Interior | Department of Agriculture | Department of Commerce | Department of Labor | Department of Health and Human Services

Department of Housing and Urban Development | Department of Transportation | Department of Energy | Department of Education | Department of Veterans Affairs

Independent Establishments and Government Corporations

ACTION
Administrative Conference of the U.S.
African Development Foundation
American Battle Monuments Commission
Appalachian Regional Commission
Board for International Broadcasting
Central Intelligence Agency
Commission on the Bicentennial of the
   United States Constitution
Commission on Civil Rights
Commission of Fine Arts
Commodity Futures Trading Commission
Consumer Product Safety Commission
Environmental Protection Agency
Equal Employment Opportunity Commission
Export-Import Bank of the U.S.
Farm Credit Administration
Federal Communications Commission
Federal Deposit Insurance Corporation
Federal Election Commission
Federal Emergency Management Agency
Federal Labor Relations Authority
Federal Maritime Commission

Federal Mediation and Conciliation Service
Federal Reserve System, Board of Governors of the
Federal Retirement Thrift
   Investment Board
Federal Trade Commission
General Services Administration
Inter-American Foundation
Interstate Commerce Commission
Legal Services Corporation
Merit Systems Protection Board
National Aeronautics and Space Administration
National Archives and
   Records Administration
National Capital Planning Commission
National Credit Union Administration
National Foundation on the Arts and Humanities
National Labor Relations Board
National Mediation Board
National Railroad Passenger
   Corporation (AMTRAK)
National Science Foundation
National Transportation Safety Board
Nuclear Regulatory Commission

Occupational Safety and Health Review
   Commission
Office of Personnel Management
Panama Canal Commission
Peace Corps
Pennsylvania Avenue Development Corporation
Pension Benefit Guaranty Corporation
Postal Rate Commission
Railroad Retirement Board
Resolution Trust Corporation
Securities and Exchange Commission
Selective Service System
Small Business Administration
Smithsonian Institution
State Justice Institute
Tennessee Valley Authority
U.S. Arms Control and Disarmament Agency
U.S. Information Agency
U.S. Institute of Peace
U.S. International Development
   Cooperation Agency
U.S. International Trade Commission
U.S. Postal Service

SOURCE: Office of the Federal Register, *United States Government Manual, 1987–88* (Washington, D.C.: Government Printing Office, 1987), p. 21.

later before the British established a civil service system, recruiting government careerists on a merit system from the upper classes.

The United States Constitution says nothing about a bureaucracy. It gives the president the power to "require the opinion of the principal officers in each of the Executive Departments" and to appoint the heads of those departments. One of George Washington's first acts (in 1789) was to ask Congress to establish the departments of *State, Treasury,* and *War* and the office of the Attorney General. The Post Office was created in 1792. The entire staff of the first State Department consisted of the secretary, a chief clerk, seven other clerks, and a messenger boy. In 1800, the entire federal government (excluding the military) consisted of fewer than 3000 bureaucrats.[5]

Our earliest presidents were able to appoint federal employees on the basis of political support. This practice of widespread political patronage was called the **spoils system,** taken from the phrase, "To the victor belong the spoils." President Andrew Jackson followed this idea in 1828–1836 in appointing many supporters from among the "plain people." Abraham Lincoln made greater use of the spoils system than any other president up to that time. But as the tasks expected of bureaucrats became more complex and corruption grew, pressures for reform increased.

The Civil Service System

In 1881, President James Garfield was assassinated by a disappointed (not to mention crazy) office seeker. The new president, Chester Arthur, backed by public outrage over the murder, sup-

---

 ★ Bureaucrat-ese

Bureaucracies tend to produce their own language—call it bureaucrat-ese—here's just a small sampling:

1. *"unlawful or arbitrary deprivation of life"* (otherwise known as "killing"). The National Association of English Teachers awarded its Doublespeak Award to the U.S. Department of State for coming up with this new, improved word for murder.

2. *"premature impact of the aircraft with the terrain below"* (translated into English as "crash"). The Federal Aviation Administration used this phrase in a report about an accident in which 180 people were killed.

3. *"to eventuate a movement in retrograde"* (also called a "retreat"). When General Douglas MacArthur was "overwhelmed" by Chinese forces at the Yalu River in Korea, he was not contemplating a simple retreat: "Should the Red Hordes continue to power across the Yalu, it might not only render impossible the resumption of our offensive, but conceivably could cause us to eventuate a movement in retrograde."

SOURCE: Morris Udall, "Some Political Laughs for an Unfunny Week," *The Washington Post,* October 25, 1987.

★ Bring Back the Spoils System

. . . [A]nyone who has had a reasonable amount of contact with the federal government has encountered people who should be fired. There are, of course, some superb civil servants—maybe 10 percent of the total—who have every right to become indignant at blanket criticism of government workers. There are another 50 to 60 percent who range from adequate to good. Unfortunately, that leaves 30 to 40 percent in the range downward from marginal to outright incompetent.

Yet fewer than one percent are fired each year. This is because 93 percent are under some form of civil service and are therefore virtually impossible to fire.

Being able to fire people is important for two reasons: 1) to permit you to hire the people you want and to get rid of those you don't want, and 2) to make it possible for you to attract the kind of risk-takers who are repelled by the safe civil service and the political emasculation it entails.

The problem with achieving all this is that for years Americans have been brainwashed by textbooks that make politics sound bad and civil service sound shiny clean. I suspect it all began when the Italian and Irish immigrants took over the elective offices in Boston and the Wasps had to figure out how to salvage something for themselves. "Politicians are inept, partisan, crooked; we are able, objective and virtuous," was their refrain, and it sounded good to their friends across the Charles at Harvard, who then put it into their textbooks from whence the doctrine spread across the land.

SOURCE: Charles Peters, *Washington Monthly* (September 1976), pp. 26–30. Reprinted from Robert E. DiClerico and Allan S. Hammock, eds., *Points of View: Readings in American Government and Politics,* 2nd ed. (Reading, Mass.: Addison-Wesley, 1983), pp. 232, 234–235.

ported the *Civil Service Reform Act* (also known as the *Pendleton Act*), which was passed by Congress in 1883. The act set up a bipartisan Civil Service Commission under which government employees were chosen by a **merit system.**

At first, only about 10 percent of federal employees were covered by a civil service merit system. But the system grew under presidents such as Theodore Roosevelt, who had been a civil service commissioner. It now covers practically the entire bureaucracy. This has considerably diminished the spoils system, and only a few think that this is a bad idea (see the box on page 432). The president today fills only about 5000 patronage jobs, of which fewer than one-third are at a policy-making level.

In 1939, Congress passed the **Hatch Act** to prevent federal employees from engaging—or being forced to engage—in political campaigns. These restrictions do not prevent federal employees from putting bumper stickers on their cars, attending political rallies, and expressing political opinions. Though government employee unions have continued to push for changes in the Hatch Act, they have not been able to gain enough support in Congress because of fear the civil service would be "politicized."

A civil service position must be filled by one of the three applicants who have scored the highest on the civil service examinations. Various civil service protections have made it difficult to discharge incompetent employees or to reward efficient employees (see the box on page 435). *While weakening the spoils system the civil service has also weakened presidential control of the bureaucracy.* The bureaucrats know they will have their jobs long after the current administration passes into history.

In 1978, President Carter pushed through a law called the **Civil Service Reform Act.** The Reform Act provided for a **Senior Executive Service** (SES) for employees in the higher grades and changed the Civil Service Commission to the *Office of Personnel Management.* This provided a core of high-level federal managers who could be moved from one agency to another, who could be fired with less difficulty, and who could be rewarded for special service. The senior executive service is similar to the top civil service corps in Great Britain. It was intended to reduce the special relationships among bureaucrats, members of Congress, and interest groups that are called the *iron triangle.* The law's supporters hoped that by periodically moving bureaucrats to new agencies, they would strengthen the influence of presidents.

Today, federal bureaucrats are vitally important in our daily lives. Sargent Shriver, who has served in high federal offices, once said, "to a large extent it is the bureaucrats who make the day-to-day decisions on government action. Certainly, for most citizens, it is they who serve as the major point of contact with the government."[6] Political scientists agree. One declared that "in the important matters of our public lives we are more involved with public bureaucracy than we are with parties, elections, and legislatures."[7] In fact, there is more administrative law (such as tax regulations) issued by bureaucrats than statutory law passed by Congress. And these actions by bureaucrats affect virtually every aspect of our lives:

At the federal, state, and local levels, administrators can grant or withhold licenses and permits; design and implement programs for schools and colleges; allocate research funds; support cultural efforts; decide who receives a television channel, an air route franchise, a railroad right-of-way, or a snack bar monopoly. Bureaucrats may refuse a person admission to the United States, destroy a farmer's sick cows and chickens, deny a person a pension or ask his or her former employers and neighbors if he or she is "unfit" for a government job.[8]

STRUCTURE OF THE FEDERAL BUREAUCRACY

The federal bureaucracy is far from neatly organized. While most government agencies in Europe are labelled *bureaus,* Americans call their federal agencies by a wide array of names: department, agency, commission, bureau, authority, board, and administration. The names have little logic to them. The federal bureaucracy is not exactly organized by function. No particular reason except tradition can explain why federal dam building, for example, is done by three different agencies: the Corps of Engineers in the Department of the Army, within the Department of Defense; the Bureau of Reclamation in the Department of the Interior; and the Soil and Water Conservation Service in the Department of Agriculture.

The federal bureaucracy can be broken down into three main categories: *cabinet departments, independent agencies,* and *regulatory bodies.* There is no great consistency regarding jurisdiction and duties. For example, cabinet departments perform regulatory functions, and responsibility for some functional areas is shared by cabinet departments, independent agencies, and regulatory commissions.

U.S. Customs officials in Miami use dogs to search for drugs in luggage.

★ Trying to Fire a Bureaucrat

Edward Lafferty, an economist who had been in the federal service since 1968, came to the agency in 1973. His job centered on plotting statistical charts in a very limited sphere, and within several months it became apparent to his supervisor that Lafferty didn't measure up to even this relatively simple chore. . . .

In March 1976, Lafferty's supervisor handed him a letter of intent to terminate his employment in 30 days. Signed by a top agency official, the letter cited incompetence, insubordination, and generally abusive conduct as the causes of dismissal. The charges were documented with specific instances, testified to by memoranda from a variety of people who had dealt with Lafferty, and by an account that his supervisor had kept over a period of several months detailing the results of assignments given to Lafferty. The letter plus the exhibits ran to 60 pages. . . .

Lafferty had 15 days to reply to the charges and two days of official time off. On April 25 the agency's highest administrative officer wrote Lafferty that his reply had been considered and the decision made to terminate his employment on May 12. The letter told him he had 15 days to appeal the decision to the Federal Employees Appeals Authority.

Lafferty did appeal the case and hired a private lawyer to represent him. The agency then had to provide the Civil Service Commission with his entire file, now 103 pages long. The file, which contained a memorandum on every meeting at which the case had been discussed, was also available to Lafferty to help him prepare his defense. The appeal hearings, which took place in September 1976, lasted two days and resulted in two volumes of transcripts. The following month, the Appeals Authority issued a decision affirming the agency's dismissal action.

But over two years had elapsed since Lafferty's incompetence had first been recognized. During most of that time he continued to receive his $20,000 salary. For about a year, various highly paid administrators at the agency had been spending a significant amount of their time on the case. And Lafferty still has recourse in the courts. . . .

SOURCE: Adapted from Leonard Reed, "Firing a Federal Employee: The Impossible Dream," in Charles Peters and Nicholas Lehman, eds., *Inside the System* (New York: Holt, Rinehart and Winston, 1979), pp. 214–16.

Cabinet Departments

The **cabinet departments** created by Congress are the major agencies of the federal government. Originally, there were only three (the departments of State, War, and the Treasury); today there are fourteen. The expansion of the cabinet has been due largely to the growth of problems that rose in the federal government priorities. The raising to cabinet-level of the Department of Energy in 1977 (following the Arab oil boycott) shows the interest in this area of both the public and the government. The former Department of Health, Education, and Welfare was split into two new units in May, 1980: the Department of Education and the Department of Health and Human Services. Although President Reagan promised in 1980 to abolish both the Departments of Energy and Education, he had changed his mind by his second term.

Each cabinet department is headed by a secretary, who is appointed by the president with the consent of the Senate by a majority vote (which is usually given). Cabinet secretaries hold office as long as the president wishes. Because cabinet secretaries have large bureaucracies to manage, however, they have less loyalty to the president than do members of the executive office. *Pressures from their staff and constant involvement with their agencies may cause secretaries to act more as lobbyists for their departments than representatives of the president.* (See Figure 14.3 for the structure of one cabinet department, Commerce.)

The amount of control cabinet heads have over their own departments varies greatly. Often a department may contain strong, relatively independent bureaus. For example, the Coast Guard within the Department of Transportation and the Internal Revenue Service in the Treasury Department are fairly autonomous. Although the attorney general has authority over the FBI, which is in the Justice Department, J. Edgar Hoover's lengthy rule as director of the FBI limited the cabinet secretary's, and everyone else in government's, influence over Hoover.

The Columbia space shuttle takes off from the Kennedy Space Center in Florida in August 1989.

Independent Agencies

Independent agencies are headed by "directors" or "administrators." They report directly to the president. The function of these agencies and the roles of the directors and administrators are not easily distinguished from those of the cabinet departments. However, the agencies do not generally have as much prestige, influence, or breadth of jurisdiction as the cabinet departments. That is why the Veterans Administration lobbied in 1988, successfully, to be elevated to cabinet rank.

Some of the independent agencies of the federal government perform "housekeeping" functions. For example, the Office of Personnel Management administers the civil service system, and the General Services Administration manages the government's buildings and properties. Other agencies, like the National Science Foundation, serve particular clients. Still others carry out targeted functions, such as the National Aeronautics and Space Administration, the Central Intelligence Agency, and the U.S. Arms Control and Disarmament Agency.

FIGURE 14★3
Department of Commerce

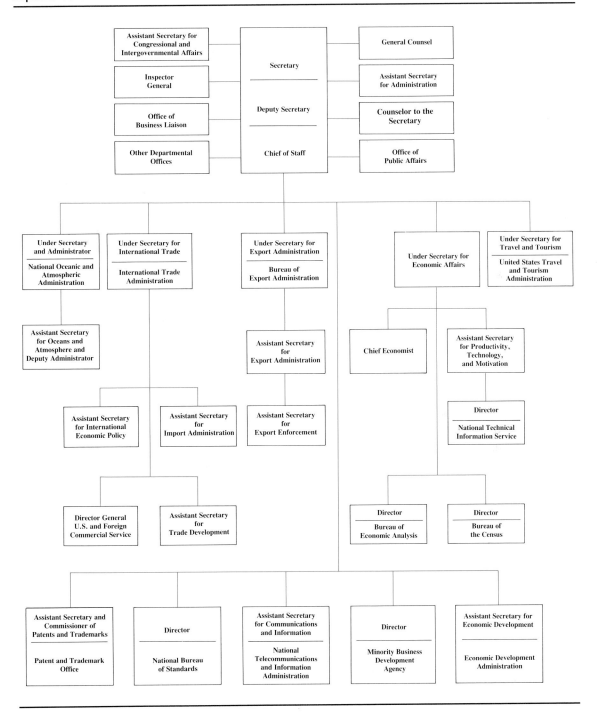

SOURCE: *U.S. Government Manual,* 1989.

Some independent federal agencies are organized as **government corporations.** This form of organization presumably gives them a little more freedom and flexibility in carrying out their responsibilities. Such federal corporations include the Tennessee Valley Authority, which was established to build dams in the valley and produce electricity; the U.S. Postal Service; and the Federal Deposit Insurance Corporation, which was set up to insure customer bank deposits against losses.

Government corporations are *unlike* private ones that sell stock and pay dividends. They are *like* private corporations in that they provide a service that could be done by the private sector, and, like a business, they charge for their services. Government corporations usually have some control over how they spend the money they earn. Sometimes government corporations are set up to manage a "sick industry." Amtrak is a government corporation running the railroad passenger line. As a necessary if unprofitable service, Congress has kept Amtrak going through subsidies, with a political assist as shown in the beginning of the chapter.

Regulatory Bodies

Regulatory boards and commissions are charged with regulating parts of the economy. They function partly like legislatures and partly like judges. Federal **regulatory bodies** issue rules and hold hearings to enforce them. They also enforce laws passed by Congress. They are governed by boards and commissions, whose bipartisan members are appointed from political parties by the president, serve staggered terms, and are confirmed by the Senate. The regulatory bodies are fairly autonomous. They do not report directly to the president, although they are subject to congressional oversight, and active presidents often have some control over them.

Among the federal regulatory bodies are the *Interstate Commerce Commission,* which regulates railroads, trucks, and pipelines; the *Federal Communications Commission,* which issues television and radio licenses; the *Securities and Exchange Commission,* which oversees the operation of the stock market; *The Federal Reserve,* which regulates the money supply; and the *National Labor Relations Board,* which oversees labor-management matters.

Captured Bodies

The federal regulatory bodies are often vulnerable to "capture" by interest groups.[9] This means they protect the interests of groups they are supposed to regulate.

Minneapolis Star and Tribune

Any governmental regulatory body can be captured in a number of ways. First, groups that are regulated by an agency influence political appointments to the agency's board by promoting people who are sympathetic to their interests. This often becomes what is known as the **revolving door;** the back-and-forth career movement between an industry and its government regulator. Appointees to regulatory boards or staffs often come from the regulated groups. This practice is justified by the argument that appointees working with the industry have the expertise needed for the job. After serving awhile, the appointees go back into a profession associated with the regulated group.

For example, a young lawyer just out of law school who wants to specialize in securities law, dealing with corporate stocks and bonds, may seek an entry-level job with the Securities and Exchange Commission. With experience and widened contacts in industry and government, the lawyer may later secure a position with a law firm that handles securities matters. Then, after building a reputation in the private sector, the lawyer may—with political support and help from the securities industry—serve a presidential appointment as a member of the Securities Exchange Commission itself. When the lawyer's term as a commissioner expires, he or she may enter a law firm or a brokerage firm as a full partner. Various laws have been passed to reduce the effect of the revolving door phenomenon, but none have had very noticeable effects.

Interest-group capture is not common to all bureaucracies at all times. It has been lessened by reducing the amount of federal regulation **(deregulation)** of industries. In the airline industry, for example, the Civil Aeronautics Board was simply abolished and federal regulations were relaxed to allow more competitive rates and services. Interest-group capture has also been reduced by the appointment of more "consumer-oriented" members to federal regulatory commissions. That, of course, depends on which political forces are most influential in a particular congress or administration. Some regulatory agencies, like the Food and Drug Administration (FDA), have traditionally been tough on the industries they regulate.

Bureaucrats

Bureaucrats are everybody's favorite punching bag. When he was running for president, former Alabama Governor George Wallace delighted audiences by complaining that Washington was dominated

★ We Need Regulation

By the late 1970s, complaints of excessive regulation had become management's all-purpose cop-out. Were profits too low? Blame regulation. Were prices too high? Blame regulation. Were inadequate funds and manpower earmarked for research and development? Blame regulation for sapping both funds and manpower. Was American industry unable to compete with foreign competitors? Blame regulation.

Regulations provide protection against the avarice of the marketplace, against shoddy products and unscrupulous marketing practices from Wall Street to Main Street. They protect legitimate businessmen from being driven out of business by unscrupulous competitors, and consumers from being victimized by unscrupulous businessmen. . . .

The extent to which we take regulations for granted in our daily lives is reflected by the confidence with which we drink our water, eat our food, take our medication, drive our cars, and perform hundreds of other tasks without thought of peril. This provides a striking contrast to the situation in many Third World nations, devoid of regulations, where those tasks can be performed only with extreme care.

SOURCE: Susan and Martin Tolchin, *Dismantling America* (Boston: Houghton Mifflin, 1983), reprinted from George McKenna and Stanley Feingold, eds., *Taking Sides: Clashing Views on Controversial Political Issues,* 4th ed. (Guilford, Conn.: Dushkin, 1985), pp. 130, 132.

by "pointy-headed" bureaucrats. He said that they could not park a bicycle correctly and suggested that their briefcases—which contained nothing but peanut butter sandwiches—should be thrown into the Potomac River. Others see bureaucracies as "rule-bound, precedent-oriented, paper-shuffling, self-protecting, experiment-resisting, conformity-rewarding, responsibility-avoiding, and delay-filled."[10] While most Americans think there are too many federal employees, and that nongovernmental employees work harder, a high percentage of those who have dealt with bureaucrats were "pleased" with that government employee.[11]

Who are the federal bureaucrats? In respect to their education, religion, income, and party identification, as well as in their political and policy views, they are typical Americans, mirroring the general public. However, considering all federal jobs (from top to bottom), women are considerably underrepresented in relation to their percentage of the total population. Blacks and American Indians are slightly overrepresented. Hispanics and Asian Americans are underrepresented.

The federal bureaucracy is not a mirror of the general population among executives and managers. Minorities and women are still severely underrepresented. As one observer has put it:

While no other large sector of the economy even approaches the success of the federal government in moving minorities and women into professional ranks, the federal civil service, nevertheless, remains distinctly divided by class, race and sex. In Washington, professionals are predominantly white, male and moderately affluent; support staff is almost entirely female, mostly black and either working class or borderline poor (at least by Washington area standards). The result of these differences is at best a condition of continuing social strain and at worst a state of near class warfare in many agencies.[12]

The people who reach the top level of the federal civil service generally start near the bottom in their agency. They usually stay in the same agency during their entire career, working their way up after twenty years or more of service. Even many political appointments are filled by career bureaucrats who have worked their way up through the ranks.

What do bureaucrats do? They do not just shuffle papers, attend meetings, and talk on the telephone. They do all sorts of things. "Bureaucrats operate bridges, investigate crimes, manage forests, program computers, arbitrate labor disputes, counsel teenagers, calculate cost-benefit ratios, operate sea-rescue cutters, run libraries, examine patent applications, inspect meat, negotiate contracts, and so on and so forth."[13]

HOW THE FEDERAL BUREAUCRACY WORKS

The federal bureaucracy is part of the executive branch, but it has been called the "fourth branch of government"—in addition to the executive, legislative, and judicial branches—because of its importance, permanence, and, often, its independence. There are different ideas of what the bureaucracy does and what it should do.

The Classic Model

The classic idea of **public administration,** the study of governmental bureaucracy, was that *policy* and *administration* were two distinctly different functions of government. The president and Congress, elected by the people, should make policy. The bureaucracy, which was not elected, should carry it out. Woodrow Wilson wrote that "administrative questions are not political questions. Although politics sets the tasks for administration, it should not be suffered to manipulate its offices."[14] The basic goal of the "science of administration" was "efficiency." Thus, according to the ideal model of bureaucracy, bureaucrats were supposed to administer policy, supply expert knowledge to the policymakers, and provide continuity in government functions. But the making of policy was to be the responsibility of elected leaders. Today, most political scientists consider this classic view incomplete and a bit naive.

More Realistic Images

The political conflicts out of which policies evolve don't stop when Congress passes a law. They continue in the administration of these policies. Often Congress has fashioned a compromise to pass a bill by putting vague language in the law. That usually leaves it to the administrators to referee the debate—on, say, auto safety standards or how clean is clean water—in applying the law. Bureaucrats may have been influential in advice and information, and even in lobbying the bill through Congress. They must often apply the law to changing political and economic situations not foreseen by those who drafted it. And with Republicans in the White House and Democrats dominating Congress, it becomes even less likely that administration will be detached from politics.

The result is that the model of a bureaucrat as a politically neutral administrator looks like a single musical note in a symphony of sounds (see the box on page 444). Bureaucrats carry other tunes as well. They can be heard playing such parts as *interest groups, policymakers,* and *budget makers.*

The Pentagon's most advanced bomber, the B-2 stealth bomber, is first revealed to the public in July 1989.

Bureaucracies as Interest Groups

Bureaucracies often act as interest groups, or as parts of interest groups, competing with other bureaucracies and other interest groups. They try to protect their "turf" (jurisdiction) and influence the decisions of Congress and the president. Former President Eisenhower called attention to such activity when he warned in his 1960 farewell address about the rising power of the *military-industrial complex.* The military bureaucracy works closely with interest groups that have a financial stake in military appropriations. Many of these groups in turn employ former military officers. Both the military bureaucracy and their interest groups work closely with the congressional committees that have jurisdiction over defense spending. These relationships form the type of sub-government or iron triangle discussed in Chapter 9. Similar triangles exist throughout the federal government.

A federal agency that enjoys national public support—as the National Aeronautics and Space Administration (NASA) did during the Kennedy and Johnson administrations—can exercise great influence over elected policymakers. Most federal agencies employ a number of people to handle public relations. Although its stated purpose is "public information," the public relations function in federal agencies is often aimed at influencing public opinion. Common Cause publicized a Department of Defense campaign—news releases, letters-to-the-editor efforts, and news conferences—on the eve of the 1984 presidential election. It aimed to build voter support for Reagan's military buildup and the Pentagon's management improvement program (in response to the public outcry about the department's paying ridiculously high prices for spare parts).[15]

★ Colonel North, Bureaucrat

Constantine Menges, who served with Ollie North in the government, describes how an aggressive bureaucrat sees his relationship to political leaders:

"In my earlier discussions with Ollie on alternative strategies in Central America, I had always insisted that the president had to have a clear understanding of what was involved, what sorts of risks lay behind different actions. North disagreed and said: 'No, we have to make the right things happen and make sure that the president goes the way we want.'

It was an echo of a phrase of Ollie's that I had always found particularly worrisome: 'We must cause this to happen.'

'No,' I'd say, 'we don't cause things to happen. The president is the one who decides what the government will do, and our job as his staff is to give him the facts and point out the alternatives so he can make an informed decision.'

'No,' Ollie would say to me, 'you're wrong. We have to box him in so there's only one way he can go—the right way.'"

SOURCE: Constantine C. Menges, "The Sad, Strange Mind of Col. North," *The Washington Post,* November 27, 1988.

Bureaucracies as Policymakers

Bureaucracies are also involved in policymaking because they exercise legislative, judicial, and executive power. For example, the Department of Agriculture has the authority to issue regulations concerning eligibility for food stamps. The Internal Revenue Service (IRS) holds hearings on individual tax cases and makes judicial findings. These legislative and judicial powers have been delegated by Congress. In exercising executive power, federal bureaucracies formulate overall long-range plans, and then make decisions concerning the day-to-day operations of large government programs.

How to divide money among competing programs involves the most serious policy decisions made in the government. Federal bureaucracies share in this decision making. Bureaucracies tend to be territorial, guarding their turf against poaching by other agencies. They even develop ideologies and enforce them internally through recruitment, indoctrination, and promotional rewards. They also tend to generate and require employee loyalty to the bureau, its territory, and its ideology. As one federal bureaucracy says about itself: "Being a Marine is not just a job" (see Chapter 16).

Bureaucratic territoriality, ideology, and loyalty as well as "iron tri-angles" are all involved in the budgeting process. To see how budget making is something more than neutral administration, look at a typical agency: the Federal Aviation Administration (FAA) in the Department of Transportation. Each year the administrator of the FAA must prepare the agency's budget for the coming year and present it to the secretary of transportation.

In Theory.   Theoretically, budget preparation, presentation, and approval might occur like this: Under the direction of the FAA administrator, the staff would prepare a budget for the entire agency. It would be presented to the secretary of transportation, who would approve it with his changes and then forward it to the Office of Management and Budget (OMB). After meetings between the OMB and the Department of Transportation, the budget, with further modifications, would be recommended for approval by the president. The president then approves the overall federal budget including the budget for the FAA. The appropriate committees in both houses of Congress hold hearings at which the FAA administrator testifies in support of the recommended budget. Finally, after more changes, Congress passes authorization and appropriation bills to provide for the next FAA budget. At each level of this theoretical budgetary process, the budget would be approved only when the decision makers were satisfied that each program was fully justified.

In Practice.   This model of the budgetary process does not exist. For one thing, budget making has tended to be based upon **incremental-ism,** in which each budget builds slowly and marginally on the last one. Decision makers have not conducted searching examinations of current programs. Instead, programs and services have usually been changed gradually, and their budgets have gradually increased. Jimmy Carter attempted to offset the effects of incrementalism through *a zero-based budgeting system,* in which each program and service in the federal bureaucracy would have to be justified anew during each annual budgetary process. The results of Carter's efforts were limited at best (see Chapter 17).

This theory of the budgetary process is unrealistic for another reason. The people who prepare budgets know they will not get all they ask for. The policymakers understand that a certain amount of "padding" will be added to a budget presented to them in expectation of cuts. The federal budgetary process becomes a game: the people who request budgets add some padding and the officials who approve the budgets attempt to find this padding and eliminate it.

Finally, the theoretical model of the federal budgetary process *does not take into account the bargaining and alliances at the various levels of decision making.* For example, while the FAA is preparing its budget, aviation groups and interested members of Congress may contact FAA officials to convince them to include certain items in the agency's budget request. When the secretary of transportation later considers the FAA budget, FAA clients (such as airlines and pilot unions) and interested congressional staff may intervene again. FAA bureaucrats may generate some of this intervention, seeking to influence the secretary's budgetary decisions. These alliances may try to influence the OMB's decisions concerning the FAA's budget.

Supposedly the administrator and other FAA officials are required to follow (and not go outside) the chain of command. In fact these officials are experienced Washington players with longstanding social and political ties to important members of Congress and interest groups. Such officials will let "friendly" representatives, client groups, and even White House staff know when their budgets are running into trouble with the OMB. They hope that these friends will intervene to influence the decisions of OMB. The fight may also be taken up in the White House and Congress with similar interventions at all of the various decision points. The federal budgetary process, then, is not a neatly divided system of administrative and political decision making.

Restraints on Bureaucracy

Clearly, bureaucracy does not operate in a vacuum. Bureaucrats are not politically impotent. They are one of a number of power centers in the policymaking process. Bureaucrats are not usually unrepresentative, unresponsive power centers operating on their own. They are part of, and influenced by, other major players in the political process.

The major restraints on bureaucracy can be found in the actions of *interest groups, media,* and *elected officials.* Examples of these informal checks abound. In early 1989, the new Secretary of the Treasury proposed a small fee on deposits in savings and loans banks as a way of raising monies needed to bail out endangered S&L's. There was an outcry in Congress over the proposal and news reports on the Bush's administration's first "blunder." The White House quickly distanced the president from the bureaucratic proposal.

These groups may serve as safeguards on bureaucratic actions or may allow administrative decisions to go unchecked because they do not have the necessary influence. As the case study of the World War II decision not to bomb the rail lines to the Auschwitz concentration

Depositors of the Sunshine State Bank in Miami, Florida wait outside the failed bank to collect their savings from the officials of the Federal Deposit Insurance Corporation (FDIC).

camp shows, their influence may not always be sufficient. Or these groups, by their inaction, may leave it to the bureaucracy to shoulder the responsibility for decisions that accurately reflect dominant political opinion.

Interest Groups

Interest groups and the competition among them can restrain arbitrary bureaucratic decisions. If a bureau becomes too client-oriented, favoring one interest group over another, the neglected interest groups may act to counter bureaucratic excesses. Their ability to influence the bureaucracy will depend on their access to policymakers, their success in publicizing their issues, and the other groups they can mobilize. Often they can operate through citizen advisory panels and public hearings. Of course, since most Americans are not represented in interest groups, competition among these groups is far from being a full public check on arbitrary bureaucracy.

Media

Another important restraint on bureaucratic power is the media. They call attention to bureaucratic arbitrariness, waste, dishonesty, and red tape. New federal laws giving the press greater access to bureaucratic decisions through "freedom of information" legislation have increased this power. Other legislation protects federal employees who go to the press and "blow the whistle" on wrongdoing or mismanagement. The restraining influence of the media is limited because reporters tend to develop good working relationships with the bureaucrats whose agencies they cover. These reporters often depend on the bureaucrats for information through press releases and "leaks."

A more basic safeguard against unchecked bureaucratic power is the constitutional authority represented in the office of the *president*, in *Congress*, and in the *courts*. Of course everything done by administrative agencies must conform to the law. That means that many bureaucratic actions can be appealed, some eventually to the courts. However, only formal orders of federal agencies can be appealed. Further, a person upset by a bureaucratic order may not be able to afford the time and expense involved in a legal appeal. Nonetheless, courts can be a formidable restraint on bureaucratic actions.[16]

The power of the American president is greater. It involves the authority to appoint, direct, and remove the people in most of the top positions in the federal agencies. And, of course, most members of the executive branch look to the chief executive as their overall boss.

But presidential authority over the bureaucracy has several limits: the restrictions on hiring and firing under the civil service system, the fact that officials in some positions including all those in the reg-

---

★ The Interagency Mouse

The problems presidents have with their bureaucracies are not always limited to major policy matters. One such example is from the Carter presidency: "When a couple of mice scampered across the President's study one evening last spring, an alarm went out to the General Services Administration, housekeeper of Federal buildings. Some weeks later, another mouse climbed up inside a wall of the Oval Office and died. The President's office was bathed in the odor of dead mouse as Carter prepared to greet visiting Latin American dignitaries. An emergency call went out to GSA. But it refused to touch the matter. Officials insisted that they had exterminated all the "inside" mice in the White House and this errant mouse must have come from outside, and therefore was the responsibility of the Interior Department. Interior demurred, saying that the dead mouse was now inside the White House. President Carter summoned officials from both agencies to his desk and exploded: 'I can't even get a damn mouse out of my office.' Ultimately, it took an interagency task force to get rid of the mouse."

SOURCE: Hedrick Smith, "Problems of a Problem Solver," *The New York Times Magazine,* January 8, 1978. Copyright © 1978 by The New York Times Company. Reprinted by permission.

ulatory bodies are appointed for fixed terms and can only be removed for cause, and the massive size and complexity of the bureaucracy make it difficult to know what's going on or to focus on a problem once it's raised (see the box on page 448). Still, the chief executive has considerable authority over the bureaucracy, particularly through budget-making power. And in some areas, the president can demand loyalty from the federal bureaucracy, although many bureaucrats have a considerable amount of independence within the jurisdiction Congress has assigned them.[17]

Congress has considerable power to keep the bureaucracy in check. It can change a law that is not being administered to its liking. It can state a law more clearly if it does not approve of a bureaucratic interpretation. Congress can cut the budget of a bureau with which it disagrees, or abolish an agency or program altogether. And it can pressure the bureaucracy in individual cases through "casework" by representatives for their constituents.

Congress could reduce the discretion of bureaucrats by specifying the details of laws when they are first passed, leaving little to be filled in by regulations. But *members of Congress may not wish to be associated with the details of a new program or law, preferring to let public complaints be directed at bureaucrats.*

In the case study none of these restraints appeared to have had much effect. The agency involved refused to modify a military policy whose enforcement had tragic consequences. On closer examination, however, the apparent bureaucratic failure to hinder the genocide of European Jews reflected broader political realities. The lack of attention by the media, the indifference of elected officials, the divisions among interest groups, and the broad popular apathy all set conditions under which it became unnecessary for a bureaucracy to make an exception to the rule.

Bureaucratic Inaction: The Refusal to Bomb Auschwitz

In the spring of 1941, Adolph Hitler ordered the "complete solution of the Jewish question" for the areas of Europe under Nazi occupation. The "solution"—the systematic extermination of almost six million Jews—was carried out through mass shootings and in six gas chambers established in Poland in late 1941.

Reports describing Hitler's plans were initially revealed in June 1942, when *The New York Times* and the British Broadcasting Corporation broke the story that 1000 Jews per day were being gassed to death at the Chelmno killing center. Responding to these revelations, American Jewish leaders began a largely unsuccessful three-year effort to persuade U.S. government officials to rescue and relocate those people threatened with extermination. A close look at one chapter in this tragedy—the War Department's refusal to bomb the Auschwitz gas chambers in 1944—may explain the cause of bureaucratic inaction.[18]

The American Response Before 1944

Soon after the first reports of the use of gas chambers and mass shootings reached the U.S. in 1942, American Jewish leaders began to campaign for the rescue of Jews not yet trapped behind the Nazi lines. The U.S. government took virtually no action.

Several factors worked against the success of Jewish leaders' appeals in this period. First, there was widespread skepticism about the reports of Nazi atrocities. The American press hesitated to give prominent coverage to the stories, because reports of German atrocities during World War I had been so exaggerated. Because of this limited press coverage, no real public outcry for action in this country developed.

Within the U.S. government, other factors worked against the campaign for rescue. In blunt terms, Allied leaders were reluctant to support rescue efforts because they saw no place to put the Jews once they were rescued. Neither British nor American State Department officials wanted Jewish settlement of Palestine (Israel) because they feared Arab unrest would develop. In addition, the U.S. Congress was unwilling to allow rescued Jews to emigrate to the United States. Driven by post-Depression fears that war refugees would steal "American" jobs, a coalition of Southern Democrats and Republicans had restricted immigration to a trickle. Roosevelt's State Department never even filled the existing quotas—which limited non-British emigrants to only 7000 per year—during the entire war.

The War Department's Rescue Policy

In this atmosphere the War Department (later renamed the Defense Department in more peaceful times), established its basic "policy" on rescue attempts. The policy was largely developed by Assistant Secretary of War John McCloy, who held responsibility for planning all War Department operations (including rescue).

The existing ad hoc, unwritten policy was that rescue missions would divert resources away from the War Department's central mission of winning the war. In January, 1944, the Department's rescue policy was set down in writing for the first time. Faced with a new rescue request by the recently created War Refugee Board (the WRB was formed in January 1944 to "coordinate" war refugee policies and rescue attempts), War Department officials met to decide how to stem what would likely be a flood of rescue proposals from this new bureaucratic agency.

The following policy emerged:

It is not contemplated that units of the armed forces will be employed for the purpose of rescuing victims of enemy oppression unless such rescues are the direct result [*emphasis added*] *of military operations conducted with the objective of defeating the armed forces of the enemy.*

Would Auschwitz meet this narrow test?

Spring, 1944: The Situation At Auschwitz

In July, 1944, plans by the Nazis to deport Jews held in Hungary to the Auschwitz concentration camp for extermination were revealed to Allied intelligence and reported in the British and American press. At Auschwitz, men, women, and children arrived by crowded box car to face gassing with hydrogen cyanide. Almost three million people died this way at Auschwitz and five other death camps.

Following these reports, calls for the bombing of the rail lines connecting Hungary and Auschwitz, as well as the camp's gas chambers and crematoria, were relayed by American Jewish leaders in July to the U.S. War Refugee Board (WRB). Letters requesting action at Auschwitz were also sent to President Roosevelt directly. Using this two-pronged strategy, Jewish leaders hoped to spur War Department action.

After some hesitation, the WRB asked the War Department in September to "consider" an air strike on Auschwitz. The War Department refused. The Department argued that they would impede its primary bureaucratic mission: to win the war. Such an air operation could not be undertaken, the War Department wrote in response, "[because] it could be executed only by diversion of considerable air support essential to the success of our forces now engaged in decisive operations." The other access point—through Roosevelt and the White House—proved

Concentration camp inmates photographed shortly before their liberation.

even less fruitful. There was never any reply from Roosevelt to the request for bombing Auschwitz.

Jewish leaders repeated their request for bombings through the WRB in November, after more extensive evidence of the killings—which numbered at least 150,000 since July. Again, the War Department refused, claiming that (1) the Auschwitz area was not a vital industrial target; and (2) that a bombing mission launched from bases in Great Britain was too dangerous, requiring 2000 miles of unescorted flight over enemy territory.

In fact, both reasons were wrong, or worse, misleading. First, the Auschwitz area clearly qualified as a vital industrial target. Why else would the department have approved an Allied bombing mission flown by 127 Flying Fortress bombers (accompanied by 100 Mustang fighters) on *August 20, 1944* to destroy factories located *less than five miles* from the camp's gas chambers and a similar mission on September 13. The reasoning behind the department's second stated objection to the WRB request that unescorted flying from Great Britain was too dangerous was also questionable. The closest Allied airbase—the airbase used to destroy industrial targets five miles from Auschwitz—was in Italy, not Great Britain.

Famine-relief efforts for Ethiopia in the 1980s were increased due to media coverage.

The Absence of Domestic Political Pressure

Clearly, rescue was not part of the War Department's mission. Yet to alter the bureaucracy's position would require pressure from other groups. But public opinion, interest groups, or elected officials would not provide the needed support.

Muted Public Opinion

As noted earlier, "The Holocaust" was reported in newspapers regularly. However, the American press did not treat the story as front page news. *Boston Globe* coverage of the killings at the Chelmno concentration camp was typical. In June, 1942, the Globe ran a story about Chelmno whose headline read "Mass Murders of Jews Pass 700,000 Mark." The story ran on page twelve. Few papers gave the story any greater prominence.

But the media's failings do not completely explain public opinion. Were Americans fearful of a new wave of immigrants? Apparently so. Four separate public opinion polls conducted in 1938, for example, found that upwards of 70 percent of Americans opposed increasing immigration quotas to help Nazi war refugees, Jews and non-Jews. Were Americans largely indifferent because they couldn't "see" the horrors of the concentration camps? The mid-1980s strong reaction to the Ethiopian famine (which was filmed) but lukewarm response to the mass murder of five million Cambodians (largely unfilmed) tends to support this view.

Limited Lobbying by Interest Groups

Because of dissenting opinions over the need for a state in Palestine, many American Jewish leaders did not join the call for resettlement of European Jews in Palestine made by pro-Zionist groups. Jewish reluctance to press the government to rescue Jews also stemmed from their concern that American Jews not be seen as placing their own religion above the national interest. As a result, the War Department and President Roosevelt heard only infrequent cries for action from influential mainstream groups such as the American Jewish Committee and B'nai B'rith.

Other groups that might have encouraged action by the War Department—through political muscle on the Congress or the White House—also failed to speak out loudly. Few Christian church leaders or liberal editorialists supported active intervention. Labor leaders, while sympathetic, were reluctant to organize their rank and file behind such proposals. More refugees, after all, potentially meant fewer jobs at home for union members.

Mixed Signals From Elected Officials

Officials in the War Department also may have found it easier to reject rescue proposals because they felt that President Roosevelt and Congress did not consider this a priority. For example, although Roosevelt created the War Refugee Board in 1944 to respond to Nazi atrocities, he gave the new agency little else: it had no power over the War or State Departments, and a budget of only $1.1 million. Roosevelt, reflecting the majority view in Congress, also acted several times to severely limit migration to the U.S. These actions, compounded by British unwillingness to accept Jews in Palestine and North Africa, left few places for rescued refugees to go. War Department officials were aware of this political "dilemma."

Conclusion

In one sense this is an easy case. A U.S. bureaucracy, the former Defense Department, faced with a clear moral question of saving people from extermination failed to act. But making a harsh judgment from the safety of history should not obscure the political forces surrounding the bureaucrats. There was too little domestic pressure for the bombing of Auschwitz and too much international pressure against it. Interest groups, the media, and elected officials, were either indifferent or unable to exert the needed influence. The British, worried about Arab unrest, pushed for a very limited rescue policy. The American public justifiably concerned about winning the war, were less justifiably concerned about increased immigration in the post-Depression economy.

With no clear direction from political leaders and insufficient domestic pressures, the bureaucracy fell back on its accepted mandate of military victory. Independent missions to save European civilians did not fall under this mandate. The department then interpreted the facts (such as distance to the target and danger to U.S. bombers) to fit the policy. But the significant factors occurred outside the bureaucracy. Jews died not so much because of what "bad" bureaucrats did, but because of what "good" people, politically, did not do.

WRAP-UP

Bureaucracy undercuts Americans' belief that we have "a government of laws, rather than of men." For most of us the bureaucracy is the government, influenced only at the edges even by the most powerful. Historically bureaucracy has developed in response to government's need to accomplish ever greater and more complex tasks. The comforting distinction between policymaking by elected authorities and policy administration by unelected bureaucrats does not exist in reality. Bureaucrats make policy in numerous ways. Even implementing policy is a form of policymaking. The restraints on bureaucracy, from the public and their representatives, may or may not work in practice, as the case study made clear.

The government needs to get its work done. That means that bureaucratic organizations, speeches aside, are likely to stay. But keeping bureaucracy responsive and responsible then becomes a major part of the government's work. For that job we cannot rely on bureaucracy on its own. Groups within and outside the government must check the power of institutions the Constitution never foresaw.

Key Terms

spoils system (p. 431)
merit system (p. 432)
Hatch Act (p. 433)
Civil Service Reform Act
  (p. 433)
Senior Executive Service (p. 433)
cabinet departments (p. 435)
independent agencies (p. 436)

government corporations
  (p. 438)
regulatory bodies (p. 438)
revolving door (p. 439)
deregulation (p. 440)
public administration
  (p. 442)
incrementalism (p. 445)

Suggested Readings

Heclo, Hugh, *A Government of Strangers* (Washington, D.C.: Brookings Institution, 1977).

Leone, Robert A., *Who Profits? Winners, Losers and Government Regulation* (New York: Basic Books 1986).

Pertschuk, Michael, *Giant Killers* (New York: W. W. Norton Co., 1987).

Radin, B. A. and W. D. Howley, *The Politics of Federal Reorganization: Creating the U.S. Department of Education* (Elmsford, N.Y.: Pergamon Books, 1988).

Trausch, Susan, *It Came From the Swamp: Your Federal Government at Work* (New York: Houghton Mifflin & Co., 1986).

Volcker, Paul, *Public Service: The Quiet Crisis* (Lanham, Md.: University Press of America, 1988).

Endnotes

[1]Charles Peters, "Firemen First or How to Beat a Budget Cut," in Peters and Nicholas Lemann, *Inside the System,* 4th edition (New York: Holt, Rinehart and Winston, 1979), pp. 227–28.

[2]H. H. Garth and C. Wright Mills, eds., *From Max Weber: Essays in Sociology* (New York: Oxford University Press, 1958), Chapter 8.

[3]Quoted in Theo Lippman, Jr., "Reagan Wit Ranked High," *Pittsburgh Press* (March 27, 1982).

[4]*The Budget for Fiscal 1990: Special Analysis* (Washington, D.C.: U.S. Government Printing Office, 1989), pp. I-2, I-11, I-12, I-13.

[5]For a history of American federal bureaucracy—and a discussion of the irony that efforts to increase popular control of government "planted the seeds of modern bureaucratic power"—see Michael Nelson, "A Short Ironic History of American National Bureaucracy," *Journal of Politics:* 44, no. 3 (August 1983), pp. 747–77.

[6]Quoted in the preface to Harry Kranz, *The Participatory Bureaucracy* (Lexington, MA: D. C. Heath, 1976), p. xiii.

[7]Eugene Lewis, *American Politics in a Bureaucratic Age* (Cambridge, MA: Winthrop Publishers, 1977), p. 8.

[8]Kranz, p. 17.

[9]Francis E. Rourke, *Bureaucracy, Politics and Public Policy,* 3rd edition (Boston, MA: Little, Brown, 1984), pp. 58–62. See also John E. Chubb, *Interest Groups and the Bureaucracy: The Politics of Energy* (Stanford, CA: Stanford University Press, 1983).

[10]See reference to Harold Laski in Lewis C. Mainzer, *Political Bureaucracy* (Glenview, IL: Scott, Foresman, 1973), p. 2.

[11]*The Washington Post,* July 16, 1983.

[12]Charles T. Goodsell, *The Case for Bureaucracy: A Public Administration Polemic* (Chatham, N.J.: Chatham House, 1983), pp. 82–88.

[13]Goodsell, p. 83.

[14]Woodrow Wilson, "The Study of Administration," reprinted in *Political Science Quarterly* (December 1941): 493–495.

[15]*The New York Times,* October 4, 1984.

[16]See Peter Woll, *American Bureaucracy* (New York: W. W. Norton, 1988), pp. 144–54.

[17]See, generally, John Hart, *The Presidential Branch* (New York: Pergamon Press, 1987).

[18]This case study is adapted from David S. Wyman, *The Abandonment of the Jews* (New York: Random House, 1984) and Wyman, "Why Auschwitz Was Never Bombed," in *Commentary,* May, 1978.

★

CHAPTER 15

The Judiciary

"Why doesn't the Supreme Court pass the school desegregation case?" asked one of Chief Justice Vinson's law clerks in 1952. *Brown* v. *Board of Education* of Topeka, Kansas had arrived on the Court's docket in 1951, but it was carried over for oral argument the next term and then consolidated with four other cases and reargued in December 1953. The landmark ruling did not come down until May 17, 1954. "Well," Justice Frankfurter explained, "we're holding it for the election"—1952 was a presidential election year. "You're holding it for the election?" The clerk persisted in disbelief. "I thought the Supreme Court was supposed to decide cases without regard to elections." "When you have a major social political issue of this magnitude, timing and public reactions are important considerations, and," Frankfurter continued, "we do not think this is the time to decide it."[1]

Judges are policymakers. Like the other two branches of government, the judiciary helps shape the nation's choices. Unlike the other branches, the courts do this by applying the Constitution and laws to the disputes brought before it. The results of this administering of the laws is not only to resolve particular conflicts in the courtroom. The courts also interpret, enforce, and actually create policies. For example, no legislative act declared that during the first months of pregnancy a state law could not deny a woman's right to an abortion. Based on its interpretation of the Constitution, the U.S. Supreme Court established that rule.

The courts also have strict limits placed on their judicial powers. Our judicial system is not self-starting. An actual case must be brought before it. Otherwise the courts cannot interpret the law, pursue criminals, or establish norms of behavior. In addition, courts are expected to follow previous decisions of past courts whenever possible. The norms of judicial behavior further insulate judges from popular pressure and constrain them from being personally involved in cases before them.

The great powers and equally severe limits placed on the judicial branch will provide the background for this discussion. The law itself is the setting in which the legal system functions. Its participants are schooled in it, exhibit great respect for its values and procedures, and think of themselves as upholding its norms. The structure of the judicial system parallels that of the law it applies and the federal system of which it is a part. The U.S. Supreme Court in its practices usually reflects the dominant norms of the political system. Whether its decisions, or those of the courts

Linda Brown was refused admission to a white elementary school in Topeka, Kansas. On her behalf the NAACP brought a class-action suit that resulted in the 1954 landmark Supreme Court decision *Brown* v. *Board of Education.*

below it, are implemented often involves judges in political conflicts testing the limits of judicial authority, as illustrated in the case of busing in Richmond, Virginia.

WHAT IS "LAW"?

Law is the set of rules of conduct established and enforced by a governing authority. The need for predictability of behavior is the basic reason for law. "To some extent and within certain degrees of freedom, the individual members of a society must be able to demand from others certain regularities of behavior, and they must also accord to others the expectation that they, themselves, will behave predictably."[2]

Law and Politics

Law is central to politics. It largely governs *how* politics is played and *why* it is played. It is used to shape the *process* by authorizing the institutions that participate and by regulating their behavior. Legislatures or attorneys or interest groups are established by law and are restricted by it, for example, in violating others' civil rights. Law is the *objective* of most political activity; the goal is usually to pass a law, influence its administration, or affect how it's interpreted by the courts.[3]

There is a considerable overlap between law and politics. As was shown in the case study on tax reform in Chapter 12, politics influences practically all of Congress's law-making functions. And as the Justice Frankfurter story makes clear, politics impinges upon how the Supreme Court conducts its affairs. In the sense that law reflects the wishes of government (and the groups influencing it), then *law is the great instrument of politics.* Law gives to political bodies a legitimacy and force that they would otherwise lack. Its authority makes regulating conduct through the political process possible. Of course, in turn, the law regulates politics and society through the judicial system.

But law is not just a product of the political system. It reflects changing customs in society, such as the evolving position of women shown by the changes in divorce and child-custody laws. Law also has a logic and a force all its own. The legal system is governed by lawyers who are trained to view law as a separate intellectual structure whose words and ideas are special. The rest of us also view the law as involving obligations to our nation and containing a sense of morality, of right and wrong. This symbolic nature of law leads to the respect and obedience most people show it.

Law can be classified in two principal ways. First, according to whom it involves and protects, it can be *civil law* or *criminal law.* Second, it can be categorized by source: *constitutional law, statutory law, administrative law,* and *judge-made law.*

Law and Whom It Involves

Civil law involves offenses—called *torts*—committed by a private individual or corporation against another. It also deals with the relationships among private individuals or corporations, such as contracts, marriages, or property ownership. Under civil law, an individual may sue another for an offense, such as negligence resulting in an automobile accident. If successful, the person who brought the suit may secure *damages* (a court award in money) or obtain a court order requiring the person who was sued to do something (for example, admit a person to a public school) or refrain from doing something (such as stop blocking a driveway).

Criminal law involves an offense against the public interest as defined by the government. This kind of offense—murder or driving while intoxicated, for example—constitutes a crime. Crimes are punishable by fine or imprisonment or both. More serious crimes can involve the death penalty. These are called *capital crimes.* Sometimes, an offense that causes injury to another person's automobile or body (such as reckless driving) can constitute both a tort and a crime. The person who commits the offense may be sued for damages in a civil case and may also have to stand trial separately for a crime.

Law and Its Sources

If law is classified according to its source, **constitutional law** is based on a constitutional provision, such as the equal protection clause in the Fourteenth Amendment to the U.S. Constitution. Second, **statutory law** consists of acts passed by a legislative body. One example is the Civil Rights Act of 1964, passed by Congress. Third, the rules and regulations issued by executive departments and agencies make up **administrative law.** The federal regulations requiring affirmative action programs are administrative law. Fourth, **judge-made law** consists of decisions and opinions by courts. It is based on the doctrine of *stare decisis,* a Latin phrase meaning "the decision should stand." That is, in judge-made law, courts give considerable weight to precedents, prior decisions, and opinions in similar cases. When no clear constitutional, statutory, treaty, or administrative law provision applies, a judge may refer back to common law cases or equity cases in basing decisions on precedents. Regardless of the source of law it is applied to cases decided by the courts.

Common law is made up of judge-made laws in actual cases. Some are English cases going back hundreds of years, and others are more recent decisions of U.S. courts. **Equity** developed when English courts found that the common law had become too rigid. Equity decisions attempted to make the common law more fair and to provide more flexible remedies. Thus, in equity, a court order can direct a person to stop doing something (with an *injunction*), rather than just awarding damages after the fact for an act or a failure to act. Today, statutory law has *codified* (spelled out) and replaced most of the early judge-made common laws and equity. But judges still make or uncover law today.

THE STRUCTURE OF THE JUDICIAL SYSTEM

The judicial system, like much of the rest of our government, is decentralized. Two factors define its structure—*jurisdiction* and *federalism.* **Jurisdiction** means the authority to interpret and apply the law. It involves both the kinds of cases a court may hear (civil or criminal, for example) and at what stage it may hear them (trial or on appeal). **Federalism** refers to our dual system of government; thus, the states and the federal government have separate, if similar, judicial systems.

Civil and Criminal Courts

Civil cases involve private disputes. Controversies stemming from divorces, antitrust matters, and wills, for example, are all civil cases. Civil cases begin with a petition or *complaint,* which states the *plaintiff's* views. (The plaintiff is the person who brings the suit.) It concludes with the remedy sought by the plaintiff, such as money or a divorce. When the petition or complaint is filed, the defendant is served with a *summons,* a notice that the suit has been filed and that an answer is required.

At pretrial conferences, trial judges bring the parties together. Agreements by the parties reduce the controversy over facts and law to a bare minimum. Trial judges also pressure the parties to settle their lawsuit. Most cases are, in fact, settled out of court.

The plaintiff in a civil case has the burden of proof: he or she must prove his or her case. This proof must convince the judge or jury by "a preponderance of the evidence," a standard less strict than the one used in criminal cases.

Criminal cases may involve **misdemeanors** (petty theft of, say, under $500), which are minor offenses generally punishable by less than one year of imprisonment. Or, they may involve **felonies** (grand theft of over $500), serious offenses that carry prison terms of one year or more.[4] Criminal cases begin with an arrest. The *accused* is *arraigned* (brought before a judge or magistrate), informed of the charge, and asked to enter a plea of guilty or not guilty. Bail is then set (or denied in some cases). A *grand jury* session in most states or preliminary hearing determines whether there is sufficient evidence to require a trial. *Plea-bargaining* between the accused and the prosecutor may result in a reduced charge in return for a plea of guilty. Prosecutors seek these pleas to reduce the number of cases that have to be tried. If there is no plea of guilty and if the charges are not dismissed, the case will go to trial with the constitutional guarantee of a jury of peers sitting in judgment. The burden of proof that falls on the government is much heavier in a criminal case. A person accused of a crime is presumed innocent until proven guilty. Thus, *the accused cannot be convicted unless the prosecutor proves the case "beyond a reasonable doubt," which, in a judicial setting, once again reflects the Constitution's suspicion of governmental power.*

In the federal system the district courts, courts of appeal, and the Supreme Court have both civil and criminal jurisdiction. This is usually true of state trial courts, but some states have established separate appellate systems for criminal and civil cases.

Trial and Appellate Courts

The U.S. Constitution created the Supreme Court but left the establishment of the other federal courts to Congress. Congress has established eleven courts of appeal and at least one district court in each state. (Some states have more than one district court, depending upon population and caseload.) Congress has also created a number of special federal tribunals, such as the Court of Claims, the Customs Court, the U.S. Court of Customs and Patent Appeals, and the Court of Military Appeals (see Figure 15.1).

Appellate judges determine whether the lower court correctly applied the law to the facts of the case, while the trial courts establish the facts. In examining the facts and in applying the law, appellate judges usually do not hear witnesses. Instead, they read the trial record and consider the lawyers' briefs and oral arguments.

Most cases are settled without a trial, usually through plea bargaining. Nine out of ten cases that go to trial are settled by trial courts without being appealed. But the losing side in a federal district court

FIGURE 15★1
Federal Court Structure and the Flow of Cases to the Supreme Court

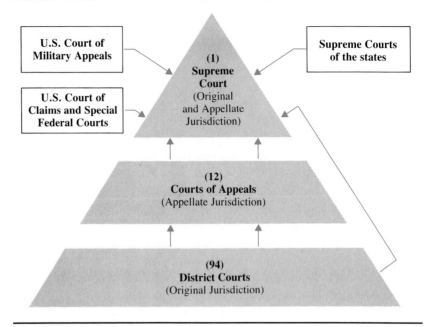

SOURCE: Adapted with permission of Macmillan Publishing Co. from *American Constitutional Law,* 3rd Edition, by Rocco J. Tresolini and Martin Shapiro. Copyright © 1972 by Rocco J. Tresolini and Martin Shapiro.

has the right to appeal. The eleven federal appeals courts serve groups of judicial districts, which are called *circuits.* Under certain circumstances, appeals from these courts may be taken to the U.S. Supreme Court, which is the "court of last resort" in the federal judicial system.

The state systems have similar levels of appellate jurisdiction. There are usually appellate courts and then a court of last resort, usually a state supreme court. Some states provide separate civil and criminal appellate courts. When a federal question is involved, an appeal may be taken from a state's highest court to the Supreme Court of the United States, if it accepts jurisdiction.

Federalism

America has a dual court system based on federalism. This means that a person may be tried for the same criminal offense in both a state court under state law, and in a federal court under federal law. For example, a person charged with the possession of crack cocaine could be tried in a state court and a federal court. Two trials do not, in this instance, constitute a *double jeopardy,* because an offense has been committed against two separate laws and two separate authorities.

The Supreme Court's *original jurisdiction*—its power to hear cases that have not gone through the lower courts—is limited. According to the Constitution, it is restricted to only cases involving "Ambassadors, other public ministers and Consuls, and those in which a State shall be a Party." Congress has further limited this original jurisdiction by providing that such cases may originate in other courts as well. Only cases between two or more states must originate in the Supreme Court. Only two percent of the Court's cases each year come to it under original jurisdiction. Most of these involve states in disputes with other states over subjects like water rights or air pollution problems such as acid rain.

THE UNITED STATES SUPREME COURT

The Supreme Court of the United States, composed of a chief justice and eight associate justices, stands at the head of the federal court system (see the box on page 465). Very few cases ever reach the Supreme Court. Of more than 10 million cases tried every year in American courts (federal and state), 4000 to 5000 petitions for review make it to the Supreme Court. Of these, the Court hears oral arguments and writes opinions in about 150 cases. The rest of the petitions are affirmed or reversed by written "memorandum orders."

Many cases that reach the Supreme Court involve constitutional issues. The majority of these cases come to the Court in the form of petitions (written requests) for a *writ of certiorari* (certiorari means to be informed of something). A writ of certiorari is an order to the lower court to send the entire record of the case to the higher court for review. Someone who has lost a case in a lower court may petition for this writ. It is granted when four justices of the Supreme Court feel that the issues raised are important enough to merit a review. The Court denies between 85 and 90 percent of all such applications. This procedure keeps control over the appeal process in the hands of the Supreme Court, allowing it to keep most decisions in the lower courts. It also enables the Court to influence the actions of lower-court judges by establishing guiding decisions on certain crucial cases.

The Court decides most cases on the basis of the record in the lower court and the written briefs filed by the lawyers. In a few important cases, the Court requires oral arguments. Afterwords, the justices meet in secret conference, presided over by the chief justice. If the chief justice is in the majority on the question of how the case

A 1958 photo of six black children who had attended Little Rock's Central High School, sitting with two NAACP officials outside the Supreme Court building (the man seated in the center is Thurgood Marshall, later to be a justice of the Supreme Court).

should be decided, he may write the majority opinion, or he may assign another justice who represents the majority to write the opinion. This power of assignment gives the chief justice considerable influence over the other justices and in shaping the final opinion. Other justices may write their own separate opinions. These may be *concurring*—in agreement with the majority opinion—or *dissenting*—disagreeing with the majority opinion. These separate opinions may be circulated among the other members of the Court for their approval. Before the Court makes a final decision, it is possible that what was at first a dissenting opinion may have gained enough support to become the majority opinion. Although only the majority opinion has the force of law, lawyers study dissenting and concurring opinions for possible arguments that might cause the Court to change its majority opinion in a future case.[5]

The Final Authority?

The Supreme Court has been prominent in American political history because it has been thought to have "final" authority over what the Constitution means. *Historically, however, a ruling of the Court has not always been the final word.* The Court itself has reversed or modified its decisions, as will be shown in the case study. If the Court interprets a law in a way Congress doesn't like, Congress will often overrule the Court simply by rewriting the statute. Amendments to the Constitution also have reversed decisions by the Court. The Court's pre-Civil War *Dred Scott* decision supporting ownership of slaves in all parts of the country was reversed by the Thirteenth Amendment outlawing slavery. An 1895 Court decision striking down the federal income tax was overcome by the Sixteenth Amendment in 1913, which allowed such taxes. More recently, an unsuccessful attempt was made to reverse the Supreme Court's ruling restricting antiabortion laws by an amendment to the Constitution.

The strength of the Court's "final" authority is also affected by the other branches of government. Congress and the president, as well as the Supreme Court, have taken their turn in interpreting vague parts of the Constitution to meet the demands of the time and the needs of those in power. The president's right to involve the country in the Vietnam war without a declaration of war would seem to fly in the face of the war-making powers given to Congress by the Constitution. Yet without a challenge by the courts and Congress, the president's interpretation stood.

★ The Supreme Court, 1989

JUSTICE	DATE OF BIRTH	APPOINTED BY	DATE APPOINTED
William J. Brennan, Jr.	1906	Eisenhower	1957
Byron R. White	1917	Kennedy	1962
Thurgood Marshall	1908	Johnson	1967
Harry A. Blackmun	1908	Nixon	1970
William H. Rehnquist, Jr. (appointed chief justice in 1986)	1924	Nixon	1971
John Paul Stevens	1920	Ford	1975
Sandra D. O'Connor	1930	Reagan	1981
Antonin Scalia	1936	Reagan	1986
Anthony Kennedy	1936	Reagan	1988

Despite this shared role in changing the Constitution, the Supreme Court, by its constant interpretation and reinterpretation of the Constitution through its rulings, breathes life into two-hundred-year-old words. A brief history of the Court will show how this has been done.

Early Years of the Court

The Supreme Court has undergone many changes in the nearly two hundred years it has existed. For its first fifty years or so, surprising as it seems today, interest in the Court was slight. No cases at all were brought to the Supreme Court in its first three years. Many leaders, such as Patrick Henry and Alexander Hamilton, refused appointments to serve as judges; and court sessions were held in such places as basement apartments.

Two landmark decisions greatly increased the influence of the Court during its initial period. The first established **judicial review,** the power not only to declare acts and laws of any state and local government unconstitutional, but also to strike down acts of any branch of the federal government. The second major decision established the principle of **national supremacy,** that the United States laws and Constitution are the supreme law of the land and that state laws that are in conflict with federal laws cannot stand.

Judicial Review and National Supremacy

The principle of judicial review was established in the case of *Marbury* v. *Madison* (1803) in which the Supreme Court for the first time struck down an act of Congress. The case shows what a shrewd politician Chief Justice John Marshall was. Marshall, the nation's fourth chief justice, was a conservative and federalist who attended only two months of law school.

Shortly before leaving office, President Adams (who had nominated Marshall to the Court) appointed a number of minor judicial officials in order to maintain the influence of his party in the coming administration of his opponent, Thomas Jefferson. When Jefferson took office, he discovered that one of the appointments, that of William Marbury, had not actually been delivered. Jefferson ordered his secretary of state, James Madison, to hold it up. Under a section of the Judiciary Act of 1789, Marbury sued in the Supreme Court to compel the appointment. Marshall was then confronted with deciding a case between his political allies and his enemy, Jefferson, who

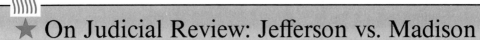

★ On Judicial Review: Jefferson vs. Madison

"Why should an undemocratically constituted body of nine elitists, who are not responsible to the people via the ballot box, be accorded the overriding power to strike down what the people want? Is not Congress, and is not the Executive equally capable of judging and interpreting the constitutionality of a proposed measure or course of action? Are they not equally devoted to the principles of government under law?"—Henry J. Abraham, on Jefferson's views, *The Judiciary,* 3d ed. (Boston: Allyn & Bacon, 1973), p. 128.

"Judiciary is truly the only defensive armor of the Federal Government, or rather for the Constitution and laws of the United States. Strip it of that armor and the door is wide open for nullification, anarchy, and convulsion."—James Madison, ibid., p. 129.

was not only president but also intent on weakening the power of the conservative Supreme Court. It was not at all clear that if the case went against him the president would obey the court.

What Marshall did was to dismiss Marbury's case, ruling that the section of the Judiciary Act under which he had sued was unconstitutional (the act allowed the Supreme Court original jurisdiction in a case not mentioned by the Constitution). By doing so he clearly asserted that the Supreme Court, on the basis of *its* interpretation of the Constitution, could set limits on the actions of Congress. The Court also supported Jefferson's argument that he did not have to make the appointment. It was a clear meshing of law and politics. Marshall asserted the right of judicial review against a law of Congress rather than against a presidential action (or inaction). How could the president object?

Another early decision established clearly that states could not interfere with the functioning of the federal government. In this landmark case, *McCulloch* v. *Maryland* (1819), the state of Maryland attempted to tax the Baltimore branch of the unpopular Bank of the United States, established by the federal government. Chief Justice Marshall, speaking for a unanimous court, ruled that the federal government "...though limited in its powers, is supreme within its sphere of action." Thus a state legislative act must give way to an act of Congress. He also found that although the Constitution did not specifically allow Congress to create a bank, Article I, Section 8 gave Congress the power to make all laws "necessary and proper" for carrying out its authority. The *implied powers* based on this clause were to be used later in broadly expanding the duties that Congress could undertake.

Then in 1857 came the famous *Dred Scott* case *(Dred Scott* v. *Sanford)*. Here, the Court ruled that a slave (Dred Scott) was not automatically free merely because his owner had taken him to a state not allowing slavery. Congress, the Court said, had no right to interfere with property rights guaranteed by the Constitution. The Court went on to say that the Missouri Compromise (1820), which had attempted to resolve the slavery issue by dividing the new western territories into slave and free parts, was invalid. In terms of constitutional development, this unpopular decision was the first time an act of Congress of any great importance was struck down by the courts. As such, the Dred Scott case marked an expansion of judicial powers.

The Court Since the Civil War

The end of the Civil War was also the end of the major political conflict that had dominated the first seventy-five years of the Republic—*states rights* versus *federal powers.* With unity achieved, rapid national growth began. The resulting economic expansion and the unrestrained growth of giant monopolies created a new demand for government regulation of the economy. The Supreme Court became more active, and judicial power was greatly enlarged. In just nine years (1864–1873), ten acts of Congress were struck down, compared with only two acts in the previous seventy-four years.

Not only was the Court more active, it was also more conservative. In the view of many, the Court became an instrument for protecting the property rights of the rich and ignoring popular demands for government regulation.

In the early twentieth century, the Court found itself up against the growing power of the executive branch. The presidency was widely felt to be the most effective place in the government to regulate the social and economic changes brought about by post-Civil War industrialization. But the Supreme Court continued to resist the expansion of state and federal regulatory power, even though much of the legislation it struck down (such as minimum-wage and child-labor laws) was favored by a majority of the American people. Between 1890 and 1936, the Court declared forty-six laws unconstitutional in full or in part.

Franklin D. Roosevelt finally caused the Court's position to change. While the Constitution does not specify how many members the Supreme Court should have, since 1869 there have been nine justices. Angered by the opposition of the "nine old men" (as he called the members of the Court) to his New Deal programs, Roosevelt sought to "pack" the Court with friendly justices. In 1937 he asked Congress to increase the Court's membership to twelve. Backed by strong public opinion on the issue, however, Congress refused to pass the needed legislation and the idea died. While the legislation was being considered, the Court began to act more favorably toward New Deal programs (known as *the-switch-in-time-that-saved-nine*). Soon vacancies on the Court changed its makeup and philosophy. Under broad interpretations of the Constitution's commerce and welfare clauses, the Court upheld Roosevelt's proposals for regulating the economy and for dealing with the Great Depression. This left the Congress and the executive free to make economic policy without judicial interference.[6]

★ Helping the President

"In this century, all chief justices served as presidential consultants. Taft pursued the broadest range of activities. He helped shape the 1924 Republican party platform and regularly advised Presidents Harding and Coolidge on everything from patronage appointments and judicial reform to military expenditures and legislation. Stone was an intimate adviser of Hoover, joining his 'Medicine Ball Cabinet,' at which policy questions as well as an exercise ball were thrown around.

"... Both the Kennedy and the Johnson administrations came to Warren for advice on judicial appointments and other matters. According to Nixon's White House aide John Ehrlichman, Burger "sent a steady stream of notes and letters to Nixon" in his campaign to reform judicial administration. Ehrlichman also claimed, though both Nixon and Burger deny, that the President and Attorney General Mitchell also sought to keep 'in touch with Burger' and openly discussed with the Chief Justice the pros and cons of issues before the Court."

SOURCE: David M. O'Brien, *Storm Center: The Supreme Court in American Politics* (New York: W. W. Norton and Company, 1986), p. 86.

The Warren Court's decisions were so bold and liberal, especially on civil rights, that calls for Warren's impeachment sprang up, even along the highway.

The Modern Court

Since 1937, Supreme Court decisions have shown three major trends. First, the Court has invalidated much less federal legislation than it had in the previous fifty years. In most of these cases the legislation struck down was not very significant. In a second area, the Court has avoided protecting private property rights. Generally the Court in the last fifty years has not been greatly concerned with guarding economic interests from government policy-making.

A third area in which the Court has shown more positive interest is increased judicial protection for civil liberties. While reducing property rights in importance, the Court has sought to preserve and protect the rights of individuals against the increased powers of the government. First Amendment freedoms of speech, press, religion, and assembly have been developed and expanded by modern Supreme Courts. With Earl Warren as chief justice (1953–1969), the Supreme Court moved in reapportionment, racial discrimination, and the rights of defendants in criminal cases.

The Warren Court (1953–69)

In decisions dealing with *reapportionment,* beginning with *Baker* v. *Carr* (1962), **the Warren Court** established the principle of "one man, one vote" for election districts. The Court ruled that districts should be drawn based on equality of population so that each citizen's vote would count as much as another's. In moving to eliminate *racial discrimination,* the Court was a leading force in cutting away racism in schooling, voting, housing, and the use of public facilities.

Another major interest of the Warren Court's decisions, the rights of criminal defendants, saw the Court throw the protection of the Bill of Rights around people accused of crimes. The Court insisted on an impoverished defendant's basic right to a lawyer; declared that illegally seized evidence cannot be used in state criminal trials; and held that a suspect must be advised of his or her constitutional right to silence, and to have a lawyer, before questioning. This last area, summed up as the *Miranda* decision (*Miranda* v. *Arizona,* 1966), is familiar to all fans of television detective series.

The Burger Court (1969–86)

The Supreme Court under Warren Burger was less activist than the Warren Court, but not as conservative as some had expected. On the liberal side, **the Burger Court** legalized abortions, declined to stop publication of the Pentagon Papers (official papers discussing plans for the Vietnam War unofficially leaked to the press), and limited capital punishment. The Burger Court also outlawed wiretapping of domestic groups without a court warrant and declined to interfere with massive busing designed to integrate schools in cities such as Boston and Los Angeles.

In more conservative directions, the Burger Court allowed local communities, within limits, to define obscenity and ban works considered pornographic. Perhaps the most important changes the Burger Court made in the precedents set under Chief Justice Warren were in the rights of the accused. Here the Court allowed the police broader powers in searching without a warrant—deciding, for example, that persons detained on minor charges (like traffic violations) may be searched for evidence of more serious crimes (like possession of drugs). The Court also permitted some illegally obtained information to be used at a trial and the police to continue their questioning after a suspect has claimed the right of silence. The Miranda decision still remains in effect.[7]

The Rehnquist Court (1986–   )

Many of these rulings aroused opposition. The 1986 appointment of William Rehnquist as chief justice came from the Reagan administration's wish for a more conservative, more restrained court. **The Rehnquist Court,** while clearly tending in a conservative direction, has less dramatically broken with the past than many predicted. In some areas like civil liberties (including the 1989 ruling allowing flag burning) the Court has zigged and zagged with little of the clear direction Rehnquist's Republican backers had hoped for (see the box on

Flag burning, and whether it should be prohibited by law, became an issue of controversy in 1989. Here, people in New York City burn flags on July 4, 1989.

Printed by permission of Mike Luckovich and Creators Syndicate.

page 473). In other instances like the 1988 case upholding the independent counsel that was prosecuting several Reagan appointees, the Court clearly disappointed the Reagan administration. After reviewing Rehnquist's first two years, a reporter for *The New York Times* concluded that the " . . . Administration has lost more of the political blockbuster cases than it has won."[8]

In part this may be a premature assessment of a Court that is likely to become increasingly conservative as its aging liberal members die or retire. In areas of civil rights, for example, the Court has clearly shifted to the right and greater restrictions on abortions appear to be coming. Any signs of moderation may also reflect the change in Rehnquist, who as an Associate Justice for fourteen years was often a lone conservative dissenter on cases. As chief justice, he now needs to play a role as team leader in moving very independent justices toward consensus on very divisive issues. That means he must compromise and persuade in order to lead the Court. Until more justices are appointed who share Rehnquist's philosophy, this is likely to mean shifting alliances and seemingly inconsistent decisions.

STRENGTHS AND WEAKNESSES OF THE SUPREME COURT

The United States Supreme Court has often been called "the least dangerous branch of government." Despite its great power of judicial review, the Court is clearly the weakest of the three branches. It must depend on the other parts of the government to enforce its decisions. Its authority to cancel actions of the other branches of the federal government is in fact seldom used and strictly limited. These limits are found both within the Court and in the political system as a whole.

Internal Limits on the Court

Most of the limits on the power of the Court are found within the judicial system, in the traditional practices of the Court. For one thing, a long-held interpretation of the Constitution requires that an *actual case* be presented to the Court for it to exercise judicial review. The Court cannot take the lead in declaring laws unconstitutional. It cannot give advisory opinions. It must wait for a real controversy, brought by someone actually injured under the law to make its way through the lower courts, meaning that years may pass after a law is put on the books before the Court can rule on it. (The Supreme Court's Dred Scott decision struck down the Missouri Compromise passed an exceptionally long thirty-seven years before.)

★ Presidents and the Court

Despite the advice they may render presidents, Supreme Court justices have a way of disappointing the president appointing them. President Eisenhower was so angered at Chief Justice Earl Warren's rulings that he called Warren's appointment "the biggest damn-fool mistake I ever made." The controversy set off by the Warren Court's activism led President Nixon to appoint Warren Burger as chief justice to replace Earl Warren when he retired in 1969. Nixon hoped Burger would inspire greater political restraint in the Court. But the Burger Court, in *U.S. v. Nixon* (1974), ruled that President Nixon had to surrender the White House tapes of his often-illegal conversations to the special Watergate prosecutor. The president, who resigned shortly afterward, was certainly not pleased by this clear example of the strength and independence of the Court.

Another important limit on the Court's actions is the practice that the Court will not attempt to resolve **political questions.** A political question is an issue on which the Constitution or laws give final say to another branch of government, or one the Court feels it lacks the capability to solve. Political questions often crop up in foreign relations. The justices of the Court lack important secret information; they are not experts in diplomacy; and they recognize the dominance of the presidency over the conduct of foreign affairs. Consequently, the current Court recently used the doctrine of political questions to avoid deciding cases concerning U.S. efforts in El Salvador.

The Court has narrowed or expanded its definition of a political question at various times. For many years, the Court used this doctrine of political questions as grounds for refusing to consider reapportionment of state legislatures and congressional districts. In 1962, however, the Court reversed its position and forced state legislatures to draw boundaries to create districts with more nearly equal populations. A political question, then, can almost be whatever issue the Supreme Court wants to avoid.

Just as the Court attempts to avoid political questions, so too it often *avoids constitutional issues.* The Court hesitates to decide a case on the basis of a constitutional question unless there is no other way to dispose of the case. The Court usually will not declare a law unconstitutional unless it sees a clear violation of the Constitution.

Thousands of demonstrators show their support for abortion during a rally on the Capitol grounds in April 1989.

In general, the Court will assume that a law is valid unless proved otherwise. Although we have stressed the role of the Court in applying the Constitution, the vast majority of cases it decides deal with interpretation of less-important federal and state laws.

A final internal limit on the Court is that of *precedent.* As has been shown, the Court generally follows previous Court decisions in cases involving the same issue. Although the Court has reversed past decisions, it often tries to be consistent with precedent even when changing the law. In the 1989 abortion case, *Webster* v. *Reproductive Health Services,* the Supreme Court did not reverse *Roe* v. *Wade* but instead modified it to allow some restrictions on abortions.

What these and the other limits on the Court's power mean is that the Court actually avoids most of the constitutional questions pressed upon it. For both political and legal reasons the Court will often duck an issue that is too controversial, on which the law is uncertain, or about which no political consensus has formed. It may simply not hear the case, or it may decide it for reasons other than the major issue involved. Knowing the difficulty of enforcing a ruling against strong public opinion, the Court generally seeks to avoid such a confrontation. This self-imposed restraint may make the use of judicial review scattered and delayed. But one can argue that *the Court has maintained its great authority by refusing in most instances to use its power of judicial review.*

External Limits on the Court

The Court is also limited by the duties the Constitution gives to other parts of the government, especially to Congress. Congress has the right to set when and how often the Court will meet, to establish the number of justices, and to limit the Court's jurisdiction. This last power has been used when Congress wished to avoid judicial involvement. For example, the bill establishing the Alaska pipeline excluded the Court from exercising jurisdiction (on possible damage to the environment) under the Environmental Protection Act. Also, Congress may pass legislation so detailed that it limits the Court's scope in interpreting the law. Finally, the Senate has the duty of approving the president's nominations to the bench which, as in the Bork confirmation, can allow the Senate to shape the political complexion of the Court. Congress has the seldom-used power to impeach Supreme Court justices.

These limits on the Court reflect the very real weaknesses of that body. With no army or bureaucracy to enforce its decisions, the court must depend on other parts of the government and all the political players to accept and carry out its decisions. (President

Andrew Jackson, violently disagreeing with a Supreme Court decision, once remarked: "John Marshall has rendered his decision; now let him enforce it!") Yet with few exceptions, the Court's decisions have been enforced and accepted. And when opposed, this weak and semi-isolated branch of government has been able to overcome resistance. Why?

Strengths of the Court

The major political strengths of the Court lie in its enormous prestige; the fragmented nature of the American constitutional structure; and the American legal profession, which acts in many ways as the Court's constituency.

The Court's *prestige* is unquestionable. Public opinion polls have shown repeatedly that the position of a judge is one of the most respected in our society. This respect is due not only to the generally high quality of the people who become judges, but also to the judicial process itself. Anyone who has seen a court in action is aware of the aspects of theater in the legal process: the judge sitting on a raised platform dressed in robes; the formal speeches addressed to "your honor"; the use of Latin phrases; the oath on the Bible. All create a heavy impression of dignity and solemnity, which often masks the fact that a judge is simply a public administrator judging controversies. The Supreme Court, which presides over this judicial system, has added prestige because it is seen as the guardian of the Constitution and often is equated with that document in people's eyes.

Another strength of the Court lies in the *fragmented nature of the American system of government.* With separation of powers among the branches of the federal government, and federalism dividing power between the states and federal government, conflict is inevitable. This division of power creates a need for an *umpire,* and the Court largely fills this role.

In acting as an umpire, however, the Court is hardly neutral. Its decisions are political (they determine who gets what, when, and how), and to enforce them it needs political support. The other political players might not give this support to decisions they strongly disagree with. Consequently, the Court's rulings generally reflect the practices and values of the country's major political forces. As an umpire, the Court enforces the constitutional rules of the game as practiced by the most powerful players.

A final source of support for the Court is the *legal profession.* There are only some 600,000 lawyers in the United States. Yet lawyers occupy all the major judicial positions, and more lawyers than any other occupational group hold offices in national, state, and city

★ The Court's Porno Movies

"The Justices take their obligation to research opinions so seriously that in one area of law—obscenity—the result has led to a lot of snickering both on and off the bench. Since 1957, the Court has tried repeatedly to define obscenity. The subject has become so familiar at the Supreme Court building that a screening room has been set up in the basement for the Justices and their clerks to watch the dirty movies submitted as exhibits in obscenity cases. Justice Douglas never goes to the dirty movies because he thinks all expression—obscene or not—is protected by the First Amendment. And Chief Justice Burger rarely, if ever, goes because he is offended by the stuff. But everyone else shows up from time to time.

"Justice Blackmun watches in what clerks describe as 'a near-catatonic state.' Justice Marshall usually laughs his way through it all.... The late Justice Harlan used dutifully to attend the Court's porno flicks even though he was virtually blind; Justice Stewart would sit next to Harlan and narrate for him, explaining what was going on in each scene. Once every few minutes, Harlan would exclaim in his proper way, 'By George, extraordinary!'"

SOURCE: Nina Totenberg, "Behind the Marble, Beneath the Robes," *The New York Times Magazine,* March 16, 1975. Copyright © 1975 by The New York Times Company. Reprinted by permission.

governments. The *American Bar Association (ABA),* with about half the lawyers in the country as members, represents the legal profession. The ABA reviews nominees to the bench, and its comments on a candidate's fitness greatly influence whether he or she is appointed. The legal profession, through the ABA, has generally supported the Court. For example, it opposed bills to curb the Court for its liberal civil liberties decisions. Because of their own commitment to law, as well as some similarity in educational and social backgrounds, lawyers generally back the Court.

The Court as a Political Institution

It should be clear by now that the Supreme Court is a *political institution* that sets national policy by interpreting the law. In applying the Constitution to the cases before it, the Court clearly makes political choices. In arriving at decisions on controversial questions of national policy, the Court's procedures may be legal; its decisions may be phrased in lawyers' language, but it is fulfilling an important political role.

"We are under the Constitution, but the Constitution is what the judges say it is," declared former Chief Justice Charles Evans Hughes. In interpreting the meaning of the Constitution, each

Supreme Court must operate within the political climate of its time. *The justices not only read the Constitution, they read the newspapers as well.* The Court cannot ignore the reaction to its decisions in Congress or in the nation, because its influence ultimately rests on the acceptance of these decisions by political and public opinion. Nor, generally, are the Court's opinions long out of line with the dominant views in the legislative and executive branches.

Judicial Activism versus Judicial Restraint

The question of how the political and legal power of the Court should be applied has centered on the use of judicial review. Should judicial authority be active or restrained? How far should the Court go in shaping policy when it may conflict with other branches of the government? The two sides of this debate are reflected in the competing practices of *judicial restraint* and *judicial activism.*

Judicial restraint is the idea that the Court should not impose its views on other branches of the government or on the states unless there is a clear violation of the Constitution. Judicial restraint (often called self-restraint) calls for a passive role in which the Court lets the other branches of government lead the way in setting policy on controversial political issues. The Court intervenes in these issues only with great reluctance. Felix Frankfurter and Oliver Wendell Holmes, Jr., are two of the more famous Supreme Court justices identified with judicial restraint. Frankfurter often argued that social improvement should be left to more appropriate parts of the federal and state governments. The Court, he declared, should avoid conflicts with other branches of the federal government whenever possible.

Judicial activism is the view that the Supreme Court should be an active, creative partner with the legislative and executive branches in shaping government policy. Judicial activists seek to apply the Court's authority to solving economic and political problems ignored by other parts of the government. In this view the Court is more than an umpire of the American political game: it is an active participant as well. The Supreme Court under Earl Warren for the most part practiced judicial activism. In its rulings on reapportionment, school desegregation, and defendants' rights, the Warren Court broadly and boldly changed national policy.[9]

It is important not to confuse judicial activism versus restraint with liberal versus conservative. Today's Rehnquist Court claims to be both restrained and conservative, believing that judges should defer to the elected branches on questions of policy. (There's an argument that the Court was more restrained in dealing with a Republi-

Chief Justice William Rehnquist (at left) is noted for his policy of judicial restraint. The justification for judicial restraint is that it leaves power in the hands of elected officials. Critics of present-day judicial restraint often charge that it is merely a cover for supporting conservative policies.

can administration than a Democratic Congress.) Although most of the recent activist justices, such as Earl Warren and Thurgood Marshall, have taken liberal positions on issues like school integration and toleration of dissent, this wasn't always so. John Marshall's court was both activist (in establishing judicial review) and conservative (in protecting private property rights). And it was the activist, *conservative* Supreme Court during the 1930s that attempted to strike down most of Franklin D. Roosevelt's New Deal program as unconstitutional. On the other side, justices Frankfurter and Holmes were political liberals. Yet both believed it was not wise for the Court to dive into the midst of political battles to support policies they may have personally backed.

PARTICIPANTS IN THE JUDICIAL SYSTEM

While the Supreme Court stands on top of the judicial system, it hardly stands alone. Those in the system all have something to do with the outcomes. And they may alter decisions or make enforcement of decisions difficult if not impossible.

In some ways a courtroom contest is similar to a boxing match. In boxing there are two fighters in a ring. Each fighter has one or more "seconds," advisers and trainers. A neutral referee enforces the rules, and judges award the decision to one of the fighters. In a lawsuit, the formal participants are similar. Litigants, the actual parties to the lawsuit, are like the fighters in the ring. The lawyers are similar to the seconds. The judge is comparable to the referee, or, if there is no jury, the fight judges. A boxing match also has informal participants. Most notably, there is an audience; in a lawsuit, public opinion also plays some role. There are reporters at boxing matches; the media is involved in lawsuits too. Each fighter has interested backers (financial or otherwise); in lawsuits, interest groups can also play a part.

Litigants, Cops, and Robbers

The litigants start the system in motion. In a criminal case, the state or federal government brings a charge against the *accused* or the *defendant.* In a civil case, the person who brings the action is the *plaintiff.* The person against whom the action is brought is the *defendant.* These are the **litigants.**

Theoretically, the courts are open to everyone. In reality, many people cannot gain access to our judicial system because they cannot afford it. Court cases are expensive; so are experienced lawyers. Consequently, most Americans do not go into court to settle their disputes or protect their rights.

The civil law courts are used primarily by middle-class Americans, while criminal law defendants are mostly poor people. Crimes of violence and against property are most numerous among young males who are poor or members of minority groups. They make up a large percentage of the unemployed in any area, they often live in crowded conditions, and they frequently feel that they are the victims of discrimination. This is an explosive combination. Thus, in urban courts, most of the felony defendants are from the lower-income classes, while the administrators of the justice system are usually middle-class whites.[10]

This difference between criminal defendants and administrators begins with the arresting officers. Police officers often fill dangerous roles that are frequently not well defined. They make policy, because they have considerable discretion in deciding whether to make an arrest and on what charge. Minorities may feel considerable hostility toward local police officers because to them the police are symbols of the power and discrimination of the dominant society. Efforts have been made to increase the minority members on police forces, but progress has been somewhat slow.[11]

Lawyers

Our judicial system requires experts. A litigant must be represented by a licensed attorney unless the party chooses to represent himself or herself personally, which is unusual. The legal process is complicated and most people turn to professionals to guide them through it. Americans spend over $35 billion annually for lawyers and their support staff. One observer was moved to say that "we Americans have more faith in laws, regulations, and litigation . . . than any society on earth." Certainly Americans depend more on law and lawyers than other countries. There are twenty-five times as many lawyers for each American as for each Japanese. This may have something to do with the fact that 120 million Japanese filed 362,000 lawsuits in one year, while 240 million Americans filed 13.2 million.[12] (See the box on page 481.)

The professional nature of the judicial system limits citizen access. A person does not need to hire a lawyer to approach a governor or a member of Congress. But a lawyer is nearly always essential to seek the assistance of the court. Judicial assistance cannot be sought informally; it can only be secured in the formal forum provided by the law—the courtroom—following established legal procedures.

Practicing lawyers in America are called *the bar* because they are admitted within the low rail, or "bar," in a courtroom, while the public must remain outside. In most states a lawyer must belong to a

635 ROBBERIES IN THE DISTRICT OF COLUMBIA

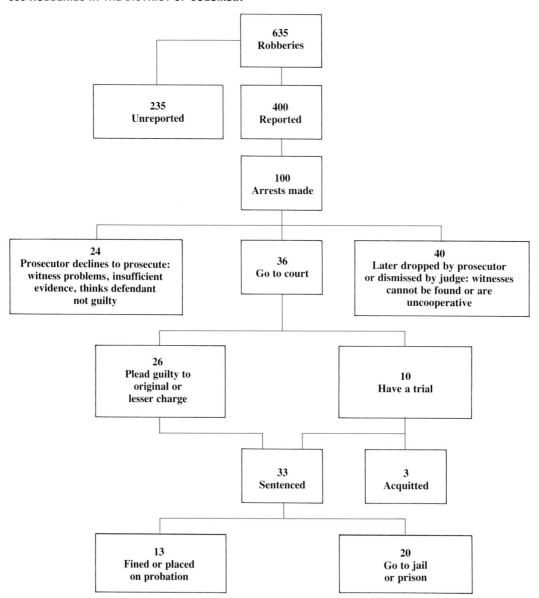

SOURCE: From Charles H. McCaghy, *Crime in American Society* (New York: Macmillan, 1980), p. 43. Derived from National Criminal Justice Information and Statistics Service, *Criminal Victimization Surveys in 13 American Cities* (Washington, D.C.: U.S. Department of Justice, 1975), p. 250; and "'Revolving Door Justice': Why Criminals Go Free," *U.S. News and World Report* (May 10, 1976), pp. 36–40. Cited in Mitchell S. G. Klein, *Law, Courts, and Policy* (Englewood Cliffs, N.J.: Prentice-Hall, 1984), p. 228.

state bar association in order to practice in the state courts. Lawyers are bound by professional codes that bar associations have developed. They are required to observe the confidentiality of the "lawyer-client relationship"; they cannot reveal what their clients say to them. They must avoid conflicts of interest—that is, they cannot represent one party in a lawsuit when they have a conflicting tie to an opposing party. Lawyers who violate the professional code can be "disbarred" by their state bar association, which means that they can no longer practice law. Bar associations not only police their membership, they also act as interest groups. They lobby state and local governments for laws that are favorable to lawyers and, presumably, to the system of justice.

Attorneys in private practice make up about 70 percent of the practicing lawyers in America. Most private lawyers are either partners in a law firm or employees of such a firm. Government lawyers work for local, state, or federal agencies. The federal government alone employs nearly 20,000 lawyers. The Justice Department is the principal federal employer of government lawyers because it is the main law office of the general public. The Justice Department includes the office of the *U.S. solicitor general,* who represents the federal government in appellate cases.

At least one *U.S. district attorney* (D.A.) is located in each state, the number depending on the state's size. U.S. attorneys are responsible for prosecuting federal crimes in their districts. They are nom-

★ Lawyers: How Many Are Too Many?

	LAWYERS		JUDGES	
	TOTAL	PER 100,000 PEOPLE	TOTAL	PER 100,000 PEOPLE
Japan	13,200	11	2,000	2
U.S.	655,000	279	27,800	12
Britain	64,100	114	28,200	50
W. Germany	47,300	77	17,000	28
France	15,800	29	4,350	8

Notes: All figures as of April 1986. Figures for judges in the United States include both federal and state judges.
SOURCE: *The Economist,* August 22, 1987, p. 32.

inated by the president and confirmed by the Senate. If senators in a state are in the same party as the president, they will usually exercise control over the appointment of a U.S. district attorney via "senatorial courtesy." Younger attorneys who hope to use the visibility of the office to launch political careers often seek these appointments.

The U.S. Supreme Court has held that, in both state and federal courts, a person charged with a crime that may result in jail is entitled to free legal counsel if he or she cannot afford to hire a lawyer.[13] Most large cities have "public defender" offices that are paid for with public funds. In rural areas, private lawyers are frequently hired to represent particular criminal defendants. In civil cases, poor people may obtain representation from legal aid offices, which are privately funded as charities. The federal government provides the *Legal Services Corporation* for free services in civil matters. Many established law firms encourage their lawyers to offer free *pro bono* service to people having difficulty affording legal representation. This is an effort at a wider distribution of services by the bar and reflects a professional ethic toward lawyers' social obligations. Still, in civil cases less than half of the people who need legal assistance actually get it. In criminal cases, the representation is often less effective than it would be if clients were able to hire a private lawyer.[14]

Public-interest lawyers who specialize in civil liberties, consumer problems, and environmental protection, such as the American Civil Liberties Union (ACLU) and Ralph Nader, perform a variety of functions. Some focus on making governmental commissions and agencies perform their jobs more responsibly. They often use legal actions not only to settle particular disputes, but also to mobilize public opinion to affect government policy-making outside the courts. Conservative law groups have formed legal foundations to battle existing liberal institutions. The Mountain States Legal Foundation fought environmental regulations, while the Capital Legal Foundation helped people bring cases against the media networks.

Judges

Judges exercise considerable discretion in determining the facts (when there is no jury), in assessing the facts, and in applying the law. Thus, who the judges are is important to how the system works.

All federal judges are nominated by the president and confirmed by the Senate. Before a judicial appointment is sent to the Senate, the nomination goes through several steps. If a senator in the state of the appointment is in the same party as the president, *senatorial courtesy* comes into play. As a rule, the U.S. Senate will not approve a nomination unless the relevant senator or senators support it. A federal district judgeship is a prestigious position. Like other federal judicial appointments, it is for life and greatly prized by lawyers. Most senators take an active part in recommending judicial appointments to presidents of their own party. They often use this as a reward to important supporters. (See the box on page 484.)

Jimmy Carter attempted to establish a system for choosing federal judges based on merit. This system, however, worked far better at the appellate level than at the district-court level, where the traditional senatorial patronage system continues to have strong influence. The Carter system did result in the appointment of more women and blacks—and liberals. President Reagan also advocated a merit system for appointing federal district judges, but allowed local U.S. senators of his own party to select them. He disbanded Carter's commission for the selection of the circuit-court judges.

After the local recommendation is determined, the names of the people being considered for a federal judicial appointment are subjected to two screening processes—one official and one private. Official screening of each prospective nominee is performed by the Federal Bureau of Investigation. The FBI makes a written report regarding the nominee's background that is available to the president, the Attorney General, and the Senate Judiciary Committee. This screening process is intended to eliminate people with questionable morals or associations. As shown in the Bork case, it may also remove people that a majority of the Senate finds have questionable politics (see the case study in Chapter 11).

The American Bar Association (ABA) conducts the private screening. A committee of the ABA looks into the qualifications of potential nominees. A finding by the ABA that a nominee is not qualified will nearly always block the nomination. This screening power of the American Bar Association, a private organization, has been criticized on the grounds that the ABA is an elite unrepresentative group.

The same factors that influence the appointment of Supreme Court justices—professional qualifications and political, representational, and ideological considerations—also have an impact on the nomination and confirmation of other federal judges. Of Jimmy Carter's federal judiciary appointees, for example, 97.8 percent were of Carter's own party. Congress can change the number of federal judgeships and can create new federal courts. When the president and a majority of the Senate are of the same party, pressure exists to create new positions, sometimes called "jobs for the boys." In 1978, for example, with a Democrat in the White House and a Democratic majority in the Senate, Congress passed an act creating 152 new federal judgeships, the largest one-time increase in history. In any eight-year period, a president is able to appoint about half of the sitting federal judges.

At the state level, judges are elected in twenty-two states, and in ten of these the elections are "nonpartisan." In a few states, the legislature selects the judges; in eight states the governor makes the appointment. Even in states where judges are elected, governors may play a dominant role by being able to make interim appointments to fill vacancies. A growing number of states use a system of merit selection. The selection process usually involves a nominating commission of lawyers, who recommend a list from which the state governor may choose. Under this "Missouri Plan," judges who are appointed—and in some other states, those who are elected, too—do not run for reelection against an opponent. Instead, they are simply required to submit themselves to the electorate for a "vote of confidence." A no-confidence vote results in removal from office.[15]

Informal Participants

Interest groups may participate informally in the judicial process in a number of ways. They may finance a **test case**—an action brought by an individual to test a law or a public official's acts. The NAACP used this tactic to great advantage during the 1950s and 1960s. This kind of activity lessens the passive, reactive nature of the courts by bringing up cases the courts are forced to decide. Interest groups also frequently file *amicus curiae* briefs with permission of the court involved. These Latin words mean "friend of the court," and they refer to groups who are not actual litigants but who may be affected by the outcome of the case and therefore wish to comment on the issues involved. Finally, interest groups often publish articles in legal journals. By publicizing legal positions they favor, groups hope to affect "professional opinion" and gain acceptance for their views among lawyers and judges.

It is unusual for public opinion to have a direct effect on judicial decisions, and this relationship cannot usually be proved.[16] But public opinion can certainly affect judicial decision making indirectly, as in the case of busing in Richmond, Virginia. Members of the executive and legislative branches are directly affected by public opinion, especially through elections. When these elected officials select judges, their choices may reflect public attitudes. Further, courts and judges have great difficulty enforcing their decisions in the face of strongly opposing public opinion.

The media can also influence the judicial process. Inflammatory news reports about a criminal case may influence jurors toward conviction. A biased or incomplete report of a decision can also affect public opinion and, thus, the degree to which people may comply with the decision.

Obeying the Law

Law (and the judicial system that uses it) operates with a blend of legitimacy and force. The legitimacy of the courts lies in the symbolism of the law in general and the Constitution in particular. The authority of government is visible in a unique way in the majesty and theatre of a court (such as the robed judge sitting on a raised platform and the use of Latin phrases). The force behind the courts lies in the police powers of the state: the threats of loss of property, prison, and even death. But *law may not always work.*

In the Prohibition Era of the 1920s, an amendment to the Constitution (the Eighteenth) outlawed the sale or consumption of alcohol. Yet this ran counter to the social habits of so many people that the law was soon widely ignored. The case study on busing shows the limits of law in bringing about social change. Its success depends on the support for the law in the community where it is being applied, and on the incentives or sanctions that authorities can bring to enforce it. The law itself may be ambiguous because of the political coalitions, both in the courts and the legislatures, needed to pass a law or render a decision in the first place.

Gaining compliance with a controversial law is surrounded by politics. And, like most political activities, the eventual impact of a law or a judicial decision remains uncertain.

Government agents seized enormous quantities of illegal beer and liquor during the Prohibition Era. Here, agents dump a number of barrels of beer into Lake Michigan.

★ CASE STUDY

Enforcing Court Decisions: Busing in Richmond

When the Supreme Court of the United States issues a decision, it often generates as many conflicts as it resolves. Nowhere is this more true than in civil rights.

School Segregation in Virginia

Soon after Robert R. Merhige took office in 1967 as a U.S. District Court Judge for the Eastern District of Virginia, he was given responsibility for overseeing the city of Richmond's plan to desegregate its school system. There was one major stumbling block. Richmond officials didn't want to integrate.[17]

Their game plan was simple. As each of their new "integration" plans were thrown out by federal courts, city and state officials would set up a new plan to "comply" with the court. Most recently community leaders had established private schools to avoid integration. The state legislature helped by providing tuition grants for these white-only schools.

The problem for Judge Merhige was that the Supreme Court had only given him the authority to overturn proposals that failed to end segregation. Merhige lacked the power to issue his own affirmative proposals to effectively integrate the schools. But Merhige would soon get this power.

Frustrated by the slow pace of school integration in Virginia, several leading civil rights lawyers challenged Virginia's latest proposed method to achieve school integration: the so-called *freedom-of-choice* plan. Under the freedom-of-choice system, black students were free to attend formerly white-only schools. However, since so many white public schools had been closed in favor of white-only private schools, civil rights lawyers argued the freedom-of-choice system should be overturned.

The Supreme Court agreed in 1968. The Court instructed the District Courts "to take whatever steps might be necessary to convert to a unitary system in which racial discrimination would be eliminated

root and branch." In Richmond, this "affirmative duty" fell on Judge Merhige.

School Busing in Richmond: Round One

One immediate problem facing the judge was that school was set to open in a few weeks yet no one could agree on the best way to integrate the schools. On one side, the Richmond School Board was proposing to expand the number of "neighborhood schools." Opposing the Board, civil rights leaders supported an extensive busing program. In their view, the school board's plans to rely on neighborhood schools to integrate a city with rigidly segregated neighborhoods was just another delaying tactic.

While agreeing that the city's plan was "totally inadequate", Merhige was uncomfortable with imposing widespread busing. Merhige wanted to strike a balance between the Supreme Court's mandate to do what is "effective" and the community's reluctance to do

Black students board a bus in Richmond.

Busing: Round Two

Judge Merhige knew that his "interim" busing plan for the 1970 school year was only a first step toward integration. The next step—an expansion of the city's busing program—meant a new round of public objections and perhaps violence. But there was another problem: white flight to the suburbs was quickly turning Richmond into a largely black community. Almost 40 percent of Richmond's white students had "disappeared" in two years. By April, 1971, Richmond had become two-thirds black.

In light of this situation, Judge Merhige began to examine a new integration plan—consolidating all the region's schools. The idea was simple. To achieve effective integration—what the Supreme Court had instructed him to do—the available "pool" of white and black students had to be expanded. Busing would take place across city-county borders. On January 10, 1972, the Judge directed Richmond and two neighboring counties to consolidate and integrate their school districts.

Reaction to Merhige's decision was predictable. Opponents argued that a federal judge lacked the authority to redraw state political boundaries, and questioned whether judges should engage in such vast and unpopular social

anything. Judge Merhige felt that he should "proceed slowly in order to give the community time to adjust."

Thus, Merhige decided to reject the radical busing plan proposed by the civil rights leaders in favor of a less extensive "interim" busing arrangement. His more limited approach also made sense given that the opening day of school was in two weeks. Yet Merhige's more moderate approach did nothing to win him support among busing opponents in Richmond. White community leaders called for his impeachment. The *Richmond News Leader,* one of Merhige's most persistent critics, suggested that his background and conduct be investigated.

Merhige recognized that *a good deal of the criticism was political showmanship.* It was easier for local politicians who privately supported desegregation to let Merhige be the fall guy than to take the heat themselves. Local leaders, Merhige recalled, "asked me to understand that they must offer public opposition for political reasons."

Less easy for Judge Merhige to contend with was the rising tide of personal attacks leveled against him. Death threats against the judge, his wife, and his young son began soon after his first busing decision. His guest house was burned to the ground. Despite a number of crank calls, he refused to take his name out of the phone book. He did, however, move his family out of Richmond and returned to the case.

planning. White suburbanites—many of whom had moved out of Richmond to escape city-wide busing—were not ready to welcome a federally mandated "invasion" of urban blacks. The *Richmond Times-Dispatch* termed Merhige's opinion "a nauseating mixture of vacuous sociological theories." Once again, Merhige found himself the target of death threats. The judge held his ground. He challenged his opponents, "We are not afraid . . . [because the threats] are not going to change one single thing, whether it's me or any other judge." But Judge Merhige was wrong about the other judges.

Merhige is Reversed

Merhige's opponents felt confident that they could win an appeal before the Fourth Circuit Court of Appeals—the Appeals Court had historically been less activist than the Judge in civil rights cases. They also expected that the Supreme Court would uphold Merhige. After all, the Supreme Court had strongly rebuked Virginia officials in recent school desegregation cases. Thus, while pursuing their appeal, local school officials began preparing for the coming consolidation.

The 4th Circuit did overturn Merhige's decision as expected, but the Supreme Court did not reverse the Appeals Court. Justice Lewis F. Powell,

Jr., because he was a former Richmond School Board member, disqualified himself from the case. The Supreme Court ended up deadlocked on the consolidation plan (four for and four against). Therefore, the Appeals Court judgment stood.

Soon after, in 1973, another case came before the Supreme Court posing the same question as the Richmond case. Faced with white flight to the suburbs and an inferior inner-city black school system, a Federal District Judge in Detroit had ordered the busing of students across existing school district boundaries. He reasoned (as did Merhige) that such boundaries "are simply matters of political conve-

nience and may not be used to deny constitutional rights."

This time the High Court responded with a firm, although close, decision on the case. By a 5–4 vote, the Supreme Court overturned the Detroit consolidation plan. A changed court, bolstered by five conservative Nixon appointments made since 1969, had sent a clear message: lower court judges had taken integration too far. Affirmative action—to redress past civil wrongs—indeed had its political (and legal) limits.

Although defeated in his attempt to consolidate Richmond-area schools, Merhige did retain control over integration of the city school system. Eventually, the community

These students are being bused across school district boundaries in an attempt to desegragate Richmond.

accepted that busing at least within the city's borders would not go away, in part because of the Judge's continued oversight.

Judge Merhige's role in the case finally ended in 1987. Finding no "overt vestiges" of segregationist intent, Judge Merhige surrendered control of busing back to the city's School Board. He noted that the program had achieved as much integration as possible given the city's predominantly black population.

Conclusion

The integration of schools taking place under a constitutional mandate has been swayed and often halted by political constraints. Public opinion does, and some would say should, change the judiciary's interpretation of the law of the land. Faced with local resistence, even a determined local judge like Merhige had to moderate his enforcement of Supreme Court decisions. And public opinion indirectly changed the nature of these decisions through the influence of politics over the appointments of justices.

This case of Richmond's schools illustrates the process. Busing for integration had to be implemented by a judge battling local political forces as well as a changing judiciary. The results, as Judge Merhige found, were often inconsistent and incomplete, reflecting national and local political choices made by courts and others.

WRAP-UP

The English philosopher Thomas Hobbes once described life without government and laws as "solitary, poore, nasty, brutish, and short." Society needs law. Law, in turn, needs government, and specifically, a judicial system, through which it is applied.

At the peak of the American judiciary sits the U.S. Supreme Court. Established by the Constitution, the Court is unique in the world in its ability to overturn the acts of popularly elected officials. Judicial review frequently places the Supreme Court and the courts below it in the middle of political battles. From civil rights to abortion, the courts have been deeply involved in shaping national policies. The restraints placed by law and practice as well as the activities of other participants have served to limit the Court's powers in controversial situations, as shown in the Richmond busing case.

Whatever the political limits on the power of the judiciary, the courts will continue as a major player. In a federal system of divided powers there is a great need for a referee to resolve disputes. The courts fill this role. In a constitutional system where laws are looked to as guides for action, there is a need to adapt traditional words to modern situations. The courts will fill this role. And in a political system where the demands of the poor and the weak are not always heard, there is a need for legally protected access to decision makers. Here, too, the courts play a role. These judicial roles will also continue to be filled with an eye to the political forces dominating the other branches of government.

Key Terms

civil law (p. 459)
criminal law (p. 459)
constitutional law (p. 459)
statutory law (p. 459)
administrative law (p. 459)
judge-made law (p. 459)
common law (p. 460)
equity (p. 460)
jurisdiction (p. 460)
federalism (p. 460)
misdemeanor (p. 461)

felony (p. 461)
judicial review (p. 466)
national supremacy (p. 466)
the Warren Court (p. 470)
the Burger Court (p. 470)
the Rehnquist Court (p. 471)
political questions (p. 473)
judicial restraint (p. 477)
judicial activism (p. 477)
litigants (p. 478)
test case (p. 484)

Suggested Readings

Baum, Lawrence, *The Supreme Court,* 2nd ed. (Washington, D.C.: Congressional Quarterly Press, 1985).

Black, Hugo, and Elizabeth Black, *Mr. Justice and Mrs. Black* (New York: Random House, 1986).

Carp, Robert A., and C. K. Rowland, *Policymaking and Politics in the Federal District Courts* (Knoxville, Tenn.: University of Tennessee Press, 1983).

Cox, Archibald, *The Warren Court* (Cambridge, Mass: Harvard University Press, 1968).

Schwartz, Herman, *Packing the Court: The Conservative Attempt to Rewrite the Constitution* (New York: Charles Scribners Sons, 1988).

Tribe, Lawrence, *God Save This Honorable Court: How the Choice of Justices Shapes Our History* (New York: Random House, 1985).

Wishman, Seymour, *Anatomy of a Jury: The System on Trial* (New York: Penguin, 1987).

Endnotes

[1] David M. O'Brien, *Storm Center: The Supreme Court in American Politics* (New York: W. W. Norton and Company, 1986).

[2] David W. Rhode and Harold G. Spaeth, *Supreme Court Decision Making* (San Francisco: Freeman, 1976), p. 2.

[3] Much of this discussion is based on Herbert Jacob, *Law and Politics in the United States* (Boston: Little, Brown and Company, 1986), Chapter One, "Law and Politics."

[4] Material for this section is taken from George F. Cole, ed., *Criminal Justice: Law and Politics,* 3rd edition (North Scituate, MA: Duxbury Press, 1980).

[5] For stories on the Supreme Court's discussions, see Bob Woodward and Scott Armstrong, *The Brethren: Inside the Supreme Court* (New York: Simon and Schuster, 1979).

[6] See Raoul Berger, *Federalism: The Founders' Design* (Norman, Oklahoma: University of Oklahoma Press, 1987), Chapters 5 and 6.

[7] See Herman Schwartz, ed., *The Burger Years* (New York: Viking, 1987).

[8] Stuart Taylor, Jr., "Rehnquist's Court: Tuning Out the White House," *The New York Times Magazine,* September 11, 1988, pp. 38–41, 94–98.

[9] For an activist judge's discussion of the concepts, see J. Skelly Wright, "Public School Deregulation," in Norman Dorsen, ed., *The Evolving Constitution* (Middletown, CT: Wesleyan University Press, 1987), pp. 44–65.

[10] See Jerold S. Auerbach, *Unequal Justice* (New York: Oxford University Press, 1977).

[11] For a good fictional account of interaction between law-enforcement officials and minorities, see Tom Wolfe, *Bonfire of the Vanities.*

[12] *The Economist,* August 22, 1987, p. 32.

[13] See Anthony Lewis, *Gideon's Trumpet* (New York: Vintage, 1966).

[14] Jacob, *Justice in America* (Boston: Little, Brown and Company, 1984), pp. 73–75.

[15] Sheldon Goldman, "Judicial Selection" in Robert J. Janosik, ed., *Encyclopedia of the American Judicial System* (New York: Scribner's, 1987), pp. 585–87.

[16] See Henry R. Glick, *Courts, Politics and Justice* (New York: McGraw-Hill, 1983), pp. 247–48.

[17] See Ronald J. Bacigal and Margaret I. Bacigal, "A Case Study of the Federal Judiciary's Role in Court-Ordered Busing," *Journal of Law and Politics,* University of Virginia, Vol. III, No. 4, Spring, 1987. The material for this case study is drawn from this article, which is excerpted from the forthcoming authorized biography of Judge Merhige by the Bacigals.

★ What difference does all this make? How does America's government with its history, players, and institutions matter to us? One way it affects us is because at the end of the day the government acts. And these activities have consequences for all of us at work, at school, and at home.

There are patterns in the fabric of this political tapestry. There is an order and a logic to the web of government activities. Yet it is a tangled process in which problems turn into issues, and then become policies and programs to later be evaluated and perhaps redone. The laws and programs government establishes, and the goals and assumptions underlying them, are called *public policy*.

Chapter Sixteen outlines the process and participants in the cycle of public policy, illustrating through environmental issues how the stages lead from one to another. Chapters Seventeen and Eighteen discuss two major arenas of policy debate. Nothing is more politically important than the economy. Economic policy, including the government's role in managing it with fiscal and monetary tools, is reviewed in Chapter Seventeen. Foreign policy in Chapter Eighteen rivals the economy in importance in times of crisis. In more relaxed periods it illustrates the same multiple actors crowding on the stage attempting to direct the course of events.

Whatever the arenas in which policies are acted upon, the politics of their creation and implementation remain lively, messy, and subject to unending debate.

PART FOUR

AMERICA'S GOVERNMENT

The Policies

Nuclear protesters
file petition

★

CHAPTER 16

Public Policy

By 1970, large numbers of Americans called themselves environmentalists. On "Earth Day"—April 22 of that year—public rallies, teach-ins, seminars, and other demonstrations were held simultaneously throughout the country to show concern about environmental issues.

Were there no pollution problems in America prior to the 1960s and 1970s? Of course there were. By and large, however, pollution had been a "quiet crisis." A small number of people, mainly naturalists and conservationists, were concerned. But environmental issues were not on the nation's agenda because not enough people had discovered a shared interest in them.

There was little public interest in environmental issues until the 1960s, and even less government attention. The problems had been building for a long time, especially following WW II, with population expansion, growth in production, and the development of new technologies. Thirty years after WW II, the population of the United States had increased by 50 percent and the Gross National Product (GNP)—total goods and services produced—had increased by 250 percent. With all sorts of new products that were not biodegradable or reusable, pollution levels had increased ten to twenty times.[1] The depletion of the nation's natural resources and the pollution of its land, air, and water became increasingly apparent.

But events alone do not create issues for decision making. Actors must be involved. With the environment, these actors included interest groups, the media, politicians, public officials, and even books. The publication of Rachel Carson's *Silent Spring* (1962) was fundamental to the development of public concern for environmental issues and the "grim specter" of pesticides.[2]

Carson's book lifted a rising tide of concern about pollution. New environmental groups, including Friends of the Earth and Environmental Action, sprang up. Existing groups became more active on pollution issues; for example, the Oil, Chemical, and Atomic Workers Union was concerned about the effects of pollution on their members at work. Many older environmental groups saw an enormous jump in membership. The Sierra Club, founded in 1892, increased its membership from 15,000 to 85,000 during the 1960s. Politicians and public officials responded to the issues, and their activities were increasingly reported by the media. By the 1960s, environmental problems became issues for America.

This very brief description of how environmental issues quickly reached the political agenda by the early 1970s raises as many questions as it answers. What is involved in the agenda-building

The disposal of toxic waste became an important issue in the 1980s. Here a scientist looks for ways to safely dispose of hazardous chemicals in New Jersey.

How politicians respond to environmental disasters has become an important part of the political agenda. Here, a fireboat battles flames on the Cuyahoga river near downtown Cleveland in the 1952 fire made famous by the fact that the river actually burned.

process? How is policy—environmental policy, for example—made and how is it adopted, implemented, and evaluated?

PUBLIC POLICY AND POLICY ANALYSIS

Public policy consists of the goals and assumptions that underlie what government does. It is a guide for government action. Put another way, policy is the "common understanding" that public officials bring to a decision and which, by repeating, they reinforce.[3] For example, a policy of cleaning up the country's water supplies will lead to numerous actions setting standards for pollutants, enforcing them, and reviewing complaints. Like individuals, governments are limited by scarce resources and by the inability to do everything at once. So policy-making means *government making choices* to do one thing rather than another, or to do less of this and a lot of that.

Policy analysis—the study of public policy—does not just examine what politicians say and how political institutions are supposed to work. It describes and explains the causes and consequences of government activity. "Policy analysis is finding out what governments do in education, health, welfare, housing, civil rights, environmental protection, natural resources, defense and foreign policy; why they do it; and whether it really makes any difference in the lives of their citizens."[4]

Policy-making is complicated, and so is policy analysis. Both are made more difficult by the fragmentation of the American political system. In the federal government, policy is made in all three branches—legislative, judicial, and executive (including the bureaucracy). Congress makes policy every time it decides to spend federal money one way rather than another. The U.S. Supreme Court made policy with its 1973 *Roe* v. *Wade* decision on abortion, holding that the government could not regulate abortions during the first trimester of a pregnancy. The executive branch, through Secretary of State Shultz, engaged in policy-making in 1988 when the State Department entered into talks with the Palestine Liberation Organization (PLO).[5]

In addition to the federal government, 50 state governments and more than 77,000 local governments make public policy. A resident of Park Forest, Illinois, for example, pays taxes to the following policy entities:

- The United States of America
- The State of Illinois
- Cook County
- Cook County Forest Preserve District
- Suburban Tuberculosis Sanitary District
- Rich Township
- Bloom Township Sanitary District
- Non-High School District 215
- Rich Township High School District
- Elementary School District 163
- Regional Transportation Authority
- South Cook Country Mosquito Abatement District

Each of these governmental bodies is responsible for developing and carrying out public policy. How? Who is involved? What is the role of the public? Answering these questions requires a look at the five principal steps involved in the policy-making process: *agenda building, policy formulation, policy adoption, policy implementation,* and *policy evaluation.*[6]

In a televised announcement in September 1989, President George Bush, shown here holding a bag of crack, declared a war on drugs and pledged that the U.S.'s drug problems would top his administration's political agenda.

AGENDA BUILDING

> *The first lesson of the [Exxon Valdez] oil spill is that it's time for this country to get serious about energy conservation. The second is that, since energy production is dangerous and even a company as well equipped as Exxon can't be counted on to maintain discipline, the government will have to do more of it—and Exxon will have no one to thank but itself. . . .*
>
> —editorial, *The Washington Post,* April 4, 1989

A government agenda is like a restaurant menu. The menu may list hotcakes and bacon but not eggs and grits, or the menu may offer all of these choices. In policy-making, the **agenda** is the list of things to be done or considered. The **issues** on the public-policy agenda are like the *dishes* on a restaurant menu.

What is an issue? Issues develop from problems. A problem is a situation that hinders or injures a particular group. Not all problems become issues, just as not all dishes are included on a restaurant menu. A problem develops into an issue when a group demands government action, when there is a disagreement about solutions, and when the alternatives involve the conflicting interests of groups. The editorial writers of *The Washington Post,* among others, tried to turn the Alaskan oil spill into an issue demanding government attention.

Just because a problem has developed into an issue, however, does not mean it will get on the official agenda for government policy-making. The importance of the government agenda is that only issues on it will be considered, in the same way a restaurant customer may choose only from the items on the menu.

How does an issue get on the agenda? The answer lies in the difference between the two kinds of agendas. The **public agenda** exists in the minds of the public. It consists of all the issues that a large part of the population believes should be acted on by government. The public agenda is an *unwritten menu;* it is *customer demand,* which restaurant owners (and public officials) ignore at their own risk.

America's war on drugs extended into Colombia, when the Bush administration sent military aid to the government of Colombia in 1989 to help them in their battle with local drug lords. Here, a car is examined after a former Colombian mayor was assassinated by members of a cocaine cartel.

In 1989, Senator Pete Wilson (second from left) introduced a bill called the "Drug War Bond Act" that would allow the Treasury Department to issue tax-free bonds to fund the national effort to eradicate drugs.

But decision makers cannot deal with all issues at once. They have limited time and budgets. They must focus on the most pressing or important or potentially solvable poblems. The **official agenda** is the set of issues that are formally before the policymakers for active consideration. It is the *written menu*. Until an issue is on the official agenda, it is not a subject of official policy-making.

For example, introducing a congressional bill or making a speech on the floor does not automatically place an issue on Congress's official agenda. Thousands of bills are introduced and thousands of speeches are made without causing the subjects to be seriously considered by Congress. Some interplay must usually occur between the public agenda—public demand—and the official agenda of government decision makers before congressional leaders reach a consensus that an issue deserves active consideration.

Every item on an official agenda is not necessarily on the public agenda. This is especially true in the judicial system, where an individual may bring before courts issues arousing little public attention. In addition, the daily policy decisions in the executive department and the bureaucracy are often made on issues of which the public is barely aware.

Governmental decision makers may refuse to let issues on the public agenda get on the official agenda. The Supreme Court may decide that a case does not involve a serious enough question to accept an appeal, or the Court may refuse to hear an issue because it is a *political question;* the Supreme Court held this position for a long time on legislative reapportionment. Congress may decide that an issue should be decided at the state rather than at the federal level, as it did for many years concerning civil rights. Government decision makers may avoid an issue on the public agenda because they feel it would be too risky to handle. Policymakers have repeatedly dodged certain issues with religious overtones, such as abortion. These issues were eventually taken into the courts.

Access to both the public and official agendas depends on the *type of issue* involved, the *actors,* and sometimes on *events.* Frequently, it depends on all three.

Type of Issue

The type of issue involved will affect agenda building. Some issues automatically get on the official agenda, such as annually proposed budgets. An issue has a far better chance of reaching the official agenda if it is acceptable to public opinion. Popular opinion may also make some issues out of bounds. Although social security was controversial when first passed, today its continuation is largely outside the boundaries of political debate, even by conservatives. Proposals to end public ownership of the Post Office are not generally debated among American policymakers.

The Alaskan oil spill by the *Exxon Valdez* in 1989 generated debate on a number of policy issues, such as environmental protection and corporate accountability.

Events

Sometimes issues that are "out of bounds" for political discussion rapidly become "in bounds" due to events. Such events might include natural catastrophes, such as a mine explosion; human acts, like a riot; technological changes, such as the growth in air travel; ecological changes, like the rural-to-urban shift in America's population; and external events, such as wars. An event may open a "window of opportunity" for action on an issue. For example, a new administration's taking office may impel change. The Alaskan oil spill on March 24, 1989 opened up the question of whether more drilling should be allowed along the western coast and in Alaskan wildlife reserves.

Actors

Events do not actually put issues on agendas; actors must be involved. Citizens may put issues on agendas; rich people have a better chance of doing this than poor people. Decision makers are more likely to consider issues raised by citizens who are more informed, wealthier, or better organized. Officials hear more about issues raised by active citizens and, as the cliché goes, "the squeaky wheel gets the oil."

The media is an important actor in agenda building, as well as a crucial intermediary between the president and the public. Lyndon Johnson examined a wide range of newspapers daily in order to learn what was being said in the media about him and his policies.

Interest groups are important actors in agenda building. Militant farmers blocking traffic with their tractors virtually force consideration of their demands. Issue activists can also be important actors. These would include environmentalists publicizing the dangers of nuclear waste disposal, consumer activists like Ralph Nader, and civil rights leaders such as Dr. Martin Luther King, Jr.

Politicians and public officials are also important actors in putting issues on agendas. Once agendas have been drawn up, these actors can become policymakers as well. They may have strong personal feelings about an issue, or they may think there is political advantage in it, or both.

As we know, the president and other public officials help to create, as well as respond to, public opinion. Congress is not a passive body forced to reflect public issues. Congress is second only to the president in creating political issues and putting them before the public for national debate.

The media can be important actors in agenda building. They may uncover and publicize scandals such as Watergate and the Iran-Contra affair. They may editorialize on public issues. In short, they bring issues to public attention. Political chemistry sometimes occurs between public officials and the media in the process. Here is how one Congressman was able to get a matter that was important to him on the official agenda of Congress:

He had been making speeches on the floor and writing the committee chairman for months, to no avail. Then an editor for a minor magazine noticed it and asked him to write an article.

The handicapped have become a powerful interest group in recent years. Here, handicapped protesters meet with a local official to discuss the installation of ramped curbs at all Chicago intersections to accommodate wheelchairs.

When the article, drawn from his speeches, appeared, the editor of an important newspaper in the district of a senior committee member picked it up and wrote a prominent editorial. That committee member, in turn, inquired of this congressman and became a leading advocate at hearings. Then the editor of another newspaper, this time in the district of another committee member, also picked it up and wrote a prominent story. That committee member called the congressman, asking for a copy of his bill, and eventually introduced it. Finally, after the chairman's initial reluctance, hearings were scheduled.[7]

As we have seen, the media does more than report news. They help determine how important the facts are and what policy actions should be taken because of this news.

POLICY FORMULATION

Workers examine hazardous wastes at Swartz Creek, Michigan, one of the worst dumps in the United States.

Once an issue gets on the official agenda, the next step is the formulation of policy. *Proposals must be developed for solving the problem.* What shall we do about pollution? How shall we reduce the waste of energy in America? The formulation process provides answers.

Policy formulation occurs in two stages. First, decisions must be made about *the type of action needed.* This involves deciding what the problem is; the problem is not a "given." Policymakers must identify and formulate it. How the question is asked can point toward the type of action required. As Charles E. Lindblom states:

Rioting breaks out in dozens of American cities. What is the problem? Racial discrimination? Impatience of the Negroes with the pace of reform now that reform has gone far enough to give them hope? Incipient revolution? Black power? Low income? Lawlessness at the fringe of an otherwise peaceful reform movement? Urban disorganization? Alienation?[8]

Second, the action on the problem must be *channeled into a particular form,* such as legislation, administrative rules, or court opinions.

Problem Solvers

All the actors involved in agenda building can also be involved in policy formulation. Not surprisingly, formulation involves much bargaining and compromising. At the national level, Congress may formulate policy. It took the lead in environmental pollution. Congress passed the Clean Air Act in 1963, and made it tougher in regard to automobile exhaust emissions in 1970. In 1970, the Water Quality Improvement Act, for cleaning up oil spills, was adopted, and the

U.S. Environmental Protection Agency (EPA) was created. The Carter years saw Congress pass the first "superfund" program for the cleanup of toxic waste dumps. While superfund and clean-water legislation was renewed in 1986, action on other environmental bills stalled as the administration put other priorities ahead of them.

The president is a leading actor in policy formulation. The Office of Management and Budget (OMB), which is part of the Executive Office of the President, is especially important in policy formulation. OMB is the final clearinghouse for the federal budget before it is approved by the president and submitted to Congress. Today, presidents also use this agency as a clearinghouse for all executive proposals—not just budget proposals—to be submitted to Congress.

Presidents favor *task forces* or *advisory commissions* to assist them in policy formulation. These task forces are usually created to handle specific issues like deficits, urban disorders, or government pay raises. Presidents sometimes appoint them for symbolic reasons. By appearing to take action through a study, presidents attempt to soothe disgruntled groups or to reassure the public. In 1988, after huge fires burned over one million acres in Yellowstone National Park, President Reagan appointed a task force to review the Forest Service's policy of letting forest fires burn. Although there had been a public outcry against the policy, the task force endorsed fires as a natural part of a forest's life cycle. They blamed the policy of *not* allowing fires in the past for the buildup of forestry growth that fueled uncontrollable fires. The task force served to delay hasty action and to keep the policy of "let it burn" as the ironic solution for the problem of forest fires.[9]

Fires rage through Yellowstone National Park in 1988. Environmental policy toward forest fires was greatly debated in that year.

Federal task forces are sent to disaster areas, like the 1989 California Bay-area earthquake pictured here, to evaluate such policy issues as disaster relief.

Often these symbolic actions to deal with pressing political problems are not very helpful in setting policy directions. When Richard Nixon created a Council on Environmental Quality in 1970, he declared that the 1970s "absolutely must be the years when America pays its debt to the past by reclaiming the purity of its air, its water and our living environment. It is literally now or never." Note that this original formulation of the problem of the environment did not include other questions. What is the proper trade-off between energy needs and environmental protection? How will environmental controls affect jobs? How much regulation of business is too much? Events of the 1970s and 1980s, such as the energy shortage and President Reagan's election, were to add other items to the first simple environmental agenda.

The original formulation of the environmental problem—how can the health and ecology of the country be better protected?—was to be revised in a more complex way. For example, in 1984, New York, Pennsylvania, and Maine petitioned the federal government to use the Clean Air Act to require power plants in the Midwest to cut down on sulphur dioxide emissions, which create acid rain. The Environmental Protection Agency took the side of the power companies, saying that more study was needed. On other environmental issues, the Reagan administration preferred to change the formulation: the question was not, "How can we better protect the environment?" but "How can we cut government spending and regulation in this arena?" This change in policy formulation had an enormous impact on environmental policy.

There are a number of ways to formulate policy. The *comprehensive* method would have taken all the aspects of environmental problems into full account initially. Other policy formulation methods are *incremental, branching,* and *invention.*

The Comprehensive Method

The ideal policy formulation would be to consider every possible solution to a problem and then choose the best one. This, if it existed, might be called the **comprehensive method.** In the real world, things don't work like this, but a discussion of the method helps explain why and how decision makers act like they do.

In 1967, President Johnson appointed the National Advisory Commission on Civil Disorders (*the Kerner Commission*) to investigate black riots occurring in many American cities that summer. Johnson asked for a comprehensive report recommending ways to prevent these disorders. The Kerner Commission immediately ran into trouble. It found that the frustrations felt by blacks in America's central cities were not just a result of racial discrimination. They also came from a lack of jobs and adequate income. Furthermore, with poor people moving into the central cities and middle-class people moving out, the tax bases of the cities were lowered. The Kerner Commission realized that a comprehensive solution meant making economic recommendations, and covered virtually every aspect of urban disorders in its 750-page report. Its findings, while widely publicized, were virtually ignored within the government. (Fred Harris served on the Kerner Commission).

The Kerner Commission experience points up some of the problems in the comprehensive method. First, policymakers usually *can't control all elements of a problem,* and are therefore not able to offer a complete solution. The Commission had little to say over how the governments or the economies of the cities concerned would function. Second, the method is difficult to use because it is *not always possible to know all the facts,* to consider all choices, and to suggest the best possible solution. Third, government policymakers are limited by the *risks* involved, such as the political response from interest groups and bureaucrats who fear their turf is being invaded.

Fourth, although the Kerner Commission never saw its conclusions acted on, if they had they would have found *unintended results,* another barrier to the comprehensive approach. Aspirin is taken for headaches though it may cause stomach bleeding. Unintended results also come from some of the government's most well-intentioned efforts. Take housing, for example:

> *Since the creation in 1934 of the Federal Housing Authority (FHA), the government has subsidized home-building on a vast scale by insuring mortgages that were written on easy terms and, in the case of the Veterans Administration (VA), guaranteeing mortgages. Most of the mortgages have been for the purchase of new homes. It was cheaper to build on vacant land, but there was little such land left in the central cities and in their larger, older suburbs. These were almost always zoned so as to exclude the relatively few Negroes and other "undesirables" who could afford to build new houses. In effect, then, the FHA and VA programs have subsidized the movement of the white middle class out of the central cities and older suburbs, while at the same time penalizing investment in the rehabilitation of the rundown neighborhoods of these older cities. The poor—especially the Negro poor—have not received any direct benefit from these programs.[10]*

Fifth, the comprehensive approach is hampered by the *difficulty of making an accurate cost-benefit analysis* of solutions. How do we quantify the value of human life? Is a program that costs $50 million

An eleven-story building in the Pruitt-Igoe housing project in St. Louis is demolished after it was declared unlivable in 1972.

justified on a cost-benefit basis if it will save one hundred lives? One thousand? One hundred thousand? How do we make a cost-benefit analysis when the goal of a program is to produce more musicians? What is the value of music? How does a policymaker weigh priorities? Which is more important: cleaning up the air or providing more jobs?

Presidents have attempted to establish a cost-benefit analysis of government policy and a comprehensive approach to policy formulation for the federal budget. Jimmy Carter favored a *"zero-based budget system."* According to this plan, each federal agency was supposed to completely justify its budget each year, starting from zero. *One problem with this system was that those who could come up with the best justification for their programs in mathematical, cost-benefit terms could prevail over those who could not.* The budget of the Department of Defense went up, while less was done about environmental pollution.

A sixth barrier to comprehensive policy formulation is the assumption that "goals" could be scientifically determined, clearly defined and stated in advance, all separate from politics. But "It is impermissible to treat goals as if they were known in advance. 'Goals' may well be the product of interaction among key participants rather than . . . some 'spook' that posits values in advance of our knowledge of them."[11] President Reagan's use of cost-benefit analysis was severely criticized on the ground that it favored business interests over harder-to-quantify social goals, such as better health and a cleaner environment. But a defender of Reagan's system asked, "What's the alternative? Flipping a coin? Consulting a ouiji board?"

He has a point. Government policy-making cannot stop because policymakers cannot formulate policy comprehensively. Inflation, unemployment, and pollution are real problems. Just because there is no perfect method of formulating policy to solve them doesn't mean that policymakers can ignore these problems. Instead, they do the best they can using three other approaches: incremental, branching, and inventive.

The Incremental Method

The **incremental method** *focuses on small changes in existing policy,* such as extending, updating, strengthening, or cutting back. Government budgetary processes are prime examples of this method. As a bureaucratic cliché goes, the best way to predict next year's budget is to look at last year's. The incremental method is the most widely used in government because it stirs up the least opposition and is the easiest way to build coalitions for support. Although the incremental method requires no jarring change at any one time, *the cumulative impact of incremental decisions can be enormous.* America's involvement in Vietnam was incremental: we first became involved through material and financial aid, then by sending military advisers, next by sending combat troops, and finally by heavily increasing combat troops. The country fell victim to the executive's failure to fully consider the consequences and costs of an indefinite and deepening American participation.

Incremental decision making is popularly known as *the science of muddling through.* Given that policy-making is complex and disorderly, the advocates of incrementalism claim that this approach is the only feasible one. It concentrates the policymaker on what he or she knows already, and sharply reduces the number of factors and alternatives that need to be analyzed. It is, in reality, the way policy is made.[12]

The Branching Method

The **branching method** of policy formulation *varies a previously established policy to meet new situations.* The Rail Passenger Act of 1970, which set up a government-sponsored private corporation to meet railroad problems, was a branching (like a tree branch) from the theme (or tree trunk) that had previously been established in the Communications Satellite Corporation, created in 1962. The law requiring environmental impact statements for new federal programs has served as a branching model for making similar advance assessments of the impacts of other federal programs before they are put into effect.

The Invention Method

Invention, also called innovation, is *the use of new ideas.* The amount of invention in government policy is very small. One reason for this is the U.S. Constitution. Its complex balancing of rival power centers makes it difficult for new ideas to run the gauntlet of approval. Another reason is that many people, especially bureaucrats, avoid taking risks or trying something new. This may be especially true of politicians facing election. Sometimes invention happens when new scientific developments require new policy forums. The Atomic Energy Commission after World War II tried to oversee the peaceful use of nuclear energy. Invention also occurs when an issue on the public and official agendas is widely recognized as a serious one but much of the public is undecided about what the policy should be. New ideas put forward by leaders are most likely to be accepted at these times. A study showed that within the federal government, almost two-thirds of the inventive policies have come from executive departments or agencies and presidential commissions and task forces; one-third have come from congressional committees. Some examples of inventive policies are the Social Security Act, the Marshall Plan, the Interstate Highway Program, revenue sharing, and the Gramm-Rudman Act.[13]

POLICY ADOPTION

When the debate ends, the main point of congressional decision, the calling of the roll, is reached. . . . Here on the floor, the ultimate policy choice is made; here the bill is accepted or rejected; here the nature of the system's output is specified. Put another way, when the roll is called, the coalitions for and against the bill are identified.[14]

Policymakers must look backward as well as forward. Backward to problems, forward to policies. Policy formulation and adoption cannot be neatly separated. Like the other steps in the process, they are interactive. In both, *decision makers must be concerned with the political effects of the alternatives being considered.*

The actual decisions in the adoption process are made by public officials such as legislators and executives. Policy adoption requires policymakers to make judgments about the facts, alternatives, risks, and probable consequences of their decisions.[15] It is usually the result of bargaining, compromise, and coalition building. The coalitions presumably reflect popular opinion because they are made by public officials who directly or indirectly answer to the voters.

Government policy-making does not just involve decisions to do something. It can also involve inaction, a decision not to do anything. Lack of action usually implies a policy in favor of the status quo. In regard to environmental issues, we have seen how both types of policy decisions—more action early, less later—have been a part of policy adoption at the federal level.

POLICY IMPLEMENTATION

A reasonable policy goal may appear much less reasonable when it has to be implemented on the ground. Meeting national clean-air quality standards for carbon monoxide and other pollutants meant drastic changes in some cities. They were required to send plans to the Environmental Protection Agency in Washington for changing their traffic patterns to reduce pollution.

Pittsburgh's plan included a rush-hour ban on cars carrying fewer than three people from one of the busiest outbound parkways in the city. The ban was announced on a Thursday, to be implemented the next Wednesday. By Friday, the state's Department of Transportation was swamped with complaints and by Saturday the ban was postponed, with EPA approval, for 90 days. Policies are, on occasion, adjusted for reality.

Once adopted, policies are like the automobiles produced by Detroit's assembly lines. They are the "output" of America's political system. But they are not the end of the line. Policies also stimulate; they are causes as well as consequences.

Policy **implementation** means putting the objectives of policy decisions into practice. Assessing the impact of these decisions is one of the goals of policy analysis. What does—or does not—happen once a government policy is adopted?

Policy is generally not self-executing; it does not implement itself. Policies usually consist of instructions to administrators who will carry out the law, rather than of direct commands to citizens. The details of any new policy are often left to those who will apply it. Therefore *implementation is not only a result of policy, it also involves making policy.* As Robert Lineberry has written, implementation is "a continuation of policy-making by other means."[16]

There are three elements in the implementation of policy. The first is *organization:* a decision must be made on which structure will be used to operate the program. This structure may be an old agency that shifts its mission to accept incremental changes in policy, or it may be a new agency, created separately or within an existing department. The second involves *interpretation:* policy goals must be trans-

Many states require car emissions testing to control the amount of pollutants released in the environment. Here, cars wait in line to be tested at an inspection center in Skokie, Illinois.

In response to an epidemic of measles in 1989 in Chicago (as well as other cities), the Cook County Department of Public Health administered free vaccine innoculations.

lated into specific rules. The third is *application:* resources must be allocated, and the rules must be applied to the specific problem. Interpretation and application offer considerable room for discretion by administrators on the ground.

One basic goal of public policy is to gain *compliance,* to influence those targeted by policy to behave in desired ways or not to behave in undesired ways. Public reaction to a new policy has an important impact on implementation. If a law benefits everyone, compliance will probably follow. If it is considered to benefit no one, it will probably not be obeyed. What about the common situation where a new policy benefits some people but is a burden to others? If a person thinks he will lose more from obedience than from disobedience, he will break the law. If he believes he will lose more through disobedience, he will obey. To bring about compliance when it is not automatic, administrators use education, persuasion, punishments, and rewards.

Actors and Implementation

The actors in policy formulation and adoption usually get involved in implementation. They include interest groups, the media, politicians, and public officials. The public officials involved in policy implementation come not only from the executive bureaucracy, but also from the legislature and the courts.

Legislators can influence implementation by looking over administrators' shoulders either through oversight powers—hearings, investigations, required reports—or by "casework." In casework, legislators intervene with administrators for constituents with complaints about a government program, such as Social Security benefits. This type of legislative intervention in specific cases, or even the threat of it, affects the way administrators implement policies. Often, administrators will be particularly interested in the opinion of legislators who serve on the committees that formulated the policy and who will have a say over whether the program continues.

Judges are also involved in policy implementation. In handling individual cases, they must interpret laws and administrative regulations. They also administer the law in naturalization proceedings, bankruptcies, and paroles. Chapter 15's case study on Richmond busing showed a judge implementing civil rights rulings over local opposition.

The bureaucracy is vital in implementing policy. Actually, bureaucrats come up with many of the ideas that become policy. They also help to sell these ideas in the executive and legislative branches. In the implementation of policy, bureaucrats often interpret the laws, filling in the details through rules and guidelines and deciding how to apply the rules in particular cases.

Bureaucratic Barriers

Harry Truman once made a prediction about the fate that was to await his successor: "He'll sit here and he'll say, 'Do this! Do that!' And nothing will happen. Poor Ike—it won't be a bit like the Army. He'll find it very frustrating."[17] Truman's point was that just because policy has been adopted does not mean it will be carried out the way policymakers intended. From outside the government, the lack of public acceptance or the resistance of political forces can block the intentions of policymakers.

There are internal reasons why policies may not be fully implemented by bureaucrats.[18] Administrators may be uncertain about orders. They may ask, "What exactly are we supposed to do?" The policy may be too difficult to implement. Administrators may wonder, "I was told what to do, but how can I do it?" Bureaucrats may simply oppose implementing a policy. President Truman is once again worth quoting: "The difficulty with many career officials in the government is that they regard themselves as the men who really make policy and run the government. They look upon the elected officials as just temporary occupants."[19] Thus, bureaucrats may delay; they may obey the letter but not the spirit of orders, suggest changes in the orders before carrying them out, go over the heads of their executive superiors to the legislative branch, and "go public" with their complaints through "leaks" to the press (see the box on page 513).

There are, of course, remedies for bureaucratic resistance to policy implementation. The policy may be spelled out in more detail. Policymakers and the media can shine the light of publicity on its implementation. Officials can discipline or transfer stubborn bureaucrats, and Congress can use its "power of the purse" to threaten an office with extinction.

Most people think that a problem has been solved once a policy has been adopted. Public attention ceases. The television crews turn off their cameras and leave, reporters shift to other matters. The excitement of debate no longer commands public attention. But if the original goals of policies are to be reached, more focus must be on implementation, not just on policy formulation and adoption.

POLICY EVALUATION

Do police patrols prevent crime? Many people think so. Some years ago the Kansas City, Missouri Police Department decided to study the question. They took an area usually covered by fifteen patrols. It was divided into thirds. In one area, all five patrols were taken away, only responding to calls for service; the second area kept its normal five patrols as a control; and the third area had its five patrols increased two to three times.

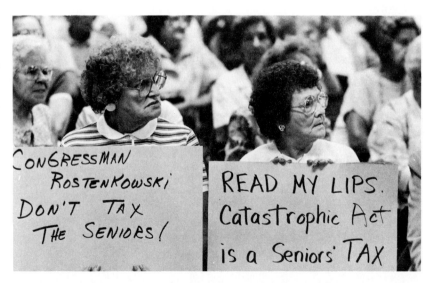

Irate senior citizens surround the car of Congressman Dan Rostenkowski in Chicago to protest his support of the controversial Catastrophic Coverage Act, an insurance medical plan that many feared would burden middle-class senior citizens with higher tax rates.

A series of surveys were taken, numerous interviews were conducted of citizens and officers, observations were made, and mountains of departmental data on crime, traffic, and arrests were collected. It was a well-planned evaluation. The result? Decreasing or increasing police patrols had no effect on crime, citizens' fears of crime, or public attitudes toward police and police services.[20]

Policy evaluation means *assessing the impacts of policy.* Outside the government, the media may play an important role in policy evaluation. Interest groups never hesitate in pointing out alleged policy defects that affect them. Individuals (through surveys, for example) and academic researchers may also be important outside actors for an evaluation.

Inside the federal government, Congress—through its committees—exercises oversight on policy, providing continuous surveillance as policy is formulated, adopted, implemented, and evaluated. The Equal Employment Opportunity Act of 1972, for example, required monitoring studies of employment so Congress could evaluate the effect of the act on women and minorities in the work force. Presidents maintain a system of evaluating policy implementation, too, often through commissions or task forces set up for this purpose.

The aim of evaluation is to provide "feedback" to assist in adjusting policy. A *"seat-of-the-pants" impressionistic evaluation* is the least useful. Review is based on fragmentary evidence ("Somebody told me that people drive up in Cadillacs to get food stamps") or bias ("Republican policies always help big business").

Operation-centered policy evaluation forcuses only on the narrow efficiency of programs: Is the program honestly run? What are its financial costs? Who receives benefits (payments or services) and in what amounts? Is there unnecessary overlap or duplication with other programs? Were legal standards and procedures followed?

Systematic evaluation is the most useful to policymakers. It is more scientific than impressionistic evaluation, yet its purposes are much broader than operation-centered evaluation. Systematic evaluation seeks to measure the extent to which policy objectives are actually achieved and what *impact* they have on society. This may include *cost-benefit* analysis which will try to balance all the benefits of a program against the actual costs. Evaluation of a policy may reveal that administrative resistance to its implementation is hurting the achievement of its goals. Or the policy may be at fault because its goals are too vague or based on a mistaken interpretation of the problem. Evaluation may also reveal undesirable and unintended side effects. New problems may also be discovered that will find their way on to the policy agenda as issues for decision makers to deal with.

Evaluation may turn out to be the start of another **policy cycle.** The evaluation, often operating as an arm of political interests, may affect public opinion, bureaucrats, and policymakers. *Back through policy formulation, adoption, implementation, and evaluation, the issues raised by evaluation may repeat the policy cycle.* The hope is

The war on drugs promises to greatly influence public policy in the 1990s. Here, neighbors against crime board up an abandoned house used by crack users in Detroit.

Reprinted with permission of Doug Marlette/*New York Newsday*.

"YOUR LIPS SAY 'NO, NO', BUT YOUR NOSE SAYS 'YES, YES'!"

that through this testing and feedback a *learning* process occurs. Problems are reinterpreted, assumptions are adjusted, implementation is corrected, organizations are modified, personnel are reassigned, new problems are discovered, and policies are changed. Of course the policy cycle may just serve to reinforce the political and institutional interests supporting the original program. The judgment about whether programs are solving problems may prove secondary. Which direction the policy cycle takes will ultimately be a political question dependent on the actors involved and their objectives, resources, and skills.

WRAP-UP

Policy-making has important consequences. It can result from and cause serious conflicts. Some people want policy-making taken "out of politics," detached from partisan forces. This is both impossible and undesirable. Government policy-making necessarily involves politics when making choices between important, often conflicting interests. Therefore, to paraphrase Clemenceau's famous statement about war and generals, policy-making is too important to be left to the "experts." The people and their representatives must have a role.

Not surprisingly, policy-making is complex. The field of policy analysis (within political science) attempts to break this process into its overlapping steps. Policy-making begins with a problem, which grows to become an issue. Some issues get on the public agenda and then on the official agenda, where they are available for decision.

Policy-making involves making choices. In policy formulation, the available choices are spelled out and considered. During the adoption stage, a set of goals or assumptions is legitimated in the political process or approved by government officials. Policy implementation is the next step. Because it involves considerable discretion, policy implementation may also be policy-making. At the evaluation stage, the results and overall impact of policy are judged. This assessment may then be fed back into the policy-making process, for this is not just an end; it is also a beginning of a policy cycle.

A frustrated bureaucrat talked about her job this way: "You can work in this building (Public Health Service) all your life and not know there are sick people outside." Buried under red tape, narrowed functions, and political maneuvering, agencies of government often turn inward, ignoring the public purposes their programs were set up to serve. Connecting government policy to solving public problems is the goal of policy-making. It also remains its major failing.

Key Terms

public policy (p. 496)

policy analysis (p. 496)

agenda (p. 498)

issues (p. 498)

public agenda (p. 498)

official agenda (p. 499)

comprehensive method (p. 504)

incremental method (p. 507)

branching method (p. 507)

invention (p. 508)

implementation (p. 509)

systematic evaluation (p. 514)

policy cycle (p. 514)

Suggested Readings

Berry, William D., and David Lowery, *Understanding United States Government Growth* (New York: Praeger, 1987).

Califano, Joseph, *America's Health Care Revolution: Who Lives? Who Dies? Who Pays?* (New York: Random House, 1986).

Peterson, Paul, Barry G. Rabe, and Kenneth K. Wong, *When Federalism Works* (Washington, D.C.: Brookings Institution, 1987).

Pressman, Jeffrey, and Aaron Wildavsky, *Implementation,* 3rd ed. (Berkeley: University of California Press, 1984).

Shuman, Howard E., *Politics and the Budget* (New York: Prentice-Hall, 1988).

Vig, Norman J. and Michael S. Kraft, eds., *Environmental Policy in the 1980s: Reagan's New Agenda* (Washington, D.C.: Congressional Quarterly Press, 1984).

Endnotes

[1] Barry Commoner, "Energy, Environment and Economics," in Gary D. Eppen, ed., *Energy: The Policy Issues* (Chicago: University of Chicago Press, 1975), p. 27.

[2] Rachel Carson, *Silent Spring* (Boston: Houghton Mifflin, 1962).

[3] Charles O. Jones, *An Introduction to the Study of Public Policy,* 3rd edition (Monterey, California: Brooks/Cole, 1984), Chapter 2.

[4] Thomas R. Dye, *Policy Analysis* (University, Ala.: The University of Alabama Press, 1976), pp. 2–3.

[5] For a discussion of political analysis as art, see Aaron Wildavsky, *Speaking Truth to Power: The Art and Craft of Policy Analysis* (New Brunswick: Transaction, 1987).

[6] This breakdown of the policy process generally follows the framework used in Charles O. Jones, *An Introduction to the Study of Public Policy,* 3rd ed.

[7] John W. Kingdom, "Dynamics of Agenda Formation in Congress," in Anderson, ed., *Cases in Public Policy-Making* (New York: Praeger, 1976), p. 36.

[8] Charles E. Lindblom, *The Policy-Making Process* (Englewood Cliffs, N.J.: Prentice-Hall, 1968), p. 13.

[9] *The Washington Post,* December 19, 1988, p. A3.

[10] Edward C. Banfield, *The Unheavenly City Revisited: A Revision of the Unheavenly City* (Boston: Little, Brown and Co., 1974), pp. 15–16.

[11]Aaron Wildavsky, "The Political Economy of Efficiency," in Austin Ranney, ed., *Political Science and Public Policy* (Chicago: Markham, 1968), p. 80.

[12]Lindblom, *The Policy-Making Process.*

[13]Grover Starling, *The Politics and Economics of Public Policy* (Homewood, Illinois: The Dorsey Press, 1979), pp. 219–20.

[14]Leroy N. Rieselbach, "Congressional Voting Decisions," in Anderson, ed., *Cases in Public Policy-Making* (New York: Praeger, 1976), pp. 122–23.

[15]See Robert A. Dahl, *Modern Political Analysis* (Englewood Cliffs, N.J.: Prentice-Hall, 1970), pp. 100–12.

[16]Lineberry, *American Public Policy* (New York: Harper and Row, 1977), p. 71.

[17]Quoted by Dennis D. Riley, *Controlling the Federal Bureaucracy* (Philadelphia: Temple University Press, 1987), p. 2.

[18]This material is taken from Morton H. Halperin, "Implementing Presidential Foreign Policy Decisions: Limitations and Resistance," in James E. Anderson, ed., *Cases in Public Policy-Making* (New York: Praeger, 1976), pp. 208–36.

[19]Harry S. Truman, *Memoirs, Vol. II: Years of Trial and Hope* (New York: Doubleday, 1956), p. 165.

[20]Jones, pp. 196–97.

★
CHAPTER 17

Economic Policy

In January 1989, President George Bush was inaugurated and the U.S. Congress began its 101st session. The political agenda facing both the legislative and executive branches included major unresolved economic problems. At the top of the list was an annual budget deficit of $140 billion. It was more or less chaperoned by a deficit-reduction law that would cut spending evenly but brutally unless Bush and Congress made more surgical cuts or came up with new revenue. One might think this made new spending almost unthinkable.

But advocates of deeply-eroded social spending called for restoring programs for the poor and homeless. Given that the income of the nation's poorest one-fifth had declined by 11 percent in eight years, and that one of every five children lived in poverty, they had their points. Beyond this, there were new, large, and expensive problems on the horizon. The federally insured savings and loan industry included walking-dead thrifts that could cost over $100 billion to close or salvage. Neglect of deadly radioactive contamination at nuclear weapons plants could cost over $80 billion to clean up. The U.S. trade deficit remained over $100 billion and signalled a loss of economic clout in the global marketplace. Latin American and African nations owed about $300 billion to U.S. banks that they probably couldn't repay. And the private sector didn't seem to be pulling its weight, with productivity down and the savings rate declining.

All these problems provided good arguments for increased spending. Yet fears about the effects of the federal deficit were already credited with helping trigger the October, 1987 stock-market crash, the biggest one-day loss in the history of the market. In a "budget summit" after the October crash, Congress and the White House had agreed on an even stricter deficit-cutting mechanism. And, of course, voters were reminded to read the president's lips: *No new taxes.*

The public, however, was comfortable with a consumer economy in the midst of one of the country's longest expansions. Low inflation, low unemployment, and record corporate profits meant reasonably prosperous times, which aided Bush's electoral victory. While some Democrats mentioned a steep boost in the gasoline tax, they also promised to let Bush make the first move on taxes and reap the political fallout. The president seemed content to leave well enough alone, and let the Federal Reserve first raise interest rates to slow inflation, and then ease rates to avoid tipping the economy into a recession.

The federal bailout of troubled savings and loan institutions became an important issue in the late 1980s.

A new president finding himself both the beneficiary and victim of economics underlines the importance of the subject to students of government. *A prosperous, fair economy is the rock on which popular government rests.* Its needs fill a large part of the government's agenda. The discussion that follows will range over different ideas about what the government's role in the economy should be, as well as what direction this role has actually taken. The budget is the arena in which most of the issues of economic policy will arise. More specific insight can be gained from how the government uses its fiscal and monetary tools to influence the economy. Finally, conclusions will be ventured on how well recent administrations have done toward the economy as a whole and in making this a more equitable society in particular. As one undergraduate concluded, "It's a mixed bag."

THE GOVERNMENT'S ROLE IN THE ECONOMY

America's economy has always been based on **capitalism.** Under this system, the means of production are privately owned by individuals rather than publicly owned by the government. Individuals and privately owned corporations may own land, natural resources, factories, and businesses. In addition to private ownership, America's economic system from the start was based on **free enterprise.** This meant that people had the right to start whatever businesses they pleased, and workers had the right to move from job to job (with the glaring exception of slaves) without government interference.

Classic Capitalism

Laissez-faire, a French phrase for "leave things alone," characterized our early economic policy. The bible of this free-enterprise philosophy was the *Wealth of Nations,* written in 1776 by a Scot, Adam Smith. Smith declared that if left alone, the "invisible hand" of competitive self-interest—the "uniform, constant, and uninterrupted effort of every man to better his own condition"—would improve society in general and the individual in particular. This philosophy was very radical in eighteenth-century England, where business expected government protection from competition. Even today, businesspeople often show ambivalence about government's role. They will declare their belief in the free competition of Adam Smith while demanding government subsidies and protection against their own competitors.[1]

The classic laissez-faire period in American history ended in 1887, when Congress established the *Interstate Commerce Commission (ICC)*. The ICC was created to regulate the railroads, which had a virtual monopoly in transportation. This new law and the *Sherman Antitrust Act of 1890* were based on the realization that not only could government action preserve monopolies, but government *inaction* could as well. These and other laws passed in the early twentieth century, particularly during Theodore Roosevelt's administration, launched the federal government on its effort to restrict the unrestricted power of American industry.

The Great Depression of the 1930s extended government's reach over the economy. It produced immense economic problems: intolerably high unemployment, millions of poor, idle factories, abandoned farms, failing banks, and stagnant foreign trade. During his famous first "100 days" in office in 1933, Franklin D. Roosevelt recommended a rush of federal activities to "jump start" the economy and to protect working people.

While he expanded government's role, Roosevelt did not embrace the socialism that Karl Marx had advocated in his book, *Das Kapital* (1867). Marx's idea of how to improve the human condition was very different from Adam Smith's. Marx advocated abolishing private property and establishing an economic system based on public ownership of the means of production. He believed that capitalism led to centralized production in monopolies and had within itself the seeds of its own destruction. To Marx, it was a virtual "scientific" inevitability that capitalist abuses would eventually destroy capitalism and replace it with socialism:

A congressman buys an apple from an unemployed man in front of the Capitol in Washington, D.C. in 1930.

> *Along with the constantly diminishing number of the magnates of capital . . . grows the mass of misery, oppression, slavery, degradation, exploitation; but with this too grows the revolt of the working class always increasing in number, and disciplined, united, organized by the very mechanism of the process of capitalist production itself. . . .*[2]

Although Roosevelt did not believe that the means of production should be socialized in America, he did support some government enterprises. The *Tennessee Valley Authority (TVA)* is a still-existing federal enterprise established to generate electricity and improve living conditions in its area. Today, the publicly owned *Corporation for Public Broadcasting,* like the TVA, competes with private enterprises and offers a "yardstick" to measure the performance of the private broadcasting companies. But the Marxist idea of public ownership has proved neither inevitable nor widespread in America.

To offer short-term assistance to the unemployed, Congress authorized the Civilian Conservation Corps in 1933 to combine two of President Franklin D. Roosevelt's favorite causes—improving national parks and employing young people. Here, CCC youths plant trees in 1934 in a national forest in Idaho that had recently been ravaged by fire.

The Mixed Economy

America today is not, however, a completely free-enterprise economy. It is a **mixed economy.** Although most property and the means of production are privately owned, the government is deeply involved in regulating the uses of private property and how private enterprises operate. Publicly owned enterprises exist on state and local levels as well. In North Dakota, there is a state-owned bank. The electricity distribution systems in some American cities are owned by city governments. There are also a number of electricity, food, and other kinds of cooperatives throughout the country that are owned by the people that they serve.

Franklin Roosevelt did not replace capitalism, he reformed it. In fact, one liberal critic of Roosevelt's policies has said that Roosevelt's "timid" efforts amounted only to "a trickle of government spending and a wholly inadequate cushion of social support . . . and the Depression hung on, arrested but not cured, until World War II arrived and swept away all inhibitions."[3] Since Roosevelt, the federal government has become a *regulatory police officer,* protecting consumers and workers against the abuses of business. The 1970s saw additional government regulation to protect the environment and promote the affirmative-action rights of minorities and women.

Franklin Roosevelt also recognized the federal government's responsibility to find jobs for idle workers. For FDR this meant creating government jobs by providing federal funds for public improvements such as new community buildings and replanted forests. In 1946, this responsibility was specifically put into law. In that year, Congress passed the *Employment Act,* committing the federal government to three basic goals, those of promoting maximum employment, maximum production, and economic stability.[4] The Act established the president's *Council of Economic Advisers,* required a regular economic report from the president, and established the *Joint Economic Committee in Congress* to review the president's economic report. Since 1946, there has been a rough consensus between conservatives and liberals that the government has a role in reducing unemployment and in holding down *inflation* (the rate of increase in the price of goods and services).

The Employment Act of 1946 was largely based on the writings of an Englishman, John Maynard Keynes. In *The General Theory of Employment, Interest and Money* (1936), he argued that unemployment resulted from inadequate spending by consumers, investors, and government.[5] *Keynes' remedy for unemployment was simple: greater spending.* If needed, he declared, government should tax the rich to provide jobs for the poor. The federal government practiced various versions of **Keynesian economics** until President Reagan took office. The Keynesian approach called for greater consumer, investor, and government spending during periods when factories were idle. Under this approach the government may also, instead of spending more money, cut taxes. This leaves more money in the hands of taxpayers, thus increasing their spending for consumer goods and investments. The government may even increase spending *and* cut taxes at the same time.

Keynesian economics also meant that government should act in times of excessive spending, especially when too much consumer money was chasing too few goods, thus producing inflation. Keynesians maintain that in such times governments should reduce total spending, by raising taxes (thus taking money from consumers and investors), by reducing government spending, or both.

The use of government's taxing and spending powers to affect the economy is called **fiscal policy.** Such fiscal policy may involve taxing less or spending more to stimulate the economy, thus decreasing unemployment. Fiscal policy may also mean taxing more or spending less to dampen the economy, thus hopefully reducing inflation.

The Supply-side Approach

In 1980, President Reagan pledged to support the non-Keynesian **supply-side theories** of UCLA professor Arthur B. Laffer. The "Laffer Curve" attempted to demonstrate that when government taxes get too high, revenues go down because investment and business were discouraged. The way to stimulate investment—and increase government revenues—was to reduce taxes sharply, especially for investors and businesses. President Reagan's first economic plan included a sharp cut in the rise of federal spending (except for defense, which was greatly increased), some reduction in regulation of business, and a restrictive monetary policy with high interest rates. Reagan declared that reduced federal domestic spending, plus increased business investment as a result of the tax cuts, would produce a balanced budget and reduced inflation by 1984.

Under this economic policy, inflation did come down—and stayed down—although at the immediate cost of a recession and increased unemployment. By 1984, unemployment had also begun to fall, reaching a fifteen-year low of 5.0 percent in 1989. An economic expansion begun in 1982 continued into 1989, making it one of the longest on record. There were still gaps in the boom. The energy-rich states of Texas and Louisiana saw the collapse of overextended real estate and banking sectors, while legislatures in both states were reluctant to boost plummeting tax revenues. However, most Americans saw themselves as beneficiaries of the Reagan Recovery and voted for his successor, George Bush. For this notable economic achievement, the supply-siders were quite willing to take credit.

FIGURE 17★1
Deficit Projections (in billions of dollars)

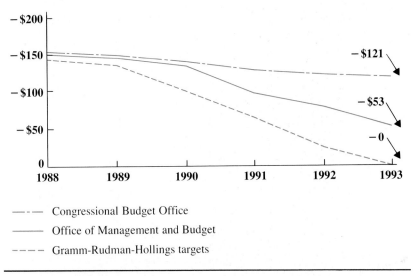

------ Congressional Budget Office

——— Office of Management and Budget

- - - - Gramm-Rudman-Hollings targets

SOURCE: David Rapp, "Is Anyone Really Trying to Balance the Budget?" *Congressional Quarterly,* November 26, 1988, p. 3380.

The major cloud on the supply-side horizon was that the annual federal deficit did not come down very fast. It went up—to an unprecedented *$210 billion* in fiscal 1985—and by fiscal 1988 still stood at $155 billion. No one saw the deficit going below $110 billion by fiscal 1990 (see Figure 17.1).[6] *The federal government financed economic recovery on borrowed money.* President Reagan was accused of adopting a strange Keynesian line by ignoring deficits and spending borrowed money to maintain prosperity. The most serious effort to limit the deficit was the Gramm-Rudman law, which set reduced target figures for the deficit each year. By 1989, however, the bill and its targets were deferred to, but their effectiveness remained in doubt.

THE BUDGETARY PROCESS

No questions on the official agenda are more automatic or more important than those of the budget. As one student of the budget put it, questions of budgeting—taxing, spending, mobilizing and apportioning resources—now take as much time on the floors of Congress as all other issues put together. Why? Because *the budget process asks and answers government's most important questions:* "How large government will be, the part it will play in our lives, whether more or less will be done for defense or welfare, how much and what sort of people will pay for services, what kind of society, in sum, we Americans want to have. . . ."[7]

President Bush, surrounded by congressional leaders, presents the 1990 budget in April 1989.

Every year, the president must propose a federal budget for the next fiscal year, which begins on October 1 and ends on September 30 of the following year. The president's responsibility for proposing the federal budget stems from the *Budget and Accounting Act of 1921*. Surprisingly, before then the president played no direct role in preparing the budget. The Secretary of the Treasury did it. The president's budgetary role increased in 1939 with the *Executive Reorganization Act.* It created the Executive Office of the President and transferred the Bureau of the Budget from the Treasury Department to the new office. A Nixon reorganization plan in 1970 expanded the duties of the budget bureau and changed its name to the **Office of Management and Budget (OMB).** The president appoints the director of OMB with Senate consent.

Preparation of the proposed budget begins more than a year before it is presented to Congress. The Council of Economic Advisers (CEA) provides the president (and OMB) with estimates of national income and future rates of unemployment and inflation. With the

CEA's estimates in mind, OMB weighs budget requests from the various federal departments. The president approves the finished product. The entire process is *incremental*—budget makers use the previous year's budget as a base, rather than beginning from the ground up each year.

The president's final budget proposals are presented to Congress. These proposals recommend total federal expenditures and taxes, and thus the overall deficit or surplus. The proposed federal budget represents fundamental national-policy decisions. The expenditure side of the budget tells "who gets what" by recommending increased spending for some government programs (such as airport security) and possibly reducing others (such as subsidized housing). The tax side of the budget tells "who pays"—individuals or corporations? rich or poor? The president's budget proposal goes on to estimate the budget's impact on the national economy, including its effect on unemployment and inflation.

Congress and the Budget

These priorities and estimates are highly political. Not surprisingly, the process does not end with the president's presentation of the budget to Congress. An old saying in Washington—"The president proposes, but the Congress disposes"—is as true for the budget as it is for other legislative proposals made by the chief executive.

However, the president does have an advantage over Congress in putting together the budget. Through OMB, the president is able to make more comprehensive decisions about total revenues, expenditures, borrowing, and the impact of the proposed budget on the economy. The president can also speak with one voice for the entire executive department when calling for public support. Congress's budgetary authority is fragmented.

The most obvious division in Congress is the one between its two chambers—the House of Representatives and the Senate—but there is additional fragmentation. Within each House, much of the power over the budget resides in numerous standing committees and subcommittees. Committees with jurisdiction over taxes—the Senate Finance Committee and the House Ways and Means committee—are separate from the appropriations committees in each body. Appropriations committees are themselves fragmented into subcommittees that deal with separate federal agencies and programs. Furthermore, appropriations bills are not supposed to be passed in either house until a separate "authorization" bill has first been passed, and these bills are handled by *other* standing committees.

Congress sought to pull together its fragmented budget power with the *Congressional Budget Act of 1974.* The act created new budget committees in both the House and the Senate. It also set up the **Congressional Budget Office (CBO),** which seeks to unify the congressional budget effort and to evaluate the president's recommended budget. It mirrors the more comprehensive approach used by the OMB. The Congressional Budget Office has recently made more accurate, and more pessimistic, predictions about the size of the deficits than the OMB.

The Budget Act calls for both houses of Congress to adopt a tentative federal budget in May of each year, projecting total revenues, expenditures, and the federal surplus or deficit. It calls for congressional adoption of a final budget in September of each year. Tax measures and appropriations bills following this should conform to this final budget.

After appropriations are made, committees of Congress exercise "oversight" on federal spending. These committees keep a wary eye on agencies. In addition, the **General Accounting Office,** an arm of Congress, audits executive departments to make sure that money appropriated by Congress is spent wisely and lawfully.

These budget procedures are activated in a whirl of politics on the part of numerous interests. Senate members may deliberately, say, vote for more defense spending than they want so that they can establish a bargaining position with the House. The House may vote for a program that members dislike but that has voters' support, calculating that lack of Senate support will allow the program to be dropped and the Senate blamed. An interest group defeated in the House will appeal to the Senate. The president's veto gives him a tool more frequently threatened than used in the bargaining—or posturing—over spending and taxes.

The complexity of the process, the intensity of its politics, and the recent huge deficits have led many to the reasonable conclusion that the budget is "out of control." *Neither the executive nor the legislative branches have seemed able to balance budget resources with the demands put on them.* Put another way, "What we desire in particular (more programs) turns out not to be what we desire in general—less total spending and lower taxes."[8] The incentives are mostly on the *particular* demands, not on the *general* controls. Without a political consensus on the "conflicting promises" that a government's budget covers, there can be little hope of controlling the budget by improved procedures. The task of control is the task of coordinating commitments. That requires both a broad agreement outside of government on what government can and cannot do, and the political will inside government to enforce that consensus (see Figure 17.2).

The Federal Government Dollar (Fiscal Year 1989 Estimate)

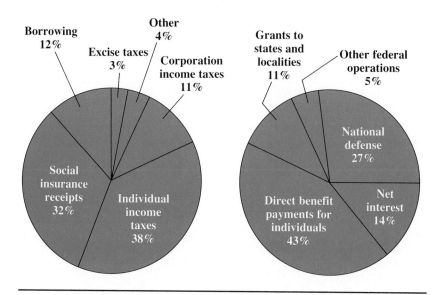

HERE IT COMES. . .   THERE IT GOES . . .

SOURCE: Office of Management and Budget, *The United States Budget in Brief, Fiscal Year 1989* (Washington, D.C.: Government Printing Office, 1988), inside cover.

FISCAL POLICY

Who government takes money from and who it gives money (or benefits) to almost describes the essence of government. Spending, taxing, and borrowing make up government's moving bottom line.

Spending

Federal spending has three general effects. First, the *fiscal effect* causes unemployment and inflation to rise or fall as a result of varied federal spending. Second, there is a *regulatory effect* of spending. For example, the federal government grants subsidies to regional airlines for service to cities that might not otherwise be served, and the Department of Agriculture has long granted subsidies to farmers who hold down production of crops such as cotton. Third, there is the *distributional effect,* by which spending can redistribute wealth from one group to another.

Usually we think that this distribution is from the wealthy to the poor. That is the object of social welfare programs like Medicaid, food stamps, and public housing. But *redistribution also goes from the not-so-wealthy in America to the more wealthy* via the route of federal subsidies. For example, a fraction of Americans own airplanes; yet those who do benefit from hundreds of millions of dollars in federal subsidies in the form of free traffic control, weather reporting systems, and airport construction. In addition, much of the costs of flights of privately owned airplanes are deducted as business expenses for tax purposes.

The deficit itself redistributes money from mostly middle-class tax payers to mostly wealthy bondholders. The deficit is paid for by issuing U.S. Treasury bonds with interest going to owners. Some 93 percent of all bonds are held by the country's richest 10 percent. This means that while Medicaid payments are reduced, interest payments

FIGURE 17★3
Federal Expenditures, 1970–1993 (estimate, in billions of dollars)

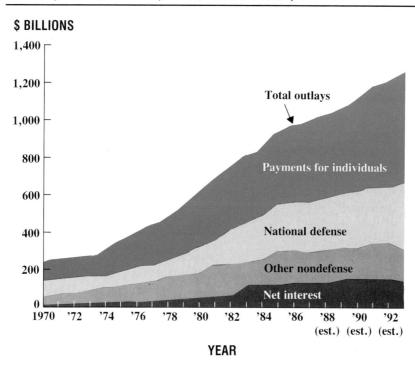

SOURCE: Office of Management and Budget, *Budget of the United States, Fiscal Year 1989: Historical Tables* (Washington, D.C.: Government Printing Office, 1988), pp. 127–31.

are increased. This includes a doubling of interest paid to foreign holders of U.S. debt between 1980 and 1987, to $23.5 billion. The deficit, it can be argued, causes redistribution without even the consolation of seeing tax dollars spent on actual government programs which might clean up the environment or feed the hungry.[9]

How the government spends our money may have a great impact on the economy, may greatly affect particular businesses and communities, and may produce dramatic changes in the distribution of wealth and income. It may also greatly affect an individual life (see the box on page 534).

Taxes

"There are 100 taxes on an egg and I don't think the chicken put them there; someplace between the hen and the table they crept in."

—Ronald Reagan

Taxes, like spending, can have three important effects (in addition to simply raising revenues). The *fiscal effect* is the impact on unemployment or inflation as money is taken from, or left with, people for consumption or investment. The *distributional effect* results from tax decisions about "who will pay the costs," these cigarette smokers or those car drivers. The *regulatory effect* of taxes may discourage or promote certain activity. A heavier tax on "gas-guzzling" cars may discourage their purchase, while a tax reduction may encourage the use of solar equipment. Taxes primarily raise money to finance the government, but they are also used for these other purposes.

How high are federal taxes? Among countries similar to the United States, only one taxes their people less. Local, state, and federal taxes take about 29 cents out of every dollar of national output in the U.S., or about $4944 per capita. Japan has a slightly lower tax rate, but most other countries—including Sweden, France, Britain and West Germany (at $5500 per capita)—tax their people more, some considerably so. Also, taxes have been increasing faster in these countries than in the United States. Federal income taxes in America are not nearly as high as they once were (see Figure 17.4).

Holding down federal income taxes has spread the tax bite, resulting in recent increases in Social Security, local, and state taxes. These taxes are largely **regressive.** They take a larger share of the income of low-income groups than they do from high-income groups. A **progressive tax,** on the other hand, takes a larger percentage of income from high-income groups than from low-income groups. A progressive tax is based on the ability to pay.

FIGURE 17★4
How Big Is Big?

The graph shows that the national, state, and local governments in the United States spend a smaller percentage of their country's resources than those in almost all other democracies with developed economies do. Only Japan spends a smaller percentage, and it, unlike the United States, has a very small defense budget. Compared with this record, the United States has a rather modest public sector.

TOTAL EXPENDITURES OF GOVERNMENT AS A PERCENTAGE OF THE GROSS DOMESTIC PRODUCT*, 1986

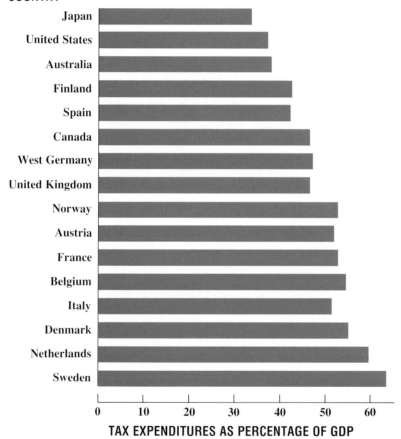

*Gross Domestic Product is Gross National Product minus the value of goods and services produced outside the country.

SOURCE: *OECD Economic Outlook* 43 (June 1988), p. 183.

The federal *income tax* was designed to be progressive: the higher the income, the higher the tax rates. That is generally not true of federal *excise taxes*—on liquor, tobacco, gasoline, and air travel—which account for about 5 percent of federal tax collections.

FIGURE 17★5
Federal Revenues, 1977–1991

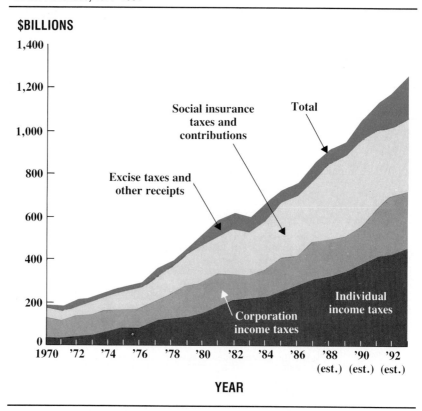

$BILLIONS

SOURCE: Office of Management and Budget, *The United States Budget in Brief, Fiscal Year 1989* (Washington, D.C.: Government Printing Office, 1988), p. 45.

The regressive federal social insurance taxes, covering Social Security and Medicare, take an even larger bite out of most Americans' paychecks. These taxes, while not fully based on the ability to pay, compose over a quarter of all federal tax collections. Maximum earnings subject to Social Security taxes in 1988 were $48,000. If a person made more than that amount, the extra earnings were not taxable for this purpose. There has also been a staged increase in the Social Security tax rate, from 6.7 percent in 1985 to 7.65 percent in 1990. So, while federal income taxes have decreased, steadily increasing Social Security taxes have eaten up much of the benefit (see Figure 17.5).

State and local taxes take a large bite out of the incomes of most Americans. While two-thirds of the states have some kind of state income tax, most states rely heavily on sales taxes, which are not based on the ability to pay. Some states exclude certain necessities, such as food and medicine, from the sales tax. But the sales tax still takes a larger percentage of the incomes of low-income citizens than it does from high-income citizens. Similarly regressive are local property taxes. Even renters are affected by the property tax, since landlords may pass these taxes on via higher rents.

The federal government also collects estate and gift taxes, custom duties, and tariffs. The theory behind estate and gift taxes is that they would reduce the unequal distribution of wealth by collecting a part of what people inherit from relatives through estates or gifts. There are a number of ways to avoid these taxes, and they have had little affect on the distribution of wealth. Tariffs and customs duties were responsible for a large portion of federal tax collections during the early years of the Republic. This is no longer true. They are now often used to regulate commerce. Tariffs, for example, increase the cost of imports, making them less competitive with American-made goods.

Income Taxes

Corporate and individual income taxes are today the most important sources of federal revenue. To pay for the Civil War, Congress enacted the first federal income tax in 1861. The tax expired in 1873. Congress next passed an income tax in 1894, but the Supreme Court declared this tax unconstitutional. The Court held that the income tax was a direct tax and therefore must be apportioned among the states on the basis of their population. In 1913, the states ratified the Sixteenth Amendment to the U.S. Constitution. It gave the federal government the power, through Congress, "to lay and collect taxes

These impressive parking lots in Newark, New Jersey in 1981 demonstrate the scope of Japanese exports to the U.S.

on income, from whatever source derived, without apportionment among the several states, and without regard to any census or enumeration." Gotcha—the modern income tax.

From the beginning, "loopholes" existed. The special tax treatment of *capital gains* was one example. A **capital gain** is the difference between the purchase price and the sale price of property, if the sale price is higher. The property involved may be real estate, corporate stock, a horse, a truck, or other personal property. This income, when the property was held for six months or more, was taxed at a lower rate than earned income. So suppose one person makes a living by making Ford cars, and another makes a living by buying Ford Motor Company stock at a lower price and selling it at a higher price. If both make $20,000 a year, the person who makes Fords will pay considerably higher federal income taxes than the person who buys and sells Ford stock. This tax difference on capital gains was removed by the 1986 tax reform. But President Bush proposed restoring a lower tax on capital gains to encourage investments and Congress found it hard to resist this popular tax cut.

★ Who Needs Government?

Senator Ernest Hollings tells this story: A veteran returning from Korea went to college on the GI Bill; bought his house with an FHA loan; saw his kids born in a VA hospital; started a business with an SBA loan; got electricity from TVA and, then, water from a project funded by the EPA. His kids participated in the school-lunch program and made it through college courtesy of government-guaranteed student loans. His parents retired to a farm on their social security, getting electricity from the REA and the soil tested by the USDA. When the father became ill, his life was saved with a drug developed through NIH; the family was saved from financial ruin by Medicare. Our veteran drove to work on the interstate; moored his boat in a channel dredged by Army engineers; and when floods hit, took Amtrak to Washington to apply for disaster relief. He also spent some of his time there enjoying the exhibits in the Smithsonian museums.

Then one day he wrote his congressman an angry letter complaining about paying taxes for all those programs created for ungrateful people. In effect, he said, the government should get off his back.

SOURCE: Jonathan Yates, "Reality on Capitol Hill," *Newsweek*, November 28, 1988, p. 12.

Of course "loopholes" lie in the eyes of the beholders, who are usually those not benefitting directly from the tax break. However, critics made several points about tax loopholes like the special treatment of capital gains. First, *if you have money, the tax laws help you make more money.* These special provisions are not available to those who do not have money to invest. Second, and not so apparent, is that these special tax provisions are actually *tax expenditures.* They have the same effect on the federal treasury as if the taxes were first collected and then paid back to particular citizens. Under a lower capital gains tax, for example, if people invested in property for over six months, the treasury paid them back by not collecting some of the taxes they would owe. Finally, *these loopholes distort the market.* People make business and investment decisions based on their tax consequences rather than their economic results. Sheltering money from the government became as important as the profit motive.

These criticisms led to the most significant modern change in federal income taxes, the *Tax Reform Bill of 1986.* The reform combined a Democratic push to close loopholes with a Republican wish for lower rates. The tax rate for individuals was cut almost in half (to 28 percent), dozens of loopholes were closed, millions of poor families no longer had to pay income taxes, and a minimum tax was set for wealthy individuals who previously had escaped paying any taxes. The effort to simplify the tax system through this reform was notably unsuccessful, as anyone filling out the new, equally complex IRS forms can testify. But a few years after this momentous reform commentators noted how little difference it had made. Business investments hadn't collapsed, as critics predicted. Tax shelters hadn't disappeared, as reformers hoped. One of the 1986 Act's creators, economist Joseph J. Minarik, concluded two years afterward, "Taxes don't make nearly as much difference in behavior as has been thought."[10] (See the case study in Chapter 12.)

Borrowing

When spending exceeds income, the federal government must borrow money. It borrows from individual and institutional lenders—and pays interest on the debt like any other borrower. The last year the federal government had a balanced budget and did not have to borrow money was 1969. By 1988 the amount of the *deficit* (or annual amount borrowed) was $155 billion, and the total debt was well over $2.6 trillion.

The first great deficits came during World War II, when the national debt rose by more than $200 billion. The government had borrowed $23 billion during World War I and some $13 billion during the 1930s Depression. The Vietnam War required borrowing, too, but not nearly as much as the slow-growth years between 1975 and 1980. During this last period, high inflation increased the costs of government, and idled workers and plants reduced the government's tax collections. President Reagan's first-term reduction in taxes and increase in defense spending, combined with high interest rates and a severe recession, pushed the national debt through the roof.

During his 1980 presidential campaign Reagan spoke of balancing the budget by 1983. In his first televised address after taking office he pointed to that year's "runaway deficit of nearly $80 billion." The $79 billion deficit in 1981 that Reagan took over from Carter would be the last he would be able to write in two digits. The average deficit for the next six years was $184 billion, ranging from a low of $128 billion in 1982 to a high of $221 billion in 1986. This more than doubled the entire federal debt that had accumulated *since the founding of the Republic* (see Figure 17.6).

This deficit has not resulted from disagreements about spending between Congress and the president. There has been little difference in their proposals over total *amounts,* just disputes on the *distribution* between defense and nondefense spending. One economist concluded, "The deficit has resulted mostly from the fact that federal revenues have consistently fallen far short of the administration's early projections."[11]

The national debt limit is set by law, and Congress every so often raises it. If the limit were not raised, the federal government could not pay its bills because it would not be allowed to borrow money. The government can only spend money it either has or is authorized to borrow. Some state constitutions require that the state's budgets be balanced. President Reagan called for a similar budget-balancing amendment to the federal Constitution. But, since he had never actually proposed a balanced budget, some dismissed his proposal as political posturing.

The huge federal deficits have created predictable responses from citizens: "My family and I have to live within our means, we can't spend more than we take in, and the government should have to also"; "Why don't they run the government like a business and balance out expenses with income?" But few families, and virtually no businesses, could get along without debt. Rather than pay cash, a family will borrow money to buy a house. A family borrows money for thirty years to buy a house, and in ten years, they sell that house and take out a new mortgage for another thirty years in order to buy a new house. They may never get out of debt. Similarly, American

FIGURE 17★6
Budget Deficit

IN DOLLARS[1] (In billions of dollars, not adjusted for inflation)

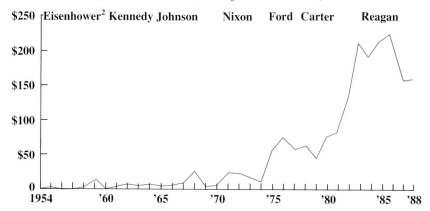

AS PERCENT OF GNP[1]

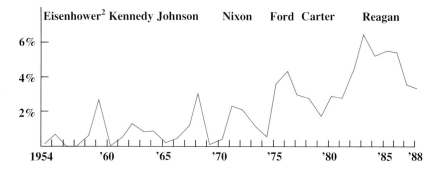

[1]The government ran a surplus in 1956, 1957, 1960, and 1969.
[2]Years are assigned to the administration in office when the fiscal year began.

SOURCE: David Rapp, "Is Anyone Really Trying to Balance the Budget?"
Congressional Quarterly, November 26, 1988, p. 3379.

business corporations have the same kind of rising debt as the federal government does.

There are, however, at least two serious problems with the present run-up in government debt. First, *the debt itself is real, growing, and has to be paid back.* It has risen relative to GNP, which means our total production of goods and services, or, in a sense, the ability to pay our debts (see Figure 17.6). Americans in the future will have to service this debt by paying taxes and transferring the goods they produce and the assets they own to lenders who are increasingly in other countries. The second consequence is that *this debt has simply raised consumption with no advance in productivity to go with it.* The funds saved on lower taxes have not gone for investments. The savings rate has fallen to a new modern low. Americans saved over 7 percent of their after-tax income from the 1950s to the 1970s. But by 1987 they were saving just 3.7 percent. Americans were consuming more and saving less, courtesy of an increasing deficit.[12]

MONETARY POLICY

In addition to fiscal policy—spending, taxes, and borrowing—the federal government affects the national economy through its influence on the money supply, its **monetary policy.**

What is money? Money is, first of all, coins and paper currency. This kind of U.S. money today is not redeemable in silver or gold, but can only be exchanged for other currency. Thus, the value of money depends on faith in the government that backs it. The value of money also depends on how much of it exists. Money is something like a commodity such as wheat. If there is a huge surplus of wheat one year, wheat will not "buy" as much money per bushel. If there is a great shortage of wheat in another year, a bushel of wheat will "buy" more money than in the year of surplus. There is no such ratio that links the supply of money so directly with its value. No one doubts, however, that if money were in unlimited supply, it would have little value. Thus, governments—ours included—control the creation of money.

Money does not just consist of coins and currency. It also consists of *demand deposits,* or *checking accounts,* which can be immediately withdrawn from banks by depositors. Coins, currency, and demand deposits together are called "M1" by economists. Today, economists also consider *time deposits* or *savings accounts* in banks (called "M2") to be money. When we speak of "money," now we must include coins and currency, demand deposits and time deposits, all of which carry out money's most important function: to serve as a medium of exchange.

The banking system is allowed by law to create money as a result of what they do with the deposits they hold. If you put $500 in a checking account, the bank does not hold that $500 until you write checks on it. Instead, the bank is required to keep only about one-seventh of the amount of your deposit as *reserves*—in the form of cash, deposits in other banks, or in government bonds. What does the bank do with the rest of your checking account money? It loans it out, charging interest. Banks, then, make a profit in two ways: by charging for checking services and, most important, by loaning money at interest. Checks written by you are deposited by their recipients in other banks, which use the accounts to loan to borrowers, who make deposits in other banks. By the time your $500 has gone through the banking system, it has swelled to around $3500 in circulation.

Since banks (plus savings and loan institutions) never have enough money on hand to pay off all depositors at once, state and federal governments have passed laws to protect depositors. The banks must be chartered before they can go into operation—state banks by state authorities, federal banks by the *Comptroller of the Currency*. Their operations are audited by the chartering authorities. Also, almost all banks have their deposits insured by the *Federal Deposit Insurance Corporation (FDIC)*. The *Federal Savings and Loan Insurance Corporation (FSLIC)* does the same thing for savings and loans. (Because of the large number of failed savings and loans, the Bush administration in 1989 proposed putting the FSLIC under the FDIC, with the savings and loans placed under tighter regulations.) These insuring federal agencies also audit and regulate the insured institutions.

The Fed

To both regulate the banks and the amount of money in circulation, Congress created the Federal Reserve System in 1913. The **Federal Reserve System**—or the *Fed*—is run by a seven-member board appointed by the president and confirmed by the Senate. Board members serve for fixed, staggered terms of fourteen years. The president also names the chairperson of the board, with Senate confirmation, for a term of four years which does not run concurrently with the president's term. Because of their long fixed terms and because they can only be removed for cause, neither the chairperson nor the members of the Board of Governors are directly controlled by the president.

The Federal Reserve System operates through twelve regional Federal Reserve Banks, owned by the member commercial banks. All national banks must belong to the Federal Reserve System. A large number of state banks, 1099 in early 1988, voluntarily belong to it. Since these member banks are among the largest in the country, they account for over three-fourths of the bank deposits in the United States.

All countries have "central banks" that regulate the **money supply.** But our central bank—the Fed—is unique. *It is both privately owned and operates almost independently of direct government control.* By contrast, the Bank of England—that country's central bank—is government owned and follows the monetary policy set by the British cabinet.

How does the Fed regulate the money supply? How does it make the money supply grow faster or slower? And what difference does it make? Answering the last question first, faster growth of money in circulation encourages consumers to buy more and businesses to invest more, because interest rates are lower and credit is easier to get. This stimulates spending, increases production, and reduces unemployment. On the other side, when growth in the money supply is slowed, consumers spend less and businesses invest less, because interest rates are higher and credit is harder to get. Thus, *tighter money supply* tends to slow down spending and reduce the rate of inflation, often leading to slowed production and higher unemployment. A *looser monetary supply* may stimulate spending and decrease unemployment, often leading to higher inflation.

The Fed affects the money supply in three ways. First, and most important, the Fed (through its "open market committee," made up of the seven-member board of governors and five representatives from district banks) may buy or sell the government bonds it owns. These and other decisions by the Fed are made in secret.

When the Fed sells government bonds (mostly to dealers in bonds who sell to banks, insurance companies, and large corporations), the purchasers pay by writing checks on their accounts in various banks. This reduces the deposits against which these banks may loan money. When the Fed sells bonds on the open market, then, it lowers or tightens money supply.

On the other hand, when the Fed buys government bonds on the open market, the people who sell such bonds deposit the sale proceeds in their bank accounts. This increases the deposits against which banks can make loans and thus *expands* the total money supply. *The Fed's open market operation is its most important monetary tool.*

Second in importance, the Fed can expand the total money supply by changing the *discount rate* it charges member banks to borrow from it. Banks have to borrow money. One place they borrow from is the Fed. By raising or lowering this discount rate, the Fed can encourage or discourage borrowing by member banks. When member banks are encouraged to borrow from the Fed, they will have more money to loan out. This increases the money supply. When they are discouraged from borrowing from the Fed, they will have less loan proceeds to loan out. This restricts the money supply.

The third and least used of the Fed's major monetary tools is its power to change the *reserve requirements* for member banks. As mentioned, banks are required to keep reserves on hand to pay demand deposits. By changing these reserve requirements for member banks, the Fed may determine what portion of demand deposits a member bank can loan out. When the Fed raises reserve requirements, member banks can loan less. When the Fed lowers reserve requirements, member banks can loan more. More loans mean greater growth in the money supply; fewer loans mean less growth.

When the Fed is expanding the money supply, interest rates inch downward. When the Fed slows growth in the money supply, interest rates inch upward. A signal of what is happening to interest rates generally comes when the largest banks in the country—such as Chase Manhattan or Citibank, both in New York—announce an increase or decrease in their *prime rate*. This is the rate of interest that banks charge their biggest and best borrowers. Ordinary borrowers usually pay more. *Interest rates* are essentially the price of money. Of course, the amount it costs to borrow money will affect how much of it is in circulation.

Monetarists

Monetarists emphasize monetary policy (some to the virtual exclusion of fiscal policy) as the most important way to manage the economy. Their famous phrase is "money matters" (in contrast to Keynesians who stressed fiscal policy over monetary policy). Led by Milton Friedman and his "Chicago School" of economists, monetarists called for an automatic annual growth rate of, say, 4.5 percent in the money supply. Friedman accused the Fed of causing inflation and worsening the business cycle by its erratic money supply policy—first supplying too much and then tightening abruptly. The Fed was a political institution, Friedman charged, preserving its own power and protecting the noncompetitive banking industry rather than giving the country the predictable money growth it needed.[13]

By late 1979, under Chairman Paul Volcker the Fed had been nudged by an inflation rate of nearly 13 percent to adopt a monetarist line. The Fed announced it would set a target for money supply and follow it no matter what happened to interest rates. What happened was that interest rates reached 21 percent and the country plunged into a deep recession. Some critics charged that the Fed's change in policy was just political protection, allowing Volcker to raise rates indirectly. It was not until the Fed loosened their reins on the money supply in mid-1982 that the economy revived.[14]

The difficulty of calculating money supply led to further disillusionment with strict monetarism by the Fed. The international flow of dollars reduced the Fed's control over supply, and the increasing use of new ways of holding money, such as money-market funds (which were neither quite checking accounts or savings accounts), made the question of "what is money" very debatable. When Alan Greenspan replaced Volcker as Chairman of the Fed in 1987, he announced that the Fed would follow a variety of indicators for setting monetary policy. Rather than just mechanically adjusting the money supply, the Fed would look at unemployment, inflation, and other indicators of the economy's health and direction before influencing interest rates. The Fed wasn't rejecting monetarism; it seemed to be absorbing it in other approaches. Greenspan's pragmatism put the Fed squarely back into the policy-making role it had probably never left.

While the Fed usually follows the monetary policy desired by the president, it does not always do so. Congress sets the limits within which the Fed must operate, but the Fed has wide discretion. Thus, it is quite possible that while the president and Congress are using fiscal policy to increase spending and decrease unemployment, the Fed might be using monetary policy to slow growth in the money supply and to bring down inflation, thereby increasing unemployment. High-level members of the Bush administration complained in mid-1989 that the Fed was over-concerned with inflation and should loosen its tight monetary policy. This is known as "Fed-bashing."

The Fed has also been accused of reflecting the wishes of bankers and causing recessions. "Recessions were induced by the federal government. In the seven recessions since World War II, the same transaction had preceded each contraction: the Federal Reserve's decision to force up interest rates to an abnormal level."[15] There is some truth in this, but it's good not to overstate the imperfect science the Fed engages in. The Fed is constantly adjusting a flow of money, correcting for past mistakes, wrong calculations, and new developments. Money supply is not "controlled" by any one force. It is, as John Maynard Keynes suggested, like water in a reservoir. The Fed can maintain the supply by pouring water into it. But other factors—rainfall, evaporation, leakage, and the habits of users—can also change the level. To all these forces the Fed must adjust.

THE RESULTS OF FEDERAL ECONOMIC MANAGEMENT

This discussion of the government's role in the economy leads to important conclusions. Inflation rates—whether hamburger costs more the next time we go to the supermarket—are not made in heaven, or down below. Unemployment—whether we get a notice

★ Guess Who's Coming to Dinner

Imagine one hundred people at the banquet seated at six tables. At the far right is a table set with English china and real silver, where five people sit comfortably. Next to them is another table, nicely set but nowhere near as fancy, where fifteen people sit. At each of the four remaining tables twenty people sit—the one on the far left has a stained paper tablecloth and plastic knives and forks. This arrangement is analogous to the spread of income groups—from the richest 5 percent at the right to the poorest 20 percent at the left.

Twenty waiters and waitresses come in, carrying 100 delicious-looking dinners, just enough, one would suppose, for each of the one hundred guests. But, amazingly, four of the waiters bring 20 dinners to the five people at the fancy table on the right. There's hardly room for all the food. (If you go over and look a little closer, you will notice that two of the waiters are obsequiously fussing and trying to arrange 10 dinners in front of just one of those five.) At the next-fanciest table, with the fifteen people, five waiters bring another 25 dinners. The twenty people at the third table get 25 dinners, 15 go to the fourth table, and 10 to the fifth. To the twenty people at the last table (the one with the paper tablecloth) a rude and clumsy waiter brings only 5 dinners. At the top table there are 4 dinners for each person; at the bottom table, four persons for each dinner. That's approximately the way income is distributed in America—fewer than half the people get even one dinner apiece.

SOURCE: William Ryan, *Equality* (New York: Pantheon Books, 1981), p. 11.

that 15 percent of us at work are being laid off—is not simply bad luck. Interest rates—whether we can afford the mortgage payments to buy a home—are not a question of fate. Inflation, unemployment, and interest rates are all affected by political decisions. Economic policy-making is not an exact science. It involves choices and conflicting interests. And when the government makes choices about the economy, all of us are affected.

How successfully has the federal government managed the economy? How well has it kept people employed while maintaining stable prices and interest rates? Has there been a closing of the gap between the very rich and the very poor? The short answer is that the government has done some of its tasks well and some not very well at all.

The Recent Record

When John Kennedy took office in 1960, the economy was stagnant, with idle industrial plants and high unemployment. In line with Keynesian economics, Kennedy took the novel step of a large tax reduction in order to "get the economy moving again." There was opposition to this idea, which would increase the federal deficit at least in the short run. Kennedy's advisers argued that the tax cut would leave more money in the hands of consumers, would stimulate private spending (he also recommended increased federal spending), and would eventually result in increased tax collections. This proved to be true.

The Kennedy years confounded those who believed that there is a "trade-off" between unemployment and inflation (if one goes down, the other must go up). Unemployment went down but prices did not go up. Then came the Lyndon Johnson years. At first, the economy functioned quite satisfactorily. But the Vietnam War, with its cost of $30 billion a year, helped to end that. Johnson wanted "guns and butter," both the increased domestic spending on his "Great Society" programs and the military spending for the war. For political reasons, he delayed asking Congress for a tax increase to pay for it all. The result was a classic case of inflation: too much spending (money) for too few goods. Prices went up.

Still, when Richard Nixon took office in 1969, the rate of inflation was only 4.8 percent, and unemployment was only 3.5 percent. Both figures were to double during his administration. Nixon tightened fiscal policy by *impounding funds* (not spending all the money Congress appropriated for particular programs) and cutting expenditures. At the same time, the Fed head, Arthur Burns, sternly restricted the growth in the money supply. The term **stagflation** was coined to describe what happened: inflation and stagnation—both unemployment and prices began to shoot upward.

After having said that he would never do so, President Nixon invoked *wage and price controls* under legislation that Congress had passed. They were later relaxed in phases, with the result that prices went back up. As the 1972 election approached, Burns loosened up on the money supply and Nixon began releasing impounded funds and increasing federal spending. As a result, things got better and Nixon was reelected.

Things generally do get better, economically speaking, at election time. Not surprisingly, when they do, incumbent presidents usually get elected again. The important thing is not whether the economy improved under the incumbent president, but that the public sees things getting better as an election draws near. A skeptic might con-

Long lines form in an unemployment office near Detroit in 1988.

clude that we could enjoy prosperity all the time in America if we could just have a presidential election every year.[16]

Nixon's successor, Gerald Ford, had to deal with the shattering decision of oil-producing countries (OPEC) to embargo oil going to the United States. This caused the price of crude oil to quadruple. Increased energy prices dampened the economy much like a government tax increase would. Worse, these "taxes" did not stay in the United States but went to foreign countries and multinational oil companies. They left behind an ever-spiraling inflation.

The economy continued to perform poorly throughout Ford's time in office—and, importantly, throughout the 1976 presidential campaign. Ford was defeated by Jimmy Carter. Carter at first primarily fought unemployment—and the rate came down to 6 percent. But inflation went up—and he switched to fight it. His increasingly conservative economic policy combined restraints on spending and slower growth in the money supply. Unemployment started back up, inflation and interest rates remained high, and the country went into a recession in the election year of 1980. In February of that year, polls showed that 70 percent of Americans disapproved of the job Carter was doing, particularly with the economy. In November, they voted him out of office.

At first the economy worsened under President Reagan. A large tax cut, mostly benefiting business and individuals in higher brackets, did not stimulate the economy sufficiently. Reagan followed the monetarists with a tight-money, high-interest-rate policy at the Fed that severely slowed the economy. Inflation, which had been as high as 12 percent under Carter, was cut by two-thirds. But the nation went into a severe recession. Unemployment shot up to 11 percent.

Long lines at the gas pumps were a common sight in the 1970s, primarily because of the actions of oil-producing countries. Oil embargos caused energy shortages which resulted in gas being sold only during certain hours of the day.

Since the government was losing around $30 billion for every percentage point of unemployment—through income tax revenues lost when people are out of work and through increased unemployment and welfare benefits—the federal budget deficit soared. Partly because of this borrowed money, and partly because the Fed reversed course and lowered interest rates, things were getting better, economically, at election time. President Reagan was resoundingly reelected in 1984.

The Twin Deficits

The twin deficits, budget and foreign trade, dominated the national economic concerns during Reagan's prosperous second term. However, these problems seemed secondary to the comfortable economic conditions workers and consumers enjoyed, especially compared to the 1982 recession. Unemployment continued to drop toward 5 percent and inflation dozed uneasily at around 4 percent. Economic growth hovered at a low 2 to 3 percent, a rate that, according to *Forbes* magazine, "only just repaired the damage of the 1982 recession" by 1988.[17] Even the budget deficit grew more slowly in 1987 and 1988, to some extent because the untouchable social security trust fund was included on the plus side of the budget ledger in a bookkeeping ploy that critics called a little slippery.

The trade deficit, which had been a surplus until 1975, grew from an already staggering $150 billion in 1985 to $175 billion by 1987. This happened despite steps taken in 1986 to lower the value of the dollar relative to other nations' currencies. This made U.S. exports cheaper and raised the prices of imports. By 1988 the trade deficit had dropped to its lowest level of growth in over three years. U.S. debt to foreign lenders went over $400 billion in 1987, keeping the U.S. as the world's number one debtor. And the stock market lost its optimism and about $1 trillion in wealth (on paper) as the Dow average dropped over 500 points, or 22 percent, on Black Monday, October 19, 1987. Besides scaring investors, the stock market crash seemed to have little effect on the economy.

Nonetheless, as President Bush succeeded President Reagan, the economy was simmering at a level to warm the incumbent party's hearts. At seven years and counting it was the longest peacetime boom without a turnaround of the business cycle in the modern era. Unemployment and inflation remained subdued, although the latter showed signs of awakening. Dissent was heard about the increased number of families below the poverty line. And some liberal economists said that incomes were being eroded by a drop in wage levels concealed by the rapid growth in families supported by two incomes. However, helped along by a huge advantage given by prosperity, Republican Bush was elected president and kept his popularity high through most of his first year in office.

Wealth and Income in America

The framers of the Constitution believed that citizens had an equal right to unequal wealth. We tend to think of this right to private ownership of property as a freedom *from* government. In fact, property rights are established and protected *by* government.[18] The founders of the United States recognized this. In *Federalist 10,* James Madison wrote that the fragmentation of government powers was specifically designed to control (among other things) "the rage for . . . an equal division of property, or any other improper or wicked project."

In America today, there is a great disparity in wealth and income between the rich and the poor. According to a study by the Federal Reserve, the wealthiest 2 percent of America's families own 30 percent of all privately held financial assets, including 50 percent of all corporate stock and 71 percent of all (tax-free) municipal bonds.[19] The Joint Economic Committee of Congress, in a 1986 report, said that the richest 0.5 percent of families in the U.S. controlled 27 percent of the wealth of the country in 1983, up from 25 percent in 1963.

Most Americans own only minimal assets, usually houses or cars that produce no income (50 percent of American families have a net worth of less than $25,000, and 33 percent have a net worth of $5000 or less). One-fifth of American families have a negative net worth— that is, they owe more than they own.

The gap between the rich and the poor grew wider during the 1980s (see Figure 17.7). In the early 1970s, in part because of the Great Society programs, fewer American families lived in poverty than at any time before or since. Since 1980 the figure has risen so that in 1986, after four years of prosperity, almost 11 percent of all families lived in poverty. This meant 32 million Americans lived in poverty, 3 million of whom worked full-time all year long. The group that now suffers the greatest poverty are children, with one out of five living below the poverty line.[20]

Politics affects poverty. Poverty is greatly influenced by government programs and benefits. According to Census Bureau figures, the poverty figure would be almost twice as high without government programs like Social Security, welfare, Medicare, and food stamps. Government programs sharply reduced economic inequality. In 1986, the poorest fifth of the population received only one percent of the country's total income, excluding government benefits and taxes. The top fifth received 52.4 percent. After counting government benefits and taxes, the lowest fifth got 4.9 percent of the income and the top fifth got 45.5 percent. Social Security alone reduced poverty among the elderly from 48 percent to 14 percent, lifting over 15 million people out of poverty.[21]

Capitalism and Democracy

F. Scott Fitzgerald once said to Ernest Hemingway, "The rich are different from you and me." Hemingway responded, "Yes, they have more money." In fact, Fitzgerald was right. The rich have more than more money. Being affluent in America means having access to the things money can buy, such as good nutrition, good health services, and good housing. It also means having a better chance of passing one's privileged economic status to one's children through things like a first-class education for them.

Economic power becomes political power in several ways. The most obvious is through campaign contributions by wealthy individuals and businesses. The "politics and money cycle" was never more candidly explained than when U.S. Senator Boies Penrose of Pennsylvania told a business group at the turn of the century, "I believe

FIGURE 17★7
Changing Shares

PERSONAL INCOME
(averaged by fifths of the population, in constant 1986 dollars)

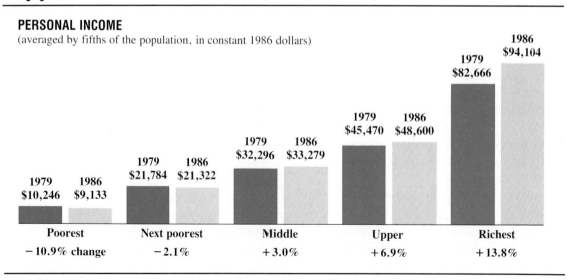

SOURCE: Leonard Silk, "Now, to Figure Why the Poor Get Poorer," *The New York Times,* December 18, 1988, p. E5.

"... RELAX, MEN ... THIS PLAN WILL LAND US A BIG FINANCIAL AID PACKAGE!..."

in a division of labor. You send us to Congress, we pass the laws under . . . which you make money; . . . and out of your profits you further contribute to our campaign funds to send us back again to pass more laws to enable you to make more money."[22]

What "laws" enable these interests to make more money? How about some of these: direct government subsidies, government regulation that limits competition, tariffs and import quotas to protect against foreign competition, relaxed environmental safety standards, and less enforcement of antitrust laws.

On the other hand, those who are not rich in America—the third of our families who are trying just to make ends meet—often seem trapped in a bind. They suffer the "hidden injuries of class," as Richard Sennett and Jonathan Cobb's book by that title has shown.[23] People are not born with true equality of opportunity. These families are hard hit by economic downturns; they often live in fear because of high crime rates in their neighborhoods; and they find that good schools, healthcare, nutrition, and housing are not available to them. Yet many poor people internalize these problems. They feel that there must be something wrong with them. Furthermore, as shown in Chapter 5, they are less likely to be listened to by government because they are least likely to vote or take part in politics.

There is a tension between capitalism and democracy. The Catch-22 of our system, *the irony of democracy,* is that those who most need the intervention of government to protect and improve their lives are the least influential politically, while those who least need government intervention are the most politically powerful.[24] Charles Beard wrote that "The device of universal suffrage does not destroy economic classes or economic inequalities. It ignores them."[25] We have never really come to grips with this "paradox." Differences in economic power produce differences in political influence that may, in turn, maintain or increase the disparity in wealth, income, and economic power.

WRAP-UP

A frustrated Harry Truman once declared his intention to hire a one-armed economist as his adviser. The former president hoped this would prevent the economist from saying, "On the other hand. . . ." Economics is not an exact science. Economists disagree about what policies should be adopted to solve the nation's economic problems. Still, making economic policy is a vital function of the federal government—a function with political input and consequences.

What the government decides about levels and purposes of taxation and spending, what happens in regard to growth in the money supply, and whether government deregulates or intervenes in the market are intense political decisions. They affect every citizen, although, of course, every citizen does not have equal influence in the decisions. Those with the most influence not surprisingly tend to receive the greatest benefits. Those with the least influence suffer accordingly.

Key Terms

capitalism (p. 520)
free enterprise (p. 520)
laissez-faire (p. 520)
mixed economy (p. 522)
Keynesian economics (p. 523)
fiscal policy (p. 523)
supply-side theories (p. 523)
Office of Management and Budget (OMB) (p. 525)
Congressional Budget Office CBO) (p. 527)

General Accounting Office (p. 527)
regressive tax (p. 530)
progressive tax (p. 530)
capital gain (p. 534)
monetary policy (p. 538)
Federal Reserve System (p. 539)
money supply (p. 539)
monetarists (p. 541)
stagflation (p. 544)

Suggested Readings

Kleinfeld, Sonny, *Staying at the Top: The Life of a CEO* (New York: New American Library, 1987).

Lekachman, Robert, *Visions and Nightmares* (New York: Macmillan Publishing Company, 1987).

Malabre, Alfred, *Beyond Our Means: How America's Long Years of Debt, Deficits and Reckless Borrowing Now Threaten to Overwhelm Us* (New York: Random House, 1987).

Niskanen, William A., *Reaganomics: An Insider's Account of the Politics and the People* (New York: Oxford University Press, 1988).

Penner, Rudolph G. and Alan J. Abramson, *Broken Purse Strings: Congressional Budgeting, 1974–1988* (Washington, D.C.: Urban Institute Press, 1988).

Sprague, Irvine H., *Bailout: An Insider's View of Bank Failures and Rescues* (New York: Basic Books, 1986).

Weidenbaum, Murray, *Rendezvous with Reality: The American Economy After Reagan* (New York: Basic Books, 1988).

Endnotes

[1] See Robert Lekachman, *Economists at Bay* (New York: McGraw-Hill, 1976), p. 209–15.

[2] See Karl Marx, *Capital* (New York: Random House/Modern Library, 1977), pp. 836–37.

[3] Robert L. Heilbroner, *An Inquiry Into the Human Prospect* (New York: W. W. Norton, 1980).

[4] For a study on how this law came to be, see Stephen K. Bailey, *Congress Makes a Law* (New York: Columbia University Press, 1950).

[5] John Maynard Keynes, *The General Theory of Employment, Interest and Money* (New York: Harcourt Brace Jovanovich, 1965).

[6] See David Rapp, "Is Anyone Really Trying to Balance the Budget?" in *Congressional Quarterly,* November 26, 1988, pp. 3379–87.

[7] Aaron Wildavsky, *The New Politics of the Budgetary Process* (Glenview, IL: Scott, Foresman and Company, 1988), p. vii.

[8] Wildavsky, p. 31. This discussion owes much to Chapter 1.

[9] Mark Shields, "And Redistribution, Reagan-Style," *The Washington Post,* December 5, 1988.

[10] *Business Week,* March 7, 1988, p. 82.

[11] Benjamin Friedman, *Day of Reckoning* (New York: Random House, 1988), p. 19. Much of this discussion is based on this work.

[12] *Ibid.,* pp. 157–58, 162.

[13] See Milton Friedman, "The Role of Monetary Policy," *American Economic Review* (March 1968): 12–17; and Milton Friedman and Anna J. Schwartz, *A Monetary History of the United States, 1867–1960* (Princeton, N.J.: Princeton University Press, 1963).

[14] See William Greider, *Secrets of The Temple* (New York: Simon and Schuster, 1987), Chapter 3.

[15]Greider, p. 393.

[16]See Edward R. Tufte, *Political Control of the Economy* (Princeton, N.J.: Princeton University Press, 1978).

[17]*Forbes,* October 31, 1988, p. 90.

[18]See Charles E. Lindblom, *Politics and Markets* (New York: Basic Books, 1977), p. 8.

[19](Update) "Survey of Consumer Finances," *Federal Reserve Bulletin* (September 1984), pp. 679–90; and "Survey of Consumer Finances, 1983: A Second Report," *Federal Reserve Bulletin* (December 1984), pp. 857–68.

[20]Friedman, pp. 161–62.

[21]*The Washington Post,* December 28, 1988 and *The New York Times,* December 28, 1988.

[22]Quoted in Fred R. Harris, "The Politics of Corporate Power," in Ralph Nader and Mark J. Green, *Corporate Power in America* (New York: Grossman Publishers, 1973), p. 11. See also Frank J. Sorauf, *Money in American Elections* (Glenview, IL: Scott, Foresman), 1988.

[23]Richard Sennett and Jonathan Cobb, *The Hidden Injuries of Class* (New York: Vintage Books, 1973).

[24]See Thomas R. Dye and L. Harmon Zeigler, *The Irony of Democracy: An Uncommon Introduction to American Politics,* 6th ed. (Monterey, CA: Brooks/Cole, 1984).

[25]Charles Beard, *The Economic Basis of Politics* (New York: Vintage Books, 1957), p. 69.

CHAPTER 18

Foreign Policy

Fifty years ago, just before World War II, the United States had an army of 185,000 men on an annual budget of less than $500 million. The America of 1939 was bound by no entangling alliances, and no American troops were based in any foreign country. The prevailing mood of isolationism reflected America's feelings of security. It was a security not brought by military power or diplomatic cunning. It was, instead, an inherited gift of geography that distanced America from her foes.

The America of a half century later possessed enormous armed forces, supported by a military budget of over $300 *billion.* Defensive alliances tied the United States to some 50 nations and placed over a million soldiers, sailors, and air force troops in more than 100 countries. U.S. forces intervened in countries from the Persian Gulf to the Caribbean, distributed huge amounts of arms to numerous friendly governments, and maintained enough nuclear capability to destroy the world several times over. Yet for all America's strength of arms and global reach, national security was neither assured nor assumed. America was far stronger and felt far less secure than she had been 50 years before.[1]

The superpower conflict with the Soviet Union was the occasion of America's great strength and great insecurity. This Cold War has taken up almost half of the twentieth century. It has occupied the central focus of American foreign policy for most of that period, and has produced its own traditions and routines. While it has warmed at times and chilled at others, it is ". . . a rivalry made all the more striking by the fact that at no point in its long history have its major antagonists actually come to blows."[2]

The thrust of American foreign policy since World War II has been to adapt to the country's new superpower status in the setting of the Cold War. The nation's actors and institutions somewhat abruptly turned to an international foreign policy without quite giving up the themes of isolationism and interventionism. *Demands on foreign policy from abroad were often secondary to domestic political needs.* This was understood by political actors from the president to the U.N. So, the coalition building found in domestic politics among separate government institutions and diverse political interests was often repeated in foreign policy. How this policy-making process can steer the U.S. toward a future where foreign commitments will be restricted by economic limits is an underlying question of this chapter.

A symbol of the Cold War between the U.S. and the Soviet Union was "Checkpoint Charlie," the border station separating West Berlin from Soviet-controlled East Berlin until the Berlin Wall came down in November 1989 as an act of Eastern European reform.

THE HISTORY OF AMERICAN FOREIGN POLICY

Foreign policy consists of a government's pattern of words and actions toward other nations, along with the goals and assumptions that underlie them. The basic purpose of any country's foreign policy is to preserve its security as a nation. Thus, foreign policy involves matters of both peace and war, as well as economics.

There have been three major themes in the history of American foreign policy: *isolationism, interventionism,* and *internationalism.*

Isolationism

In 1801, Thomas Jefferson warned America against "permanent alliances" with other countries. This spirit of **isolationism** has always been a strong strain in American public opinion and foreign policy. It was probably an appropriate stance for a young country in the last century, focused inward on its own growth and eager to avoid entanglement in European intrigues. In today's world, isolationism looks more like nostalgia for a past time.

Isolationism was strongest in America before World War I. European countries were engaged in efforts to maintain a *balance of power* among themselves: each acted to prevent other nations from becoming too powerful. These balance-of-power policies arose from their concerns for national security, nationalism, and economic interests. Until World War I, the United States was able to remain relatively aloof from European foreign policy maneuvers.

Then, in August 1914, Europe was engulfed in war. Economic and political tensions that had been building up for years were ignited by the assassination of Austria's Archduke Franz Ferdinand by a Serbian nationalist. Austria declared war on Serbia. Interests and alliances caused Germany, and later Bulgaria and Turkey, to join Austria, while France, Great Britain, and Russia lined up with Serbia. Eventually, President Wilson came to feel that the war affected America's interests. In 1917, after German submarines had endangered U.S. ships and violated what Americans felt was freedom of the seas, the U.S. declared war on Germany, Austria, and their allies. Patriotism swept the U.S.; Americans came to believe that they were engaged in a crusade "to end all wars," as Wilson put it.

Of course, World War I did not end all wars. After the war, the Senate rejected the League of Nations, which Wilson had helped create. The League, which was to be a world peace-keeping organization, was established without United States membership. The United States tried to go back to its historical isolation from affairs outside the western hemisphere. The peace imposed on Germany—including a loss of territory and a burden of war payments to the victors—helped sow the seeds of a new world conflict twenty years later.

Interventionism

This historical isolationism was not applied in our own hemisphere. In Latin America, U.S. foreign policy has been characterized by **interventionism.** During the Revolution, Americans looked forward to a Canadian revolt against Britain similar to their own. Periodically American leaders, like Theodore Roosevelt, talked about making Canada a part of the Union by having our own westward expansion take a right turn. Canada did not share the sentiment. In recent years, Canada (with whom the U.S. has the longest undefended border and biggest trade relationship of any two countries in the world) has protested economic domination by American companies, expressed concern about U.S. foreign policy (in El Salvador, for example), and objected to U.S. "acid rain." However, in 1989 the world's largest free trade agreement between two countries became effective, removing almost all trade barriers between the U.S. and Canada.

Historically, U.S. foreign policy has treated Latin America as our special province. This policy dates back to the **Monroe Doctrine,** the 1823 declaration by President James Monroe that warned European nations to stay out of the affairs of nations in this hemisphere. But the Monroe Doctrine did not limit *our* involvement there. A war with Mexico, settled in 1848, brought the independent Republic of Texas into the Union and gave the U.S. the territory that became New Mexico and Arizona. After the Spanish-American War in 1898, the U.S. seized Puerto Rico (as well as the Pacific islands of Guam and the Philippines).

From 1904 to 1934, the United States intervened militarily eight times in Latin American countries. American foreign policy paralleled the interests of American business corporations that operated there. In 1938, when all private oil holdings in Mexico were expropriated—converted to government ownership—America supported the oil companies, many of which were American, and tried to punish Mexico.

Throughout the postwar era, the United States actively intervened in Latin America. The CIA was involved in the violent 1954 overthrow of an elected leftist government in Guatemala; the U.S. mili-

A scene of destruction in Hiroshima after the U.S. dropped the atomic bomb in 1945. The U.S.'s monopoly on atomic weapons at the time made it the most powerful country in the world.

tary intervened in the Dominican Republic in 1964; and in the 1970s the CIA joined with a private American company, International Telephone and Telegraph Company (ITT) and Chilean military forces to help bring down the elected leftist government of Salvador Allende in Chile.

President Reagan's preoccupation with Central America led many to fear a revival of American interventionism. His support for the military-backed government in El Salvador, his backing of antigovernment "contra" military forces in Nicaragua, and the invasion of Grenada raised Latin American fears of American "gunboat" diplomacy. It also put the U.S. at odds with the most important country in the region, Mexico. The effort to fight the Sandinistas would eventually lead to illegal funds going to Nicaragua and the most serious scandal of Reagan's administration—the Iran-Contra affair.

Internationalism

World War II brought American foreign policy into an era of **internationalism.** With most of the developed countries devastated by the war, America became the most powerful nation on earth. Our own country had not been touched by war; our factories and farms retained their full productive capacity. In addition, during the war, American scientists aided by refugees from Nazi Germany had produced a new, unbelievable force, the atomic bomb. This new bomb had destroyed the Japanese cities of Hiroshima and Nagasaki. Having a monopoly on the bomb for a number of years after the war added to U.S. influence.

In the postwar period, the American foreign policy of internationalism was characterized by the goals of **recovery** and **containment**—economic recovery for Western Europe and Japan, and containment of communism. These two goals came creatively together in the Marshall Plan of 1947. Under the leadership of Harry S. Truman and George C. Marshall, the noted army general who was now Truman's secretary of state, the United States launched the **Marshall Plan** to provide massive aid to help Western Europe recover. With General Douglas MacArthur acting as an enlightened military governor, Japan also started on the road to economic recovery and democracy. At the same time, America and its former ally, Russia, increasingly saw each other as rivals. The United States saw Russia's seizure of control over Eastern Europe as evidence of its intention to spread communism throughout the world. The Communist-engineered coup in Czechoslovakia in 1948, bringing that country behind the Iron Curtain, was for many the final proof.

China increased the fear. Our wartime ally, Chiang Kai-shek, headed an autocratic regime that had fallen to Marxist forces led by Mao Tse-tung. Bitter arguments over "Who lost China" erupted in the United States. Chiang Kai-shek's forces took over the independent island of Taiwan, where they set up the separate government of Nationalist China. America broke off relations with mainland China, refusing to recognize Mao's government. These ties were not renewed until the 1970s, when Richard Nixon visited China. Jimmy Carter reestablished full diplomatic relations in 1979.

The renewal of diplomatic relations with China was marked by President Nixon's visit to China in 1972.

In the early 1950s, Senator Joseph McCarthy of Wisconsin made political capital out of an intense anticommunist campaign. His "red-baiting"—making untrue charges that Communists were rampant within the U.S. government—helped launch a period of fearful anticommunism at home and vigorous Cold War abroad. Truman's secretary of state, Dean Acheson, and Eisenhower's secretary of state, John Foster Dulles, viewed communism as an ideological, aggressive force ruled from Moscow. Both pursued a hard-line policy of containment, the application of counterforce to every Soviet effort to expand. As outlined by George Kennan in his famous July 1947 article in *Foreign Affairs,* first setting forth containment policy, communism would flow into "every nook and cranny" unless resisted.[3] In the midst of this Cold War, the reaction to the 1950 North Korean invasion of South Korea was predictable. With United Nations backing, the United States plunged into a war that resulted in the deaths of 35,000 American soldiers by its end in 1953.

The Cold War was still a strong factor in American policy when John F. Kennedy assumed office. He approved an invasion of Cuba in 1961 (by Cubans) that ended in disaster at the "Bay of Pigs." He more successfully countered Russia during the Cuban missile crisis when it was discovered that the Soviet Union had placed offensive missiles on the island, only 90 miles from the United States. His "quarantine" of Cuba, restricting Soviet ships from docking, forced Russia to withdraw its missiles after taking the world to the "brink" of a nuclear war between the superpowers.

Direct American involvement in Vietnam had begun in the mid-1950s, after the colonial French forces (backed by large amounts of American aid) had been defeated at Dien Bien Phu by Ho Chi Minh's Communists, who were fighting for their independence. The Geneva Accords attempted to settle the conflict by guaranteeing the Vietnamese free elections to choose their own government. But Eisenhower feared that the Communists would win, so he sent military aid and advisers to help the newly formed South Vietnamese government undercut the Geneva agreements.

American involvement in Vietnam escalated rapidly when Lyndon Johnson took office. Kennedy had sent 16,000 military "advisers" to Vietnam. But by 1967, more than 500,000 Americans were fighting in Vietnam. As casualties mounted, public opinion turned against Johnson. Antiwar sentiment, at first restricted to a small number of liberals and students, soon spread throughout the country. The Tet offensive in early 1968 demonstrated that the North Vietnamese were far from being militarily defeated, despite U.S. government optimism. In March 1968, Johnson ordered a partial

Soviet Premier Nikita Khrushchev succeeded Joseph Stalin during the Cold War years and made efforts to lessen tensions between the Soviet Union and the United States. However, his handling of the Cuban Missile Crisis in 1962 encouraged his oust from power.

bombing halt to encourage negotiations and shocked the nation by announcing he would not run for reelection. (See Chapter 13.)

Richard Nixon and his National Security Assistant, Henry Kissinger, followed a twofold policy in Vietnam. While pursuing harsh military action, including massive bombing attacks on the North, they also negotiated with representatives of North Vietnam and gradually withdrew troops. Finally, in January 1973, a truce was signed. Almost all American troops were withdrawn. The government we had supported soon collapsed, and the government of North Vietnam controlled South Vietnam and unified the country.

Post-Vietnam Policy

The period after Vietnam was an unsettled time. Americans were increasingly distrustful of foreign interventions that might lead to wars. Communism was no longer seen as monolithic—the serious split between the Soviet Union and the People's Republic of China undercut that assumption. Partly to take advantage of this split and to "play the China card" against the Soviet Union, the United States moved toward closer ties with China pushed by President Nixon's trip in 1972.

The 1970s saw the Middle East become an even more vital focus of U.S. policy—both because of its oil wealth and because of the close relationship between the United States and Israel. The United States had supported Israel beginning with President Truman's recognition of the new state in 1948. As more Jews fled persecution, first from the Nazis, then from other parts of the world, Israel was frequently fighting with its Arab neighbors and the Palestinians (led by the Palestinian Liberation Organization—PLO) who claimed a right to the land.

With the increased importance of Arab oil, American policymakers tried to balance their conflicting interests by seeking a stable peace in the Middle East. They had only a few successes. Jimmy Carter helped Egypt and Israel negotiate a bilateral peace at Camp David in 1979, after thirty-one years of hostility. About this time, the Shah of Iran, whom we had long supported, was overthrown. The religion-based government of Ayatollah Khomeni held a number of American diplomats hostage. U.S. relations with the fundamentalist government remained hostile during the seven year Iran-Iraq war that ended in 1988.

President Reagan's support of Israel's 1982 invasion of Lebanon didn't help U.S.-Arab relations, nor did the brief and tragic stationing of U.S. Marines in Beirut. By the end of Reagan's second term, the PLO's announced recognition of Israel's right to exist and denun-

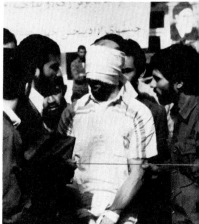

Foreign relations with the Middle East were plagued by acts of terrorism. At left, the U.S. Embassy in Beirut was bombed in 1983. Below, seeking the return of U.S. hostages taken by groups in Lebanon remains an unsolved problem.

ciation of terrorism led to U.S. discussions with the PLO and perhaps a new chapter in U.S.-Middle East relations. But the international terrorism so often connected to Palestinian groups did not seem to end and American hostages remained captive in Lebanon.

Initially, Reagan's foreign policy returned to an acceptance of an east-west confrontation with Russia and greater interventionism in this hemisphere: new military bases in Honduras, stepped-up aid to El Salvador in its fight against leftist guerillas, and strong backing for the contra military forces in Nicaragua. The U.S. Central Intelligence Agency secretly mined Nicaragua's harbor and was found out. Underlying U.S. activities was a clear policy, only slightly overstated by the president in March 1983: "The Soviet Union is the focus of evil in the modern world."[4]

This world view did not stop somewhat contradictory moves toward accommodation. In almost every particular, Reagan's foreign policy "started out by confronting the world with a hard-line, aggressive ... set of policies, or pronouncements, that in nearly every instance gave way to compromise and at least outward accommodation."[5] Carter's grain embargo on the Soviets was cancelled and the blockage of equipment to build a Soviet-European gas pipeline was reversed.

The most important impulse toward warmer relations between the superpowers came from Soviet domestic changes. Propelled by economic discontent, a liberal leader who took power in Moscow pledged to lighten Russia's expensive military burdens and remove many bureaucratic controls. By Reagan's second term, moderating Soviet behavior under its new leader, Mikhail Gorbachev, was apparent in their withdrawal from Afghanistan, the easing of restrictions on dissent, and greater tolerance of liberalization in Eastern

European states such as Poland. In December, 1987, Reagan and Gorbachev signed an agreement eliminating short-range nuclear missiles in Europe, the first actual reduction in the two sides' missile forces. As George Bush entered office, some observers, Ronald Reagan among them, were trumpeting the "end of the cold war." Others, including the new president, were more skeptical.

Increasingly, U.S. foreign policy was forced to react to the changing economic conditions the country faced. The phrases from newspaper headlines encapsulated the changes: the trade deficit, the budget deficit, the weakened dollar, the decline in American productivity, and the rise of economic powers of the Pacific Rim and in the integrated European Economic Community. All these reinforced the primary point that *the U.S. was no longer in harmony with international markets. It was consuming more than it produced and investing more than it saved.* To maintain this, flows of foreign capital were needed. Yet an eventual adjustment by the U.S. seemed both inevitable and inevitably painful. It remained for the foreign policy of President Reagan's successors to oversee this adjustment and to adapt policy to it.[6]

As the U.S. entered the 1990s, there was no chance that the United States would return to its pre-World War II isolationism. Yet foreign policy was increasingly strained by domestic and world economic problems and U.S. reliance on ever-expensive armaments. Power was increasingly spread multilaterally among European and Asian nations, but the political obligations and stresses continued to follow a bipolar line of tension between the Soviets and the Americans.

WHO MAKES AMERICA'S FOREIGN POLICY?

During the Vietnam War, Senator Frank Church (D-Idaho) quoted the distinguished columnist Walter Lippman in arguing with President Lyndon Johnson for a negotiated settlement. The president glared at Church and said, "Frank, the next time you want a dam in Idaho, you just go to Walter Lippman for it."[7]

Like other policies, foreign policy issues reach the political agenda primarily because of the influence of events and actors. Unlike other political issues, foreign actors may have a major role in formulating the American foreign policy agenda. The unprecedented decision of Egypt's late President Anwar Sadat to visit Jerusalem in 1978 was an important influence on America's policy in the Middle East. Mikhail Gorbachev's stunning public relations campaigns of the late 1980s made it necessary for U.S. administrations to respond to his arms control proposals. On the other hand, when the Soviet Union invaded Afghanistan, foreign policy decision makers in our country felt they had to respond with such actions as the Moscow Olympic boycott and grain embargo.

Who are America's foreign policy actors and decision makers? Who influences foreign policy-making? As with domestic policy, public officials, interest groups, the media, and the public are all involved in making America's foreign policy.

The President

The U.S. Constitution and historical practice make the president preeminent over foreign policy. As we have seen, *these constitutional powers give the president far greater control over foreign policy than he has over domestic policy.* As a result of these formal constitutional powers, the president has three primary political resources to bolster his position over foreign policy: *information control, personal diplomacy,* and *crisis management.*

Information Control

The president has unparalleled access to information sources needed for decision making. The president names the heads of the principal foreign policy bureaucracies, and they are primarily loyal to him. They report directly and regularly to the president but only irregularly to relevant congressional committees. Presidents can often withhold information from Congress based on *executive privilege.* This doctrine means that the president and his principal aides cannot be forced to testify before Congress or reveal their papers if that would damage national security or the confidentiality of advice to the president. Executive privilege has been a widely used shield. Nixon's national security adviser, Henry Kissinger, once argued that because of the president's executive privilege, he (Kissinger) could not be required to go before the Senate Foreign Relations Committee to explain how the year's foreign military aid funds had been divided. The information available to the president about events and trends abroad are among his most important resources for directing American foreign policy.[8]

The president's closest aide on foreign policy matters is the **national security adviser,** who heads the staff of the National Security Council. As the coordinator in the White House on foreign policy matters, the NSC adviser has often battled the Secretary of State for influence with the president. Even a strong Secretary of State like George Shultz had to admit in late 1986 that during the Iran-Contra affair American ambassadors in the Middle East were ignoring the chain of command in the State Department and reporting directly to

Current Secretary of State James Baker with President and Mrs. Bush.

One of Jimmy Carter's greatest achievements as president came with the signing of the Camp David Accords between Egypt and Israel in 1978.

NSC staff members like Oliver North. With James Baker as a powerful Secretary of State, the expectation was that President Bush's NSC advisor, Brent Scowcroft, would not take this kind of initiative (see the box on page 566).

Personal Diplomacy

The U.S. Supreme Court has held that the president is the "sole organ" of the federal government in dealing with other nations.[9] Usually, such negotiations are carried on by members of the executive branch under the president's authority. In recent years, however, presidents have often engaged in "personal diplomacy." Jimmy Carter took a major role in the 1978 Camp David summit negotiations between Egypt's President Sadat and Israel's Prime Minister Begin. Reagan took office less convinced that personal diplomacy would work. However, at the unsuccessful Reykjavik, Iceland summit of 1986, President Reagan met Premier Gorbachev with only two weeks preparation and, once there, tried to personally negotiate the elimination of all nuclear weapons. While sympathizing with the president's desire to "cut out the middle men," even Reagan supporters were puzzled at his performance.

If diplomacy results in treaties, they must be submitted to the Senate for ratification, but nothing requires the president to involve the Senate in negotiations leading up to a treaty. Furthermore, modern presidents have sometimes entered into **executive agreements**—

understandings between the president and the head of a foreign government—without submitting them for ratification as treaties. Such executive agreements have been used in recent years to establish military bases in foreign countries. According to one estimate, between 1946 and 1976 the U.S. entered 7201 executive agreements, far more than the number of treaties signed during the same period. Some of these can be very important, such as the agreements reached after World War II between the allies on the future of Eastern Europe.

Crisis Management

As commander in chief, the president can resist military attacks on our country without waiting for a formal declaration of war. Presidents have also assisted friendly nations when they have come under attack. For example, Reagan sent arms and other assistance to the Afghan rebels following Soviet support of the Afghan government. This presidential power is not unlimited. Foreign events and actors cannot always be predicted. America cannot always impose its will abroad, or sometimes can only do so at too great a cost.

The president's power in foreign policy is also limited by public opinion. Especially today, after Vietnam, Watergate, and the Iran-Contra affair, there is far less willingness to support any president's foreign policy initiatives. However, in times of crisis this constraint seldom operates in the short run. *Once a president puts a policy into motion, it is difficult for public opinion, or Congress, to reverse it.* The president, especially one skilled in mass communications, can usually steer public opinion in his direction. As one early practitioner of the art (Teddy Roosevelt) put it:

> *People used to say to me that I was an astonishingly good politician and divined what the people are going to think. . . . I did not "Divine" how the people were going to think; I simply made up my mind what they ought to think, and then did my best to get them to think it.*[10]

The Foreign Policy Bureaucracy

The president has bureaucratic help in maintaining his dominance. He needs it. In foreign policy, the president must be like a juggler, keeping several balls in the air at once. Issues in one part of the world do not subside in importance just because other issues somewhere else in the world become more pressing. Who advises the president on foreign policy? One answer might be, "everybody who gets a chance." But in our system of government, there are certain formal offices and bureaucracies established for this purpose.

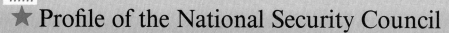

★ Profile of the National Security Council

Origin: Established under Harry S Truman in 1947.

Duties: To coordinate the policies of the Department of State, the Department of Defense, and the Central Intelligence Agency, assess national-security needs, and make recommendations to the president.

Members: The president, vice-president, secretary of state, secretary of defense, director of the Central Intelligence Agency, chairman of the Pentagon's Joint Chiefs of Staff, counselor to the president, White House chief of staff and deputy chief of staff, and the national-security adviser.

Staff: About 130 persons, including 65 professionals with a variety of geographic and technical specialties.

Budget: $5.4 million in fiscal 1990.

SOURCE: The White House Press Office, 1989.

The State Department

The U.S. secretary of state is today the ranking cabinet official in the executive branch. He is the head of the State Department and, at least formally, the principal foreign policy adviser to the president. The State Department maintains 150 embassies and missions overseas and some 140 consular posts. Yet its budget is one of the Cabinet's smallest, some $2.2 billion in 1990, less than one percent of the $282 billion requested for the military.

The State Department is involved in the *formulation, adoption,* and *implementation* of foreign policy. To assist with the formulation and adoption of foreign policy, it gathers and interprets foreign "intelligence." As one of those implementing foreign policy, the State Department handles negotiations with foreign countries and international organizations, coordinates the activities of the government overseas, and represents U.S. interests—including the protection and promotion of U.S. businesses in foreign countries.

The top positions in the State Department are filled by political appointees, including twenty-one assistant secretaries. Under them are members of the **foreign service,** specially trained career people who serve in key positions in the State Department and in embassies abroad. Traditionally, these diplomats were drawn from elite Ivy League schools, which gave the service a white, male, upper-class tone. The ranks have long since been opened to a more representative sampling of the country's population.

Most modern presidents have complained about the State Department. President Kennedy said that trying to get it to act was like "punching a bowl of jelly."[11] The State Department is said to be slow to make decisions, lacking in imagination, and bureaucratically self-protective. Many in Congress see the "striped pants types" as too likely to favor foreign countries' views for diplomatic reasons, rather than being "tough" in standing up for U.S. security and economic interests.

These problems are partly the result of serious organizational problems within the department. The State Department is organized in two overlapping ways. It is organized by *world regions,* with separate bureaus for Europe, Latin America, Africa, and so on. The State Department is also organized by *functions;* there are separate bureaus within the department for administration, congressional relations, international organizations (including the United Nations), and research. In getting "clearance" on a policy paper, the State Department checks with all bureaus that might have an interest before taking an official stance on it. This takes time and sometimes produces a bland "committee" decision.

Adding further to the State Department's problems have been the growth of other executive agencies that cut into the foreign-policy turf. Placed in the position of advocating costly foreign aid programs, and required to report on a crisis in the Middle East or some discouraging Soviet threat, the State Department has often been labeled *The Bureau of Bad News.* Unlike other government agencies, the State Department operates at a critical disadvantage, because it has no **domestic constituency** to lobby for its programs.

The result of all this has been *the decline of the State Department's predominance over foreign policy since World War II.*[12] Many organizational reforms have been tried, with limited success, to reverse this trend. The problem may be more basic. It may lie in very different perspectives toward foreign policy.

The State Department seeks the orderly conduct of diplomacy, reconciling other countries' interests with our own. This means building a consistency and logic into relationships between countries. Political leaders, on the other hand, want "to manage foreign affairs in a way that will do the least damage to a government's domestic standing."[13] This may include election-year rhetoric, which can please domestic interest groups and change policy drastically when a new administration takes power. The perceptions of foreign policy held by democratic leaders and professional diplomats may differ so widely because their needs and objectives differ so much.

This was apparent after the 1989 killing of Chinese students in Beijing. State Department officials stressed maintaining good relations with the world's most populated country, while congressmen reflecting outraged constituents demanded immediate sanctions.

The Defense Department

People often speak of the "Pentagon" when they mean the Defense Department. This is because the Department's headquarters is housed in a massive five-sided building on the Virginia shores of the Potomac River. A visitor searching for a particular office inside often wishes for a golfcart to negotiate the wide, endless halls. The Defense Department's housing reflects its organizational problems. It has been criticized for mismanagement and for "gold plating" high-technology weapons that contribute very little to national security.[14] A mid-1980s House Appropriations Committee study found that the combat readiness of conventional forces had actually deteriorated despite the rapid increase in spending.

The Department of Defense is a relatively young agency. It was organized in 1947 by the integration of the army, navy, and air force under one secretary of defense. Until that time the military services had been operating relatively separately, reporting directly to the president. Today, under the secretary of defense, a number of assistant secretaries preside over such functional areas as financial management, intelligence, telecommunications, and congressional affairs. Remaining within the department are the separate and semi-autonomous departments of the army, navy, and air force, headed by civilian secretaries who report to the secretary of defense. The rivalries among the services continue.

Within the department, with even more autonomy, are the **Joint Chiefs of Staff**—the military commanders of the army, navy, air force, and the Marine corps. The specific mission of the secretary of defense is to coordinate national security policy with foreign policy, while that of the Joint Chiefs of Staff is to put the military aspects of the policy into effect. The Joint Chiefs of Staff maintain close relationships with relevant congressional committees, with a network of civilian organizations (such as the Association of the U.S. Army, which promotes the interests of that branch of the armed services), and with private corporations engaged in contract defense work. *Thus, while the tradition of civilian control of the military is technically preserved, the military establishment is very involved in influencing the formulation and adoption of policy, not just its implementation.* In 1986, the power of the Joint Chiefs was concentrated in the group's Chairman, who is now General Colin Powell. This was

Diplomatic relations with China remains a foreign policy issue for the 1990s. The massacre of Chinese students during pro-democracy demonstrations in Beijing in 1989 stirred debates over the extent of U.S. investment and aid.

aimed at breaking a gridlock among the services, which increased waste and duplication.

The secretary of defense's influence, like that of the secretary of state, may depend on his relationship with the president. Reagan's former defense secretary, Caspar Weinberger, a long-time friend and associate, had great influence with him, convincing him not to cut Defense appropriations. President Reagan's tendency to see foreign policy problems in military terms also enhanced the department's standing in the field. But Defense has some advantages in influencing foreign policy, regardless of who heads the Defense Department (see the box on page 404 in Chapter 13).

The special role of Defense in making foreign policy derives from four basic sources. First, in the missile age, the Defense Department deals with awesome concepts: "second strike capability," the ability to inflict unacceptable damage on an enemy after having suffered a first attack; and "mutually assured destruction," the idea that the ability to destroy each other ensures no attack will occur. Thinking about the unthinkable leads one to rely on experts when stakes are so high.

Second, the Defense Department is influential in foreign policy because of the huge sums of money it spends and spreads out among a great many states and congressional districts. *Unlike the State Department, Defense very definitely has a domestic constituency.* Upon leaving office, President Eisenhower warned about the growing strength of what he called the **military-industrial complex.** This term refers primarily to private organizations and corporations that work closely with the Defense Department and whose economic interests are strongly supported by influential lobbyists. Defense industry labor unions are also a part of this complex; for example, the United Auto Workers union lobbied in favor of additional MX missiles, which meant jobs for its members.

Third, *military matters are more quantifiable* than most of the foreign policy issues with which the State Department deals. These "hard" numbers, unlike the "soft" State Department alternatives, often give military recommendations greater standing in the policy-making process. As one authority has put it, "Perhaps defense decisions—so heavily involved with troop commitments, weapons procurements, and resource allocation—lend themselves more easily to the appearance of order, rationality and cost-benefit analysis than do the less quantifiable and more subtle means of diplomatic discourse." Thus, the Defense Department's ability to provide numbers has been " . . . one more stepping stone to increase its importance in foreign policy."[15]

Finally, the Defense Department can "symbolically appeal" to patriotism. For the general public and for some in Congress, the military is identified with national pride, its soldiers and sailors risking their lives for their country. This sets the Defense Department apart from other executive agencies and gives it an advantage in influencing foreign policy. On the other hand, diplomats don't march in parades.

The Intelligence Establishment

During World War II, the Office of Strategic Services (OSS), headed by William "Wild Bill" Donovan, performed almost legendary spying and sabotage operations for the United States. After the war, OSS was replaced (in 1947) by a permanent intelligence organization, the *Central Intelligence Agency (CIA)* which was given the mission of both gathering and interpreting intelligence.

The CIA is not the only intelligence organization in the federal government. Both the Defense and State Departments have their own intelligence bureaus, as does each branch of the armed services. Also in the Defense Department is the *National Security Agency (NSA),* which was established to gather intelligence by using modern technology, including satellites, electronic surveillance, and code-breaking devices.

A large number of CIA employees are engaged in research and in analyzing "overt" intelligence—information gained from public sources. The CIA also uses sophisticated electronics to gather intelligence information. This overt part of the CIA's work has generally been noncontroversial. However, the "covert" or secret operations of the CIA have been severely criticized in recent years. These operations involve spying as well as so-called "dirty tricks." Without specific authorization by law, the CIA has tried to overthrow governments, bribe officials, and assassinate foreign leaders. It has also illegally involved itself in domestic surveillance of American citizens. Congress and former Presidents Ford and Carter took steps to end the illegal activities of the Central Intelligence Agency, to curtail its covert operations, and to bring it under tighter executive and congressional control. Both houses of Congress have established special committees to oversee CIA activities.

Yet, whether because of these restrictions or the ineffectiveness of the agency itself, the quality of U.S. intelligence has come under repeated criticism. Nearly all modern presidents have complained at one time or another about their inability to get enough information to make foreign policy decisions. Kennedy, for example, blamed the CIA for the Bay of Pigs invasion of Cuba, which our government organized and financed under the mistaken assumption that it would result in a general uprising—a major miscalculation of intelligence. Reagan blamed the previous administration's budget cuts for the lack of warning when a suicide truck loaded with TNT killed 230 Marines in Beirut on October 23, 1983. Of course, these incidents may have just reflected *presidents seeking political protection through the usual route of blaming bureaucrats.*

Clearly, an effective intelligence capacity is needed. Just as clearly, much of what intelligence does conflicts with traditional democratic concepts of a free press, public disclosure of information, and civil liberties. Further restricting the CIA from engaging in "dirty tricks" or covert operations altogether might eliminate many of these points of conflict. But much of this tension between a publicly accountable democracy and secret intelligence operations is and likely will prove an inevitable part of the present U.S. role in the world.

The National Security Council

The president's ability to maintain control over all the foreign policy bureaucracies is limited in at least two ways. First, as has been shown, *growing numbers of participants* in the policy-making process limit the president's control. So many people are involved, and there is such an overwhelming flow of information, that it is increasingly difficult to stay on top of it all. Second, *the executive bureaucrats involved in foreign policy have their own constituencies and interests* to which they are loyal. Their loyalty to the president may be secondary.

To improve the president's ability to coordinate advice from various officials, and to integrate "domestic, foreign, and military policies relating to the national security," the National Security Act of 1947 created the National Security Council (NSC). The president's national security adviser heads the NSC staff. Inevitably, as seen earlier, some rivalry develops between the president's national security adviser and other foreign policy bureaucracies.

Presidents generally have preferred to use their own White House staff to quickly make foreign policy decisions and to implement them. Before he took office, Henry Kissinger wrote about the freedom of action that a president could gain in avoiding the foreign policy bureaucracies. "One reason for keeping the decisions to small groups," he wrote, "is that when bureaucracies are so unwieldy and when their internal morale becomes a serious problem, an unpopular decision may be fought by brutal means, such as leaks to the press or Congressional committees."[16] Once in government, Kissinger had a reputation for repeatedly leaking information to the press.

The other side of the coin was shown in the Iran-contra affair during President Reagan's second term. Here the president's national security adviser, members of the NSC staff, and CIA officials arranged to sell arms to Iran in order to gain the release of American hostages held by Iranian allies in Lebanon. The money from the sales were then used to fund anticommunist contras fighting to overthrow the Nicaraguan government. All this violated congressional resolutions and legal restrictions on the supply of U.S. arms to the contras, eventually leading to the trial of Colonel Oliver North in 1989. Trafficking with Iran directly contradicted the president's public policy of not negotiating with terrorists, leading one Reagan backer to remark, "It's like suddenly learning that John Wayne had secretly been selling liquor and firearms to the Indians."[17]

More to our point, *Iran-contra underlined the danger of a small group of officials secretly formulating and implementing foreign policy.* Both the Secretaries of State and Defense had protested the NSC officials' actions in the Iran-contra affair, with no obvious effect. President Reagan either gave tacit approval for the operation or, as he claimed, knew nothing about it. Either way, the NSC's actions illustrated its own failure to unify the government's foreign-policy machinery.

Other Foreign Policy Bureaucracies

The *Agency for International Development (AID)* is attached to the State Department but operates with some autonomy. Its job is to oversee U.S. development aid and much of our military assistance to other countries. Foreign aid has never been popular in this country. Policymakers support it as a tool of diplomacy that, in crude terms, can be used to reward friends and punish enemies. It also underlines America's moral obligation to help less-developed countries on the assumption that this will help to produce a more secure world. Some advocates of foreign aid to developing nations have suggested that all industrial nations should allocate at least one percent of their gross national products for this purpose, partly through private donations and partly through governmental appropriations. The United States has not come near this level of assistance (see Figure 18.1).

FIGURE 18★1
Foreign Aid

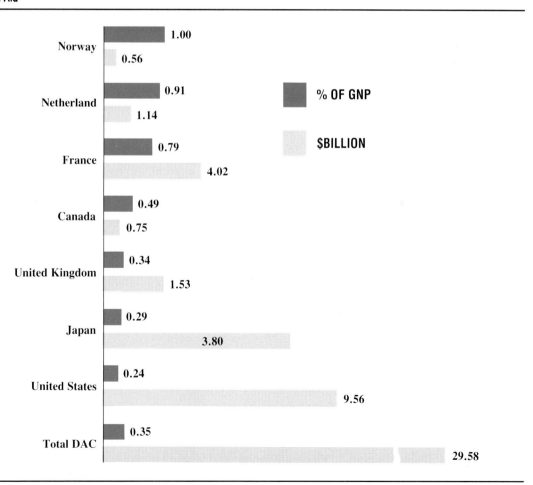

SOURCE: OECD *Observer,* no. 46, March 1988, p. 22.

While the U.S. gives foreign aid to other countries in times of need, policymakers generally use foreign aid to reward friends and punish enemies. Here, Armenian earthquake victims in need of help gather their things in 1989.

America's humanitarian concerns can be demonstrated by AID's reaction to natural disasters such as the Armenian earthquake. However, foreign aid, like the diplomacy it serves, is seldom given for selfless reasons. Most of AID's budget, in fact, stays in this country. Recipient nations must use most of their foreign aid for purchases from U.S. suppliers. Foreign arms sales, which are handled through the Pentagon, have also resulted in the United States becoming one of the great arms sellers of the world. Between rewarding friends, developing foreign markets, and helping U.S. producers, very little of the aid budget is wasted on foreign "giveaways."

The United States Arms Control and Disarmament Agency (ACDA) is housed in the State Department. Its director's job is to advise the secretary of state and the president on agreements furthering arms control. But the Defense Department, the Joint Chiefs of Staff, and key members of Congress have probably had more impact on U.S. arms control policy than has this weak agency that is charged with the responsibility. Congress has been especially assertive in arms control in recent years.

The *United States Information Agency (USIA),* attached to the State Department, has the responsibility for spreading information abroad that is favorable to the image and policies of the United States government. It also administers the international radio system, "Voice of America." A key tension in USIA's activities is whether what they're doing is journalism or propaganda.

With the rise in importance of trade and economics, the federal bureaucracies involved in foreign policy are not just those whose missions obviously concern foreign policy and national security. The *Department of the Treasury* gets involved in foreign policy matters relating to America's balance of payments and to international monetary negotiations. The *Department of Commerce* is deeply concerned with international trade and promoting the sale of American products. Likewise, the *Department of Agriculture* promotes agricultural sales abroad. The *Department of Justice* supervises immigration and naturalization matters and attempts to control traffic in illegal drugs.

In the Executive Office of the President, a trade negotiator with "ambassador" status aids the president on trade matters. The *U.S. Trade Representative (USTR)* achieved new importance under Clayton Yeutter in the Reagan administration, as the United States began to lose its dominance in the global market. The 1989 trade agreement with Canada and the fights with the European Economic Community over meat imports focused attention on the USTR. The threat of sanctions against Japan put Bush's Trade Representative Carla Hills in the position of balancing congressional demands for action against broader interests pushing for good relations with Japan.

Congress

In October 1987, the Senate passed a $3.6 billion authorization bill to finance the operations of the State Department for the coming year. During the debate on the measure, eighty-six amendments were adopted. One called on the president to seek reimbursement from those nations whose ships were being protected by the U.S. Navy in the Persian Gulf. Another demanded that the chief executive close the offices of the Palestine Liberation Organization (PLO). Still another condemned Chinese persecution of Tibetan nationalists. A final bit of congressional dissatisfaction came when Congress made its deepest cut in thirty years in the State Department's operating budget.[18]

The formal foreign policy powers of Congress are plainly stated in the Constitution: the power to declare war and raise and support armies; the "power of the purse" through its control over federal expenditures; investigative and oversight powers to call executive officials to account; the law-making power; and for the Senate, the power to ratify treaties and confirm appointments. Clearly, the framers of the Constitution intended the control of foreign policy to be shared by the president and the Congress.[19] Or, as the noted presidential scholar Edward S. Corwin phrased it: "The Constitution is an invitation to struggle for the privilege of directing American foreign policy."

There is considerable difference, however, between the formal powers of Congress in the field of foreign policy and its actual influence in that area. Congress is at a disadvantage in dealing with the president in foreign policy for four principal reasons. First, Congress is often hampered by *a lack of unbiased information.* It must depend largely on executive sources, which often neatly package the information to support a single policy alternative. Second, because of various committees involved, Congress does not have the *organizational capability* to prepare a unified alternative on a given issue. Congress usually comes into the foreign policy picture after the various alternatives have been considered, privately and internally, by the executive branch. Congress, then, is asked to react to a chosen action.

Third, unlike the president, *Congress usually cannot act quickly.* It is, indeed, a "deliberative" institution—often *very* deliberate. Each house is coequal. Each contains numerous semiautonomous committees and subcommittees having partial jurisdiction over foreign policy issues. For example, when Congress drafted a trade bill in 1986, six standing committees played a significant role. As Barry Goldwater joked on retiring from the Senate: "If this is the world's greatest deliberative body, I'd hate to see the worst."

Finally, Congress is at a disadvantage in that it is made up of 535 elected officials who are expected to speak, to some degree, for *local rather than national interests* if they hope to be reelected; "Afghanistan's not in my district," as a legislator might put it. The president, on the other hand, can speak for the entire nation.

The more urgent a foreign policy issue is, the more influence a president has and the less Congress has. Congress seldom takes the initiative in foreign policy. Congress is better at helping to end a policy, such as our involvement in the Vietnam War, than it is at helping to start a policy. And Congress is more influential on foreign policy when the decisions concerning an issue stretch out over a period of time.

From Roosevelt to Nixon, the pendulum of foreign policy power swung widely toward the president and away from the Congress. But during Richard Nixon's administration, the pendulum began to swing the other way. At that time, Congress passed the *Case Act,* which required the president to report the details of any agreement to Congress, even if it did not have the formal status of a treaty. The

War Powers Act, passed over Nixon's veto, sought to limit the president's power to involve America in military hostilities for more than sixty days without formal congressional approval.

Congress used the full range of its powers in its frequent battles with President Reagan over foreign policy. It employed its investigative authority to expose Iran-contra. The power of the purse was turned on and off toward Central American policy. Laws were passed restricting trade to South Africa. Informal congressional visits and use of the media bolstered Cory Aquino's forces in the Philippines. Approval of Reagan's nominee for CIA director was withheld by the Senate because of his involvement in Iran-contra.

By the end of Reagan's tenure, it was clear that even a strong president could not restrain Congress's involvement in foreign relations. The Bush administration spoke of **bipartisanship** in foreign policy, which critics denounced as a weak form of "coalition government." In an unusual move, the administration in April 1989 informally allowed several congressional committees "an informal legislative veto" in giving them the right to override legislation providing assistance to the contra forces in Nicaragua.[20]

Congress's *entrepreneurial staff* increasingly contained foreign policy experts and acted as the driving force behind many legislative initiatives, especially in the Senate. Lobbyists representing constituencies and parts of public opinion alienated from administration policy looked for comfort from Capitol Hill. As long as the executive branch's foreign policy stirs up domestic dissent, Congress is likely to continue its assertiveness.

Interest Groups

In 1985, on the eve of a visit by the Saudi Arabian head of state, 64 senators signed a letter declaring their "deep concern" and "serious reservations" over arms sales to Saudi Arabia. This was widely seen as an effort by AIPAC, the American-Israel Public Affairs Committee, to block the sales. In the 1984 elections AIPAC had organized contributions of $1.82 million to Senate races. One interesting aspect of the AIPAC effort is that these two-thirds of the Senate were opposing a sale that had yet to be announced by the Administration.[21]

Like domestic policy, foreign policy is not neutral, either in causes or consequences. The results of foreign policy often hurt some groups and help others. Not surprisingly, interest groups attempt to influence foreign policy decisions. These groups include foreign corporations and even foreign governments.

Interest groups active in the foreign policy field fall into seven major categories. First, there is organized *labor.* The AFL-CIO, for example, has been consistently opposed to foreign imports because it feels they reduce domestic jobs.

Business groups, including the U.S. Chamber of Commerce and the National Association of Manufacturers, probably have more influence on American foreign policy than any other domestic interest groups. Some American multinational corporations, such as Exxon, are bigger and more powerful than most of the nations of the world.

Third, *agricultural groups* usually support free trade because, as exporters, they feel that if America's agricultural surplus is to be sold abroad, the country must buy things in return. Fourth, *veterans' groups* like the American Legion and the Veterans of Foreign Wars are active in backing a strong American military capability.

Fifth, *ethnic groups* seek to influence America's foreign policy. In Greek-Turkish disputes, for example, a number of members of Congress will support Greece, responding to the lobbying of Greek-American groups. Sixth, *religious and ideological groups* include peace groups, such as the National Council of Churches and the Society of Friends (Quakers), that support a freeze on nuclear weapons. There are pro-military and anticommunist groups, such as the Reverend Jerry Falwell's Moral Majority.

Finally, many *foreign governments,* through their Washington embassies, employ U.S. consultants to lobby Congress and the executive branch on trade and other policies. This representation does not come cheap. Michael Deaver, a former Reagan aide, was paid $105,000 by the Canadian Government to deal with the issue of acid rain. He had begun his public administration firm with a $2 million-a-year contract from South Korean government sources. George Bush's former chief of staff (when he was vice-president) received $250,000 for one month's work representing the Japanese government.[22]

The Mass Media

A former American diplomat remembers the advice he received as a young foreign-service officer: "Never write a telegram you would be unwilling to see on the front page of *The Washington Post.*"[23] The media do not just report on what the U.S. government says and does abroad. They often go beyond official announcements, frequently contradict them, and investigate events on their own. In the Vietnam War, for example, media accounts did not jibe with the official statements and were eventually instrumental in turning U.S. public opinion against the war. By their very nature, diplomacy and the press are often adversaries. Diplomats prefer quiet understandings. The press needs newsmaking visuals.

The government is justifiably anxious to keep much of its foreign policy activity secret. Difficult negotiations might be made more difficult if there were day-to-day reports in the press on the details of the discussions. But in the past, secrecy has often been used to avoid adverse public opinion, as when former President Nixon ordered an invasion of Cambodia, or when the Pentagon prohibited press coverage of the 1983 Grenada invasion to prevent any unfavorable reports. (See the case study in Chapter 13.)

The president and the foreign policy bureaucracy also use the media to influence public opinion. Presidents can produce or withhold information or preempt television time for major statements. Senior officials can call press conferences and issue official statements whenever they want to—and these receive coverage. Officials can favor some journalists with interviews and "leaks" while punishing others by withholding information. The president's people can float "trial balloons"—especially through leaks from a "highly placed source"—to gauge reaction to various policy alternatives.

The president and his top foreign policy officials have the upper hand over the media. They can dominate the news, give events the "spin" most favorable to them, and restrict information or appearances when these don't serve their interests. The media can be an important influence on policymakers, but only when the information it reveals is acted on by others involved in the formulation, adoption, and implementation of foreign policy.

Public Opinion and Participation

A political scientist wrote once: "If a fight starts, watch the crowd because the crowd plays the decisive role."[24] Whether the public gets involved or not in foreign policy fights can in many cases determine who wins or loses. An example of the use of public opinion by a dissenting policymaker to change foreign policy occurred in the Philippine elections.

In 1986, Senator Richard Lugar (R-Indiana), Chairman of the Senate Foreign Relations Committee, was convinced that President Ferdinand Marcos of the Philippines had stolen an election victory from Cory Aquino. The president and his White House advisers wanted to stick with Marcos. With support from State Department dissenters, Lugar made the rounds of the Sunday television talk shows and gave speeches around the country charging Marcos with widespread corruption. This play to public opinion through the media undermined the administration's position, changed the balance of forces inside the administration, and eventually changed the policy.[25]

Public opinion in the foreign policy field, as reflected in opinion polls, by interest groups, and by elections, can often be decisive. One historian has said, "Looking back through history, one can almost count on one's fingers the numbers of occasions when American statesmen made major decisions that they thought contrary to the public will."[26]

Clearly, some members of the public are more interested in policy than others. About 30 percent of the American public is called the *mass public,* a group that is only rarely interested in foreign-policy issues. Another 45 percent might be called the **attentive public,** because they are aware of major foreign-policy developments. The remaining 25 percent of the American public might be called **opinion makers,** since they are knowledgeable about foreign affairs and communicate their opinions to others.[27]

What is the relationship between the president and public opinion in foreign policy matters? On one extreme, Seymour Lipset wrote, "The President makes public opinion, he does not follow it."[28] Of course Lipset was writing about Lyndon Johnson in 1966, who a couple of years later strayed too far from public opinion on Vietnam and was forced into early retirement. On the other extreme is the view that public opinion serves as a "dictator" of foreign policy. It is true that when the public is extremely upset, as it was when President Nixon ordered the invasion of Cambodia in 1970, it can act as

Public opinion plays an important role in foreign policy making in the U.S. Here, protestors march against the interventionist policies of the Reagan administration.

a powerful critic and can even dictate policy. This, however, is probably as rare as modern presidents ignoring public opinion.

It is probably more accurate to think of public opinion as an *accomplice* to the president in foreign-policy matters; the president and the public are mutually influenced by each other. The president can lead and, especially in crises, his influence is likely to prove decisive. But the public will set the limits. Former President Reagan's ideological instincts were often restrained by the caution of the public. In regard to defense and arms control, he may have followed as much as led public opinion. When Reagan first took office in 1981, the public, like him, favored more money for defense and a harder line toward the Soviets. By his second term, the public narrowly favored defense and strongly supported arms control with the Russians. That may have had something to do with the direction Reagan took—reducing the defense build-up and reaching arms agreements with the Soviets.

Usually, the mass public is more interested in domestic problems than in foreign issues, but this is also increasingly true of the attentive public and the opinion makers. Since the Vietnam War, these better-informed members of the American public have become increasingly aware of the limits on America's ability or need to reshape the world, and have become more concerned about domestic problems. U.S. public opinion, for instance, opposed any Reagan policy that threatened to more deeply involve the U.S. in civil wars in Central America.

Those who criticize the idea of greater public participation—on the grounds that the general public is not well-informed on foreign-policy matters—are often the same people who feel "national security" dictates that foreign policy should be carried on largely in secret. Elites who dismiss the public's ability to deal with foreign policy feel that vital information should be withheld from it. This, in turn, keeps the general public uninformed. The attitude blames the victim—the general public—for being poorly informed, when it is the leaders who withhold information from the public.

The goal of leaders ought to be a well-informed public that cannot be stampeded by fear or prejudices to accept a foreign policy not in the national interest. The alternative is scary:

In a democracy armed to the teeth with nuclear weapons, public noninvolvement is a terrifying danger and not a desirable goal. An 'irresponsible public' is one that is kept in the dark most of the time, leaving it to the 'experts' to run the show. Such a public is manipulable, apathetic, and panic-prone, in sharp contrast to an informed public that feels it must share responsibility for its own future with its leaders.[29]

The Vietnam War changed the way a generation of Americans feel about U.S. involvement in foreign affairs. Here, a Vietnam veteran visits the Vietnam Veterans Memorial in Washington, D.C.

THE U.S. AND INTERNATIONAL ORGANIZATIONS

The United States carries out its foreign policy in and through a number of international organizations. It belongs to more than 200 of them. The most important are the *Organization of American States (OAS)*, the *World Bank*, the *North Atlantic Treaty Organization (NATO)*, and the *United Nations*.

The **OAS** is a regional organization made up of the United States and Latin American nations. The United States has dominated the organization (in 1988 providing about two-thirds of its budget) and has used it in recent years to bolster the governments of Latin America against internal enemies. The United States has also used the OAS to organize sanctions, such as the condemnation of Panama's General Noriega for upsetting his country's 1989 elections and dealings in the drug trade. The United States has been less successful in getting OAS support in its attempt to isolate the Sandinista regime of Nicaragua. Similarly, the United States stood alone in 1982, when it backed Great Britain's fight with Argentina over control of the Falkland Islands.

Founded in 1944 at the Bretton Woods (New Hampshire) conference on the international finance system, the *International Bank for Reconstruction and Development (IBRD)*, known as the **World Bank,** had 151 nation-members and a major role in development assistance to the Third World in 1989. The bank had started as an instrument for channeling funds to war-devastated Europe. But by 1960, it was the major source of money for large development projects to the poorer nations. It brought expertise and a banker's disciplined approach to its lending practices. However, the increasing financial problems of its aid recipients brought changes to the World Bank. Some one quarter of the bank's recent loans were *bailouts*—restructurings of debt that the developing countries had little or no hope of repaying. Congress acted in 1987 to boost the bank's loan capital and commit the United States to 20 percent—about $70 million a year—of the new funds. The Reagan administration pushed for loans to the private sector, as opposed to the governments of less-developed countries, on the grounds that this most effectively promoted economic growth.[30]

NATO links the United States and Western European countries in a military alliance. In 1949, when it was founded, NATO marked America's break from its isolationist past and its commitment to contain communism in Europe. The *Warsaw Pact* integrates the military operations of Eastern European countries with the Soviet Union in a similar military alliance. In recent years, the U.S. has pressed European nations like West Germany (which were growing economically faster than America) to pay more of the costs of NATO. Soviet leader Gorbachev's late-1988 announcement of a phased withdrawal of 500,000 Russian troops from Eastern Europe led to further questioning of the size and cost of NATO forces. The NATO countries, after initial disagreement, were able to match the Soviet reductions with proposals of their own. Supporters point out that NATO has seemingly deterred the Soviet invasion it was set up to prevent, and thus must be deemed a success of American foreign policy.[31]

The **United Nations (UN)** is a universal representative peacekeeping organization. As World War II ended, there was a strong feeling that the failure of the United States to become a member of the League of Nations after World War I had contributed to the outbreak of World War II. Whether this was true or not, the U.S. and its allies pushed for the establishment of the UN as soon as World War II was over. Its location in New York City was aimed at keeping the U.S. involved.

The United Nations operates through a General Assembly, a Security Council, and four other major organs (the Economic and Social Council, the Trusteeship Council, the International Court of Justice, and the Secretariat). The Security Council was originally seen as an executive committee for the UN, with its permanent members being the big powers, each of whom has a veto on council matters. The veto, usually exercised by the out-voted Soviet Union, considerably reduced the council's effectiveness. In the 1950s and 1960s, the General Assembly greatly expanded to include the developing nations, which won their independence from former colonial powers.

The United Nations, which maintains no regular peacekeeping force, depends on volunteer forces furnished from time to time by member countries. Similarly, its financial base depends on voluntary contributions. The United States provides considerably more funds to the UN than any other nation.

The United Nations has not enjoyed strong popular support in America in recent years, particularly because of the increasing aggressiveness of the African and Asian countries in the General Assembly. Jeane Kirkpatrick, as Reagan's first-term UN Ambassador, became a favorite of the American Right and the Republican party because of her hard-line anti-Soviet and anti-Third World statements. Congress, cheered on by the Reagan administration, cut its contribution of one-quarter of the UN budget back to 20 percent in 1985.

Since then *the UN has staged a comeback.* The author of the congressional cutback, Senator Nancy Landon Kassebaum (R-KS), was the leader of a Senate message sent to Reagan in 1988 to restore UN cuts because of budgetary reform and more responsiveness to U.S. concerns. The UN's increasing role in settling disputes like the Soviet occupation of Afghanistan, the Iran-Iraq war, and South Africa's control of Namibia enhanced its image. The UN revival was capped in 1988 when the Nobel Peace Prize was awarded to its peace-keeping forces. Despite the recent U.S. desire to have the UN involved in the Middle East, drug traffic, and terrorism, this country remained $402 million behind in UN dues.[32]

FOREIGN POLICY AND THE FUTURE

As the 1990s dawned, America's foreign policy carried with it an expectation of continued internationalism and, probably, interventionism. U.S. interests seemed to extend to every place on the globe, especially where it appeared to our policymakers that there was a threat of Soviet influence. Yet the ascent of Gorbachev in Moscow and the mellowing of Reagan's second term led to a substantial reduction in tensions. Positive steps like the Russian withdrawal from Afghanistan, the reduction in Soviet troop strength in Europe, and the liberalization of Kremlin restrictions on the media and migration contributed to the warming. The smiles and handshakes between presidents and premiers symbolized the improvement.

In other global arenas such as development assistance, the United States continued to reject Third World demands for more sharing of power and resources by the industrial nations. Instead, the U.S. emphasized private trade and investment in these countries rather than government aid. With domestic budget problems preventing any large increase in aid, this may have made an ideological virtue out of necessity. In Central America, despite a rising tide of opposition in Congress and efforts by Latin American nations for a negotiated settlement, the U.S. continued its muted efforts to moderate the government of Nicaragua. The Reagan administration ignored peaceful overtures from Fidel Castro in Cuba, and supported the government of El Salvador as it weathered a storm of leftist guerrilla warfare. In Africa, the 1988 agreement to withdraw Cuban troops from Angola and South African troops from Namibia, with the eventual independence of the latter, was justifiably heralded as a victory for American persistence.

The Bush and Reagan administrations worked for closer cooperation with Japan and Western Europe. Economic policies, including the low American dollar that raised the price of European exports to

The Soviet withdrawal of troops from Afghanistan in 1988 was a key step in the lessening of tensions between the Soviet Union and the U.S.

Debate over U.S. involvement in Third World countries, including the world's poorest continent, Africa, promises to continue in the 1990s.

the U.S., irritated relations with Western Europe. But ties were generally close, especially with Margaret Thatcher's equally conservative British government. The U.S.-Soviet warming was greeted enthusiastically by NATO countries, many of whom believed that Reagan had made too much of the Soviet threat in the first place. *Both superpowers seemed to parallel each other in their increasing attention to domestic economic problems and their relative loss of power in the world.* Even as the Soviet Union increased in military strength, its weaknesses seemed more apparent.

Mikhail Gorbachev, the political superstar of the late 1980s, was very open about the many problems he faced. Western observers wondered whether Gorbachev's reform of *glasnost* (political openness in society and in culture) and *perestroika* (an economic restructuring for efficient delivery of goods) could be achieved. A huge, inert state bureaucracy protected jobs that depended on Gorbachev's changes not coming too fast. Short-term reforms seemed to mean fewer, not more, goods on the store shelves. Free elections in 1989 revealed more dissent to the regime. Unemployment was reported publicly. Nationalism caused sparks of rebellion among the restless peoples of Georgia, Estonia, Latvia, and Armenia. After the Armenian earthquake in 1988, Gorbachev often appeared more popular abroad than in his own country. Certainly the relaxation of tensions with the West served the priorities of his domestic agenda.

For its part, the United States faced challenges to its position in the world. Yet America confronted its dilemma without the same clear-cut direction Gorbachev offered the Soviets. The U.S.'s altered position can be summed up by a simple contrast. In 1945, the U.S. produced half the world's economic product. On a planet devastated by war, the U.S. reigned supreme. Forty years later the U.S. was producing less than a fifth of a world economy that had grown five times. With many more independent nations, U.S. political power had probably declined even more.

These changing economic conditions confronted the U.S. with a basic foreign policy dilemma. Despite the clear reduction in the U.S. share of world economic strength, the country's massive global foreign and military obligations have remained essentially unchanged for over twenty-five years. What Professor Paul Kennedy has called "imperial overstretch" simply meant that the nation's military burdens are far larger than the financial resources it has to maintain them. *Bringing the country's commitments into balance with its economic power is the essential adjustment that America's foreign policy of the future will be called on to make.*[33]

The record so far is not reassuring. Essentially, the United States has gone into debt to bridge the gap between its commitments abroad, its living standards at home, and its inability to afford both. Protectionism through quotas or informal pressures on allies, along with devaluing the dollar, have been the main responses to the trade deficit. Huge increases in defense spending have been the response to extensive foreign policy commitments and our allies' unwillingness to assume more of the burden. Unprecedented deficits have bridged the gap between a government unwilling to spend less or tax more. A host of domestic problems have risen to plague our mature economy, including a decline in productivity, a decrease in the savings rate, the rise of corporate debt, and a relative industrial and agricultural decline. All of these affect the American capacity to act on the world stage.

WRAP-UP

In the best of times, the American political system has been justly criticized for making foreign policy difficult. Its institutional fragmentation and wide public participation are not likely to lead to a foreign policy marked by coherence and consistency. Elections, lobbyists, political parties, mass media, federalism, congressional subcommittees, and PACs are only some of the factors more likely to paralyze decision making than to enable policy to adjust to uncontrollable changes in the world.

Yet the openness and dispersion of political power may also provide hope for a new foreign policy. Winston Churchill once referred to democracy as a raft—it never sinks but your feet are always wet. The very unstructured, market-oriented nature of society may leave the process of adapting American international relations to changed circumstances in the hands of any number of decentralized decision makers. Whatever such a process may lack in coherence, it may compensate for by also avoiding the rigidity of a more centrally directed adjustment. It will, however, like any great national change, still require smart politicians.

Key Terms

foreign policy (p. 555)
isolationism (p. 555)
interventionism (p. 556)
Monroe Doctrine (p. 556)
internationalism (p. 557)
recovery (p. 558)
containment (p. 558)
Marshall Plan (p. 558)
national security advisor (p. 563)
executive agreements (p. 564)
foreign service (p. 566)
domestic constituency (p. 567)

Joint Chiefs of Staff (p. 568)
military-industrial complex (p. 570)
bipartisanship (p. 577)
attentive public (p. 580)
opinion makers (p. 580)
OAS (Organization of American States) (p. 582)
World Bank (p. 582)
NATO (North Atlantic Treaty Organization) (p. 582)
United Nations (UN) (p. 583)

Suggested Readings

Brzezinski, Zbigniew, *Game Plan: How to Conduct the U.S.-Soviet Contest* (New York: Atlantic Monthly Press, 1986).

Bundy, McGeorge, *Danger and Survival: The Political History of the Nuclear Weapon* (New York: Random House, 1989).

Cohen, William S. and George J. Mitchell, *Men of Zeal: The Inside Story of the Iran-contra Hearings* (New York: Viking Penguin, 1988).

Isaacson, Walter and Evan Thomas, *The Wise Men: Architects of the American Century* (New York: Simon & Schuster, 1986).

Lehman, John F. Jr., *Command of the Seas: Building the 600 Ship Navy* (New York: Charles Scribners Sons, 1989).

Woodward, Bob, *Veil: The Secret Wars of the CIA* (New York: Simon & Schuster, 1989).

Endnotes

[1]Stephen E. Ambrose, *Rise to Globalism,* 5th edition (New York: Penguin Books, 1988), Introduction, p. xi.

[2]John Lewis Gaddis, *Inquiries Into the History of the Cold War* (New York: Oxford University Press, 1987), p. 20.

[3]Barton Gellman, *Contending with Kennan* (New York: Praeger, 1984), Chapter 5.

[4]Ambrose, p. 314.

[5]Henry Grunwald, "Foreign Policy Under Reagan II," *Foreign Affairs:* 63, no. 2 (Winter 1984/1985), pp. 219–39.

[6]See John D. Steinbruner, ed. *Restructuring American Foreign Policy* (Washington, D.C.: The Brookings Institution, 1989), Chapters 1 and 2.

[7]I. M. Destler, Leslie H. Gelb, and Anthony Lake, *Our Own Worst Enemy* (New York: Simon and Schuster, Inc., 1985), p. 62.

[8]See Cecil V. Crabb, Jr. and Pat M. Holt, *Invitation to Struggle,* 3rd ed. (Washington, D.C.: Congressional Quarterly Press, 1989), pp. 18–19.

[9]See *United States* v. *Curtiss-Wright Export Corp., 299* U.S. 304 (1936).

[10]Crabb and Holt, p. 20.

[11]See Arthur Schlesinger, Jr., *A Thousand Days* (Boston: Houghton Mifflin, 1965).

[12]See Barry Rubin, *Secrets of State: The State Department and the Struggle Over U.S. Foreign Policy* (New York: Oxford University Press, 1985).

[13]David D. Newsom, *Diplomacy and the American Democracy* (Bloomington: Indiana University Press, 1988), p. 26.

[14]James Fallows, *National Defense* (New York: Random House, 1981).

[15]Howard Bliss and M. Glen Johnson, *Beyond the Water's Edge: America's Foreign Policies* (Philadelphia: J. B. Lippincott Company, 1975), pp. 165–66.

[16]Henry A. Kissinger, "Bureaucracy and Policy-Making: The Effects of Insiders and Outsiders on the Policy Process," in Morton H. Halperin and Arnold Kanter, eds., *Readings in American Foreign Policy* (Boston: Little, Brown, 1973), p. 89.

[17]See James Schlesinger, "Reykjavik and Revelations: A Turn of the Tide?" in William G. Hyland, ed., *The Reagan Foreign Policy* (New York: New American Library, 1987), pp. 254–55.

[18]Crabb and Holt, p. 39.

[19]In regard to Congress and foreign policy, generally, see Fred R. Harris and Paul L. Hain, *America's Legislative Processes: Congress and the States* (Glenview, IL: Scott, Foresman, 1983), pp. 395–99.

[20]David S. Broder, "The High Cost of 'Coalition Government,'" *The Washington Post,* April 9, 1989, B-7.

[21]James A. Nathan and James K. Oliver, *Foreign Policy Making and the American Political System,* 2nd ed. (Boston: Little, Brown, 1987), p. 263.

[22]See *The New York Times,* January 12, 1989, and Nathan and Oliver, p. 273.

[23]Newsom, p. 58.

[24]E. E. Schattschneider, *The Semi-Sovereign People* (New York: Holt, Rinehart and Winston, 1961), p. 3.

[25]See Hedrick Smith, *The Power Game,* pp. 82–83.

[26]Ernest R. May, "An American Tradition in Foreign Policy: The Role of Public Opinion" in William H. Nelson, ed., *Theory and Practice in American Policy* (San Francisco: W. H. Freeman and Company, 1978), pp. 23–25.

[27]Barry B. Hughes, *The Domestic Context of American Foreign Policy* (San Francisco: W. H. Freeman and Company, 1978), pp. 23–25.

[28]Quoted in Ralph B. Levering, *The Public and American Foreign Policy, 1918–1978* (New York: William Morrow and Company, 1978), p. 152.

[29]Daniel Yankelovich, "Farewell to 'President Knows Best,'" *Foreign Affairs,* 57, no. 3 (1978):692.

[30]*Editorial Research Reports,* October 7, 1988, p. 498.

[31]David P. Calleo, *Beyond American Hegemony: The Future of the Western Alliance* (New York: Basic Books, 1987).

[32]*Congressional Quarterly Weekly Report,* September 17, 1988, pp. 2578–79 and *The New York Times,* January 11, 1989.

[33]Paul Kennedy, *The Rise and Fall of the Great Powers* (New York: Random House, 1987), Chapter 8.

★

THE DECLARATION OF INDEPENDENCE

The Unanimous Declaration of the Thirteen
United States of America

When in the Course of human events, it becomes necessary for one people to dissolve the political bands, which have connected them with another, and to assume among the powers of the earth, the separate and equal station to which the Laws of Nature and of Nature's God entitle them, a decent respect to the opinions of mankind requires that they should declare the causes which impel them to the separation.—We hold these truths to be self-evident, that all men are created equal, that they are endowed by their Creator with certain unalienable Rights, that among these are Life, Liberty and the pursuit of Happiness.—That to secure these rights, Governments are instituted among Men, deriving their just powers from the consent of the governed,—That whenever any Form of Government becomes destructive of these ends, it is the Right of the People to alter or to abolish it, and to institute new Government, laying its foundation on such principles and organizing its powers in such form, as to them shall seem most likely to effect their Safety and Happiness. Prudence, indeed, will dictate that Governments long established should not be changed for light and transient causes; and accordingly all experience hath shown, that mankind are more disposed to suffer, while evils are sufferable, than to right themselves by abolishing the forms to which they are accustomed. But when a long train of abuses and usurpations, pursuing invariably the same Object evinces a design to reduce them under absolute Despotism, it is their right, it is their duty, to throw off such Government, and to provide new Guards for their future security.—Such has been the patient sufferance of these Colonies; and such is now the necessity which constrains them to alter their former Systems of Government. The history of the present King of Great Britain is a history of repeated injuries and usurpations, all having in direct object the establishment of an absolute Tyranny over these States. To prove this, let

Facts be submitted to a candid world.—He has refused his Assent to Laws, the most wholesome and necessary for the public good.—He has forbidden his Governors to pass Laws of immediate and pressing importance, unless suspended in their operation till his Assent should be obtained; and when so suspended, he has utterly neglected to attend to them.—He has refused to pass other Laws for the accommodation of large districts of people, unless those people would relinquish the right of Representation in the Legislature, a right inestimable to them and formidable to tyrants only.—He has called together legislative bodies at places unusual, uncomfortable, and distant from the depository of their public Records, for the sole purpose of fatiguing them into compliance with his measures.—He has dissolved Representative Houses repeatedly, for opposing with manly firmness his invasions on the rights of the people.—He has refused for a long time, after such dissolutions, to cause others to be elected; whereby the Legislative powers, incapable of Annihilation, have returned to the People at large for their exercise, the State remaining in the meantime exposed to all the dangers of invasion from without, and convulsions within.—He has endeavored to prevent the population of these States; for that purpose obstructing the Laws for Naturalization of Foreigners; refusing to pass others to encourage their migrations hither, and raising the conditions of new Appropriations of Lands.—He has obstructed the Administration of Justice, by refusing his Assent to Laws for establishing Judiciary powers.—He has made Judges dependent on his Will alone, for the tenure of their offices, and the amount and payment of their salaries.—He has erected a multitude of New Offices, and sent hither swarms of Officers to harass our people, and eat out their substance.—He has kept among us, in times of peace, Standing Armies without the Consent of our legislatures.—He has affected to render the Military independent of and superior to the Civil power.—He has combined with others to subject us to a jurisdiction foreign to our constitution, and unacknowledged by our laws; giving his Assent to their Acts of pretended Legislation.—For quartering large bodies of armed troops among us:—For protecting them, by a mock Trial, from punishment for any Murders which they should commit on the Inhabitants of these States:—For cutting off our Trade with all parts of the world:—For imposing Taxes on us without our Consent:—For depriving us in many cases, of the benefits of Trial by Jury:—For transporting us beyond Seas to be tried for pretended offenses:—For abolishing the free System of English Laws in a neighboring Province, establishing therein an Arbitrary government, and enlarging its Boundaries so as to render it at once an example and fit instrument for introducing the same absolute rule into these Colonies:—For taking away our Charters, abolishing our most valuable Laws, and altering fundamentally the Forms of our Governments:—For suspending our own Legislatures, and declaring themselves invested with power to legislate for us in all cases whatsoever.—He has abdicated Government here, by declaring us out of his Protection and waging War against us.—He has plundered our seas, ravaged our Coasts, burnt our towns, and destroyed the lives of our people.—He is at this time transporting large armies of foreign Mercenaries to complete the works of death, desolation and tyranny, already begun with circumstances of Cruelty & perfidy, scarcely paralleled in the most barbarous ages, and totally unworthy the Head of a civilized nation.—He has constrained our fellow Citizens taken Captive on the High Seas to bear Arms against their Country, to become the executioners of their friends and Brethren, or to fall themselves by their hands.—He has excited domestic insurrections amongst us, and has endeavored to bring on the inhabitants of our frontiers, the merciless Indian Savages, whose known rule of warfare, is an undistinguished destruction of all ages, sexes and conditions. In every stage of these Oppressions We have Petitioned for Redress in the most humble terms: Our repeated Petitions have been answered only by repeated injury. A Prince whose character is thus marked by every act which may define a Tyrant, is unfit to be the ruler of a free people. Nor have We been wanting in attentions to our British brethren. We have warned them from time to time of attempts by their legislature to extend an unwarrantable jurisdiction over us. We have reminded them of the circumstances of our emigration and settlement here. We have appealed to their native justice and magnanimity, and we have conjured them by the ties of our common kindred to disavow these usurpations, which would inevitably interrupt our connections and correspondence. They too have been deaf to the voice of justice and of consanguinity. We must, therefore, acquiesce in the necessity, which denounces our Separation, and hold them, as we hold the rest of mankind, Enemies in War, in Peace Friends.—

We, therefore, the Representatives of the United States of America, in General Congress, Assembled, appealing to the Supreme Judge of the world for the rectitude of our intentions do, in the Name, and by the Authority of the good People of these Colonies, solemnly publish and declare, That these United Colonies are, and of Right ought to be Free and Independent States, that they are Absolved from all Allegiance to the British Crown, and that all political connection between them and the State of Great Britain, is and ought to be totally dissolved; and that as Free and Independent

States, they have full Power to levy War, conclude Peace, contract Alliances, establish Commerce, and to do all other Acts and Things which Independent States may of right do.—And for the support of this Declaration, with a firm reliance on the protection of divine Providence, we mutually pledge to each other our Lives, our Fortunes and our scared Honor.

THE CONSTITUTION OF THE UNITED STATES OF AMERICA

We the People of the United States, in Order to form a more perfect Union, establish Justice, insure domestic Tranquility, provide for the common defence, promote the general Welfare, and secure the Blessings of Liberty to ourselves and our Posterity, do ordain and establish this CONSTITUTION for the United States of America.

ARTICLE I

Section 1

All legislative Powers herein granted shall be vested in a Congress of the United States, which shall consist of a Senate and House of Representatives.

Section 2

(1) The House of Representatives shall be composed of Members chosen every second Year by the People of the several States, and the Electors in each State shall have the Qualifications requisite for Electors of the most numerous Branch of the State Legislature.

(2) No Person shall be a Representative who shall not have attained to the Age of twenty-five Years, and been seven Years a Citizen of the United States, and who shall not, when elected, be an Inhabitant of that State in which he shall be chosen.

(3) [Representatives and direct Taxes[1] shall be apportioned among the several States which may be included within this Union, according to their respective Numbers, which shall be determined by adding to the whole Number of free Persons, including those bound to Service for a Term of Years, and excluding Indians not taxed, three fifths of all other Persons.][2] The actual Enumeration shall be made within three Years after the first Meeting of the Congress of the United States, and within every subsequent Term of ten Years, in such Manner as they shall by Law direct. The Number of Representatives shall not exceed one for every thirty Thousand, but each State shall have at Least one Representative; and until such enumeration shall be made, the State of New Hampshire shall be entitled to choose three, Massachusetts eight, Rhode-Island and Providence Plantations one, Connecticut five, New York six, New Jersey four, Pennsylvania eight, Delaware one, Maryland six, Virginia ten, North Carolina five, South Carolina five, and Georgia three.

(4) When vacancies happen in the Representation from any State, the Executive Authority thereof shall issue Writs of Election to fill such Vacancies.

(5) The House of Representatives shall choose their Speaker and other Officers; and shall have the sole Power of Impeachment.

Section 3

(1) The Senate of the United States shall be composed of two Senators from each State, [chosen by the Legislature][3] thereof, for six Years; and each Senator shall have one Vote.

(2) Immediately after they shall be assembled in Consequence of the first Election, they shall be divided as equally as may be into three Classes. The Seats of the Senators of the first Class shall be vacated at the Expiration of the second Year, of the second Class at the Expiration of the fourth Year, and of the third Class at the Expiration of the sixth Year, so that one-third may be chosen every second year; [and if Vacancies happen by Resignation, or otherwise, during the Recess of the Legislature of any State, the Executive thereof may make temporary Appointments until the next Meeting of the Legislature, which shall then fill such Vacancies].[4]

(3) No person shall be a Senator who shall not have attained to the Age of thirty Years, and been nine Years a Citizen of the United States, and who shall not, when elected, be an Inhabitant of that State for which he shall be chosen.

(4) The Vice President of the United States shall be President of the Senate, but shall have no Vote, unless they be equally divided.

(5) The Senate shall choose their other Officers, and also a President pro tempore, in the Absence of the Vice President, or when he shall exercise the Office of President of the United States.

(6) The Senate shall have the sole Power to try all Impeachments. When sitting for that Purpose, they shall be on Oath or Affirmation. When the President of the United States is tried, the Chief Justice shall preside: And no Person shall be convicted without the Concurrence of two thirds of the Members present.

(7) Judgment in Cases of Impeachment shall not extend further than to removal from Office, and disqualification to hold and enjoy any Office of honor, Trust or Profit under the United States: but the Party convicted shall nevertheless be liable and subject to Indictment, Trial, Judgment and Punishment according to Law.

Section 4

(1) The Times, Places and Manner of holding Elections for Senators and Representatives, shall be prescribed in each State by the Legislature thereof; but the Congress may at any time by Law make or alter such Regulations, except as to the Places of choosing Senators.

(2) The Congress shall assemble at least once in every Year, and such Meeting shall [be on the first Monday in December,][5] unless they shall by Law appoint a different Day.

---

[1] The Sixteenth Amendment replaced this with respect to income taxes.

[2] Repealed by the Fourteenth Amendment.

[3] Repealed by the Seventeenth Amendment, Section 1.

[4] Changed by the Seventeenth Amendment.

[5] Changed by the Twentieth Amendment, Section 2.

Section 5

(1) Each House shall be the Judge of the Elections, Returns and Qualifications of its own Members, and a Majority of each shall constitute a Quorum to do Business; but a smaller Number may adjourn from day to day, and may be authorized to compel the Attendance of absent Members, in such Manner, and under such Penalties as each House may provide.

(2) Each House may determine the Rules of its Proceedings, punish its Members for disorderly Behavior, and, with the Concurrence of two thirds, expel a Member.

(3) Each House shall keep a Journal of its Proceedings, and from time to time publish the same, excepting such Parts as may in their Judgment require Secrecy; and the Yeas and Nays of the Members of either House on any question shall, at the Desire of one fifth of those Present, be entered on the Journal.

(4) Neither House, during the Session of Congress, shall, without the Consent of the other, adjourn for more than three days, nor to any other Place than that in which the two Houses shall be sitting.

Section 6

(1) The Senators and Representatives shall receive a Compensation for their Services, to be ascertained by Law, and paid out of the Treasury of the United States. They shall in all Cases, except Treason, Felony and Breach of the Peace, be privileged from Arrest during their Attendance at the Session of their respective Houses, and in going to and returning from the same; and for any Speech or Debate in either House, they shall not be questioned in any other Place.

(2) No Senator or Representative shall, during the Time for which he was elected, be appointed to any civil Office under the Authority of the United States, which shall have been created, or the Emoluments whereof have been increased during such time; and no Person holding any Office under the United States, shall be a Member of either House during his Continuance in Office.

Section 7

(1) All Bills for raising Revenue shall originate in the House of Representatives; but the Senate may propose or concur with Amendments as on other Bills.

(2) Every Bill which shall have passed the House of Representatives and the Senate, shall, before it becomes a Law, be presented to the President of the United States; If he approve he shall sign it, but if not he shall return it, with his Objections to that House in which it shall have originated, who shall enter the Objections at large on their Journal, and proceed to reconsider it. If after such Reconsideration two thirds of that House shall agree to pass the Bill, it shall be sent, together with the Objections, to the other House, by which it shall likewise be reconsidered, and if approved by two thirds of that House, it shall become a Law. But in all such Cases the Votes of both Houses shall be determined by Yeas and Nays, and the Names of the Persons voting for and against the Bill shall be entered on the Journal of each House respectively. If any Bill shall not be returned by the President within ten Days (Sundays excepted) after it shall have been presented to him, the Same shall be a Law, in like Manner as if he had signed it, unless the Congress by their Adjournment prevent its Return, in which Case it shall not be a Law.

(3) Every Order, Resolution, or Vote to which the Concurrence of the Senate and House of Representatives may be necessary (except on a question of Adjournment) shall be presented to the President of the United States; and before the Same shall take Effect, shall be approved by him, or being disapproved by him, shall be repassed by two thirds of the Senate and House of Representatives, according to the Rules and Limitations prescribed in the Case of a Bill.

Section 8

(1) The Congress shall have Power To lay and collect Taxes, Duties, Imposts and Excises, to pay the Debts and provide for the common Defense and general Welfare of the United States; but all Duties, Imposts and Excises shall be uniform throughout the United States;

(2) To borrow money on the credit of the United States;

(3) To regulate Commerce with foreign Nations, and among the several States, and with the Indian Tribes;

(4) To establish an uniform Rule of Naturalization, and uniform Laws on the subject of Bankruptcies throughout the United States;

(5) To coin Money, regulate the Value thereof, and of foreign Coin, and fix the Standard of Weights and Measures;

(6) To provide for the Punishment of counterfeiting the Securities and current Coin of the United States;

(7) To establish Post Offices and post Roads;

(8) To promote the Progress of Science and useful Arts, by securing for limited Times to Authors and Inventors the exclusive Right to their respective Writings and Discoveries;

(9) To constitute Tribunals inferior to the supreme Court;

(10) To define and punish Piracies and Felonies committed on the high Seas, and Offenses against the Law of Nations;

(11) To declare War, grant Letters of Marque and Reprisal, and make Rules concerning Captures on Land and Water;

(12) To raise and support Armies, but no Appropriation of Money to that Use shall be for a longer Term than two Years;

(13) To provide and maintain a Navy;

(14) To make Rules for the Government and Regulation of the land and naval Forces;

(15) To provide for calling forth the Militia to execute the Laws of the Union, suppress Insurrections and repel Invasions;

(16) To provide for organizing, arming, and disciplining the Militia, and for governing such Part of them as may be employed in the Service of the United States, reserving to the States respectively, the Appointment of the Officers, and the Authority of training the Militia according to the discipline prescribed by Congress;

(17) To exercise exclusive Legislation in all Cases whatsoever, over such District (not exceeding ten Miles square) as may, by Cession of particular States, and the Acceptance of Congress, become the Seat of the Government of the United States, and to exercise like Authority over all Places purchased by the Consent of the Legislature of the State in which the Same shall be, for the Erection of Forts, Magazines, Arsenals, dock-Yards, and other needful Buildings;—And

(18) To make all Laws which shall be necessary and proper for carrying into Execution the foregoing Powers, and all other Powers vested by this Constitution in the Government of the United States, or in any Department or Officer thereof.

Section 9

(1) The Migration or Importation of such Persons as any of the States now existing shall think proper to admit, shall not be prohibited by the Congress prior to the Year one thousand eight hundred and eight, but a tax or duty may be imposed on such Importation, not exceeding ten dollars for each Person.

(2) The Privilege of the Writ of Habeas Corpus shall not be suspended, unless when in Cases of Rebellion or Invasion the public Safety may require it.

(3) No Bill of Attainder or ex post facto Law shall be passed.

(4) No Capitation, or other direct, Tax shall be laid, unless in Proportion to the Census or Enumeration herein before directed to be taken.[6]

(5) No Tax or Duty shall be laid on Articles exported from any State.

(6) No Preference shall be given by any Regulation of Commerce or Revenue to the Ports of one State over those of another; nor shall Vessels bound to, or from, one State, be obliged to enter, clear, or pay Duties in another.

---

[6]Changed by the Sixteenth Amendment.

(7) No Money shall be drawn from the Treasury, but in Consequence of Appropriations made by Law; and a regular Statement and Account of the Receipts and Expenditures of all public Money shall be published from time to time.

(8) No Title of Nobility shall be granted by the United States: And no Person holding any Office of Profit or Trust under them, shall, without the Consent of the Congress, accept of any present, Emolument, Office, or Title, of any kind whatever, from any King, Prince, or foreign State.

Section 10

(1) No State shall enter into any Treaty, Alliance, or Confederation; grant Letters of Marque and Reprisal; coin Money; emit Bills of Credit; make any Thing but gold and silver Coin a Tender in Payment of Debts; pass any Bill of Attainder, ex post facto Law, or Law impairing the Obligation of Contracts, or grant any Title of Nobility.

(2) No State shall, without the Consent of the Congress, lay any Imposts or Duties on Imports or Exports, except what may be absolutely necessary for executing its inspection Laws: and the net Produce of all Duties and Imposts, laid by any State on Imports or Exports, shall be for the Use of the Treasury of the United States; and all such laws shall be subject to the Revision and Control of the Congress.

(3) No State shall, without the Consent of Congress, lay any duty of Tonnage, keep Troops, or Ships of War in time of Peace, enter into any Agreement or Compact with another State, or with a foreign Power, or engage in War, unless actually invaded, or in such imminent Danger as will not admit of delay.

ARTICLE II

Section 1

(1) The executive Power shall be vested in a President of the United States of America. He shall hold his Office during the Term of four Years, and, together with the Vice-President, chosen for the same Term, be elected, as follows:

(2) Each State shall appoint, in such Manner as the Legislature thereof may direct, a Number of Electors, equal to the whole Number of Senators and Representatives to which the State may be entitled in the Congress; but no Senator or Representative, or Person holding an Office of Trust or Profit under the United States, shall be appointed an Elector.

[The Electors shall meet in their respective States, and vote by Ballot for two persons, of whom one at least shall not be an Inhabitant of the same State with themselves. And they shall make a List of all the Persons voted for, and of the Number of Votes for each; which List they shall sign and certify, and transmit sealed to the Seat of the Government of the United States, directed to the President of the Senate. The President of the Senate shall, in the Presence of the Senate and House of Representatives, open all the Certificates, and the Votes shall then be counted. The Person having the greatest Number of Votes shall be the President, if such Number be a Majority of the whole Number of Electors appointed; and if there be more than one who have such Majority, and have an equal Number of Votes, then the House of Representatives shall immediately choose by Ballot one of them for President; and if no Person have a Majority, then from the five highest on the List the said House shall in like Manner choose the President. But in choosing the President, the Votes shall be taken by States, the Representation from each State having one Vote; A quorum for this purpose shall consist of a Member or Members from two-thirds of the States, and a Majority of all the States shall be necessary to a Choice. In every Case, after the Choice of the President, the Person having the greatest Number of Votes of the Electors shall be the Vice-President. But if there should remain two or more who have equal Votes, the Senate shall choose from them by Ballot the Vice-President.][7]

(3) The Congress may determine the Time of choosing the Electors, and the Day on which they shall give their Votes; which Day shall be the same throughout the United States.

(4) No person except a natural born Citizen, or a Citizen of the United States, at the time of the Adoption of this Constitution, shall be eligible to the Office of President; neither shall any Person be eligible to that Office who shall not have attained to the Age of thirty-five Years, and been fourteen Years a Resident within the United States.

(5) In case of the Removal of the President from Office, or of his Death, Resignation, or Inability to discharge the Powers and Duties of the said Office, the same shall devolve on the Vice-President, and the Congress may by Law provide for the Case of Removal, Death, Resignation or Inability, both of the President and Vice-President, declaring what Officer shall then act as President, and such Officer shall act accordingly, until the Disability be removed, or a President shall be elected.[8]

(6) The President shall, at stated Times, receive for his Services, a Compensation, which shall neither be increased nor diminished during the Period for which he shall have been elected, and he shall not receive within that Period any other Emolument from the United States, or any of them.

(7) Before he enter on the Execution of his Office, he shall take the following Oath or Affirmation:—"I do solemnly swear (or affirm) that I will faithfully execute the Office of President of the United States, and will to the best of my Ability, preserve, protect and defend the Constitution of the United States."

Section 2

(1) The President shall be Commander in Chief of the Army and Navy of the United States, and of the Militia of the several States, when called into the actual Service of the United States; he may require the Opinion in writing, of the principal Officer in each of the executive Departments, upon any subject relating to the Duties of their respective Offices, and he shall have Power to Grant Reprieves and Pardons for Offenses against the United States, except in Cases of Impeachment.

(2) He shall have Power, by and with the Advice and Consent of the Senate, to make Treaties, provided two-thirds of the Senators present concur; and he shall nominate, and by and with the Advice and Consent of the Senate, shall appoint Ambassadors, other public Ministers and Consuls, Judges of the supreme Court, and all other Officers of the United States, whose Appointments are not herein otherwise provided for, and which shall be established by Law: but the Congress may by Law vest the Appointment of such inferior Officers, as they think proper, in the President alone, in the Court of Law, or in the Heads of Departments.

(3) The President shall have Power to fill up all Vacancies that may happen during the Recess of the Senate, by granting Commissions which shall expire at the End of their next Session.

Section 3

He shall from time to time give to the Congress Information of the State of the Union, and recommend to their Consideration such Measures as he shall judge necessary and expedient; he may, on extraordinary Occasions, convene both Houses, or either of them, and in Case of Disagreement between them, with Respect to the Time of Adjournment, he may adjourn them to such Time as he shall think proper; he shall receive Ambassadors and other public Ministers; he shall take Care that the Laws be faithfully executed, and shall Commission all the Officers of the United States.

Section 4

The President, Vice President and all civil Officers of the United States, shall be removed from Office on Impeachment for, and Conviction of, Treason, Bribery, or other high Crimes and Misdemeanors.

---

[7]This paragraph was superseded in 1804 by the Twelfth Amendment.

[8]Changed by the Twenty-fifth Amendment.

ARTICLE III

Section 1

The judicial Power of the United States, shall be vested in one supreme Court, and in such inferior Courts as the Congress may from time to time ordain and establish. The Judges, both of the supreme and inferior Courts, shall hold their Offices during good Behavior, and shall, at stated Times, receive for their Services a Compensation which shall not be diminished during their Continuance in Office.

Section 2

(1) The judicial Power shall extend to all Cases, in Law and Equity, arising under this Constitution, the Laws of the United States, and Treaties made, or which shall be made, under their Authority;—to all Cases affecting Ambassadors, other public Ministers and Consuls;—to all Cases of admiralty and maritime Jurisdiction;—to Controversies to which the United States shall be a Party;—to Controversies between two or more states;—[between a State and Citizens of another State];[9]—between Citizens of different States;—between Citizens of the same State claiming Lands under Grants of different States, and [between a State, or the Citizens thereof, and foreign States, Citizens or Subjects].[10]

(2) In all Cases affecting Ambassadors, other public Ministers and Consuls, and those in which a State shall be Party, the supreme Court shall have original Jurisdiction. In all the other Cases before mentioned, the supreme Court shall have appellate Jurisdiction, both as to Law and Fact, with such Exceptions, and under such Regulations as the Congress shall make.

(3) The trial of all Crimes, except in Cases of Impeachment, shall be by Jury; and such Trial shall be held in the State where the said Crimes shall have been committed: but when not committed within any State, the Trial shall be at such Place or Places as the Congress may by Law have directed.

Section 3

(1) Treason against the United States, shall consist only in levying War against them, or in adhering to their Enemies, giving them Aid and Comfort. No Person shall be convicted of Treason unless on the Testimony of two Witnesses to the same overt Act, or on Confession in open Court.

(2) The Congress shall have Power to declare the Punishment of Treason, but no Attainder of Treason shall work Corruption of Blood, or Forfeiture except during the Life of the Person attained.

ARTICLE IV

Section 1

Full Faith and Credit shall be given in each State to the public Acts, Records, and judicial Proceedings of every other State. And the Congress may by general Laws prescribe the Manner in which such Acts, Records and Proceedings shall be proved, and the Effect thereof.

Section 2

(1) The Citizens of each State shall be entitled to all Privileges and Immunities of Citizens in the several States.

(2) A Person charged in any State with Treason, Felony, or other Crime, who shall flee from Justice, and be found in another State, shall on demand of the executive Authority of the State from which he fled, be delivered up, to be removed to the State having Jurisdiction of the Crime.

(3) [No Person held to Service or Labor in one State, under the Laws thereof, escaping into another, shall, in Consequence of any Law or Regulation therein, be discharged from such Service or Labor, but shall be delivered up on Claim of the Party to whom such Service or Labor may be due.][11]

Section 3

(1) New States may be admitted by the Congress into this Union; but no new State shall be formed or erected within the Juris-diction of any other State; nor any State be formed by the Junction of two or more States, or Parts of States, without the Consent of the Legislatures of the States concerned as well as of the Congress.

(2) The Congress shall have Power to dispose of and make all needful Rules and Regulations respecting the Territory or other Property belonging to the United States; and nothing in this Constitution shall be so construed as to Prejudice any Claims of the United States, or of any particular State.

Section 4

The United States shall guarantee to every State in this Union a Republican Form of Government, and shall protect each of them against Invasion; and on Application of the Legislature, or of the Executive (when the Legislature cannot be convened) against domestic Violence.

ARTICLE V

The Congress, whenever two-thirds of both Houses shall deem it necessary, shall propose Amendments to this Constitution, or, on the Application of the Legislatures of two-thirds of the several States, shall call a Convention for proposing Amendments, which, in either Case, shall be valid to all Intents and Purposes, as part of this Constitution, when ratified by the Legislature of three-fourths of the several States, or by Conventions in three-fourths thereof, as the one or the other Mode of Ratification may be proposed by the Congress; Provided that no Amendment which may be made prior to the Year One thousand eight hundred and eight shall in any Manner affect the first and fourth Clauses in the Ninth Section of the first Article; and that no State, without its Consent, shall be deprived of its equal Suffrage in the Senate.

ARTICLE VI

(1) All Debts contracted and Engagements entered into, before the Adoption of this Constitution, shall be as valid against the United States under this Constitution, as under the Confederation.

(2) This Constitution, and the Laws of the United States which shall be made in Pursuance thereof; and all Treaties made, or which shall be made, under the Authority of the United States, shall be the supreme Law of the Land; and the Judges in every State shall be bound thereby, any Thing in the Constitution or Laws of any State to the Contrary notwithstanding.

(3) The Senators and Representatives before mentioned, and the Members of the several State Legislatures, and all executive and judicial Officers, both of the United States and of the several States, shall be bound by Oath or Affirmation, to support this Constitution; but no religious Test shall ever be required as a Qualification to any Office or public Trust under the United States.

ARTICLE VII

The Ratification of the Conventions of nine States, shall be sufficient for the Establishment of this Constitution between the States so ratifying the Same.

DONE in Convention by the Unanimous Consent of the States present the Seventeenth Day of September in the Year of our Lord one thousand seven hundred and Eighty seven and the Independence of the United States of America the Twelfth. In Witness whereof We have hereunto subscribed our Names.

Go. WASHINGTON
President and deputy from Virginia

---

[9]Restricted by the Eleventh Amendment.

[10]Restricted by the Eleventh Amendment.

[11]This paragraph has been superseded by the Thirteenth Amendment.

AMENDMENT I[12]

Congress shall make no law respecting an establishment of religion, or prohibiting the free exercise thereof; or abridging the freedom of speech, or of the press; or the right of the people peaceably to assemble, and to petition the Government for a redress of grievances.

AMENDMENT II

A well regulated Militia, being necessary to the security of a free State, the right of the people to keep and bear Arms, shall not be infringed.

AMENDMENT III

No Soldier shall, in time of peace be quartered in any house, without the consent of the Owner, nor in time of war, but in a manner to be prescribed by law.

AMENDMENT IV

The right of the people to be secure in their persons, houses, papers, and effects, against unreasonable searches and seizures, shall not be violated, and no Warrants shall issue, but upon probable cause, supported by Oath or affirmation, and particularly describing the place to be searched, and the persons or things to be seized.

AMENDMENT V

No person shall be held to answer for a capital, or otherwise infamous crime, unless on a presentment or indictment of a Grand Jury, except in cases arising in the land or naval forces, or in the Militia, when in actual service in time of War or public danger; nor shall any person be subject for the same offense to be twice put in jeopardy of life or limb; nor shall be compelled in any criminal case to be witness against himself, nor be deprived of life, liberty, or property, without due process of law; nor shall private property be taken for public use without just compensation.

AMMENDMENT VI

In all criminal prosecutions, the accused shall enjoy the right to a speedy and public trial, by an impartial jury of the State and district wherein the crime shall have been committed, which district shall have been previously ascertained by law, and to be informed of the nature and cause of the accusation, to be confronted with the witnesses against him; to have compulsory process for obtaining witnesses in his favor, and to have the Assistance of Counsel for his defense.

AMENDMENT VII

In Suits at common law, where the value in controversy shall exceed twenty dollars, the right of trial by jury shall be preserved, and no fact tried by a jury, shall be otherwise reexamined in any Court of the United States, than according to the rules of the common law.

AMENDMENT VIII

Excessive bail shall not be required, nor excessive fines imposed, nor cruel and unusual punishments inflicted.

AMENDMENT IX

The enumeration in the Constitution, of certain rights, shall not be construed to deny or disparage others retained by the people.

AMENDMENT X

The powers not delegated to the United States by the Constitution, nor prohibited by it to the States, are reserved to the States respectively, or to the people.

AMENDMENT XI[13]

The Judicial power of the United States shall not be construed to extend to any suit in law or equity, commenced or prosecuted against one of the United States by Citizens of another State, or by Citizens or Subjects of any Foreign State.

AMENDMENT XII[14]

The Electors shall meet in their respective states and vote by ballot for President and Vice-President, one of whom, at least, shall not be an inhabitant of the same state with themselves; they shall name in their ballots the person voted for as President, and in distinct ballots the person voted for as Vice-President, and they shall make distinct lists of all persons voted for as President, and of all persons voted for as Vice-President, and of the number of votes for each, which lists they shall sign and certify, and transmit sealed to the seat of the government of the United States, directed to the President of the Senate;—The President of the Senate shall, in presence of the Senate and House of Representatives, open all the certificates and the votes shall then be counted;—The person having the greatest number of votes for President, shall be the President, if such number be a majority of the whole number of Electors appointed; and if no person have such majority, then from the persons having the highest numbers not exceeding three on the list of those voted for as President, the House of Representatives shall choose immediately, by ballot, the President. But in choosing the President, the votes shall be taken by states, the representation from each state having one vote; a quorum for this purpose shall consist of a member or members from two-thirds of the states, and a majority of all the states shall be necessary to a choice. [And if the House of Representatives shall not choose a President whenever the right of choice shall devolve upon them, before the fourth day of March next following, then the Vice-President shall act as President, as in the case of the death or other constitutional disability of the President.][15]—The person having the greatest number of votes as Vice-President, shall be the Vice-President, if such number be a majority of the whole number of Electors appointed, and if no person have a majority, then from the two highest numbers on the list, the Senate shall choose the Vice-President; a quorum for the purpose shall consist of two-thirds of the whole number of Senators, and a majority of the whole number shall be necessary to a choice. But no person constitutionally ineligible to the office of President shall be eligible to that of Vice-President of the United States.

AMENDMENT XIII[16]

Section 1
Neither slavery nor involuntary servitude, except as a punishment for crime whereof the party shall have been duly convicted, shall exist within the United States, or any place subject to their jurisdiction.

Section 2
Congress shall have power to enforce this article by appropriate legislation.

---

[12]The first ten amendments were adopted in 1791.

[13]Adopted in 1798.

[14]Adopted in 1804.

[15]Superseded by the Twentieth Amendment, Section 3.

[16]Adopted in 1865.

AMENDMENT XIV[17]

Section 1

All persons born or naturalized in the United States, and subject to the jurisdiction thereof, are citizens of the United States and of the State wherein they reside. No state shall make or enforce any law which shall abridge the privileges or immunities of citizens of the United States; nor shall any State deprive any person of life, liberty, or property, without due process of law; nor deny to any person within its jurisdiction the equal protection of the laws.

Section 2

Representatives shall be apportioned among the several States according to their respective numbers, counting the whole number of persons in each State, excluding Indians not taxed. But when the right to vote at any election for the choice of electors for President and Vice-President of the United States, Representatives in Congress, the Executive and Judicial officers of a State, or the members of the Legislature thereof, is denied to any of the male inhabitants of such State, being twenty-one years of age, and citizens of the United States, or in any way abridged, except for participation in rebellion, or other crime, the basis of representation therein shall be reduced in the proportion which the number of such male citizens shall bear to the whole number of male citizens twenty-one years of age in such State.

Section 3

No person shall be a Senator or Representative in Congress, or elector of President and Vice-President, or hold any office, civil or military, under the United States, or under any State, who, having previously taken an oath, as a member of Congress, or as an officer of the United States, or as a member of any State legislature, or as an executive or judicial officer of any State, to support the Constitution of the United States, shall have engaged in insurrection or rebellion against the same, or given aid or comfort to the enemies thereof. But Congress may by a vote of two-thirds of each House, remove such disability.

Section 4

The validity of the public debt of the United States, authorized by law, including debts incurred for payment of pensions and bounties for services in suppressing insurrection or rebellion, shall not be questioned. But neither the United States nor any State shall assume or pay any debt or obligation incurred in aid of insurrection or rebellion against the United States, or any claim for the loss or emancipation of any slave; but all such debts, obligations and claims shall be held illegal and void.

Section 5

The Congress shall have power to enforce, by appropriate legislation, the provisions of this article.

AMENDMENT XV[18]

Section 1

The right of citizens of the United States to vote shall not be denied or abridged by the United States or by any State on account of race, color, or previous condition of servitude.

Section 2

The Congress shall have power to enforce this article by appropriate legislation.

AMENDMENT XVI[19]

The Congress shall have power to lay and collect taxes on incomes, from whatever source derived, without apportionment among the several States, and without regard to any census or enumeration.

AMENDMENT XVII[20]

The Senate of the United States shall be composed of two Senators from each State, elected by the people thereof, for six years; and each Senator shall have one vote. The electors in each State shall have the qualifications requisite for electors of the most numerous branch of the State legislatures.

When vacancies happen in the representation of any State in the Senate, the executive authority of such State shall issue writs of election to fill such vacancies: *Provided,* That the legislature of any State may empower the executive thereof to make temporary appointments until the people fill the vacancies by election as the legislature may direct.

This amendment shall not be so construed as to affect the election or term of any Senator chosen before it becomes valid as part of the Constitution.

AMENDMENT XVIII[21]

Section 1

After one year from the ratification of this article the manufacture, sale, or transportation of intoxicating liquors within, the importation thereof into, or the exportation thereof from the United States and all territory subject to the jurisdiction thereof for beverage purposes is hereby prohibited.

Section 2

The Congress and the several States shall have concurrent power to enforce this article by appropriate legislation.

Section 3

This article shall be inoperative unless it shall have been ratified as an amendment to the Constitution by the legislatures of the several States, as provided in the Constitution, within seven years from the date of the submission hereof to the States by the Congress.

AMENDMENT XIX[22]

The right of citizens of the United States to vote shall not be denied or abridged by the United States or by any State on account of sex.

Congress shall have power to enforce this article by appropriate legislation.

AMENDMENT XX[23]

Section 1

The terms of the President and Vice-President shall end at noon on the 20th day of January, and the terms of Senators and Representatives at noon on the 3rd day of January, of the years in which such terms would have ended if this article had not been ratified; and the terms of their successors shall then begin.

Section 2

The Congress shall assemble at least once in every year, and such meeting shall begin at noon on the 3rd day of January, unless they shall by law appoint a different day.

---

[17]Adopted in 1868.

[18]Adopted in 1870.

[19]Adopted in 1913.

[20]Adopted in 1913.

[21]Adopted in 1919. Repealed by Section 1 of the Twenty-first Amendment.

[22]Adopted in 1920.

[23]Adopted in 1933.

Section 3

If, at the time fixed for the beginning of the term of the President, the President elect shall have died, the Vice-President elect shall become President. If a President shall not have been chosen before the time fixed for the beginning of his term, or if the President elect shall have failed to qualify, then the Vice-President elect shall act as President until a President shall have qualified; and the Congress may by law provide for the case wherein neither a President elect nor a Vice-President elect shall have qualified, declaring who shall then act as President, or the manner in which one who is to act shall be selected, and such person shall act accordingly until a President or Vice-President shall have qualified.

Section 4

The Congress may by law provide for the case of the death of any of the persons from whom the House of Representatives may choose a President whenever the right of choice shall have devolved upon them, and for the case of the death of any of the persons from whom the Senate may choose a Vice-President whenever the right of choice shall have devolved upon them.

Section 5

Sections 1 and 2 shall take effect on the 15th day of October following the ratification of this article.

Section 6

This article shall be inoperative unless it shall have been ratified as an amendment to the Constitution by the legislatures of three-fourths of the several States within seven years from the date of its submission.

AMENDMENT XXI[24]

Section 1

The eighteenth article of amendment to the Constitution of the United States is hereby repealed.

Section 2

The transportation or importation into any State, Territory, or possession of the United States for delivery or use therein of intoxicating liquors, in violation of the laws thereof, is hereby prohibited.

Section 3

This article shall be inoperative unless it shall have been ratified as an amendment to the Constitution by conventions in the several States, as provided in the Constitution, within seven years from the date of the submission hereof to the States by the Congress.

AMENDMENT XXII[25]

Section 1

No person shall be elected to the office of the President more than twice, and no person who has held the office of President, or acted as President, for more than two years of a term to which some other person was elected President shall be elected to the office of the President more than once. But this Article shall not apply to any person holding the office of President when this Article was proposed by the Congress, and shall not prevent any person who may be holding the office of President, or acting as President, during the term within which this Article becomes operative from holding the office of President or acting as President during the remainder of such term.

Section 2

This article shall be inoperative unless it shall have been ratified as an amendment to the Constitution by the legislatures of three-fourths of the several States within seven years from the date of its submission to the States by the Congress.

AMENDMENT XXIII[26]

Section 1

The District constituting the seat of Government of the United States shall appoint in such manner as the Congress may direct:

A number of electors of President and Vice-President equal to the whole number of Senators and Representatives in Congress to which the District would be entitled if it were a State, but in no event more than the least populous State; they shall be in addition to those appointed by the States, but they shall be considered, for the purposes of the election of President and Vice-President, to be electors appointed by a State, and they shall meet in the District and perform such duties as provided by the twelfth article of amendment.

Section 2

The Congress shall have power to enforce this article by appropriate legislation.

AMENDMENT XXIV[27]

Section 1

The right to citizens of the United States to vote in any primary or other election for President or Vice-President, for electors for President or Vice-President, or for Senator or Representative in Congress, shall not be denied or abridged by the United States or any state by reasons of failure to pay any poll tax or other tax.

Section 2

The Congress shall have power to enforce this article by appropriate legislation.

AMENDMENT XXV[28]

Section 1

In case of the removal of the President from office or of his death or resignation, the Vice-President shall become President.

Section 2

Whenever there is a vacancy in the office of the Vice-President, the President shall nominate a Vice-President who shall take office upon confirmation by a majority vote of both Houses of Congress.

Section 3

Whenever the President transmits to the President pro tempore of the Senate and the Speaker of the House of Representatives his written declaration that he is unable to discharge the powers and duties of his office, and until he transmits to them a written declaration to the contrary, such powers and duties shall be discharged by the Vice-President as Acting President.

Section 4

Whenever the Vice-President and a majority of either the principal officers of the Executive departments or of such other body as Congress may by law provide, transmit to the President pro tempore of the Senate and the Speaker of the House of Representatives their written declaration that the President is unable to discharge the powers and duties of his office, The Vice-President shall immediately assume the powers and duties of the office as Acting President.

---

[24] Adopted in 1933.

[25] Adopted in 1951.

[26] Adopted in 1961.

[27] Adopted in 1964.

[28] Adopted in 1967.

Thereafter, when the President transmits to the President pro tempore of the Senate and the Speaker of the House of Representatives his written declaration that no inability exists, he shall resume the powers and duties of his office unless the Vice-President and a majority of either the principal officers of the executive departments or of such other body as Congress may by law provide, transmit within four days to the President pro tempore of the Senate and the Speaker of the House of Representatives their written declaration that the President is unable to discharge the powers and duties of his office. Thereupon Congress shall decide the issue, assembling within forty-eight hours for that purpose if not in session. If the Congress, within twenty-one days after receipt of the latter written declaration, or, if Congress is not in session, within twenty-one days after Congress is required to assemble, determines by two-thirds vote of both houses that the President is unable to discharge the powers and duties of his office, the Vice-President shall continue to discharge the same as Acting President; otherwise, the President shall resume the powers and duties of his office.

AMENDMENT XXVI[29]

Section 1
The right of citizens of the United States, who are 18 years of age or older, to vote shall not be denied or abridged by the United States or any state on account of age.

Section 2
The Congress shall have power to enforce this article by appropriate legislation.

PROPOSED AMENDMENTS: (EQUAL RIGHTS AMENDMENT)[30]

Section 1
Equality of rights under the law shall not be denied or abridged by the United States or by any State on account of sex.

Section 2
The Congress shall have the power to enforce, by appropriate legislation, the provisions of this article.

Section 3
This amendment shall take effect two years after the date of ratification.

(D.C. VOTING RIGHTS)[31]

Section 1
For purposes of representation in the Congress, election of the President and Vice President, and article V of this Constitution, the District constituting the seat of government of the United States shall be treated as though it were a State.

Section 2
The exercise of the rights and powers conferred under this article shall be by the people of the District constituting the seat of government, and as shall be provided by the Congress.

Section 3
The twenty-third article of amendment to the Constitution of the United States is hereby repealed.

Section 4
This article shall be inoperative, unless it shall have been ratified as an amendment to the Constitution by the legislatures of three-fourths of the several States within seven years from the date of its submission.

---

[29] Adopted in 1971.

[30] Approved by Congress in 1972 and sent to the states for ratification. On October 6, 1978, Congress voted to extend the deadline for ratification from March 29, 1979, to June 30, 1982, marking the first time the ratification period was ever extended. The ERA was approved by 35 out of 38 states necessary for ratification.

[31] Proposed Amendment passed by Congress and sent to the states for ratification on August 28, 1978.

GLOSSARY

The number(s) within the parentheses refers to the chapter(s) where the term is found.

A

active-passive presidents the amount of energy brought to the job by a president in categories created by James David Barber. **(13)**

administrative law the rules and regulations issued by executive departments and agencies. **(15).**

affiliates local broadcast stations with contracts to major networks. **(6)**

Agency for International Development (AID) supervises U.S. foreign aid and military assistance given to other nations. **(18)**

agenda a list of things to be done or considered. **(16)**

agenda setting the creation of national priorities by elite institutions, telling people what they should think about in order to ensure stability and moderation. **(5, 6)**

agents of socialization elements that alter our opinions, including families, schools, peers, the media, and our experiences. **(5)**

amicus curiae Latin words meaning "friend of the court" referring to individuals or groups who are not actual litigants in a case but who may be affected by the outcome. **(15)**

Arms Control and Disarmament Agency (ACDA) one of the State Department bodies advising the secretary of state and the president on arms control matters. **(18)**

Articles of Confederation first form of the national government, which created a "league of friendship and perpetual union" among the sovereign states. **(1)**

attentive public 45 percent of Americans who are aware of major foreign policy issues and developments. **(18)**

B

Baker v. *Carr* **(1962)** the Supreme Court decision in 1962 that ruled that malapportionment of a state legislature was a justiciable question. Courts could decide legislative apportioning matters that had previously been considered "political" issues. **(3, 11)**

balance of power the actions of nations to prevent other nations from becoming too powerful. **(18)**

balancing the weighing of individual interests and interests of government in keeping order. **(4)**

ballot fatigue having so many officials to vote for at each level of government that people get turned off. **(7)**

bar, the title for practicing lawyers in America because they are admitted within the low rail, or "bar," in a courtroom. **(15)**

benign quotas a classification designed to help a group by making up for past discrimination. **(4)**

bicameral legislature a legislature made up of two houses. **(1, 2)**

block grants grants that provide federal funds for broad functions but allow state, local, and tribal officials to exercise greater discretion in their specific uses of the funds. **(3)**

branching policy formulation method modifying a previously established policy to meet new situations. **(16)**

broad constructionist one who believes the federal government possesses both express and implied powers. **(3)**

Brown v. Board of Education **(1954)** a landmark Supreme Court case holding that racially segregated schools are inherently unequal. **(4, 10)**

Budget Act of 1974 enabled Congress to propose a coherent alternative to the president's budget based on an examination of all spending and tax measures and the overall needs of the economy. **(12)**

bureaucracy a large administrative system with the basic characteristics of job specification, hierarchy of authority, a system of rules, and impersonality. **(14)**

C

cabinet department a federal agency, such as the Department of Defense, headed by a secretary whose appointment is confirmed by the Senate and who reports directly to the president. **(14)**

Campaign Reform Act of 1974 a law that limits contributions and spending in federal campaigns, requires all candidates for federal office to disclose all the financial aspects of their campaigns, and provides a public financing system for presidential campaigns. **(7)**

canvassing sending workers of candidates door-to-door to talk directly with voters. **(7)**

capital crimes serious crimes that can involve the death penalty. **(15)**

capital gain the difference between the purchase price and sale price of property, if the sale price is higher. **(17)**

capitalism America's economic system, in which the means of production are privately owned by individuals and corporations rather than publicly owned by the government or some government unit. **(17)**

capture a phenomenon in which regulatory bodies protect the interests of groups they are supposed to regulate. **(14)**

Case Act a nonbinding congressional resolution passed in 1971 requiring the secretary of state to submit all executive agreements to Congress to end secret commitments with foreign nations. **(13, 18)**

casework constituent service or helping constituents solve individual problems or claims. **(11)**

caucus a gathering of all the members of the party serving in the House or Senate. **(12)**

census a means of counting individuals that can be used to determine both the universe and a sampling size and composition. **(5)**

chief diplomat the constitutional power given to the president to negotiate and sign treaties with foreign countries. **(13)**

chief executive the head of government who ensures that laws are faithfully executed. **(13)**

civil disobedience breaking the law in an open, deliberate, nonviolent manner. **(10)**

civil law involves offenses, called torts, committed by a private individual or corporation against another or relationships among private individuals or corporations. **(15)**

civil liberties rights of freedom of speech, petition, assembly, and press that protect citizens against governmental actions that would interfere with their participation in a democratic political institution. **(4)**

Civil Rights Act of 1964 law prohibiting discrimination in public places, in voting, and in jobs that empower the executive to enforce it. **(10)**

civil rights the protections granted in the Constitution recognizing that all citizens must be treated equally under the law. **(4)**

Civil Service Reform Act of 1978 created a Senior Executive Service for employees in the higher grades, which provided a core of high-level executive managers who could be held accountable for their actions and would be rewarded for exemplary service. The hope was that this would blunt the effects of the "iron triangle." **(14)**

class action suits people bring a case to court not only for themselves but on behalf of everyone in a similar situation. **(4)**

clear and present danger doctrine rights such as freedom of speech cannot be restricted unless the words used create a clear and present danger that evil will result before there is time for a full discussion. **(4)**

closed primary party voters may only choose among candidates of their own party. **(8)**

cloture method of ending a filibuster by a vote of three-fifths of the Senate membership. **(12)**

Cold War the superpower conflict between the United States and the Soviet Union from 1945 to the present. **(18)**

commander-in-chief the constitutional power granted the president to appoint and promote officers of the armed forces and to "make" war; used in various conflicts without a formal congressional declaration of war. **(13)**

commerce clause Article I, Section 8 of the Constitution, which gives Congress exclusive power to regulate commerce "among the several states." **(3)**

common law made up of judge-made laws in actual cases. **(15)**

comparable worth demand for equal pay for different jobs that are equivalent. **(10)**

complete incorporationists those who believe that because of the Fourteenth Amendment, every provision of the Bill of Rights should be applied to the states. **(4)**

comprehensive policy formulation method consideration of every possible solution to a problem and the choosing of the best one. **(16)**

compulsory referendum usually involves a proposed state constitutional amendment that must be referred to a popular vote by the state legislature. **(3)**

concurrent powers powers shared and exercised by the federal and state governments. **(3)**

concurring opinion justices' separate opinions that agree with the Supreme Court majority opinion but disagree on the means of reaching that conclusion. **(15)**

conditionality the ability of Congress to prevent the president from having free rein in foreign policy by adding restrictions and prohibitions. **(13)**

conference committee appointed to resolve differences in versions of bills passed by the House and Senate. **(12)**

confirmation power the constitutional authority of the Senate to approve or reject presidential nominees. **(2, 12)**

Connecticut Compromise agreement at the Constitutional Convention in 1787 between the Virginia, New Jersey, and Hamilton plans that created a federal union. **(1)**

consent of the governed consent to be governed by the majority without restricting inalienable rights. **(1)**

conservatives individuals who desire a more limited role for government, fearing bigness might take away individual liberties. **(5)**

Constitution the fundamental and supreme law of a society. **(1)**

constitutional law based on a constitutional provision. **(15)**

construction, management, and decline the three chronological states of political regimes. **(13)**

containment the policy of keeping communism from expanding from its post-World War II borders, typified by the Marshall Plan. **(18)**

convention method provides for nomination by

a vote of party delegates who have been elected for that purpose. **(8)**

cooperative federalism a descriptive term for the relationship today between the states and the national government. **(3)**

cost-benefit analysis placing the cost of a projected policy over the benefits that would accrue and determining the value of the policy in light of potential trade-offs. **(16)**

Council of Economic Advisors the three-member body that advises the president on national economic developments. **(13)**

courtesy and accommodation the congressional norm, which means that a member of Congress should be courteous to other members, should be cooperative and willing to compromise where principle and back-home sentiment will allow, should help a colleague and expect to be helped in turn, should refrain from excessive partisanship, should not push the use of formal rules to the limit, and should keep his or her word. **(11)**

covert operations the secret operations of the CIA that include attempted overthrows of unfriendly governments, subversion of foreign officials, and other operations generally criticized by non-pragmatists. **(18)**

cracking splitting up an opponents' supporters into minorities in a number of districts to weaken their influence. **(11)**

criminal law involves an offense serious enough to be against the public interest as defined by the government. This kind of offense constitutes a crime. **(15)**

crisis management the ability of the president to move quickly to solve international crises because of his powers as commander-in-chief. **(18)**

D

dealignment declining loyalty to both parties among voters. **(8)**

defendant the accused in a criminal case. **(15)**

deficit amount borrowed by the federal government exceeding income. **(17)**

delegate legislators those who believe that their role is to represent what the "folks back home" want in Congress. **(11)**

demand deposits money that can be immediately withdrawn from banks by depositors. **(17)**

democratic process a process by which citizens have the right to select their governmental leaders. **(1)**

direct mail specialists people who use census data and polling information to target computer-produced letters to voters. **(7)**

direct primary election an election in which the voters of the party, rather than the leaders or delegates, decide the party candidate to be nominated. **(8)**

dissenting opinion a justice's opinion disagreeing with the majority opinion of the Supreme Court. **(15)**

distributional effect of federal spending government policies that redistribute wealth from one group to another. **(17)**

distributional effect of taxes results from tax decisions about "who will pay the costs," more or less from some taxpayers as compared with others. **(17)**

district plan reform of the electoral college system that would allow the unit rule to be used only by districts within a state, not on a statewide basis. **(7)**

doctrine of incorporation the means whereby the courts have been including the guarantees of the Bill of Rights into the Fourteenth Amendment, thus applying those rights to the states. **(4)**

E

ear to the ground an unscientific means of measuring public opinion by informally talking to individuals and asking questions to get a general "sense" of public feelings. **(5)**

elastic clause constitutional provision that enables Congress to "make all laws which shall be necessary and proper for carrying into execution the foregoing powers . . ." Also called the "necessary and proper clause." **(3)**

electoral college a constitutionally constituted group of electors from each state, equal to each state's congressional representation, who are pledged to a particular presidential and vice-presidential candidate and who vote for the winning candidate in each state. **(2, 7)**

Equal Rights Amendment proposed by Congress in 1972, it states: "Equality of rights under the law shall not be denied or abridged by the United States or by any state on account of sex." It failed ratification by the required number of states. **(10)**

equity developed when English courts found that common law had become too rigid. Equity decisions attempt to make common law more fair and to provide more flexible remedies without permanent damage. **(4, 15)**

excise tax federal tax on liquor, tobacco, gasoline, telephones, and air travel. Items taxed are considered to not be necessities. **(17)**

exclusionary rule the exclusion of certain illegally obtained evidence against a defendant. **(4)**

exclusive powers powers reserved solely to the national or state governments. **(3)**

executive agreement an understanding between the president and the head of a foreign government not subject to the Senate for ratification as a treaty. **(13, 18)**

executive function carrying out or enforcing the laws. **(2)**

Executive Office of the President established in 1939 to advise and assist the president, including the White House staff, Office of Management and Budget, the Council of Economic Advisers, and the National Security Council. **(13)**

executive privilege the withholding of information by the president and his principal aides using the claim of damage to national security should the information be revealed. **(12, 18)**

express or stated powers powers specifically given to the federal government in the Constitution. **(3)**

expropriate to convert property to government ownership. **(18)**

F

face-to-face interview the most reliable method of conducting an interview. **(5)**

fairness doctrine the requirement that controversial views on controversial issues be presented in the media. **(6)**

federal grants-in-aid federal funds provided to lower levels of government for the accomplishment of specific purposes. **(3)**

Federal Reserve System created by Congress in 1913 to both regulate the banks and the amount of money in circulation. **(17)**

federal system a system in which sovereignty, or governmental power, is divided by constitution between a central, national government and individual regional or state government. **(1, 3)**

federalism a principle that calls for political authority to be distributed between a central government and the governments of the states. **(2)**

Federalist, The a series of newspaper articles in New York written by James Madison, Alexander Hamilton, and John Jay that carefully stated the political philosophy and arguments of the Federalists in support of adopting the Constitution. **(1)**

felonies serious offenses that carry prison terms of one year or more. **(15)**

filibuster an attempt to "talk a bill to death"; it may be used by senators to prevent a final vote on a bill or other measures. **(12)**

First Continental Congress the first truly national organization meeting in Philadelphia that drew up a list of grievances to be presented to King George III. **(1)**

fiscal effect of federal spending causes unemployment and inflationary pressures on prices to rise or decline as a result of greater or reduced federal spending. **(17)**

fiscal effect of taxes may increase or decrease unemployment or inflation as money is taken out of the hands of consumers or left in their hands for consumption and investment. **(17)**

fiscal federalism the intertwined finances of the various levels of government. **(3)**

fiscal policy the use of governmental taxing and spending powers to affect the economy. **(17)**

fiscal power the power of the purse held by Congress based on Article I, Section 8 that gives Congress the power to "lay and collect taxes" and on Section 9, which states that "No money shall be drawn by the Treasury, but in consequence of appropriations made by law." **(12)**

focus group a small group of targeted voters who are interviewed. **(7)**

foreign policy the patterns of words and actions of one nation to others including goals and assumptions. **(18)**

Foreign Service specially trained non-clerical career officials who serve in key positions in the State Department and in foreign embassies. **(18)**

Fourteenth Amendment constitutional amendment adopted after the Civil War; its key phrases of "due process" and "equal protection" have been used by the courts to both extend and increase protections granted in the Bill of Rights. **(4)**

fourth branch of government although a part of the executive branch, the bureaucracy, because of its importance and independence, has developed an extraconstitutional significance. **(14)**

franking privilege free postage for members of Congress for official business. **(11)**

free enterprise the right of people to start or invest in whatever business or other enterprise they please, and the right of workers to move from job to job as they please without government interference. **(17)**

G

gerrymandering the drawing of boundary lines in a way that favors particular candidates, incumbents, or parties. **(11)**

glasnost openness in society and culture in the Soviet Union, instituted by Soviet Premier Gorbachev. **(18)**

government corporations a type of independent agency with a greater amount of flexibility than cabinet departments. These are unlike private corporations in that no dividends are paid, but are like private corporations in that they charge for their services. Examples include the U.S. Postal Service and the Tennessee Valley Authority. **(14)**

Gramm-Rudman Act of 1985 law requiring five years of federal deficit reductions of $36 billion a year, resulting in a balanced budget by fiscal 1991. **(12)**

grassroots campaigns interest group membership floods representatives with appeals to back a certain position. **(9)**

H

Hamilton Plan plan presented to the Philadelphia Convention in 1787 that would base U.S. government on a British model with an elected monarch. **(1)**

Hatch Act of 1939 congressional attempt to detach federal employees from politics by forbidding employees from engaging in political activities. **(14)**

head of government an individual with actual political responsibilities and powers. **(13)**

head of state an individual who represents the nation at symbolic and ceremonial occasions. **(13)**

horizontal federalism interstate obligations, relations, and dealings. **(3)**

human rights fundamental rights of people who should be treated the same. They are so basic that they cannot be sold, given up, or taken away. **(1)**

I

impeach (the power to) the power of the House of Representatives to charge any officer of the executive or judicial branches of the federal government, including the president. **(12)**

impeachment formal accusation by a majority vote in the House of Representatives. **(2)**

implied powers powers inferred from those specifically granted. **(3)**

in-party the party with more of its own members in important government positions. **(8)**

incremental policy formulation method making small changes in existing policy. **(16)**

incrementalism the gradual change of programs and services leading to gradual increases of program budgets. **(14)**

incumbency already holding an office. **(2, 11)**

independent agencies agencies that have functions similar to those of cabinets and their heads, called directors or administrators, that report directly to the president, but do not have as much prestige as cabinets. **(14)**

independents Americans who are not significantly tied to either the Republican or Democratic party. **(8)**

inevitable discovery exception it holds that when evidence obtained by an illegal search would inevitably have been discovered without police error or misconduct, the evidence is admissible. **(4)**

inflation the rate of increase in the price of goods and services. **(17)**

information control the president has unparalleled access to many sources of information and can also withhold information by his own prerogative. **(18)**

initiative allows voters to propose a law by securing a sufficient number of signatures on a petition. **(3)**

injunction in equity, a court order directing a person to stop doing something that violates someone else's rights. **(4, 15)**

institutional loyalty a norm dictating that members of Congress should be loyal to their own house against the other and to Congress against any real or perceived encroachment from the president, the bureaucracy, or the judiciary. Members should also avoid public criticism of Congress and refrain from behavior that might bring Congress, or their house, into disrepute. **(11)**

interest rates essentially, the price of borrowing money. **(17)**

internationalism the involvement of the United States around the world as a result of World War II, typified by recovery and containment. **(18)**

interventionism the involvement of nations in the internal affairs of others for a variety of reasons. **(18)**

invention policy formulation method the use of new ideas. **(16)**

iron triangle the special networks consisting of interest groups, bureaucrats, and key congressional members that develop into subgovernments. **(9, 14)**

irony of democracy those who most need the intervention of government to protect and improve their lives are the least influential politically. **(17)**

isolationism a nation's desire to avoid foreign involvement. **(18)**

issue-oriented groups interest groups that offer their members benefits other than material ones. **(9)**

J

Joint Chiefs of Staff the heads of the various uniformed services who decide on specific strategies and tactics to put military aspects of national policy into effect. **(18)**

judge-made law consists of decisions and opinions by courts. **(15)**

judicial activism the view that the Supreme Court should be an active, creative partner with the legislative and executive branches in shaping government policy. Activists seek to apply the Court's authority to solving economic and political problems ignored by other parts of the government. **(15)**

judicial function interpreting the laws. **(2)**

judicial restraint the idea that the Court should not impose its views on other branches of the government or on the states unless there is a clear violation of the Constitution. This creates a passive role in which the Court lets the other branches of government lead the way in setting policy on controversial political issues. **(15)**

judicial review the courts' authority not only to declare acts and laws of any state and local government unconstitutional, but also to strike down acts of any branch of the federal government. Literally, the authority to say what the Constitution means. **(2, 15)**

jurisdiction the authority to interpret and apply the law. **(15)**

K

Keynesian economics based on the writings of John Maynard Keynes, which argue that unemployment results from inadequate spending by consumers, investors, and government. The remedy for unemployment is greater government spending. If necessary, the government should tax the rich in order to provide jobs for the poor. **(17)**

L

lack of political efficacy a lowered sense that government will respond to the needs of the voter. **(7)**

laissez-faire a French phrase meaning roughly "leave things alone," which characterized early American government economic policy. **(17)**

landmark decision one that involves major changes in the law. **(4)**

law the set of rules of conduct established and enforced by a governing authority. **(15)**

legal direct action self-help efforts to directly affect conditions that people want changed. Action is aimed at directly motivating the targets of the action. **(10)**

legislative function passing laws. **(2)**

liberals individuals who see an increased governmental role in regulation and service to solve society's complex problems. **(5)**

limited government a government that does not violate standing law or act arbitrarily, controlled primarily by a social contract or constitution which is limited by the rights and liberties of the governed. **(1, 2)**

line-item veto the authority of some state governors to veto a particular item in an appropriation bill without having to veto the whole bill, a power not available to the president who must accept or reject the entire bill. **(3, 13)**

litigants the parties to a lawsuit. **(15)**

litigation the process of bringing lawsuits. **(9)**

lobbying the effort to influence governmental decisions. **(9)**

M

majority leader of the House second-ranking majority party leader in the House **(12)**

majority leader of the Senate principal leader of the majority party in the Senate and the nearest equivalent to the Speaker of the House. **(12)**

majority opinion the majority view of the Supreme Court on a case. **(15)**

majority party the party with the greatest number of members in each house. **(12)**

majority vote one more than half of all votes cast. **(8)**

majority whip of the House assists the Speaker and majority leader to coordinate party positions on legislation, pass information and directions between the leadership and other party members, make sure party members know when a particular vote is coming, try to persuade wavering representatives to vote with the leadership, and conduct informal surveys to check the likely outcome of votes. **(12)**

malapportionment an imbalance in the population of congressional districts. **(11)**

Marbury v. *Madison* **(1803)** landmark Supreme Court decision that established the principle of judicial review. **(15)**

mark-up session a meeting in which decisions are made concerning amendments and final wording of a bill. **(12)**

Marshall Plan the economic assistance given to Europe to provide recovery from World War II and make communism less appealing. **(18)**

mass public the 30 percent of the American public that is only sporadically interested in foreign policy matters. **(18)**

McCone Commission Report the 1965 report prompted by racial unrest and violence in the United States in cities in the 1960s; it was generally ignored. **(10)**

McCulloch v. *Maryland* **(1819)** Supreme Court decision that first recognized the doctrine of implied powers. It declared that a conflicting state legislative act must give way to an act of the U.S. Congress that is in accord with the Constitution. **(3, 15)**

media chains companies that combine different media in different cities under one owner. **(6)**

media means of communications that permit messages to be made public. **(6)**

merit system the process of competitive hiring of federal employees to remove political influence. **(14)**

military-industrial complex the statement by President Eisenhower in his farewell address in 1961 concerning a close relationship between the military bureaucracy and defense contractors. **(14, 18)**

minority Leader principal leader of the minority party in each house of Congress. **(12)**

misdemeanors minor offenses generally punishable by less than one year of imprisonment. **(15)**

mixed economy most property and the means of production are owned by individuals and private corporations, but the government is deeply involved in controlling and regulating how private property may be used and how private enterprise may be allowed to function. **(17)**

modern political machine an issue-oriented organization using the technologies of fund raising and direct mail campaigns to influence voters. **(8)**

monetarists economists who emphasize monetary policy as the most important way to manage the economy. **(17)**

monetary policy the effect the federal government has on the economy through its influence on the money supply. **(17)**

money coins and currency, demand deposits, and time deposits—all of which serve as mediums of exchange. **(17)**

Monroe Doctrine a declaration in 1823 warning European nations to stay out of the Western hemisphere. **(18)**

mutually assured destruction the idea that the ability to destroy one's adversary and vice versa ensures that no attack will occur. **(18)**

N

National Advisory Commission on Civil Disorders also called the Kerner Commission, it was appointed following the riots of 1967 and blamed whites for many of the racial problems in cities. As African Americans became frustrated, the nation polarized between whites and blacks. **(10)**

National Security Council a body that assists the president in national military and foreign policies. **(13)**

nationalist one who believes that there must be a sovereign and "solid coercive union" that could unite the states, regulate trade, and provide for a common army. **(1)**

networks agencies that produce and sell programs with advertising to local broadcasting stations. **(6)**

New Jersey Plan the plan presented by Thomas Patterson at the Philadelphia Convention that called for a stronger central confederation with a weaker central government, benefitting the smaller states. **(1)**

news leak a means by which the president or some other White House official can distribute non-attributable information to test public reaction. **(13)**

news management government control of information going to the public through television, radio, and newspapers. **(6)**

Nineteenth Amendment it was adopted in 1920, giving women the right to vote. **(10)**

norms informal unwritten rules or standards of conduct that have developed over the years in Congress. **(11)**

North Atlantic Treaty Organization (NATO) a defensive military organization of the United States, Canada, and Western European nations set up in 1949. **(18)**

O

Office of Management and Budget the Office sets federal budget priorities and oversees all agencies in the executive branch. **(13)**

Office of Personnel Management the current name of the Civil Service Commission, changed by the Civil Service Reform Act of 1978. **(14)**

official agenda the set of issues that are formally before the policymakers for active consideration. **(16)**

oligarchy the rule of the many by the few. **(9)**

open primary allows voters, whether registered Republicans, Democrats, or Independents, to choose to vote either in the Democratic or Republican primary. **(8)**

opinion leaders individuals who receive media messages and pass them on to others. **(5)**

opinion makers Americans who are generally knowledgeable about foreign affairs and who communicate their opinions to others. **(18)**

order judicial action that requires someone to take a specified action to ensure someone else's rights. **(4)**

Organization of American States (OAS) a regional organization of the United States and Latin American states, sometimes dominated by the United States. **(18)**

overt intelligence the research and analysis of information gained from public sources. **(18)**

P

packing drawing up a district so that it has a large majority of a candidate's supporters to ensure a "safe" seat. **(11)**

paradox of democracy those who most need the government to improve their lives participate the least and are the least influential. **(7)**

partial incorporationists those who see the due process language of the Fourteenth Amendment as meaning that the states must obey some parts of the Bill of Rights, mainly those procedures guaranteeing a fair trial. **(4)**

party elites party organization officials. **(8)**

party-in-the-electorate citizens who identify themselves with one or another party label. **(8)**

party organization the permanent party machinery with its elected officials. **(8)**

party parity equality of voter identification with the two major parties. **(8)**

party platform statement of what the party promises to do if it controls the government. **(8)**

party realignment a permanent shift in the ratio of Democratic and Republican voters. **(8)**

party-in-government public officials who hold office under a party label at the federal, state, and local levels. **(8)**

patronage the power to appoint supporters to public jobs. **(8)**

Pendleton Act an 1883 congressional act, also known as the Civil Service Reform Act, that set up a bipartisan Civil Service Commission to choose government employees under a merit system. **(14)**

perestroika Soviet restructuring of the economy for a supposed efficient delivery of goods. **(18)**

plaintiff the person who brings the action in a civil case. **(15)**

platform planks portions on specific issues by the party in the platform. **(8)**

pluralism competition and compromise between interest groups, which then make policy with the government by simply giving approval to these decisions. **(9)**

plurality vote at least one more vote than any other candidate. **(8)**

pocket veto presidential refusal to sign a bill within ten days of congressional adjournment. **(13)**

policy adoption the act of making policy choices. **(16)**

policy analysis the study of public policy, which describes and explains the causes and consequences of government action. **(16)**

policy evaluation assessing the impact of policy, performed by the actors as well as by those affected. **(16)**

policy implementation placing policy decision objectives into operation. **(16)**

policy process the procedure that includes everything from putting issues on the public agenda to evaluating their implementation. **(9)**

political action committees (PACs) organizations set up to legally solicit campaign contributions. **(9)**

political consultants professionals skilled at using media, polls, the mails, computers, and organization to win elections for those who hire them. **(7)**

political education the means by which students in schools are indoctrinated in a specific ideology, including the traditions of the government. **(5)**

political efficacy the degree to which people believe that being politically active can make a difference. **(5)**

political machine an old-style city organization led by political bosses and characterized by patronage with a dash of corruption. **(3)**

political movements these movements are characterized as flexible and unstable, advocates of major change, and mobilizers of as many people as possible. **(10)**

political participation the right to take part in or influence political decisions that reflect the community will while protecting human rights. **(1)**

political party a group organized to run candidates in elections in order to control government. **(8)**

political socialization how people learn and form opinions about politics from various agents. **(5)**

politicos members of Congress who are both delegates and trustees depending on the importance of principles involved and the intensity of constituency feelings about an issue. **(11)**

politics the process by which people seek to secure and preserve their share of power or authority. **(1)**

positive-negative presidents a categorical definition of presidents by James David Barber based on how they perform in office. **(13)**

precinct the smallest geographical unit of American party organization. **(8)**

President of the Senate the vice-president of the United States. **(12)**

President pro tempore a largely honorary position in the Senate given to the senior member of the majority party; ranks after Speaker of the House in succession to the presidency. **(12)**

presidential power the power to persuade based both on formal powers as well as political skills. **(13)**

prime rate the rate of interest banks charge their biggest and best borrowers. **(17)**

prior restraint the action of government to not allow expression to be uttered or printed, rather than punishment after the fact. **(4)**

private attorneys general organizations created to support rights of individuals and groups. They act for groups bringing court cases against the government or against other groups. **(4)**

Proclamation of 1763 a British royal decree that limited American colonial expansion to the West. **(1)**

progressive tax a tax that takes a larger share of the income from high-income groups than it does from low-income groups. It is related to ability to pay. **(3, 17)**

proportional representation each district has more than one representative, and each party that receives a certain number of votes gets to send a proportionate number of representatives to the legislature. **(8)**

protest referendum people petition for a popular vote on whether a measure passed by a legislative body should be approved or repealed. **(3)**

public administration the business of making government work, implying a separation of politics and administration. **(14)**

public agenda all the issues that a large part of the population believes should be acted on by government. **(16)**

public interest groups organizations that seek to represent the general public in the policy-making process. **(9)**

public policy the goals and assumptions behind government action. **(16)**

Q

quorum one more than half the members of either house of Congress needed to operate. **(12)**

R

random sample the random selection of interviewees in a certain geographic area that gives each member of the universe an equal chance to be chosen. **(5)**

ratification the process by which special state conventions agreed to the Constitution. Today, the process by which states agree to constitutional amendments. Also, the authority of the Senate to approve or reject treaties. **(1, 2)**

reapportionment changing legislative district lines to reflect the rearrangement of state population. **(3)**

recall a reverse election in which people may remove public officials before the end of their terms by petition and popular vote. **(3)**

recovery the return to productivity of war-torn Europe and Japan after World War II, brought about by massive American aid. **(18)**

red baiting making charges that communists are in the American government. Sometimes called McCarthyism. **(18)**

regressive tax a tax that takes a larger share of the income of low-income groups than of high-income groups. It is not related to ability to pay. **(3, 17)**

regulatory bodies groups, such as the Federal Communications Commission, headed by boards or commissions that are subject to confirmation by the Senate. They do not report to the president. **(14)**

regulatory effect of federal spending the federal government granting subsidies in return for compliance with government regulations. **(17)**

regulatory effect of taxes the use of taxing policy to either discourage or promote certain activities. **(17)**

representative sample the people selected for an interview are chosen in such a way that their views accurately reflect those of the universe. **(5)**

republic representatives chosen by citizens to carry out the will of the people in a government. **(1)**

reserve requirements monetary reserves that banks are required to keep on hand to pay demand deposits. **(17)**

reserved powers the Tenth Amendment reserves to the states or the people all powers not delegated to the central government. **(2)**

residual power presidential powers that are not specifically delegated to the president in the Constitution but are necessary for the successful conduct of activities. **(13)**

revenue sharing a system of distributing to state, local, and tribal governments a set percentage of federal tax dollars with only limited strings attached. **(3)**

revolving-door lobbying the practice of former government officials immediately being employed in companies they had dealt with while in government. **(9)**

revolving-door phenomenon the career movement from an industry to its governmental regulator. **(14)**

Reynolds v. *Sims* **(1964)** the Supreme Court decision that established the "one person-one vote" principle for both houses of state legislature. **(3)**

Roe v. *Wade* **(1973)** the Supreme Court decision that held a woman has a right to an abortion during the first three months of pregnancy and that no state can interfere with this right. **(10)**

roll call ballot of the party delegates at a convention. **(8)**

S

safe seats districts or states in which incumbent members of Congress win reelection by more than 60 percent of the general election vote. **(11)**

scientific poll the means of using a properly assigned sampling of a universe, asking carefully designed questions free from bias, and correctly evaluating results. **(5)**

selective exposure the means by which individuals ignore certain news items based on their preconceptions.

selective perception the distortion of a message by a recipient based on preconceptions. **(5)**

selectivity the willingness of media to report certain things and ignore others. **(6)**

senatorial courtesy the Senate will not usually confirm a person's appointment to any federal office if the senators of the president's political party from the state of the nominee refuse to endorse the confirmation. **(12)**

seniority length of service determines committee chairs in Congress and rankings within the congressional committees. **(11)**

separation of powers the principle that the powers of government should be separated and put in the care of different parts of government. **(2)**

Shays's Rebellion uprising of farmer-debtors in New England to halt the foreclosing of mortgages and the taking of land and cattle. **(1)**

single-issue groups issue-oriented groups that are concerned only about one issue. **(9)**

single-member district electing one representative at a time from each district to Congress. **(8)**

Sixteenth Amendment the constitutional amendment which gave the federal government, through Congress, the power to levy an income tax. **(17)**

social contract an implied agreement by all citizens with all citizens where certain liberties and rights are given up by individuals for the common good. **(1)**

social insurance taxes taxes which fund Social Security and Medicare. **(17)**

socialization how we learn our society's traditions and values and how we accept our own cultural patterns. **(5)**

sound bites media events that reduce a candidate's daily message to a brief, catchy phrase, usually with an attractive visual. **(7)**

***South Carolina* v. *Baker* (1988)** the Supreme Court decision ruling that tax exemptions on municipal bonds were not based on the Constitution and could be restricted by Congress. **(3)**

Speaker of the House principal leader of the majority party in the House and presiding officer of the House; follows the vice-president in line of succession to presidency. **(12)**

Special Assistant for National Security Affairs the official title of the National Security Adviser, who is the prime foreign-policy adviser to the president. **(18)**

specialization and reciprocity once assigned to a committee or subcommittee, a member of Congress is expected to become expert in that area. Members are also involved in the mutual recognition of the expertise of other members, particularly members of the committee with jurisdiction over the matter being considered. Legislators seek guidance on how to vote from their party's members on the committee specializing in the area. **(11)**

spin control the ability of the president and his agents to put the best possible interpretation on events for reporters' benefits. **(13)**

spoils system the practice of rewarding political supporters with federal appointments— sometimes called "patronage." The term derived from the expression "to the victors belong the spoils of the enemy." **(14)**

standing committee a permanent congressional committee. **(12)**

stare decisis a Latin phrase meaning "the decision should stand." **(15)**

State of the Union address a power given the president in Article II, Section 3 of the Constitution for an annual assessment of national conditions and goals. **(13)**

statutory law a law that consists of acts passed by a legislative body. **(15)**

straw poll an unscientific measurement of public opinion that is unreliable because the sample is not scientific. **(5)**

strict constructionist one who believes the federal government operates only on express or stated powers. **(3)**

Students for a Democratic Society (SDS) an organization founded by graduate students at the University of Michigan in the 1960s to help develop radical alternatives to what they saw as an inadequate society. **(10)**

suburbanization rapid population shifts to the suburbs. **(3)**

supply-side economics based on the theories of Arthur B. Laffer, who argues that when government taxes get too high, revenues go down because investors and businesspeople are discouraged. The way to stimulate investment and business and increase revenues is to reduce taxes sharply, especially for investors and business. **(17)**

supremacy clause the statement in Article VI of the Constitution that the Constitution and the laws of the central government are supreme to state laws. **(2, 3)**

suspect classification categories for which the burden of proof is on the government, which must show them to be necessary. **(4)**

T

tariff a tax on foreign imports. **(12)**

Tax Reform Act of 1986 combined the Democratic concept of closing loopholes with the Republican plan for lower tax rates. **(17)**

test case action brought by an individual to test a law or a public official's acts. **(15)**

theocracy the rule of God administered by his representatives with no separation of church and state. **(1)**

Tonkin Gulf Resolution a nonbinding congressional measure in 1964 that gave the president an almost blank check to pursue the war in Vietnam. **(13)**

tracking polls taken nightly by telephone, these can measure the daily effect of events, advertisements, debates, and mistakes and allow next-day corrections in a campaign. **(7)**

trustee legislators those who believe their role is to vote as their judgment and conscience demand. **(11)**

two-party system a system in which two political parties are nationally competitive. **(8)**

U

unit rule the practice by which all of a state's electoral votes are cast for the candidate who receives the most popular votes in that state. **(7)**

unitary government a system in which all governmental power is vested in the central, national government. **(3)**

United Nations a universal peacekeeping organization operating through a General Assembly, a Security Council, and other component parts. **(18)**

United States Information Agency (USIA) a unit of the State Department disseminating favorable information overseas through Voice of America, Radio Free Europe, and other means. **(18)**

United States Trade Representative (USTA) a person who is part of the Executive Office of the president with ambassador status and who advises the president on trade matters. **(18)**

Universal Voter Registration Act proposed by former President Carter in 1977, this would have allowed voters to register and vote simply by showing proper identification at the polls on election day. **(7)**

universe the particular public or population whose opinion is to be sampled in a scientific poll. **(5)**

urbanization rapid population shifts to the cities. **(3)**

V

veto presidential rejection of a congressional bill, which cannot then become law until approved by a two-thirds vote in both houses of Congress. **(13)**

Virginia Plan the plan presented by James Madison at the Philadelphia Convention that called for a stronger central government and benefitted the larger states. **(1)**

voluntary referendum the state legislature may decide to refer a legislative proposal to the people rather than take action on the measure itself. **(3)**

voter targeting using census and voting patterns to identify groups that are likely to support a candidate. **(7)**

voting cues members of Congress get indications of how to vote from those whose opinions they trust. **(11)**

Voting Rights Act 1965 law appointing federal examiners to stop discrimination in voter registration in the South. **(10)**

W

War Powers Act of 1973 a congressional act recognizing the power of the president to order military action for defense, but requiring the president to report to Congress within forty-eight hours after committing any armed forces to foreign combat and to terminate any such troop commitment within sixty days unless approved by Congress. **(12, 13, 18)**

welfare clause a constitutional provision that says Congress has the power to provide for "the general welfare of the United States." **(3)**

Wesberry **v.** *Sanders* **(1964)** Supreme Court decision that required all congressional districts to be approximately equal in population. **(11)**

White House staff those closest to the president who control the day-to-day operations of the White House and intercede with the media. **(13)**

wire services specialized agencies that gather, write, and sell news to the media that subscribe to them. **(6)**

Women's Liberation Movement established in the 1970s as women increasingly recognized their own inequality in society. **(10)**

World Bank the common name for the International Bank for Reconstruction and Development founded in 1944 to provide development assistance originally to war-ravaged Europe and today to the Third World. **(18)**

writ of certiorari an order to a lower court to send the entire record of the case to a higher court for review. **(15)**

Z

zero-based budget system each agency must justify its budget each year, harming those agencies that can not use cost-benefit analysis to their favor. The purpose is to reduce incrementalism. **(14, 16)**

zone of privacy shielding individuals from government intrusion into their thoughts, religious beliefs, and some actions. **(4)**

ACKNOWLEDGMENTS

PHOTOGRAPHS AND CARTOONS

Unless otherwise acknowledged, all photos are the property of Scott, Foresman and Company. Page positions are as follows: (T)top, (C)center, (B)bottom, (L)left, (R)right, (INS)inset.

Front cover background: Jimmy Carter Library **Front and back cover photos, clockwise from top:** Diana Walker/*Time Magazine,* John McDonnell/*The Washington Post,* AP/Wide World, Kaluzny/Gamma-Liaison, AP/Wide World, Tannenbaum/Sygma, Eli Reed Distributed by Magnum Photos **Chapter 1: 1** Antonio Suarez/*Time Magazine* **2** Illustration from *History Of North America,* by Reverend Cooper, New York Public Library, Astor, Lenox and Tilden Foundations **3** The Colonial Williamsburg Foundation **4** Library of Congress **5L** The Franklin Institute, Philadelphia **5R** Private Collection **6** John Carter Brown Library, Brown University **8** Library of Congress **9** The Illustrated London News, Nov. 29, 1856 **10** Historical Pictures Service, Chicago **14** Culver Pictures **17** After a painting by Alonzo Chappel, Published by Johnson, Fry & Co., NY, 1866. Chicago Historical Society **21TR** Roger Butterfield **21BR** Culver Pictures **29** Brown Brothers **Chapter 2: 32** Paul Conklin **33** Ira Wyman/Sygma **36T** Viriginia Museum of Fine Arts, Richmond, Gift of Col. and Mrs. Edgar Garbisch **36B** U.S. Bureau of Printing and Engraving **37** AP/Wide World **40** AP/Wide World **49** U.S. Bureau of Printing and Engraving **51** Copyrighted, Chicago Tribune Company, all rights reserved, used with permission. Photo by Ernie Cox, Jr. **53** UPI/Bettmann Newsphotos **Chapter 3: 57** Courtesy Media Services, Texas House of Representatives **58** Scott Thode/*U.S. News & World Report* **60** AP/Wide World **63** Owen Franken/Stock Boston **65** AP/Wide World **69** AP/Wide World **71** Courtesy, Nebraska Legislature, Unicameral Information Office **73** Courtesy, County Clerk, Cook County, Illinois **78** Courtesy, Mayor's Office of Public Information **80** Michael D. Sullivan/TexaStock **84** J. L. Atlan/Sygma **88T** Martin A. Levick **88B** Copyright 1981 by Herblock in *The Washington Post* **Chapter 4: 92** Alice Hargrave/Gamma-Liaison **93** UPI/Bettmann Newsphotos **95L** AP/Wide World **95R** AP/Wide World **98** AP/Wide World **100L** Photograph by Dorothea Lange, War Relocation Authority, The National Archives **100R** Library of Congress **102** Harkel/Gamma-Liaison **103** © 1985, Drawing by Lorenz/*The New Yorker Magazine,* Inc. **104** © 1969 *The Des Moines Register.* Reprinted with permission. **105** AP/Wide World **108** Gamma-Liaison **111L** Elliott Erwitt/Magnum Photos **111R** © *LOOK Magazine*/Library of Congress **112** UPI/Bettmann Newsphotos **113** AP/Wide World **Chapter 5: 123** AP/Wide World **124** Ralf-Finn Hestoft/Picture Group **125** Ken Heinen **126** Reprinted by permission of United Feature Syndicate, Inc. **127** Brig Cabe/*Insight Magazine* **128** AP/Wide World **134** UPI/Bettmann Newsphotos **135** AP/Wide World **137** Max Winter/Picture Group **143** © 1988, Drawing by Lorenz/*The New Yorker Magazine,* Inc. **146** © 1984 by Herblock in *The*

Washington Post **149** Lionel J. M. Delevingne/Stock Boston **150** Paul Conklin **152** Sarah Buffum/*Time Magazine* **Chapter 6: 156** AP/Wide World **157** Bill Fitz-Patrick/The White House **158** © 1981, *Raleigh News & Observer,* Reprinted by permission, Los Angeles Times Syndicate. **160** Steve Starr/Picture Group **163** AP/Wide World **167T** AP/Wide World **167B** AP/Wide World **168** Michael Evans/The White House **169** Mike Clemmer/Picture Group **173** Alex Webb/Magnum Photos **175** Courtesy, *NATIONAL ENQUIRER* **176** AP/Wide World **Chapter 7: 180** The Bettmann Archive **181** Cynthia Johnson/*Time Magazine* **183** NYT Pictures **185** Paul Conklin **190** Copyrighted, Chicago Tribune Company, all rights reserved, used with permission. Photos by Jerry Tomaselli. **192** AP/Wide World **193** Paul Conklin **195** AP/Wide World **197** Gamma-Liaison **198** AP/Wide World **201** UPI/Bettmann Newsphotos **203** AP/Wide World **205** AP/Wide World **Chapter 8: 209** AP/Wide World **210** Cartoon by Thomas Nast, from *Thomas Nast,* by Albert Bigelow Paine, **211** Cartoon by Thomas Nast, from *Thomas Nast,* by Albert Bigelow Paine. **216** Constantine Manos/Magnum Photos **217** AP/Wide World **221T** Owen Franken/Stock Boston **221B** AP/Wide World **224** AP/Wide World **229** © Jonathan Kirn/Picture Group **232** R. Maiman/Sygma **236** Y. Hemsey/Gamma-Liaison **239** Joe Wrinn/NYT Pictures **240** Dennis Brack/Black Star **Chapter 9: 244** Paul Conklin **247** Gene Bassett/*The Atlanta Constitution* **249** UPI/Bettmann Newsphotos **254** AP/Wide World **257T** Steve McCurry/Magnum Photos **257B** National Rifle Association **268** UPI/Bettmann Newsphotos **270** Lyndon Baines Johnson Library **274** Terry Ashe/Gamma-Liaison **275** AP/Wide World **Chapter 10: 280** Timothy A. Murphy/*U.S. News & World Report* **282** James H. Karales © 1965, *LOOK Magazine,* Library of Congress **284** The Bettmann Archive **285** Carl Andon/Black Star **286** AP/Wide World **287** UPI/Bettmann Newsphotos **290** UPI/Bettmann Newsphotos **291** Lyndon Baines Johnson Library **293** Los Angeles Times Photo **295** H. Simmons/Plus 4 **296** Brown Brothers **297** UPI/Bettmann Newsphotos **298T** UPI/Bettmann Newsphotos **298B** UPI/Bettmann Newsphotos **301** Fred Ward/Black Star **302** Lee Lockwood/Black Star **305** Steve Shapiro/Sygma **Chapter 11: 311** Supreme Court Historical Society **312** James K. W. Atherton/*The Washington Post* **315** AP/Wide World **320** AP/Wide World **328** AP/Wide World **331** Ken Regan/Camera 5 **335** Paul Conklin **340** Diego Goldberg/Sygma **342** UPI/Bettmann Newsphotos **344** AP/Wide World **Chapter 12: 349** UPI/Bettmann Newsphotos **355** AP/Wide World **358** Wally McNamee/*Newsweek*/Woodfin Camp & Associates **363** Courtesy Howard E. McCurdy, *An Insider's Guide to the Capitol,* Washington, D.C. The American University, 1977. Art by Susan Lee. **364** UPI/Bettmann Newsphotos **373** Cathleen, Curtis/*The Washington Times* **378** AP/Wide World **381** UPI/Bettmann Newsphotos **382** AP/Wide World **Chapter 13: 386** Market/Gamma-Liaison **387** Cornell Capa/Magnum Photos **388** Lyndon Baines Johnson Library **394** The Franklin D. Roosevelt Library **397** Jimmy Carter Library **401** George Tames **406** Miguel Solis/Sygma **409** The National Archives **413** AP/Wide

World **415** AP/Wide World **416** AP/Wide World **419** Randy Taylor/Sygma **420** C. Johnson/Gamma-Liaison **Chapter 14: 428** © 1979 Locher. Reprinted by permission: Tribune Media Services **434** James Kamp/Black Star **436** NASA **439** *Minneapolis Star and Tribune* **443** AP/Wide World **444** Brad Markel/Gamma-Liaison **447** AP/Wide World **451** AP/Wide World **452** Sebastiao Salgado/Magnum Photos **Chapter 15: 456** Steve Liss/*Time Magazine* **457** Carl Iwasaki/*Life Magazine* © Time Inc. **464** UPI/Bettmann Newsphotos **470** AP/Wide World **471L** © 1989 Mike Lukovich/*The Atlanta Constitution* **471R** Donna Ferrato/Black Star **474** AP/Wide World **478** Cynthia Johnson/Gamma-Liaison **485** UPI/Bettmann Newsphotos **487** Richmond Newspapers, Inc. **488** Richmond Newspapers, Inc. **Chapter 16: 493** Ken Chen/Gamma-Liaison **494** Frank Fournier/Contact Press Images/Woodfin Camp & Associates **495** John Chiassion/Gamma-Liaison **496** *Cleveland Plain Dealer*/AP/Wide World **497** Dennis Brack/Black Star **498** AP/Wide World **499** Keith Jewel **500** B. Nationa/Sygma **501L** Lyndon Baines Johnson Library **501R** Copyrighted, Chicago Tribune Company, all rights reserved, used with permission. Photo by George Thompson. **502** Fred Ward/Black Star **503** Seattle Times/Gamma-Liaison **504** R. Maiman/Sygma **506** AP/Wide World **510** Copyrighted, Chicago Tribune Company, all rights reserved, used with permission. Photo by Mario Petitti. **512** Copyrighted, Chicago Tribune Company, all rights reserved, used with permission. Photo by Karen Engstrom. **514L** Nigel Dickson **514R** Reprinted with permission of Doug Marlette/*New York Newsday* **Chapter 17: 518** Susan Meiselas/Magnum Photos **519** CINNCINATTI POST/Sygma **521** UPI/Bettmann Newsphotos **522** U.S. Forestry Service **525** Dirck Halstead/Time Magazine **533** Jean-Pierre Laffont/Sygma **545T** Jean-Pierre Laffont/Sygma **545B** Tony Korody/Sygma **549** Reprinted by permission: Tribune Media Services **Chapter 18: 553** Stuart Franklin/Magnum Photos **554** Hans Verhofen/Focus/Woodfin Camp & Associates **557** Bernard Hoffman © 1945/*Life Magazine* © Time Inc. **558** AP/Wide World **559** UPI/Bettmann Newsphotos **561L** Fouad/Sygma **561R** A. Mingam/Gamma-Liaison **564L** Bill Fitz-Patrick/The White House **564R** Larry Downing/Woodfin Camp & Associates **569** Abbas/Magnum Photos **574** Alexandra Avakian/Woodfin Camp & Associates **580** Tennenbaum/Sygma **581** AP/Wide World **585L** Stuart Franklin/Magnum Photos **585R** Peter Jordan/Gamma-Liaison

LITERARY, FIGURES, AND TABLES

Chapter 1: 24 "Principal Plans Before The Constitutional Convention" from *The American Federal Government* by John H. Ferguson and Dean S. McHenry, 14th ed. Reprinted by permission of McGraw-Hill Book Company. **28** Herbert J. Storing, *The Complete Anti-Federalist.* Chicago: The University of Chicago Press, 1981. **Chapter 2: 41** Linda Greenhouse, "What's a Lawmaker to Do About the Constitution?" *The New York Times,* 1988. **47** From *An Introduction to American Government,* 5/e by Erwin L. Levine and Elmer E. Cornwell, Jr. Copyright © 1972 by Macmillan Publishing Company. Reprinted with permission. **50** From *The Basics of American Politics,* 5/e by Gary Wasserman. Copyright © 1988 by Garry Wasserman. Scott, Foresman and Company. **Chapter 3: 59** From *The New Federalism,* Second Edition by Michael D. Reagan and John G. Sanzone. Copyright © 1972, 1981 by Oxford University Press, Inc. Reprinted by permission. **70** Robert Hanley, "Jersey Takeover of School District Is Begun By State," *The New York Times,* 1988. **78** Mike Royko, *Boss: Richard J. Daley of Chicago.* New York: E. P. Dutton & Co., Inc., 1971, pp. 126–27. **82** From *The Wall Street Journal,* February 21, 1989. Copyright © Dow, Jones & Co., Inc. **Chapter 5: 123** Excerpt from "Marchers Protest 'Legal Lynching,'" AP Newsfeatures, August 26,

1989. **130** From "The Opinions of Children" from *Index to International Public Opinion* by E. H. Hastings & P. K. Hastings, Editors. Copyright © 1982 Survey Research Consultants International, Inc. Reprinted by permission. **133** From *What Americans Really Think* by Barry Sussman, p. 69. Copyright © 1988 by Barry Sussman. Reprinted by permission of Pantheon Books, a division of Random House, Inc. **135** From "Am I Reading the Papers Correctly?" by Woody Allen, *The New York Times,* 1/28/88. Copyright © 1988 by The New York Times Company. Reprinted by permission. **136** "Conservative and Liberal," *Public Opinion,* Nov./Dec., 1988, p. 30. Reprinted with the permission of the American Enterprise Institute for Public Policy Research. **145** Jane Mayer and Doyle McManus, *Landslide: The Unmaking of the President,* 1984–1988. Boston: Houghton Mifflin Co, 1988, p. 44. **151** from *What Americans Really Think* by Barry Sussman, p. 217. Copyright © 1988 by Barry Sussman. Reprinted by permission of Pantheon Books, a division of Random House, Inc. **Chapter 6: 159** "Audiences Reached by Leading Media, 1987," *Nielsen Television Index* of 1986–1987. Reprinted by permission of Nielsen Media Research. **165** From *Reporters and Officials: The Organization and Politics of Newsmaking* by L. V. Sigal, 1973, pp. 122–24. Reprinted by permission of D. C. Heath & Company. **170** "Dealing With The Media" from "Annals of Television: Shaking the Tree" by Thomas Whiteside, *The New Yorker,* March 17, 1975, p. 46. Copyright © 1975 The New Yorker Magazine, Inc. Reprinted by permission. **172** From *What Americans Really Think* by Barry Sussman, p. 214. Copyright © 1988 by Barry Sussman. Reprinted by permission of Pantheon Books, a division of Random House, Inc. **Chapter 7: 187–88** From *Why Americans Don't Vote* by Frances Fox Piven and Richard A. Cloward, pp. 5, 19. Copyright © 1988 by Frances Fox Piven and Richard A. Cloward. Reprinted by permission of Pantheon Books, a division of Random House, Inc. **Chapter 8: 218** From *The Party's Just Begun: Shaping Political Parties for America's Future* by Larry J. Sabato, p. 245. Copyright © 1988 by Larry J. Sabato. Scott, Foresman and Company. **220** "Party Identification Through 1984," *Public Opinion,* April/May, 1984, p. 32 and "Party Identification Through 1987," *Public Opinion,* Nov/Dec, 1987, p. 22. Reprinted by permission of American Enterprise Institute for Public Policy Research. **222** From *Gallup Opinion Index,* Feb. 1966, p. 14 and *The Gallup Poll,* 1987. Reprinted by permission of American Institute of Public Opinion. **225** From *Parties in Crisis: Party Politics in America,* 2/e by Ruth K. Scott and Ronald J. Hrebenar. Copyright © 1984 by John Wiley and Sons. Reprinted by permission. **228** From *Party Politics in America,* 6/e by Frank J. Sorauf and Paul Allen Beck, p. 78. Copyright © 1988 Scott, Foresman and Company. **236** From "The Convention: A Made-for-TV Event?" from *The New York Times,* February 28, 1986. Copyright © 1986 by The New York Times Company. Reprinted by permission. **Chapter 9: 252** From "A Few Interest Groups" from *Encyclopedia of Associations,* 1985, 19th Edition. Copyright © 1984 by Gale Research Inc. Reprinted by permission'. **269** Bill Keller, "The Veterans' Lobby as an 'Iron Triangle'." *Congressional Quarterly Weekly Report,* 1984, pp. 1627–34. **272** From *Man of the House: The Life and Political Memoirs of Speaker Tip O'Neill* with William Novak. Copyright © 1987 by Thomas P. O'Neill, Jr. Reprinted by permission of Random House, Inc. **Chapter 11: 316** From *Congressional Quarterly Weekly Report,* November 12, 1988, pp. 3293–95. Copyright © 1988 Congressional Quarterly Inc. Reprinted by permission. **318** From *The American Elections of 1982* by Thomas E. Mann and Norman J. Ornstein, pp. 155, 160 & 165. Reprinted with the permission of the American Enterprise Institute for Public Policy Research, Washington, D.C. **323** Robert L. Lineberry, *Government in America.* Glenview, IL: Scott, Foresman and Company, 1989, p. 387. **324** "Twelfth Congressional District of New York, 1950s" by Anthony Lewis, *The New York Times,* 11/27/60. Copyright © 1960 by The New York Times Company. Reprinted by permission. **329** From *Common Cause News,* March 2, 1989, pp. 5 & 6 and March 28, 1989, p. 5. Reprinted by permission. **332** From "Senators' 1987 Honoraria Receipts," *Congressional Quarterly Weekly Report,* June 11, 1988, pp. 1572–

73. Copyright © 1988 Congressional Quarterly Inc. Reprinted by permission. **337** Morris Udall, *Too Funny to be President.* New York: Henry Holt and Co., Inc., 1988. **338** From "Presidential Arm Twisting," *The New York Times,* 7/26/85. Copyright © 1985 by The New York Times Company. Reprinted by permission. **339** From *At the Margins: Presidential Leadership of Congress* by George C. Edwards, III, p. 18. Copyright © 1989 Yale University Press. Reprinted by permission. From *Congressional Procedures and the Policy Process,* 3/e by Walter J. Oleszek. Copyright © 1989 Congressional Quarterly Inc. Reprinted by permission. **367** Tim Hackler, "What's Gone Wrong With The U.S. Senate?" *American Politics,* 1987, pp. 7–8, 11. **370** Ross K. Baker, *Friend and Foe in the U.S. Senate.* New York: The Free Press, 1980, pp. 244–45. **374** From *America's Democracy: The Ideal and the Reality,* 3/e by Fred R. Harris. Copyright © 1986, 1983, 1980 by Fred R. Harris. Scott, Foresman and Company. **377** Donald Riegle, *O Congress.* New York: Doubleday & Company, Inc., 1972, pp. 98–99. **Chapter 13: 390** From "Public Approval of Reagan Through 8 Years," *The New York Times,* January 13, 1989. Copyright © 1989 by The New York Times Company. Reprinted by permission. **404** David A. Stockman, *The Triumph of Politics.* New York: Harper & Row, Publishers, Inc., 1986. **409** Larry Berman, *The New American Presidency.* Boston: Little, Brown and Company, 1987. **414** From *Showdown at Gucci Gulch* by Jeffrey H. Birnbaum and Alan S. Murray, p. 172. Copyright © 1987 by Jeffrey H. Birnbaum and Alan S. Murray. Reprinted by permission of Random House, Inc. **417** Robert L. Lineberry, *Government in America.* Glenview, IL: Scott, Foresman and Company, 1989, p. 447. **Chapter 14: 431** Morris Udall, *Too Funny to be President.* New York: Henry Holt and Co., Inc, 1988. **432** "A Kind Word for the Spoil System" by Charles Peters, *The Washington Monthly,* September 1976. Reprinted by permission of the author. **440** From *Dismantling America* by Susan J. Tolchin & Martin Tolchin. Copyright © 1983 by Susan J. Tolchin and Martin Tolchin. Reprinted by permission of Houghton Mifflin Company. **444** From "The Sad, Strange Mind of Col. North" by Constantine C. Menges, *The Washington Post,* 11/27/88. Copyright © 1988 The Washington Post. Reprinted by permission. **448** From "The President and the Mouse" by Hedrick Smith, *The New York Times,* 1/8/78. Copyright © 1978 by The New York Times Company. Reprinted by permission. **Chapter 15: 462** Adapted from *American Constitutional Law,* 3/e by Rocco J. Tresolini and Martin Shapiro. Copyright © 1972 by Rocco J. Tresolini and Martin Shapiro. Reprinted with permission of Macmillan Publishing Company. **467** Henry J. Abraham, *The Judiciary,* 3/e. Dubuque, Iowa: Wm. C. Brown Company Publishers, 1973. **469** David M. O'Brien, *Storm Center: The Supreme Court in American Politics.* New York: W. W. Norton & Co., 1986. **476** From "Behind the Marble, Beneath the Robes" by Nina Totenberg, *The New York Times,* 3/16/75. Copyright © 1975 by The New York Times Company. Reprinted by permission. **480** Adapted from *Crime in American Society,* 2/e by Charles McCaghy and Stephen A. Cernkovich. Copyright © 1987 by Charles McCaghy and Stephen A. Cernkovich. Reprinted with permission of Macmillan Publishing Company. **Chapter 16: 513** C. Northcote Parkinson, *Parkinson the Law.* Boston: Houghton Mifflin Company, 1980. **Chapter 17: 524** From "Is Anyone Really Trying to Balance the Budget?" by David Rapp, *Congressional Quarterly,* November 26, 1988, p. 3380. Copyright © 1988 Congressional Quarterly Inc. Reprinted by permission. **531** Adapted from "How Big Is Big" from OECD Economic Outlook 43, June 1988, p. 183. Reprinted by permission of Organization for Economic Cooperation and Development. **534** Jonathan Yates, "Reality on Capitol Hill," *Newsweek,* November 28, 1988. Copyright © Jonathan Yates. **543** William Ryan, *Equality.* New York: Pantheon Books, 1981, p. 11. **548** From "Now, to Figure Why the Poor Get Poorer" by Leonard Silk, *The New York Times,* 12/18/88. Copyright © 1988 by The New York Times Company. Reprinted by permission.

★
INDEX

Monroe Doctrine, 556
Moore, Sara Jane, 177
Moral Majority, 141, 190, 256, 578
Morison, Samuel, 20
Morton, Rogers, 170
Mothers Against Drunk Driving (MADD), 259
Motion Picture Association, 261
Mountain States Legal Foundation, 482
Movements, political. *See* Political movements
Moynihan, Daniel Patrick, 132
Multiplier effect, 184
Municipal bonds, 81
Mutiny Act, 4, 5

N

NAACP. *See* National Association for the Advancement of Colored People (NAACP)
Nader, Ralph, 250, 256, 287, 482, 501
Nagasaki, 557
Naisbitt, John, 148
NAM. *See* National Association of Manufacturers (NAM)
Napolitano, Joe, 195
NASA. *See* National Aeronautics and Space Administration (NASA)
National Academy of Sciences, 269
National Advisory Commission, 294
National Advisory Commission on Civil Disorders, 504–5
National Aeronautics and Space Administration (NASA), 436, 443
National Association for the Advancement of Colored People (NAACP), 117, 251, 259, 283, 289, 343, 484
National Association of English Teachers, 431
National Association of Manufacturers (NAM), 251–52, 268
National Association of Realtors, 190, 275
National Catholic Conference, 256
National chairperson, 231
National Conference of Catholic Bishops, 256
National Conference of State Legislatures, 258
National conventions, 235–37
See also Political parties
National Corn Growers Association, 255
National Council of Churches, 256, 578

National Education Association (NEA), 253
National Enquirer, 175
National executive, 23
National Farmers Organization, 255
National Farmers Union, 254
National figure, 163
National Governors Conference, 85, 258
National Guard, 118
National Journal, 88
National judiciary, 23
National Labor Relations Board (NLRB), 356
National League of Cities, 85
National legislature, 23
National Municipal League, 258
National Opinion Research Center, 151
National Organization for Women (NOW), 117, 251, 297, 298
National party organizations. *See* Political parties
National Republican Congressional Committee (NRCC), 274
National Rifle Association (NRA), 257, 268
National Science Foundation, 321, 436
National Security Act, 572
National security advisor, 563
National Security Agency (NSA), 570
National Security Council (NSC), 405, 418, 563, 566, 571–72
National Socialist Party of America, 93–94, 104, 120
National supremacy
and states' rights, 46
and Supreme Court, 466–68
National Unity party, 215
National Woman Suffrage Association, 297
Native Americans, 79–80
NATO. *See* North Atlantic Treaty Organization (NATO)
Natural rights, 9
Navajo, 79
Nazis, American, 93–94, 104, 120
Nazism, 450–53, 557
NBC, 159, 162
NEA. *See* National Education Association (NEA)
Near v. *Minnesota,* 101
Negative advertising, 195, 197
Networks, television, 159–60
Neustadt, Richard, 401
New Deal, 84, 126, 356, 396, 397, 469, 478
New Federalism, 86–88, 89
New Frontier, 301
Newhouse Publications, 161

New Jersey Plan, 24, 25, 26, 30
New Left, 301
New Partnership, 87
News, 162–64
See also Mass media
News management, 167
Newsweek, 159, 160, 169, 174
New Yorker, The, 161, 170
New York Times, 160–61, 165, 174, 344, 450, 472
Nicaragua, 307, 412, 418, 421, 557, 561, 583
Nightmare on Elm Street, 130
Nixon, Richard M., 40, 55, 86–87, 132, 141, 167, 170, 173, 195, 219, 220, 266, 298, 343, 356, 357, 359, 360, 389, 398, 399, 405, 407, 408, 409, 411, 413, 414, 416, 465, 469, 473, 488, 504, 525, 544, 545, 558, 560, 576, 577, 580
NLRB. *See* National Labor Relations Board (NLRB)
Nominations, and campaigns, 234
Nonaligned, 223–25
Noriega, Manuel, 583
Norms, and Congress, 328
North, Oliver, 55, 359, 405, 444, 572
North Atlantic Treaty Organization (NATO), 583–84, 585
Northwest Ordinance, 17
NOW. *See* National Organization for Women (NOW)
NRA. *See* National Rifle Association (NRA)
NRCC. *See* National Republican Congressional Committee (NRCC)
NSA. *See* National Security Agency (NSA)
NSC. *See* National Security Council (NSC)
Nuclear-freeze movement, 141

O

OAS. *See* Organization of American States (OAS)
Obscenity, and Supreme Court, 476
Occupation
and political opinions, 140
and voting, 191
O'Connor, Sandra Day, 44–45, 465
Office of Management and Budget (OMB), 403–4, 445–46, 503, 525, 526
Office of Strategic Services (OSS), 570
Official agenda, 499
Officials, elected. *See* Elected officials